AF573740

Stanford's Sailing Companion

Capt F S Campbell & Capt R J F Riley

STANFORD MARITIME LONDON

Stanford Maritime Limited
Member Company of the George Philip Group
12-14 Long Acre London WC2E 9LP

First Published 1972
Second Edition 1973
Third Edition 1976

Printed in Great Britain by
Lowe & Brydone (Printers) Ltd, Thetford, Norfolk

NOTE
The Publishers, while exercising the greatest care in compiling this publication, do not hold themselves responsible for the consequences arising from any inaccuracies therein.

ISBN 0 540 07162-5

Contents

Preface

During the course of several years' work in publishing charts and nautical text books for the sailing public, as well as lecturing at Evening Classes, many suggestions have been received for improving and furthering our services. One, which frequently recurs, has been for the publication of a book, the contents of which would clearly and concisely cover the day-to-day requirements of the cruising yachtsman.

It is with this in mind that the SAILING COMPANION has been compiled and, as its name implies, we trust that the content will be a worthwhile 'companion' during your forthcoming passages.

The first thirteen chapters cover all the theoretical and practical aspects of coastal navigation. Each chapter has also been carefully amplified to deal with the various problems which beset yachtsmen and which are often left unanswered.

Times of High Water at Dover are listed on a separate card for ease of reference. The interval from High Water, Dover, of the time of high water at individual ports is also listed as well as the Spring and Neap Rises. The time of high water at any port in the U.K. and of those on the Continent of Europe between Ijmuiden and Lezardrieux is thus readily obtainable and for a considerable period of time.

Entrance details are listed for the main yachting harbours and there are also tables listing the facilities. This latter table may appear to be rather brief but harbour developments in the provision of additional moorings, alongside berths and marinas are proceeding at such a pace that it was considered best just to list what was basically available.

Customs and Coastguard information has been included together with the necessary addresses and requisite forms. Sections of Admiralty Notices to Mariners, which are particularly relevant to yachtsmen, have also been given full coverage.

Terrestrial Tables have been included but Celestial ones omitted. In the opinion of the authors, position finding by celestial observation is both unnecessary and inaccurate in the coastal waters surrounding the U.K., English Channel and Southern North Sea. In these areas one is either within visual range of terrestrial marks or 'covered' by radio beacons from which accurate 'fixes' can be obtained. '*Sights*', taken from the deck of a small heaving craft do not give the accuracy which is necessary in confined coastal waters.

Finally, the authors would like to thank those many Yacht Club Secretaries, Harbour Masters and others too numerous to mention who have co-operated so ably both in providing information and giving advice on the material to be used.

No book on this subject can claim to be conclusive and any advice on the inclusion of additional and viable information will be welcomed.

1973

F.S.C.
R.J.F.R.

CHAPTER 1

Definitions

Every trade has its tools: every skill its own particular jargon, a language made up of words and definitions which must be as familiar to those who use them as the craftsman's tools come naturally to his hand. So it is with coastal navigation.

In any navigational publication certain words and phrases tend to repeat themselves. It is important that their import is completely understood. The definitions which follow should be read carefully and absorbed one by one. It will not then be necessary to ponder, or to refer back, when the words to which they refer are encountered. Some are definitions which the reader may not have had to consider before, even during school days.

Angular Measure

To prompt the memories of those who have forgotten how to measure angles a table is given below:

60 seconds (or 60″)	=	one minute (or 1′)
60 minutes (or 60′)	=	one degree (or 1°)
A right angle	=	90°
4 right angles	=	360° which is a full circle

Angular measure can be translated into terms of distance. Consider the diagram below. It represents a segment of a circle, the angle at B being 30°. The length of the arc AC has a measurement: 30° of arc. Whether the radii – AB or CB – needs to be measured in inches or miles, provided our maths is good enough, we could calculate the linear length of the arc AC. Consequently, if we chose, we could describe the length of the arc in degrees, minutes and seconds, or as a distance.

Fig. 1.1

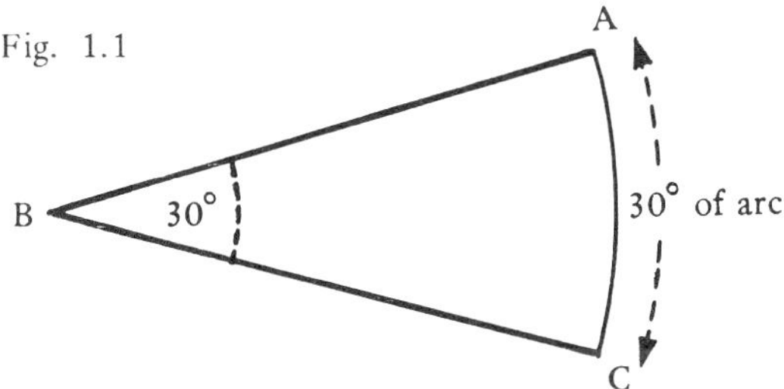

The Earth

The earth is, for all practical purposes, a sphere. We know it is not round, but, at this stage, it is convenient to consider it so. A globe of the earth is covered with a network of lines, both vertical and horizontal. They are a pattern of great and small circles. Some method of defining position at sea has to be used, in the same way as the National Grid system is adopted in this country to define position on an ordnance map. Our global network, consisting of circles named parallels of latitude and meridians of longitude, is the system adopted by mariners generally to achieve the same object.

Fig. 1.2

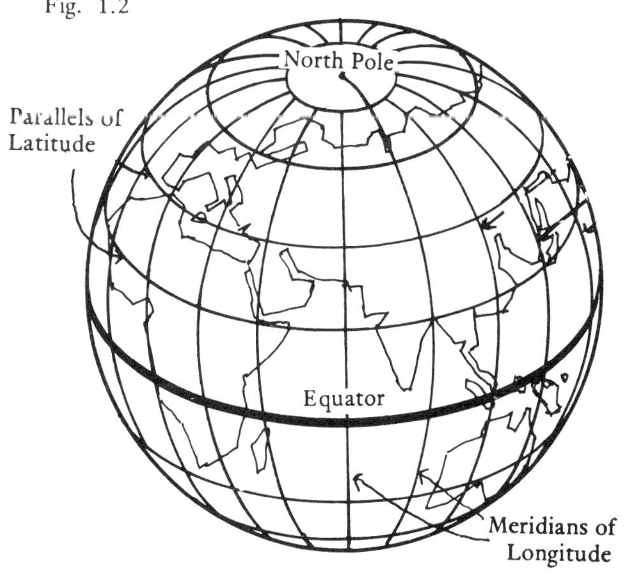

A Great Circle

A circle drawn on a sphere is defined as a great circle when its plane passes through the centre of the sphere. It may be drawn in any direction, as the figure indicates, and provided it is a perfect circle whose plane fulfils the stated condition, it will be a great circle.

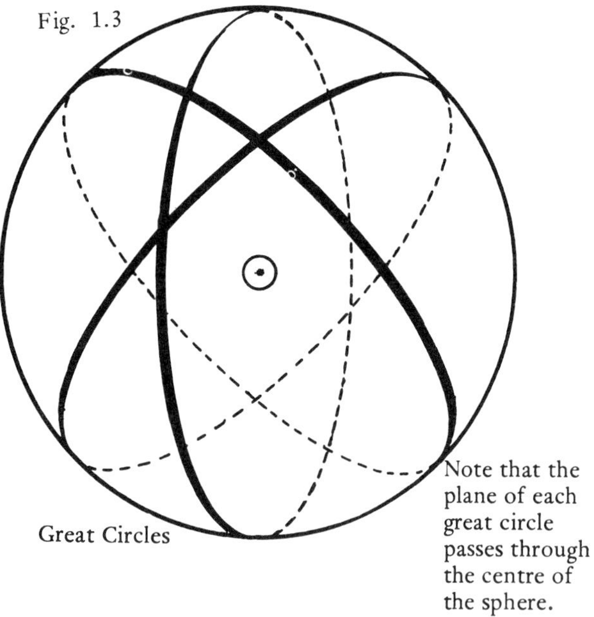

A great circle drawn through two positions on the surface of a sphere will give the shortest possible distance between them. Ships and aircraft frequently navigate on great circle routes for obvious reasons.

Small Circles (Fig. 4)

When a circle is drawn on a sphere and its plane does **not** pass through the centre, it is known as a small circle.

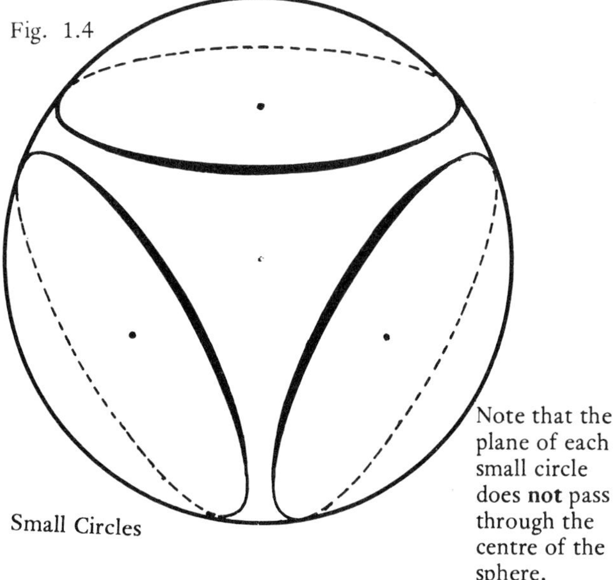

The Equator

The equator is the circle which divides the earth in half horizontally. It is a great circle and it is sometimes defined as the zero circle of latitude, which is to say that any position on it has 0° of latitude. Throughout its circumference it is exactly 90° of arc from the poles.

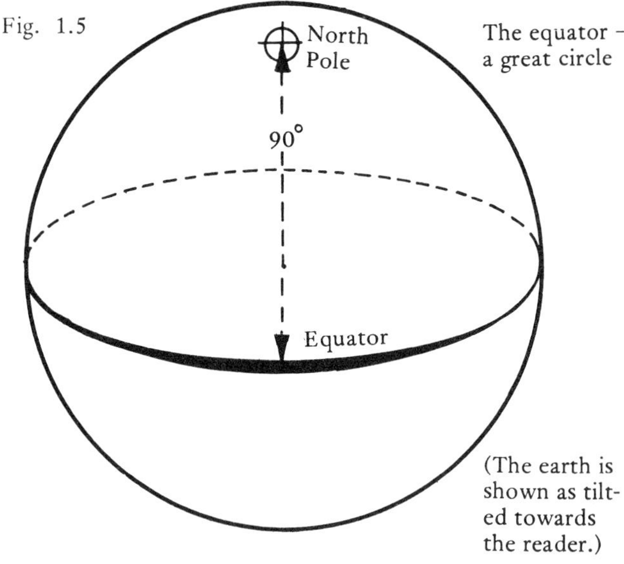

A Parallel of Latitude.

A parallel of latitude is a small circle drawn on the earth, equidistant from the equator throughout its circumference. All places on such a circle will have the same 'latitude'. For convenience and to assist the eye, parallels of latitude are usually drawn on a globe to represent latitude at precise intervals both north and south of the equator. They are drawn horizontally across the chart at convenient points. It will be appreciated later that the latter are of considerable assistance to the navigator.

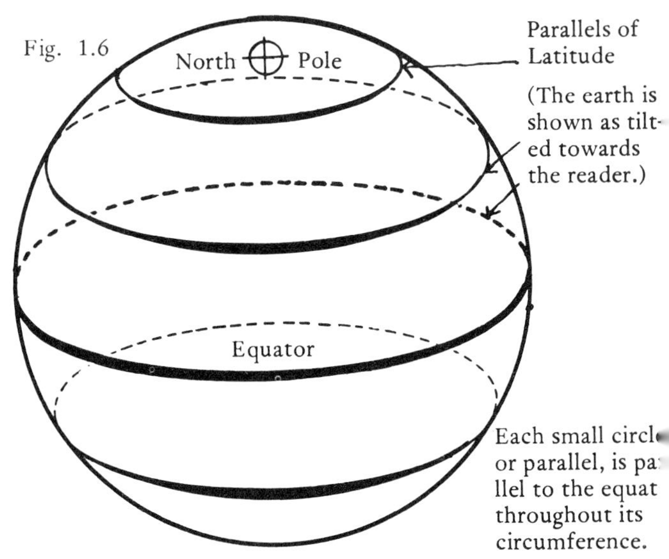

Latitude

Why do we need to bother about a precise definition of latitude? Or indeed of longitude? The reason is simply this: if we understand the definition we are half-way to one sure method of noting position at sea. When at sea, we accept that latitude and longitude combined will fulfil our needs when wishing to define position, and with great precision if need be.

So let us simplify this definition, and as we proceed the word 'latitude' will become more meaningful. For ease of definition we will call it the 'vertical measurement'; it defines the angular measurement of a place from the equator either northwards or southwards. Precisely defined, it is the angular measurement, measured up or down a meridian (which is to say, vertically on the globe), of a parallel of latitude, either north or south of the equator.

Fig. 1.7

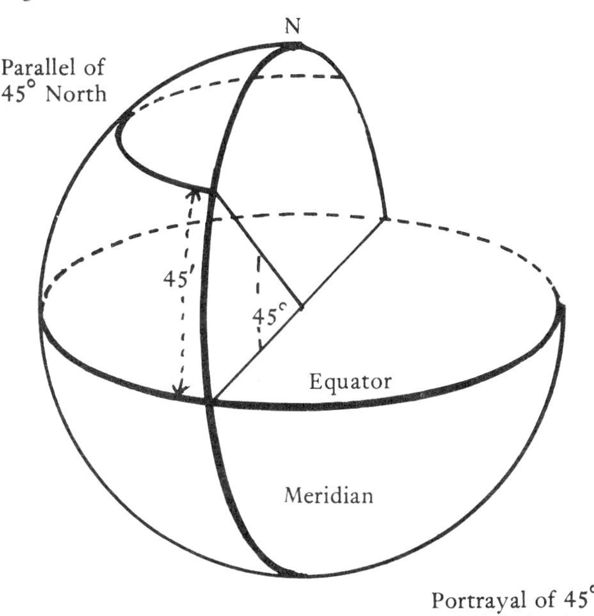

Portrayal of 45° North latitude

What does all this mean? Simply this: the latitude or vertical measurement of a place may be found by drawing a small circle on the globe, ensuring that it passes through the place in question and is parallel to the equator. If it were feasible, a line might then be drawn from the centre of the earth outwards to the equator. Vertically over the first line another line may be drawn from the centre of the earth to the small circle already drawn, which is a parallel of latitude. The angle at the earth's centre subtended by these two lines will be the latitude required.

In practice it is merely a matter of reading the latitude from the vertical margins on the appropriate chart, because latitude scales are printed on them.

Latitude is measured from the equator in degrees, minutes and seconds. The suffix: north, or south, is added to define whether the latitude is north or south of the equator.

Meridians

Meridians are great circles which pass through the poles. They are the vertical lines on a globe of the earth, and indeed those shown on charts. Note on a globe how they all converge on the poles and how each is perpendicular to the equator. It is convenient in navigation to regard, and to draw, them as 'half' great circles, drawn to the poles on the side of the earth on which one is navigating, but not beyond.

Fig. 1.8

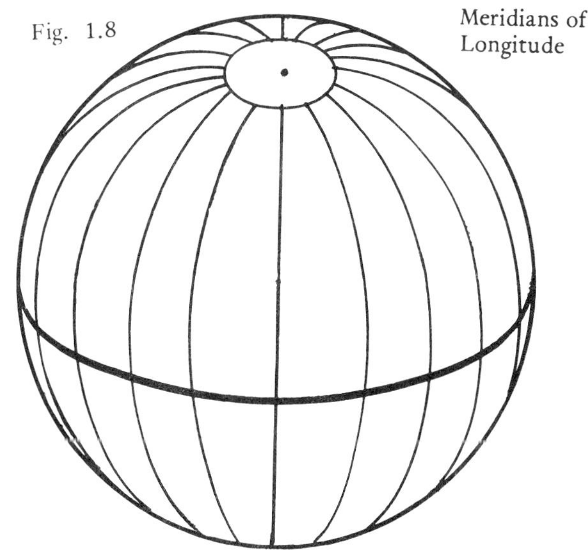

Meridians of Longitude

Longitude

The definition of latitude must of course be followed by that of longitude because the combination of these two co-ordinates gives us our precise position on the chart.

Longitude is the horizontal measurement used to define position. The words latitude and longitude are so similar in sound that at first glance it may be thought they have similar definitions. Well - nearly, but not quite. The poles provide us with the means of defining latitude; we define the equator exactly half way between them and measure from that. The earth provides no similarly convenient datum from which we can measure longitude.

Much of the early research into astronomical and navigational problems was carried out in the old observatory at Greenwich. It was perhaps natural for the scientists of that day to decide that, if only for their own convenience, longitude should be measured from the meridian which passed through their observatory. No one has yet seen fit to change this system.

Longitude, using the definition of text books, is the angular distance east or west of the prime (Greenwich) meridian, measured along the equator to the meridian passing through the position whose longitude it is desired to define. It is also correct to say that it is the angle at the centre of the earth produced between a line drawn outwards to the equator at the Greenwich meridian and another outwards to the equator at the meridian which passes through the position needed.

Fig. 1.9

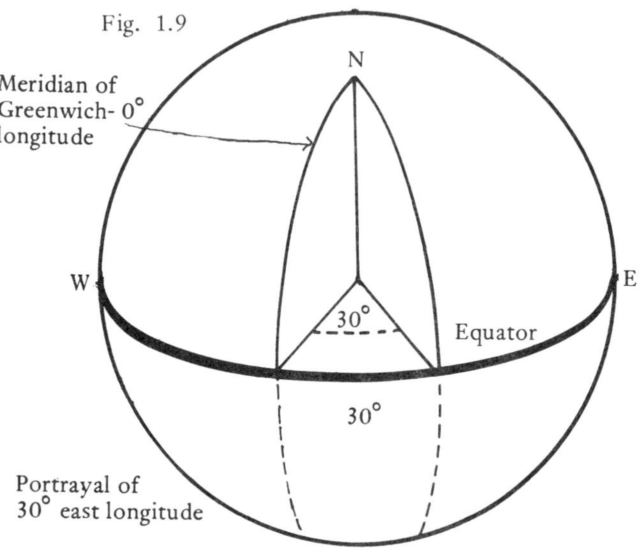

These austere definitions may be meaningful to some. No doubt the 'some' will be in the minority, so here is an explanation. Described simply, if it is desired to find the longitude of a place on the globe, one commences by drawing two half-great circles on it; they must be drawn as meridians. One must pass through the Greenwich Observatory and the other through the position whose longitude is needed. Measuring outwards from the centre of the globe to the equator, if lines are then drawn to each of the meridians, an angle is produced. This angle at the centre of the earth is the longitude needed.

Longitude is measured from 0° (at Greenwich) to 180° eastwards, and from 0° to 180° westwards. Longitude which is measured eastwards is called east: if it is measured westwards, west. East and west longitude meet on the meridian which is precisely opposite that of Greenwich. It is the well known Date Line.

Here again, in practice, one does not need to attempt such a tortuous undertaking as that described above. Nevertheless, the definition is necessary so that it is precisely understood what is meant by the word: longitude. In practice it is merely a matter of reading the longitude from the horizontal margins on the appropriate chart, where longitude scales are always printed.

The Nautical, or Sea, Mile.

Distance at sea is related to our other means of measurement; angular measure. On land we may decide to measure in miles, or kilometres, or even ells and, provided everyone knows the standard unit of measurement adopted, it is of little real consequence which unit is chosen. This is not good enough for use at sea. Linear measurement has to be meaningful to the navigator, and capable of being related to angular measurement — and it is.

The nautical mile is defined, again austerely, as the length of an arc on the earth's surface produced by an angle of one minute at the centre of curvature, which is the centre of the earth. If, then, one could draw an angle of one minute at the centre of the earth and extend this angle in any direction to the earth's surface, the distance between the two points thus produced would be one nautical mile.

This is not accurate enough for navigational purposes. We know that the earth is flattened slightly at the poles and so it is not a perfect sphere. Consequently, if we accept this definition, the length of a nautical mile would be a little longer at the poles than it would be at the equator. This fact is realised and, to overcome it, an average between the two is taken, so that navigators may be spared complicated computations. The nautical mile is accepted internationally as being one of 6,076 ft. (1.852 metres).

It is desirable to ponder on the following statement: the 'angle of one minute at the centre of curvature' may be produced on a scale of latitude. It is the difference, shall we say, between latitude 55° 12′ 0″ N., and 55° 13′ 0″ N., the difference between these two latitudes being one minute of arc. Further, it must be applicable on latitude scales for any place on earth. This very useful fact means that in practice the nautical mile may be taken to be the distance on the earth's surface represented by one minute of latitude, but **not** longitude. Latitude scales being printed on navigational charts, the navigator has a ready made scale of measurement.

Nautical measurements, all of which are related to the nautical mile, are given below. They should be memorised so that they are as familiar as yards, feet and inches.

6 feet	=	1 fathom
100 fathoms	=	1 cable
10 cables	=	one nautical mile
1 Int. naut. mile	=	6,076 feet.
1 knot	=	a unit of velocity equal to one nautical mile per hour

From the last definition, it should be noted how wrong it is to use the expression 'knots per hour'.

Why Longitude Scales cannot be used for Measuring Distance. (Figs. 1.10(a) and 1.10(b)).

Why, it is sometimes asked, can we not use the longitude scales on charts for measuring distances? Latitude and longitude scales on charts have more or less the same appearance; are they not the same?

To seek the answer we must return to a previous definition: a nautical mile is the length of an arc on the earth's surface which is subtended by an angle of one minute at the centre of the earth. We can produce this arc of one minute at any place on the surface of the earth, vertically, obliquely or horizontally and, for all practical purposes, the result will be the same: one nautical mile.

Let us produce this arc on the equator, both vertically and horizontally.[Fig.1.10(a)] Vertically on the latitude scale it will be identical to one minute of latitude. Horizontally on the longitude scale it will be equal to one minute of longitude. So far, so good, but if we move away from the equator, either northwards or southwards, disconcerting things commence to happen.

All the way to the poles, the length of one minute of latitude will remain the same - one nautical mile. The parallels of latitude on the globe give visual proof of this. All are equidistant from each other.

The meridians of longitude behave very differently. They converge as the poles are approached. Inevitably the linear distance between them decreases as they converge. They fulfil the requirements of angular measure but, away from the equator, it can no longer be said that one minute of **longitude** is equal to one nautical mile. In fact, the actual length of a minute of longitude has been reduced from one nautical mile at the equator to a **half** a nautical mile in latitude 60°N. [Fig.1.10(b)].

Here then is the reason: On the longitude scale at any point on earth, except the equator, one minute of longitude is **not** equal to one nautical mile.

Fig. 1.10(a)

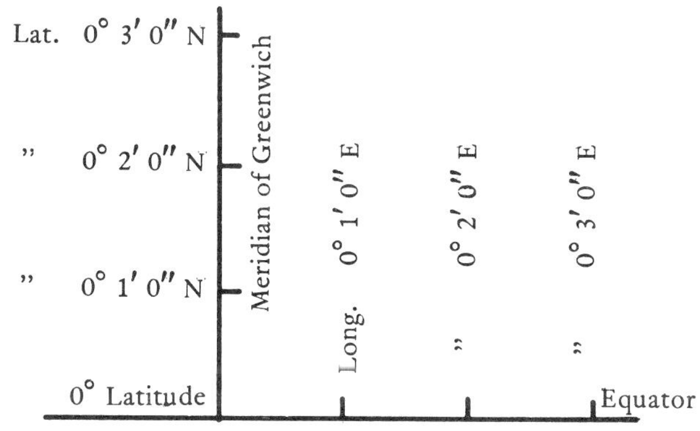

Fig. 1.10(b)

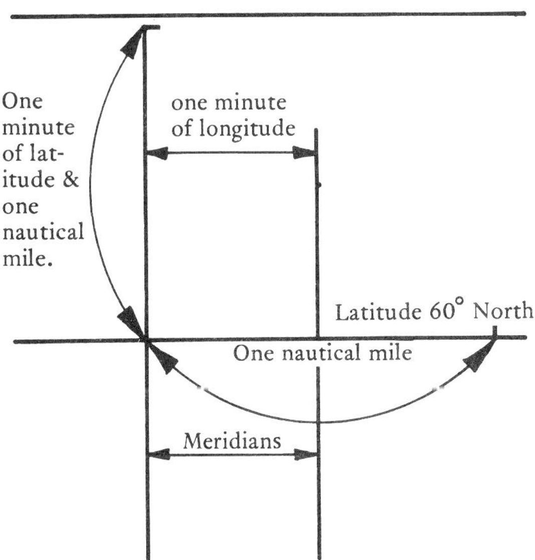

CHAPTER 2

Charts and Navigational Publications

There is a trite old saying: a little learning is a dangerous thing. It contains a great deal of truth. Insufficient knowledge of how to 'read' charts can easily lead one into trouble at sea. The intention in this chapter is not to baffle the reader with science, but only to make him so familiar with charts that he will be able to read one as easily as he does his daily paper.

Let us start at the beginning. If one pauses to think about the matter, it will be appreciated that it is not possible to project the earth's surface, which is round, on a flat surface such as a chart without some distortion occurring. Hydrographers, the people who make charts, have various means by which they can overcome this problem. Of these a system called Mercator Projection has the greatest number of advantages to mariners, and consequently it is the most widely used. The advantages are complex and subtle. Let us accept that they are real, and leave things at that.

The principles upon which a Mercator chart is based are interesting. To understand them it is helpful to imagine a cylinder of paper wrapped round a globe, so that the paper is touching the globe at the equator. (Fig. 2.1). Now let us imagine that the meridians are detached from the globe, bent backwards and transferred to the inner side of the paper tube. The meridians will now appear as vertical parallel lines. Only at the equator will their distance apart be a true representation of the distance which separated the meridians on the globe.

We must further tax our imagination: let us detach the paper from the globe and lay it flat. Now we will draw a line across it to represent the equator.

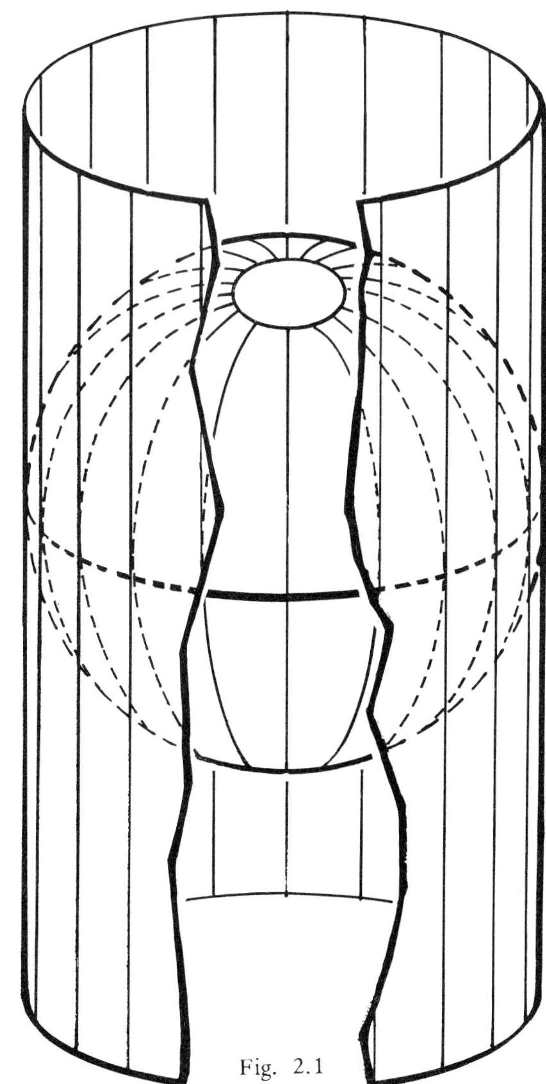

Fig. 2.1

Of one thing we are certain: that portion of our chart which touched the globe at the equator is a true representation of the earth's surface. The remainder is not. Further, as we move away from the equator either up or down our 'chart' - that is, if latitude is increased either northwards or southwards - distortion or misrepresentation, in an east-west direction must increasingly occur. Here we must note one important point: at and in the vicinity of the poles, where all meridians meet on the globe, it will be impossible to portray them using Mercator Projection. The scale would reach infinity. Polar navigators must and do use charts based upon another method of projection.

To overcome the deliberate distortion, which is brought about by portraying the meridians as vertical parallel lines, when we know that in fact they are not, a simple device is used. The **length** of each degree of latitude is progressively increased, commencing at the equator and continuing into the very high latitudes. The **amount** by which they are increased in length is directly proportionate to the amount by which the meridians have been expanded. Putting it another way, as the meridians are opened out horizontally, so is our 'chart' stretched vertically. Fig.2.2 is an example of what is done.

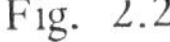

Fig. 2.2

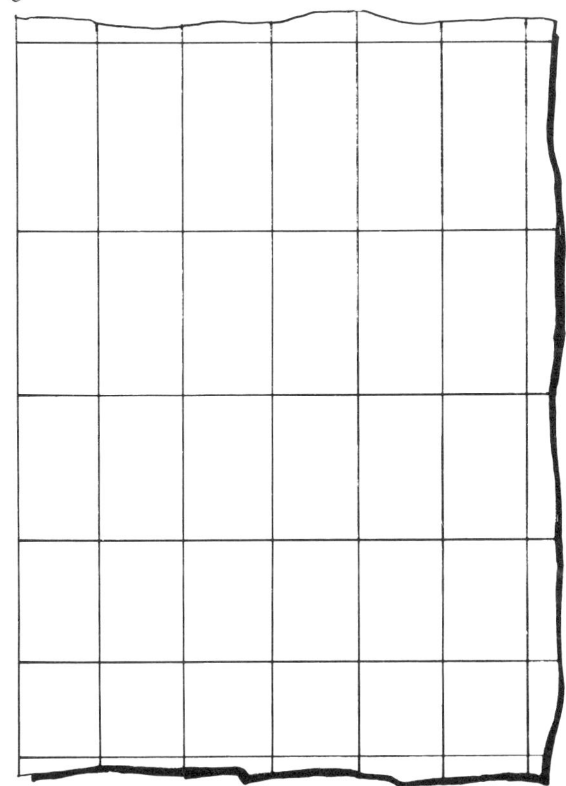

Proportion has been preserved. The chart can now be used on a flat surface. Areas some distance away from the equator will appear larger than they do on the globe. No matter: we can navigate on it. Land masses too in the greater, or higher, latitudes will appear to be much larger than the true scale representation on the globe. Again: no matter. Their portrayal will be faithfully in proportion to the sections of the chart in which they appear

For all practical purposes we shall work on charts based upon Mercator Projection, whoever the publisher may be. There will be exceptions to this but, unless quite a lot is known about charts already, it will not be apparent and it is not desirable to clutter the mind with material which can be at best merely of academic interest.

The reader may consider the foregoing explanation superfluous to his needs; one of greater interest to professionals than to amateurs. This is not strictly true and an anecdote may prove the point. The author once served under a senior naval officer who, whenever he was asked a question of a task in hand, invariably barked: I don't care how you do it - DO IT! A great deal used to be achieved by his junior officers: they learned fast, the hard way. It is true to say that without some spur to make a man undertake research into a subject, he will accept a limited number of bare facts. Beyond a certain point, presumption by an author may well be resented. No book can provide a built-in spur, so the author must anticipate his readers' questions and answer them where possible. Those who are eager to get to grips with practical chartwork should not regard the explanation of the Mercator Projection as unwanted ballast; it may well preclude some of the questions which spring to mind when working on charts.

Chart Scales

If a man intends to go walking in the New Forest he will choose a large scale map which shows streams, footpaths, rides and a profusion of detail which, read carefully, will give him a mind-picture of his projected outing before he starts. On the other hand, if he has to motor from Lancashire to Norfolk he will select a road map having a much smaller scale. Detail will necessarily be confined to that which is important to him, because the area it covers will be large.

So it is with charts. They vary in scale very widely, always with the particular needs of navigators in mind. For convenience, seamen divide them into three groups: large scale, small scale and 'plan' charts. The latter are plans of ports.

Large scale charts are used for sailing coastwise and for entering ports. They show relatively small areas in considerable detail. Obviously the amount of detail included which may be of value to the navigator will vary directly as the scale of the chart.

Small scale charts generally depict large areas of ocean, or coastline, or both. Only important detail can be shown on them. Their value is real to the navigator who is proceeding for a considerable distance. They permit him to plan his route, often from departure point to destination. For instance, in planning a voyage from Rye to Ushant, a small scale chart of the English Channel would prove most useful. These charts are also used for deep sea navigation where large scale charts would be quite unnecessary.

Charts for yachtsmen

It is probably true to say that, in the waters encompassed by this volume, most small boat sailors use the two brands of charts discussed below. First, we have the Admiralty series published by the Hydrographic Office whose excellence cannot be exceeded. Secondly, in those areas for which Stanford charts are published, the Stanford range. There are others available and they too are of high quality but for the benefit of yachtsmen it will suffice here to discuss the peculiar qualities of these two brands. Arguments have always ranged back and forth about what charts are most suitable for off-shore work but this is entirely a matter of individual preference.

New style Admiralty charts and the metric system.

Although it will be some years before all home waters are covered by the new metric charts, surveying and subsequent publication of new charts is well under way.

To obtain full details of the new metric symbols and colouring used on the new chart, all yachtsmen should purchase the book titled 'Symbols and Abbreviations' used on Admiralty Charts which is obtainable from all Admiralty Chart stockists.

The title of a chart is placed in an area which is not needed for navigation.

The number of a chart, which can be related to chart indices, is always given. On Admiralty charts it is printed in bold type in the top left and bottom right margins. On Stanford charts it is printed on the outer face when folded.

The number of a chart, together with the title, must always be quoted when ordering.

Fig. 2.4

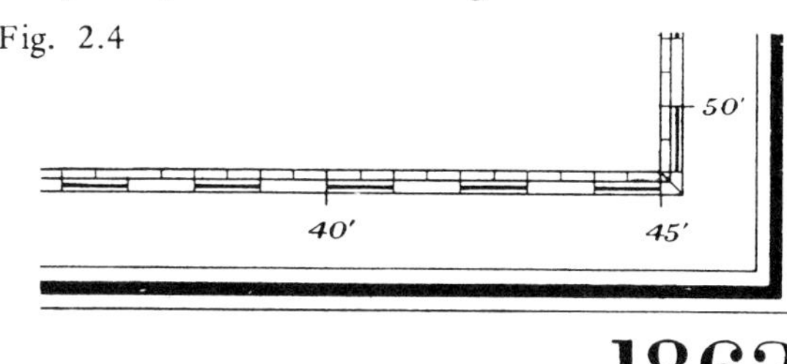

Terrestrial information is minimal. It is confined to those features on land which may be of value to the navigator.

Latitude scales are printed on the left and right margins of the chart. It may be permissible for chartmakers to divide one minute of latitude into 2, 5, 6 or even 10 divisions. On certain charts the scale may be so small that it is impractical to print scales even in divisions of one minute. Readability has to be constantly borne in mind. Thus in the latter case divisions may represent 5 or even 10 minutes of latitude but the reader may rest assured that, what ever graduations are used, the mariner is never left in doubt by the publisher.

Fig. 2.3.

Fig. 2.5

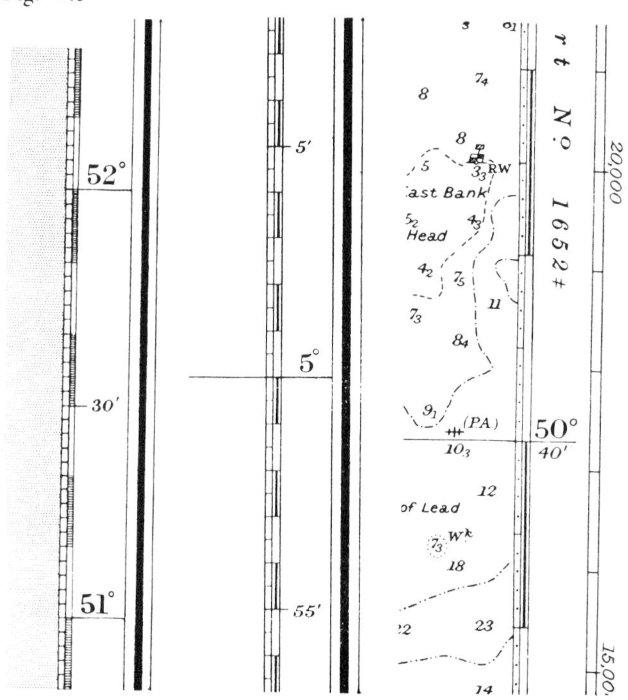

It has already been explained that the latitude scales on a chart provide the means of measurement, one minute of latitude on a Mercator chart being equal to one nautical mile. These scales, therefore, can be regarded as immovable rulers which are always ready to hand.

While retaining the same basic principles, Stanford charts approach the problems of measurement in a slightly different manner. The scales will be found to have one minute of latitude as their minimum divisions. A separate horizontal scale of latitude and distance is printed within the body of the chart, both nautical miles and cables being produced in it. When using a Stanford chart this is the scale to which measurement should be referred.

Fig. 2.6

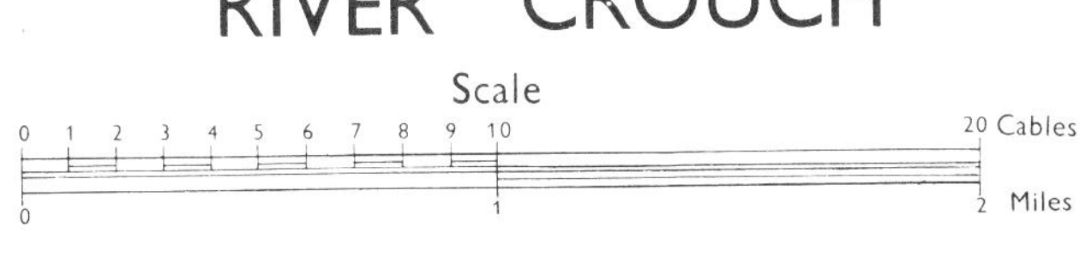

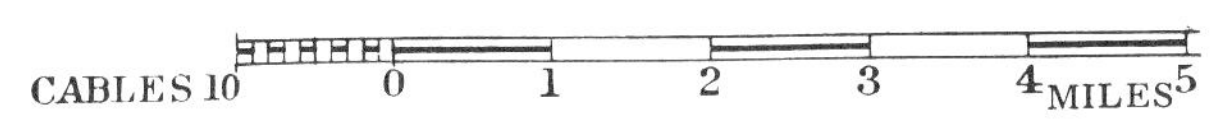

There is of course no reason why the navigator should **not** use the latitude scales in the margins for measuring distance on a Stanford chart. It becomes necessary to estimate by eye distances under one mile but this in no way invalidates its use in practical chartwork.

Longitude scales are printed on the upper and lower margins of the chart. It will be found that, what ever system of divisions is used on the latitude scale, the same system will be adopted in the longitude scale.

Parallels of latitude and meridians of longitude are produced as horizontal and vertical lines across the whole area of chart. On large scale charts, such as are mainly used by yachtsmen, they appear as a very open form of latticework. They can be produced at any latitude, or at any longitude, but in fact are drawn in a manner which it is considered will prove most helpful to navigators. As will be appreciated in a later chapter, they will be found most useful in practical chartwork.

Soundings, or the depth of the sea at any point, are given by printing the appropriate depth in number form at numerous positions on the area of sea. (See Fig.2.7). It may be taken that where a depth is given, a survey vessel has taken a sounding at that point. Where none is shown it means that, while no sounding has been taken for survey purposes, it is reasonable to assume that surrounding soundings give a fair indication of the depth of water to be expected.

All charts without exception state clearly beneath their titles whether the recorded soundings are given in fathoms or feet. On opening any chart this is one of the first things which must be determined. Woebetide the man who, sailing in relative shallow waters, mistakes soundings for fathoms when they are in fact feet.

The style of Stanford Charts being slightly different from that of Admiralty charts, in that wide use is made of insets - chartlets of ports printed within the body of the chart - a slight variation occurs. Although of course the system of recording soundings is identical to that defined above, it will be found that on the main body of the chart soundings are given in fathoms and on the insets they are given in feet. As metrication is gradually introduced there will be no difference between them. The yachtsman is left in no doubt whatsoever regarding the quantitative value of the soundings he may be using.

Fathom lines, or depth contours, indicate those areas of sea which have equal depth and have the very considerable value of drawing to the attention of the navigator areas which he may wish to avoid. They preclude the necessity of his meticulously scanning every sounding on the chart.

Fig. 2.7

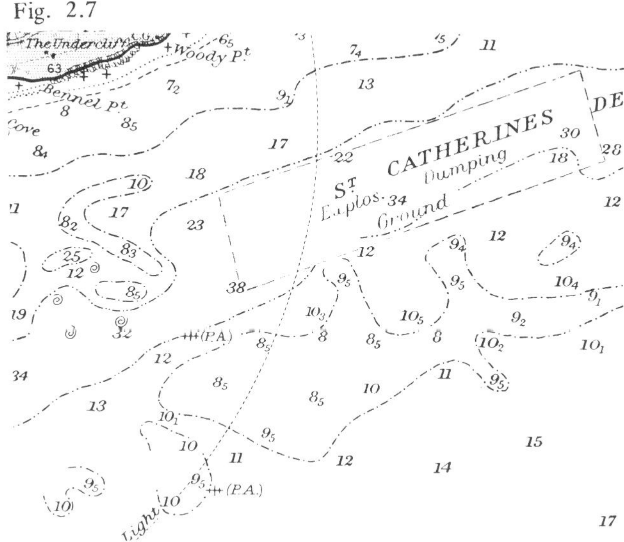

When printing Admiralty charts the Hydrographic Office must consider the needs of all shipping, from small craft to the present day monster merchant ships, and so considerable use of fathom lines is made. Stanfords do not print fathom lines above that required for the 5 fathom contour. As these charts are produced for yachtsmen there is common sense in this. After all, how many of us wish to anchor in depths of 5 fathoms or more, or are worried so long as we have 30 feet plus beneath our keels?

Compass Roses, words used by seamen to define the mariners' compasses which are printed in convenient positions on charts, provide one of the means by which direction can be obtained. The compass rose illustrated in Fig. 2.8 has an outer 'true direction' rose and an inner 'magnetic direction' rose, a common and useful style widely used by the Hydrographic Office. On some charts, the true ring only is shown with an arrow radiating out from the centre to the point of magnetic variation. Their use is fully described in Chapter 5.

Fig. 2.8

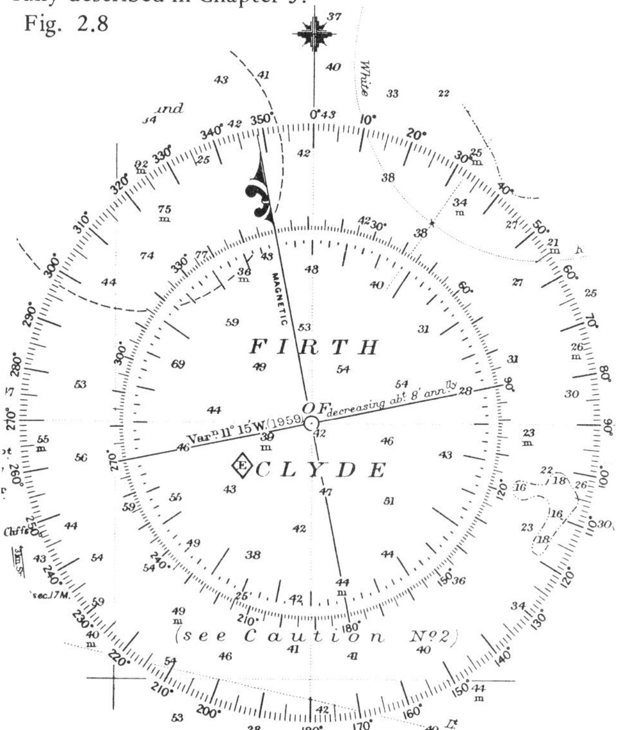

Only magnetic compass roses are printed on Stanford charts, a policy which is quite deliberate since these charts are used almost exclusively by yachtsmen. Yachtsmen, almost without exception, use the magnetic rose only, as the system meets their specific needs.

Lighthouses, lightvessels and buoys all have their distinctive symbols on charts. The navigator's eye is drawn to them by the use of colour over-printing in all cases.

On an Admiralty chart a lighthouse is shown as a black star with a magenta overprint: on a Stanford chart it is indicated by a black dot with a red overprint. Each system has equal merit.

Lightvessels are always printed as tiny drawings of these vessels, buoys are produced using a similar device. For both lightvessels and lightbuoys the Hydrographic Office use magenta overprinting, where Stanfords use yellow overprinting for white lights and red overprinting for red lights.

The actual position of a lightvessel or buoy is indicated in most cases by a tiny circle on the waterline of the sketch of a lightvessel or buoy. It must be remembered that, when navigating, it is from these tiny circles one must calculate and not from the centre of the symbols themselves.

Radiobeacons, wherever they may be located, always have a red circle round them. Usually the words 'radio beacon' are spelt out in full alongside them, or the abbreviation 'Ro. Bn.' will be found.

Tidal information printed on any chart varies according to the publisher. Admiralty charts are supported by a number of Hydrographic Office publications which are indisputably the most authoritative in this country, therefore beyond certain information which relates to the direction and rate of tidal streams, information is minimal.

In certain sea areas directional arrows are shown to indicate the average direction of the flood and ebb streams. Printed against them information about spring and neap rates may be found. In addition to these, on most Admiralty charts of British coastal waters there are tables which give more comprehensive information. Lettered symbols printed at certain selected points on the chart may be related to these tables and from them the direction and rate of tidal streams throughout the whole tidal cycle may be extracted. Full information on the use of this system will be found in Chapter 4.

Fig. 2.9

Tidal Streams referred to H.W. at GREENOCK

Hours	A 55°48'9N. 4°58'1W. L.63			B 55°43'0N. 4°55'5W. L.55			C 55°45'0N. 5°13'3W. L.63			D 55°39'9N. 5°25'2W. L.62			E 55°32'9N. 4°56'7W. L.61		
	Dirⁿ	Rate (kn) Sp.	Np.	Dirⁿ	Rate (kn) Sp.	Np.	Dirⁿ	Rate (kn) Sp.	Np.	Dirⁿ	Rate (kn) Sp.	Np.	Dirⁿ	Rate (kn) Sp.	Np.
Before HW Greenock 6	000°	0·1	0·1	233°	0·1	0·1	Tidal Streams are weak and irregular			040°	0·3	0·2	048°	0·3	0·2
5	027°	0·2	0·1	343°	0·2	0·1				030°	0·3	0·2	059°	0·3	0·2
4	054°	0·2	0·1	027°	0·2	0·1				017°	0·3	0·2	055°	0·2	0·1
3	030°	0·2	0·1	027°	0·4	0·2				330°	0·3	0·2	083°	0·2	0·1
2	024°	0·1	0·1	023°	0·4	0·3				297°	0·3	0·2	106°	0·3	0·2
1	120°	0·1	0·1	017°	0·4	0·2				243°	0·3	0·2	Slack		
H.W.	139°	0·1	0·1	009°	0·3	0·2				225°	0·4	0·3	215°	0·3	0·2
After H.W. Greenock 1	257°	0·1	0·1	Slack						215°	0·5	0·3	253°	0·3	0·2
2	279°	0·2	0·1	193°	0·3	0·2				205°	0·4	0·3	277°	0·2	0·1
3	217°	0·2	0·1	198°	0·3	0·2				194°	0·3	0·2	238°	0·3	0·2
4	265°	0·4	0·2	196°	0·5	0·3				121°	0·1	0·1	246°	0·2	0·1
5	272°	0·2	0·1	196°	0·7	0·4				062°	0·2	0·1	Slack		
6	Slack			204°	0·2	0·1				044°	0·3	0·2	064°	0·2	0·1

Hours	F 55°43'5N. 4°59'1W. L.57			G 55°24'8N. 5°24'2W. L.60			H 55°00'31N. 5°03'79W. L.67			I 55°21'2N. 5°00'6W. L.59			J 55°15'1N. 5°37'2W. L.56		
	Dirⁿ	Rate (kn) Sp.	Np.	Dirⁿ	Rate (kn) Sp.	Np.	Dirⁿ	Rate (kn) Sp.	Np.	Dirⁿ	Rate (kn) Sp.	Np.	Dirⁿ	Rate (kn) Sp.	Np.
Before HW Greenock 6	072°	0·3	0·2	343°	0·5	0·3	135°	0·6	0·4	231°	0·1	0·0	095°	2·5	1·5
5	046°	0·6	0·4	359°	0·6	0·3	148°	0·6	0·4	353°	0·1	0·1	093°	3·2	2·0
4	026°	0·7	0·4	003°	0·5	0·3	163°	0·8	0·5	005°	0·3	0·2	091°	3·3	2·0
3	044°	0·6	0·4	010°	0·4	0·3	156°	0·8	0·5	354°	0·3	0·2	088°	2·5	1·6
2	037°	0·4	0·3	032°	0·3	0·2	167°	0·6	0·4	354°	0·4	0·3	076°	0·5	0·3
1	016°	0·3	0·2	094°	0·2	0·1	180°	0·3	0·2	005°	0·4	0·3	282°	1·0	0·6
H.W.	018°	0·2	0·1	157°	0·2	0·1	289°	0·3	0·2	066°	0·3	0·2	276°	2·1	1·3
After H.W. Greenock 1	257°	0·4	0·3	175°	0·4	0·3	313°	0·6	0·4	109°	0·4	0·3	273°	3·0	1·9
2	235°	0·9	0·5	183°	0·6	0·4	336°	1·0	0·6	136°	0·6	0·4	270°	3·3	2·0
3	215°	0·9	0·6	192°	0·6	0·4	343°	1·1	0·7	217°	0·4	0·2	268°	2·4	1·5
4	209°	0·8	0·5	201°	0·4	0·3	345°	0·8	0·5	231°	0·5	0·3	262°	1·3	0·8
5	152°	0·4	0·2	228°	0·1	0·1	028°	0·3	0·2	233°	0·4	0·2	118°	0·5	0·3
6	085°	0·2	0·1	339°	0·4	0·2	126°	0·5	0·3	225°	0·2	0·1	097°	1·8	1·1

Stanford charts being largely self-supporting, a greater amount of tidal information will be found on them. A table of 'tidal constants' is produced which is related to all ports used by yachtsmen in the area encompassed by the chart. By relating these constants to the Dover high water predictions (see chapter 4), high water at any of the listed ports may be readily obtained.

Stanford tidal stream information is given in twelve chartlets, each one being of the chart itself, all of which are grouped together within the body of the chart. Again based upon Dover predictions, on them will be found the direction and rate of tidal streams for each hour of the tidal cycle over the whole body of the chart.

Areas which dry out at low water, always of particular interest to yachtsmen, are produced in styles which necessitate familiarising oneself with the range of chart abbreviations if misreading is not to occur.

Beaches which are alternately covered and uncovered by tidal waters are indicated by black speckles, and soundings will be indicated in the following manner:—

Fig. 2.10

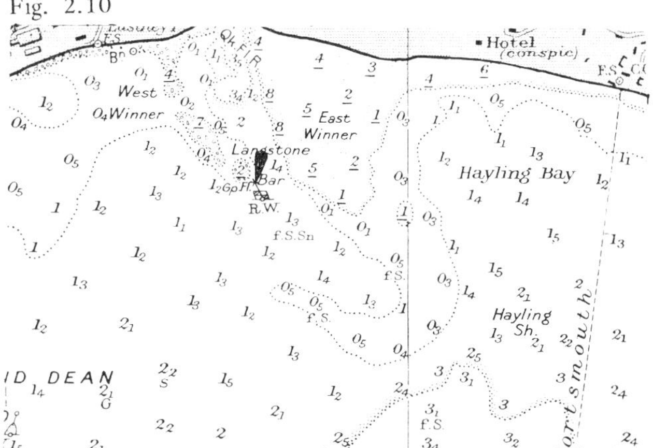

The bar beneath a sounding indicates that the area will dry out at Chart Datum to the height indicated.

The nature of foreshores varying widely and the styles of producing these variations having of necessity to indicate each one, the yachtsman should familiarise himself with them.

Fig. 2.11 **The Coastline**

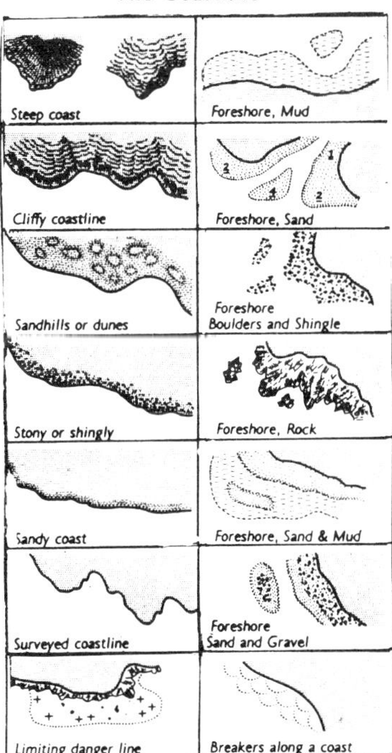

N.B. The above was extracted from Kandy publication Coastal Navigation — Notes for yachtsmen, by Watkins.

General chart abbreviations. If charts are not to be cluttered with information spelt out at length, a code of abbreviations is essential. In a great number of cases the abbreviations are self evident. The complete range is published on Admiralty Chart No. 5011 and a working knowledge of them removes unnecessary anxiety.

Use of colour wash. The most remarkable feature of a Stanford chart is the almost flamboyant use of colour wash, a system which is quite deliberate. We, whose time for leisurely poring over charts is usually limited to periods in harbour, may gain reassurance at sea from the striking use of colour coding. If, for instance, our position is in a bright blue area on the chart we know without further need for affirmation that we have no worries about depth of water under our keels.

Insets. On all Stanford charts insets are widely used. They portray, in large scale, ports which come within the orbit of the chart on which they are printed. They will be found to be adequate for a yachtsman's needs when entering and leaving port, although no pretence is made to emulate the comprehensive style to be found in Admiralty plan charts.

Tracks on Stanford Charts. Those tracks which from time to time will probably be needed by yachtsmen to sail from one place to another are printed as red lines, together with their courses. These tracks are recommended routes drawn up by experienced seamen and the yachtsman would be well advised to use them when the occasion arises.

Sailing Directions on Stanford Charts. Brief sailing directions are produced for those ports encompassed by the chart. These directions supplement that information which may be 'read' from the insets to which they refer. When a yacht has left her mooring she is 'committed' and, until the open sea is reached, there is no time to study peculiarities of restricted waters. In these sailing directions are essential features which a yachtsman can, and should, commit to memory before sailing.

Sundry Information on Stanford Charts. Summarised information is given regarding the systems of buoyage which a yachtsman may encounter, together with tables which from time to time are needed. Necessarily abbreviated due to the limitations of space available on the reverse side of the charts this sundry information is nevertheless valuable because it must necessarily include important information and exclude that of secondary importance.

Correction of Charts. It will readily be appreciated that features in the navigational world change. As examples, a buoy may be moved to a new position; a survey may indicate soundings different from those shown on charts; the characteristic light of a lighthouse may be changed; a vessel may sink in shallow water and become a hazard to shipping; and so on. For his own safety, and at the very least to avoid being confounded from time to time, the prudent mariner keeps himself up to date with such change. A chart is only a **guide** to safe navigation.

Notices to mariners. The Hydrographic Dept. of the Ministry of Defence is the British authority which publishes changes such as those outlined, as they are announced. As it becomes available, the information is collated, printed and issued weekly as Admiralty Notices to Mariners. Numbered from 1 to 52 for each week of the year, they are paper booklets. In them will be found complete details of all corrections which should be made to Admiralty and, of course, other charts, and to Admiralty publications. No. 1 in each year contains all corrections published to date and so, besides being a thick booklet, it is also a valuable one.

Within these weekly editions, Notices to Mariners are numbered. They indicate the number of the correction for the year in question. Notices which are of a temporary nature are given the suffix (T) after the notice number. Those of a preliminary nature, giving mariners advance notice of changes which will shortly be made, carry the suffix (P).

Notices to Mariners are obtainable free on request from Admiralty chart depots and other similar agencies. Mercantile Marine offices also stock them as do British consulates abroad. The impression will be gained that they are fairly easy to obtain but it is unfortunate that a certain negative aspect must be introduced. Catering for their own known demand it may well be found that these agencies although prepared to help one, have expended their available stock, or they do not have the numbers one seeks. This apparent difficulty in obtaining Notices to Mariners may be a reason why many yachtsmen do not bother about them. Another is, and it must be said, ignorance of their very existence.

Certain private agencies will, on request, obtain and despatch Notices to Mariners, thereby obviating the difficulties outlined above.

Correction of charts by chart correcting agencies. Many yachtsmen have their charts corrected by professional chart correctors. This is a highly satisfactory method, **provided** thereafter the charts are kept up to date with corrections as they are announced. In a considerable number of cases this is not done and so it can occur that a chart may be out of date within a week or so of it being returned. Perhaps these yachtsmen consider that, administered shortly before the season starts, one jolly good dose of chart corrections will last them through until the next season. Put simply, it will not.

For the correction of Admiralty charts it will usually be found that main chart depots have their own chart correcting department. Many chart correcting establishments replace Admiralty charts with new ones if more than about six corrections are needed.

Having brought his charts up to date by this means a yachtsman should give serious thought to correcting his own charts.

Correction of charts by yachtsmen. As the years progress, more and more small boat sailors are becoming almost professional in their outlook. There are a number of indications of this and one is the fact that a number of them now correct their own charts. Keeping charts in good order and up to date appears to be becoming a matter of pride, and a realisation of its importance. Correcting charts is well within the ability of all and, as relatively few charts are carried, it is not excessively time-consuming for the busy man. Apart from the weekly Notices to Mariners he needs a mapping pen, violet waterproof ink, a parallel ruler and one or two geometry instruments. In return for very little time and financial outlay, he is given the assurance that, so far as it is possible to be, he is up to date with all changes in the navigational world which affect his charts. Such assurance cannot be dismissed lightly.

Taken from the Admiralty Notices to Mariners, Weekly Edition, No. 32 of 1967, there follows a typical chart correction.

> 1395 NORTH SEA – GERMANY – EAST FRISIAN ISLANDS – Ackumer Ee – Approach – wreck removed; light-buoy withdrawn. The dangerous wreck (53°49′30″N., 7°20′45″E. Approx.) and the Qk.Fl.G. light-buoy close W. are to be expunged.
> Charts (Last correction). – 3761, (1350/67) – 3347, (1175/67) – 1405, (1351/67).
>
> Hamburg Notice 2915/67.

It will be appreciated that if such a correction is not made to charts when it is announced, a mariner navigating in the area may be subjected to confusion and worry. Where is the buoy? Is my position in doubt? Is the wreck still there, although the buoy has been washed away?

As with all notices of this nature, the content is so complete that no yachtsman can fail to understand it, but certain features need explanation. The notice number is given first: 1395. Following the content of the notice, it will be seen that certain chart numbers are quoted. The chart numbers are those Admiralty charts which are affected by the notice.

It is important that corrections to charts are inserted neatly. Endeavour should be made to emulate the style and size of the printing already on the chart. Where a notice requires an addition to be made to a chart, abbreviations are detailed within the notice. Permanent corrections should be made in ink; temporary and preliminary corrections in pencil. A correction having been made, it must be carefully checked for accuracy. Chart corrections issued through Admiralty Notices to Mariners almost take one by the hand: detail is complete and, apart from knowledge of charts generally, previous experience is not necessary. It is so simple, so valuable and, with care, one cannot go wrong.

The correction having been made, the notice number must be inserted in the lower margin of the chart on the left hand side. Typically, the record of notices from which corrections to the chart have been made appear as in Fig. 2.12 opposite.

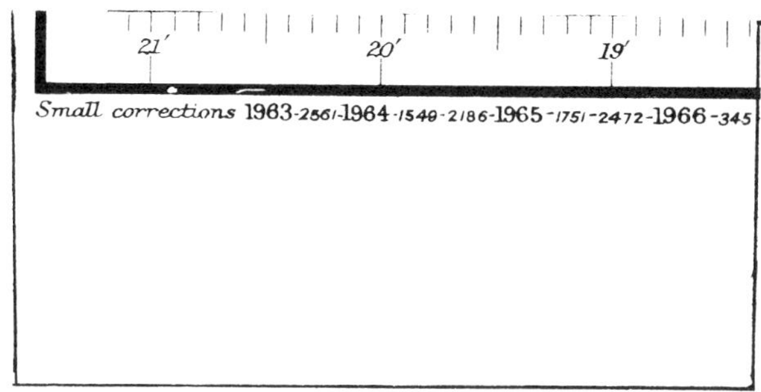

Fig. 2.12.

Referring again to the quoted notice, the bracketed numbers following the chart numbers will have been noted. These indicate the last previous notice announced by the Hydrographic Office for the chart indicated. This is valuable information. By reference to the chart margin it gives an immediate check upon whether the chart has been corrected to date. The reference to the Hamburg notice indicates the source from which the Hydrographic Office obtained the information.

What, one may ask, should one do in the case of correction of Stanford charts? Naturally one cannot expect Stanford chart numbers to be quoted in a Hydrographic Office publication but in practice no problems arise. The area affected by any notice is given precisely and so no difficulty in determining which Stanford charts are affected occurs. In all other respects, what is applicable to Admiralty charts is equally applicable to Stanford charts.

Purchasing charts. Selecting wine in a restaurant, the average man does not wish to emulate the nonchalant, cork-sniffing sophisticate, but neither does he wish to put himself completely in the hands of the wine waiter. Undoubtedly, wine waiters, like chart stockists, genuinely desire to help him make a sound choice. It remains difficult for the diner to rid himself of the feeling that it is in the interest of the wine waiter to cause him to spend just a little more money than he had intended. The purchaser of charts, never having had to make selections in this field before, must undergo similar misgivings.

Fortunately vintage plays no part in the quality of charts and making a sound choice is fairly easy if one knows how to go about it. Costing £1 upwards each, one does not want to come away with an armful of charts when a dozen or less would have sufficed. All large chart stockists, whether Admiralty agents or chandlers, carry the 'key' for Stanford charts and the Catalogue of Admiralty Charts and other publications, Hydrographic Office reference number N.P.131. They will be produced on request and so, with the maximum limits of ones intended cruising area firmly in mind, choice becomes a fairly simple task.

The Stanford key is simple. The limits of these charts, with numbered references, are drawn on an outline of the shores of Great Britain and the continent. The titles of the chart numbers quoted are printed in an accompanying list.

The Admiralty publication is a large, thick, paper-backed book which is extremely comprehensive. Not unlike a world atlas in book form, the coastlines of the world are drawn in outline and the limits of Admiralty charts are shown on them. Each chart outline is given the chart number to which it refers. With this number one may then refer to a later section which, amongst other considerable detail, gives the title of the chart.

For the sea areas encompassed by this volume it is wise to first select the Stanford chart or charts which will meet requirements. For those who do not intend to voyage far, it could well be found that a single Stanford chart will meet their needs. Nevertheless it is common practice for yachtsmen to support these charts with a few from the Admiralty series, if only to give them a feeling of greater security at sea. In any event it is wise to scan the Admiralty series chart coverage for the appropriate sea area. It may then be considered that certain ones may prove valuable supplementation to those Stanford charts purchased. It is desirable to ask to see the charts which may be considered suitable. The variation in the scales of Admiralty charts is so extensive that, without actually scanning the charts, it is difficult to decide whether or not they may be of value.

Economic factors should never compel a person to buy fewer charts than he considers he needs. As a broad principle it is wiser to have too many charts of an area than too few but, if the guidance given here is followed, money will not be spent needlessly. Practice charts and those made of thin paper which are intended as cruising guides only should never be used for navigation.

Nautical Publications. It is always necessary to support one's chart outfit with certain publications. This volume containing considerable information, the question may be posed: which supplementary publication is it desirable to obtain? Some people collect books as others collect stamps but, here it will be considered which publications are highly desirable to carry in addition to this one, assuming one intends cruising coastwise. The accuracy and completeness of detail in publications produced by the Hydrographic Office cannot be exceeded by any other publisher and the purchase of the following should seriously be considered.

Admiralty Sailing Directions.

Some 75 volumes of the Admiralty Sailing Directions encompass the world. Typically, their titles are 'English Channel Pilot' and 'North Sea Pilot'. Each Pilot describes in considerable detail general information about the sea area, the coast and all ports encompassed by the volume. Additional information too extensive to summarise here is also included and there is a strong case for a yachtsman making space in his bookshelf for the volume appropriate to his cruising grounds.

The details of all volumes available will be found in the Admiralty Chart Catalogue to which previous reference has been made.

Admiralty List of Lights.

Thirteen volumes of the Admiralty List of Lights give in great detail information about every navigational light and sound fog signal in the world. British yachtsmen would be interested in Volume A, British Isles and North

Coast of France. No other publication gives the detail about lights and lighthouses which, in many situations at sea, it is important that the mariner has to hand. This remark similarly applies to sound fog signals.

Small light-buoys are not included, no doubt because there are far too many of them. Details regarding light-buoys must be obtained from the appropriate Stanford chart or the largest scale Admiralty chart. The 'Pilots' also make reference to them in cases where their mention is essential in giving sailing directions.

Admiralty Tidal Stream Atlases – Pocket Editions.

As a useful supplement to that information given on Stanford charts, the pocket editions of the Admiralty Tidal Stream Atlases may be considered. Their value is not only in their clarity, but in particular to the man who sails a considerable distance, or crosses to the continent. The hourly tidal stream pattern for a whole sea area may be seen at a glance. Details of these booklets will be found in chapter 3.

CHAPTER 3

Visual Navigational Aids and Air Fog Signals

Lighthouses

These may be tall and sited near sea level, like Wolf Rock lighthouse, or high on a cliff and relatively short, similar to the one on Lizard Head. The latter type usually have coastguard's cottages clustered round their base. Those around our coasts are usually constructed of stone or brick, but not necessarily so: steel latticework is a variation. Their colour is always such that, for recognition purposes, they are thrown into relief against their backgrounds when viewed from seaward. Those painted in single colours are commonly black, red or white. Alternatively they may be a combination of two distinctive colours in stripes or chequers.

The lanterns they support contain their characteristic light: characteristic in the sense that at night each lighthouse exhibits a light which cannot be confused with other lights in the area. Characteristic lights of lighthouses are exhibited from sunset to sunrise and, in some instances during the day in foggy weather. Some powerful lights show in addition, and from the same lanterns, a weak continuous light which is visible at relatively short range. This 'bonus' light can prove most useful when sailing close inshore. First, it tells that one is fairly close to it and secondly, needing a bearing urgently, one does not have to wait for the sometimes momentary appearance of the characteristic light. Certain important lighthouses exhibit fog detector lights which are used for the automatic detection of fog by day and night. One of these would appear to the observer at sea as a small, intense, bluish-white light sweeping back and forth below the level of the main light.

Fig. 3.1

Fig. 3.2

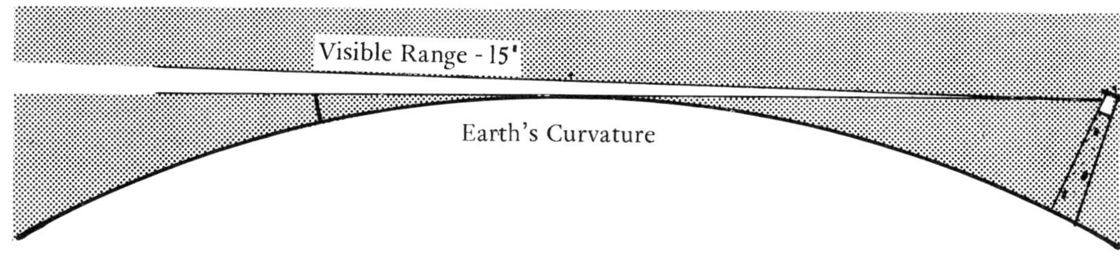

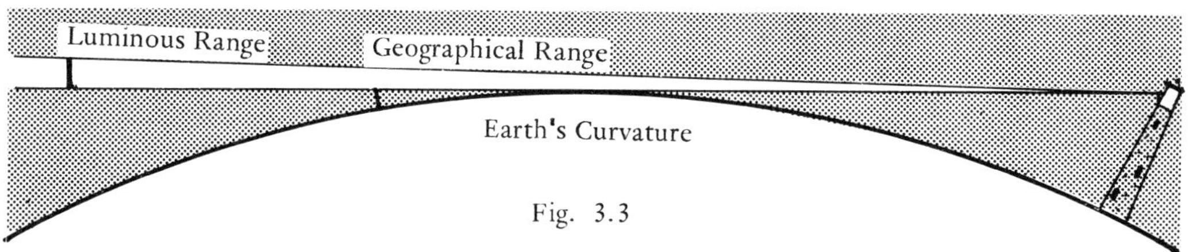

Fig. 3.3

The height of a lighthouse, which is invariably printed on Stanford charts and the largest scale Admiralty ones, is measured from the centre of the lantern to the average level of high water during spring tides. The height between low and high water being any quantity up to 35 feet around our shores, this fact can affect the maximum range at which a light will be seen. The extremely high level from which the height of a lighthouse is calculated introduces a safety factor. If the tide is **below** that level, and there is a considerable likelihood that it will be, when first sighting a light the mariner is led to believe that he is slightly closer to the light than, in fact, he is.

The range of a light, as published on charts, is the maximum range in nautical miles at which it will be seen on a dark, clear night. It assumes that the height of eye of the observer is 15 feet above sea level. This quaint anachronism goes back to the days of sail. It was then assumed that the average height of eye of an observer on the poop deck of a sailing vessel was 15 feet. If the observer's eye is higher than 15 feet, the visible range of a light will be increased: if it is lower, it will be decreased.

When sailing around the arc of maximum visibility of a light it will be seen to be just dipping below the horizon. Use of this 'dipping distance' can be made to ascertain the distance of the vessel from the light by using the dipping tables published in the various nautical tables, for example the 'Geographical range table' in the Admiralty List of Lights. Their use is simple; the observer merely taking the height of the light off the chart and with his own height of eye, printed across the top of the table, traces down until opposite the height of the light, printed down the side of the table, when the distance off will be found accurate to within half a mile. Combine this distance with a bearing of the light and the position of the vessel can be fixed with reasonable accuracy.

The Admiralty List of Lights gives two ranges for all lights which are of sufficient intensity to be seen at horizon range: first its **luminous range** which is the maximum distance at which a light can be seen, not taking into account elevation of the light, or the observer, or the curvature of the earth. It is determined by the intensity of the light and the conditions of visibility prevailing at a given time: second, its **geographical range** which is the maximum distance at which light from a navigational light can be seen, taking into account refraction, the curvature of the earth, the height of the light and that of the observer.

The value of the information to the mariner is this: it tells him not only at what (geographical) range he may expect to sight a light but also whether he may expect to see its 'loom' before it appears above the horizon, and with what intensity. It indicates to him what penetration a light possesses. Further, given the range of atmospheric visibility as stated in weather reports, or by the mariner's own observation, reference to a diagram in the Admiralty List of Lights will give him the range at which certain lights may be seen in the prevailing conditions. The value of this and other detailed information is far greater than that which can be summarised here: this publication only gives all the information about lights which the mariner should have in his possession.

On a clear night the 'loom' or beam, of a powerful light may be seen even though the light itself is not visible above the horizon. It would appear like a searchlight sweeping across the horizon at intervals corresponding to the characteristic of the light. Using care, it is entirely practicable to take a compass bearing of a loom, but one must always bear in mind that this is only an approximate bearing of the light itself.

It is as well to know that in the navigational world a light whose characteristic is defined as flashing has a period of darkness greater than its period of light in any one cycle. An occulting light is one which has a period of light greater than its period of darkness. From this definition it will be seen that, in any one cycle, a light may be visible for a number of seconds and provided its period of darkness is greater than its period of light, it will be defined as a flashing light. To a landsman a flash is a short, sharp illumination. In this context a seaman applies a different definition.

Main light abbreviations used on charts.

Gp.Fl.	Group Flashing	A group of flashes shown at regular intervals.
Occ.	Occulting	A steady light which, at regular intervals is eclipsed.
Gp.Occ.	Group occulting	A steady light which, at regular intervals is eclipsed two or three times.
F.	Fixed.	A steady light.
F.Fl.	Fixed & Flashing	A fixed light which, at regular intervals, shows a single flash of greater intensity than the fixed light.
F.Gp.Fl.	Fixed & Group Flashing	A fixed light which, at regular intervals shows two or more flashes of greater intensity than the fixed light.
Qk.Fl.	Quick Flashing	A light which flashes rapidly and continuously.
Int.Qk. Fl.	Interrupted Quick Flashing.	A light which flashes rapidly and continuously with, at regular intervals a total eclipse.
Fl.	Flashing	Showing a single flash at regular intervals. Period of light always less than period of darkness.
Iso.	Isophase	Light with equal durations of light and darkness
Alt.	Alternating	Light which shows different colours in succession on same bearing.

A light must be assumed to be white unless otherwise stated.

A typical chart description is that of the Casquets Lighthouse off Alderney.

Gp.Fl.(5) 30 sec. 120 ft. 17m.

This abbreviated description, like the majority of chart abbreviations, is self-evident. It indicates that a group of five white flashes are shown every 30 seconds. The height of the focal plane of the light is 120 feet above mean high water spring tide level and, assuming the mariner's eye is 15 feet above sea level, it will be seen at a maximum range of 17 miles on a dark, clear night. This of course is near minimal information; for a complete description it is essential to refer to the Admiralty List of Lights.

Most lights have limited arcs of visibility and a simple example of this is the fact that they are invariably obscured on their landward sides. Some have coloured sectors which warn mariners of local hazards. This type of information will be found on Stanford charts and on the largest scale Admiralty charts of the area. The following diagram is of the Nab Tower Lighthouse and its associated sectors.

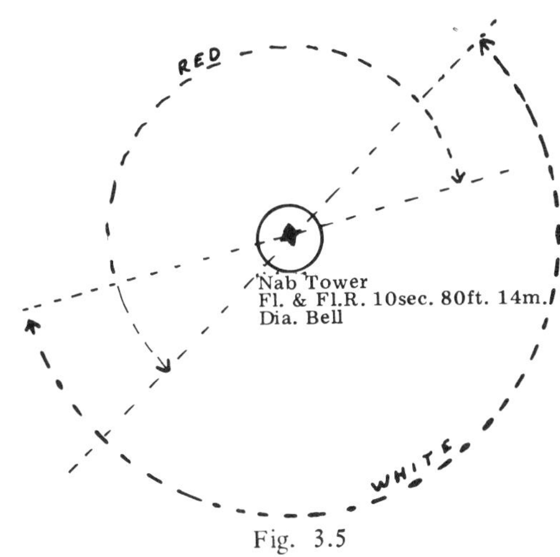

Fig. 3.5

It is important to remember that, as in the case of arcs of visibility, all bearings of lights are given from seaward. They are the bearings a mariner himself would take.

Beacons

Varying very considerably in size and type, being lit or unlit, beacons may be sited anywhere where some form of permanent visual navigational aid is desirable. They may be found on coastlines, on reefs and shoals and on permanent foundations in waterways. Except where sited in a much frequented river or channel, when lit they are generally unwatched.

A TYPICAL BEACON MARKING A REEF

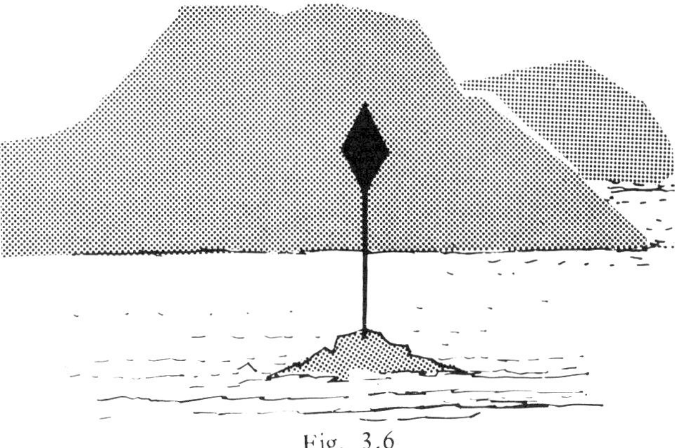

Fig. 3.6

Leading Marks and Lights.

When the entrance to a harbour, river or inland waterway has a narrow, deep-water channel, for which the penalty of deviating from its course is to run aground, buoys may be supplemented by leading marks and lights. Visible from seaward and sited on shore in line with the centre of the channel, two beacons are placed at a suitable distance apart, one behind the other. The rear one is higher than the other. If lit, their lights will be of such characteristics that one light will be distinctive from the other. A common combination is where one is a fixed or occulting light and the other is flashing.

Usually shown on charts as beacons, they are readily recognised by a line drawn through them and continued down the length of the channel to seaward. The customary notation is 'Leading lights in line bearing . . . .' on the bearing line. These bearings are given as **true** on the Admiralty chart and magnetic on the Stanford chart.

Leading Marks

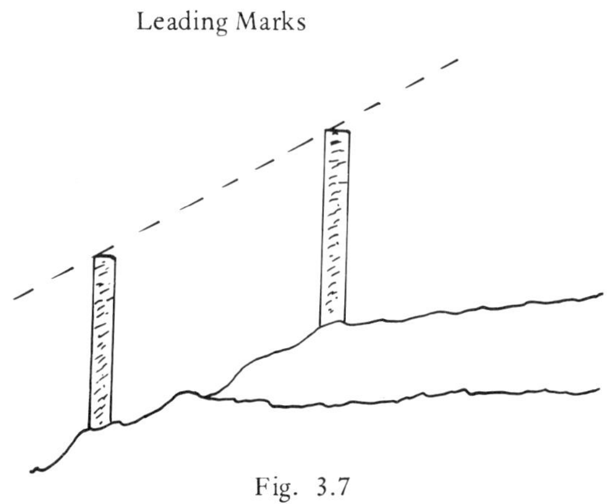

Fig. 3.7

Lightvessels

Lightvessels, the majority of which come within the jurisdiction of Trinity House, may well be reduced in numbers in coming years. Their enormous initial cost coupled with spiralling running costs have caused authorities to seek less costly alternatives.

They are invariably sited in positions where hitherto it has been impractical to build a permanent structure. Up to this time such positions have been of sufficient importance to shipping generally to warrant an easily recognised floating object by day and a powerful light by night under the constant vigilance of keepers. Typical sites are in an estuary at the entrance to an important ship channel, in the vicinity of a hazard round which considerable sea traffic must pass, or merely an offshore focal point for shipping.

Their construction varies little and by day they are easily recognised by the lantern on a structure amidships, usually referred to as the characteristic topmark.

Lightvessel

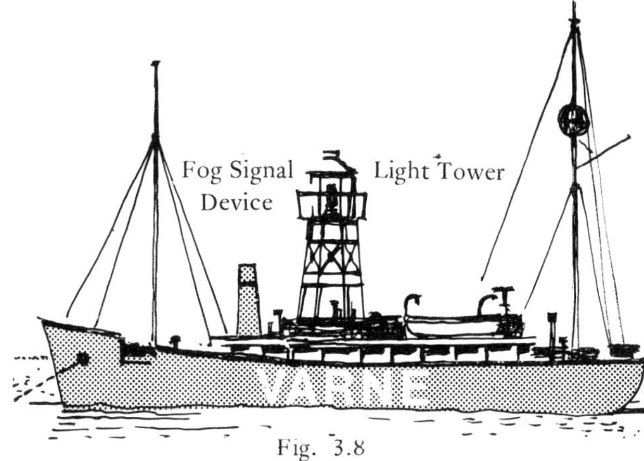

Fig. 3.8

Listed below are features common to all lightships of which mariners should be aware:

(a) Details of all features, functions and service provided by lightvessels will be found in the Admiralty List of Lights. This does not include radio services which are listed elsewhere in this volume.

(b) Lightvessels are painted red in England and Scotland and black in Ireland. Their names are painted in bold white letters on their sides.

(c) The elevation given in the Admiralty List of Lights is measured from the waterline to the centre of the lantern.

(d) At night an all-round white light is exhibited on the forestay, 6 feet above the rail. This is termed the riding light which, in conjunction with the characteristic light, indicates the direction in which a lightvessel is swung.

(e) If for any reason a light vessel is unable to display her characteristic light, the riding light only will be shown.

(f) If for any reason a lightvessel is not in her correct station by day she will show two black balls, one forward and one aft and the international code flag signal LO will be hoisted where it can best be seen. Her characteristic light will not be shown and her fog signal discontinued.

(g) All lightvessels round the coast of the United Kingdom show their characteristic light by day during foggy weather.

(h) There have been collisions with light vessels due to craft making insufficient allowance for tidal streams in their vicinity, and other unseamanlike reasons and there is a permanent Notice to Mariners in existence warning mariners to take great care when navigating in their vicinity.

(i) Lightvessels may be withdrawn from station without notice for repairs. Sometimes it is not possible to replace them with a relief vessel but where possible, buoys will be laid as a temporary measure. Reference should always be made to Notices to Mariners.

(j) Watch buoys, which are can-shaped buoys painted red with the word 'Watch' painted on their sides in white letters, are often moored close to lightvessels. These buoys are established to give the lightvessel crews immediate visual checks on the position of their vessel.

Like all floating navigational aids, lightvessels give the mariner a visual indication of the direction of the tidal stream; in the case of the latter it is due to the fact that they normally ride head to tide. Hence the yachtsman is given a check on any tidal stream for which he may be making an allowance in his course. A check on direction of tidal stream, but not on rate. When at anchor, a vessel lying head to the tidal stream is termed 'tide rode'; one which is lying head to wind, 'wind rode'. If a strong wind with a weak tidal stream prevails, a vessel may lie partly athwart the tidal stream, thus the tidal check here described must be used with caution.

Lanby Buoys

A Lanby buoy is a large automatic navigational buoy and, pending satisfactory trials, it is probable that certain lightvessels will be replaced by such buoys. Anchored to the seabed, the base is round and 40 feet in diameter. This base supports a conical superstructure 12 feet in height, which has a diameter of 15 feet at its base. The superstructure is surmounted by a lattice mast at the top of which is the main light beacon. The light is 40 feet above the sea, giving a luminous range of 22 miles. A powerful fog signal is also part of its equipment.

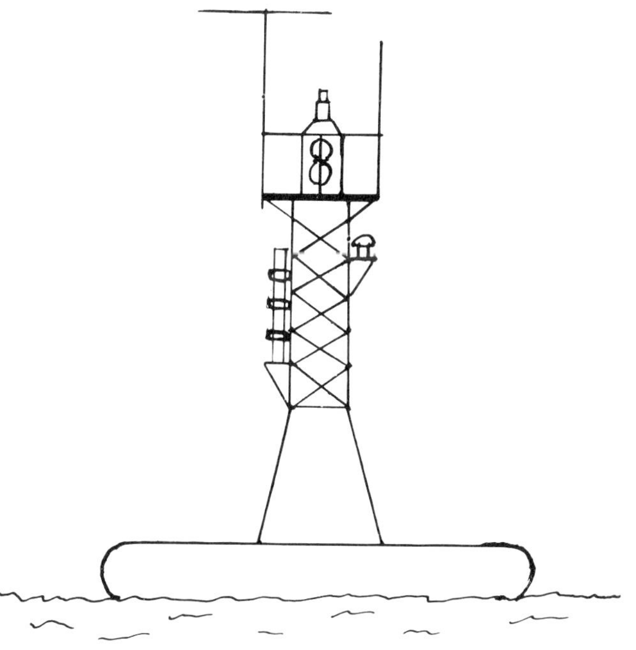

Fig. 3.4

For Colour Diagram of the Lateral System, see page 233

Similar buoys are also widely used on the American coast and are reported as being able to ride out storms of hurricane intensity without shifting moorings. Their future in these waters perhaps depends upon rendering them sufficiently reliable to fit them with marine radio direction-finding beacons and Racon equipment which is standard on many lightvessels.

Light Towers

As in the case of Lanby buoys, light towers are relatively new in the navigational scene. One of the first of its kind was built in Newhaven harbour, towed out to the position of the Royal Sovereign lightvessel and sunk on to the sea bed. Thus one more lightvessel is withdrawn. Considerably more expensive than Lanby buoys, all functions capable of being carried out by a lightvessel, can be performed by such unmanned towers.

Buoyage

It must be remembered that the only complete guide to buoys in any area is the largest scale Admiralty chart for that area. In the Stanford area the Stanford range of charts gives identical information. Where necessary for the purpose of giving sailing directions, the Admiralty Pilots make reference to buoys.

The Uniform System of Buoyage.

Prior to 1937 each country had its own system of buoyage and this tended to lead to confusion on the part of mariners. During that year an international conference was held, in which the maritime nations present agreed upon a standardisation of the basic shapes, colours and light characteristics of buoys, and their purport. It is called the Uniform System of Buoyage. Within the Uniform System there are two methods, or styles, of buoyage the Lateral System and the Cardinal System.

The Lateral System.

This system is used both off-shore and in waterways throughout the British Isles. It is also used in important waterways on the coasts of France and the Netherlands.

To understand the system it is necessary to memorise the following rules:

(a) The term 'Starboard Hand' refers to that side of the channel which will be on the right hand side of the navigator when he is going with the main stream of flood tide, or when entering a river, harbour or inland waterway from seaward.

(b) The term 'Port Hand' refers to that side which will be on the left hand of the navigator in the same circumstances.

To appreciate the significance of these rules one must be familiar with the direction of the main stream of flood tide round the British Isles and this is best conveyed diagramatically, see figure below.

An easy way to remember the direction of this flow is to recall that it is from Lands End in two directions towards Dover. The first direction is eastwards up the English Channel and thence to Dover; the second is right round the British Isles and ultimately south to Dover.

On page 21 will be found the plan of a bay, a river entrance in which a 'middle ground' swatch divides the channel, and the upper reaches of the channel. All are idealistic and imaginary. Thereon is indicated what types of buoys might be used to mark such a channel.

MAIN STREAM OF FLOOD TIDE – BRITISH ISLES

Fig. 3.9

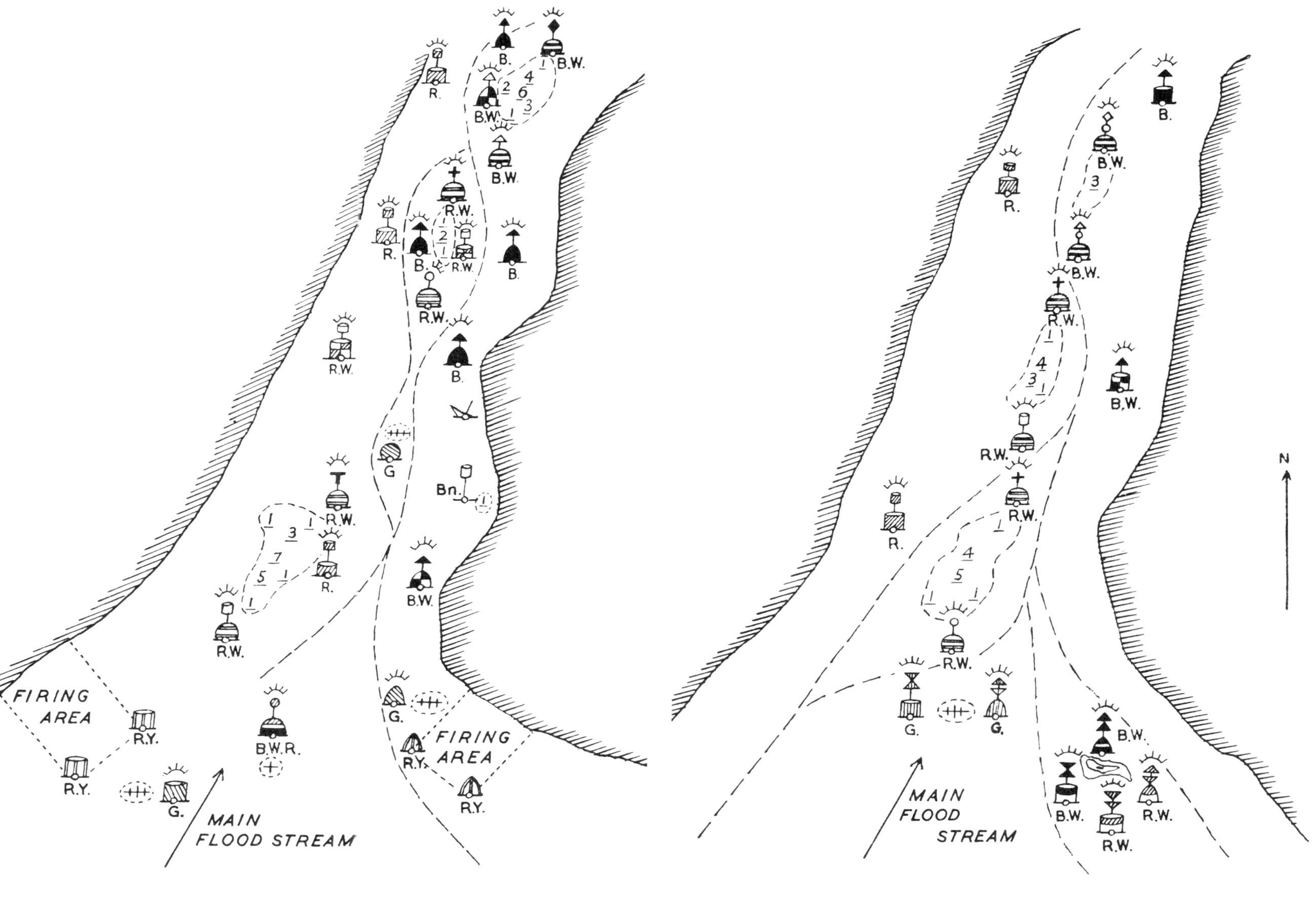

INTERNATIONAL BUOYAGE SYSTEM—LATERAL

Fig. 3.10(a)

INTERNATIONAL BUOYAGE SYSTEM—CARDINAL

Fig. 3.10(b)

Summarised in detail below are all important buoys used in the lateral system. Also included (elsewhere) is a coloured insert of these and other buoys which, it is suggested, a yachtsman may remove and either fix it over his chart table or keep it handy in his craft for reference if and when necessary.

BUOYS USED IN THE LATERAL SYSTEM

Buoy	Shape & Colour	Topmark if any	Light if any
Starboard hand	Conical B or B.W. Cheq.	Black cone, point upwards. Black diamond, but not at entrance to channel.	Fl. Gp.Fl. (3) Gp.Fl. (5)
Port hand	Can R. or R.W. Cheq.	Red Can. Red 'T' but not at entrance to channel.	Gp.Fl. (2) or (4) or (6) Fl.R. Gp.Fl. (2)R Gp.Fl. (3)R Gp.Fl. (4)R
Middle ground	Spherical		Lights will be distinctive, red or white. Rhythm will indicate which side to leave them. (See port and starboard pattern above.)
	Leave to starboard B.W.H.S.	Outer end: black cone point upwards. Inner End: black diamond.	
	Leave to port – R.H.W.S.	Outer end: red can Inner end: red 'T'	
	Leave either hand – R.W.H.S.	Outer end: red sphere. Inner end: red St. George's cross.	
Mid - channel	Usually pillar, but shape must be distinctive from other channel buoys. B.W.V.S. or R.W.V.S.	Any distinctive shape, other than can, or cone (point upwards) or sphere	Optional but distinctive from other lights marking sides of channel

Port or starboard buoys may, in addition to their topmarks, be numbered or lettered or named to facilitate recognition. If numbered or lettered such sequence will commence from seaward; odd numbers will be on the starboard hand and even numbers on the port.

Buoy	Shape & Colour	Topmark if any	Light, if any
Landfall	Optional	No topmark but usually supports trellis pillar surmounted by light.	Flashing character
Isolated Danger	Spherical Black or red with narrow horizontal white band	Sphere painted black or red, or half-black and half-red divided horizontally.	White or red flashing character
Danger area (Naval or Military)	Optional R.Y.V.S. with letters 'DZ' on sides.	–	Nil
Outfall or spoil ground	Optional Yellow and black divided horizontally	–	Optional usually red
Watch, sited near light vessels	Can Red, with name of lightvessel in white letters followed by 'Watch'	–	Nil
Cable Used by cable ships – keep clear	Optional Red or Black	–	Nil
Quarantine ground	Optional Yellow	–	Nil

Withies

Withies are a type of 'buoy' which yachtsmen encounter far more than seamen on deep-sea vessels. Usually used in the relatively shallow reaches of rivers and waterways, they are merely stakes driven into the seabed to delineate navigable water from shoal water.

Wreck-marking buoys and vessels.

For a number of years after the last war the number of off-shore wrecks constituted a real hazard for mariners generally. In recent years their numbers have been reduced to an almost negligible quantity. Removal by explosives and natural settling into the seabed have often accounted for this.

Dangerous wrecks which may be a hazard to shipping are marked by buoys. It must be remembered that a cartographer may define a wreck as dangerous whether it has five or fifty feet over it at low water. This is because he must take into consideration all shipping and some modern vessels have very deep drafts indeed. There is no way for a yachtsman to know just how much water may be over a wreck which is marked as dangerous on the chart. He must, therefore, obey the advice of the buoy which marks it unless he has certain knowledge of the depth of water over the wreck. It will be seen that if, due to exigencies which he could not forsee, he passes over the position of a dangerous wreck, the chances of his incurring hull damage are not very great.

In British waters the types of wreck marking buoys used to indicate dangerous wrecks are determined by the rules of the lateral system of the International System of buoyage; thus conical, can or spherical buoys may be used to indicate to the mariner on which hand they may be safely passed.

Wreck-marking vessels are seldom encountered. They are usually used in or near ship channels.

Types of buoys and vessels.

The colour of both buoys and vessels is always green and the word 'Wreck' is painted boldly in white on their sides.

To be passed on the mariner's starboard hand:

BUOY - Conical. If lighted it will give three green flashes every 10 or 15 seconds.

VESSEL - Three green lights displayed vertically on one end of a horizontal cross yard. By day green balls replace the green lights.

To be passed on the mariner's port hand.

BUOY - Can. If lighted it will give two green flashes every 10 seconds.

VESSEL - Two green lights displayed vertically on one end of a horizontal cross yard. By day green balls replace the green lights.

To be passed on either hand:

BUOY - spherical. If lighted it will give an occulting green light.

VESSEL - Two green lights displayed vertically on each end of a horizontal cross yard, which is to say 4 lights in all. By day green balls replace the green lights.

The Cardinal System of Buoyage (See colour diagram on page 234)

Yachtsmen intending to cross the channel will very probably pass buoys belonging to the Cardinal System and so they should make themselves familiar with its code, it being entirely different from the Lateral System.

The Cardinal System is widely used on the coasts of France to mark the positions of reefs and other off-lying dangers. A buoy marking such a hazard will be stationed to the north, south, east or west of it, the colours and topmark indicating in which quadrant it has been placed. With the knowledge of where the buoy has been placed in relation to the danger, the mariner will be able to determine its position and so steer clear of it. Off-shore dangers are generally marked with buoys belonging to the Cardinal System.

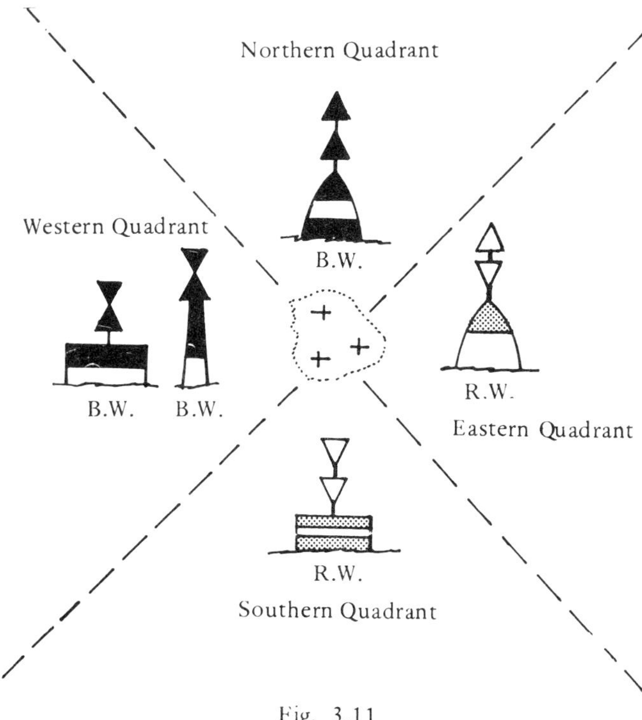

Fig. 3.11

Using the Lateral System fairly frequently, the yachtsman fairly quickly becomes familiar with it, but this cannot be said of the Cardinal System. Indeed, the writer himself quite often has to refer to a publication to decide the particular import of a buoy belonging to the latter system. This is a further reason why the coloured insert giving the types of buoys of both systems should be kept at hand, ready for use, in a craft crossing to the continent.

General remarks about buoyage systems.

It should be appreciated that, although authorities must adhere to the basic rules when planning a buoyage system, they will give a variation in the buoys of each basic shape calculated to give maximum assistance to the mariner. Within the code, therefore, a certain basic shape – say, can – may be varied: black buoys may be interspersed with chequered ones; each may or may not be given a number or letter; topmarks may or may not be used and, if used, their types may be varied. Further, it must not be assumed that, in a port where night navigation is common, every channel buoy will be lighted. It may be decided that a **sufficient** number of buoys will be lighted to enable vessels to traverse its reaches in safety.

If a ship channel is fairly wide it may be considered adequate to mark certain sections of it with mid-channel (pillar) buoys only, or vary port hand buoys with starboard hand buoys as may be expedient in various sections of the channel. If it is not necessary in the interests of safety for both sides of a channel to be buoyed, then quite possibly it will not be so. It must be borne in mind that port authorities and Trinity House keep one criterion in mind: the safe conduct of all shipping and small craft. A stranger to a port may idly decide that the buoyage provided for that port was not very cleverly worked out. No doubt if he knew more about the local conditions and hazards – or absence of the latter – he would reach the same conclusions as the authorities.

A seaman's attitude towards buoys.

Buoys generally must be regarded as **aids** to navigation; never as irrefutable evidence, by their presence, that the position of a craft is determined beyond doubt. Consequently the mariner who is navigating in a buoyed area cannot absolve himself from determining his position by other more reliable means when practicable.

Buoys are relatively small and vulnerable. They depend upon moorings to retain them in the position in which they have been established. Gales occasionally cause buoys to drag their moorings, particularly those in exposed positions; large vessels may sometimes collide with them. It may fairly be said that buoys are almost always in their correct positions, particularly those in close proximity to a port, but just occasionally they are not. Some readers may have been faced with an empty sea in place of a friendly, reassuring buoy: after a long sea passage during which dead-reckoning has played a major part in navigation, this can be most disconcerting.

British authorities are quick to restore errant buoys to their correct position, but it may be that some days elapse between routine checks on the positions and condition of out-of-the-way buoys. Faulty buoys are usually spotted fairly quickly by passing ships, but they do not always report the faults. For this and the former reason, it may be a short while before the authorities receive a report of this nature; even more likely if it is merely a characteristic light which has developed malfunction or has become extinguished. A report being received, the tenders which undertake the maintenance and restoration of buoys are not always immediately available. Nevertheless, we sail in an area of the world in which floating navigational aids are maintained at a very high standard. The writer can recall foreign waters where the standard is alarmingly low.

It often occurs that a navigator must put a 100% degree of reliance upon the position of a buoy. Needs must in a considerable number of cases. Yet this should not be done when alternatives exist, in the form of terrestrial bearings and fixes. The implication here is not that the navigator should constantly fix his position, using shore bearings, in a well-buoyed channel or area. This course need only be adopted when he, as an alert and observant seaman, has reason to doubt the information imparted to him by buoys. It **does** mean that he must constantly relate his position to terrestrial objects by eye whenever possible, and endeavour to reconcile his observations with that information he gleans from his charts.

Buoy recognition.

It will be readily appreciated that, when approaching a buoy from afar in daylight, its various features will appear in an order which may be regarded as their degree of importance.

1. Its shape, which tells the mariner on which side it should be passed.

2. Its topmark, which may distinguish it from other similar buoys in the area.

3. Its colour, which serves as a further distinguishing mark. The reservation must be made that weathering often makes colour identification of buoys difficult.

4. Its name or number if any, which would give final confirmation of the precise buoy which has been sighted.

If doubts exist when you sight a buoy, and it is important to know which buoy it is, it should be closed for further identification.

At night no confusion about which buoy has been sighted should arise. Those buoys which are lighted exhibit distinctive characteristics which can be related to the information given on charts.

It is worth mentioning here the occasional situation which may occur when a yachtsman is approaching a port at night. From seaward, at some distance, he may be faced with an array of winking buoys and a plethora of fixed and flashing lights from the town behind them, which have no pattern, no message and certainly no invitation. On the chart it may look easy; in practice it appears forbidding. This channel-less superabundance of lights may cause him to stand off the port until daylight. Often such a course is unnecessary. The closer the buoys are approached, the more their pattern will be revealed until, at the entrance to the channel, there will probably be no doubt about its direction.

Lateral System in Continental ports

Continental ports, although conforming to the Lateral System already outlined, often give the impression that styles of buoys are not quite the same as our own. A conical buoy may be slightly narrower, slightly taller than its British counterpart; occasional unfamiliar variations in topmarks may be noted. The strangeness of all the eye encounters in foreign ports further disturbs the assurance of a few yachtsmen. Usually this minor dilemma is very short lived, just as driving on the right on continental roads is daunting, but only at the outset.

Radar reflectors.

Both off-shore and channel buoys may be fitted with radar reflectors. These are so designed to give maximum response on the plan position indicator (screen) of a radar set, From what ever direction a radar transmission may emanate, the reflector will return the radio wave directly back to the transmitter/receiver aerial. Where none is fitted a radar 'echo' of a buoy may be small or difficult to recognise, due to the shape and size of the buoy, or the state of the sea.

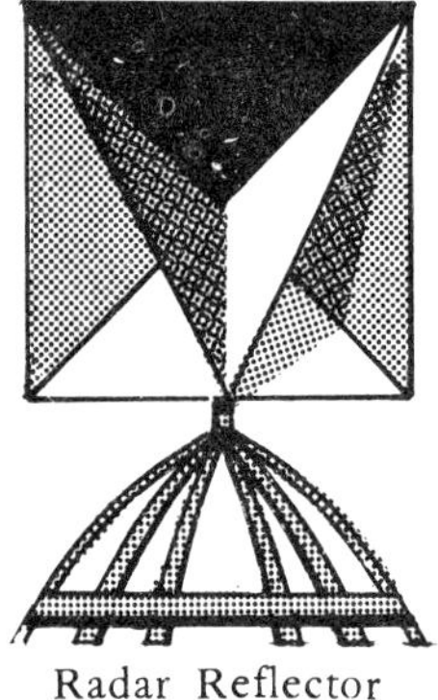

Radar Reflector

Fig. 3.12

Sailing in the vicinity of buoys.

Far more efficiently than all the tidal diagrams and atlasses, a buoy in a tideway will give visual evidence of the set and drift of the tidal stream in its vicinity. The buoy will have a wake, and the wake will indicate the direction in which the stream is setting. From the passage of water past the buoy one should be able to fairly gauge its rate. This is valuable information and, varying slightly at each buoy passed, as it may well do, observations of this nature should be automatic to the yachtsman.

If a yachtsman must pass close to a buoy, he should pass under its lee. There is in all of us something of the daring, swash-buckling adventurer whose thrills, perhaps unfortunately, are often reduced to pastimes such as seeing how close we can sail to a buoy without actually touching it. The skill required to pass a buoy within inches on its lee side is equal to that required on its weather side. In the latter case, particularly in a racing tidal stream or a stiff breeze, there is a risk of scraped paint, a dented hull or even a capsize. The calculated, justifiable risk presents itself frequently and oft times unexpectedly at sea and the mature yachtsman is content with this knowledge.

Air Fog Signals.

Fog signals operate during periods of reduced visibility, both by day and by night. A table listing those types commonly used is given opposite. The value of this knowledge is in the awareness of what type of signal it is expected to hear. The types of fog signals are usually given in abbreviated form on large scale charts.

It must be borne in mind that air fog signals cannot be implicitly relied upon. Extraordinary phenomena have been experienced in fog and for this reason the Hydrographic Office gives the following warnings to mariners:

1. Air fog signals are heard at greatly varying distances because the behaviour of a sound wave in air depends upon the state of the air. Similarly the apparent direction of a fog signal can be misleading.

2. When an air fog signal is a combination of high and low notes, one of the notes may be inaudible at times.

3. Occasionally there are areas in the vicinity of a fog signal in which the note is totally inaudible.

4. A station may not be aware that there is fog a short distance away, and so the fog signal will not be sounded.

5. Some fog signals take a little time to start up after signs of fog have been seen.

It should be noted that details of fog signals on all charts are minimal. Full details may be found in the Admiralty List of Lights.

Fog signals on buoys.

The fog signals of both bell-buoys and whistle-buoys may be operated by either mechanical or compressed air devices, or by wave action. No chart indicates to the mariner which method is used. Generally, buoys fitted with fog signals in open waters are operated by wave action; those in consistently smooth water as, for example, a sheltered waterway, are operated by mechanical means.

First, it must be remembered that mechanical devices can become defective. Secondly, when the fog signal of a buoy depends upon wave motion, the frequency with which fog signals are emitted will largely depend upon the state of the sea. It can occur that when the sea is smooth, no fog signal is emitted. It may be said of non-automatic bell and whistle buoys that no message to mariners was ever more dolefully or weirdly emitted.

The owner of a power craft whose engine and exhaust noise is considerable should, when listening for a fog signal, cut power from time to time. It is improbable that a distant fog signal would be heard over the noises generated inboard.

Fog signal	Chart abbreviation	Operated by	Note emitted and detail
Diaphone	Dia.	Compressed air	Powerful low note terminating in what is usually called a grunt.
Siren	Siren	Compressed air	A medium-powered high or low note, or a combination of both.
Reed	Reed	Compressed air	Low-powered high 'piping' note. May be operated by hand in which case the power will be small
Typhon	Ty.	Compressed air	Powerful medium-pitched note, similar to the note emitted by ships using compressed air sirens.
Nautophone	Naut.	Electricity	Note similar to that emitted by a reed.
Electric fog horn	Elect.	Electricity	Powerful, medium pitched note.
Gun	Gun	Gun	Acetylene gun giving a bright flash.
Explosive	Explo.	Explosion in mid-air.	—
Bell	Bell	Mechanically or by wave action	Varying note and power. Irregular when actuated by wave action.
Gong	Gong	As for Bell	As for Bell.
Whistle	Wh.	Compressed air or steam.	Low power and low note.
Whistle on buoy	Wh.	Compressed air by wave action.	Irregular low note of low power.

CHAPTER 4

Tides

The rises and falls of the level of the sea are known as tides. They are caused by the gravitational forces of the moon, and to a lesser extent, the sun. Their rhythmic pattern is directly related to the unvarying movement of the moon in its orbit round the earth. Much being known about the factors which produce and influence tides, the times of their occurrence may be predicted.

The gravitational forces of the moon, which is the nearest heavenly body to the earth, act upon the earth as a whole. That is to say, upon the solid mass of the earth itself, the non-rigid waters of the earth, and even the atmosphere surrounding it. These forces are greatest upon the face of the earth which presents itself to the moon at any given time.

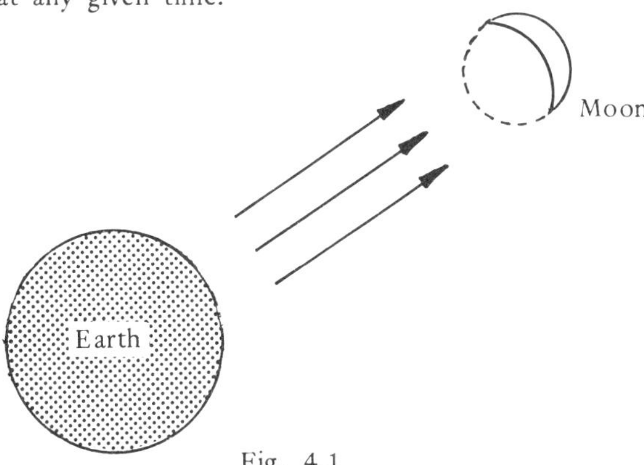

Fig. 4.1

The reasons for this are twofold. It is that area of the earth's surface which is closest to the moon, and it presents itself at right angles to the forces to which it is exposed. Within this area the rigid earth only minimally responds to the moon's gravitational pull but the non-rigid waters of the earth are perceptibly raised.

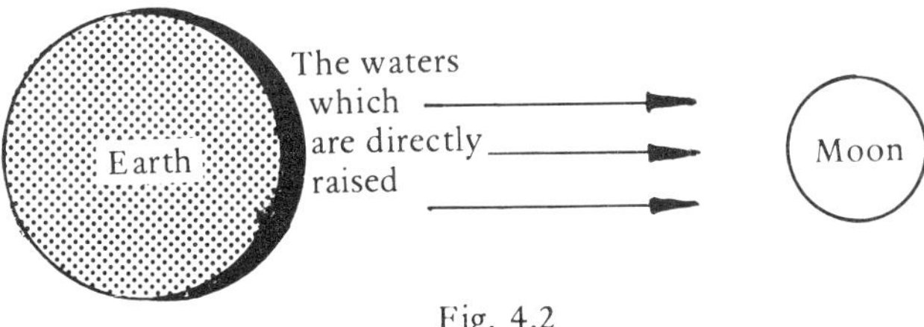

Fig. 4.2

At the same time the **earth itself** is fractionally being pulled towards the moon. The most startling effect of this is that the waters on the opposite side to the moon tend to get 'left behind'.

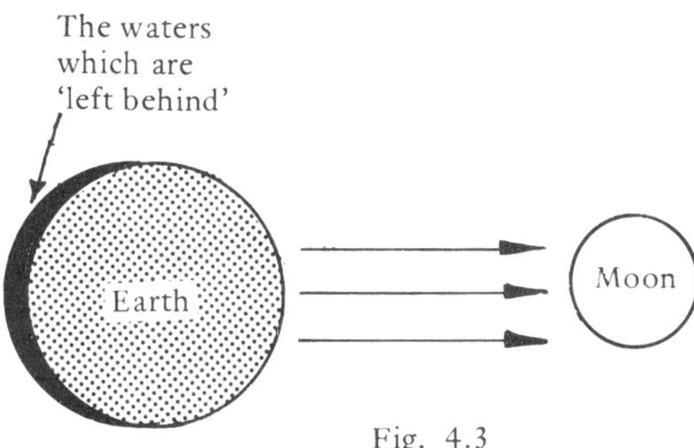

Fig. 4.3

From the two effects above described, which occur simultaneously, a raising of the seas occurs on sides of the earth which are diametrically opposite each other.

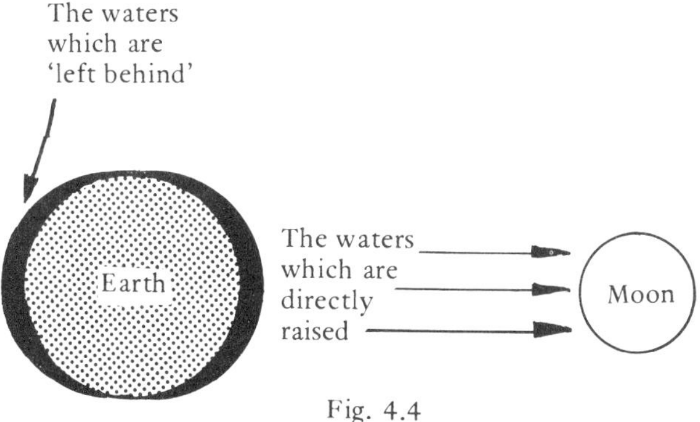

Fig. 4.4

A similar, but less marked effect is caused by the sun. It is less because although the sun is very much larger than the moon, its distance from the earth is considerably greater. Consequently its gravitational pull is much weaker. The lesser gravitational pull of the sun is superimposed upon that of the moon.

When the sun, moon and earth are in transit, the moon's and sun's gravitational forces combine. The effect is to raise the seas a little higher than usual.

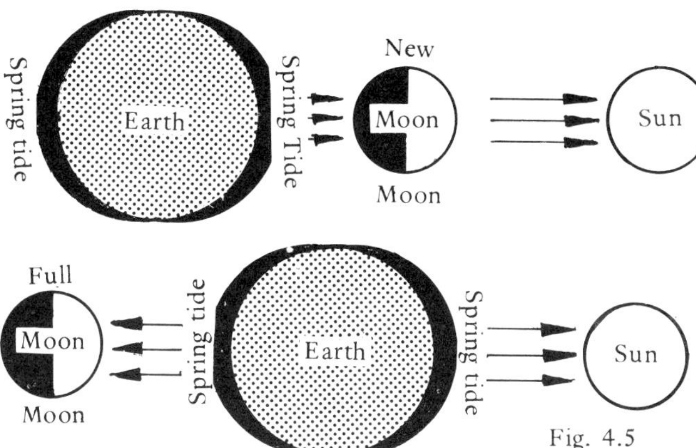

Fig. 4.5

Note that whether the moon is on one side of the earth or the other, the gravitational effect is the same.

These combined tide-raising forces, which have the effect of raising the seas a little higher than usual, produce what are known as spring tides. They are always associated with new and full moon.

When lines drawn through the sun and moon from the earth form a right angle, the tide-raising forces of each acts in opposition to each other. The moon's tide-raising forces, being stronger, have the greatest effect upon the oceans and seas but they are reduced by those of the sun.

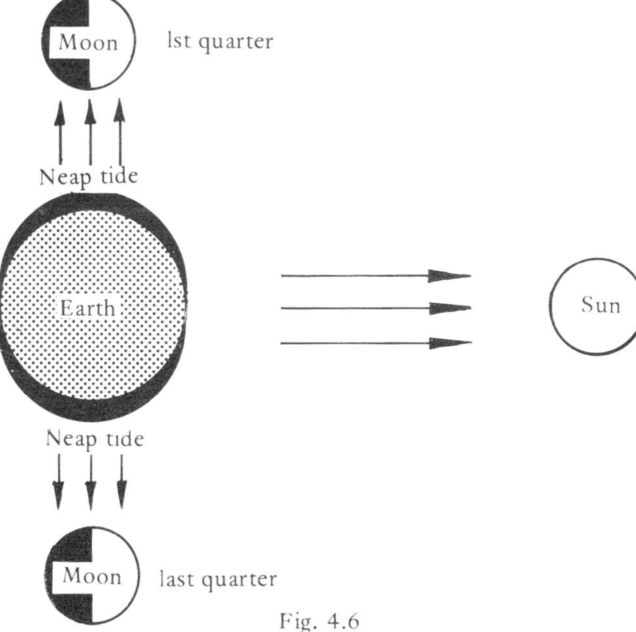

Fig. 4.6

Whether the moon is on one side of the earth or the other, note how the tide-raising forces of the moon are opposed by those of the sun. Note also that in both cases only half the moon is visible from the earth. One is known as the first quarter and the other, the last quarter.

When either condition is extant the tide-raising forces of the moon are lessened by those of the sun. Consequently the seas are not raised as high as usual and neap tides are produced.

Between spring tides and neap tides a gradual transition from one type to the other occurs, as the moon, sun and earth assume gradually changing aspects to each other.

The tides as we know them.

Although the tide-raising forces described will act upon any expanse of water on earth, their effect upon diminutive lakes and rivers is negligible. It is upon the centres of the vast expanses of sea – the Pacific, Indian and Atlantic Oceans – where their consequences are most marked. In these areas the sea level may be raised as much as 6 feet.

It is evident that if an expanse of water in the centre of an ocean is alternatively raised and lowered, oscillations from such upheavals must occur throughout the length and breadth of that ocean. These tidal oscillations, or tidal waves, may be likened to the outward movement of ripples created when one drops a pebble in the centre of a pool Thus it is believed that tidal waves flow from some central point in the oceans, shorewards in all directions. The arrival of a tidal wave on any shore will produce a high water in that area.

Just as waves steepen - increase in amplitude - as they move shorewards on a gradually shelving beach, so do tidal waves increase in amplitude as the relatively shallow waters surrounding continents is encountered. A tidal oscillation may be increased in amplitude from 5 feet to 6 feet in mid-Atlantic to about 20 feet around our shores. If the tidal wave is, at the same time, flowing into a gradually narrowing gulf this will further increase the amplitude. In the upper reaches of the Bristol Channel, for instance, rises of 36 feet may be encountered.

In fact a tidal wave causes an oscillation in the sea level. It rises above sea level, falls below it and then returns to its natural level. A tidal oscillation may thus be defined as a time interval occurring between the sea being at its ordinary level, through one complete oscillation and returning to ordinary level again.

It is also, shall we say, the difference in time between the occurrence of one high water and the next.

Fig. 4.7

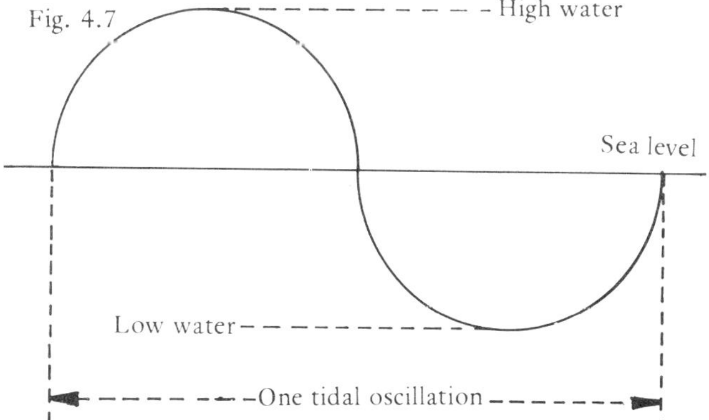

When tidal oscillations occur.

One lunation, or lunar month, is a period of approximately 29½ days. This is the time that elapses between one full moon and the next. A lunar day is one of very nearly

24 hours 50 minutes. It may be defined as the period elapsing between successive passages of the moon over a single meridian on the earth. In consequence the oceans of the world are being subjected to the tide-raising forces of the moon once every 24 hours 50 minutes.

The reader may assume from the last paragraph that in all large sea areas two tidal waves are being generated once every lunar day. In fact this is not so in all cases. The shape of oceans, seas, and their basins, and astronomical phenomena, have a direct effect upon tidal waves. Diurnal tides, those which occur **once** per lunar day, are experienced in certain areas of the world, notably in the Pacific Ocean and the Mediterranean Sea.

In the Atlantic Ocean and its adjacent sea areas, for the reasons given, **two** tidal waves occur every lunar day. These are called semi-diurnal tides and we who sail around our shores are very much concerned with them. If we experience two tidal oscillations per lunar day, then a period of about 12 hours 25 minutes will elapse between successive tides. It will be similarly true to say this of two successive high waters, or two successive low waters.

Spring and neap tides.

The effect of spring tides is to increase the amplitude of a tidal oscillation. Higher high waters and lower low waters are experienced at these times.

Neap tides decrease their amplitude and so lower high waters and higher low waters occur.

Local tides.

Superimposed upon the pattern of diurnal and semi-diurnal tides, in certain areas local tides may be experienced. These bear only small relation to the patterns already described. Again, the contours of the sea boundaries and the shape of the sea basins will dictate whether these extraordinary phenomena will occur. A good example of local tides is on our own doorstep, in the Southampton area. Tide tables indicate that four high waters and two low waters occur every lunar day. Tides of this nature are almost impossible to predict by rule-of-thumb methods often used by mariners. Areas where local tides are found are relatively rare.

The effect of Meteorological conditions upon tides.

Every mariner should be aware that the effect of weather upon tides can be considerable. A strong wind blowing steadily over a sea area for a protracted period will produce a surface current. If this occurs in confined tidal waters such as the English Channel and the North Sea, it will effect the times and heights of tides and generally disturb tidal predictions. If, for example, a steady northerly wind blows in the North Sea for a few days, a banking-up of water will occur in the Dover area, the amount being directly proportionate to the strength of the wind and its duration. It will cause both high and low waters in the southern North Sea to be greater than those predicted. It was precisely these conditions which, in 1953 during a period of very high spring tides, caused extensive flooding in the Thames Estuary and the Low Countries. Predicted high water levels were increased by as much as 9 feet.

Other meteorological conditions can affect tides, usually to a minor degree; it is the one outlined which the alert mariner may recognise. He will not be dismayed if, in similar circumstances to those described, predicted tidal patterns appear to be wrong. One must not assume that predictions may occasionally be totally disrupted. High waters and low waters may be advanced or retarded by as much as an hour. Heights may vary by a foot or more. More often than not, that is all.

A necessary admonition.

From what has been written here the reader will have the impression that, for the most part, semi-diurnal tides follow a regular pattern; that successive high waters follow each other at intervals of 12 hours 25 minutes. It may be assumed, for example, that between successive high and low waters, 6 hours 12½ minutes will almost invariably elapse.

Tide tables will indicate that the intervals between successive high and low waters are seldom that stated above, although they often approach it. Different ports have different intervals. Once again astronomical phenomena and the shape of the coastline and sea basin in each area for which predictions are given play a part in apparently putting the tides a little out of step.

Nevertheless, for rough calculations such as are frequently made by seamen the intervals defined are a good rough guide. When planning a passage for the following day it is useful to know that if high water occured at midday, then tomorrow it will be about 50 minutes later than midday.

Definitions.

It must be borne in mind that 'tide' refers to a vertical movement of the sea. One must resolve, therefore, never to use the words 'high tide' and 'low tide' when referring to the **state** of a tide. The proper terms are 'high water' and 'low water'.

Chart Datum.

The contours of the sea bed can be likened to those of a valley. The valley being filled with water, and a lake thus formed, as the surface is traversed varying depths of water will be found. So it is with the seas. It is essential that, on charts portraying the oceans and seas, the varying depths are faithfully recorded.

We know that the sea level is constantly being raised and lowered by tides. Indeed, on our own shores the height difference between low and high water may be 20 feet to 30 feet. How then can the depth of water be recorded at any point so that it is meaningful to the mariner? It is achieved by selecting an arbitrary level which is so low that tides will seldom fall below it. When scanning the soundings in an area one can say with truth that the depth of water will almost certainly not be lower than 'chart datum' - the name given to the low level selected - as printed on the chart and it will probably be greater. This is a valuable safety factor. Obviously one must, in the vast majority of cases, add the height of tide to chart datum to find out what the true depth of water will be. Chart Datum has usually been taken as Mean Low Water Springs. It has been found, however, that on several days per year the tide will fall below this level and, on new charts, surveys are based on Lowest Astronomical Tide

(L.A.T.) which is the lowest predictable tide under normal atmospheric conditions. When studying a chart one should refer to the datum to see which has been used in the survey. See note at end of this chapter.

The following tidal terms are best referred to Fig. 4.8:—

M.S.L.	Mean sea level
M.H.W.S.	Mean high water spring tides
M.L.W.S.	Mean low water spring tides
M.H.W.N.	Mean high water neap tides
M.L.W.N.	Mean low water neap tides
H.W.F. & C.	High water full and change, an obsolescent reference once used in tidal predictions.

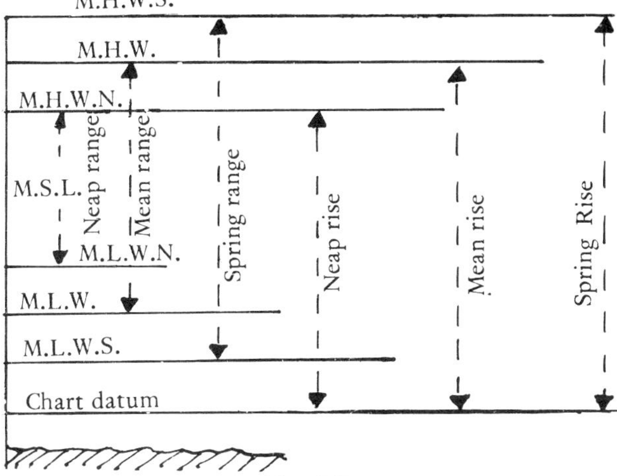

Fig. 4.8

Range of tide. The difference in feet and inches between high and low water heights.

Duration of tide. The difference in time between the occurrence of high water and the following low water or, conversely, the time of low water and the following high water. The duration of rise and fall are not usually identical.

Height of tide. The height of the water level above chart datum at any instant.

Rise of tide. The height of highwater above chart datum.

Spring rise. The difference in feet and inches between chart datum and mean high water springs.

Spring range. The difference in feet and inches between the levels of mean low water springs and mean high water springs.

Neap rise. The difference in feet and inches between the levels of chart datum and mean high water neaps.

Neap range. The difference in feet and inches between the levels of mean low water neaps and mean high water neaps.

Flood tide. A rising tide. **Ebb tide.** A falling tide.

The rate of rise and fall of tides.

The rate of rise and fall of a tide is not uniform. Between both low and high water, and high and low water, it commences slowly, accelerates to a maximum at half-tide and decelerates thereafter. The 'stand' of a tide occurs when there is no perceptible vertical movement of water.

This whole phenomenon is best described graphically and Fig. 4.9 should be studied. A duration of a tide of 6 hours is portrayed for simplicity. Although one-hour time intervals are equidistant on the semicircle, note how horizontal lines drawn through them to the 'tide pole' indicate drastically different rises in successive hours. Note also that in the first and last hours: in the second and fifth: in the third and fourth hours of the tide, the rate of rise and fall is uniform.

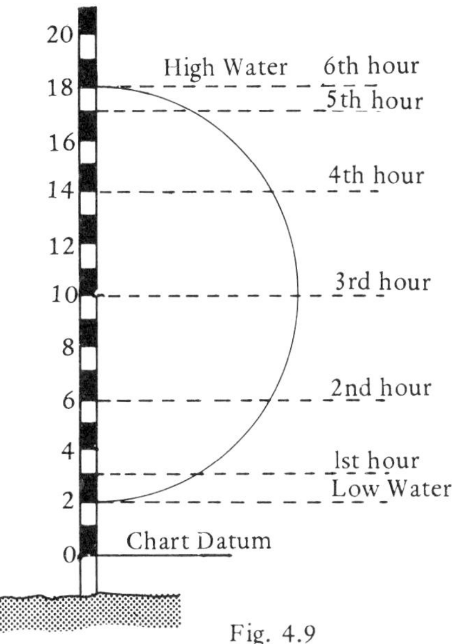

Fig. 4.9

Tide poles.

In tidal waterways and harbours used by shipping, tide poles are occasionally encountered. They often have the appearance of stout baulks of timber projecting vertically from the water. Boldly graduated in feet so that they may be read at a distance - sometimes the feet are painted alternately in black and white - the reading at water level indicates the exact height of water above chart datum. It has already been stated that tidal heights are not always those which have been predicted and so the information imparted by tide poles is valuable in that it is not a prediction: it is a visual statement of fact.

'Tide poles' are occasionally painted on dock walls. These sometimes merely serve to indicate the depth of water at the entrance to an enclosed dock, perhaps a dry-dock, and so it is unwise to assume that such graduations relate to rise of tide above chart datum, unless one has local knowledge.

To find when spring and neap tides occur.

In these waters spring tides occur approximately 1½ days after the occurrence of both full and new moons: neap tides the same period after the first and last quarters of the moon. It need be of only passing interest to remark here that these time lags are connected with the movement of the moon, and apparent movement of the sun round the earth.

Of immediate interest to the yachtsman are the **dates** on which these phenomena occur. When afloat he must know whether he can expect spring or neap ranges of tide. The quickest and simplest way of finding out is to scan any complete table of tidal predictions for a port in the area. If he notes the dates on which the highest high waters occur he will establish the days on which spring tides will be experienced. Similarly the lowest high waters will reveal when neap tides may be expected.

The prediction of tidal phenomena.

Tidal predictions are published annually in a fairly wide range of nautical publications and other lesser media. Diaries and calendars produced for sale to a local nautical community often reproduce tidal predictions for a specific port. The latter have value to seamen who do not venture far from the port for which predictions are given.

Yachtsmen who cruise beyond the confines of their own home port need tidal information for sundry ports and, although the Admiralty Tide Tables are the most valuable for mariners generally, many yachtsmen who can cruise only occasionally during the summer months find them a little baffling. Other tide tables, produced commercially, are regarded similarly and all these tables must be renewed annually. It may be fairly said that the scope and range of such tables are better suited to the needs of professional seamen and to a relatively few yachtsmen.

To roughly estimate the time of low water.

The approximate time of low water at any port may be obtained by adding, or subtracting, 6 hours to or from the nearest high water. This rule-of-thumb method makes it imperative that a yachtsman allows in his mental calculation for the fact that low water **could** occur up to one hour after, or before, any low water time he calculates. Occasionally this variation may be exceeded. In practice the yachtsman will find that his rough and ready calculation is sufficiently accurate for general needs. It remains necessary for him to assimilate the general remarks upon tidal behaviour which follow later in this chapter.

To roughly estimate the height of low water.

A yachtsman who uses a rule-of-thumb method to assess the time at which low water will occur **must** assume that low water heights will be those produced on his charts: in fact, chart datum. In a considerable number of cases, particularly during neap tides, low water heights will be as much as 3 or 4 feet above datum, but it would be unwise for him to assume this without real knowledge and experience. Very occasionally low water heights during spring tides may be minimally less than datum, and this fact cannot be overlooked.

Tidal streams, or tidal currents.

So far only the vertical movement of the sea has been discussed, yet it is evident that to achieve considerable vertical movement, lateral flow must occur.

The beginner must understand the manner in which the direction of a tidal stream is defined. Any direction extracted from nautical publications generally, and navigational charts, is a statement of the direction in which seawater **flows**. Hence a tidal stream given a direction, or set, of 120° indicates it is flowing in that direction.

During a period of spring tides when the range of tide - which, it will be recalled, is the vertical measurement between the heights of high and low water - is greatest, the lateral flow must obviously achieve a maximum rate. During neap tides when the range is often markedly less, a minimum rate will be encountered. It can be said, therefore, that spring tides are synonymous with large ranges **and** relatively fast flowing tidal streams. In the same way, neap tides indicate tidal currents of lesser velocity.

In some areas of the world neap ranges are great, and their associated spring ranges even greater, so in such areas neap ranges may be swift and spring rates more swift. Although there are better examples elsewhere in the world, in the upper reaches of the Bristol Channel one can experience neap ranges of about 30 feet and so, even during a period of neap tides, tidal streams have quite a marked velocity there.

Just as tidal times and heights can from time to time be rendered a little inaccurate, mainly by meteorological conditions, so can tidal streams be similarly affected. It must never be forgotten that predictions remain what they are - **forecasts** of tidal heights. Published tidal streams are obtained by observing the average flow of tidal currents in sundry selected positions during a considerable number of observations. From this advice the reader must not assume that he will frequently encounter dismayingly capricious tidal streams. Occasionally he will find that the set is slightly different from that which is indicated in his tidal stream atlas; a tidal stream may commence a half an hour earlier or later than expected: or the strength of the stream will be a little different from that which is foretold. Greater variations **can** occur, but only occasionally, and these are more likely in winter when variations in weather are frequent and pronounced - and most yachts are laid up.

Where to find tidal stream information.

Information relating to offshore tidal streams in British and continental waters may be obtained from a considerable number of sources but, for yachtsmen, the three following are considered the most useful:

1. **Admiralty Tidal Stream Atlases.**

Of great value to yachtsmen are the Admiralty **Pocket** Tidal Stream Atlases. All being of handy size as indicated, these divide the British Isles and the near shores of the **continent** into 12 areas. A booklet is produced for each area. Each contains 13 identical charts which give the rates and the directions of tidal streams for each hour of the tidal cycle. All information is referred to Dover high water times, which are published in this volume, and a full explanation how to use the system is contained in each booklet. See Fig. 4.10.

2. **Stanford charts.**

Within a box on the face of every Stanford chart a group of 12 chartlets is produced. Each chartlet is uniform and portrays the sea area covered by the chart on which it is printed. The tidal information contained therein is almost identical to that produced in the Admiralty Pocket Tidal Stream Atlases and it has equal value. They too are referred to Dover high water predictions. (See Fig. 4.11).

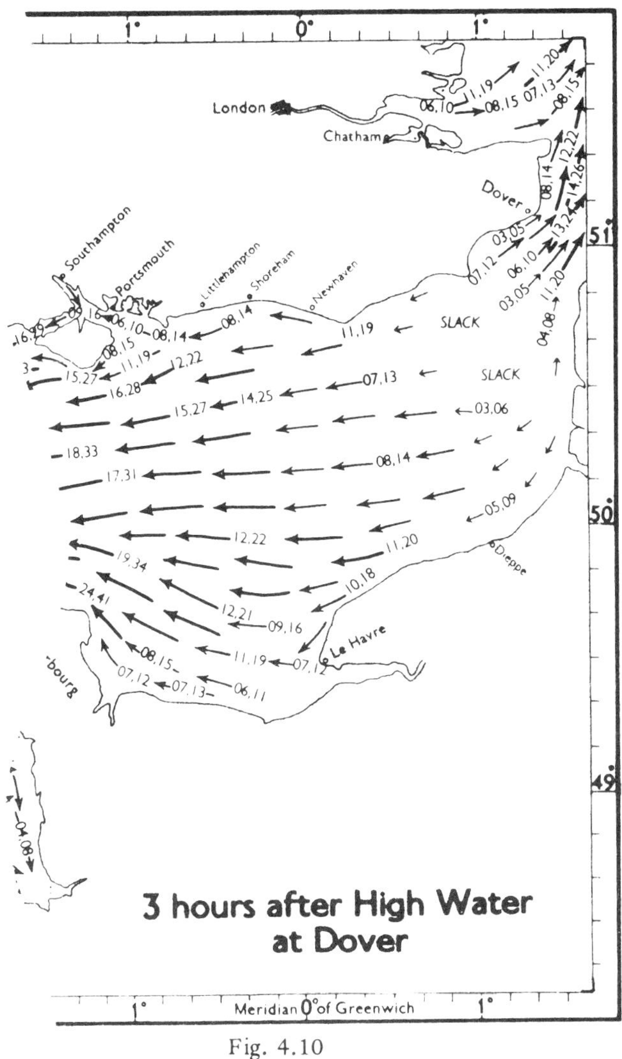

Fig. 4.10

3. **Admiralty large scale charts.**

Most large scale Admiralty charts of sea areas in home waters include tables of tidal stream information for selected positions. (See Fig. 2.9. Page 10).

The Standard Port to which the information refers is always printed above the tables, it is not necessarily Dover. At the head of each column of tidal stream predictions is a lettered symbol and, alongside it, the geographical position on the chart where a duplicate of this symbol will be found. The tidal stream information in each individual table relates to the streams which may be expected in the vicinity of the lettered symbol.

To use these tables the yachtsman must first seek a lettered symbol on his chart which is nearest to the area in which he is navigating. The letter will indicate which column of predictions to use. It remains for him to determine how many hours before or after high water at the Standard Port his local time occurs and then from the table, the spring or neap tidal direction and rate may be extracted.

This system has limitations. It is not immediate visual indication of the behaviour of tidal streams in an area.

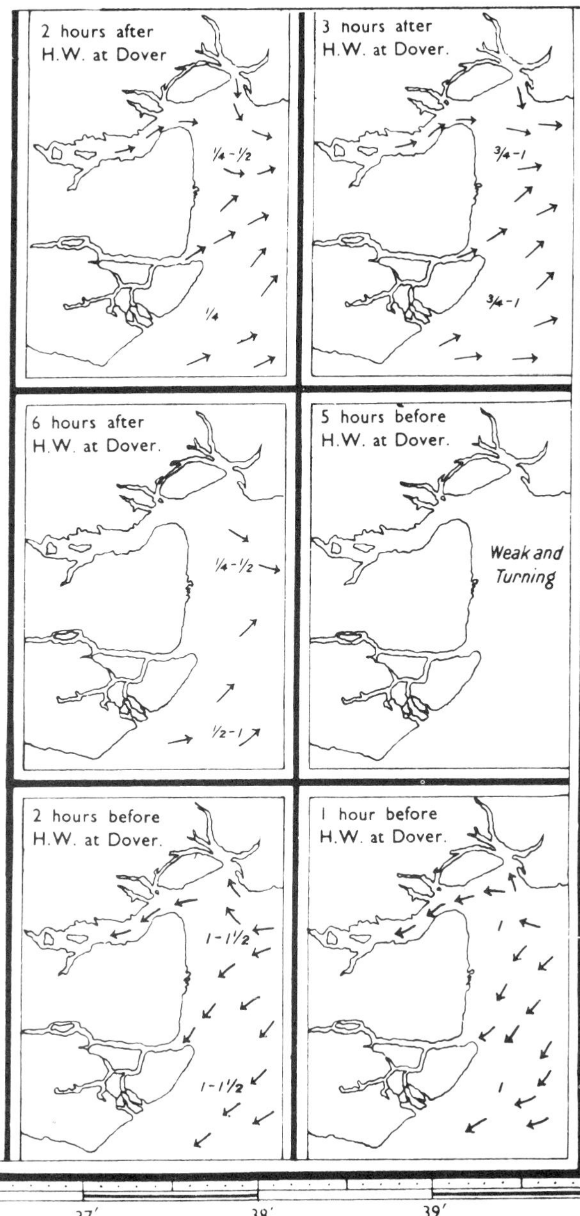

Fig. 4.11

Valuable to mariners in the absence of more specific information, it should be regarded as a competent general guide. As Admiralty charts are supported by many authoritative and comprehensive publications, the shortcomings of the system are wholly negated.

Tidal Stream information for rivers and harbours.

1. **Admiralty Sailing Directions. (Pilot's).**

In the Admiralty Sailing Directions detail is always included relating to features peculiar to the approaches of all ports. Where directions to mariners are given about the manner in which they should approach ports, where necessary, information about local tidal sets and rates is included.

2. **Plan and large scale Admiralty charts.**

Large scale Admiralty charts frequently include brief information relating to tidal currents in confined waters.

3. **Stanford charts.**
The port information which is published on the reverse side of all Stanford charts always includes advice about tidal streams at the entrance to and within ports.

General information relating to tides and tidal streams.

The more practical experience a yachtsman gains with tides, the better he will be able to comprehend that which is written in this chapter. Until he gains that experience, the following remarks should prove helpful.

1. If a port is in an estuary or at the mouth of a river, it is probable that the duration of ebb flow will exceed that of the flood; put another way, the outflow of river water will probably augment the ebb and retard the flood, so the period of ebb will be prolonged and that of the flood will be shortened.
2. A period of heavy rain will increase the volume of river water, just as a prolonged drought will decrease it. It is likely that a river in spate will lengthen the normal duration of ebb flow, and increase its rate. Drought conditions will probably produce the reverse effect.
3. Prolonged strong onshore winds in an estuary can produce a building-up of water within the estuary, if it has a reach of a few miles. This could increase the predicted depths of water, particularly in the upper reaches.
4. A high barometer causes depths of water to be slightly less than predicted heights, whereas a low barometer has the reverse effect. Differences created in this way should not normally exceed one foot.
5. A yachtsman must do his homework with tides before sailing, and do it thoroughly. When under way he should have the broad pattern of tides and tidal streams in his mind.
6. In restricted waters the good seaman will endeavour to be in the most shallow area on a rising tide, even though this may sometimes mean that he must delay progress towards his destination to achieve it.
7. Unless a yachtsman is familiar with the area in which he is navigating, it could never be regarded as excessively cautious if he allows a generous margin of water beneath his keel.
8. It is sometimes sensible to anchor and wait for the strength of a tidal stream to diminish, rather than to fight it and make negligible headway over the ground.

Conclusion.

Inevitably there will be the purists to whom the general advices contained within this chapter are suspect: those who are not entirely convinced that safety and simplicity can go hand in hand at sea. In the interests of safety at sea the authors are convinced that yachtsmen desperately need a simple and understandable means by which they can obtain and deal with tidal phenomena. The authors have long felt that all other books available to yachtsmen really cater for professionals and no more than 10% of yachtsmen. They hope that what is written here will be of real service to the remaining 90%

Additional Note on Chart Datum

Correspondence received at the Hydrographic Office in Taunton from yachtsmen and others indicates that, in the minds of some, the adoption of Lowest Astronomical Tide (L.A.T.) as Chart Datum causes confusion. It is hoped that the following remarks will be instructive to yachtsmen generally.

Hitherto Chart Datum was the approximate mean level of low water spring tides, MLWS. But due to astronomical effects at certain times of the year, not infrequently low water fell below this level in many areas. It was an undesirable feature. After all, mariners should reasonably expect that charted soundings are the lowest they will encounter in normal conditions. In addition the system could create misunderstanding in the minds of some seamen. Lack of understanding can lead to errors, and errors at sea often contain risk. Although the Admiralty has always used a precise and simple code in their tide tables to indicate when tidal preditions have to be *subtracted* from charted soundings, it was recognised that a change to a *lower level of charted soundings,* a reduced Chart datum, was desirable in the interests of seamen generally. This is to say, desirable in the sense that a seaman would then reasonably expect that almost every tidal height prediction in the Admiralty Tide Tables has to be added to Chart Datum, and only in very rare cases would it need to be subtracted. So it was determined to use approximate L.A.T. as Chart Datum for the future. It is the lowest level capable of being predicted in normal meteorological conditions.

In 1968 the Admiralty commenced metrication of their charts, and so their 'new look' charts show soundings – and other heights – in metres. New Admiralty charts are easily recognised by the wide use of colour wash on them: old ones are plain white. As old charts are withdrawn and replaced, so is the Chart Datum reduced to the approximate level of L.A.T. It can be said, therefore, that all Admiralty charts which show soundings in fathoms and feet use the old Chart Datum, and those which give soundings in metres have approximate L.A.T. as their datum. Stanford charts have yet to be modernised and so, as with old style Admiralty charts, they use the old Chart Datum.

Tidal predictions in the Admiralty Tide Tables have been calculated from approximate L.A.T. for the last three years – but how many yachtsmen are aware of that? This similarly applies to all tide tables obtainable from other sources, because they merely quote Admiralty predictions. Practically, these predictions are correct for the new style Admiralty charts, but not for the old ones. Whilst demanding caution of any mariner, in this latter comment there is no cause for dismay. It merely means that, on *any* charts giving soundings in fathoms and feet, datum is probably 1 to 4 feet below the soundings on the chart, an amount not usually measurable by modern sounding equipment suitable for use in small craft.

In any case, if yachtsmen take the seamanlike precaution of reading the tidal information and data on any large scale chart used, they should not have doubts about the datum to which soundings are referred. Naturally, on the new Admiralty charts the yachtsman must expect to see soundings indicating slightly less water in shallow areas than have hitherto been shown, and drying areas which have apparently increased in size. But of course nothing has materially changed, and a cartographer is unable to lower the sea level at the stroke of a pen. He is in fact adding a safety factor to Admiralty charts.

CHAPTER 5

Compass Work

It has been said before and it is worthwhile repeating here: a yachtsman's compass is the most important single item of equipment in his craft.

This being acknowledged, it is both dismaying and saddening to the writer that of all the gear and paraphernalia both necessary and dear to the heart of the small boat sailor, in so many cases it is his compass about which he knows the least.

The subject can be deep and baffling to the amateur. This chapter is intended to impart to him sufficient knowledge and know-how to enable him to regard his compass, and all the little problems it brings in its train, with confidence.

Magnetism, magnets and the magnetism of the earth.

Since early history it has been known that certain ferrous ores, which are those containing iron, have the property of being able to attract other particles of a like material to them. It has also been known that pieces of such ore, when freely suspended, will settle in a certain direction. As science and knowledge of the subject progressed it was found that, by relatively simple means, a piece of hard iron could be so wrought and treated that it would permanently retain its properties of attraction. So magnets as we know them were born. They may be wrought in a number of shapes but the type with which we must concern ourselves here is the 'bar' magnet. Some of these can be needle-like and very small indeed.

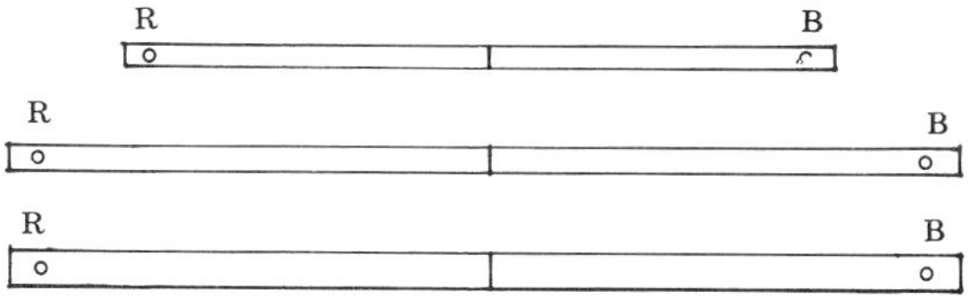

Fig. 5.1

In an artificially produced bar magnet it is assumed that the points of attraction, known by convention as 'poles', are located close to, but not at, its ends. Again by convention, one is named the red pole and the other the blue. To facilitate the work of those who use magnets the ends are usually painted accordingly.

It is assumed that 'lines of force' emerge from the red pole and enter the blue in the following manner:–

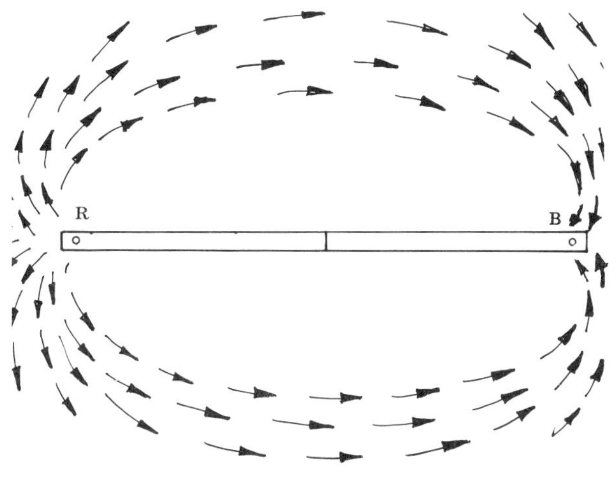

Fig. 5.2

Perhaps a school experiment may be recalled, whereby fine iron filings being placed on a piece of paper, a magnet is placed beneath them. Slight vibration of the paper causes the filings to align themselves with the lines of force, much in the pattern of that produced above. Such lines of force are termed a magnetic field.

If the reader cares to experiment with two bar magnets he can prove to himself one of the fundamental laws of magnetism: that different poles attract and like poles repel one another. Lay one magnet on a table and, using cotton, centrally suspend the other one over it. If the suspended magnet is lowered until both are close enough to interact upon one another - placed in each other's magnetic fields - the suspended one will come to rest parallel to the other, yet with opposing poles.

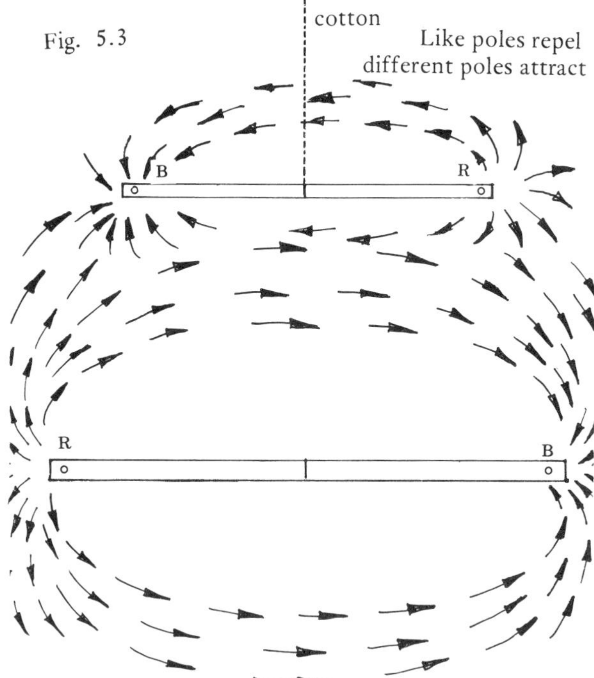

Fig. 5.3

The earth itself has identical properties to those of a magnet and, for compass work, it is regarded as one. If the earth is substituted for the large bar magnet used in the last experiment, and the needle magnets in the average compass card for the small one, it will be readily understood why a boat's compass possesses directional force.

Research tends to indicate that the lines of force of the earth's magnetic field are such as would be produced by a relatively short, extremely powerful, bar magnet at the centre of the earth which has its blue pole pointing in a northerly direction. One end of the axis of this imaginary bar magnet emerges at a point on the earth's surface in the Hudson's Bay area in the northern hemisphere. The other is in the locality of South Victoria Land in the southern hemisphere. The emergence of this axis produces, in the areas stated, what we know as the magnetic poles.

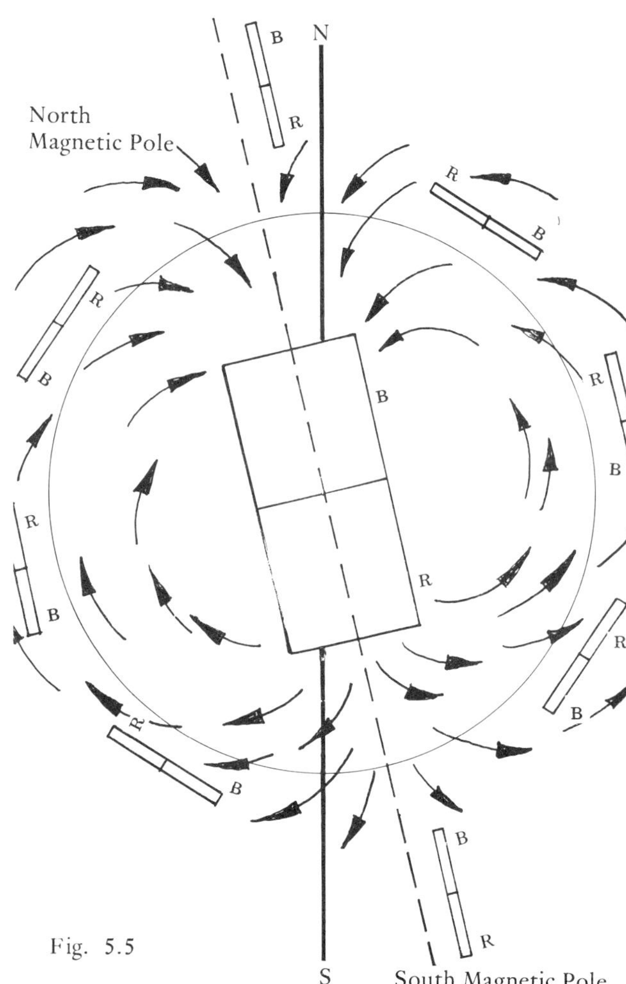

Fig. 5.5

Given access to the necessary magnets, another illuminating experiment could be conducted. The requirements are a large bar magnet and a tiny needle magnet. If the needle magnet is centrally suspended with fine cotton over the other, its behaviour will be identical to the suspended magnet in the former experiment. It will come to rest with its poles opposing those of the other. Much more important here, it will come to rest parallel to the lines of force in the magnetic field in which it is placed. Proof that this is so will be obtained by moving the needle magnet towards one end or the other of the large magnet. It will tilt downwards, aligning itself with the lines of force in the locality in which it is placed.

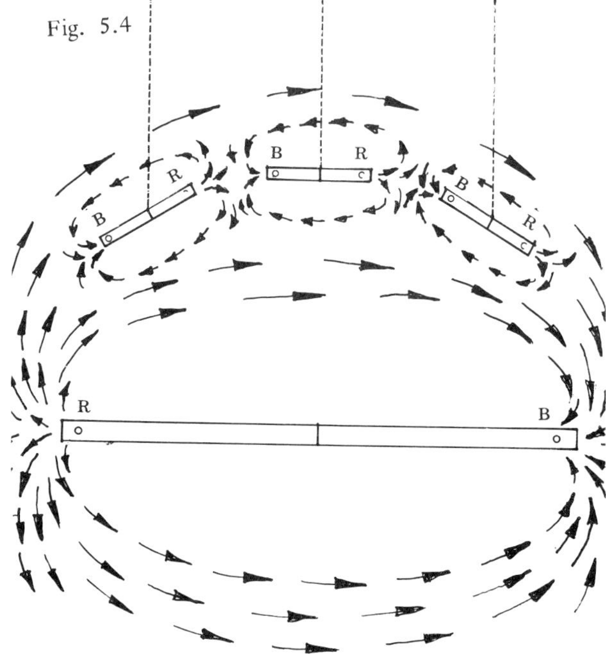

Fig. 5.4

As will be realised from a study of Fig. 5.5, a freely suspended magnetic needle, such as one of those found in a compass card, which is placed in the earth's magnetic field will align itself with the lines of force present in the locality in which it is situated. In so doing it will point to both the north and the south magnetic poles. Again by convention, it is only north-seeking – note that: north **seeking** – or red end which is regarded in compass work. Yes, of course it would be more explicit to refer to both ends, but reference to one end automatically implies reference to the other, and it is more simple.

Referring again to Fig. 5.5, it will be seen that roughly in the vicinity of the equator a magnetic needle will lie parallel to the surface of the earth. In the vicinity of the magnetic poles it will lie vertically. In intermediate latitudes it will tilt downwards towards the magnetic pole of the hemisphere in which it is situated. The seaman is naturally concerned with the 'horizontal component' (Fig. 5.6) of this phenomenon. It must obviously be greatest at the equator and non-existent at the magnetic poles.

Fig. 5.6

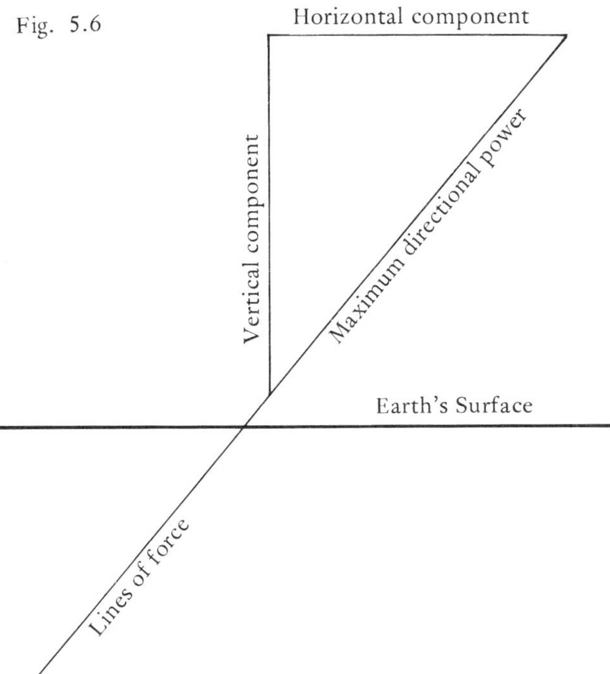

An example of the angle of incidence of lines of force with the earth's surface in the middle latitudes. Only the horizontal component, considerably less than the maximum directional power, will give the compass directional power.

It will now be understood why a magnetic compass is useless at the magnetic poles and why, for navigational purposes in those areas, more sophisticated means of obtaining direction must be adopted. It is fortunate that the magnetic poles are located in areas well away from the main sea lanes of the world. The writer would like to be able to state that the positions of the magnetic poles are fixed as arbitrarily as the geographical poles themselves but, to confuse the issue still more, they move very slightly year by year in an unknown path.

The magnetic compass.

A boat's compass, or more accurately the permanent magnet or magnets attached to the underside of its card, is a refinement of the tiny bar magnet whose behaviour in the earth's magnetic field has been discussed.

In large magnetic compasses, instead of using one bar magnet, four or six may be used, all being precisely parallel to each other. It has been found that, by arranging compass magnets in this way, the directional power of a compass is increased. A compass with this ability to 'hunt', or return to, magnetic north quickly, is said to have 'dead beat' qualities.

Due to the inherent difficulties in manufacturing small compasses which have dead beat properties a different system is widely used. A ring magnet, circular as its name implies, is attached to the underside of the card. It is magnetised in such a way as to have identical properties to the larger dead beat compasses.

The compass card is mounted on a frictionless pivot located centrally in the compass bowl. It is so designed that, by giving the card a low centre of gravity, at rest it will always remain horizontal. This is to prevent it from tilting downwards in its endeavour to align itself more nearly to the earth's lines of force in intermediate - and our own - latitudes.

The accuracy of the pivot is such that, the compass being tilted by dynamic forces, the card will remain horizontal. To assist the action of the pivot, the compass bowl is invariably mounted in gymbals. In a boat this combination is essential.

Although these devices are sufficient to keep the card level in all conditions, the sometimes violent action of a boat will cause the compass card to gyrate and vibrate sharply unless means are adopted to dampen down this movement. Dampening is effected by filling the compass bowl with a mixture of water and alcohol, the latter being used for its anti-freeze properties.

The axis of the compass needles, or the magnetised sections of the ring magnet, is accurately aligned with the north point printed on the card itself. Consequently the north - south line on the compass card will align itself with the earth's lines of force always provided no other magnetic influence is present to deflect the compass card.

Fig. 5.7

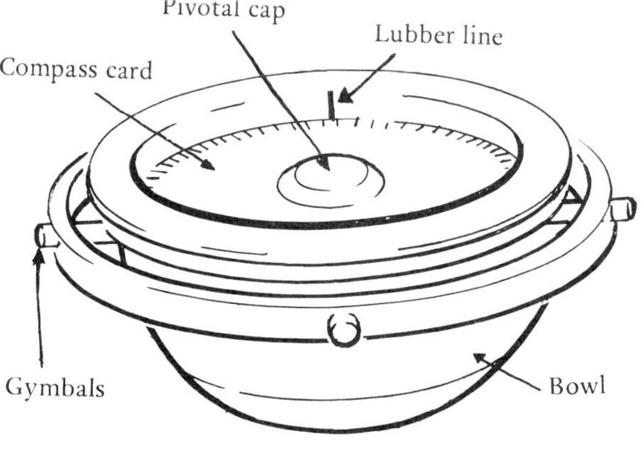

Mariner's compass

The periphery of modern compass cards is graduated in degrees from 0° at the north point, clockwise through 360°. Small compasses such as are generally used on yachts and similar craft have cards graduated in 2° or 5° steps for greater clarity.

A line or a fine wire, known as the lubber's point or lubber line, is painted or affixed vertically on the inner side of the compass bowl. This line indicates the direction of the boat's head, thus it is essential so to mount the compass that the axis of the compass bowl, indicated by the lubber line and guide marks on the bowl's exterior, is accurately aligned in the fore and aft line of the boat. The lubber line being close to the compass card, the boat's head, or heading, may be read at a glance.

Direction at sea.
When a boat is out of sight of land the horizon appears as a circle with the boat at its centre and, no matter where the boat moves, the circle remains constant. To point a boat in a certain direction a mariner must have some constant line of reference, some datum, to which he can relate direction. Otherwise he may go round in circles. The datum is provided by the axis of the compass needles which is indicated by the north point on the compass card.

Each of the following directions can be described by referring them to compass north:

Boat's head or heading. The direction in which the boat is heading.

The Course. The direction in which the boat is being steered.

A Bearing. The direction of an object from the boat. The initiate may now be a little confused, particularly if he hitherto believed that the north point on a compass pointed to geographical north. He is about to learn that in addition to taking into account the magnetism of the earth itself, before he can determine true direction from his compass he must take into account another elusive factor.

Variation.
Variation is the angle produced between the true meridian, which is to say, true north, and the direction of earth's lines of force, usually referred to as the magnetic meridian. If this angle is known it becomes a simple matter for the navigator, aware that his compass will line itself up with the magnetic meridian, to apply 'variation' to his compass to determine his true direction.

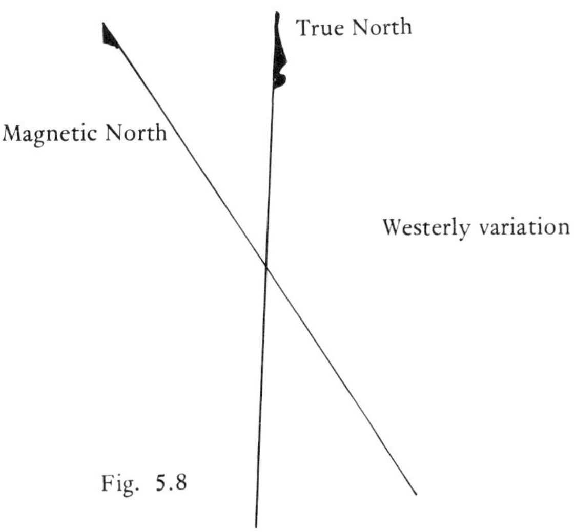

Fig. 5.8

The amount of variation differs widely in various parts of the world. It changes only when a craft changes its position. No matter in what direction a boat is heading, the variation remains the same.

When magnetic north lies to the west of true north the variation is called westerly and when it lies to the east it is called easterly.

Special charts are published by the Admiralty which give the amount of variation in localities throughout the world. On these charts all places having the same amount of variation are linked together by lines, known as isogonic lines, and given the position for which variation is required, extracting the required information from them is a simple matter. These charts are usually used by deep-sea mariners and it is not necessary for yachtsmen to buy them as the same information is promulgated in a different way on large scale charts.

Variation is always given on large scale charts within the compass roses printed upon them in the following manner:

Fig. 5.9

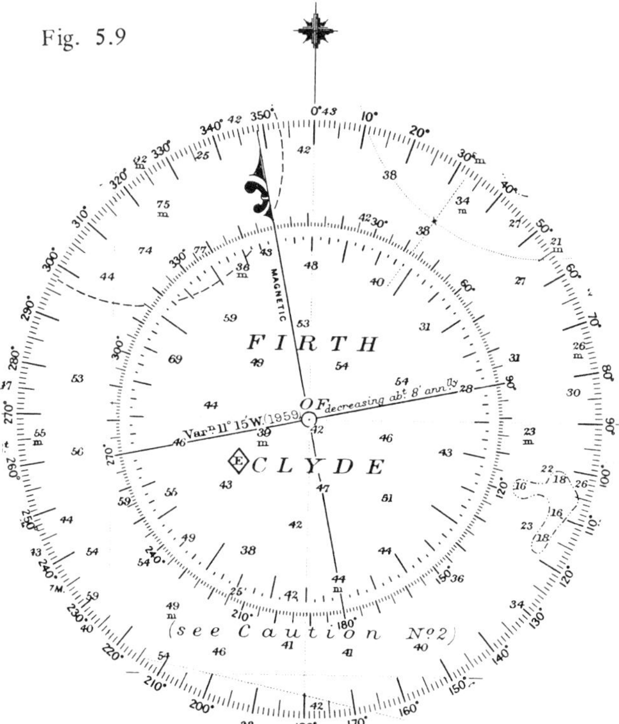

It should be noted that the variation is given for a certain year and following it is information indicating by how much the variation in that place increases or decreases annually. This secular change, as it is known, occurs because of the slight movement of the magnetic poles. To bring the variation up to date this correction must be applied where necessary.

Example: Given the following information on a chart, find the correct variation for 1971. Var'n. 7° 50'W. (1954) decreasing ab't 10' ann'ly.

1954 variation	7° 50'W.
Annual change (17 years x 10') -	2° 50'
1971 variation	5° 0'W.

In practice one would do this type of calculation mentally and take the result to the nearest degree. It must be remembered that, variation being different in diverse localities, one must always extract variation from the compass rose nearest to the area in which one is sailing.

The inner compass rose in Fig. 5.9 will have been noticed, together with the fact that its north point indicates a direction different from the true north point on the outer rose. It is a magnetic compass rose and is offset by the amount of variation in that area If, then, a mariner wishes to take off a course for which the error of variation is already allowed, he may use this magnetic compass rose. Note also that on Stanford's charts only the magnetic rose is printed.

Deviation.

Every piece of ferrous metal in a boat will possess some magnetic properties to a greater or lesser degree. The magnetic field created by a steel hull will be considerable. Each piece of ferrous metal used in the construction of a composite boat will produce its own magnetic field. Every item of equipment made of ferrous metal will possess similar properties. Electrical equipment too may manifest like characteristics.

Of these magnetic fields, which may be present in considerable numbers, some will be negligible and some will not. Certain fields may create a 'pull' on the compass in one direction, others may pull in another. Some will cancel each other out and others combine to produce stronger fields. A number may be far too distant from the compass to have any effect upon it. The yachtsman will not be concerned with this possible profusion of magnetic fields but only in the resultant, or total, affect upon his compass if any.

It is not necessary here to delve deeply into a subject which is profound and complex. It nevertheless remains essential that the yachtsman has a basic understanding of the manner in which the resultant of his craft's magnetic field may affect his compass.

Deliberately over-simplifying, let it be assumed for the sake of convenience that the effect of ferrous metal in a boat is to produce a total magnetic field whose red pole is in the bow and blue in the stern. We shall now study what effect this magnetic field would have on the boat's compass.

On a westerly course the red pole of the boat will attract the blue pole of the compass card and in so doing will cause compass north to be deflected to the right, or eastwards. If the boat heads on an easterly course the compass card will be deflected to the westward.

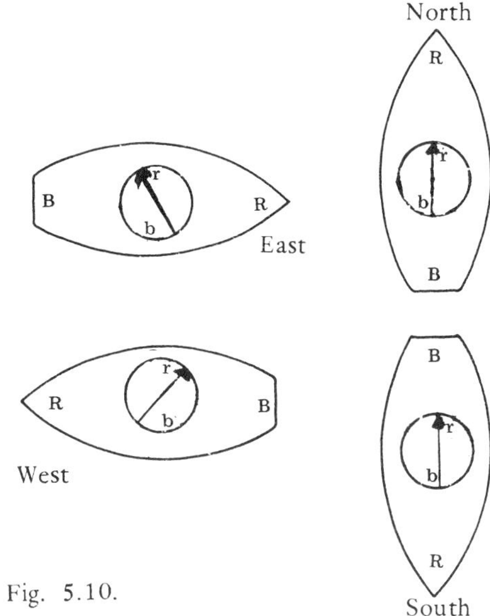

Fig. 5.10.

On a northerly heading, the poles of the boat will be in line with the poles of the compass and so there will be no deflection of the compass card. This will similarly apply on a southerly heading.

In this simple but by no means typical illustration, maximum deflection of the compass card was experienced on easterly and westerly headings and none on north and south headings. It will now be apparent that the deflection of the compass card caused by the magnetic properties of a boat is a variable quantity. The amount of deflection if any will entirely depend upon the direction in which a boat is heading. It will have two maxima and two minima and at intermediate compass headings it will vary between maximum and minimum. In the illustration it was assumed that the lines of force were in a fore-and-aft direction: in the majority of boats they will probably not be so and there are no means by which one can find out where they do lie. All one can do is to find out what the deflection on various headings is and make due allowance in one's courses.

The deflection of the compass card away from magnetic north is called **deviation** and is named in the same manner as variation. That is to say, if compass north is deflected to the west of the magnetic meridian, the deviation is called westerly. If it is deflected to the east it is called easterly.

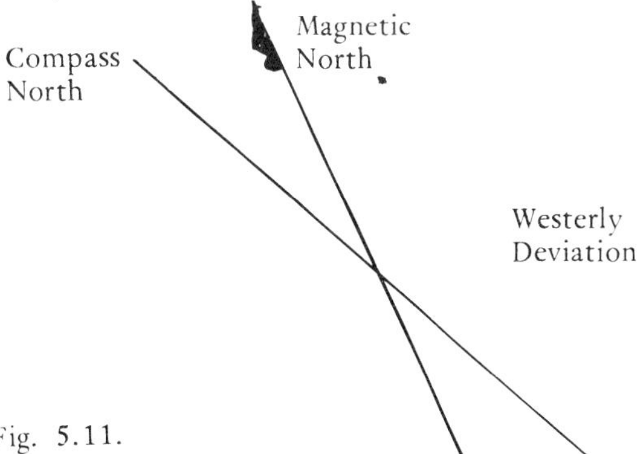

Fig. 5.11.

It will now be seen that although deviation has something in common with variation in that it is an error of the compass, in fact it is very different from it. It will change in amount with every change in the direction of the boat's head. Without a table from which the mariner may extract the deviation for every compass heading, it will be impossible to apply it.

Compass error.

When both variation and deviation have to be considered at the same time, as for instance when converting a true course taken off the chart into a compass course by which a mariner can steer, it is customary to combine the two mathematically. The resultant is known as total error or, more commonly, compass error.

Example. Variation 15°E., deviation 5°E. = 20°E. compass error.

Rule. Same names - add.

Example. Variation 10°W., deviation 3°E. = 7°W. compass error.

Rule. Different names - subtract and name the result the same as the greater.

The majority of yachtsmen prefer to 'work magnetic', which is to say they extract their courses from the magnetic compass roses on their charts. This eliminates the need to apply variation in their course calculations, it only remaining for them to apply compass deviation if any.

The affects of variation and deviation on a compass.

To clearly understand the affect of variation and deviation upon a compass it should prove helpful to study the following diagram. It portrays a boat steering 300° by her compass with the variation 10°E, and the deviation 20°E.

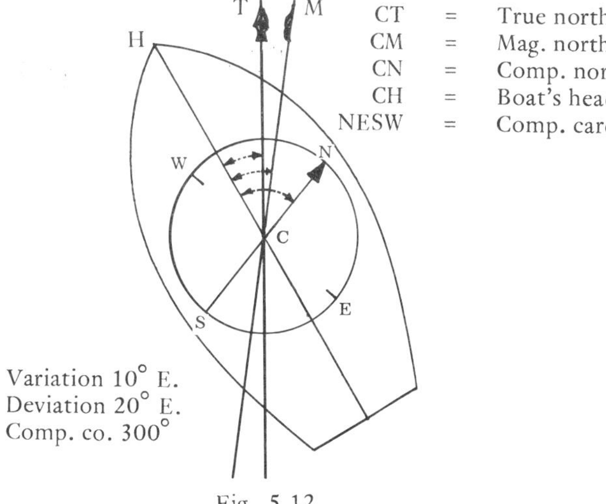

Fig. 5.12

Explanation.

Angle TCM	=	**Variation**, which is the angle between the true and magnetic meridians.
Angle MCN	=	**Deviation**, which is the angle between the magnetic meridian and compass north.
Angle TCN	=	**Compass error**, the angle between the true meridian and compass north.
Angle TCH	=	**True course**, the angle between the true meridian and the boat's head.
Angle MCH	=	**Magnetic course**, the angle between the magnetic meridian and the boat's head.
Angle NCH	=	**Compass course**, the angle between north and the boat's head.

Construction.

(a) The true meridian is drawn as a vertical line.

(b) The magnetic meridian is drawn to the left or right of the true meridian as appropriate, the angle between them representing the amount of variation.

(c) Compass north is drawn to the left or right of the magnetic meridian as appropriate, the angle between them representing the amount of deviation.

(d) The compass heading is drawn the appropriate number of degrees to the right of compass north.

(e) The outlines of the compass card and the boat are then completed.

Notes.

The variation being easterly in this case, note how the magnetic meridian has been produced to the right of the true meridian. Similarly, easterly deviation has been shown by drawing compass north to the right of the magnetic meridian. This is in conformity with the rules given previously and is reiterated here:

Variation is named easterly when the magnetic meridian lies to the eastward, or to the right, of the true meridian and westerly when it lies to the left.

Deviation is named easterly when compass north is deflected to the eastward, or to the right, of the magnetic meridian and westerly when it is deflected to the left.

A complete appreciation of Fig. 5.12 will lead to a full understanding of the inter-related factors governing course correction. The method of construction is given and, using one's own choice of variation, deviation and compass course, one may assist learning by practice with this diagram.

Correction of courses and bearings.

If error is present in a compass it is essential to know how to apply it. Must it be applied to the right, or to the left? Added, or subtracted? Similarly, bearings taken with a compass which is known to have errors must be corrected before they can be drawn on the chart. Which way must the error be applied?

Here we have one of the small, recurring, yet important problems with which a small boat sailor in deep waters is faced: the conversion of true or magnetic courses and bearings into compass courses and bearings: in reverse, the conversion of compass and bearings into magnetic or true ones.

50 - 50 may be considered good odds. A guess has a 50% chance of being correct. The need for accuracy in these calculations is best appreciated by considering the case of a yachtsman who, on a certain compass heading, has 5°W deviation in his compass. If he allows this error the wrong way he will steer 10° off course. In thick weather the consequences could be serious.

The basic requirement is a simple, fool-proof system, perhaps aided by a jingle or catchword by which means the mariner may, without reference to written aids, correct his courses and bearings immediately and with assurance.

There are many such systems and the majority have merit. One should avoid a system which he personally cannot readily assimilate. For this reason some choose one method and some another. Having chosen a system it is wise to forget all others due to the possibility of confusion. The adopted system should be accepted in its entirety: attempts to further simplify or improve can also lead to confusion.

One such system the writer can recommend is the memorisation of the CERM and MELC rules, the application of which is described below.

To convert a compass course or bearing into a magnetic course or bearing.

Memorise	CERM (call it 'Serm')
Expanded	Compass Easterly Right Magnetic
Expanded again	From compass to magnetic allow easterly to the right.
And again	When converting a compass course or bearing into a magnetic course or bearing, allow easterly deviation to the right.

If CERM indicates that easterly must be allowed to the right, then westerly must be allowed to the left.

To convert a magnetic course or bearing into a compass course or bearing.

Memorise	MELC (call it 'MELK')
Expanded	Magnetic Easterly Left Compass
Expanded again	From magnetic to compass allow easterly to the left.
And again	When converting a magnetic course or bearing into a compass course or bearing, allow easterly to the left.

If MELC indicates that easterly must be allowed to the left, then westerly must be allowed to the right.

The occasional yachtsman may wish to 'work true', thereby emulating the style of his deep-sea brethren. Having read the above he may ask himself why he should use a rule which is primarily devised for the application of deviation alone and not total, or compass, error.

None but the brave —. He may change the catchwords to CERT (**C**ompass **E**asterly **R**ight **T**rue) and TELC (**T**rue **E**asterly **L**eft **C**ompass). Identical rules and previous explanations will apply.

In applying any rule of this type, until one has become thoroughly familiar with it, he will find it helpful to imagine himself in the centre of a large compass looking outwards to the compass card's graduations. The way he must apply the correction, either left or right, will then be readily apparent.

Examples of the CERM and MELC rules.

(a) Given compass course 120°, deviation 4°E., find magnetic course. CERM dictates easterly deviation to right, therefore magnetic course is 124°.

(b) Given compass bearing 256°, deviation 6°W., find magnetic bearing. CERM dictates westerly deviation to left, therefore magnetic bearing is 250°

(c) Given magnetic course 177°, deviation 3°W., find compass course. MELC dictates westerly deviation to right, therefore compass course is 180°.

(d) Given magnetic bearing 309°, deviation 5°E., find compass bearing. MELC dictates easterly deviation to left, therefore compass bearing is 304°.

CHAPTER 6

Finding the Deviation

Whether a man commands a 1 tonner or a 1,000 tonner, only by comparison can he find the deviation in his magnetic compass. Comparison, that is to say, between what a distant object bears by that compass and what it **should** bear. Those who are conversant with celestial navigation have, in addition to terrestrial objects, almost every visible celestial body at their disposal to achieve this end. The small boat sailor is almost invariably restricted to the use of terrestrial objects.

In practice there are two cases to consider:—

(a) Swinging a boat to determine deviations on all compass headings. The term 'swinging' in this context is a seaman's term for carrying out a check for deviation on selected headings through 360°. Obviously it entails swinging a boat right round the compass.

(b) When sailing on a certain course, the mariner wishes to check his deviation on that course.

Details of the manner in which (a) may be achieved are explained below, (b) is carried out by all ships, large and small, if magnetic compasses are carried, perhaps once during every watch and at every alteration of course. This practice is almost non-existent in the off-shore sailing community, not due to negligence but because of inherent difficulties, lack of suitable opportunities and the limitations of the craft involved.

Putting the matter into perspective.

It must be emphasised that, in the opinion of the writer, the most satisfactory method of finding the deviations which may be present in a magnetic compass is to enlist the services of a compass adjuster. Compass makers and certain large retailers of compasses have at least one adjuster on their staff. For a small fee, plus expenses, he will find the deviations if any are present, reduce them by the use of corrector magnets if they tend to be large, and produce a table of deviations for use in the boat.

The above advice has even greater validity in the case of yachts constructed partially or wholly of steel which when at sea may be heeled over for lengthy periods. In these circumstances another constituent of deviation called heeling error may be introduced. The assessment and correction of heeling error is best left to the professional.

In craft in which it has been established that deviations are present they can and often do change over a long period. They may well alter if any structural changes involving iron or steel, or electrical equipment, are made. Possessing a craft in which compass deviations are known to exist, the prudent yachtsman will cause his compass to be checked for deviations once annually and carefully assess whether he should take a similar course after alterations or additions are made to his craft. He must bear in mind that a simple decision such as the removal of an outboard motor from its sea-stowage under a bunk to a position under a side bench in his cockpit could affect a compass sited within the cockpit. Many parallel cases could be cited, even that of an ill stowed iron frying pan, but it will suffice here to draw the attention of the reader to the general problem.

Corrector magnets are small bar magnets specially made for the reduction of deviations. Suitably sited they will produce an equal and opposite effect to the magnetic properties of a boat. Provision is made in the design of certain good compasses for their introduction where necessary. Where no provision is made, compass adjusters may affix them to the boat's structure in the vicinity of a compass where they would appear as tiny tubes serving no apparent purpose. The purchaser of a second-hand boat should be aware of these facts. An amateur should never manipulate existing magnets or introduce new ones. The reduction of deviations is strictly a matter for a professional.

The contents of this chapter are simplified, yet all described methods of determining deviations are entirely practical. Just how much one can simplify a fairly complex subject is a daunting decision to make. A knowledgeable motorist can service and carry out repairs to his car, **until** some totally baffling defect is experienced. At this point he will have to call in a motor engineer. The amateur yachtsman must be prepared, very occasionally, to experience some completely puzzling problem in relation to his magnetic compass and if this occurs he would be wise to consult a compass adjuster.

Deviation and types of compasses used by yachtsmen.

Hand-bearing compass. It is invariably assumed that hand bearing compasses have no deviations in them. This is a fair assumption, always provided they are used on deck in a position which is not close to potentially magnetic materials. For this reason they need not come into the deliberations which follow.

Dual-purpose compass. This type, which will have suitably large graduations, is usually mounted on the coach roof, a position which is clearly visible from the steering position. It will be so designed that it may be read from both a horizontal and a vertical position. The whole horizon being visible from such a site, bearing sights will be mounted on it so that it may be used for taking bearings.

Steering compass. A steering compass may be mounted in any position which is readily seen from the steering position. Such a site may be in a wheelhouse, in a midship cockpit or within the well of a sailing craft. As the requirement of the helmsman is the main consideration when siting such a compass, its position will in all probability render the task of finding deviations in it a little less easy. In craft where this type of compass is used, a hand-bearing compass is invariably used for navigational purposes. Unless a steering compass is sited by a person who is aware of the inherent problems, too often it may be fixed in a position decided only by the needs of the helmsman. The admonitions (d), (e) and (f) under the heading 'Preparation of a boat for the swing' must be taken into consideration and an ill-placed compass resited if necessary. Sometimes the position of a steering compass becomes a matter of compromise, between the position which would minimise possible deviations and that which is most suitable for the helmsman.

An assessment of the problems.

The inherent difficulties in keeping a small craft on course in a seaway make it necessary for the small boat sailor to keep errors of the compass in perspective. On a calm sea a large ship can be steered precisely on course for protracted periods and therefore due allowance must be made for an error of even 1°. In similar conditions the helmsman of a small craft cannot possibly achieve such accuracy and it would be almost ludicrous for him to make allowance for a similar error. What, it may be asked, is the amount of error which the yachtsman may regard as negligible? Errors of 2° or under may be regarded as minimal in small boats and in normal circumstances can be ignored.

Can the yachtsman envisage whether his deviations are likely to be large, relatively small or negligible? Only very rough guides can be given. It is a fair assumption that glass fibre or wooden boats with minimal ferrous metal in their construction and equipment, and well-placed electronic equipment where carried, may have negligible deviations in their compasses. At the other end of the scale, steel-hulled craft will almost certainly produce deviations of such magnitude that they cannot be ignored. In a boat made of non-magnetic materials, if an inboard motor is located beneath the well and a steering compass is sited in close proximity, deviations may be produced. In this latter case deviations may vary, depending upon whether the motor is running or is stopped. Summing up, for the remainder of composite craft both large and small, it would be seamanlike to check for compass deviations because, in various parts of the boat's structure, there could well be unsuspected magnetic materials.

Preparation of a boat for the swing.

Before attempting to swing a boat for deviations, the following conditions should prevail.

(a) It should be a fairly calm day and there should be no marked lop on the water.

(b) If the boat is going to be swung in a tideway, a period near slack water should be chosen.

(c) The boat should be in sea-going trim and upright.

(d) If practicable, no permanently positioned ferrous metal should be within 4 feet of the compass.

(e) No radios or electronic equipment should be within 5 feet of the compass.

(f) Loose gear made of ferrous metal should be in its sea stowage well clear of the compass.

(g) Electric wiring near the compass should be twin-flex and twisted to neutralise its magnetic properties.

The swing.

Swings for determining deviations have common factors; in any method adopted the principle remains the same. A distant fixed object is selected and its magnetic bearing is determined by one means or another. On a series of equidistant headings round the compass the boat is steadied and a bearing of the distant object is taken. Such headings should not be more than (say) 30° apart, a spacing which would give twelve separate observations. Obviously, the more observations taken the better and 12 observations should be regarded as a minimum. Each heading, and the compass bearing of the distant object on it, has to be recorded for later evaluation. Every endeavour should be made to achieve accuracy with the bearings: near enough is certainly not good enough in such an important undertaking.

Dual purpose compasses - first method.

A yacht mooring or a small buoy is chosen, the position of which can be determined from the chart, and the craft moored to it. A distant charted object such as a promontory, a lighthouse or a beacon three or more miles away is selected and the magnetic bearing of it from the buoy extracted from the chart. With a large oar to both propel the craft round the buoy and to hold it steady when required, the swing may be commenced.

On any convenient selected heading the craft is steadied. A carefully taken bearing of the distant object is obtained. Both the boat's heading and the bearing is recorded. At the pre-determined, equidistant intervals round the compass this procedure is followed. In a manner described later, the information thus produced may be evaluated.

Even more accurate results may be obtained from this method if suitable conditions exist in a yacht marina. Using warps between piers it is possible to rigidly hold a craft on successive headings.

Dual-purpose compasses - second method.

Although it may not be possible to hold a craft on a series of headings throughout a swing, similar results may be achieved although the craft is under way throughout. It entails manoeuvring her in very nearly the same position during the swing, steadying her when necessary. By relating position to objects near at hand - a moored boat, a channel buoy, a jetty - the boat's position will not materially change.

The distant object should be no less than 5 miles away in this case and, although it may be judged that an accurate magnetic bearing of it cannot be obtained, an alternative exists which renders recourse to the chart unnecessary. One should proceed as follows: the swing should be conducted on the lines previously described and, on completion, the total of all compass bearings calculated. This total must be divided by the number of bearings taken and the quotient will be the magnetic bearing required.

Dual-purpose compasses - third method.

Opportunities to swing a craft for compass deviations when under way occasionally occur when leading beacons in line (see chapter 3) or points in transit (see page 47) provide a precise magnetic bearing upon which a craft may be manoeuvred throughout a swing.

Steering compass only - the one practical method.

Two or three methods are propounded by which the yachtsman may himself determine the deviations in a compass he uses for steering alone. It is the conviction of the writer that the method which follows, based upon a method used by compass adjusters, is the only one which should be attempted by the amateur. Other methods can at best give results which lack the desired accuracy.

The problem.

Bearings taken from the compass, for which it is required to obtain the deviations, have to be obtained, and the only feasible method of determining what they are is by using a subsidiary device called a pelorus. With this one can find the relative bearing of the distant object, which is to say the bearing in relation to the boat's head. At the moment a bearing by pelorus is taken, if the boat's head by compass is noted, it is simply a matter of adding together the relative bearing and the compass heading to determine the compass's bearing of the distant object.

The following figure portrays a boat whose true heading is 050° when the relative bearing of an object is found to be 077°.

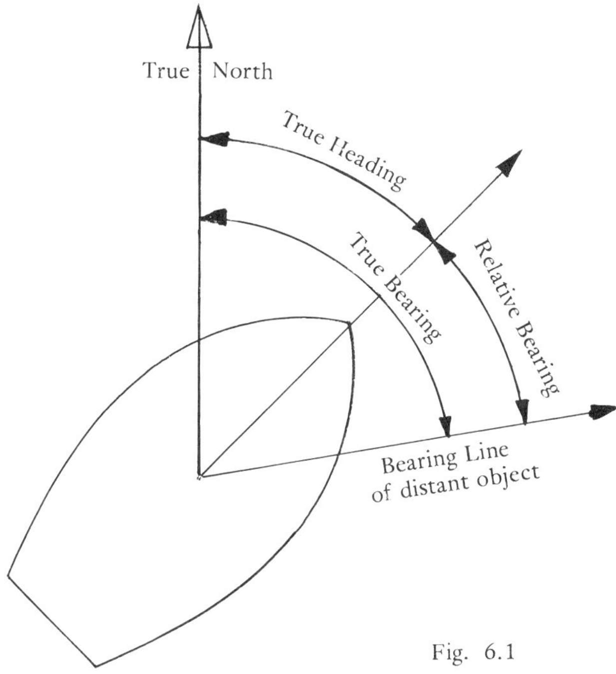

Fig. 6.1

A Pelorus.

A pelorus is a bearing ring, an azimuth circle, graduated in degrees on its periphery from 0° to 360°. Sight vanes are mounted over it which pivot about its centre. If the sight vanes are lined up with an object for which a relative bearing is needed, the bearing may be read directly from the disc. For a few pounds a pelorus may be purchased from some large chandlers but consideration may be given to constructing one's own.

PELORUS

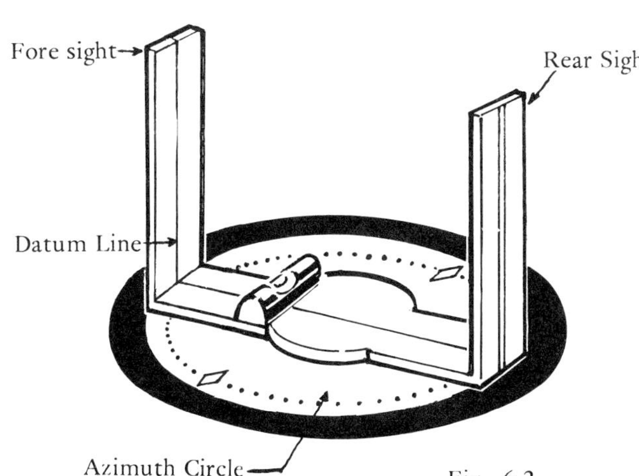

Fig. 6.2

Constructing a pelorus.

The bearing ring may be made of metal or plastic and degrees from 0° to 360° inscribed on it. An entirely practical alternative is to draw the bearing ring on a card and glue it to a wooden disc. The sights can be made of transparent rigid plastic. Vertical lines drawn centrally on the fore and rear sights will be necessary, together with a corresponding line on the horizontal section. It will be evident that great care must be taken to locate the sights centrally on the disc, to ensure that the bush of the bearing is vertical and has no play in it, and to ensure that the fore and rear sights are precisely vertical to the horizontal section.

Setting up a pelorus

A pelorus must be so fixed in a position on the deck that its 0° - 180° line is accurately placed in, or parallel to the fore and aft line of the craft. Evidently, if this is not achieved then any relative bearing taken with it will be inaccurate. Boat builders of repute work extremely accurately and it may be said that a straight, fore-and-aft member of a boat's superstructure is precisely parallel to the keel. If, then, one's boat has such sections they may be used to line up the pelorus.

The case of a craft whose superstructures do not provide such convenient lines for reference must be considered. Provided the upperworks of one's boat allow us such a method, the fore-and-aft line may be defined in the following way:—

Using a piece of string, one end is held at the apex of the bow. With a piece of chalk tied to the other end and the string kept taut chalk marks are made on both the port and starboard sides of the boat against the hull. Using the reference marks thus produced, two arcs of precisely equal radius are scribed. A straight line drawn through the two points of intersection of these arcs will be in the exact fore-and-aft line of the boat. Where a mast defeats this method, the after side of the mast, at deck level, may be used as the datum point for scribing the first radius.

Fig. 6.3

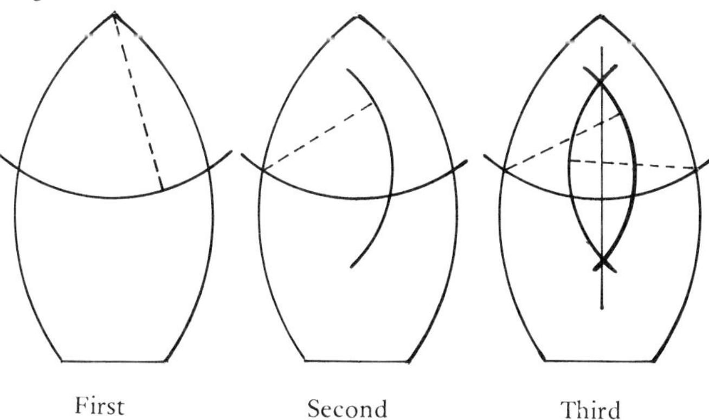

Determining the compass bearing from a pelorus bearing.

Two people are needed, one the helmsman who cons the boat and reads the steering compass for the benefit of the other who takes the bearings by pelorus.

Their object must be to take a relative bearing by pelorus when the craft is on the desired heading; how they co-operate in this undertaking is largely a matter of choice. It is suggested that the one who is reading the steering compass calls ON to the other when the correct heading is achieved. It is helpful if he keeps repeating ON as long as the boat's head remains on the required heading, and OFF when the boat's head wanders. The repetition of ON gives the bearing-taker time – time to ascertain the bearing, because good bearings are not obtained in a split second.

The relative bearing obtained from the pelorus is applied in the following manner:—

Examples

(a)	Heading by steering compass		120°
	Relative bearing of distant object	+	073° (by pelorus)
	Compass bearing of distant object		193°
(b)	Heading by steering compass		300°
	Relative bearing of distant object	+	227° (by pelorus)
			527°
	Reject 360°	-	360°
	Compass bearing of distant object		167°

The above calculations can be done mentally, or by rapid calculations on scrap paper.

Summing up, this method of finding the deviations is not so straightforward as those described for use with a dual-purpose compass but it should be equally as accurate and well within the competence of the average yachtsman.

Steering compass only - an occasional case.

On fairly large craft, sometimes of unusual design, two fixed compasses may be carried. One is for navigational purposes and therefore is on deck and the steering compass may be in the wheelhouse. Deviations in the steering compass may be found by first determining those present in the 'standard' compass. Thereafter, careful comparison between the two compasses on a series of heading through 360° will give the differences, if any, between them. These differences, and the deviations known to be in the standard compass, can be used to calculate the deviations present in the steering compass.

The production of a deviation card.

A table of deviations, generally known as a deviation card, must be carried in a craft whose compass is known to have deviations present in it. The production of one is quite straightforward and, armed with the series of headings upon which bearings have been taken, together with the corresponding compass bearings, one may proceed homewards with the intention of completing the work at a suitable opportunity.

First, one must draw up a table of results in the following form:—

(a) Compass heading	(b) Comp. brg. of object	(c) Mag. brg. of object	(d) Deviation E. or W.
000°	126°	124°	2°W.
030°	124°	124°	Nil
060°	120°	124°	4°E.
090°	118°	124°	6°E.
120°	117°	124°	7°E.
150°			
Etc.			

Column (a) is self-explanatory. In column (b) one must enter the compass bearing of the distant object on the various headings. Column (c) is the magnetic bearing of the distant object and will, therefore, be constant on all headings. It is column (d) which will at first cause mystification because in it one must determine and name the deviations.

More than one method is available for naming deviations but the writer tends to favour the following one:

Memorise:	TROEE (Loosely pronounced TRUE)
Expanded:	When True is to the Right of Observed, the Error is East.
Expanded again:	When the true bearing (or the magnetic bearing) is to the right of the observed bearing (that is, the compass bearing) the compass error (or deviation) is easterly.
For us:	If the magnetic bearing of the distant object is to the right of the compass bearing, the deviation must be named easterly. If it is to the left it must be named westerly.

Column (d) may now be completed. The amount of deviation against each heading will be the difference between the bearings in columns (b) and (c). The deviations must be named according to the above rule.

The deviations must now be transferred to squared paper in the form of a graph.

Fig. 6.4

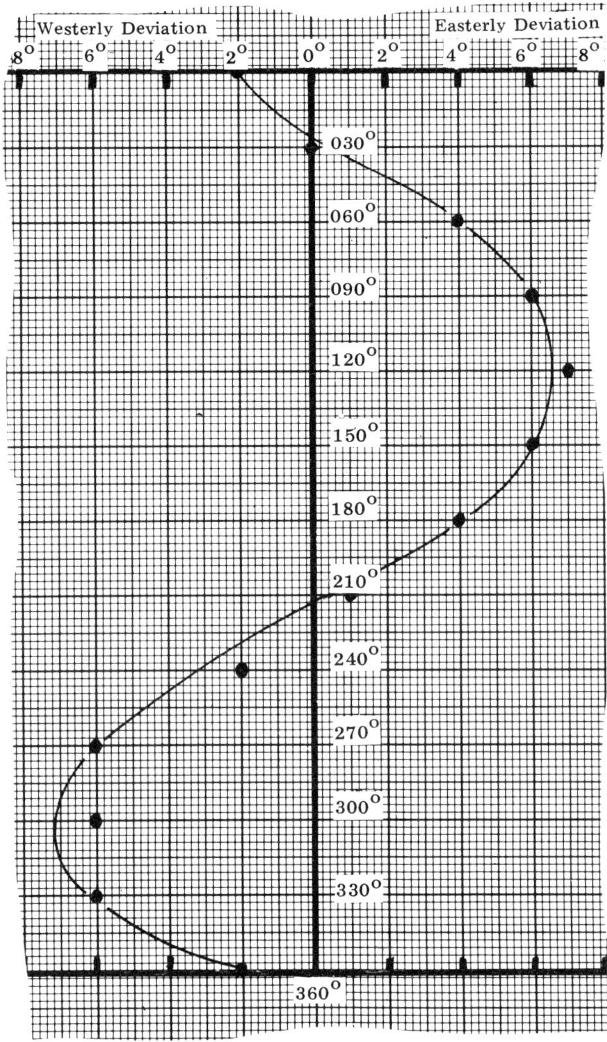

To construct the graph, one commences by drawing a line down the centre of the squared paper to represent the periphery of the compass card as a straight line. Equidistant marks are made on this line, the number being equal to the number of headings upon which bearings were taken. Against each mark the appropriate compass heading is written, commencing with 0° - north - uppermost.

To the left of the line, one or more small squares must be allowed for each degree of westerly deviation. On the right of the line the same procedure must be adopted for easterly deviations.

It remains to transfer the deviations to the graph. Each one is entered on the horizontal line corresponding to the compass heading upon which it was taken, to the right or left of the line as appropriate. These various deviations must now be joined together in a sweeping, even curve. It is quite possible that one or two deviations will not coincide with the natural curve; they would be bearings in which error has occurred. These divergent deviations which would, if included in the curve, destroy its symmetry, should be ignored. The curve being completed, it will give in graph form the deviation for every compass heading.

It is neither seamanlike nor practical to carry such a graph on a boat and so the valuable information it imparts must be transferred to a Deviation Card which may be pinned over one's chart table for easy reference. From the graph, deviations may be extracted for as many compass headings as one chooses. It is proposed that deviations at 10° intervals will prove entirely adequate. Deviation Cards are invariably produced in this form:

DEVIATION CARD

Compass	Deviation	Magnetic
000°	2°W	358°
010°	2°W	008°
020°	1°W	019°
030°	Nil	030°
040°	1°E	041°
050°	3°E	053°
060°	4°E	064°
070°	5°E	075°
Etc.	Etc.	Etc.

A Deviation Card may be used for transposing compass courses into magnetic ones and vice versa. Interpolation is of course necessary if courses fall between the steps given.

Checking a deviation during passage.

As has already been intimated, seldom is this procedure carried out by yachtsmen during a passage due to the inherent difficulties involved. Even then it can only be carried out when a dual-purpose compass is carried. A check on the deviation of such a compass may be obtained by taking transit bearings of terrestrial objects and it must be said that such transits are infrequently encountered.

A transit bearing occurs when two objects are in transit - in line - with the observer's eye.

A compass bearing being obtained when the objects are in transit, this may be compared with the magnetic bearing extracted from the chart. The difference between the bearings, named using the TROEE rule, will give the deviation on the compass course at that time.

Two well-defined headlands are ideal for this form of check but many other charted objects will serve equally as well: a lighthouse with an off-shore rock; a beacon with a church spire; leading beacons; and so on.

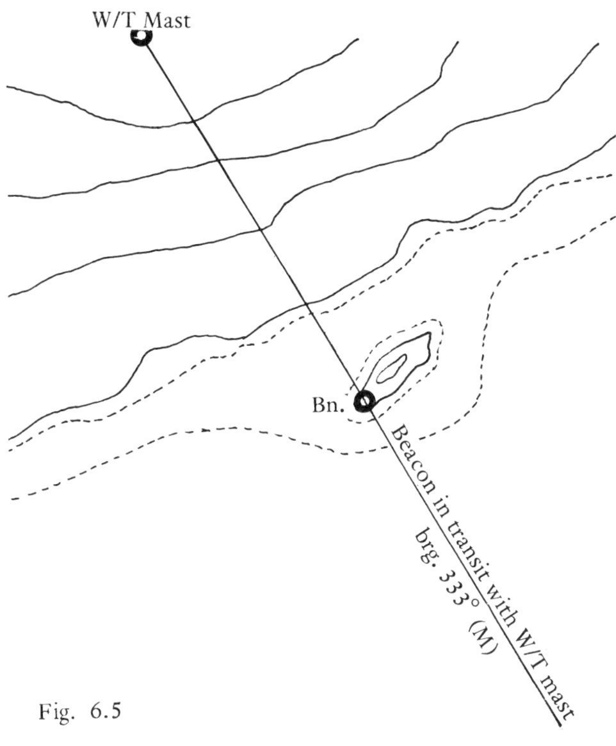

Fig. 6.5

Naturally the closer together such objects are, the less the degree of reliance can be placed upon the transit. For example, there would be little point in endeavouring to obtain a transit bearing from two closely adjacent piers outside a harbour. For the reasons given in chapter 3, buoys should only be used for transit purposes when the need is very great.

Systems of course and bearing correction.

First system— for craft with steering compass and hand bearing compass.

Bearings. This yachtsman will use his hand-bearing compass for bearings and, because he will use it in a position which can be considered reasonably free of possible magnetic influences, he will assume that every bearing he takes is a magnetic one. He will apply these bearings directly to his chart, using the magnetic compass rose.

Courses. Possessing an up to date Deviation Card for his steering compass he will extract magnetic courses from his chart and translate them into compass courses directly from his Deviation Card. In reverse, he can still utilise the Deviation Card.

If this yachtsman does **not** have a Deviation Card for his compass because he has not troubled to find out whether or not there are deviations in his compass he is taking a possibly grave risk. He can only assume that there are no deviations present. Such a lofty assumption is best enjoyed within sight of land in clear weather.

Second system - for craft with dual-purpose compass

We will assume that the owner of this craft prefers to 'work magnetic'. Further, that he has a Deviation Card for the compass.

Bearings. He will apply the CERM and MELC rules to any bearings he takes, thereby obtaining magnetic bearings. He will apply to bearings the deviation which he is allowing on the course he is steering. The reader must ponder upon and absorb the content of the last statement as it is highly important. A deviation is produced by a yacht being on a certain heading: therefore any bearing taken with her dual-purpose compass will contain the error of deviation appropriate to that heading. One cannot and must not refer a bearing to his deviation card.

Courses. He will adopt identical methods to those described for courses in the first system.

It should be appreciated that if this owner has taken no steps to ascertain whether or not deviations are present in his compass, both his bearings and courses may contain undetermined error.

Third system - 'working true'.

There are many arguments in favour of 'working true' and those yachtsmen who have traversed long distances may well prefer to do so even when on short sea voyages. The method of working true is explained in chapter 5: both the first and second systems explained above may be adapted to it.

Buying a compass.

If the reader intends sailing coastwise or crossing the channel he would be well advised to obtain the best compass available which is suited to his craft. While quite willing to agree that there are some high quality ex-service compasses in use which have been bought for a song, the writer is firmly of the opinion that, broadly speaking, in the field of compasses the best are those which cost the most.

The yachtsman who finds himself having to economise when fitting out his boat should, whatever misgivings he experiences, still purchase the best compass available. In the swinging seventies there are many items of equipment which are now regarded as standard equipment, yet yachtsmen managed extremely well without them 10 and 20 years ago. There is, to the writer's mind, no agony of decision in choosing between one or two really good compasses on the one hand and a cheap compass plus a moderately priced echo sounder on the other.

Boat builders, yacht chandlers of repute and experienced yachtsmen are the people to whom the initiate should refer before buying a compass. The type he buys will be governed by the type of craft he owns and, to a small extent, the style of compass with which he considers he will be most at home.

Sailing grids are preferred by many yachtsmen, particularly in smaller sailing craft. Instead of holding the craft to a compass heading in the traditional manner, which needs unremitting concentration and is a strain on the eyes in certain circumstances, the sailing grid makes the task easier. The rotatable grid being suitably lined up for the correct compass heading, steering the course resolves itself into maintaining parallel lines on the grid parallel to corresponding lines on the compass card.

Compasses for steel-hulled craft.

Many good compasses have built-in corrector magnets as a standard fitment. In steel-hulled craft this refinement becomes almost essential but, to repeat a former warning, the manipulation of corrector magnets should not be attempted by the amateur.

Removing an air bubble from a compass.

It is fairly common for an ageing but efficient compass to develop an air bubble, perhaps due to minute leakage of its water/alcohol content, or evaporation through the sealed joints of the compass's components.

Every liquid-type compass has a tapped screw in its bowl. The writer has occasionally removed air bubbles by holding the compass with its screw uppermost. With a hyperdermic syringe filled with distilled water and the screw removed, he has restored the compass bowl to capacity, thus eliminating the air bubble. The use of other devices will occur to yachtsmen, but one must bear in mind that water cannot merely be poured into the tiny aperture: it has to be injected.

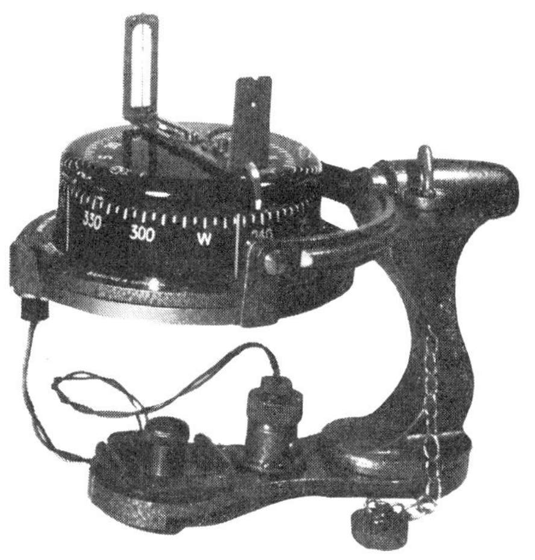

Dual Purpose Compass

Steering Compass

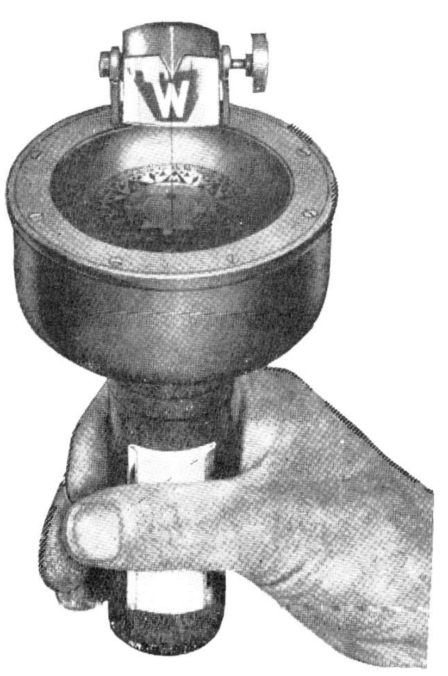

Hand Bearing Compass

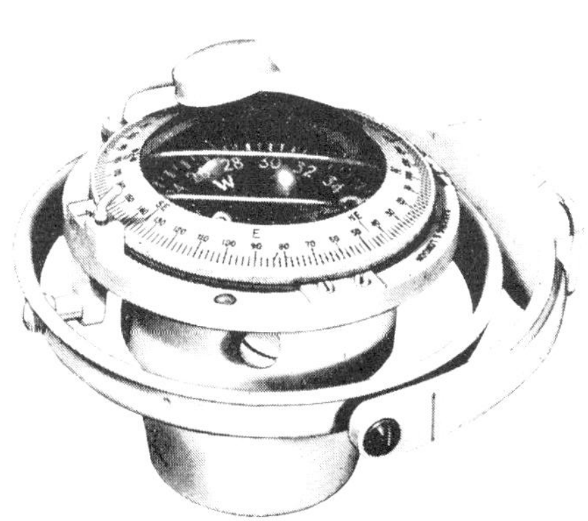

Sailing Grid

Fig. 6.6.

CHAPTER 7

Chartwork

It is simple truth that yachtsmen must navigate their craft in conditions which, at best, are never really easy and at times are extremely difficult. Put another way, the cramped conditions in the average yacht or motor cruiser do not lend themselves to precise work on a chart and the elements make the task infinitely more onerous.

This, of course, is well known by the old hand but the beginner sometimes feels that there may be something lacking in himself if the results he obtains are less than those for which he had hoped. It is well to keep matters in perspective. All the various means by which the mariner may determine the position of his craft are best practised in large vessels. A method of fixing position entirely practicable on a deep sea vessel in almost all conditions may be wholly impracticable in a small yacht sailing in a stiff breeze. The writer gains the impression that the occasional yachtsman is diffident about his excursions into the navigational field because he does not appreciate the magnitude of the task with which he is from time to time presented. He might ask himself: in these conditions, in these waters, could a Chichester do better?

Distance recording.

A study of the various methods of fixing position which follow will highlight the fact that some of them depend upon distance sailed, or run, for their accuracy. Estimating the speed of one's craft through the water, and from this computing the distance run, can be surprisingly inaccurate. When navigating off-shore a patent log is essential. This is a mechanical or electronic instrument for recording distance run: the type is not important, but what is, is that a mariner has something to give him distance run which is more accurate than his own judgement.

Estimated time of arrival - (E.T.A.)

On passage, whether a yachtsman is sailing between buoys under a mile apart or making for some distant destination he should calculate his E.T.A. at the position for which he is making. Obviously this has greater validity during periods of low visibility and when out of sight of land, but it is a practice which should be adopted in all conditions. Scribbling on the edge of the chart is one way to produce E.T.A.'s but, to save time, Time, Speed and Distance Tables are printed on pages 217 and 218. Entering the tables with boat's speed and distance to go, one can extract the sailing time required. This, added to the time of obtaining the last known position, will give the E.T.A. at the point for which one is making.

Too frequently one hears of dismaying happenings which need never have occurred if this seamanlike habit had been adopted. For example, sailing from buoy to buoy in a channel in fog, if it is not known when the next buoy should be sighted, it is quite possible to sail past the buoy without sighting it. It causes one to sail on, still searching for it, when it is in fact astern. Due to the omission of this practice, the writer once grounded in the Thames Estuary.

Notation on the chart.

On completion of a passage it should be possible for a knowledgeable stranger to 'read' from a yachtsman's chart the track followed from departure point to destination. It should be evident, in part, what factors influenced his decisions from time to time.

Good habits can be acquired just as easily as bad ones and one should resolve not only to adopt the order of work propounded in the various worked examples in this chapter but to adopt the following simple code throughout.

(a) Always - **always** - note the time against every bearing, every position whether absolute or dead-reckoning, every alteration of, or adjustment to, course. Time required to do this is negligible yet if it is not done one is unable to refer back with confidence to a previous projection. This is often necessary, particularly when position may be in doubt.

(b) Against every course drawn on the chart its direction should be noted using the following code:-

A true course	020° or 020° (T). If a course or bearing is given no suffix it is assumed to be a true one but either system is correct
A magnetic course	020° (M).
A compass course	020° (C).

If the navigator has to apply to a course either compass error or deviation it is helpful to note against the course line both the course extracted from the chart and the compass course.

(c) A bearing or position line should be given a single arrow feather, like this:-

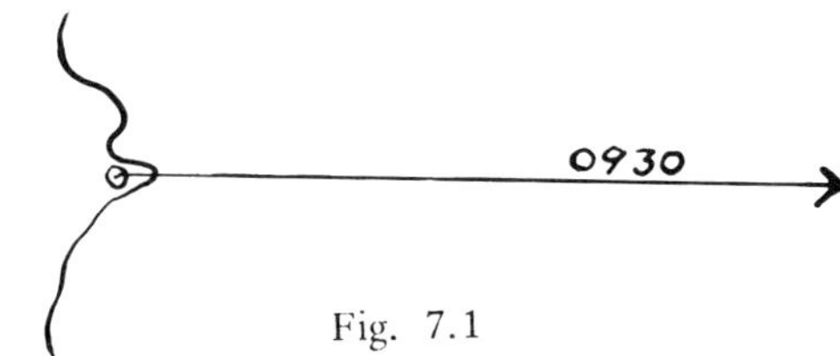

Fig. 7.1

(d) A 'transferred position line' should be given a double arrow feather, like this:-

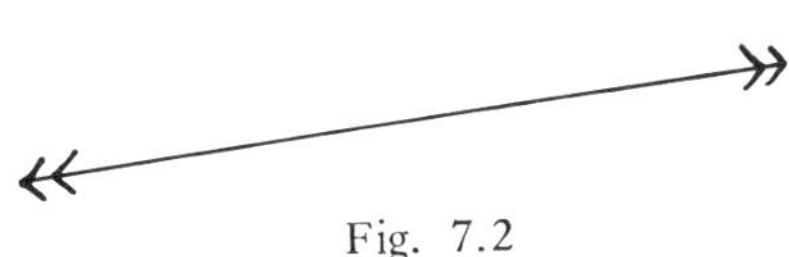

Fig. 7.2

These feathers greatly assist a navigator in his deliberations if they are added at the same time as the bearing or position line is drawn on the chart. That this system is seldom used is known by the writer but any device which saves time spent in head-scratching is sound. Clearly it is in this category.

(e) When an absolute position has been obtained it should be ringed in the following way:-

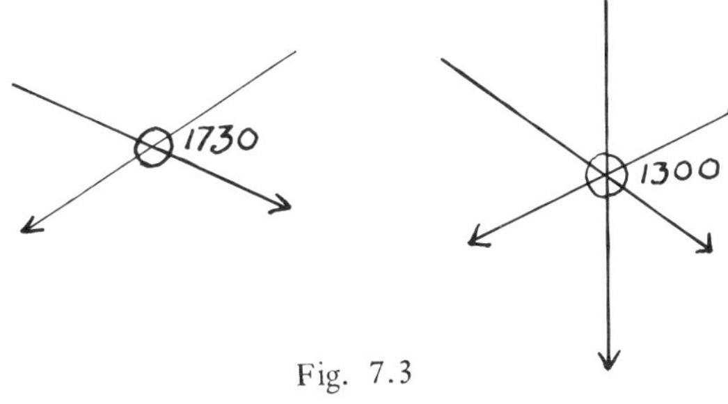

Fig. 7.3

(f) A dead-reckoning position should be shown as a cross, as follows:-

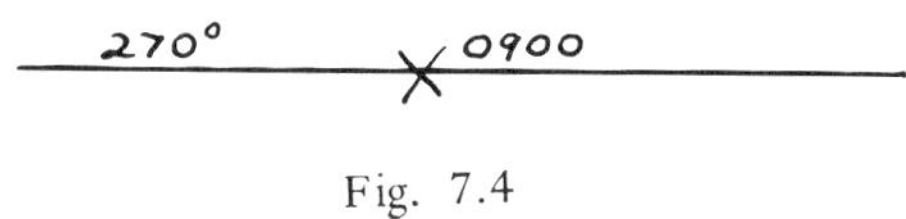

Fig. 7.4

(g) When ever a fix - the seaman's term for an absolute position - or a bearing has been obtained, or an alteration of course is made, or a dead-reckoning position is noted on the chart, the patent log should be read and its reading noted on the chart as follows:-

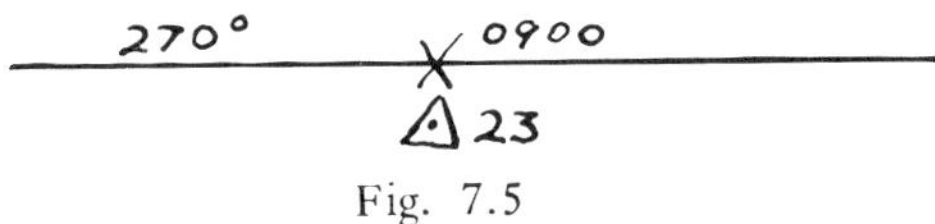

Fig. 7.5

Equipment requirements.

Parallel rulers.

First and foremost comes the parallel ruler which is essential for almost all work on a chart. The seaman has a choice of types and the one he buys is a matter of personal preference.

Captain Field's Improved.

Made in boxwood or plastic, as illustrated, 'walking' them across a chart needs a little practice but they are perhaps the most widely used.

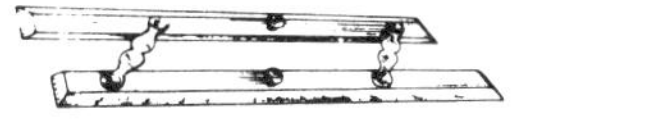

Fig. 7.6

Graduated as a protractor, this facility is more generally used by deep-sea men who 'work true', referring courses and bearings to the true meridian. When 'working true' the protractor graduations may be used by placing the ruler, closed, across a meridian on the chart with the graduations uppermost. Keeping the index on the lower edge of the ruler on the meridian, the ruler is rotated until the required course or bearing on the graduated scale coincides with the meridian. This is a quick and accurate means of determining a course or bearing, obviating the necessity of using the true compass rose, but for the average yachtsman who 'works magnetic' its value is for the most part lost.

Roller-type ruler.

Made of brass, boxwood or plastic, it will probably be considered by the beginner that this type is easier to use as, the ruler being set on the compass rose in the direction required, it can be rolled across the chart to the place of work. It is considered by many that this type of ruler does not lend itself to chartwork in small craft at sea.

The Douglas Protractor.

Made of celluloid and completely different from the types of ruler described above, this combines the function of both parallel ruler and protractor. Wholly unfairly, it is sometimes spurned as a poor man's device, yet it lends itself to work on charts in confined spaces. It is small and it grips the chart well, a virtue when boat movement is considerable. Instructions for it's use are supplied.

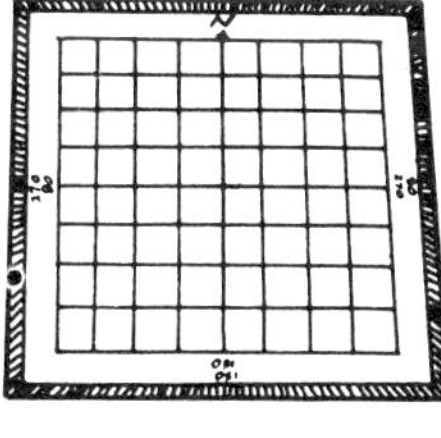

D OUGLAS PROTRACTOR.

Fig. 7.7

Dividers.

Necessary for measuring distance on charts, the most simple nautical type will suffice. Those intended for geometry have needle-like points and should not be used. Two pairs are desirable, one 6 in. and one 4 in.

Magnifying glass.

No matter how good one's eyes, a magnifying glass is essential for studying detail on charts. The larger the glass, the better.

Illuminated magnifying glasses may be purchased in motor accessory shops and these have their value on a boat during night hours.

Pencils.

One should use high quality B, or 2B pencils **only**.

Rubber.

Best quality India rubbers are most suitable for chartwork.

Compasses.

Simple brass compasses of the cheapest type, in which a stub of pencil may be inserted, will from time to time justify their presence amongst chart equipment.

Protractor.

A celluloid, school-type protractor, though seldom needed, is a valuable item to carry.

Care of charts.

Stanford charts being so folded that they may be stowed away neatly almost anywhere in a yacht (provided they are kept in a polythene waterproof bag) present no problems of preservation when they are not in use.

Admiralty charts usually have one fold, sometimes two, but rarely more. Intended primarily for big ship use, it is assumed that they will be stowed flat in their original folds in the drawers of a chart table. The **only** way to stow these charts on small craft is to maintain the original creases and roll them up. A yachtsman's whole stock of Admiralty charts can often be rolled up together, placed in a polythene bag and stowed out of harm's way.

When using charts, because of the confined space available to the yachtsman, he usually has to fold them. Again, the folds in Stanford charts can be used to advantage; not so in the case of Admiralty charts One can only adjure the yachtsman to fold Admiralty charts methodically when necessary, returning them to their original folds before stowing them away. Haphazardly folded damp charts have a considerably reduced life-span.

The use of drawing pins to hold down a chart to the table may seem a sensible course. The reader is advised against it. They restrict free movement of a parallel ruler and they damage the charts.

These are methods which may be adopted in normal conditions. The lone yachtsman in heavy weather may consider reducing the size of his working chart by folding it to manageable dimensions and sealing it in a waterproof polythene bag. Suitable types may be purchased in yacht chandlers. Sitting on it so that it is handy for reference, chart, compass and good seamanship could suffice in preventing him from getting into serious navigational difficulties.

A series of 'musts'

One must always use the largest scale chart available.

One chart must be used at a time and unwanted ones stowed away.

A double check on calculations must be carried out when transferring a position from one chart to another and a fix obtained as soon as possible after the transference has been carried out.

The nearest compass rose must always be used.

The seaman must determine whether the soundings on the chart on which he is working are given in fathoms or feet or; for the future; metres.

Charts must be cleaned off after use. Failure to do so will cause the pencil lead to become ingrained in the chart.

B and 2B pencils do not need to be used heavily to obtain clear definition hence they must be used lightly. Ineradicable lines, commonly known as tramlines, are the result of excessive pressure on pencils.

Every care must be taken to keep charts dry. The removed dripping hat, the towel handy for drying one's hands and the other towel laid along the front edge of the chart table do much to prevent sodden charts.

To plot a position as a latitude and longitude.

Latitude.

One edge of the parallel ruler is placed along a convenient parallel of latitude, or along the top or bottom border of the chart. Near enough is not good enough; the parallel ruler must be exactly parallel to the horizontal line upon which it is laid. The ruler is moved until its upper edge reaches the required latitude on the vertical marginal scale. The ruler being held firmly in position with one hand, a fine pencil line is drawn at the correct point on the scale. This method gives visual assurance that the precise latitude required is found. Retaining the parallel ruler in position, another line a few inches long is made in the vicinity of the longitude required. A glance at the longitude scale will indicate where this latter line must be drawn.

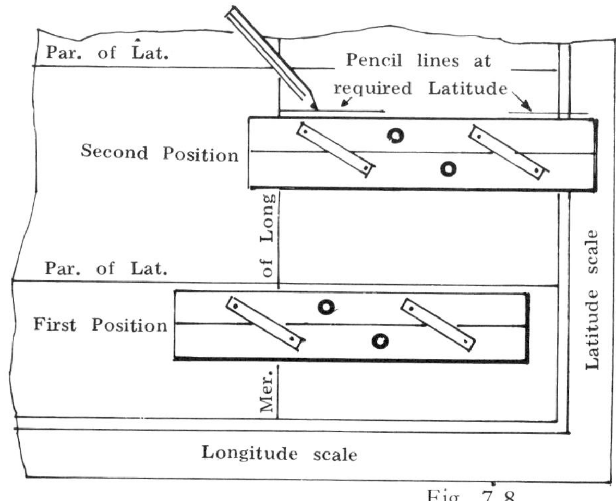

Fig. 7.8

Longitude.

Using the dividers **only**, and working on the longitude scale on the upper or lower margin of the chart, the distance between a convenient meridian of longitude and the required longitude is measured. With this measurement on the dividers, and in the position of the latitude already drawn, the longitude can be determined. With one point of the dividers on the meridian, the position where the other point meets the line of latitude already drawn gives the longitude. Thus position expressed as a latitude and longitude may be found.

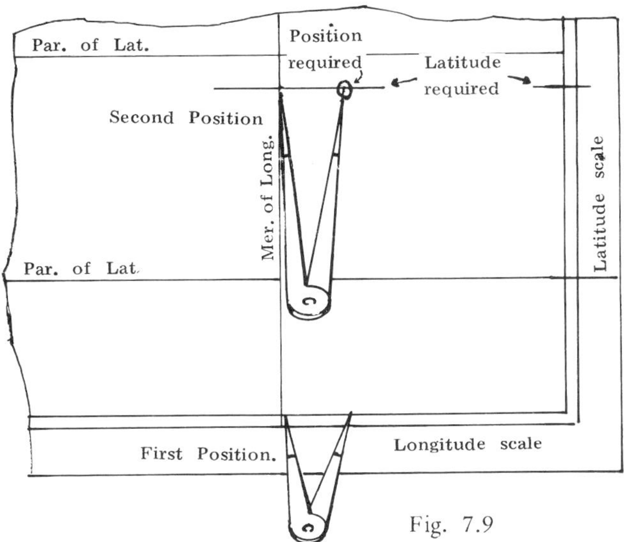

Fig. 7.9

Notes.

The writer has noted many methods by which yachtsmen arrive at the same answer. It cannot be over-emphasised that sound, workmanlike methods greatly assist accuracy.

To find the latitude and longitude of a position.

In this case it is customary, because it is both accurate and quick, to use dividers throughout.

Latitude.

With the dividers held vertically in relation to the chart, the distance between the position and the nearest parallel of latitude is measured. Moving the dividers to the left or right hand margins, the latitude may be read directly from the scale.

Longitude.

The dividers being held horizontally, the distance between the position and the nearest meridian of longitude is measured. Transferring the dividers to the upper or lower margins of the chart, the longitude may be extracted.

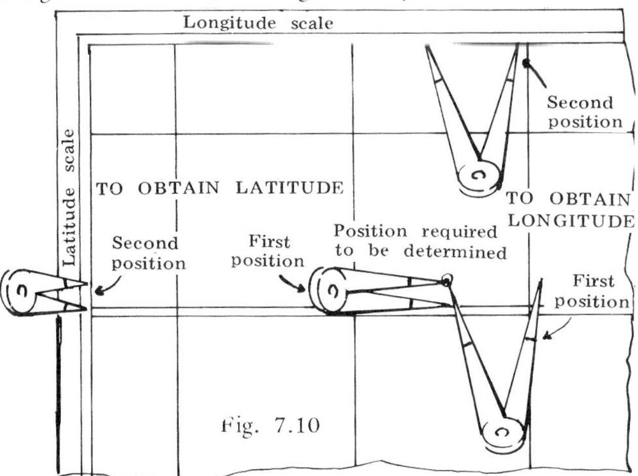

Fig. 7.10

Note.

Except when absolute precision is necessary, as for instance when correcting a chart, it is not usual to quote seconds when defining latitude and longitude. Thus position 50° 25′ 30″ N., 6° 12′ 30″ W., would in all probability be referred to as 50°26½′N., 6°12½′ W.

To plot a position by reference to some known object or place.

In coastal waters it will often be found more convenient, and it will have more immediate impact upon the recipient, if position is expressed in the following way:–

150° Dungeness LH 4 miles

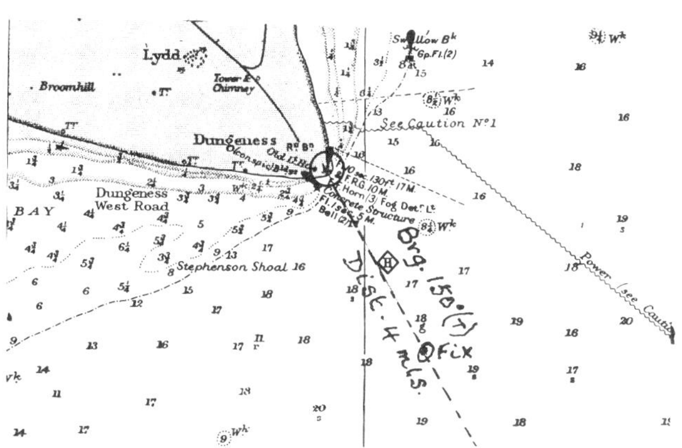

Fig. 7.11

Order of work.

Using a parallel ruler, join the position of Dungeness lighthouse and the boat's position with a pencil line. Move the parallel ruler to the nearest compass rose and, with its edge coincident with the centre of the rose, read the bearing. With the dividers, span the distance between the two points and read off the exact distance from the nearest latitude scale.

Note

It should be remembered that the position must be defined as a range and bearing from the lighthouse: note how simple it is to read from the compass rose the reciprocal bearing which is 330°.

When wishing to read a bearing or course off a compass rose it is good seamanlike practice to draw a line right across the compass rose when the ruler is in place, making sure that the line passes through the centre. The ruler may then be removed and not until that point of time need the bearing or course be read. This method gives an immediate visual check that the course or bearing has been read correctly, and it saves time.

To find the course and distance from one position to another.

Example.

Find the course and distance from a position 2 miles, 160° from Beachy Head LH to the R.Sovereign LV.

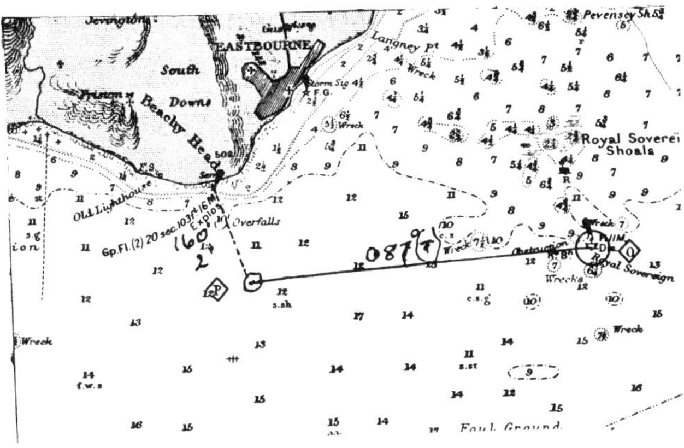

Fig. 7.12

Order of work.

(a) Plot the position from Beachy Head LH.

(b) Using the parallel ruler, draw a line from this position to the R.Sovereign LV.

(c) Holding the ruler firmly to the chart so that the direction is not lost, 'walk' it carefully to the nearest compass rose and read off the course.

(d) Using the dividers, measure the length of the course line and relate the distance produced on the dividers to the latitude scale on Admiralty charts and to the latitude and distance scale on the appropriate Stanford one.

Note

If the distance to be measured is greater than the maximum spread of the dividers, one should put a convenient measurement on them - 5,10 or 15 miles - and 'leg off' the distance along the course line. The final short leg may be measured separately and added to the distance already measured.

Drawing a course to pass a certain distance off.

When making a passage coastwise it is usual to decide before sailing what courses will be steered. It is then necessary to decide at what distance headlands and similar marks will be passed. A study of the chart will give the prudent distance in each case. So that the course lines may be drawn, it is customary to scribe round each object a circle which has a radius equal to the distance at which it is desired to pass it.

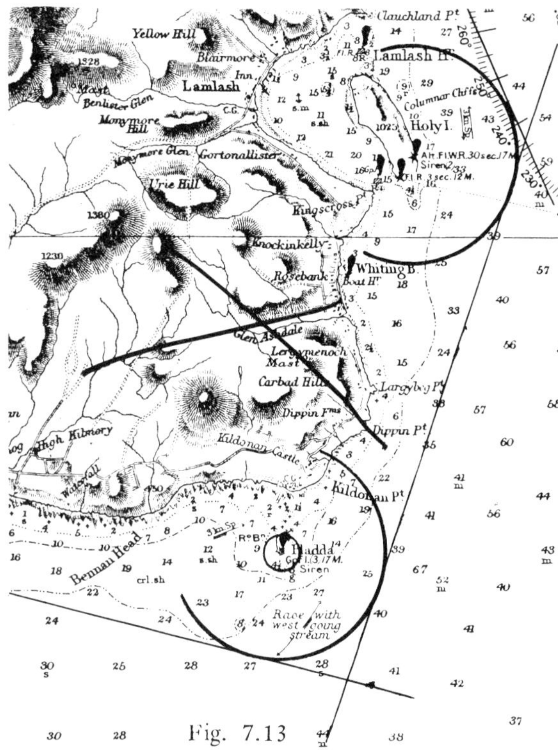

Fig. 7.13

inding the course to steer to counteract the ffect of a tidal stream.

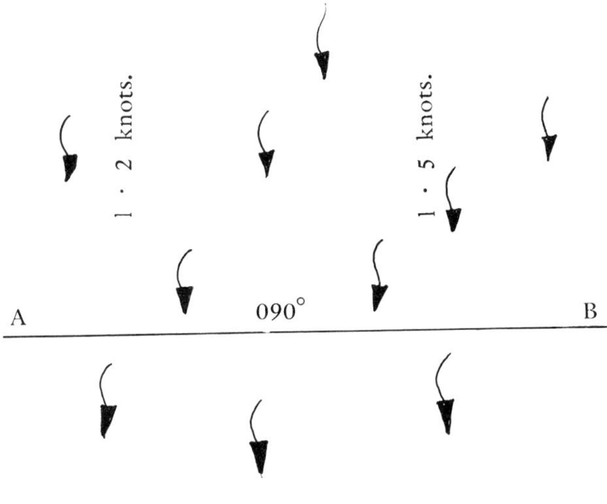

Fig. 7.14 .

In the above diagram a yachtsman intends sailing from A to B which is a course of 090°. Provided he steers a good course and there is no external influence to upset his calculation, he will in due course arrive at B. **But** - there is a tidal stream setting 180° and, though he may steer 090°, inevitably his craft will be carried to the southward. Obviously, to arrive at B he must steer a course somewhat to the northward of 090°. His problem is to find **what** course. Let us project this yachtsman's problem.

Example.

Find the course to steer to **make good** a course of 090°, allowing for a tidal stream setting 180° at 2 knots. Boat's speed 6 knots.

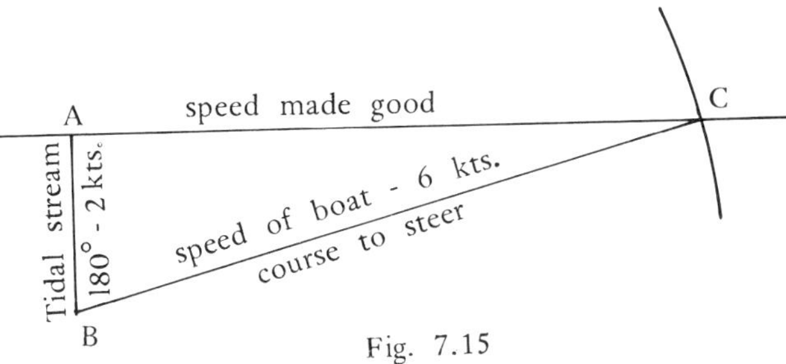

Fig. 7.15

Order of work.

(a) Select a point on the course line, A in this example.

(b) From A draw a line to represent the direction of the tidal stream.

(c) With 2 miles, the rate of the tidal stream, set on dividers, produce point B this distance from A.

(d) The tidal stream having been plotted for one hour, it must be considered how far the boat will travel **through the water** in one hour. It is 6 miles. With this distance on the dividers, one point is placed on B and an arc described. Where this arc bisects the course line produces point C.

(e) Join B and C.

Explanation.

The line BC gives the course to steer to counteract the effect of the tidal stream. It will be found to be 071°.

Though heading 071°, the craft will in fact progress along the line AC. In one hour she will cover the distance represented by AC which is 5·7 miles.

To further elucidate the problem, consider the triangle XYZ in Fig.7.16. Were no tidal stream experienced during the hour under discussion, steering 071° the yachtsman would arrive at Y. But a tidal stream was experienced and, though he steered 071°, the tidal stream washed him to the southward. In fact its effect was to cause him to arrive at Z.

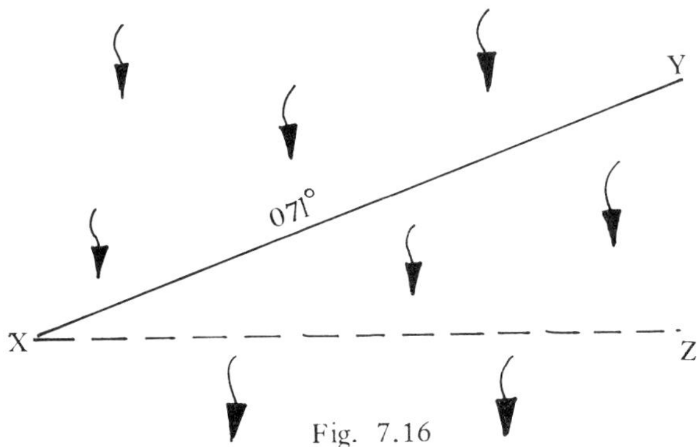

Fig. 7.16

Note

When producing a current triangle, if the tidal stream or current is calculated for one hour, the boat's speed must be calculated proportionately, i.e., for the same period. There is no reason why the navigator should not use a two - or even a three-hour interval, **provided** the same multiple is used for both the speed of the craft and the rate of the tidal stream. The larger the triangle produced, the greater accuracy achieved. But if this is done it must be remembered to **divide** the length of AC by the multiple used to find the distance made good in one hour.

For clear definition the terms 'speed through the water' and 'speed over the ground' are used. Speed through the water is self-evident, yet it must be remembered that the whole body of water through which the boat is sailing is itself moving over the sea bed. 'Speed over the ground' is 'speed made good', both of which are terms used to define progress over the sea bed - the ground. It is equally as common and expressive to speak of 'course over the ground' or 'course made good'.

Example.

Find the course to steer to make good a course of 250°, allowing for a tidal stream setting at 120° at 1½ knots. Boat's speed 5 knots. Also find the speed over the ground.

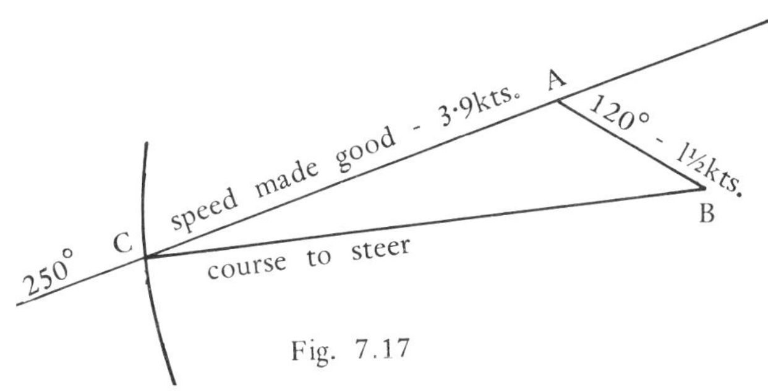

Fig. 7.17

Explanation.

The order of work is identical to that in the previous example. Though directions have changed, which causes one to pause for orientation, the basic triangle remains the same. BC will again be the course to steer to counteract the effect of the tidal stream; it will be found to be 263°. AC, a distance of 3·9 miles, gives the boat's speed over the ground as 3·9 knots.

Note.

Quite cheap plastic devices may be purchased which, by the manipulation of a rotatable dial and cursor, will solve these triangles in a matter of seconds without the need to resort to drawing them on the chart.

To find the course and speed made good when under the influence of a tidal stream.

It often occurs that a boat may be merely sailing a course, making no allowance for a tidal stream which is known to be present. An example of this occurs when a yachtsman is sailing close hauled. This is not the time to make due allowance in one's course for a tidal stream; it is purely a matter of making the best possible progress to windward. For navigational purposes the yachtsman must have a means by which he can determine his course and speed made good.

Example.

A yachtsman is steering 090° and is under the influence of a tidal stream setting 070° at 1 knot. Boat's speed is 5 knots. Find the course and speed made good over the ground.

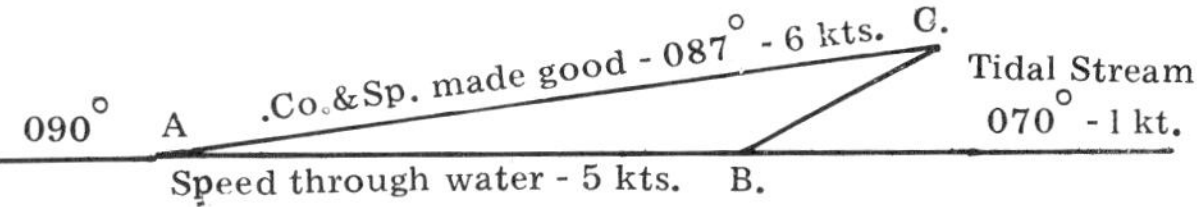

Fig. 7.18

Order of work.

(a) Select a point on the course line, A in this example.

(b) Measure along the course line the distance sailed in one hour (boat's speed)and produce point B.

(c) From point B project the set of the tidal stream, and its rate, so producing point C, The rate, it will be recalled, will be the distance the tidal stream sets in one hour.

(d) Join A and C.

Explanation.

During the period the boat has progressed along AC and the direction of AC will be her course over the ground; or course made good. The distance between A and C will be the speed made good in one hour.

Note.

Two current triangles have now been described. Both appear similar but there is a vast difference between them. This difference must be crystal-clear in the yachtsman's mind. To counteract the effect of a tidal stream the tidal stream must be drawn from point A in the triangle. To find the course and speed made good when **no** allowance is being made, the tidal stream must be projected from point B.

Leeway.

Leeway being the amount, measured in degrees of the compass, by which a boat is blown off course, it may be regarded as self-evident but in chartwork it is not.

The amount of leeway a boat will make is not a factor which can be determined by the application of a standard formula; it will vary in amount according to the following conditions:—

(a) The underwater hull form of the craft.

(b) The hull and sail area presented to the wind.

(c) The strength of the wind.

(d) The angle between the fore and aft line of the craft and the direction of the wind.

(e) The speed through the water.

(f) The state of the sea.

This formidable list will not dismay the experienced yachtsman. It is intended to impress upon the beginner the fact that leeway is one of the most elusive factors with which he must contend.

How much leeway?

Beginners often ask **how much** leeway a boat will make. The variables listed earlier are sufficient reason in themselves to indicate that it is impossible to give a general answer. An owner has to learn from experience what amount of leeway his craft will make in varying conditions. Possessing a certain type of craft, he may glean some useful information from her builders or from owners of other craft of the same design.

Although the amount of leeway made by power craft will be considerably less than that experienced in sailing craft, an owner cannot assume that it is a factor which he can totally ignore. A fresh breeze on the beam of a motor cruiser with high topsides and only a moderate turn of speed will certainly produce leeway. Again the variables listed must be applied but it will be evident that in such a craft, steaming into the teeth of the wind or directly downwind, leeway will be non-existent.

Leeway is defined as the angle between a boat's fore and aft line and her wake. Fig 7.19 best describes this definition.

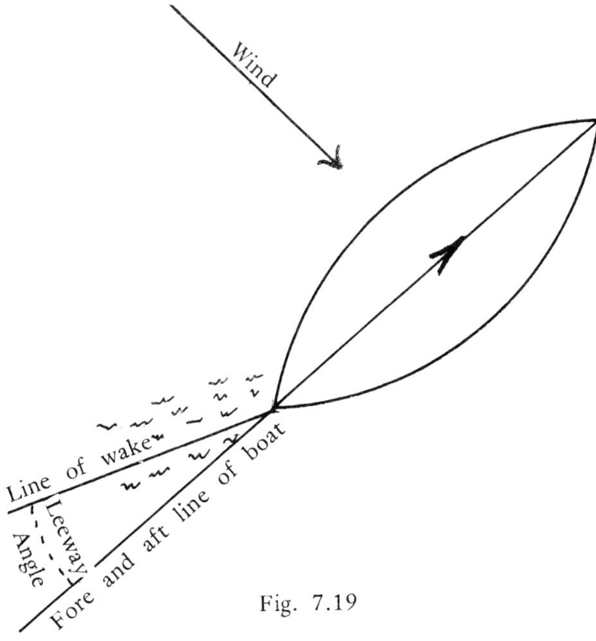

Fig. 7.19

If this angle can be determined at sea, a close approximation of the actual leeway being experienced may be obtained. Those who mistrust their ability to fairly accurately guess the angle between the fore and aft line and the wake can utilise a hand-bearing compass to obtain it.

Unfortunately, as wind strength increases, and consequently the amount of leeway, the sea surface becomes increasingly disturbed and when this occurs the turbulence of the wake is often lost within a few feet of the transom. If scraps of white paper are placed in the wake over the transom they will remain visible for a considerable distance. In adverse conditions they will provide a means of determining leeway.

How close to the wind will she sail?

When planning a passage, knowledge of how close to the wind a craft will sail is useful information. Owners of racing yachts know almost precisely the weatherly qualities of their craft; those who are lucky enough to possess sophisticated electronic 'masthead computers' may read off from their dials the desired information. For the remainder, which is the vast majority, this sailing angle has to be found by trial and error. It is common to attribute to sailing craft qualities which they do not possess, much in the way that motorists usually believe their cars will do more miles to the gallon than they actually do.

The sailing angle may be found by relatively simple means. Given a good sailing breeze, the craft is brought up to the wind on one tack or the other. She must be sailed 'full and by', which is to say that careful balance must be found between maximum progress through the water and the nearest course to the wind. The compass course on this tack being noted the craft is then laid over on the other track. The same procedure is adopted on it and the compass course noted.

The sailing angle is found by calculating the angle between the two courses. Half of this angle will be the sailing angle. It will be noted that the precise direction of the wind is not required, which is just as well because determining the direction of the wind is not always easy. Yet this exercise, executed for a different reason, produces as a bonus the wind direction.

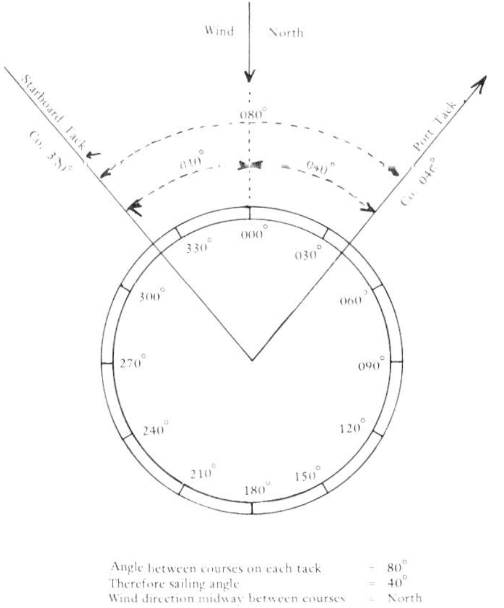

Angle between courses on each tack = 80°
Therefore sailing angle = 40°
Wind direction midway between courses = North

Fig. 7.20

The problems.

Two conditions have to be considered.

(a) To find the **course to steer**, making due allowance for leeway.

(b) To find the **course made good**, allowing for leeway.

The apparent similarity of these conditions, at least when spelled out as they are here, tend to make students lose sight of the marked difference between them.

Condition (a) occurs when a yachtsman, wishing to **make good** a certain course, is calculating the course he must steer; within his course he includes an allowance for leeway.

Condition (b) is extant when he has been sailing 'by the wind' on a compass course which he has not previously calculated. This can occur when clawing to windward. He notes the compass course he is steering and, to find what course he is **making good**, he applies to his course an allowance for leeway.

Examples.

(a) A yachtsman wishes to **make good** a course of 220°(M). The wind is SE'ly and he estimates that his craft will make 6° of leeway. If the deviation in his compass is 4°W., what compass course must he steer?

Fig 7.21

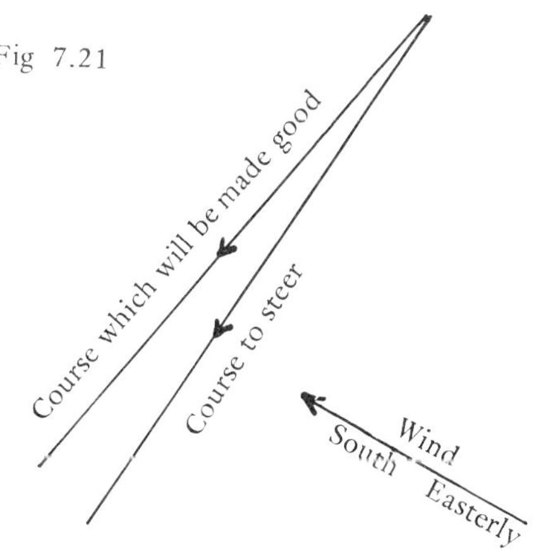

Course to be made good	220°(M)
Leeway	- 6°
Mag;course to steer	214°(M)
Deviation	4°W(MELC)
Comp.co.to steer	218°(C)

Note that leeway has been allowed **towards** the wind, which is minus in this case.

(b) A yachtsman is sailing close hauled and he notes that his course is 055°(C). The wind is SE'ly and he estimates his craft will make 7° of leeway. If the deviation on this heading is 3°E., find the magnetic course he is making good.

Fig. 7.22

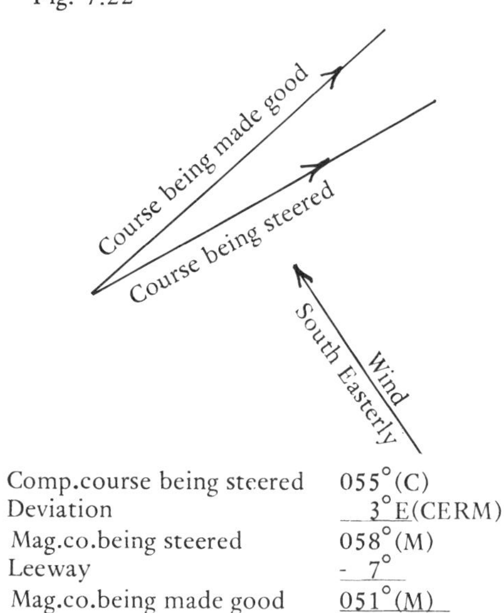

Comp.course being steered	055°(C)
Deviation	3°E(CERM)
Mag.co.being steered	058°(M)
Leeway	- 7°
Mag.co.being made good	051°(M)

Note that leeway has been allowed **away from the wind**, which is minus in this case.

The reader should note carefully that there is an exact reversal of work between one condition and the other. If he has a little difficulty in assimilating the application of leeway, he may gain solace from the fact that at sea, when conditions as they exist are clearly apparent, it is improbable that he will make a foolish error.

Dead-reckoning.(D.R.)

On passage when it is not possible to determine a boat's position by observation, it is of considerable importance that an estimation of the boat's position be recorded on the chart at regular intervals. Such estimations, called dead-reckoning positions, must take into consideration courses steered, distances traversed, the effect of tidal streams or currents, and leeway.

Dead-reckoning, invariably referred to as D.R., can thus be defined as the best estimation of the boat's position at any time. Seldom will it coincide with one's true position and the more experience obtained in making these calculations, the less D.R. positions will vary from true ones. Indeed, the skill of a navigator may be assessed according to the quality of his D.R.'s.

Dead-reckoning is necessarily calculated from the last known position, usually referred to as the departure position. The intervals between D.R. positions will vary according to circumstances. For example, sailing coastwise with no means of fixing position available, hourly intervals may suffice in normal conditions. Crossing the channel in similar conditions 2 hourly intervals may be adequate. Again, a power boat with a greater turn of speed should have her D.R. positions recorded at more frequent intervals.

As a matter of interest, in the Royal Navy dead-reckoning has a slightly different meaning. In Admiralty manuals Estimated Positions (E.P.) is the equivalent of our D.R. However, all other traditional seamen accept the definition given here.

It must again be stressed that the plotting of regular D.R. positions, when means by which regular absolute positions cannot be obtained, is highly important. The majority of yachtsmen are generally aware of this but it appears to the writer that some merely pay lip-service to this necessary navigational procedure.

Example.

From a position 110° Dungeness LH 4 miles a boat steers 070° (C) for two hours. Deviation 4°E. Boat's speed 6 knots. Tidal stream setting 210° at 1½ knots. Boat estimated to be making 5° leeway in N'ly breeze. Find the D.R. position.

Fig. 7.23

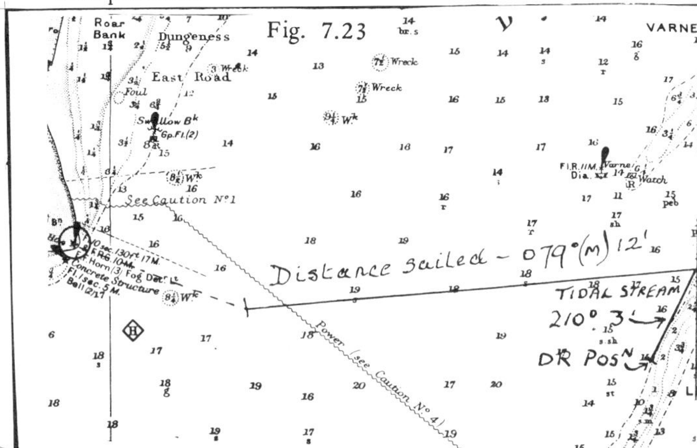

Calculation necessary before projection on chart.

Compass course being steered	070°(C)
Deviation	4°E.(CERM)
Mag. course being steered	074°(M)
Leeway for N'ly breeze	+ 5°
Mag. course being made good	079°(M) (thro' the water)

Order of work.

1. Correct the course for deviation.

2. Allow the leeway **away** from the wind.

3. Lay off the course of 079° (M) and, with the dividers, measure along the course line the distance run in 2 hours; 12 miles.

4. From this position lay off the tidal stream for 2 hours; 210°, 3 miles.

5. The position thus found is the D.R. position of the boat after 2 hours.

Note

This is a simple example. During a passage the tidal stream may turn in another direction or be reduced in rate; the wind may freshen or change in direction; the boat may alter course. These and other factors must all be taken into consideration.

In the sailing ships days a log book had to be a far more efficient record of factors affecting a D.R. position than is necessary in the large, power-driven vessels of today. From the detail recorded in their log books the 'Day's Work' could be extracted. 'Day's Work' is a quaint old term which referred to the work, in terms of progress made, of a vessel. All those factors which influenced the progress of a sailing vessel had to be included and from them the D.R. position of the vessel calculated. The reader may agree that there is no real difference between the needs of an old time sailing ship and a modern sailing yacht.

Perhaps due to the real difficulties inherent in sailing and navigating small craft, a number of yachtsmen appear to keep an inadequate record of their 'Day's Work'. Only when the need of a good D.R. position becomes paramount is it brought home to them that they have been guilty of what many would call a cardinal sin. It may be argued that the keeping of proper records in the form of a log book is expecting too much of a small boat sailor: it **cannot** be argued that there is no time to make appropriate jottings for D.R.purposes on the chart.

Dead-reckoning - tacking to windward.

When tacking to windward in sight of land in clear weather many yachtsmen do not usually keep a constant plot of their track. The length of their tacks may be governed by caprice, a desire to keep clear of a large ship in the vicinity or other similar reasons. From time to time they will obtain a position by shore bearings and not concern themselves very much with what occurred in the intervening periods.

Out of sight of land, as for example when crossing the channel, such methods would be utter folly. A constant dead-reckoning plot has to be kept. Positions obtained from a radio direction finder should support, not replace, such a plot.

To keep a constant dead-reckoning in difficult conditions when beating to windward in the open sea is tedious and trying, yet necessary. One seeks for methods other than the traditional one. Perhaps the purchase of expensive electronic equipment which will almost, but not quite, produce a D.R. position for the yachtsman. Or the possibility of carrying out extended tacks which will reduce considerably the number of times one may have to go about, and what of the probability that certain ebb and flood tidal streams will cancel themselves out; will this not reduce the work involved? Each alternative to the old and tried method produces its own problems, and, if one is not prepared to tack away into the blue and hope for the best, he can only resolve to do the best possible with the proven method.

In effect the navigator produces the material for dead-reckoning before he commences tacking to windward. A preliminary example will assist comprehension:

Example.

A yacht in a northerly breeze is on the port tack and making 5 knots. She sails 40° to the wind and is making 5° leeway. A tidal stream is setting 110° at 1½ knots. Find the course and speed being made good.

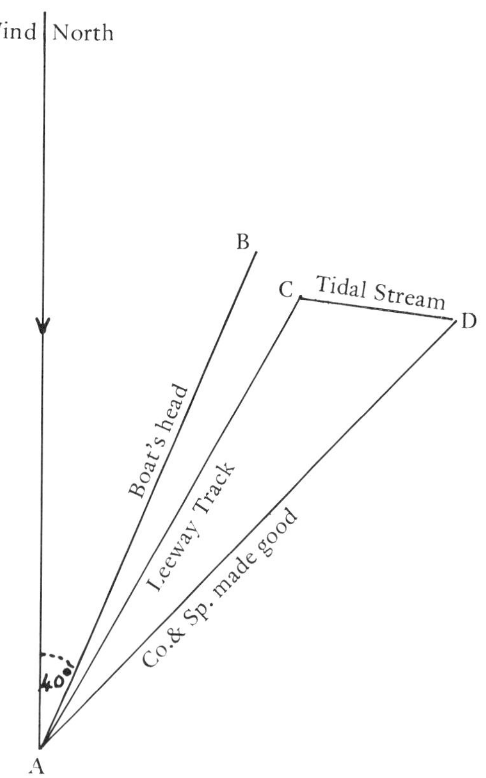

Fig. 7.24

Order of work.

(a) Draw in the wind direction and mark point A.

(b) 40° to the right of the wind draw in AB which is the course of 040°. Note that this has been determined from knowledge of how close to the wind the yacht will sail.

(c) Draw in the leeway track which is 5° down-wind from the course.

(d) From A measure along the leeway track the distance the yacht will sail in 1-hour, 5 miles in this case, and produce point C.

(e) From point C project the set and rate of the tidal stream for 1 hour, 110°, 1½ miles and produce point D.

(f) Join A and D. The direction and length of this line, will give the course and speed the yacht is making good in 1 hour.

Let us now consider the case of a yacht leaving a south coast port intending to head due south for some point on the coast of France. With the wind emanating from the direction in which it is desired to proceed, the yachtsman will have to beat to windward. He knows the weatherly qualities of his craft and he wants to know what course and speed he will make good on both tacks. A complete example is used here.

Example.

A yacht off the south coast of England wishes to tack to a position on the coast of France due south of his position. The wind is south. She will sail 35° to the wind and will make 5 knots and 7° leeway when beating on either tack. The tidal stream is setting 240° at 1 knot. Find the course and speed she will make good on both tacks.

Fig. 7.25

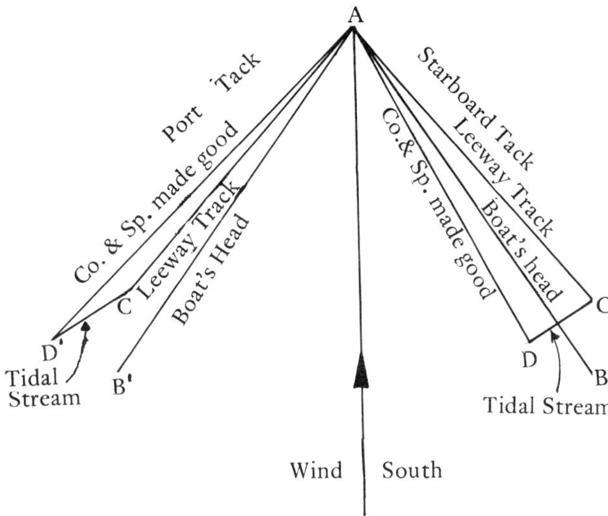

Order of work.

(a) Determine the position of the yacht, A.

(b) Draw in the wind direction which is south.

(c) Since the yacht will tack 35° off the wind, produced AB and AB[1] 35° on either side of the wind to represent both tacks.

(d) Produce leeway tracks for each tack, 7° to leeward of each tack course line.

(e) From A measure along **both** leeway tracks the distance the yacht will sail in 1 hour, 5 miles, and produce points C and C'.

(f) From both C and C' project the set and rate of the tidal stream for 1 hour, 240°, 1 mile, and produce point D and D'.

(g) Join A and D. Join A and D'. The direction and length of these lines will give the individual course and speed being made good on both tacks.

Note

It is desirable to project this type of diagram in a part of the chart away from the area in which one is working, otherwise the chart becomes cluttered with a profusion of incomprehensible lines.

It must be emphasised that such a diagram will be valid only for the conditions of wind and tide used in producing it. Any change in wind strength or direction, or tidal stream direction and rate, must necessarily cause the navigator to re-draw the diagram taking into consideration the changed conditions. It is fortunate when one can project such diagrams in the knowledge that the tidal element can be ignored because it is negligible, but it is an unfortunate fact that this happy state of affairs seldom occurs in home waters.

At the commencement of an extended beat to windward it may from time to time be considered profitable, in terms of accuracy of a D.R.plot, to spare a little while at the outset to undertake the experiment explained earlier under the heading, 'How close to the wind will she sail?'. It will give both an accurate wind direction and the yacht's sailing angle under prevailing conditions of wind and sea.

The examples given have assumed that the yachtsman wished to sail directly into the wind. More often than not this will not be so but the plotting method does not vary so long as a yacht must tack to reach her destination to windward.

When the wind does not emanate from the direction in which it is desired to progress, inevitably a yacht will make good progress on one tack and poor progress on the other, as is evidenced in the following diagram;

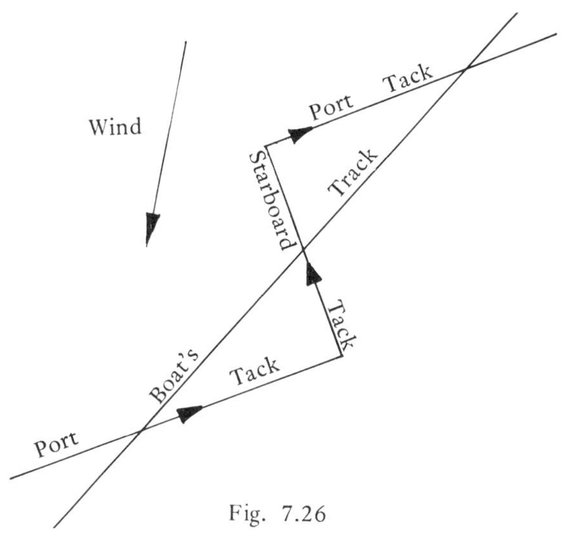

Fig. 7.26

In these cases the method usually adopted is to commence working to windward on the most favourable tack. In the event the wind changes in direction either one way or the other in such a manner as to improve the slant, so much the better. Should such a wind change adversely affect the slant at least it can be said that, the wind change coming in the first tack, maximum progress towards one's destination was made while the opportunity offered.

Tacking within limits.

It is not desirable, and sometimes it is not possible, for a yacht to deviate too far from her intended course line when tacking. Hence it is common to decide in advance how far to port and starboard of the course line it is desirable to tack. That is to say, tacking limits are imposed. As an example, in Fig. 7.27 is portrayed the projection on the chart of a yachtsman whose course line is 060°. He has decided to limit his tacks to within 3 miles of his course line. It is assumed that the wind is 055°.

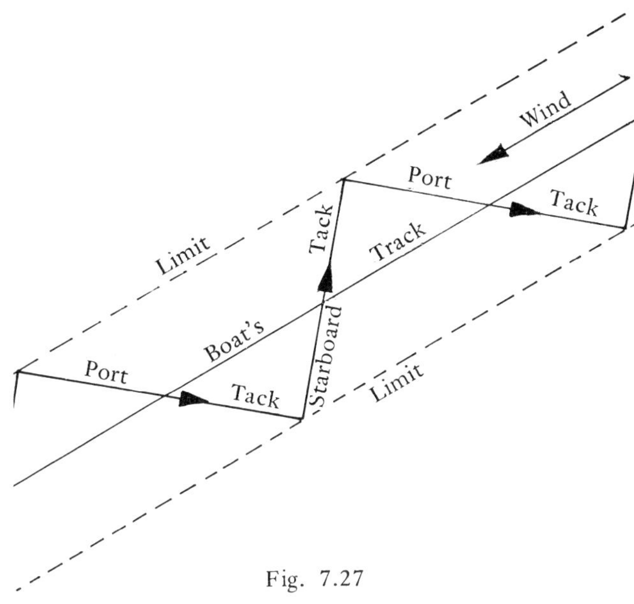

Fig. 7.27

Tacking along a coast with a charted object visible ahead, a yachtsman may decide that, while an imposition of a limit to seaward is not necessary, he does not wish to approach the coast closer than a certain distance. Such a situation can be met by determining a bearing of the object beyond which it is not intended to go. The bearing being achieved, he must go about on to the other tack.

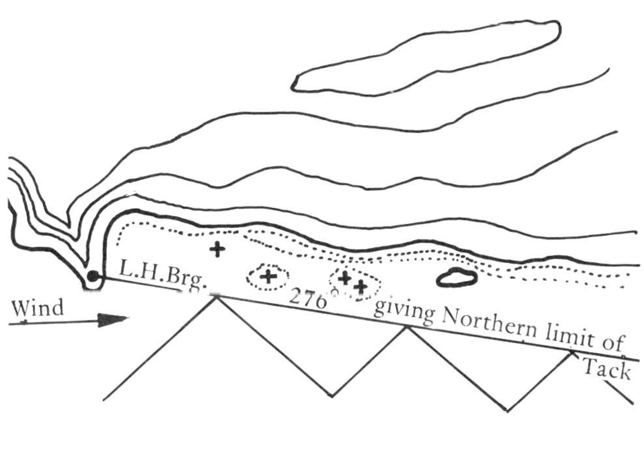

Fig. 7.28

When tacking towards a not too distant destination, and there are navigational reasons why later tacks must be shortened, a 'corkscrew' tack may prove useful. In these conditions it is likely that a charted object is at one's destination - a lighthouse, a headland, pier heads - which will assist greatly in ensuring that the yachtsman keeps within his self-imposed limits.

Example.

Intending to use a corkscrew tack in making for headland X which bears 280°, he decides that 7° limits either side of his track are required.

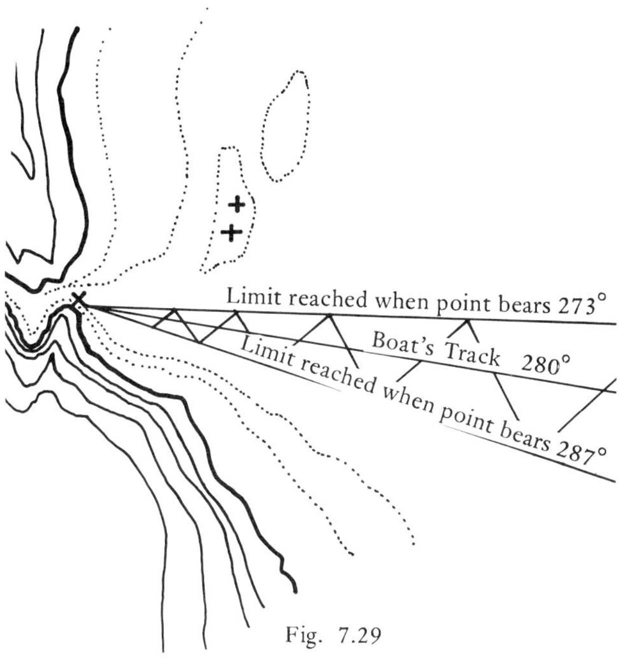

Fig. 7.29

Order of work.

(a) The bearing of the headland is drawn on the chart which then becomes his intended track.

(b) From the headland he projects on his chart two lines, or limits, one 7° greater than the bearing and one 7° less, that is 287° and 273°.

Explanation.

He will keep a constant check on the bearing of the headland as he works towards it. When on the port tack, as soon as the bearing reaches 273° he will go about and proceed on the other tack until it reaches 287°. Thereby, using his bearing compass alone, he will safely work towards his destination.

Summing up the navigational problems in tacking to windward.

The calculation of courses and speeds made good on various tacks for D.R. purposes is not difficult but it is time-consuming and difficult to carry out in the confines of the average small yacht. Depending upon prevailing conditions the lone yachtsman may find it beyond him because of the time required, yet in the waters for which this publication is intended it **must** be carried out if undue risks are to be avoided.

It will have been noted that, following the projection to the letter, it is time alone which decides when the yachtsman should go about on to the other tack - not distance by log, yet distance by log should be closely followed. The triangles are calculated assuming a certain speed through the water and if there is a variation in speed the information produced by the triangles will be in error.

No doubt there are those who will decide to rely upon radio direction finding alone to determine position in these conditions. The writer reiterates that D.F. provides a useful adjunct to the methods outlined. These adventurous few should not fail to appreciate the strengths and limitations of D.F.

Single position lines and position circles.

When off-shore it is often found that, no matter how diligently the coast is scanned, only one recognisable object is visible. The yachtsman wants to have some idea of his position; what should he do? Should he delay matters in the hope that other objects which he can relate to his chart come into view? The emphatic answer is; take a bearing of it.

The value of a single bearing, which is a position line, is not always fully appreciated by the amateur. In ways which will be explained, a single position line can be combined with other factors. Even assuming no other factors are available, the single position line tells the navigator that he is **somewhere** on the line produced. This information alone is of considerable value. As a last resort he can estimate his distance off the object taken, thereby obtaining a position although it will be a somewhat sketchy one. It is most likely that a position so obtained will be more accurate than a D.R. position.

A single bearing, or position line.

The commonest form of position line in coastal navigation is the single bearing. In the following diagram the navigator has taken a visual bearing of Bardsey Island Lighthouse which he finds to be 080°(M). Using his parallel rulers he has transferred this bearing from the nearest compass rose to the position of the lighthouse and has drawn a line from it to seaward.

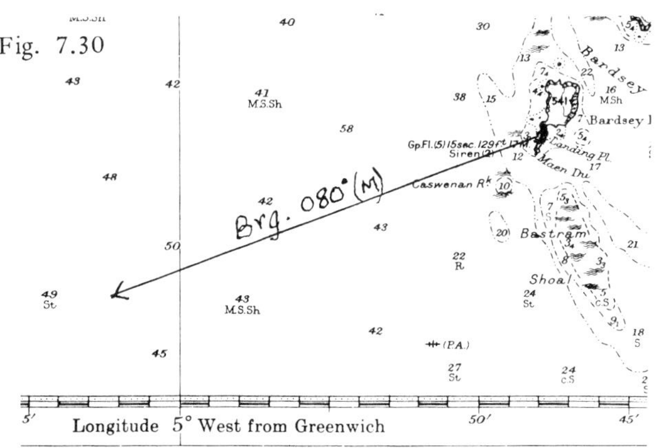

Fig. 7.30

Position line from points in transit.

It sometimes occurs that two charted objects appear in line - in transit - and without the necessity of taking a bearing a position line may be produced on the chart.

The following diagram portrays a situation where a yachtsman has sighted New Romney Church in line with Old Romney Church. With a ruler he has drawn a line through both churches and extended it to seaward. He knew that at the moment the two churches appeared in transit, he was **somewhere** on the line he produced on his chart, and he did not need to take a bearing.

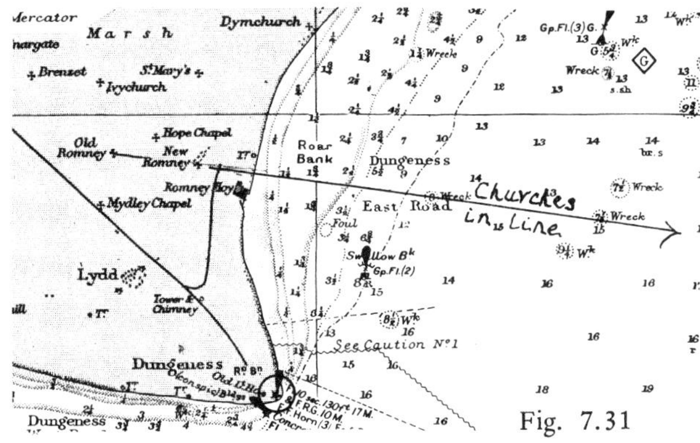

Fig. 7.31

Position line from a single radio bearing.

Bearings taken by a radio direction finder are discussed in detail in Chapter 8. Suffice it to remark here that, although a single radio bearing may appear to have everything in common with its visual counterpart, this is not the case. Certain potential errors have to be considered. A single radio bearing may be used with caution when close to the transmitting station.

Below is portrayed the case of a mariner who has taken a radio bearing of the Nab Tower radio beacon. Having translated it into a compass bearing he finds it is 310°. In the same manner as described for other compass bearings, he has projected the position on the chart.

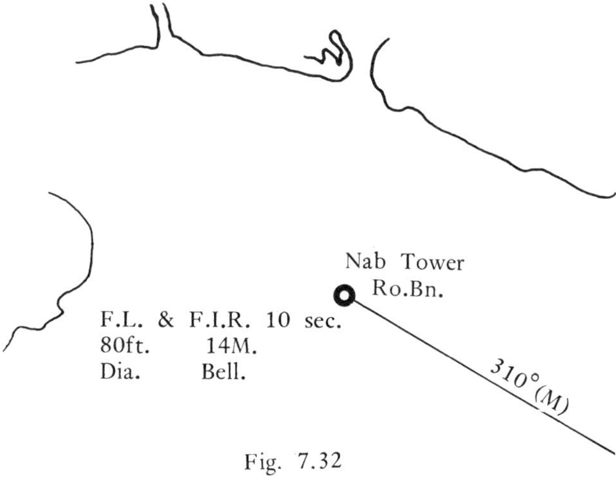

Fig. 7.32

Clearing bearings.

Approaching a coast which has off-lying dangers, from time to time the mariner requires some means by which he can ensure that during his progress shorewards, he does not hazard his craft by approaching a danger too closely.

Clearing bearings are the answer. Bearings taken from his chart before he is in the vicinity of a danger will give him the assurance he needs. It is a matter of choosing a charted object **behind** the off-lying danger and drawing a bearing seawards from it. If the bearing is so drawn that it clears the hazard, by using his bearing compass the mariner may himself clear the hazard.

For the approaches to ports and anchorages many clearing bearings are given in the Admiralty Sailing Directions. Some charts include such information but there is no reason why the yachtsman should not determine and use his own. Two examples of clearing bearings are given below.

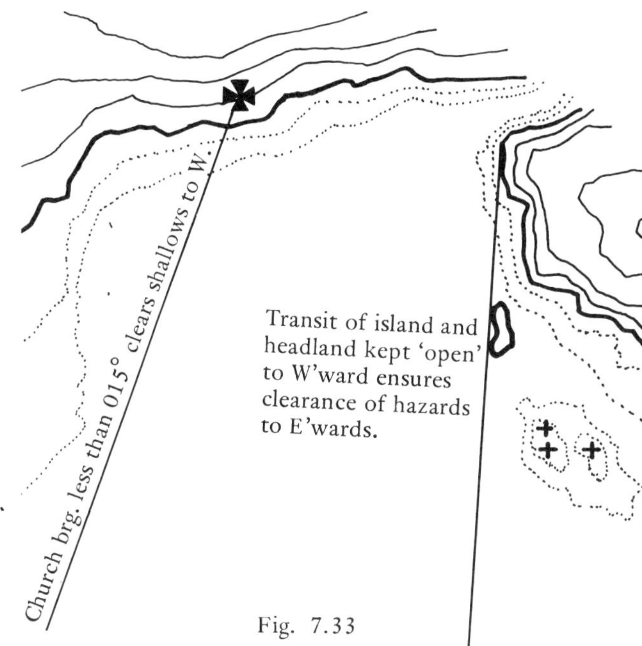

Fig. 7.33

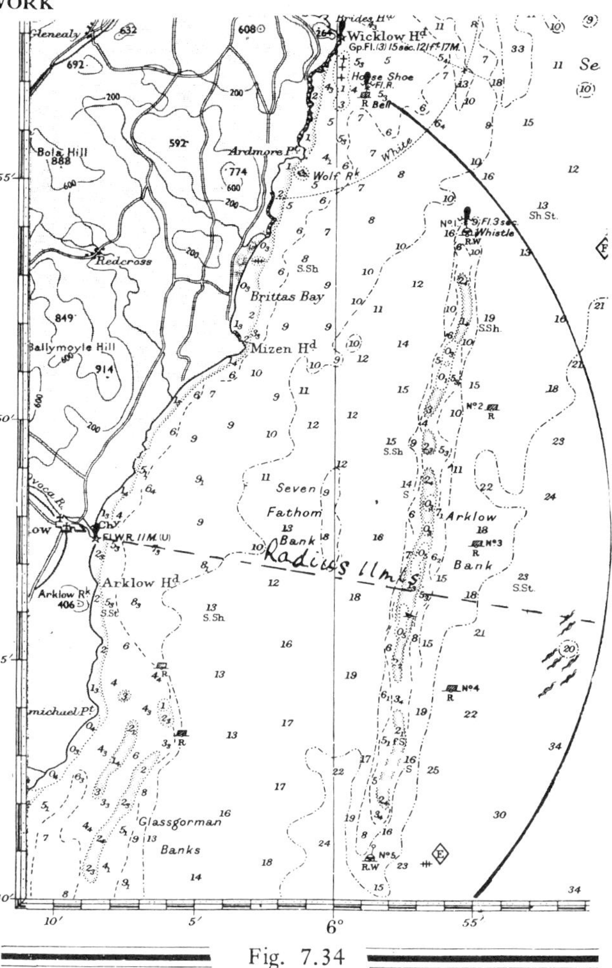

Fig. 7.34

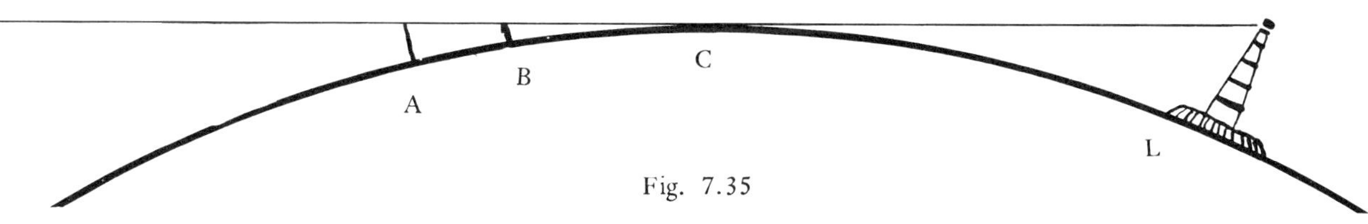

Fig. 7.35

A single position circle.

When a circle is drawn on a chart and it can be said that a boat's position is somewhere on the periphery of that circle, it is known as a position circle. In all respects it has the same value as a single position line.

Position circle from the dipping range of a light.

When the maximum geographical range of a navigational light is given on the chart, or elsewhere, assuming the height of eye of the navigator is 15 feet, a circle may be described round the light using the range as a radius. Sailing away from the light, when it dips below the horizon it will be known that the position of the boat is somewhere on the position circle produced. Sailing towards the light, when it appears above the horizon the same conclusion may be made.

Theoretical and practical aspects of the dipping bearing.

In chapter 3 it has been explained that the published geographical range of a navigation light is calculated assuming the height of eye of the observer is 15 feet above sea level. If his height of eye is greater than 15 feet the light will be seen at a greater distance; if less it will be seen at a lesser distance. Before distance off a dipping light can be accurately determined, any variation from 15 feet in height of eye must be taken into consideration.

The easiest way to calculate this is to refer to a well known table, 'Distance of the sea horizon' which is produced on page 216. Such a table simply gives the distance of the sea horizon when viewed from various altitudes. Consider the following sketch:—

The range of the light L is published as 21 miles. At ship A, where the height is 15 feet, it will come into view at the published range. At boat B, with a height of eye of only 5 feet, the charted range of the light will be reduced by the distance between A and B. We can calculate this distance from the table as follows:—

Distance of the sea horizon from A (15′) (AC in sketch)	=4·45miles
Distance of the sea horizon from B (5′) (BC in sketch)	=2·57miles
Thus distance AB, or the reduction in the range of the light	=1·88miles

For navigational purposes it suffices to call this result 2 miles, so the light would be sighted at a range of 21 miles - 2 miles = 19 miles.

It should be noted that whatever the range of the light L, the reduction in visibility range will, assuming there is no change in height of eye, remain constant. This is useful information. This yachtsman has merely to deduct 2 miles from the charted range of most navigational lights to determine their dipping or rising range. It is a 'constant' which could easily be memorised.

The writer now wishes to introduce what he regards as sanity into a simple subject which tends to be made a theoretical one. He has long felt that the fore-going, which can be read in most text books in one form or another, is more applicable to large vessels than to the relative cockle shells we sail.

Let the reader consider this; he has already been advised in effect that in most small boats the affect of height of eye is to reduce the range of the light. He has also learned in chapter 3 that this range is calculated for M.H.W.S. tides. There is a great likelihood that when he needs to consider the range of a light the height of tide will be lower than this very high level. Perhaps considerably lower. Such effect can only be to **increase** the height, and therefore the range, of the light.

We thus have two factors which affect the range of the light; one decreases it and the other increases it. The effect of the former is greater than that of the latter but both are rather small. Let us cut right across all this theory. The writer advises any small boat sailor to forget all theory in this matter and assume charted range of lights whenever they need to be considered, which is seldom in any case. What is a mile or so of error when one may be 20 miles off shore?

Fixing the position.

Fixing position at sea using conventional methods may be obtained by combining two or more position lines, or two or more position circles, or by a combination of position lines and position circles.

If two simultaneously obtained position lines cross each other, their point of intersection must be the required position. A third, and even a fourth, position line will confirm or refute the evidence of position provided by two position lines. They will also give the seaman greater faith in the results obtained. These facts will be revealed in the examples which follow. The remarks here apply equally to position circles.

Position by cross bearings.
A two-bearing fix.
Example:

Off the south coast of England, bearings were taken as follows:

Beachy Head LH	351° (M)
R.Sovereign LV	086° (M)

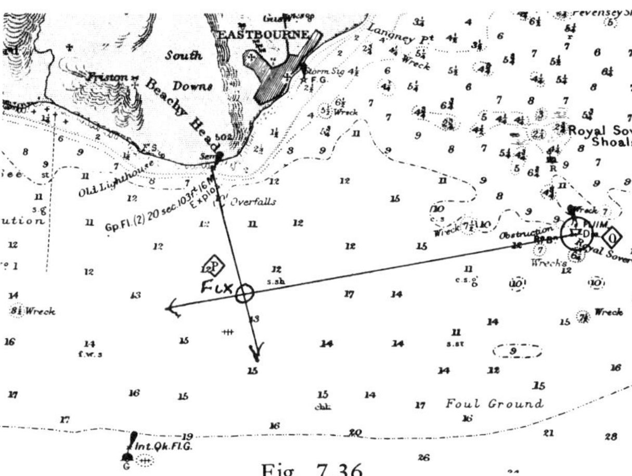

Fig. 7.36

Both bearings being position lines, the navigator knows that, assuming no errors have occurred, his position must be where the bearings cross. The position will be inaccurate if any of the following occurred:—

(a) **Error due to inaccurately reading the compass bearing.** Two conditions may cause this. First, the navigator may have difficulty in holding his hand bearing compass steady: patience and practice is needed. Secondly, a slight swinging of the compass card will render it difficult to read the correct bearing and often the mean, or average, bearing has to be judged. Again, this needs practice. Both these conditions usually occur in adverse weather conditions.

(b) **Faulty projection.** Carelessness will be the probable offender. As all work on a chart should be checked for accuracy, the answer to this type of error is in oneself. Considerable movement of the craft will make projection difficult but this is a reason, not an excuse, for error. It too can be overcome by checking results.

(c) **Incorrect application of deviation where applicable.** Deviation allowed the wrong way, for instance to the right instead of the left, will produce a wholly erroneous position because incorrect bearings will be drawn on the chart.

(d) **Use of incorrect deviation, where deviation is applicable.**
Incorrect deviation, although applied correctly, will produce similarly erroneous results as mentioned in (c) above.

Ideally, the two bearings of a fix of this type should have an angle of near 90° between them. As the angle between them increases, or decreases, the accuracy of a two-bearing fix must be increasingly suspect. If the angle between bearings is very small or very large, small errors in bearings will produce disproportionately large errors in fixes so obtained.

In the examples below the positions marked A are intended to indicate the true positions obtained from accurate bearings. Those marked B are produced by the alteration by a mere 2° in only one of the bearings in each case.

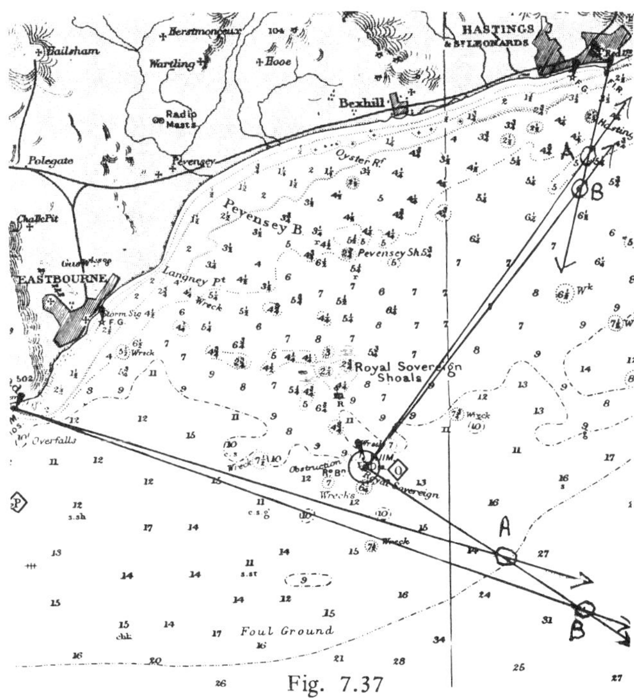

Fig. 7.37

A Three - or Multi-bearing fix.
As has already been implied, a three-bearing (or more) fix has considerably greater value than one obtained from two bearings only, and it should always be obtained where possible. If errors have occurred they will become apparent in the projection.

Example.
Off the south coast of England bearings were taken as follows:

Beachy Head LH	312° (M)
Eastbourne FG	350° (M)
R.Sovereign LV	083° (M)

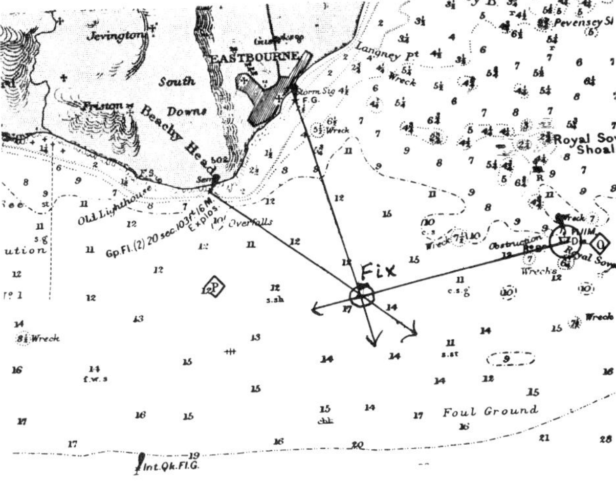

Fig. 7.38

The projection in Fig.7.39 indicates **what would** have appeared on the chart if the navigator had taken faulty bearings and he had read them as follows:

Beachy Head LH	315° (M)
Eastbourne FG	348° (M)
R.Sovereign LV	087° (M)

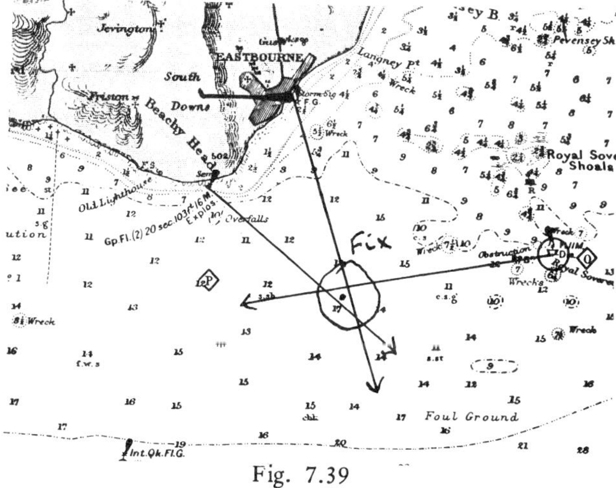

Fig. 7.39

Note.
Triangles produced from slightly faulty bearings such as in this example are known as cocked hats, for obvious reasons. Provided the triangles are small it is customary to assume that the position is in the centre of the cocked hat. Of course it will not be the precise position but it will be very near to it. When large cocked hats are produced one should re-take the bearings. The great advantage of the three or more bearing fix is that the **magnitude** of any error is made apparent to the navigator. Even gross errors may not be readily apparent in a two-bearing fix.

The writer once had the misfortune to sail with an officer who, when coasting, invariably showed by his fixes that the vessel was always on the course line as long as he was on watch. More intriguing still, his three- and four-bearing fixes were always perfect; never a cocked hat. The obvious was ultimately proved; every one of his fixes was 'cooked' and in fact he never took a bearing. He did not last long.

It is hoped that this true anecdote will indicate to the reader that, even in ideal conditions,seldom will he obtain the perfect multi-bearing fix. On ships both large and small, all kinds of factors contribute to a craft leaving her track and to the production of the imperfect fix.

Identifying terrestrial objects by use of a fix.

It can be irritating to a navigator who has taken, say, three bearings for a fix only to find that one of them is obviously wrong. Not wrong because he has taken a bearing incorrectly but because he cannot identify on the chart one of the objects he has taken. This may happen in the case of a prominent hilltop; it appears jutting and bold to the observer yet it cannot be related to the summits indicated on the chart.

Such a promontory can often be identified by first fixing the position with those bearings which are known to have been recognised correctly on the chart. Then with the bearing of the unknown object on the parallel ruler, a line may be drawn shoreward from the fix. It may well be found that the line passes through or near an object marked on the chart not previously recognised as the object being taken.

The running fix, or transferred position line.

From time to time it occurs that only one recognisable terrestrial object is available when it is desired to obtain a fix. This happens more frequently at night when only navigational lights are visible. In these circumstances a well known method of fixing position is available; the running fix. For reasons which will be explained, it cannot be defined as an **absolute** fix but nevertheless it is a valuable method.

So that the principle of this method of fixing position may be readily understood, it is desirable that the term 'transferred position line' be clearly defined.

Example.

At 0800 hours, from a boat steering 070° at 4 knots, a headland bears 000°. Lay off the bearing and project a position line for 0900 hours. See Fig. 7.40.

Order of work.

(a) Lay off the bearing.

(b) From any position on the position line thus produced, lay off the boat's run for 1 hour; 070°, 4 miles.

(c) Through the point of termination of the run, draw a position line parallel to the bearing.

Explanation.

It is true to say that the boat was on the position line drawn at 0800 hours. It will be equally true to say that provided the run has been accurately assessed, she will be on the second, or transferred, position line at 0900 hours.

Note the three other dotted projections of the run between 0800 and 0900 hours. They establish the reality that no matter what position is chosen on the position line from which to draw the run, the transferred position line is in no way affected.

Two facts have been established; first, that a transferred position has similar value to an absolute one in that it may be said that a boat is **somewhere** on that line at the time for which it is drawn; secondly, it is of no consequence from what point on the position line the run is drawn. With these points cleared up the running fix may be described.

Example.

From a boat steering 090° at 5 knots, at 1700 hours a lighthouse bore 030° and at 1800 hours it bore 340°. Find the position at 1800 hours.

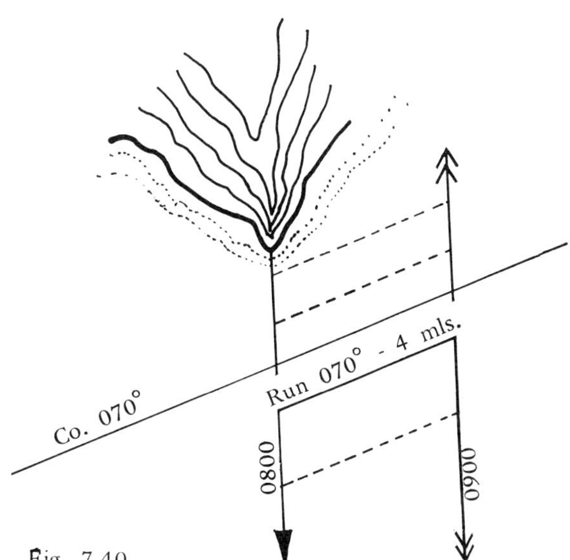

Fig. 7.40

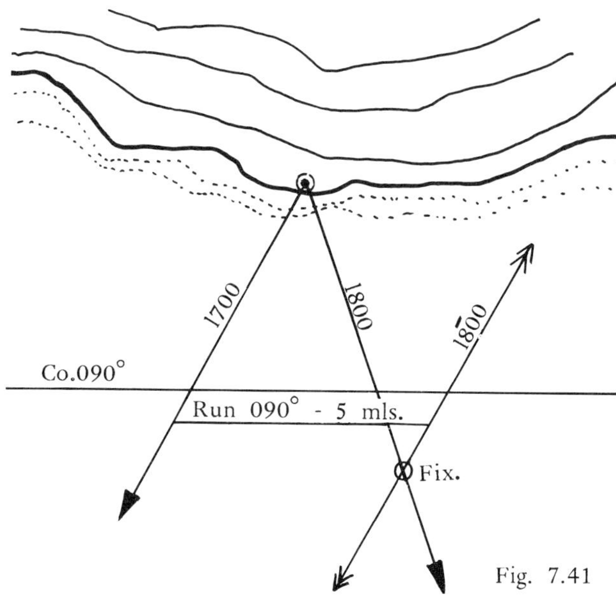

Fig. 7.41

Order of work.

(a) Lay off the first bearing.

(b) From any point on the first bearing lay off the course and the distance run between 1700 and 1800 hours.

(c) Through the point of termination of the run laid off in (b), draw a line parallel to the first bearing. This is the transferred position line.

(d) Lay off the second bearing.

(e) Ring the point of intersection between the transferred position line and the second bearing, it being the boat's position.

Explanation.

It can be assumed that at 1800 hours the boat was on the transferred position line. It is known that she was on the position line produced by the second bearing which was taken at that time. Obviously the position must be where these two lines meet.

Caution.

There is one weakness in this method of fixing position. The accuracy of a fix so obtained will largely depend upon the navigator's assessment of the course and distance sailed between the bearings. If the run he allows is inaccurate then the transferred position line will be incorrectly drawn; if that is not accurate, then any position obtained from it will be in error.

Note

The boat's course line inevitably crosses the bearings in these problems. Instead of separately projecting the boat's run between bearings, it is common to use the course line already drawn on the chart for this purpose. When one is thoroughly familiar with this method of fixing position there is no reason why one should not do so but it may tend to confuse the beginner.

It is not necessary always to use the same terrestrial object for bearings. When coasting it sometimes occurs that one object disappears in the haze or dips below the horizon and, a short while afterwards, another comes into view. If bearings of both are obtained they may be combined as a running fix.

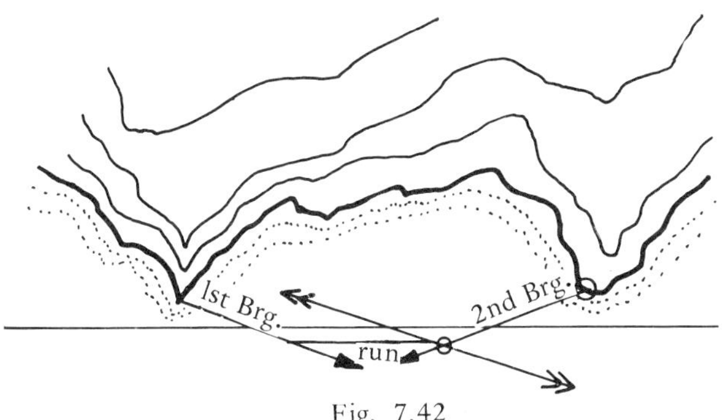

Fig. 7.42

Running fix under the influence of a tidal stream.

If a boat is under the influence of a tidal stream at the time a running fix is needed, due allowance must be made for it.

Example.

From a boat steering 090° at 5 knots, at 1700 hours a lighthouse bore 030° and at 1800 hours it bore 340°. During the period the boat was under the influence of a tidal stream setting 240° at 1½ knots. Fix the position at 1800 hours.

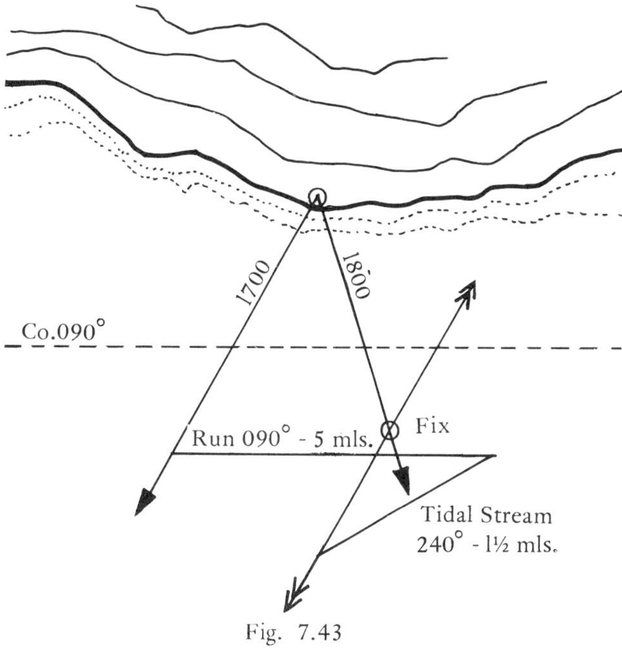

Fig. 7.43

Order of work.

(a) Lay off the first bearing.

(b) From any point on the first bearing, lay off the course and distance run between 1700 and 1800 hours.

(c) From the point of termination of the run, project the tidal stream experienced during the period between bearings.

(d) Through the point of termination of the tidal stream, draw in the transferred position line parallel to the first bearing.

(e) Lay off the second bearing. The point of intersection with the transferred position line will be the boat's position.

Explanation.

As previously indicated, in a running fix it is essential that, for accuracy of the fix, the run between bearings is faithfully projected. In the example the boat made a course over the ground as indicated by the dotted line. Only by considering the run and the tidal stream separately can the course and distance **over the ground** be determined.

Leeway and the running fix.

That course which is being made good **through the water** is that which must be applied to the chart and **not** the course being steered.

Summing up the running fix.

In terms of usage by mariners, the running fix is a close runner up to the fix by cross bearings, notwithstanding its limitations.

For the reasons which follow, the greater the speed of the boat, the more accurate a running fix is likely to be:

The change in bearing of the object taken is more quickly achieved.
It is generally more easy to steer a good course at a greater speed.
The time between bearings will be less, thus potential errors in computation of course, speed and tidal stream will be less marked.
The amount of leeway being made will be less.

A sailing craft tacking in light winds may have to go about between bearings, and her low speed will accentuate the affect of any tidal stream upon her course. These conditions would render it difficult to determine the run over the ground between bearings and the yachtsman must consider the desirability of using a running fix in these or similar conditions.

The yachtsman and the fix by 4-point bearing.

Some of the methods of fixing position passed on to the small boat sailor by his big-ship brethren are limited in their application to small craft. Knowledge of their existence is useful as it may be possible to apply them from time to time. Nevertheless the amateur yachtsman should be constantly aware that, being unable to apply certain navigational principles, it may be the limitations of his craft which render it so and not his own short-comings as a navigator. One such method which comes to mind is clearly in this category; the 4-point bearing.

Fix by 4-point bearing.

The application of the 4-point bearing fix is simplicity itself. Nevertheless, it entails maintaining a steady course between bearings, much in the manner that a pilot of a bomber used to have to maintain a steady course during the final stage of a bombing run. Any deflection from the course for whatever reason renders the bombing run, and the 4-point bearing run, null and void.

In Fig. 7.44, triangle ABC is an equilateral triangle, therefore angles A and B are 45° and sides AB and BC are of equal length. If the navigator takes a bearing of the object when it is 4 points on the bow (which is the obsolescent way of saying 45°), and again when the object is abeam, the distance traversed between the two bearings must be the distance off when point B is reached.

Explanation.

The patent log reading being taken at A and again at B, the difference between the readings will give the distance off the object taken at B. The effect of a tidal stream will render almost meaningless the assumptions in this problem as in these conditions distance run between bearings will not be

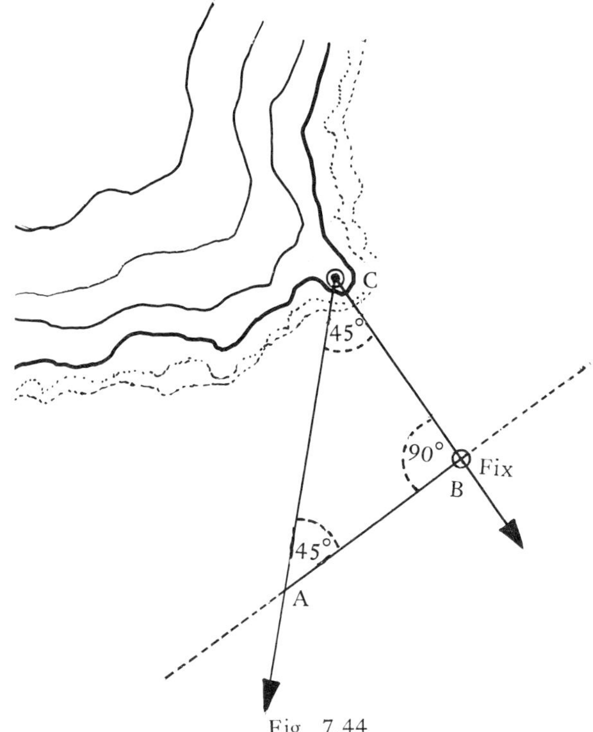

Fig. 7.44

distance off. While not absolutely essential it is nevertheless highly desirable that the boat is heading in the direction she is making good, consequently the effect of an allowance being made for leeway between bearings introduces an issue which tends to complicate what is intended to be a very simple method of fixing position. The writer would advise that if the craft is making leeway, or if she is sailing under the influence of a tidal stream, it is better to treat the two bearings as those needed for a running fix and proceed accordingly.

Let it be reiterated that occasions do present themselves when the sailing fraternity can profitably take advantage of this method of fixing position. Running free during a period of slack water is obviously a case in point. Owners of power boats will also appreciate that, given tidal streams of low velocity, they will frequently be able to utilise the fix by 4-point bearing.

Fix by doubling the angle on the bow.

Another method of fixing position which is closely allied to the fix by 4-point bearing is doubling the angle on the bow. All the limitations described in the case of the fix by 4-point bearing have equal validity in this method.

The advantage of doubling the angle on the bow is that, a boat approaching a headland or off-lying danger, the distance she will pass off it will be determined **before** she reaches it. Thus in this respect such a fix has greater value than the fix by 4-point bearing.

In Fig. 7.45 triangle ABC is an isosceles triangle. Angles A and C are equal and sides AB and BC are of equal length. If a bearing is taken from a boat sailing from D to E when the headland is 30° on the bow, and again when it is double that amount, 60°, the yachtsman can say that the distance run between the bearings is the distance off at the time of taking the second bearing. Thus a fix is obtained before the headland is closely approached. It does not have to be 30° and 60°: it could be 25° and 50°, or 34° and 68°: the requirement is to double the angle on the bow. Proof of this would require an excursion into geometry which is not necessary here.

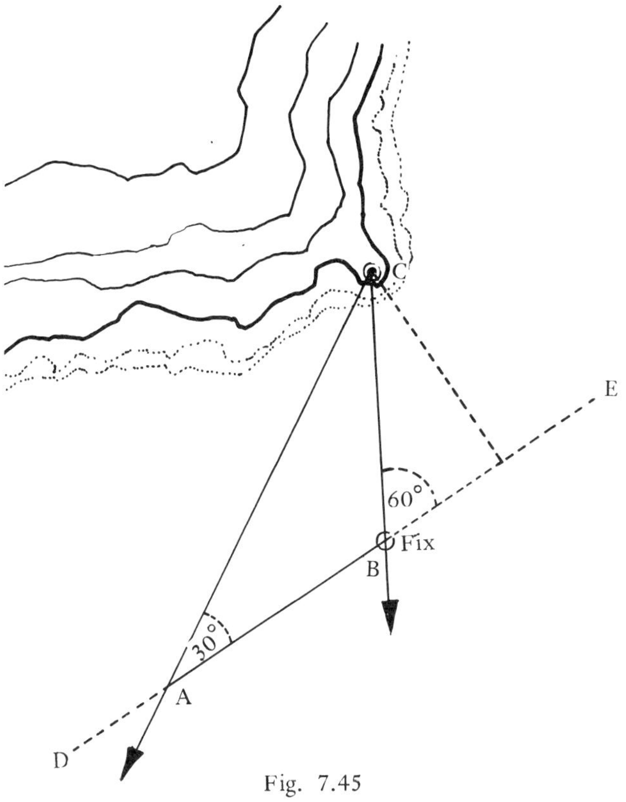

Fig. 7.45

Where a hand bearing compass is carried, in addition to a compass used for steering only, such a method cannot be used and it is proposed that, provided one's craft lends itself to such an arrangement, permanent sight vanes be established on the coach roof or, failing this, an index point on the coach roof coupled with bearing markers on the guard rails. Such vanes can be tiny and unobtrusive and can be used as sights for taking relative bearings. The number of relative bearings capable of being taken will be limited to the number of vanes it is decided to establish. A suggested pattern is outlined in Fig.7.46 below, but it must be remembered that, when using such sights, the boat **must** be steady on her course.

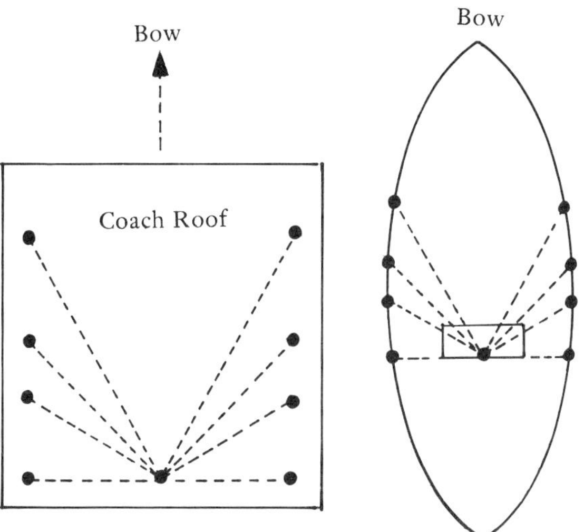

Markers at 30°, 45°, 60°, & 90° on each side in both cases.

Fig. 7.46

Determining angles on the bow.

For those who possess craft of such a type that they can take advantage of the simple types of fix outlined above, it remains for them to determine how angles on the bow may be found in their particular craft.

For those who use dual-purpose compasses the problem is easy. It will simply be a matter of calculating from the course being steered the number of degrees to the left or right of it.

Example.

From a boat on a compass course of 040° it is desired to know when the compass bearings of a distant object will be, first when it is 30° on the port bow and second, when it is 60°

Compass course	040°	Compass course	040°
Port bow - deduct	30°	Port bow - deduct	60°
First bearing	010°	Second bearing	340°

Application.

When the above compass bearings are achieved, the distance object will be 30° and 60° on the port bow respectively.

Transit and bearing.

A transit offering itself to the navigator, one single compass bearing of another object will provide a fix. Opportunities of fixing position so simply should never be neglected.

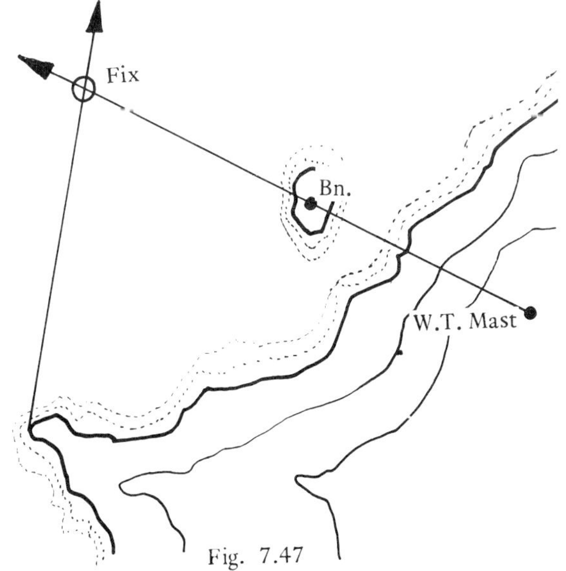

Fig. 7.47

Maximum range of light and a bearing.

A navigational light seen to be dipping below or rising above the horizon is known to be at maximum visibility range and a position circle may be described round the lighthouse using the range of the light as a radius. If a bearing of a light is taken at this time the point of intersection of the position circle and the bearing will provide a position.

Example.

A lighthouse whose charted range is 16 miles is seen to dip below the horizon bearing 290°. Height of eye 15′. Fix the position.

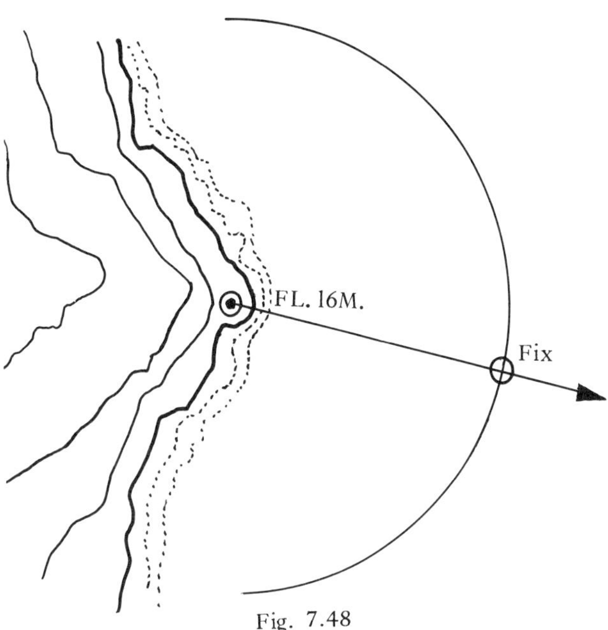

Fig. 7.48

Order of work.

(a) Using a radius of 16 miles on a pair of compasses, describe a circle round the light.

(b) Lay off the bearing.

Sounding and bearing.

Example.

Cap Gris Nez Lighthouse was observed to bear 120° at the same time as a sounding gave 20 fathoms. Fix the approximate position.

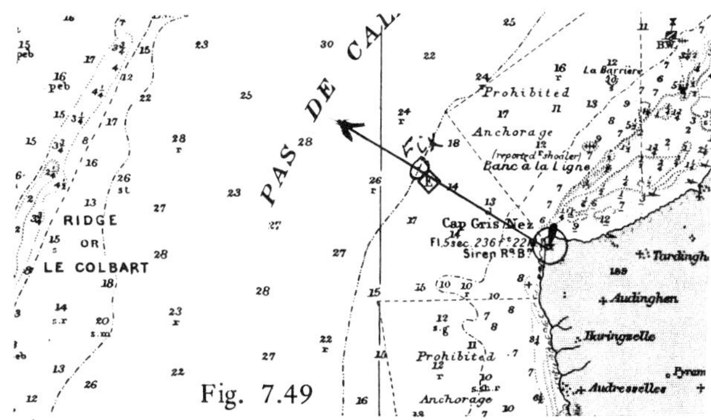

Fig. 7.49

Order of work.

(a) Lay off the bearing of the lighthouse.

(b) The sounding being 20 fathoms, it may be taken that where the bearing crosses the 20 fathom line is the approximate position.

Note

Although it is seamanlike to obtain a sounding at the same time as a single bearing is obtained, in the areas in which we navigate the seabed can be particularly unhelpful. Too often it is found that considerable areas show the same sounding, so that in these cases not even an approximate position may be obtained by this method. Again, rise of tide should be deducted from the sounding where necessary.

Line of sounding.

If a craft is on a steady heading, a series of soundings may be taken over an interval of two or three hours, or more. The times and soundings being recorded, it is sometimes possible to relate this line of soundings to soundings on the chart which produce a similar pattern. If this can be achieved, an approximate position may be obtained.

Example.

In thick weather, some distance to the westward of Pte.du Haut Banc L.H., a craft is estimated to have a course and speed over the ground of 102° at 6 knots. She commences taking soundings at 0700 hours and continues doing so at 15 minute intervals for the next 2½ hours. The soundings recorded are :—

0700	0715	0730	0745	0800	0815	0830	0845
13	11	24	19	16	10	10	8

0900	0915	0930
10	10	5 fathoms.

Find her approximate position at 0930 hours.

Order of work.

(a) A long strip of paper is utilised. It is folded once, lengthwise.

(b) On its folded edge, using the same scale as that of the chart being used, intervals are marked corresponding to the distance traversed between each sounding. In this case the distance between each mark will be 1½ miles.

(c) Against each mark the appropriate time and sounding is written.

(d) With the strip of paper folded over the edge of the parallel ruler, and the ruler being set in the direction of the course being made good, the problem then resolves itself into finding a pattern of soundings on the chart corresponding to that on the strip of paper.

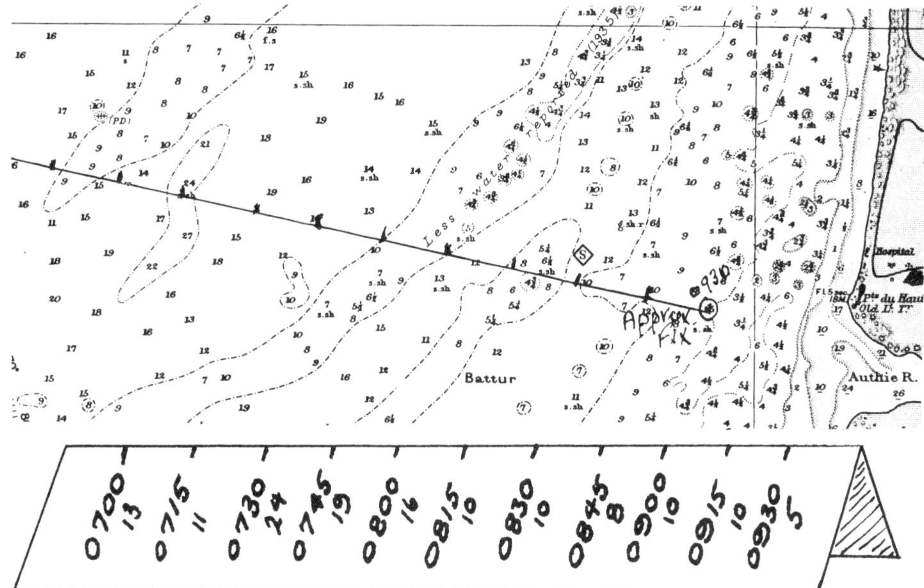

Fig. 7.50

(e) If a satisfactory relation between soundings on chart and paper strip can be found, it may be assumed that the approximate position at 0930 hours is the position of the sounding obtained at that time.

Note

From a practical point of view, it is extremely improbable that a yachtsman who depends upon a hand lead line for his soundings would undertake the above arduous task, even if he had the crew and the time. It is quite feasible for those who possess echo-sounding apparatus.

Ideally, an area with a distinctive pattern of soundings having a pronounced variation in depth is necessary to produce satisfactory results. In the English Channel and southern North Sea there are few sections of the sea bed which produce a sufficiently useful pattern of soundings. Nevertheless, this is a method of obtaining an approximate position. When position is in serious doubt no means of determining position should be overlooked.

It will be appreciated that, if necessary, the rise of tide above chart datum should be deducted from soundings taken so that they may be related to the chart.

The sextant and coastwise navigation.

The sextant is of course primarily designed for those who engage in celestial navigation. It can prove useful from time to time in terrestrial navigation too. The yachtsman who though not conversant with celestial navigation, nevertheless owns a sextant, increases the number of methods by which he can fix his position.

A sextant is a precision instrument which is capable of measuring angles between two objects in any plane, vertical, horizontal or oblique. Those sextants used by professionals will measure an angle to an accuracy of 10″ of arc. A plastic one, which can be bought for a few pounds, usually is capable of being read to 2′ of arc. The latter type should not be spurned as an expensive toy as yachts have been navigated across the great oceans with them.

Provided a sextant is capable of measuring an angle to within 1 degree, it will suffice for the needs of the coastwise navigator. As any angle measured has ultimately to be projected on the chart, and a compass rose on a chart is graduated in degrees, greater accuracy is unnecessary.

Position by vertical sextant angle and a bearing.

In a right angled triangle, given the length of one side and one of the lesser angles, it is possible to calculate one of the other sides. To relate this fact to the problem in question, given the height of a lighthouse (one side) and the angle at the observer subtended between the lantern of the lighthouse and sea level (one of the lesser angles) it is possible to calculate the distance of the observer from the lighthouse.

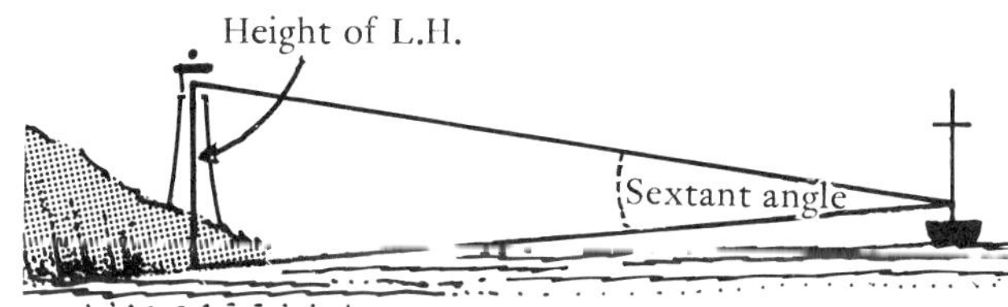

Fig. 7.51

It is not necessary to calculate the distance off. On page 215, and in many nautical publications, will be found a table, 'Distance by vertical sextant angle'. Entering the table, with the vertical angle as obtained from the sextant and the height of the lighthouse from the chart, the distance off may be extracted.

Example.

Cap Gris Nez lighthouse (236 feet) is observed to bear 070° and subtends a vertical angle of 1° 29′. Fix the position.

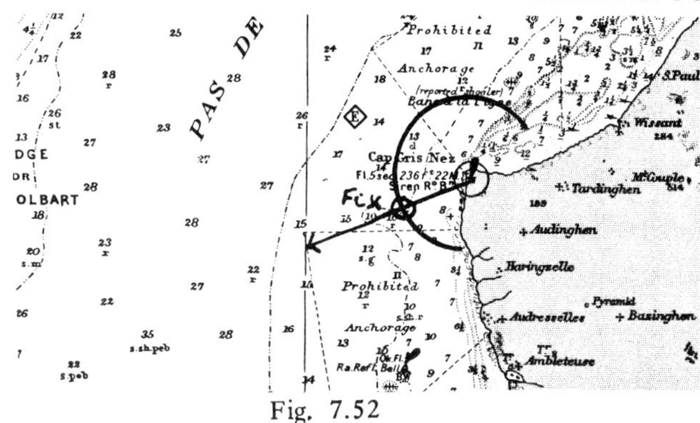

Fig. 7.52

Order of work.

(a) The table is entered with the angle $1^\circ\ 29'$ and height 236 feet. Distance off will be found to be 1·5 miles.

(b) Using a radius of 1½ miles an arc is described round the lighthouse.

(c) The bearing is drawn in. The point of intersection of the bearing with the arc is the position required.

Note

When measuring the sextant angle of a lighthouse it must be remembered that the height is measured from M.H.W.S. to the centre of the focal plane, which is the centre of the lantern.

The height being measured from M.H.W.S., if the tide level is below this point the effect will be to increase the apparent height of the lighthouse. As this has the effect of increasing the angle measured, it has the subsidiary effect of giving the navigator the impression that he is a little closer to the lighthouse than he in fact, is. As this gives him a slight safety factor, height of tide is always disregarded in these problems.

This method of determining distance off can be used to advantage in many instances. Consider, for example, the yachtsman endeavouring to weather a headland but he does not wish to close it within a certain range. He may set an angle on his sextant equivalent to that which will be produced at the minimum range he allows himself. Though he may alter course frequently as he works windward, he has only to glance through his sextant from time to time to find whether or not he is outside or inside the minimum range at which he desires to round the headland.

Fix by horizontal sextant angles.

The great value of fixing position by horizontal sextant angles is that it is achieved without the need of compass bearings, calculations or the need to refer to tables. In the confines of a small craft the small amount of geometry required for its execution becomes something of a trial but it remains very much worth while.

The angles required need a degree of accuracy which only a sextant will provide. It is sometimes propounded that if compass bearings are used, and the angles between the compass bearings calculated, satisfactory horizontal angles may be obtained. This is probably valid on large ships with large compasses but is totally irrelevent in small craft, which carry relatively small compasses.

Relating geometry to the practical aspects of navigating in small craft, it can be said that if the horizontal angle between two terrestrial objects can be found, a circle of position may be projected on the chart. Such a position circle will pass through the positions of the two objects used and the position of the observer. Further, if two such position circles can be projected in such a manner that their circumferences cross, evidently the observer's position must be at a point of intersection of the position circles.

Example.

Points A, B and C are recognisable objects on shore. By sextant, the angle between points A and B is found to be 55° and that between B and C is 37°. Fix the position.

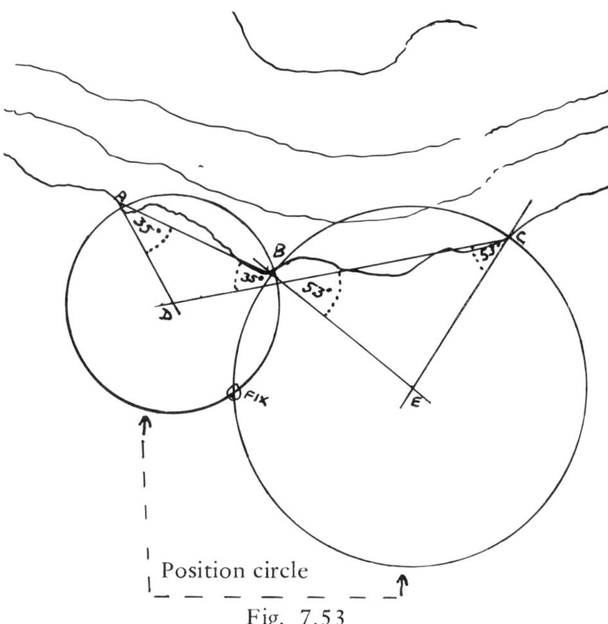

Fig. 7.53

Order of work.

(a) With pencil lines join A and B, and B and C.

(b) Subtract each angle from 90°, producing angles of 35° and 53° respectively.

(c) From position A, using the line AB as the base line, produce an angle of 35° on the same side of the line as the observer. Produce the same angle, in the same way, from position B. These two lines will cross each other at D.

(d) Treat the angle of 53°, which is that relating to positions B and C, in the same manner as described in (c). Name the point at the intersection of the produced lines E.

(e) Point D is the centre of a circle whose circumference will pass through A, B and the position of the observer. The circle may be described.

(f) Point E is the centre of a circle whose circumference passes through B, C and the position of the observer

(g) The observer's position occurs where the position circles cross.

Note

There are sound geometrical reasons, considered by the writer to be extraneous in this publication, why circles of position may be produced in this way.

It occasionally occurs that the angle between two of the objects exceeds 90°. In this case 90° must be subtracted from the angle and the resultant angles projected on the opposite side of the base line from the observer in the following manner:

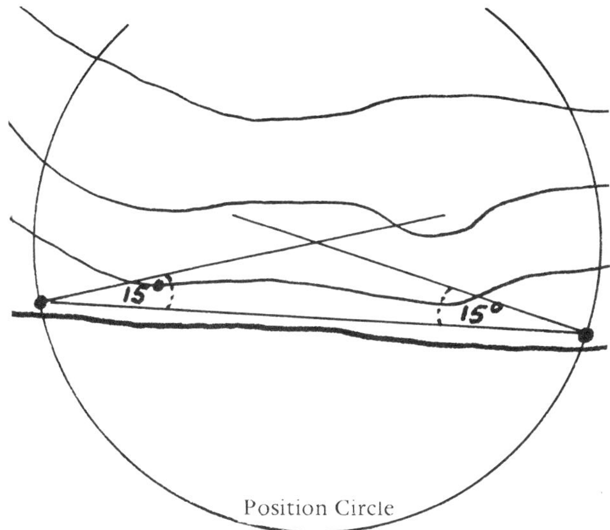

Projection of horizontal angle of 105°
Position Circle

Fig. 7.54

In order to avoid an erroneous result the three objects should be on or near the same straight line, or the centre object should be nearer to the observer than the other two, or the boat inside a triangle formed by the three objects.

The Station Pointer.

A station pointer is a rather costly piece of navigational equipment which will solve the fix by horizontal sextant angles without the necessity of resorting to the use of protractor and compasses. It comprises a circular protractor which has one fixed and two movable arms capable of being set to the observed horizontal angles. The problem then resolves itself into the manipulation of the instrument so that the arms bisect the three objects taken. The position occurs at the central hole in the station pointer.

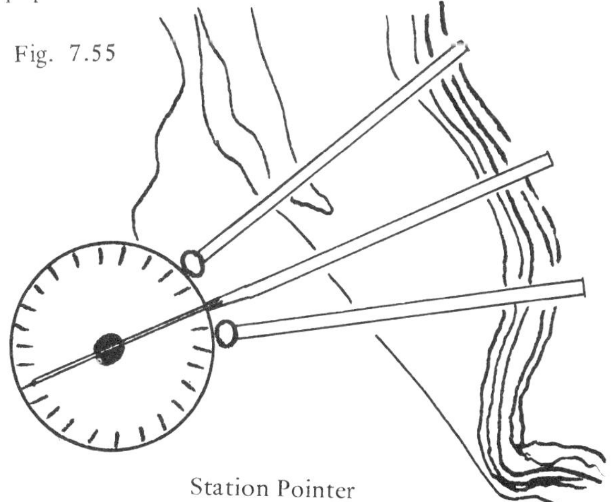

Fig. 7.55

Station Pointer

Although cheap plastic versions of the station pointer are available, the writer would not propose the purchase of one by a yachtsman. A Douglas Protractor or a piece of semi-transparent paper will produce the same result. It is simply a matter of drawing the angles either on the face of a Douglas Protractor, or on a suitable piece of paper. Manipulation of either, in the manner described above, will produce the required position.

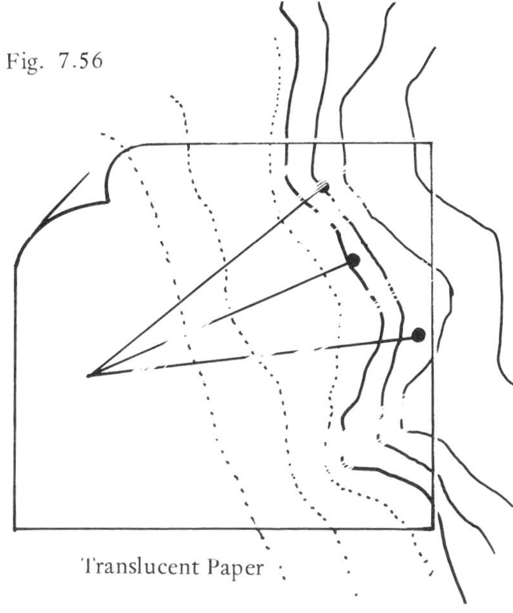

Fig. 7.56

Translucent Paper

Anchor bearings.

It is sometimes necessary for a yachtsman to anchor in a tideway. In these circumstances the possibility of a dragging anchor cannot be ignored. It is fortunate if he has been able to anchor in close proximity to a fixed object such as a pile, a buoy or a pier; any change in range from such a convenient point of reference becomes immediately apparent to him. It is not always so.

Large ships rely upon compass bearings taken both ahead and on the beam. The bearings are checked at regular intervals for any sign of dragging and there is no reason why yachtsmen should not adopt such a system. Generally speaking, small craft tend to anchor inshore or at least where the shore or a river bank is in fairly close range. As **beam** bearings are the ones which indicate any movement of the craft down-stream it is valuable to note two objects on shore which are in line. They need not be capable of being related to the chart. A certain house in line with a tree in the background will suffice. Even a small movement downstream will be immediately apparent by the change in such a transit bearing. One's head occasionally poked on deck confirms or otherwise how well one's anchor is holding. At night any convenient lights may be used in a similar way.

Failing any method of the nature described being available, one should not forget the old and tried method of dropping a weighted line - a hand lead line - on the bottom. Holding the line taut, if it assumes a slant towards the bow it is time to pay out more cable or shift berth.

The "Elingamite".

In 1902, in fog, the steamship 'Elingamite' foundered. She met her end on one of the lonely Three Kings Islands which are some miles to the northward of the northern tip of New Zealand. Forty-five lives were lost.

Bound from Sydney and making towards the passage between the Three Kings Islands and New Zealand, she ran into poor visibility during the final 20 hours of her life. During this period celestial sights were unobtainable. It is likely that her Master intended to pass midway between the mainland and the islands, a passage some 30 miles wide. She literally collided with the West King at 10.00 a.m. on the day in question: she had been running on D.R. since the previous noon.

During the critical 22 hours after the last celestial fix was obtained the evidence indicates that her patent log was fouled at least once by weed. It seems probable that the distance recorded was less than actually traversed through the water. Some 4 hours before foundering, due to the onset of dense fog, her Master ordered a reduction in engine revolutions to give a calculated speed of 4 knots. Did the changed engine revolutions produce the required 4 knots - or more? It is likely that she was some miles ahead of her D.R. position and this may have contributed to the tragedy.

The area is notorious for strong tides. Her Master had considerable experience of them. Based upon previous experience he assumed the tidal stream was setting in a southerly direction. In fact it was setting in a direction almost the reverse of that assumed. Worse still, he adjusted his course to counteract the effect of the assumed south-setting stream. Not only was the tidal stream setting the 'Elingamite' to the northward at perhaps 4 or 5 knots but he was in addition steering to the northward of his course. As land was approached during the final hours, no doubt the full effect of the tidal stream was felt.

One can imagine the effect upon her course during those last hours. Visibility was almost nil. The tidal stream was near athwart her course - that is to say, across - at a rate more than equal to her forward speed through the water. She may have been making a course 50° or more to the northward of that which it was believed she was making.

It is easy to be wise after an event. No one can know what factors her Master considered other than the obvious ones. Hindsight is valuable only in the sense that it may provide object lessons for those who indulge in it. There was undoubtedly an element of 'By guess and by God' in the conditions experienced - and those which are experienced by small boat sailors. With better luck the 'Elingamite' may have been carried past the islands, to one side or the other. Then she may have finished up, virtually anonymous like most ships, in a knacker's yard many years later. In this story there are lessons for us all.

CHAPTER 8

Radio Aids

The old saying, 'You don't get what you don't pay for', is hardly one a person would expect to apply to accuracy of position at sea. It is natural to associate such nautical precision with navigational prowess, yet in the field of radio aids to navigation the assertion is unquestionable. If a yachtsman is willing and able to make a very considerable cash outlay he can obtain almost instantaneous positions of incredible accuracy. Wishing to use these aids, yet unwilling to make any expenditure on them, he must accept a degree of potential error in position which will cause him to ponder whether he would do better to rely upon his own ability to calculate reasonably good dead reckoning positions.

At the costly end of the scale we have the Decca Navigator, a quite remarkable instrument which requires considerable electrical power. Widely used by coastal shipping, it will produce positions in home waters having an average margin of error of a mere 2 cables. The bargain basement offers us Consol, a system of value to aircraft hundreds of miles out in the Atlantic. With possible errors being up to 10 miles in daytime and 20 or more miles at night, it is necessarily of questionable value to the off-shore sailor.

Between these two extremes there is radio direction finding apparatus which compromises on both cost and accuracy. That the compromise is well worth while is affirmed by the number of yachtsmen who possess radio direction finding equipment. The system requires a yachtsman to take certain basic precautions and he must clearly recognise its limitations. These conditions being accepted, he may obtain positions of reasonable accuracy which, in moments of need, will amply repay him for his cash outlay.

D/F sets available for use in small craft.

A considerable variety of D/F sets have become available for use on small craft in recent years, the majority designed with the recognition that electric power supplies are often non-existent. Some are wholly portable, others have portable aerials connected to permanently mounted radio receivers and the remainder require permanent mountings for both receiver and aerial.

A cursory glance through pamphlets advertising D/F sets will indicate that they vary widely in price. Those capable of assessing the qualities in design and function of sets, recognising that maximum accuracy and reliability are criteria to be sought, appear to be of the opinion that these criteria are more likely to be found in sets which are in the higher price range.

D/F aerials.

All D/F sets are a combination of a Radio receiver and a special aerial. D/F receivers may vary in quality and design, but all are capable of receiving signals in what is usually known as the M/F band. It is in the type of aerial, and the manner in which the aerial is utilised, where the most marked differences in D/F sets occur.

There are two types of D/F aerial in common use:

(a) The loop aerial which must be given a permanent mounting.

(b) The 'ferrite rod' aerial, which may be permanently mounted or portable.

The loop aerial is usually mounted on deck in a craft's fore and aft line and is capable of being rotated in its mounting. The axle or spindle projects through to the cabin below, from which position the aerial may be revolved by a wheel or other suitable device. Coupled to the drive wheel is a pointer which has an associated fixed dial. The dial, being graduated from 0°, the dead-ahead position, through 360°, on it the pointer will indicate the relative direction in which the loop is pointing.

A ferrite rod aerial comprises a coil with a rod shaped piece of ferrite as its core. Both are encased in a non-magnetic material. The combination of coil and ferrite rod provides the means by which, given equal sensitivity, an aerial of considerably less dimensions than the traditional loop aerial may be used. Such a compact aerial lends itself to use in a variety of ways. It may be permanently mounted above or below decks, or held in the hand, or incorporated within a hand-held set which is itself rotated.

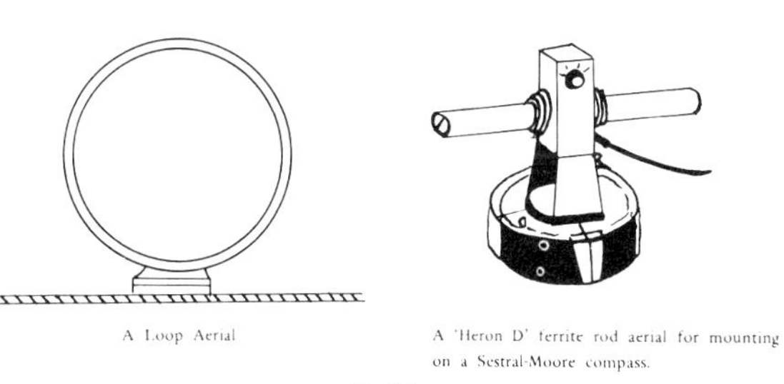

A Loop Aerial

A 'Heron D' ferrite rod aerial for mounting on a Sestral-Moore compass.

Fig. 8.1

Aerials of either type, having the same basic qualities, produce results in radio reception of a peculiar yet never-varying nature. It is this characteristic which is utilised in radio direction finding. Depending upon the angle between the axis of the aerial and the direction of an in-coming radio signal, such a signal may or may not be heard.

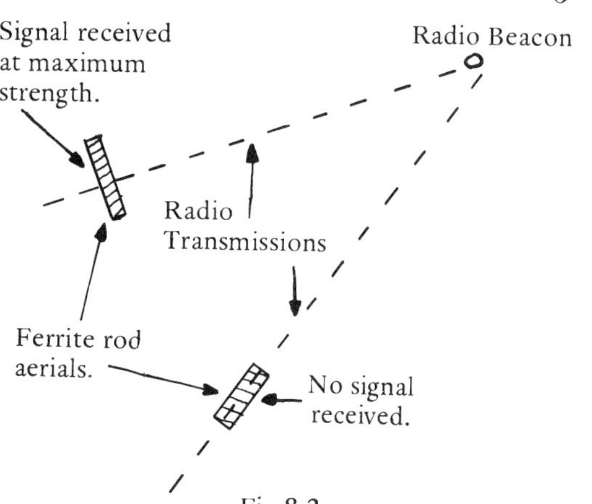

Fig.8·2

If a D/F aerial is rotated through 360°, two areas will be found in which no signal is received. This is understandable: these aerials have two sides. The two areas, usually termed nulls, will be quite sharply defined in a well designed set. An aerial being rotated and a null being approached, the signal strength will quite rapidly fall away to inaudibility and just as rapidly regain strength as rotation is continued. These nulls occur when the axis of an aerial is directly presented to a transmitting station, thus if the direction of a null can be determined, the direction from which an incoming signal emanates may be found.

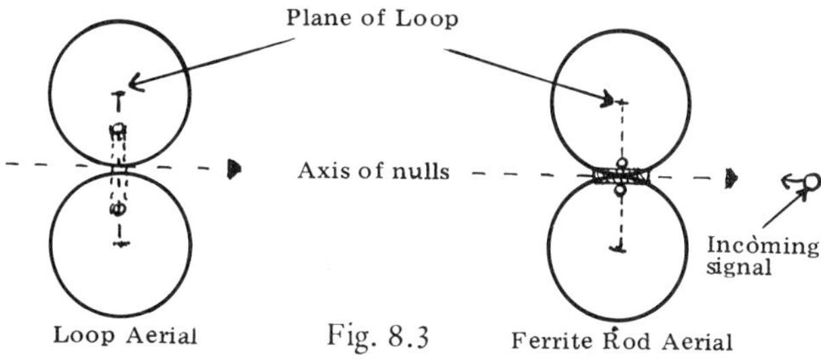

Fig. 8.3

At first glance the two polar diagrams in Fig. 8.3 appear technical and obscure but a study of them will quickly reveal their purport. There being two 'sides' to any such aerial, their qualities can be represented as a perfect figure of eight. The circles in each diagram indicate the strength of received signal at varying angles to the axis of the aerials. It should be noted how sharply defined are the null areas in each case and how the axis of the nulls indicate the direction of the received signal.

Necessary installation precautions.

Not unlike the manner in which errors of deviation may be introduced into a magnetic compass, so can errors be produced in D/F sets. Such errors are known collectively as quadrantal error. The name arises from the fact that they are at a maximum in each quadrant of relative bearing and non-existent on the port and starboard beams, ahead and astern.

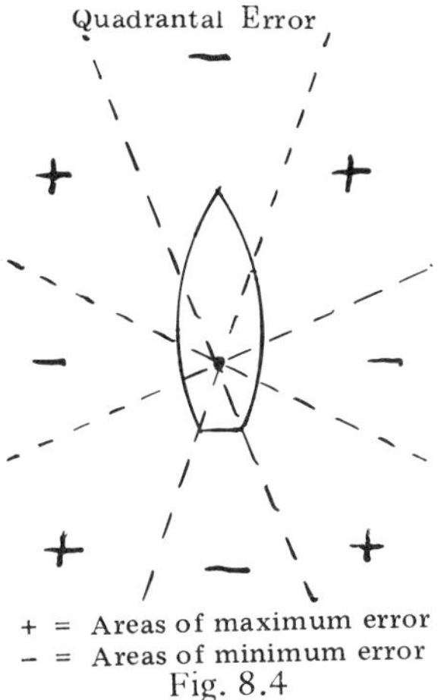

Fig. 8.4

What ever the construction of the craft and what ever type of set is used, it is essential to take certain precautions to neutralise or minimise known potential sources of quadrantal error.

Neutralisation of rigging.

In a craft where rigging is secured to a metal hull, or chain plates are so fitted to the hull or deck that there is a continuity of metal between the rigging on port and starboard sides, a 'closed loop' will be formed. Vertical closed loops of this type will produce serious quadrantal error.

The removal of such a source of error is simply a matter of breaking the loops by introducing insulators into them, thereby destroying continuity. The easiest way to do this is to substitute all lower splice rigging thimbles with insulated dead-eyes. These, or specially insulated rigging shackles which will achieve the same purpose, are fairly easily purchasable.

Neutralisation of wire guard rails.

Wire guard rails which, in a like manner, produce a closed loop will similarly produce quadrantal error although generally of less magnitude. Again the loops must be broken. First, insulated dead-eyes or shackles must be fitted as necessary and secondly, some form of insulation must be introduced where wire guard rails pass through metal stanchions. Sundry methods may be adopted to achieve this and the fitting of P.V.C. sleeves to the offending sections of guard rail immediately comes to mind.

Siting of D/F aerials – general.

It is generally recommended that a D/F aerial should not be used, or sited, within 6 feet of a metal mast, or within 3 feet of wire rigging, even though any closed loops have been broken. Fixed aerials should be fitted in the fore and aft line in metal hulled craft.

Vertically disposed aerials connected to radio sets used for general purposes are one more source of potential quadrantal error. It is not implied here that any permanent means of neutralising such error need be taken. It will suffice to disconnect any such aerial from its set while a D/F set is being operated. This, incidentally, is a precaution which can easily be overlooked: the reader should ever be mindful of it.

In general, it being impractical to give guidance in every possible case, it would be sensible for the yachtsman not to operate a D/F aerial in close proximity to any mass of metal, particularly if it is vertically disposed.

Siting of D/F aerials — metal hulled craft.

Metal hulled craft will produce quadrantal error and it would be impossible to operate a D/F aerial below the deck line of such craft. The aerial must be sited or used as high above the hull as possible. It is unlikely that this action will remove all quadrantal error but it will be reduced to relatively small quantities.

Siting of aerials - craft of wooden or glass fibre construction.

Provided the precautions already described have been taken, craft of wooden or glass fibre construction should not produce quadrantal error in a D/F set. Portable aerials, or sets, may be used above or below decks in a position which is most practicable for the operator in a seaway.

Suppression of electrical equipment.

Just as electrical components in a car engine will interfere with reception by a car radio, so will similar equipment in a yacht interfere with radio reception in a D/F set. All good sets are so designed that 'background' noise is kept to a practical minimum. It remains necessary to take steps to suppress electrical interference which may be produced within the craft. The makers of engines and other equipment frequently include the suppression of potential causes of radio interference in their design but, if they do not, it would be wise to write to them requesting advice on how suppression may be achieved.

Obviously the removal of a D/F set as far as practicable from the source of radio interference will assist greatly but this is not always possible. As a last resort, it should not be overlooked that the stopping of the engine, or whatever equipment is producing the interference, will remove the interference entirely.

Marine radiobeacons.

Marine radiobeacons are transmitters which are established on coast lines throughout the world. They are specifically intended for use by all vessels fitted with D/F equipment. Perhaps the greatest concentration of them is to be found in the British Isles and their near continental shores. Let the reader be in no doubt that this is mainly because the need is real in the sometimes treacherous, sometimes dangerous waters in which we sail.

British and continental marine radiobeacons transmit on radio frequencies between 285 and 315 kHz, a band which is covered by all D/F sets. The majority transmit continuously but a small number provide a fog service only.

In the British Isles and on the continent the characteristic signal of each beacon is standardised as follows:

Identification signal transmitted 3 to 6 times	22 seconds
Long dash lasting for	25 seconds
Identification signal transmitted once or twice	8 seconds
Silent period of at least	5 seconds
One unit transmission	60 seconds

The identification signal comprises 2 letters transmitted in the Morse Code. The speed of transmission is slow and it is not necessary for a yachtsman to gain proficiency in the code, provided he has temporarily memorised the character of the signals for which he is listening.

Grouping of Marine radiobeacons.

The considerable number of marine radiobeacons using a relatively small frequency band have caused the authorities to adopt a system of frequency-sharing. Only by the adoption of such a system can a wholly satisfactory service, in terms of quality of received signal, be rendered to mariners. In effect, grouping means that any number of marine radiobeacons up to a maximum of six may use the same radio frequency. Of course, beacons using a common frequency do not all transmit at the same time. If frequency-sharing is adopted, time-sharing is essential.

When beacons are grouped, a complete cycle of transmissions of all beacons in the group is taken to be 6 minutes. One by one each beacon transmits a unit transmission as outlined above. It will be seen that if 6 beacons are grouped, being allowed one minute of transmission time, each will follow in rotation until the cycle is completed. As long as transmissions continue the cycle will be repeated again and again.

It does not necessarily follow that, wherever beacons are grouped, a group will contain 6 beacons. Any number between 2 and 6 may be found to be sharing a common frequency but whatever the number of beacons in a group, the complete cycle of transmission will always be 6 minutes. In all cases an easily understood pattern is used and, in any table listing such beacons, the precise order of transmissions is given. To use a simple example, if 3 beacons are grouped, each will be allowed 2 unit transmissions in each 6 minute cycle: the order would probably be 1, 2, 3, 1, 2, 3.

Apart from the fact that this system gives a more satisfactory service for mariners in an area where a considerable number of beacons are found, it provides a facility. Many of the beacons which have been grouped will be found to have a common locality and so, wishing to use beacons of the same group, it is not necessary for the mariner to re-tune his D/F set for each beacon he has selected for use. Yet another advantage is that, a series of radio bearings being obtained which are linked closely in terms of time, a yachtsman does not have to take into consideration distance run between bearings.

It must be emphasised that the primary object of grouping is to minimise radio interference under all conditions: the navigational advantages to mariners which the system provides can be regarded only as useful bonuses. An appraisal of many groups of radiobeacons may indicate that it contains one or even two which are so far removed from the rest that they could not possibly be used in conjunction with the remainder. In such cases it may be said that the primary object is achieved but a percentage of the bonus is absent. Of course, the relatively recent re-grouping of English Channel marine radiobeacons puts equal emphasis on these navigational advantages and yachtsmen in that area reap the benefit.

Aero-marine radiobeacons.

Some radio beacons have locations which are such that they can prove equally advantageous to both ships and aircraft. In occasional instances authorities have established beacons which provide facilities for both. From a practical point of view this fact is only of passing interest to the yachtsman and, in the lists of marine radiobeacons on pages 88 to 95, they are included without special reference to their dual function.

Aero-radiobeacons.

It is common knowledge that radio direction finding is widely used by aircraft. Many of the beacons they use, called aero-radiobeacons, are sufficiently near a coastline to prove of value to mariners. Using the M/F band, their identification signals are either 2 or 3 letters transmitted in the Morse Code, followed by a long dash which is the tuning signal. Although these beacons transmit individually, which is to say they are never grouped, their transmissions are continuous during their hours of service. This fact is a distinct advantage to mariners as bearings of them may be obtained whatever the state of visibility.

Primarily intended to meet the peculiar needs of aircraft, their location is often such that they do not have the uninterrupted transmission path of a marine radiobeacon situated on a coastline. The peculiarities of terrain between transmitter and boat-borne receiver may sometimes have the effect of 'bending' transmissions. This will be described later. A bent transmission produces a wholly erroneous bearing and so aero-radiobeacons must be selected with caution.

Only minimal detail of these beacons is available to mariners, a fact which may from time to time prove a small embarrassment to yachtsmen, but this in no way detracts from their overall value. For instance, they cease transmission from time to time for routine servicing but such periods are not always promulgated to mariners. Should a beacon alter its identification signal, or shift its position or be withdrawn, the information may not be immediately available to the small boat sailor.

Potential errors in received signals.

Night effect.

During the period from one hour before sunset to one hour after sunrise there is a considerable likelihood that bearings of radiobeacons will be subject to 'night effect' errors. This effect may manifest itself in a fluctuation in received signal strength, or a null will be found to be indefinite or blurred. It is generally found that provided the range of the transmitter does not exceed 25 miles 'night effect' is negligible. Some advise that 50 miles is the nearer figure.

Coastal refraction.

If the path of a radio transmission passes along a coastline, or crosses it at an oblique angle, signals may be deflected away from or towards that coastline. The mariner must guard against this error by selecting beacons carefully

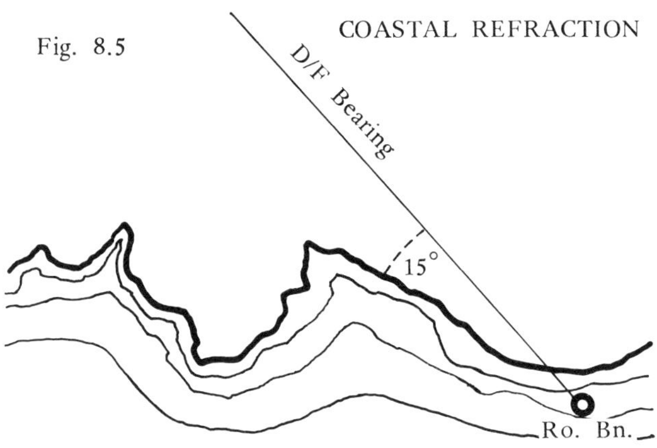

Do not take a bearing if the angle of inclination to the coast is 15° or less.

and avoiding those in which the angle of inclination to the coast is 15° or less.

Hill scatter.

When high land intercedes between beacon and D/F set, 'hill scatter' may produce an error in bearings. Marine radiobeacons usually being situated on a shore line, this effect need seldom be considered when they are being utilised but it assumes greater importance in the case of those aero radiobeacons which are situated some distance inland. The nearer the beacon is to high land, the more likelihood of error.

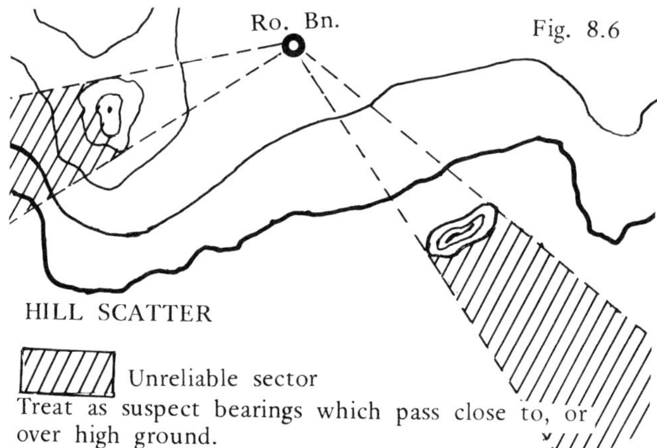

Treat as suspect bearings which pass close to, or over high ground.

Heeling error.

A yacht being heeled over due to the effect of wind, if she carries a fixed D/F aerial, that too will be angled over. In these circumstances, a factor known as heeling error will be introduced into D/F bearings. Identical in effect to quadrantal error, the only practical way to deal with heeling error is to nullify it. This is achieved naturally and unconsciously when using a hand-held set because it will be used vertically, and this must equally apply to a set which has a hand-held aerial. Certain fixed aerials may be mounted in gymbals which in their own mechanical way overcome the possibility of the introduction of this error. In cases where heeling error cannot be counteracted by those means here described, it would be sensible to bring a sailing craft up into the wind during a period in which D/F bearings are being obtained.

Selection of radiobeacons.

(a) The yachtsman should select three or more beacons whenever possible.

(b) He should use grouped marine beacons when available, for ease of operation, or use two or more grouped beacons in conjunction with other marine or aero radiobeacons.

(c) The selection of beacons should give the widest spread possible between bearings, consistent with their availability.

(d) The distance from selected beacons should not exceed the published ranges of those beacons. When through personal experience, or the experience of other yachtsmen, it is known that useful bearings may be obtained from certain beacons at ranges in excess of their published ranges, such latitude must be used with caution.

(e) It must be borne in mind that one degree of error in bearing produces a lateral error of one mile at a range of 60 miles. In this there is obviously a dictum that one must always choose the nearest beacons.

(f) Any beacon which may produce coastal refraction or hill scatter must be excluded.

(g) The possibility of night effect must be borne in mind.

To take a D/F bearing.

The yachtsman's first and most important step is to carefully calculate his D.R. position. This is essential on two counts:—

(a) From it he can calculate which radiobeacons will supply him with the most useful bearings.

(b) Recalling that two nulls will be obtained from any radiobeacon, this prerequisite will usually indicate to him quite clearly which null he must use. The nulls are, after all, 180° apart.

He should then plot this position on a chart which has sufficient scope to give him coverage of the radiobeacons he may decide to use. Again with this position he should refer it to the chartlets, which are associated with the lists of radiobeacons published at the end of the chapter. Guided by the advice contained in the foregoing paragraph under the heading, 'Selection of radiobeacons', he may then decide what radiobeacons he should use.

If his D/F set gives him relative bearings of radiobeacons, he will find it helpful first to determine from his chart what the approximate relative bearings of selected beacons will be. Such rough bearings will indicate to him the directions in relation to his craft - and indeed himself - from which the signals will emanate. Should his set include an integral compass, rough compass bearings may be extracted from the chart in place of relative bearings.

So to his first bearing. Having tuned the set to the required frequency, he would be well advised to use earphones, or a signal-strength meter where fitted, in preference to a loud speaker. Using the set's bearing pointer as his guide, he must rotate the aerial until it is roughly at right angles to the bearing of the beacon. The incoming signal will be at maximum strength in this position and he must now listen for and identify the call sign of the beacon. This being achieved and the tuning signal having commenced, he may then turn the aerial towards the direction of the radiobeacon until the signal can no longer be heard. So far, so good: he has found the null: slight movement to the left and right of the null position will indicate to him from his bearing pointer the precise direction of the null, and therefore the radiobeacon.

He must not expect to precisely identify the null position on all occasions. Background noise increases with range and D/F sets tend to vary in their ability to keep unwanted but inherent 'fuzz' to a minimum. Further, if an incoming signal is weak, the null will not be clearly defined. Thus it may be found that an area of no-signal, a null, is spread over an arc of a few degrees. This situation may be overcome by observing two bearings, one on each side of the null, at which the signal has the same strength. The true null will lie midway between these two bearings.

The first bearing having been obtained, the operation has to be repeated for each selected radiobeacon, the set being re-tuned if and when necessary. The time having been noted and the patent log read, the yachtsman may then evaluate his bearings.

Note

All sets fitted with loop aerials, and some of those fitted with ferrite rod aerials, give bearings which are relative to the boat's head. With these it is necessary to note the precise reading of the steering compass at the moment a D/F bearing is obtained. This may call for considerable agility on the part of the lone yachtsman in certain conditions. Two people being available, it is customary for the D/F operator to call STOP or NOW at the moment of obtaining a bearing, whereupon the other notes the compass reading. Some portable sets, and other types which have portable aerials, may be fitted with integral compasses. Such a facility allows the operator to read directly from the compass the bearing of the radiobeacon at the moment the null is found.

It has been found that hand-held sets may best be used by firmly holding them against the hip, the integral compass then being viewed from above. As the aerial is contained within the set and the set itself must be rotated, the body may be rotated as necessary. This method of operation tends to minimise the small, irritating, often jerky movements which, inherent in yachts at sea, can make the task of obtaining good bearings more difficult.

Some sets are fitted with a 'sense' circuit which will resolve the question of which null to use, in which case the maker's directions for operation should be followed. A yachtsman possessing a D/F set in which no sense device is fitted, it remains to consider an isolated case with which the writer earnestly hopes the yachtsman may never be confronted. It is that in which a marine radiobeacon is situated on an off-lying island, or an off-shore lighthouse, or a lightvessel and the D.R. position of the craft is seriously in doubt. He may well be confounded. Which null must he choose? Either could be the correct one. In these circumstances it is recommended that a series of bearings of the beacon be taken while the craft is under way. The alteration in bearing of the beacon, left or right, will quickly indicate in which direction the beacon lies and therefore which null to use.

When in mid-English Channel and a series of bearings is being obtained, it is wise never to select bearings only from one side. That is, only from the French side, or only from the English side. There are good geometrical reasons for this. Two or three bearings from the English side, coupled, say, with a single bearing from the French side will, when projected on the chart, confirm or refute the presence of an error just possibly common to all bearings taken - compass error. This advice has equal application in other cases when a craft is more or less surrounded by beacons.

Undoubtedly the ear has to be practiced in readily identifying a D/F signal from background noise. The unpracticed yachtsman may well decide that the arc of a null is wider than would be found by a trained operator, hence the exhortation in any publication of this nature for the amateur to obtain as much practice as possible. An example of ear-training is found in the case of a radio operator who can, from two or more morse transmissions, identify and read one of them although the other continues their confounding cacophony throughout. There is nothing really clever in this: it just requires practice. Like radio direction finding.

Projection of D/F bearings on the chart.

Bearings having been corrected for compass error, and quadrantal error if necessary, they must then be laid off on the chart. Almost certainly a cocked hat will be produced. If it is excessively large the bearings should be taken again. Assuming it is of manageable proportions, it remains for the yachtsman to decide his most probable position. The following guide lines should assist him.

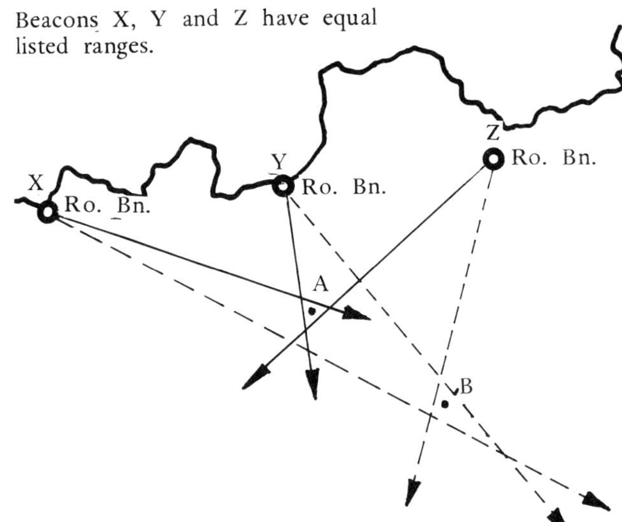

In equilateral triangle 'A' bias position towards bearing of nearest station.

In isosceles triangle 'B' bias position towards shorter side.

Fig. 8.7

(a) If the cocked hat produces an equilateral triangle, it may be assumed that the position is in its centre (but see (c) below).

(b) If an isosceles triangle is formed, it should be assumed that the position is closer to the shorter side.

(c) The position should be biased towards the bearing for which the ratio, distance from beacon: nominal range, is the least.

Use of a single D/F bearing.

Although a single D/F bearing should be treated with suspicion if no other data is available to confirm or deny its accuracy, at close range - say, at 5 miles or less, - good results can be obtained and a fair degree of reliance may be put on its accuracy. Yachtsmen have obtained good positions by running fix from successive single D/F bearings but this fact in no way invalidates the exhortation that seamen must regard radio aids purely as AIDS.

It should not be overlooked that a sounding taken at the same time as a single D/F bearing will give an approximate position, provided the contours of the seabed run nearly at right angles to the bearing. Frequently the depth contours in home waters provide no useful pattern to benefit the mariner.

Use of two D/F bearings

Generally speaking, it is inadvisable to use only two beacons for position-finding; too frequently no other means are available to check the accuracy of bearings so obtained. This being said, when no other means of obtaining position is offered it is sensible to take into consideration such bearings if only as a comparison for a D.R. position.

Cross bearings from two beacons taken at regular intervals could well prove useful if a succession of results indicates that there is a satisfactory continuity in position and distances run by patent log between 'fixes' agree with the results on the chart.

Calibration - the detection of quadrantal error.

No set should be used for navigational purposes until steps have been taken to ascertain whether or not quadrantal error is present. It has been said that, provided certain steps are taken, this error should prove negligible on wooden and glass fibre craft. Possessing such a craft, this advice is not intended to indicate that the yachtsman is absolved from taking this primary step.

All too sparsely round the British, Irish and continental coasts, radiobeacons specifically intended for the calibration of D/F sets have been established. Perhaps sparsely for yachtsmen, yet satisfactory for naval and merchant ships which are, after all, the prime consideration. It is possible that this paucity is one reason why, as the writer believes, few D/F sets on small craft have been properly calibrated. Another reason is no doubt because calibration consumes valuable time. When considerable expenditure has been made on a D/F set, is it not common sense to render that set capable of producing good fixes, whatever the temporary inconvenience?

The diversity in types of D/F sets, coupled with a similar non-uniformity in the manner in which magnetic compasses are utilised, render a full explanation of the calibration method to be adopted for every set impractical. The basic method is described here. This general knowledge, coupled with the advices in instructional hand-books which are invariably supplied with D/F sets, should suffice for the yachtsman to carry out satisfactory calibration of his set where necessary.

Error, negligible and otherwise.

Before considering calibration it is expedient that the yachtsman should be aware of the amount of D/F error which may be regarded as negligible. It is the writer's firm opinion that quadrantal errors of less than 2° may be ignored. His reasons are purely practical. If it is accepted, as it surely must be, that the movement of a small craft in a seaway is such that it is impossible to guarantee the accuracy of a visual bearing nearer than ± 2°, it cannot be assumed that greater accuracy will be obtained from radio bearings.

A quick and practical check for the presence of quadrantal error.

It is quite unnecessary for the yachtsman to sail his craft to a calibration beacon (q.v.) to find whether or not his D/F set should be calibrated. He may tune his D/F set to any beacon or radio station which transmits continuously - BBC2, Daventry, 200 kHz (1500m) is one such station - and readily determine the desired information. Pegwell Bay, Chichester Harbour, Salcombe; it does not really matter where his craft happens to be lying.

Tuning to the selected beacon or station, he must take D/F bearings at intervals of no more than 20° through 360° of relative bearing. If the D/F bearings so obtained do not vary **from each other** by an amount of more than 2°, he may assume that quadrantal error in his D/F set is negligible. It goes without saying that if it does he must take steps to calibrate his equipment using traditional methods.

This simple experiment can be used for another valuable purpose: the determination of the most suitable operating position for a hand-held set or hand-held aerial. Finding that quadrantal errors in one operating position are of a magnitude which he cannot ignore, he may select another position and carry out a further swing. The value of experimentation on these lines will be readily appreciated.

Calibration by professionals.

Some manufacturers of D/F sets will, for a fee, undertake to calibrate D/F sets of their manufacture. As in the case of the determination and reduction of deviations in a magnetic compass, professionals carry out the task with speed, dexterity and accuracy. It is probable that a yachtsman may have more faith in the findings of a professional, rather than those he may obtain for himself.

Calibration beacons.

Calibration beacons are usually located on coastlines which allow ships - but not necessarily yachts - to manoeuvre in relatively sheltered water during calibration of D/F equipment. They transmit at low power in the M/F band at an effective range which does not usually exceed 5 miles. This giving them small value as navigational aids, they are omitted from most charts. Their unit transmissions have much the same character as those of marine radiobeacons but, when operating, they differ in that there is no break in their transmissions. Marine radiobeacons may in certain cases perform the dual function of radiobeacon and calibration station and when this occurs separate frequencies will probably be used.

There are relatively few calibration beacons available for use. Seldom do large ships calibrate their D/F equipment and no doubt it is considered that the number provided is sufficient for demand. From the yachtsman's point of view, this would appear to pose problems. It is improbable that he would consider sailing 100 or more miles in a direction in which he perhaps does not wish to sail, merely to calibrate his D/F set. Even then, many of the beacons transmit 'on request' and this has to be arranged and the service paid for. For this reason details of calibration stations are not included in the lists of radiobeacons. Details of them will be found in Admiralty List of Radio Signals Volume II.

D/F calibration requiring both visual and radio bearings of a radio transmitter, and calibration beacons not being the only ones which will meet these needs, the yachtsman does not have to go to the amount of inconvenience and trouble outlined above. In fact, any marine radiobeacon which gives a continuous service will meet his requirements, provided he can take visual bearings of the aerial from which the transmissions emanate. Periods of silence during normal continuous transmissions will of course prolong the operation a little but this has to be accepted.

Yachtsmen should also consider the additional value of the constantly transmitting aero radiobeacon. Should the aerial mast of such a beacon be visible from an estuary, or similar stretch of quiet water, the beacon can be used for calibration. Yachtsmen in the Southampton area will probably be aware that a certain mast at Fawley is that belonging to Fawley aero radiobeacon and is often used for calibration. There may be others elsewhere within the area encompassed by this volume but they are unknown to the writer.

Carrying out the swing for calibration.

The craft has to be swung in a small circle within sight of the radiobeacon at a range of about 3 miles. At intervals of about 10° radio bearings of the beacon must be taken and the boats head by compass noted at the moment each bearing is taken. As each radio bearing is obtained, a visual bearing must also be taken of the beacon. As quadrantal error can only be recorded relative to the boat's head, the intention in calibrating is to ascertain errors all round the boat: **not** all round the compass. Two people are required when calibrating; one to take D/F bearings and the other to con the craft, to note headings by steering compass and to take the necessary visual bearings.

A method of recording and evaluating bearings is described below. It assumes that the D/F set produces relative bearings. This method is applicable to craft carrying dual-purpose compasses and to those which use a combination of steering compass and hand bearing compass.

(c) When completing column D, if a hand bearing compass is used it will be assumed that the bearing so obtained will be a magnetic one. If a dual purpose compass is used, bearings may have to be corrected for the deviations recorded in column B.

(d) Column E may be completed by subtracting column D from column C, adding 360° as and when necessary.

(e) Quadrantal error is the difference between the recordings in columns E and F. It is always recorded as a plus or minus quantity which is to say that, all data being evaluated and collated, the sign will indicate to the D/F operator how he must apply the quadrantal error to bearings.

Homing Beacons.

Widely used by aircraft, it is unfortunate for the small boat sailor that so few of these most valuable beacons have been established for marine purposes. Indeed, there is only one, located at Boulogne, within reasonable sailing distance of the British Isles. A radio receiver capable of receiving broadcasts on the M/F band is all the equipment required to use them.

A homing beacon has a published bearing line, usually the centre of an approach channel to a port, and two sectors on either side of it in which different morse letters will be heard. Boulogne homing beacon, for instance, has a beam width of 5° centred about the correct approach bearing. Within this beam a continuous series of dashes will be heard. If a yacht is northward of the beam the morse symbol for A will be apparent and if to the southward, that for N. In fog what more could a yachtsman ask?

A	B	C	D	E	F	G
Boat's head by steering compass.	Steering compass deviation.	Magnetic heading.	Magnetic bearing of beacon by dual-purpose compass or hand-bearing compass.	Relative bearing of beacon	Relative D/F bearing.	Quadrantal error.
120°	4°W	116°	053°	297°	292°	+5°

Note

(a) Columns A, D and F must be completed during calibration. The remainder may be completed afterwards.

(b) Column C is produced by applying the deviation (where present) to headings in Column A.

Ranging Beacons.

Signals transmitted by radiobeacons can, for ranging purposes, be synchronised with sound signals emitted from the site of the beacon. This is possible because the speed through the atmosphere of sound and radio signals is vastly different. At short ranges such as are being considered here, it can be taken that a radio signal will be heard at the moment it is transmitted; a sound signal emitted at that same instant will be heard later, how much later depending directly upon the distance of the mariner from the station.

Again unfortunately, within our area there is only one such ranging beacon at the Cloch Point Lighthouse in the Firth of Clyde. Details of services of this beacon are included later in the section listing radiobeacons.

The system is to use the spoken word by radio telephony on frequencies capable of being received by D/F receivers. It is quite simple. It tells the mariner that at the moment he hears a certain sound emission of the fog horn, his range from it will be that which is stated. Thereafter increasing ranges are spoken. That range which is being spoken at the moment the blast is heard will be the mariner's range from the station.

Homing on aero and marine radiobeacons.

It is possible to 'home' on any aero or marine radiobeacon, indeed on any other station whose transmissions are capable of being received by a D/F set. Provided the yachtsman keeps the radio bearing of the beacon dead ahead, and he corrects his course as necessary from time to time to maintain the bearing ahead of his craft, he is bound to finish up at the beacon on which he is homing - or more probably on that section of the beach which coincides with his homing bearing. This is one of the dangers of homing in thick weather and regular soundings is the method which immediately comes to mind to guard against such a misfortune.

When homing on a beacon located on a light vessel, or a similarly isolated position, in thick weather it is advisable to maintain the bearing of the beacon a few degrees on one bow or the other. This precaution will prevent an unexpected collision.

Consol.

Consol is a long range radio aid to navigation which was originally established for the benefit of aircraft approaching the British Isles from the western shores of the Atlantic Ocean. It has tended to be superseded by more accurate radio aids which serve the same purpose. Requiring no more than a marine radio receiver, Consol still has value to many mariners who for various reasons are unable to install the specialised radio equipment required for other systems.

Notwithstanding its low degree of accuracy, Consol has value to yachtsmen many miles out in the Atlantic who may not have had 'sights' for some days. For some trawlermen unable to afford a Decca Navigator, who yet must from time to time find a selected fishing ground, it provides a rather rough substitute. Other cases also come to mind.

Due to its possible margins of error, it should never be used for coastal navigation or for making landfalls. This being said, the yachtsman for whom this volume is intended will readily appreciate that there are few occasions when he can use Consol to good advantage. The cruising grounds of yachtsmen vary very widely and so that each may decide for himself whether or not he can use Consol to advantage, the diagrams in Fig.8·8 are produced.

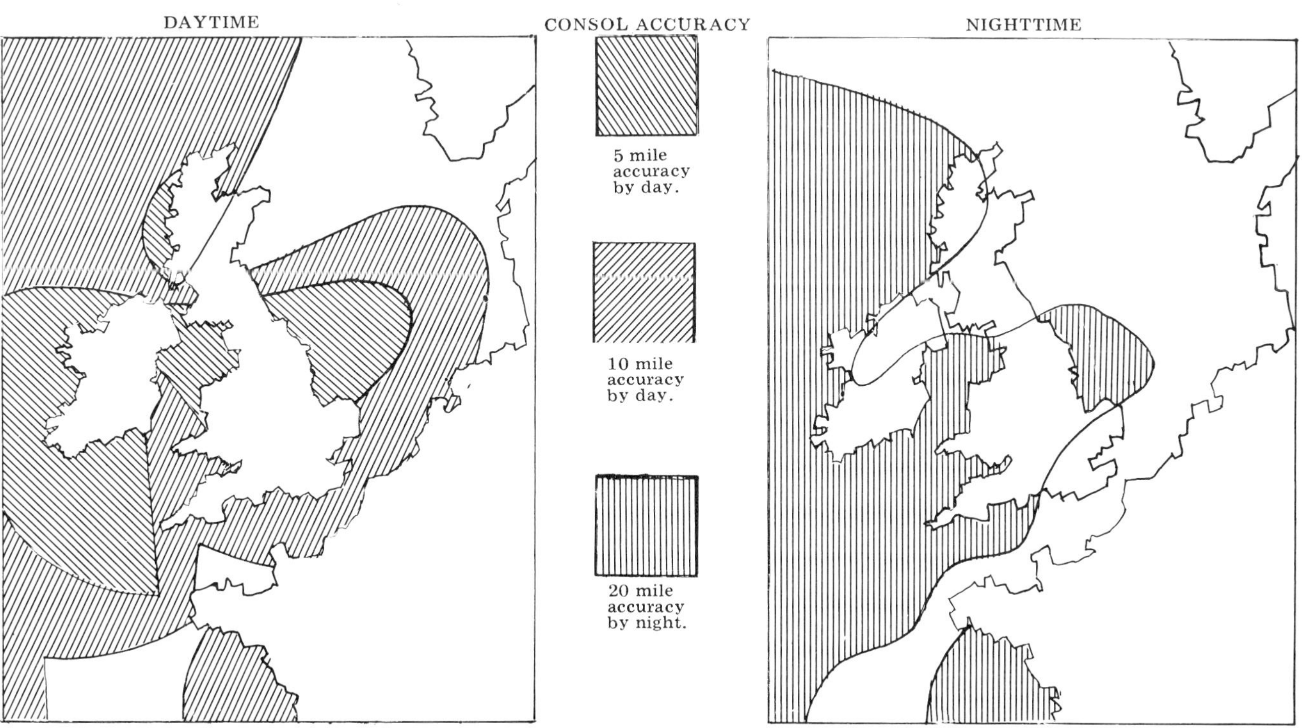

Absence of shading does not imply absence of error.

Fig. 8.8

2188B Stavanger (Varhaug). 58° 37′ 32″ N. 5° 37′ 49″ E.

CONSOL BEACON

FREQUENCY: 319. A1. 1.5 kW.
CHARACTERISTIC: Period 1 min.

LEC (- — - - - — - — -)	5.8 sec.
Long dash (—)	19.2 sec.
Silent	2.5 sec.
Directional Signals	30.0 sec.
Silent	2.5 sec.
Period	60.0 sec. (1 min.).

BEACON SERVICE: Continuous.
DIRECTIONAL SIGNALS: See A.L.R.S. Vol. V.

2075M Bushmills. 55° 12′ 20″ N. 6° 28′ 02″ W.

CONSOL BEACON

FREQUENCY: 266. A1. 2.0 kW.
CHARACTERISTIC: Period 40 sec.

MWN (— — - — — — -)	2.5 sec.
Silent	0.5 sec.
Long dash (—)	4.0 sec.
Silent	1.0 sec.
Directional Signals	30.0 sec.
Silent	2.0 sec.
Period	40.0 sec.

BEACON SERVICE: Continuous, except for maintenance periods (1600-1615 daily, and 1100-1200 on Wednesdays).
DIRECTIONAL SIGNALS: See A.L.R.S. Vol. V.
REMARKS: Aero-marine. The signal TEST (— - - - - —) may be transmitted in addition to the above signals while adjustments are taking place; bearings taken at such times may be unreliable.

2220K Ploneis (Quimper). 48° 01′ 06″ N. 4° 12′ 55″ W.

CONSOL BEACON

FREQUENCY: 257. A1. 2.0 kW.
CHARACTERISTIC: Period 40 sec.

FRQ (- - — - - — - — — - —) twice	10 sec.
Directional Signals	30 sec.
Period	40 sec.

BEACON SERVICE: Continuous, except for maintenance period (0730 – 0745).
DIRECTIONAL SIGNALS: See A.L.R.S. Vol. V.
REMARKS: Aero-marine. The signal TEST (— - - - - —) may be transmitted in lieu of the identification signal while adjustments are taking place; bearings taken at such times may be unreliable.

2231L Lugo (Otero del Rey). 43° 14′ 53″ N. 7° 28′ 56″ W.

CONSOL BEACON

FREQUENCY: 285. A1. 1.5 kW.
CHARACTERISTIC: Period 1 min.

LG (- — - - — — -)	5.0 sec.
Silent	2.5 sec.
Directional Signals	30.0 sec.
Silent	2.5 sec.
Long dash (—)	17.5 sec.
Silent	2.5 sec.
Period	60.0 sec. (1 min.).

BEACON SERVICE: Continuous.
DIRECTIONAL SIGNALS: See A.L.R.S. Vol. V.

Consol signals can be received by any M/F radio receiver and by D/F sets. The signals emanate from beacons located at Stavanger in Norway, Bushmills in N. Ireland, from one station in Spain, Lugo. Each station comprises a directional aerial system the radiation pattern of which consists of alternate sectors of dots and dashes. The sectors are approximately 15° in width and are separated by an equisignal which is heard as a short, steady note. This whole pattern is rotated once in each cycle. It then reverts to its original position and the rotation is commenced again.

Listening to a Consol station's transmissions, the yachtsman will hear a 3-letter call sign transmitted slowly in the Morse Code, followed by a long dash and thereafter a series of dots followed by dashes or, perhaps, dashes followed by dots. The number of dots and dashes counted in any one keying cycle will, by relating them to special charts or tables, indicate to the observer his bearing from the transmitter to which he is listening. At this point the reader, whether at home or afloat, may care to tune in to one of these stations to relate what is written here to practice. He will find the radio frequencies and other related information on page 84.

To find position by Consol.

Methods of evaluating the findings.

One may use special Consol charts which have lattice over-printing or tables published by the Hydrographic Office from which, having entered them with the several dot and dash counts, bearings of the various stations may be extracted. For sound reasons which it is not necessary to discuss here, the off-shore yachtsman is advised to use Consol charts.

Reception of Signals.

A marine receiver having a vertical aerial is recommended for best results. A D/F set may be used but, while there is an advantage to be gained from doing so, the operator must guard against unwittingly introducing errors into his findings. The advantage comes when another radio station is broadcasting on a frequency sufficiently close to that of the Consol beacon to interfere with its reception. Turning the D/F aerial so that one of the nulls points at the interfering station, it will be silenced. Correctly, the D/F aerial should be used for Consol reception at a point of maximum strength of received signal, which will be midway between the nulls. If to silence an interfering station entails bringing a null sector to within 20° of the bearing of a Consol station, errors in the counting of characters may result.

Operation.

The first requirement is to carefully calculate the yacht's D.R. position and plot it on the appropriate Consol chart. The chart itself will indicate which Consol beacons must be used in any given area.

The set being tuned to the frequency of the first beacon and the call-sign identified, the operator waits for the continuous signal. The completion of the continuous signal is the indication that the cycle of dots and dashes will follow. He then carefully counts, the number of dots and dashes heard. A total of 60 morse characters should be identified in each cycle but in practice they seldom, if ever, are. As the equi-signal point is approached, the Morse characters fade to a point when they can no longer be heard. The equi-signal point being passed, the characters gradually come into evidence again. The radio receiver must not be blamed for this; it is a natural phenomenon which must be expected. It may be resolved as follows:

Examples.

Characters heard: 38 dots and 14 dashes.

38 + 14 = 52 characters
60 - 52 = 8 characters lost to the ear.

Therefore, the true count was in fact 42 dots and 18 dashes.

Characters heard: 54 dashes and no dots.

54 + 0 = 54 characters
60 - 54 = 6 characters lost to the ear.

Therefore, the true count was in fact 57 dashes and 3 dots.

It will be noted that in each case the total of the observed count has been subtracted from 60. Half the difference has been added to each of the dot and dash counts.

A study of the Consol charts being used will now emphasise the importance of a good D.R. position. It will be found that the corrected counts can be related to each of several sectors on the chart, Fortunately they are usually sufficiently far apart to render the D.R. position sufficient indication to the mariner which sector to use. The sector being identified, it then becomes a simple matter of relating the counts to the lattices on the chart which will be found to be individually marked with the count number and type of character.

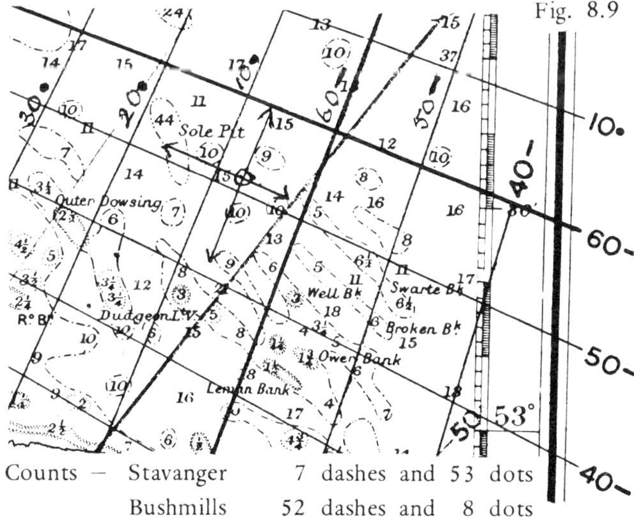

Fig. 8.9

Counts — Stavanger 7 dashes and 53 dots
Bushmills 52 dashes and 8 dots

Note

Perhaps lacking the expertise of many, the writer has found it helpful to tap with his finger during the count. Assisting concentration when the morse characters are clearly heard, he finds it particularly helpful when the signal begins to fade as the equi-signal is approached and again when it re-appears. It is in the penumbral sound zone, when the operator is trying to distinguish the weak Consol signals from background noise and other signals that all find the greatest difficulty.

One should never accept as satisfactory evidence the findings from one cycle only. A series of counts must be taken. Each succeeding count will serve to affirm the true count. This operation has much in common with radio direction finding in that aural practice, again and again and again, is the only means by which really satisfactory results will be achieved. No doubt it has occurred to the reader that when margins of error are discussed, they are necessarily related to those errors which an experienced operator may expect. What of us: we weekend sailors? Is it not sensible to assume that if through negligence we have not practiced as much as we might, the errors we may encounter could possibly be greater than those published as possible ones.

It may be found that as the morse characters fade on approach of the equi-signal, it is somewhat easier to follow their fade into nonentity, than to follow the corresponding emergence from inexistance of the following signal. Certainly, this has been the experience of the writer from time to time, in the absence of practice. The answer to it is, again, practice.

For the yachtsman who considers that in his particular case there is advantage to be gained from the Consol system, he is advised that Admiralty Consol charts are listed in Section VI of the Admiralty Chart Catalogue. The system is also described in considerable detail in the Admiralty List of Radio Signals, Vol. V and in H.M.S.O. publication C.A.P. 59., "Consol, a Radio-aid to Navigation".

Sundry Radio Aids to Navigation.

A yachtsman will from time to time encounter reference to devices which are obviously radio aids to navigation, yet he may be ignorant of what they are. He may wonder whether there are systems amongst them which he can profitably use. There follows a brief description of various radio aids which may prove of interest to him.

The Decca Navigator System.

Of all radio aids devised for coastal and landfall navigation, the Decca Navigator is by far the most accurate. Not being purchasable outright, the cost of hire of the ship-borne receiver is prohibitive for all but a very few yachtsmen and it demands considerable electrical power.

'Chains' of transmitting stations have been established in various areas throughout the world and the coverage in the British Isles and on continental shores is excellent. A chain comprises a Master station and two or three 'slaves'. The signals from any one chain are received at one and the same time by the ship-borne receiver and are translated into readings on dials which are constantly available. These readings are referred to special charts having lattice over-printing. The lattices are numbered in a manner which relate them to the dial readings, so position finding is simply a matter of taking the dial readings and, where all are coincident on the appropriate lattice chart, the required position occurs.

Loran.

The name is produced from a definition of the system which is a Long Range Navigational Aid. Combining the function of Consol and a system something akin to the Decca Navigator, it gives a fairly high degree of accuracy over the sea up to 600 nautical miles. Loran chains have been established in all the major sea areas.

Radar.

Radar is an electronic device, both very costly and demanding considerable electrical power for its function, which will with extreme accuracy give the range and bearing of an object on which its directional aerial is 'aimed'. The aerial usually being rotated electronically at a constant speed, coastlines, ships, and indeed any other object from which a radar 'echo' may be obtained, will be constantly displayed on a circular screen which has much in common with a television screen. Definition on this screen, called the Plan Position Indicator, is confined to areas of light and darkness, the light areas being those from which radar echoes are obtained.

It is well for the yachtsman to be aware of the limitations of radar. A large solid object which presents itself at right angles to a radar transmission will reflect the signal well and so it will show clearly on the radar screen. If the object is angled to the signal, a portion of the transmission will 'skate off' the object and a lesser echo will be returned, making definition correspondingly poorer on the screen. Absorbent materials give a poorer response than solid ones. The sail of a yacht which is dry will probably give little or no response, where a wet one will be recognisable. Echoes from waves will produce what is commonly known as grass on a radar screen and the larger the waves, the greater amount of grass on the screen. Small echoes such as are produced by small craft at sea may well be totally unrecognisable from the 'grass'. Herein lies the reason why it is a sound precaution to hoist a radar reflector aloft when sailing in deep waters, whether the weather be thick or clear; whether it be daytime or night-time.

Racon.

A Racon beacon is one established for use by ships fitted with radar. The beacon is automatically triggered by the transmissions of a radar set and so it becomes apparent on a radar display. A variation is the use of a separate frequency. The set being tuned to the correct frequency, a response on the radar screen usually called the Racon flash, will appear to the exclusion of other echoes. In both cases accurate ranges and bearings of Racon will be obtained.

Ramark

Ramark, having much in common with Racon, transmits independently. Instead of producing a range, it shows as a flash across the radar screen from own ship's position to the Ramark beacon. Thus a bearing of it is produced.

Radio Beacons

In order that yachtsmen may readily extract information relating to aero and marine radiobeacons which are suitable for their use, the sea areas encompassed by this volume are divided into four sections.

1. **English channel and Dover Strait Area**: From the North Foreland area to the Scilly Isles on the English coast, and from Zeebrugge (Belgium) to La Rochelle (Bay of Biscay) on the continental coast.
2. **North Sea Area**: From the Thames Estuary to the Farne Islands on the English coast and from Zeebrugge (Belgium) to the northern extremity of Germany on the continental coast.
3. **Irish Sea Area**: Land's End northwards to the Isle of Arran, the whole of Ireland and all off-lying islands.
4. **Scottish Area**: All Scotland, including off-lying islands.

Each area is listed separately, in the above order, in the pages which follow. At the end of this volume four chartlets have been produced. Each chartlet portrays one of the above areas, and they show the positions of all listed radiobeacons. The lists of radio beacons and these chartlets are intended to be used together.

Explanation of lists of marine radiobeacons.

Those radiobeacons which are grouped together are bracketed by a vertical bar. In a small number of cases grouped radiobeacons are spread over two areas. Where this occurs the group is published in the lists for both areas. For example, Zeebrugge is grouped with Nieupoort. The former is in the English Channel and Dover Strait area, the latter in the North Sea area, thus this grouping is published for both areas.

Column 1. The Admiralty reference number. Geographical order of radiobeacons has been preferred to facilitate use, hence they are not in numerical order. These numbers can be referred to the Admiralty List of Radio Signals, Volume 2.

Column 2. RC = marine radiobeacon. Aero RC = aero radiobeacon.

Column 3 & 4. The name of the radiobeacon together with its geographical local in latitude and longitude.

Column 5, 6 & 7. The frequency on which the radiobeacon transmits, its call sign in letters, and their morse equivalents. The latter facility is introduced to assist those unfamiliar with the morse code.

Column 8. The operational range of the radiobeacon, beyond which it should not normally be used. Where two ranges are given, the greater of the two is the day range and the lesser the night range.

Column 9. Where radiobeacons are grouped, this column indicates the sequence within the group that each radiobeacon transmits.

Column 10. 'Cont' indicates continuous transmissions, day and night: 'Fog only' is self-explanatory, as is 'Day'.

Column 11. The number of minutes after each hour at which the radiobeacon transmits a 'unit transmission'. The figure zero indicates the hour.

Inclusion in lists of aero radiobeacons.

It will be noted that those aero radiobeacons which have value to mariners have been included within the lists of marine radiobeacons. It may be noted by experienced yachtsmen that their number has been greatly reduced. This has been at the instigation of the Admiralty: consistent with adequate 'coverage' by beacons of all types, those aero radiobeacons whose radio reception by mariners has been in any way suspect have been eliminated.

As these radiobeacons come within the jurisdiction of the Air Ministry, full information is not available to mariners. Sufficient information is provided for their use but the mariner is unable to refer to any ministry publication to obtain further detail than is here produced. Any alteration in this minimal information is published in the Weekly Admiralty Notices to Mariners.

It should be borne in mind that occasionally the geographical location of an aero radiobeacon is altered and there may be some delay before this information appears in Admiralty Notices to Mariners. This would similarly apply to any other alteration which may be introduced.

Other radio direction finding facilities.

The few directional and range finding radiobeacons available to yachtsmen in home waters are published, together with all necessary detail for their use.

Use of the information within this book.

1. Determine one's approximate position and refer to the appropriate chartlet.
2. Determine from the chartlet those marine and aero radiobeacons which are nearest and which will be most likely to be of value.
3. Using a large scale chart, first produce one's D.R. position upon it and locate those radiobeacons which have been selected as being of probable value.
4. Select a minimum of three radiobeacons which are at a distance not exceeding their published operational range.
5. Refer to the appropriate list of radiobeacons and extract from it the information required before attempting to operate one's radio direction finding equipment.

ENGLISH CHANNEL & DOVER STRAIT AREA – MARINE RADIO BEACONS

North Foreland to the Scilly Isles & Oostende to La Rochelle

Admir. ref. no.	Type	Name	Latitude and Longitude		Freq. KHz	Call Sign	Morse	Miles Range	Sequence	Continuous or fog service	No. of minutes after each hour
0141	RC	North Foreland Lt.	51°22′28″N	1°26′51″E	301.1	NF	-. ..-.	50	–	Cont.	0, 1. 2. 3. etc.
		Dover Strait Group									
0142	RC	Falls Lt. V.	51°18′06″N	1°48′30″E	305.7	FS	..-. ...	50	1	Cont.	0, 6, 12, 18, etc.
0139	RC	Tongue Lt. V.	51°30′39″N	1°23′05″E	305.7	GU	--. ..-	30	2	Cont.	1, 7, 13, 19, etc.
0223	RC	W. Hinder Lt. V.	51°23′00″N	2°26′20″E	305.7	WH	.--	20	3	Cont.	2, 8, 14, 20, etc.
0217	RC	Oostende	51°14′14″N	2°55′54″E	305.7	OE	--- .	30	4	Cont.	3, 9, 15, 21, etc.
0823*	RC	Dyck Lt. V.	51°03′02″N	1°51′55″E	305.7	DK	-.. -.-	20	5	Cont.	4, 10, 16, 22, etc.
			*During summer months the Lt. V. is replaced by a buoy with no radio beacon facilities.								
0143	RC	E. Goodwin Lt. V.	51°13′00″N	1°36′18″E	305.7	GW	--. .--	30	6	Cont.	5, 11, 17, 23, etc.
0215	RC	Nieuport, W. Pier Lt.	51°09′24″N	2°43′05″E	296.5	NP	-. .--.	5	4, 5	Fog-cont.	3, 4, 9, 10, etc.
0219	RC	Zeebrugge Mole	For details see North Sea Area							Clear	03, 33, 03, 33, etc.
0825	RC	Calais, Jettée Est Lt.	50°58′21″N	1°50′32″E	313.5	CL	-.-. .-..	5	–	Cont.	0, 1, 2, 3, etc.
		Channel East Group									
0833	RC	Bassurelle Lt. V.	50°32′50″N	0°57′48″E	310.3	UL	..- .-..	50	1	Cont.	0, 6, 12, 18, etc.
0149	RC	Royal Sovereign			310.3	RY	.-. -.--	50	2	Cont.	1, 7, 13, 19, etc.
0837	RC	P. d'Ailly			310.3	AL	.- .-..	50	3	Cont.	2, 8, 14, 20, etc.
0829	RC	Boulogne, Jettée S.W. Lt.	50°43′56″N	1°35′10″E	310.3	BO[1]	-... ---	20	4	Cont.	3, 9, 15, 21, etc.
0827	RC	C. Gris Nez	50°52′10″N	1°35′04″E	310.3	GN	--. -.	30	5	Cont.	4, 10, 16, 22, etc.
0147	RC	Dungeness	50°54′46″N	0°58′40″E	310.3	DU	-.. ..-	30	6	Cont.	5, 11, 17, 23, etc.
			[1] Unreliable 000°–090°								
0831	RD	Boulogne Directional Beacon	For details see page 96								
0001	RC	Nab Tower Lt.	50°40′03″N	0°57′04″W	312.6	NB	-. -...	20	1, 4	Fog only	0, 3, 6, 9, etc.
0849	RC	Cherbourg, Fort de l'Ouest Lt.	49°40′30″N	1°38′52″W	312.6	RB	.-. -...	20	3, 6	Cont.	1, 4, 7, 10, etc.
0023	RC	Breaksea Lt. V.	For details see Irish Sea Area								
0845	RC	Port en Bessin Rear Lt.	49°21′00″N	0°45′36″W	312.6	BS	-... ...	5	–	Cont.	0, 1, 2, 3, etc.

ENGLISH CHANNEL AND DOVER STRAIT AREA – MARINE RADIO BEACONS

North Foreland to the Scilly Isles and Oostende to La Rochelle

Admir. ref. no.	Type	Name	Latitude and Longitude		Freq. KHz	Call Sign	Morse	Miles Range	Sequence	Continuous or fog only	No. of minutes after each hour
		Channel Centre Group									
0007	RC	Portland Bill Lt.	50°30′49″N	2°27′19″W	291.9	PB	.--. -...	50	1	Cont.	0, 6, 12, 18, etc.
0003	RC	St. Catherine's Pt. Lt.	50°34′31″N	1°17′48″W	291.9	CP	-.-. .--.	50	2	Cont.	1, 7, 13, 19, etc.
0839	RC	C. d'Antifer Lt.	49°41′04″N	0°09′55″W	291.9	TI	- ..	50	3	Cont.	2, 8, 14, 20, etc.
0841	RC	Le Havre Lt. V.	49°31′55″N	0°09′05″W	291.9	LH[2]	.-..	20	4	Cont.	3, 9, 15, 21, etc.
0843	RC	P. de Ver	49°20′28″N	0°31′09″W	291.9	ER[1]	..-.. .-.	20	5	Cont.	4, 10, 16, 22, etc.
0847	RC	P. de Barfleur	49°41′44″N	1°16′03″W	291.9	FG	..-. --.	70	6	Cont.	5, 11, 17, 23, etc.
			[1] Note different morse signal.								
			[2] Replaced by Lt. buoy during summer fitted with low power radiobeacon as follows:								
					296.5	BG	-... --.	5–10	–	Cont.	0, 1, 2, 3, etc.
0167	RC	Corbière	49°10′53″N	2°14′20″W	305.7	CB	-.-. -...	20	2	Cont.	1, 3, 5, 7, etc.
–	RC	Cap Frehel	Not yet established		305.7	–	–	20	1	Cont.	0, 2, 4, 6, etc.
–	RC	Elizabeth Castle, Jersey	49°10′37″N	2°07′30″W	287.3	EC	-.-.	5	–	Cont.	Decisions yet to be made
		Channel West group									
0013	RC	Eddystone Lt.	50°10′48″N	4°15′52″W	298.8	DY	-.. -.--	20	1	Fog only	0, 6, 12, 18, etc.
0011	RC	Start Pt. Lt.	50°13′19″N	3°38′28″W	298.8	SP	... .--.	70	2	Cont.	1, 7, 13, 19, etc.
0159	RC	Casquets Lt.	49°43′23″N	2°22′33″W	298.8	QS	--.- ...	50	3	Cont.	2, 8, 14, 20, etc.
0853	RC	Roches Douvres Lt.	49°06′28″N	2°49′04″W	298.8	RD	.-. -..	70	4	Cont.	3, 9, 15, 21, etc.
0856	RC	Île Vierge	48°38′24″N	4°34′06″W	298.8	VG	-... .-	70	5	Cont.	4, 10, 16, 22, etc.
0015	RC	Lizard Lt.	49°57′35″N	5°12′04″W	298.8	LZ	.-.. --..	70	6	Cont.	5, 11, 17, 23, etc.
0857	RC	Pointe de Creach, Île d'Ouessant[1]	48°27′36″N	5°07′48″W	308.0	CA	-.-. .-	100	6	Cont.	5, 11, 17, 23, etc.
0199	RC	Eagle I.	For details see Irish Sea Area						1		
0179	RC	Mizen Head	For details see Irish Sea Area						2		
0063	RC	Mull of Kintyre	For details see Irish Sea Area						3		
0017	RC	Round I. Lt.	49°58′42″N	6°19′20″W	308.0	RR	.-. .-.	200/100	4	Cont.	3, 9, 15, 21, etc.
0197	RC	Tory I.	For details see Irish Sea Area								
			[1] Bearings reported unreliable between d'Ouessant and Casquets (1963)								

ENGLISH CHANNEL & DOVER STRAIT AREA – MARINE RADIO BEACONS

North Foreland to the Scilly Isles & Oostende to La Rochelle

Admir. ref. no.	Type	Name	Latitude	Longitude	Freq. KHz	Call Sign	Morse	Miles Range	Sequence	Continuous or fog only	No. of minutes after each hour
0859	RC	Pointe St. Mathieu Lt.	48°19′50″N	4°46′17″W	289.6	SM	··· ——	20	1, 3, 5	Cont.	0, 2, 4, 6, etc.
0875	RC	St. Nazaire, Pointe de St. Gildas Lt.	47°08′06″N	2°14′40″W	289.6	NZ	—· ——··	35	2, 4, 6	Cont.	1, 3, 5, 7, etc.
0865	RC	Eckmühl Lt. Pointe de Penmarc'h	47°47′55″N	4°22′26″W	303.4	ÜH	··—— ····	50	1	Cont.	0, 6, 12, 18, etc.
0883	RC	Les Baleines Lt. Île de Re'	46°14′40″N	1°33′40″W	303.4	BN	—··· —·	50	2	Cont.	1, 7, 13, 19, etc.
0863	RC	Île de Sein NW Lt.	48°02′36″N	4°51′59″W	303.4	SN	··· —·	50	3	Cont.	2, 8, 14, 20, etc.
0879	RC	Île d'Yeu Main Lt.	46°43′06″N	2°22′54″W	303.4	YE	—·—— ·	100	4	Cont.	3, 9, 15, 21, etc.
0871	RC	Île de Groix, Pen Men Lt.	47°38′50″N	3°30′30″W	303.4	GX	——· —··—	50	5	Cont.	4, 10, 16, 22, etc.
0873	RC	Belle Île, Goulphar Lt.	47°18′40″N	3°13′40″W	303.4	BT	—··· —	100	6	Cont.	5, 11, 17, 23, etc.
0877	RC	Île du Pilier Lt.	47°02′37″N	2°21′32″W	298.8	PR	·——· ·—·	10	–	Cont.	0, 1, 2, 3, etc.
0881	RC	Les Sables d'Olonne, Tour de la Chaume Lt.	46°29′39″N	1°47′45″W	291.9	SO	··· ———	5	–	Cont.	0, 1, 2, 3, etc.
0885	RC	La Pallice*	46°09′45″N	1°14′21″W	287.3	LP	·—·· ·——·	5	–	Cont.	0, 1, 2, 3, etc.
0887	RC	La Rochelle, Tourelle Richelieu Lt.	46°08′55″N	1°10′22″W	291.9	RE	·—· ·	5	–	Cont.	0, 1, 2, 3, etc.

*At tower on Railway Station

NORTH SEA AREA – MARINE RADIO BEACONS

Thames to the Farne Islands & Zeebrugge to Rote Kliff, Germany

Admir. ref. no.	Type	Name	Latitude and Longitude		Freq. KHz	Call Sign	Morse	Miles Range	Sequence	Continuous or fog only	No. of minutes after each hour
0137	RC	Sunk Lt. V.	51°51'00"N	1°35'00"E	312.6	UK	..- -.-	10	1	Cont.	0, 1, 2, 3, etc.
0131	RC	Smiths Knoll Lt. V.	52°43'30"N	2°18'00"E	287.3	SK	... -.-	50[1]	1	Cont.	0, 6, 12, 18, etc.
0229	RC	Goeree Lt.	51°55'32"N	3°40'11"E	287.3	GR	--. .-.	50	2	Cont.	1, 7, 13, 19, etc.
0125	RC	Dudgeon Lt. V.	53°15'30"N	1°13'30"E	287.3	LV	.-.. ...-	50	3	Cont.	2, 8, 14, 20, etc.
0135	RC	Outer Gabbard Lt. V.	51°59'23"N	2°04'38"E	287.3	GA	--. .-	50	4	Cont.	3, 9, 15, 21, etc.
0127	RC	Cromer Lt.	52°55'27"N	1°19'06"E	287.3	CM	-.-. --	50	5	Cont.	4, 10, 16, 22, etc.
0225	RC	N. Hinder Lt. V.	51°39'18"N	2°33'00"E	287.3	NR	-. .-.	50	6	Cont.	5, 11, 17, 23, etc.
			[1] Range temporarily reduced to 25 miles UFN								
0219	RC	Zeebrugge Mole Lt.	51°20'54"N	3°12'15"E	296.5	ZB	--.. -...	5	1, 2	Fog cont. Clear	0, 1, 6, 7, etc. 0, 30, 0, 30, etc.
0215	RC	Nieuwpoort	See English Channel & Dover Strait Area								
0237	RC	Ijmuiden Front Lt.	52°27'47"N	4°34'34"E	294.2	YM	-.-- --	20	1, 4	Cont.	0, 3, 6, 9, etc.
0231	RC	Hook of Holland	51°58'54"N	4°06'50"E	294.2	HH	....	20	2, 5	Cont.	1, 4, 7, 10, etc.
0243	RC	Eierland	53°10'58"N	4°51'24"E	294.2	ER	. .-.	20	3, 6	Fog only	2, 5, 8, 11, etc.
0245	RC	Terschellingerbank Lt. V.	53°28'54"N	4°46'12"E	308.0	TG	- --.	100/70	1	Cont.	0, 6, 12, 18, etc.
0258	RC	TW/EMS Lt. V.	54°10'00"N	7°20'48"E	308.0	EM	. --	50	2	Cont.	1, 7, 13, 19, etc.
0257	RC	Borkumriff	53°47'30"N	6°22'08"E	308.0	BF	-... ..-.	50	3	Cont.	2, 8, 14, 20, etc.
0279	RC	Deutsche Bucht Lt. V.	54°10'42"N	7°26'48"E	308.0	DB	-.. -...	50	4	Cont.	3, 9, 15, 21, etc.
0241	RC	Texel Lt. V.	53°09'05"N	4°23'54"E	308.0	HK	.... -.-	50	5	Cont.	4, 10, 16, 22, etc.
0275	RC	Elbe No. 1 Lt. V.	54°00'00"N	8°06'35"E	308.0	EL	. .-..	50	6		
0247	RC	Ameland Lt.	53°27'01"N	5°37'36"E	298.8	AD	.- -..	20	1, 3, 5	Fog only	0, 2, 4, 6, etc.
0259	RC	Borkum Little Lt.	53°34'49"N	6°40'04"E	298.8	BE	-... .	20	2, 4, 6	Cont.	1, 3, 5, 7, etc.

NORTH SEA AREA – MARINE RADIO BEACONS

Thames to the Farne Islands and Zeebrugge to Rote Kliff, Germany.

Admir. ref. no.	Type	Name	Latitude and Longitude		Freq. KHz	Call Sign	Morse	Miles Range	Sequence	Continuous or fog only	No. of minutes after each hour
0264	RC	Wangerooge Lt.	53°47′27″N	7°51′31″E	291.9	WE	.–– .	30	1, 3, 5	Cont.	0, 2, 4, 6, etc.
0277	RC	Helgoland Lt.	54°11′01″N	7°52′57″E	397.2	DHE	–..	60	–	Cont. except 0600–0700	–
0287	RC	Rote Kliff Lt., Sylt	54°56′52″N	8°20′30″E	301.1	RF	.–. ..–.	20	1, 3, 5	Cont.	0, 2, 4, 6, etc.
0123	RC	Spurn Lt. V.	53°33′31″N	0°14′18″E	303.4	SL	... .–..	50	1	Cont.	0, 6, 12, 18, etc.
0105	RC	I. of May	See Scottish Area								
0111	RC	Tynemouth North Pier Lt.	55°00′52″N	1°24′05″W	303.4	TJ	– –.–	70	3	Cont.	2, 8, 14, 20, etc.
0095	RC	Kinnairds Hd.	See Scottish Area								
0119	RC	Flamborough Hd. Lt.	54°06′58″N	0°04′51″W	303.4	FB	..–. –...	70	5	Cont.	4, 10, 16, 22, etc.
0087	RC	N. Ronaldsay	See Scottish Area								
0115	RC	Sunderland 257°–786m From Roker Pier Lt.	54°55′11″N	1°21′46″W	294.2	KP	–.– .––.	20	1, 3, 5	Fog only Fog. cont.	0, 2, 4, 6, etc. 1, 3, 5, 7, etc.
0117	RC	The Heugh Lt.	54°41′48″N	1°10′30″W	294.2	HS	– ...	20	2, 4, 6	Cont.	0, 2, 4, 6, etc.
0109	RC	Longstone Lt. Farne Is.	55°38′38″N	1°36′32″W	289.6	LT	.–.. –	20	1, 3, 5	Cont.	0, 2, 4, 6, etc.
0103	RC	North Carr Lt. V.	See Scottish Area								

IRISH SEA AREA – MARINE RADIO BEACONS

Land's End to the Isle of Arran and the Irish Coast

Admir. ref. no.	Type	Name	Latitude and Longitude		Freq. KHz	Call Sign	Morse	Miles Range	Sequence	Continuous or fog only	No. of minutes after each hour
0183	RC	Tuskar Rk. Lt.	52°12′09″N	6°12′23″W	296.5	TR	— .—.	50	1	Cont.	0, 6, 12, 18, etc.
0033	RC	Skerries Lt. .	53°25′15″N	4°36′25″W	296.5	SR	... .—.	50	2	Cont.	1, 7, 13, 19, etc.
0029	RC	South Bishop Lt.	51°51′10″N	5°24′35″W	296.5	SB	... —...	50	3	Cont.	2, 8, 14, 20, etc.
0185	RC	Kish Bank Lt.	53°18′42″N	5°55′21″W	296.5	KH	—.—	50	4	Cont.	3, 9, 15, 21, etc.
0021	RC	Lundy I. North Lt.	51°12′03″N	4°40′34″W	296.5	NL	—. .—..	50	5	Cont.	4, 10, 16, 22, etc.
0051	RC	Cregneish, I. of Man	54°04′55″N	4°45′52″W	296.5	CN	—.—. —.	50	6	Cont.	5, 11, 17, 23, etc.
0001	RC	Nab Tower	See English Channel & Dover Strait Area								
0849	RC	Cherbourg	See English Channel & Dover Strait Area								
0023	RC	Breaksea Lt. V.	51°20′12″N	3°17′45″W	312.6	BK	—... —.—	30	3	Cont.	1, 4, 7, 10, etc.
0045	RC	Pt. of Ayre, High Lt. I. of Man	54°24′57″N	4°22′02″W	305.7	PY	.——. —.——	10	2, 4, 6	Cont.	1, 3, 5, 7, etc.
0041	RC	Walney Island Lt.	54°02′54″N	3°10′33″W	289.6	FN	..—. —.	20	1, 3, 5	Cont.	0, 2, 4, 6, etc.
0047	RC	Douglas, I. of Man, Victoria Pier Lt.	54°08′50″N	4°28′00″W	289.6	DG	—.. ——.	20	2, 4, 6,	Fog only	1, 3, 5, 7, etc.
0189	RC	South Rock Lt. V.	54°24′28″N	5°21′55″W	301.1	SU	... —..	20	2, 4, 6	Cont.	1, 3, 5, 7, etc.
0191	RC	Mew Island Lt.	54°41′55″N	5°30′45″W	294.2	MW	—— .——	20	1, 3, 5	Cont.	0, 2, 4, 6, etc.

IRISH SEA AREA – MARINE RADIO BEACONS

Land's End to the Isle of Arran and the Irish Coast

Admir. ref. no.	Type	Name	Latitude and Longitude	Freq. KHz	Call Sign	Morse	Miles Range	Sequence	Continuous or fog service	No. of minutes after each hour
0059	RC	Pladda Lt., I. of Arran	55°25′30″N 5°07′04″W	289.6	DA	—.. .—	20	1, 3, 5	Fog only	0, 2, 4, 6, etc.
0199	RC	Eagle Island Lt.	54°16′59″N 10°05′31″W	308.0	GL	——. .—..	100/70	1	Cont.	0, 6, 12, 18, etc.
0179	RC	Mizen Head Lt.	51°26′55″N 9°49′05″W	308.0	MZ	—— ——..	200/100	2	Cont.	1, 7, 13, 19, etc.
0063	RC	Mull of Kintyre Lt.	55°18′39″N 5°48′06″W	308.0	KR	—.— .—.	100/70	3	Cont.	2, 8, 14, 20, etc.
0017	RC	Round I.	For details see English Channel Area					4		
0197	RC	Tory I.	55°16′21″N 8°14′55″W	308.0	TY	— —.——	100/70	5	Cont.	4, 10, 16, 22, etc.
0857	RC	Pte de Creach	For details see English Channel Area					6		
0192	RC	Altacarry Head Lt. Rathlin Island	55°18′04″N 6°10′12″W	287.3	AH	.—	30	2, 4, 6	Cont.	1, 3, 5, 7, etc.

SCOTTISH AREA – AERO & MARINE RADIO BEACONS

Scottish coasts including Hebrides, Orkney & Shetland Isles

Admir. ref. No.	Type	Name	Latitude and Longitude	Freq. KHz	Call Sign	Morse	Miles range	Sequence	Continuous or Fog only	No. of minutes after each hour
0123	RC	Spurn Lt. V.	See North Sea Area					1		
0105	RC	I. of May	56°11′04″N 2°33′11″W	303.4	LM	·—·· ——	100/70	2	Cont.	1, 7, 13, 19, etc.
0111	RC	Tynemouth	See North Sea Area					3		
0095	RC	Kinnairds Hd. Lt.	57°41′52″N 2°00′08″W	303.4	KD	—·— ——·	100/70	4	Cont.	3, 9, 15, 21, etc.
0119	RC	Flamborough Hd.	See North Sea Area					5		
0087	RC	N. Ronaldsay Lt. Orkney Is.	59°23′24″N 2°22′48″W	303.4	NR	—· ·—·	100/70	6	Cont.	5, 11, 17, 23, etc.
0109	RC	Longstone Lt.	See North Sea Area					1, 3, 5		
0103	RC	North Carr Lt. V.	56°18′20″N 2°32′03″W	289.6	CR	—·—· ·—·	10	2, 4, 6	Fog only	1, 3, 5, 7, etc.
0101	Aero RC	Leuchars	56°22′15″N 2°52′00″W	251.5	LU	·—·· ··—	100	–	Cont.	–
0099	RC	Abertay Lt. V.	56°27′25″N 2°41′07″W	294.2	AY	·— —·——	20	1, 3, 5	Fog only	0, 2, 4, 6, etc.
0097	RC	Girdleness Lt.	57°08′19″N 2°02′50″W	287.3	GD	——· —··	30	2, 4, 6	Cont.	1, 3, 5, 7, etc.
0093	Aero RC	Kinloss	57°39′02″N 3°34′42″W	370.0	KS	—·— ···	50	–	Cont.	–
0091	Aero RC	Wick	58°26′49″N 3°03′42″W	344.0	WIK	·—— ·· —·—	50	–	Cont.	–
0085	Aero RC	Sumburgh, Shetland Is.	59°52′05″N 1°16′18″W	351.0	SUM	··· ··— ——	100	–	Cont.	–
0089	RC	Stroma. Swilkie Pt. Lt.	58°41′47″N 3°06′55″W	298.8	OM	——— ——	30	1, 3, 5	Cont.	0, 2, 4, 6, etc.
0083	RC	Bressay Lt. Shetland Is.	60°07′15″N 1°07′11″W	298.8	BY	—··· —·——	20	2, 4, 6	Fog only	1, 3, 5, 7, etc.
0069	RC	Barra Hd. Lt. Berneray	56°47′05″N 7°39′11″W	291.9	BD	—··· —··	200/70	2	Cont.	1, 7, 13, 19, etc.
0079	RC	Sule Skerry Lt.	59°05′00″N 4°24′23″W	291.9	LK	·—·· —·—	100/70	4	Cont.	3, 9, 15, 21, etc.
0081	RC	Muckle Flugga North Unst Lt. Shetland Is.	60°51′20″N 0°53′00″W	291.9	MF	—— ··—·	100/70	5	Cont.	4, 10, 16, 22, etc.
0075	RC	Butt of Lewis Lt.	58°30′56″N 6°15′43″W	291.9	BL	—··· ·—··	150/70	6	Cont.	5, 11, 17, 23, etc.
0077	RC	Cape Wrath Lt.	58°37′28″N 4°59′32″W	305.7	CW	—·—· ·——	30	1, 3, 5	Cont.	0, 2, 4, 6, etc.
0071	RC	Rona Lt.	57°34′42″N 5°57′27″W	305.7	NA	—· ·—	20	2, 4, 6	Cont.	1, 3, 5, 7, etc.
0073	RC	Eilean Glas Lt.	57°51′22″N 6°38′29″W	301.1	LG	·—·· ——·	30	1, 3, 5	Cont.	0, 2, 4, 6, etc.
0067	RC	Oigh Sgeir Lt.	56°58′08″N 6°40′48″W	301.1	OR	——— ·—·	20	2, 4, 6	Cont.	1, 3, 5, 7, etc.
0057	RC	Cloch Pt. Lt. (Clyde)	Range-finding beacon. For details see page 96							

DIRECTIONAL RADIOBEACONS

2213B **Boulogne.** 50°44′24″N. 1°35′47″E.
Site: 094° 6,550 ft. from Dihue Carnot LH.
Frequency: 289.6 kHz.
Range: 5 miles.

Characteristic:

Northward of beam:	A (·—) etc.
On beam:	Continuous long dashes. (Beam width 5°).
Southward of beam:	N (—·) etc.
Bearing line:	101°30′ towards radiobeacon.
Beacon service:	Continuous.

2220T **Lorient – Lohic LH.** 48°01′06″N. 4°12′55″W.
Site: At lighthouse.
Frequency: 294.2 kHz.
Range: 10 miles.

Characteristic:

Northward of beam:	A (·—) etc.
On beam:	Continuous note. (Beam width 2°).
Southward of beam:	N (—·) etc.
Bearing line:	060°30′ towards radiobeacon.
Beacon service:	Continuous.

RANGE FINDING RADIOBEACON. (Fog services only).

0057 **Cloch Point LH.** 55°56′32″N. 4°52′40″W.
Frequency: 301.1 kHz.
Range: 10 miles

Air fog signal : Siren (2): Period 50 sec. 2 blasts of 1.5 sec. in quick succession.

Characteristic of R/T emission: 50 sec.

The following preliminary speech:

"Cloch Point Lighthouse speaking. At the instant when you hear through the air the commencement of the second blast of this fog signal, your distance in cables from this Lighthouse is as stated on the radio . . . ."

This is followed by counting in speech, in cables, from one to thirty. (Note – 10 cables = 1 nautical mile).

CHAPTER 9

Meteorology

Not very long ago a family was lost off the south coast in their small yacht. Although their intention had been to obtain the BBC weather forecast for coastal waters before sailing, due to an oversight they missed it. Apparently they did not wish to cancel a day's sailing on the off-chance that a gale may have been forecast and so they sailed. In fact a gale was forecast for that day.

This tragedy, like many similar ones, lends point to the advice that no small boat sailor should venture beyond sheltered waters without having obtained a current weather forecast for his area. Compliance with this exhortation **in itself** does not provide sufficient knowledge for his needs but even the most casual cannot, for his own safety, neglect this single imperative requirement.

No meteorologist would claim that a forecast he produces is an indisputable portent of weather to come. Those uninformed people who malign him fail to appreciate that he works with elemental factors and not predictable tangibles. The experienced yachtsman is neither furious nor dismayed if a weather forecast proves to be wrong. Like other seamen, he has a working knowledge of elementary meteorology, culled mainly from his own experience. He has a sheet anchor to fall back on.

He takes appropriate action **before** the onset of bad weather, so far as it is possible for him to do so. That bad weather is imminent is indicated to him by a weather report or by his knowledge of simple meteorology. His action may be to delay or to cancel sailing from a port. Being at sea, it may be to scurry for sheltered water, or to give himself sea room, snug down, shorten sail and generally prepare to ride out a blow. None of these or similar actions would imply timidity in these circumstances. The yachtsman must pit his wits against the elements. He may suffer bruised knuckles; he may experience what is called a near thing; but seldom does the experienced seaman emerge second-best from such encounters.

Before commencing a voyage the wise man will thus be in possession of the following:

1. A current weather forecast for his sea area.

2. A rudimentary knowledge of single-observer weather forecasting.

Weather Forecasts

(General Remarks)

BBC Forecasts.

For the purposes of weather forecasting, the sea areas round the British Isles are divided in the manner shown in the diagram on page 106. It will be seen that each one is named. It is these names, and these areas, to which announcers make reference when broadcasting weather forecasts for shipping.

Wind velocity is always referred to the Beaufort Wind Scale (see page 107) which, numbering wind strengths from 0 to 12, is a readily understandable code. All weather reports and all seamen use the scale when referring to wind velocity and so the yachtsman must make himself familiar with it. With practice he will find it easier to relate wind strength to the Beaufort scale, rather than to miles per hour. One readily becomes familiar with the unvarying pattern of BBC weather forecasts. Full details of these services, including gale warnings, will be found within this chapter.

Other weather forecasts.

The BBC is by no means the only authority which provides weather reports for seamen, although theirs are the most easily obtained. Authorities in ports throughout Great Britain will give by telephone actual weather conditions prevailing in their localities. Local forecasts may be obtained, by telephone or by writing, from sundry meteorological offices. Yachtsmen who carry a radio-telephone have the means by which they may obtain even more forecasts. All necessary information relating to these services will be found within this chapter.

Single Observer Forecasting.

Though a seaman may be well versed in meteorology and weather lore, no forecast he makes from his own observations can be valid for more than five or six hours. He will make no claim to a greater degree of accuracy than the meteorologists but his short-term forecasts are more likely to be right than wrong. This being said, it follows that he is much less likely to be badly caught out by a change in weather than the man who relies upon official forecasts only.

Of the sundry factors which the professional forecaster has at his disposal, only three are of practical use to the off-shore sailor:

1. An aneroid barometer, from which he may obtain the atmospheric pressure and, more important to him, whether its tendency is to rise or fall.

2. The direction and strength of the wind which in itself occasionally gives portent of weather to come.

3. Cloud formation and movement. Of these three features, this is more often the most reliable single foretoken of future weather.

The synoptic chart, or weather chart.

Awareness of the above three factors has little or no practical value if one has no knowledge of weather systems and patterns in the British Isles. Some newspapers publish daily weather charts produced by the Meteorological Office for both the Atlantic Ocean and the British Isles which are of interest to the knowledgeable. In recent years television meteorologists have probably done most to make the man in the street familiar with weather charts and trends in our weather. If one can read a synoptic chart intelligently one is halfway to understanding why past, present and future weather trends occur.

The main feature on these maps is a visual indication of the distribution of atmospheric pressure throughout the area. Places which have the same pressure are joined together by lines called isobars. The isobaric structure in any area at any given time will itself produce the weather pattern in that area. If one can assess the **future** movements of isobars one possesses the main tool of a forecast.

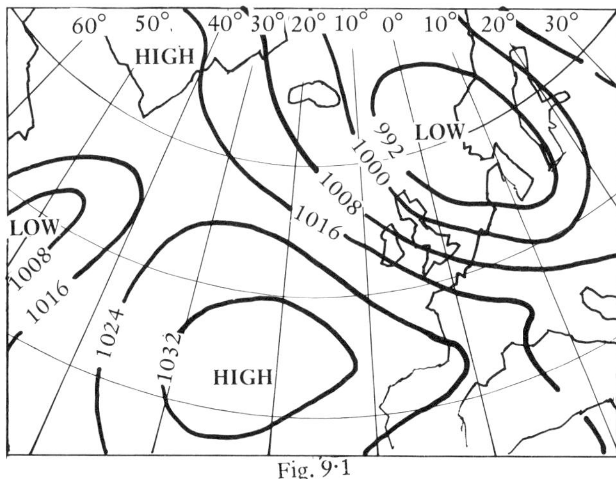

Fig. 9·1

In Fig. 9.1 note how each isobar has the barometric pressure in millibars alongside it. Note the similarity to contours on an ordnance map which indicate gradient. Their visual likeness is not the only feature they have in common. Closely spaced land contours indicate steep gradients: closely spaced isobars portray steep **pressure** gradients, which in turn produce strong winds. Conversely, widely spaced isobars, usually referred to as a weak or shallow gradient, indicate light winds.

If local weather systems did not occur to give us the myriad variations which we experience throughout the year the isobars over the Atlantic area might ideally appear as in Fig. 9·2

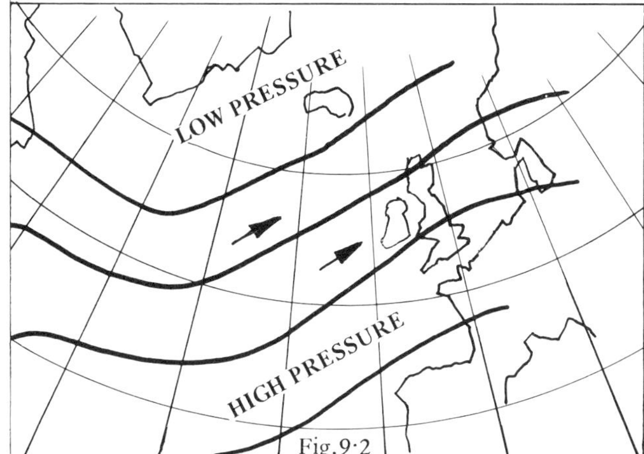

Fig. 9·2

Wind direction is broadly that in which isobars lie. Whether it will blow one way along the isobars, or the other, will be decided by pressure distribution according to an easily-understood pattern. The basic Atlantic pressure distribution accounts in part for the fact that our prevailing winds emanate from a westerly point. Local weather systems forming far to the westward of the British Isles tend to move eastwards in the general direction of these isobars. Such systems frequently disrupt the above basic isobaric pattern to a point when it is seldom recognisable.

Depressions or lows

It is well known that depressions, or lows, usually bring unsettled weather with them. Both names allude to air pressure and in particular to a body of air whose pressure is lower than that of the surrounding air. Lows are temporary phenomena with a life span seldom exceeding more than a few days. They may move fast and their rate

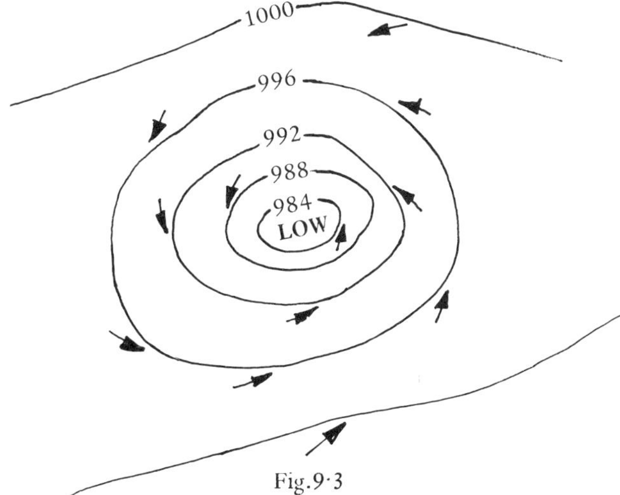

Fig. 9·3

of progression often reaches 40 knots in winter. Their form and 'depth' vary so widely that one can only talk of a 'model' one in any brief description. If one understands the features of a model depression, the features of all other types are more readily comprehended.

Figure 9.3 indicates a simple depression in the northern hemisphere. Broadly following the direction of the isobars round the low, the wind is moving in an anti-clockwise direction round it. This is the never-varying behaviour of wind circulating round a low in the northern hemisphere. Swirling round the low, much in the manner of water round the waste pipe in a bath, the wind angles inwards in its endeavour to fill the central low.

In fact the lows we experience do not usually possess this simple form. A model low would appear on a synoptic chart in the form shown in Fig. 9.4, a pattern which requires elucidation.

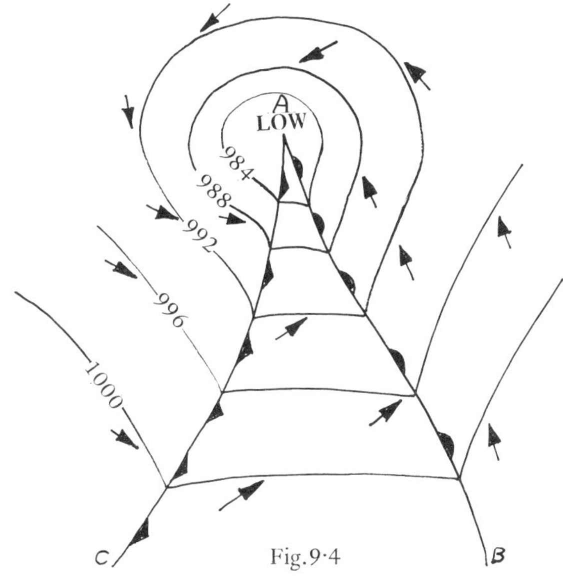

Fig.9·4

Our low is still in evidence and the wind circulating round it is anti-clockwise in direction. There are, however, 'fronts' associated with this depression. The thick line AB reaches from the centre of the low in a southerly direction. The rounded nodules define it as a 'warm front'. The air to the east, or right, of this front is relatively cold: that to the left of it is relatively warm. In concert with the low as it progresses in a north-easterly direction, this warm front will tend to sweep in a similar direction. The thick line AC is a 'cold front', indicated by the triangular nodules produced upon it. The air to the left of it is relatively cold, hence the name. The isobars defining our model low and its associated fronts do not possess the same symmetry as those isobars which are not associated with fronts. They change direction at the fronts, sometimes quite sharply. Recalling that wind direction tends to follow that of the isobars, it follows that wind change may often be associated with fronts and it may at times be quite marked. The passing of a front over an observer thus often heralds a wind change; in reverse, such a wind change may indicate to him the passing of a front.

As the age of this model depression increases, the two fronts tend to come together. This merger commences at the centre of the low and progresses outwards, as if a zip fastener were slowly drawing the fronts together.

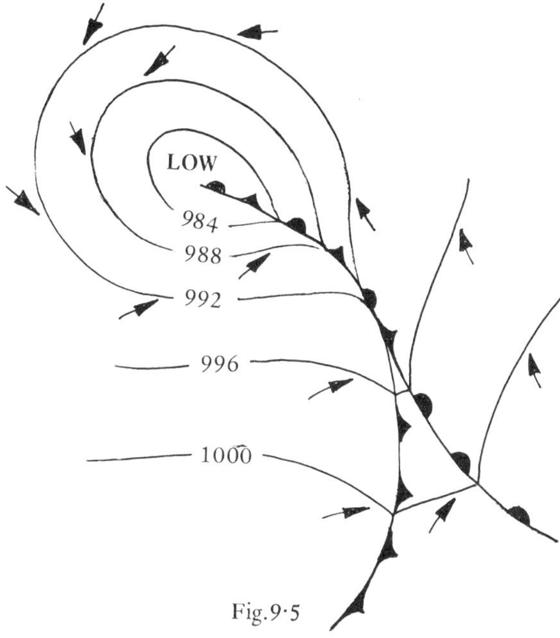

Fig.9·5

The bodies of cold air to the left and right of the fronts are joining together, undercutting the warm air between them. The warm air is lifted from surface regions, a phenomenon called an occluding process. The two fronts having merged into one, it is then referred to as an occluded front, and is recognisable on a weather chart by a pattern of alternate triangles and nodules. Occlusion having been completed, the depression decays. Pressure rises in the central area and the whole phenomenon dies.

Weather associated with a model low and its frontal systems.

There being a basic behaviour of lows and fronts in our area, it follows that there must be a corresponding weather pattern associated with them. The majority of well-delevoped Atlantic low pressure systems pass in an east-north-easterly direction on a track which takes them to the north and west of Scotland. For this reason a fairly recognisable pattern over the British Isles often manifests itself. Fig. 9.6 portrays the passage of a model low, and its associated fronts in four stages. The three weather features which we ourselves can observe are, in relation to the passage of our model low, elucidated separately. They describe the weather a yacht in position Y might experience.

Many hours before the approach of the warm front, high cloud will probably give precursory signs of a weather change for the worse. Streaky cirrus clouds, changing to cirro-stratus, will tell their story. A gradual lowering of the cloud base will be noted, alto-cumulus with alto-stratus succeeding the earlier high clouds.

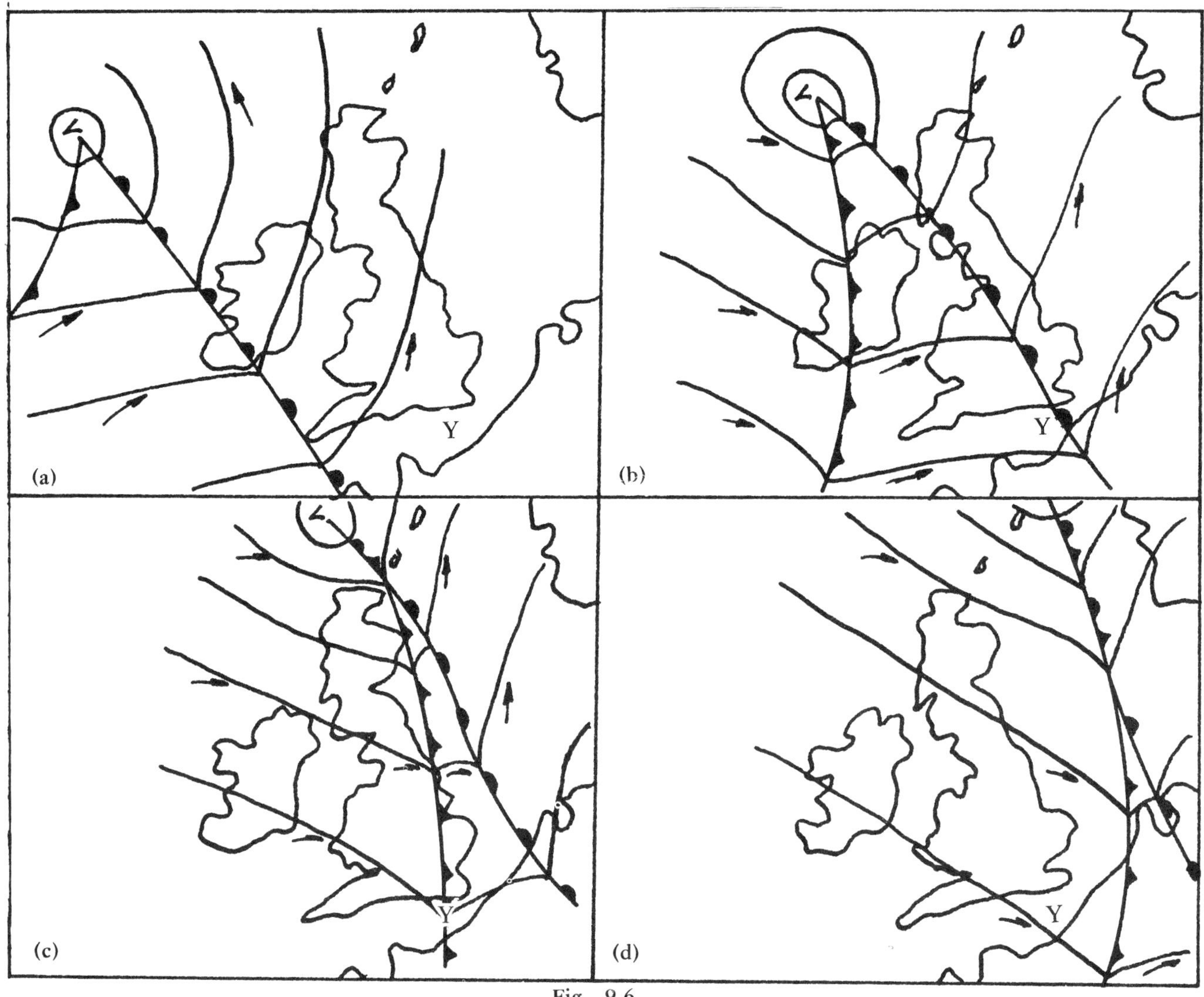

Fig. 9.6

Fig. 9.6(a)

A gradual fall in the barometer reading will be noted. The wind will be south, or even south-east, perhaps fitful at first but gradually increasing in strength. Middle cloud forms will be replaced by strato-cumulus and nimbus. Light rain at first will be replaced by more constant, probably heavier rain.

Fig. 9.6(b)

At this point the barometer will cease to fall. Note that in this isobaric formation the isobars between the fronts are roughly parallel to the track of the depression. Although the barometer is at its lowest point, it will remain steady for a little while. The wind having been strong from a southerly point hitherto, at the passing of the warm front it will veer to the south-west or west and remain fairly constant in velocity. Constant driving rain with cumulo-nimbus cloud may be experienced, probably with scud (fracto-cumulus cloud).

Fig. 9.6(c)

At the passage of the cold front a perceptible rise in barometric pressure will be noted. The wind will probably veer sharply to a west or north-westerly point, this change perhaps being accompanied by fierce rain squalls. A breaking of the cloud may be seen, perhaps with the occasional glimpse of the sun.

Fig. 9.6(d)

The barometer will rise steadily. Occasional squalls, with rain of diminished intensity may occur, but the weather will obviously be improving. The cloud base will gradually rise and cloud forms indicative of more settled weather will replace the earlier storm clouds.

Observations on the model depression.

This weather pattern is not uncommon in the British Isles. The winds associated with it will probably be stronger in the immediate vicinity of the low but its intensity may be such as to produce gale force winds far removed from it, in the English Channel.

Depressions may take considerably different tracks from the one outlined previously. Some may pass up the English Channel, or over the north of France, or even double back in a westerly direction. As the isobars, and therefore the winds, of a depression retain certain basic qualities, it will be appreciated how vastly different will be the wind changes over the U.K. when associated with a depression passing north-eastwards over northern France.

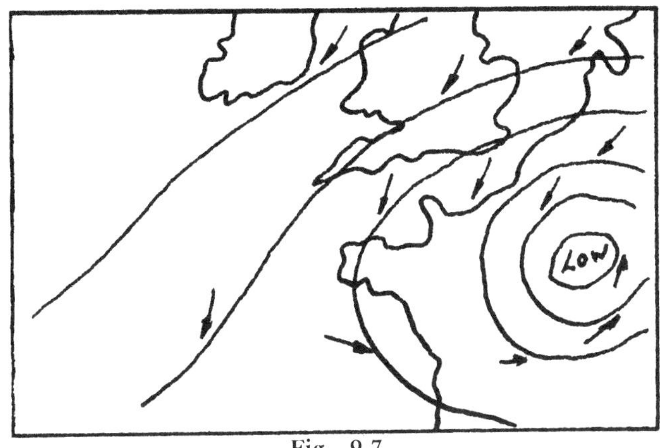

Fig. 9.7

Bearing in mind that depressions generally adopt a north-easterly track, it is often helpful to take into consideration the weather forecasts for areas other than one's own. It can often be said that weather to the **westwards** of an observer could well prove to be that which he will experience in the foreseeable future. Thus it may be wise for a yachtsman in the Dover area to note the forecast for both Wight and Portland areas. They could give him some indication of what his future movements should be.

High pressure systems.

An anti-cyclone, or high, is evidenced by a centre of relatively high pressure around which the isobars are roughly concentric. A most important feature of them is their wind circulation: in the northern hemisphere it revolves **clockwise** around them. Where depressions tend to preserve their own peculiar features throughout their life, highs are often an extension of a general area of high pressure. It may be said that highs tend to be larger than lows, are slower moving and their pressure gradients are less marked. Highs often being associated with fine weather, their frequently weak pressure gradients produce fairly light winds.

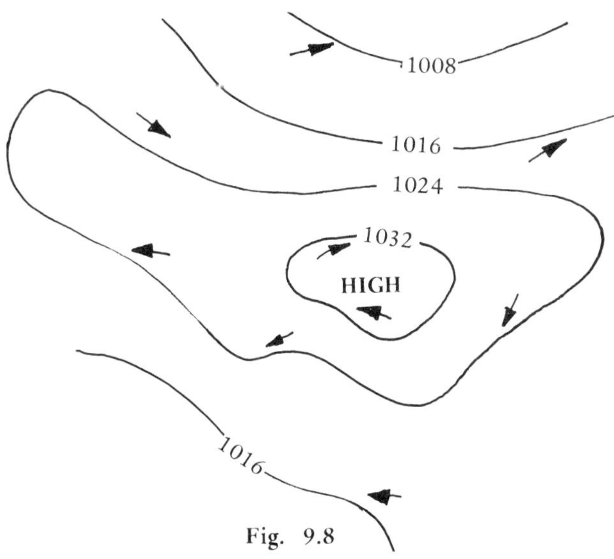

Fig. 9.8

Buys Ballot's Law.

In the last century Buys Ballot defined in the form of a law a meteorological fact. The law states that, when facing the wind in the northern hemisphere, the area of lowest pressure will lie on the observer's right. It must be said that it is only approximately true but its remarkable simplicity is often of value to the seaman. The thoughtful reader will recognise it as verification of the fact that winds form an anti-clockwise circulation round a depression and clockwise round an anti-cyclone.

General features of British weather.

The guide lines to weather which follow, inadequate as they must inevitably be, will give the off-shore sailor some indication of weather trends in general and British weather trends in particular. Emphasis is deliberately made upon bad weather. The majority of yachtsmen spend more of their time at sea in summer, a period when the blanketing statements of weather forecasters relating to settled weather are more likely to be heard. They must however, be aware of what can, and of times does, occur to make their summer cruises uncomfortable and perhaps very worrying experiences. These comments will, perhaps above all, highlight the fact that in weather there are infinite variables.

If one relates the following remarks about barometer

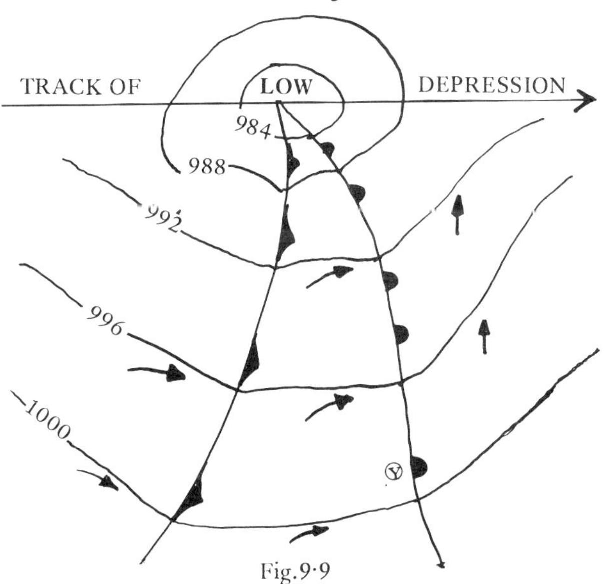

Fig.9·9

A yacht stationary in position Ⓨ will probably have a steady barometer until the cold front passes.

movement to the direction in which isobars lie, as for instance in the model depression described earlier, they will be more readily understood.

The **change** in barometric readings is usually of greater value to the seaman than the reading itself. Change indicates the presence of a pressure gradient and in turn gradient indicates wind, although not necessarily of gale force. An observer cannot assume that a steady barometer is proof that wind, even of gale force, will not be encountered. If the movement of the isobars is parallel to the direction in which they lie, then the barometer will remain steady, though a pressure gradient is present.

A low barometer is not a sure indication of strong winds. Again it will depend upon the formation of the isobars. If their gradient is weak, winds may be only moderate. It may occur that when the barometer eventually begins to rise the movement is sharp and severe winds may occur. For example, the writer experienced weather in the North Sea in winter when the barometer gradually fell to a point seldom encountered outside the centre of a hurricane. For many hours the wind and sea were moderate, yet when the barometer eventually rose it rocketed upwards and storm force winds occurred.

Gales may occur although only a shallow depression is in the area. If an anti-cyclone is in the path of the low it will slow down or deflect or stop its movement. 'Highs' often being slow moving or stationary, they have the property of being able to block the progress of a low. The low may 'press' against the high and the isobars associated with each system will be compressed. This compression will steepen the pressure gradient and so produce strong winds which could last for a protracted period.

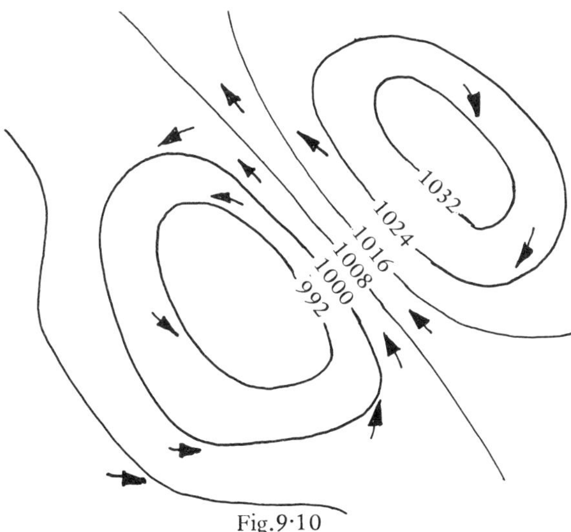

Fig.9·10

Around the British coasts it is more likely that a gale from a southerly direction will occur with a falling barometer, and one from a north-westerly direction when the barometer is rising. The majority of depressions passing to the north and west of the British Isles, it may be said that during their passage the tendency of the wind will be to **veer**, from a southerly point, through west to a north-westerly point. This is valuable information to a yachtsman.

Of the three weather features capable of being observed by the average yachtsman – barometer, wind and cloud – probably clouds provide the most reliable means of determining sometime beforehand if foul weather may be experienced. Upper cloud, sometimes fast-moving, is more often than not an indication of unsettled weather to follow. Cirrus and cirro-stratus cloud often provide the first indication that, perhaps hundreds of miles away to the west, a frontal system is approaching.

It cannot always be assumed that the gradual thickening of high and middle cloud heralds the approach of a low. Close observation of associated barometer and wind trends will probably give the observer an indication of weather to follow. Obviously if he is in doubt it would be seamanlike to prepare for a blow, even if one does not materialise.

After a day of clear skies, the sun settling low in the west behind an emergent cloud bank may give the first indication of adverse weather up to fifty miles away. Such clouds, in the absence of the sun to emphasise their presence, might otherwise go unnoticed for an hour or more. Small cumulus cloud is often associated with fine weather. During a settled period it tends to form after sunrise over both land and sea and dissipates after sunset. Large, towering cumulus clouds occasionally produce showers and sometimes local squalls.

In the English Channel during summer, thunder storms are frequently a feature during or after a fairly long spell of settled weather. They are produced by minor troughs which move northward from France. These, in common with other thunderstorms, tend to be an afternoon or evening feature, rather than a morning one. Ragged alto-cumulus is often a sign that thunderstorms may occur.

Of particular interest to yachtsmen is the frequent 'funnelling' of wind which occurs in straits, long bays and along coastlines. The effect may be likened to the waters of a stream which increase in velocity when narrows are encountered and accelerate when their path is deflected by a bank. In a like manner, though the wind is steady in direction, it may be deflected in the vicinity of headlands and cliffs, or funnelled in a slightly different direction with increased velocity in a bay or strait. It may have been noted by some that the wind in the straits of Dover often follows the direction of the straits, although the south-westerly point from which it emanates is not precisely that of the direction of the straits.

Land and sea breezes (see Glossary) produce individual features. The effect of a sea breeze during the afternoon may be to deflect the direction of the existing wind, and perhaps to accelerate or decelerate its force. In still, settled weather a land breeze in the early hours of the morning may afford the means by which a yachtsman may obtain offing. As these breezes disappear shortly after sunrise it is the early bird who is well off shore, and ideally placed to catch any wind which blows, before gentle zephyrs are the only wind movements in evidence close inshore.

Fog is a feature which the single observer afloat cannot really foresee. Although frequently associated with

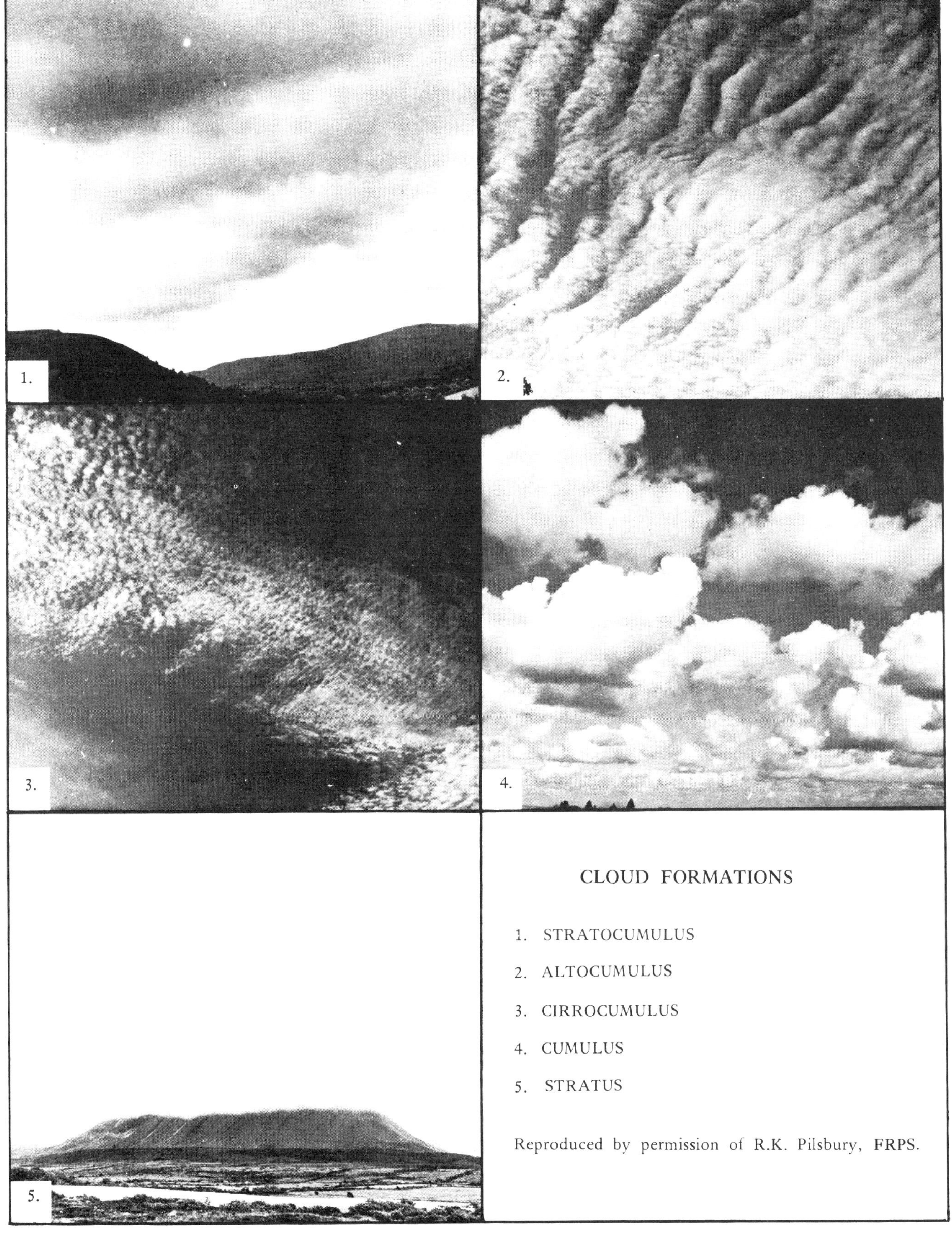

CLOUD FORMATIONS

1. STRATOCUMULUS
2. ALTOCUMULUS
3. CIRROCUMULUS
4. CUMULUS
5. STRATUS

Reproduced by permission of R.K. Pilsbury, FRPS.

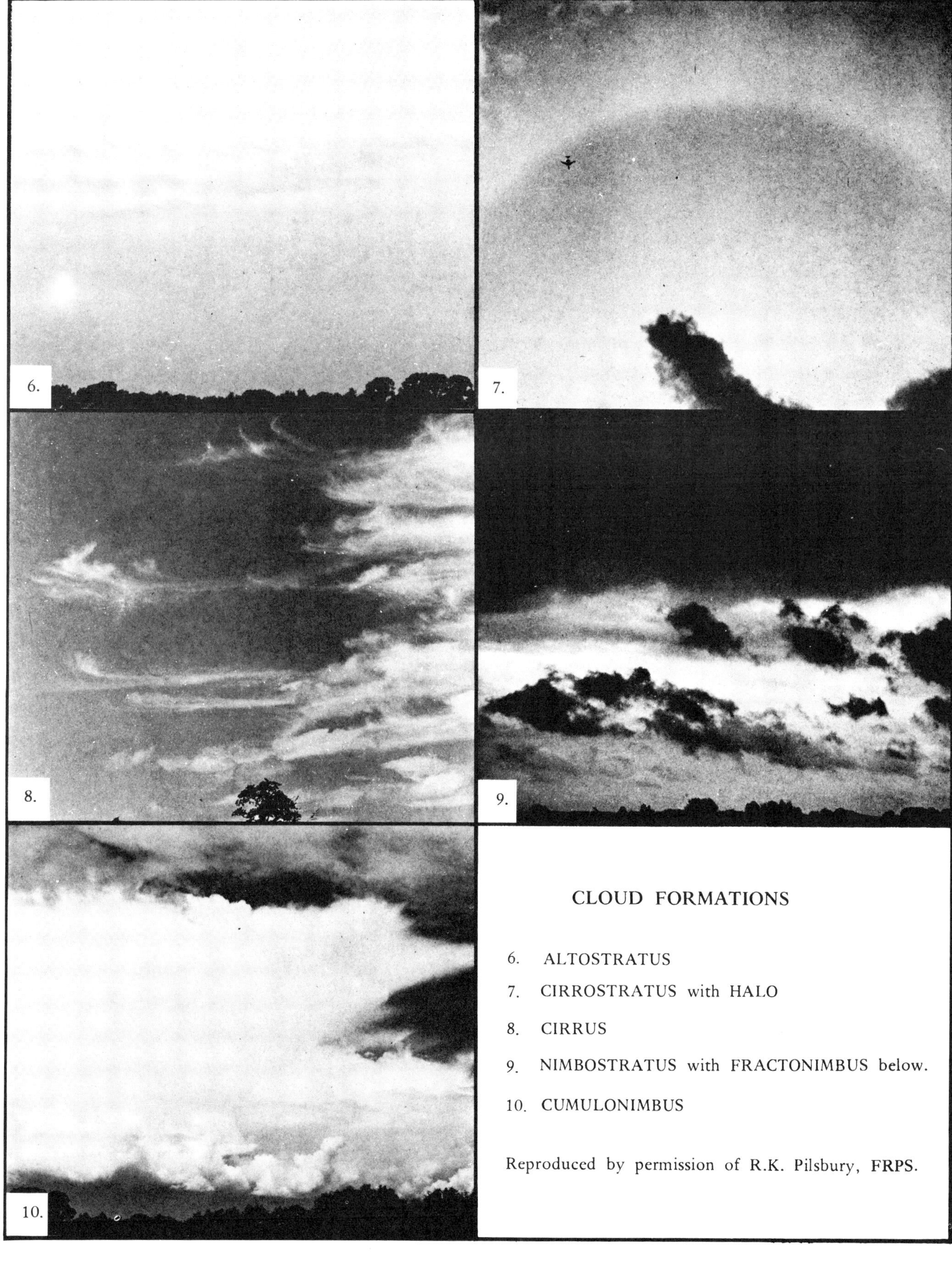

CLOUD FORMATIONS

6. ALTOSTRATUS
7. CIRROSTRATUS with HALO
8. CIRRUS
9. NIMBOSTRATUS with FRACTONIMBUS below.
10. CUMULONIMBUS

Reproduced by permission of R.K. Pilsbury, FRPS.

high pressure weather systems, it is not necessarily so. Neither can one say that, with wind being in evidence, fog will not occur. Its pending occurrence may be indicated to the yachtsman by a reduction in visibility, or a haziness around lights at night. Weather forecasts are the yachtsman's only reliable means by which he may foretell the onset of fog.

Glossary of Meteorological terms.

Anemometer. An instrument for measuring wind velocity.

Angle of indraft. Wind does not follow the precise direction of associated isobars. The angle at the earth's surface between the wind direction and an isobar is known as the angle of indraft.

Anticyclone, or high. An area of high pressure characterised by its 'closed' isobars. Its central area is the point of highest pressure.

Aurora Borealis. Commonly known as the northern lights and more often seen in the north of the British Isles than the south, it is a product of electric energy in the upper atmosphere. An observer tends to associate it with clear winter nights, it appearing to him as luminous arcs and bright streamers of light on the northern horizon.

Backing. A wind which changes direction in an anticlockwise manner is said to be backing.

Clouds. A visible assemblage of minute particles of water or ice, or both, in free air.

High clouds. Those between 16,000 and 45,000 feet.

Cirrus (Ci). Detached cloud in the form of white, fibrous filaments. They may be white patches, or narrow bands. Those having a tufted appearance indicating wind at high altitude are known by seamen as mare's tails.

Cirrocumulus (Cc). This thin cloud may be in the form of a white patch, sheet or layer, without shading. Sometimes it has a rippled appearance and is composed of very small elements.

Cirrostratus (Cs). Transparent, whitish cloud veil of fibrous or smooth appearance of the type which generally produces halo phenomena.

Medium clouds. Those between 7,000 and 23,000 feet.

Altocumulus (Ac). Greyish white, or white, or grey in colour, it may be a patch, sheet or a layer of cloud of rounded masses or rolls. Often of regularly arranged, small elements.

Altostratus (As). Greyish or bluish cloud sheet or layer of streaked, fibrous or uniform appearance.

Low clouds. From earth's surface to 7,000 feet.

Nimbostratus (Ns). A grey cloud layer, thick enough to blot out the sun. Often rendered diffuse by continually falling rain or snow.

Stratocumulus (Sc). Perhaps grey or whitish, or both grey and whitish, it may be a patch, sheet or layer of cloud which invariably has dark parts. It is non-fibrous and composed of tessellations, rounded masses, rolls, etc.

Stratus (St). Although it may occasionally appear in ragged patches, it is usually a grey cloud layer with a fairly uniform base. It may produce drizzle or snow grains.

Cumulus (Cu). Detached, thick cloud with a vertical development having a sharp outline. It appears as rising mounds, domes or towers. Their bases are usually grey and horizontal while the billowing upper regions are sunlit and white.

Cumulonimbus (Cb). Heavy, dense cloud with considerable vertical development in the form of a mountain or towers. Its upper portion is often flattened in anvil form but may be fibrous or streaked. The base is usually very dark, sometimes with low, ragged cloud merged with it. It may well produce local rain.

Cold front. The boundary line between the relatively cold air at the rear of a depression and the warm sector.

Cold sector. That part of a depression which is characterised by its region of relatively cold air at the earth's surface.

Depression, or low. An area of low pressure possessing a system of closed isobars, the point of lowest barometric pressure being at its centre.

Dew. Horizontal surfaces which are cooled by radiation at night produce a cooling of the air in their immediate vicinity. This cooling produces condensation and water droplets are deposited.

Dew point. The lowest temperature to which air can be cooled without causing condensation.

Front. The boundary lines on the earth's surface or in the air masses above it between cold and warm air masses.

Gust. A fluctuation in the strength of the wind. It is mainly caused by friction of the wind on ground surfaces which in turn produces air turbulence and eddies.

Hail. Small pieces or balls of ice, often associated with thunderstorms, which fall from cumulo-nimbus clouds.

Isobars. The lines on a weather chart which join together places of equal barometric pressure.

Isotherms. Lines on a weather chart which join together places of equal temperature.

Katabatic and anabatic winds. Air masses at the top of a gradient which, cooled to a greater degree than those in the valley, become heavier and flow down the slope under the influence of gravity produce a katabatic wind. Air which moves up a slope through the convection of heated air is referred to as an anabatic wind.

Line squall. Usually recognisable some miles away as a long, low, black cloud, it usually heralds the approach of a cold front. Associated phenomena may be a sharp rise in barometric pressure, a perceptible drop in temperature and a change in wind direction. As it passes overhead, violent squalls with heavy rain, hail or thunder may well be experienced.

Land and sea breezes. A hot summer sun will cause land to heat up more rapidly than the sea. On a shore line this will cause a slight drop in pressure over the land, air will flow towards the area of lowered pressure and a sea breeze will occur. Mid-afternoon is a period when such a phenomenon will usually be most marked.

At night the sea loses what heat it has absorbed from the sun during the day more slowly than the land. During calm weather the effect is to set up a gentle land breeze which is usually most marked before sunrise.

Occlusion, or occluded depression. When the advancing cold air at the rear of a depression has completely lifted the air in the warm sector from the earth's surface, an occlusion is said to have occurred.

Precipitation. Any particles of water or ice which fall from clouds. Rain, drizzle, snow and hail are common forms.

Ridge. The extension outwards in any direction of the isobars denoting an anticyclone on a weather chart.

Scud. An expressive seaman's term for fracto-cumulus cloud. This is the low, racing cloud which is often seen beneath rain clouds in bad weather.

Secondary. An offshoot depression which owes its existence to an established parent. Usually forming at a point of instability on the warm front of a major depression, its isobars may form an extension of existing ones. It may develop and form a 'break-away' depression in which case it will probably produce its own pattern of closed isobars.

Shower. In meteorology the word shower refers to short periods of rain between which a clearance of the sky occurs. The term 'occasional precipitation' may appear to have an identical definition but it denotes periods of rain which may last up to half an hour, the type of periodical rain usually associated with cloudy or overcast weather.

Sleet. Precipitation of wet snow and rain.

Snow. Loose formation of ice crystals having a branch formation which can vary considerably in size.

Squall. A wind gust which appreciably increases the mean wind speed for a duration of several minutes. Squalls are associated with fronts and large convective clouds.

Thunder and lightning. Lightning is a discharge of static electricity, evidenced by an enormous flash between two clouds, or between a cloud and the ground. There is only one type of lightning: that which the landsman calls fork lightning is true lightning: his sheet lightning is merely a reflection on cloud surfaces of lightning not visible to the observer.

Thunder is the sound produced by the sudden and violent expansion of air along the path of a lightning flash. A flash may be as much as two miles in length and so the sound of the associated thunder takes varying periods to reach an observer. This, often coupled with echo effects, produces the well known rumbling.

Thunderstorms. Most thunderstorms form in cumulonimbus cloud but thick, unstable medium cloud may also produce them. Weather associated with them is squalls whose onset may be sudden and violent, intense hailstorms and heavy rain. Temporary wind strengths of force 9 and above are not unknown in them and it is a point of interest that our occasional tornadoes are produced by them.

Trough. This may be defined as a line drawn through the centre of a depression at right angles to the path in which it is advancing. A depression advancing towards an observer, the barometer will fall as the trough approaches and, having passed, will rise again as the trough moves away.

Veering. A wind which changes direction in a clockwise manner is said to be veering.

Warm front. The boundary between the cold air in front of a depression and the warm sector.

Warm sector. That part of a depression which is characterised by its region of relatively warm air on its equatorial side.

Wedge. The pattern of wedge-shaped isobars which are sometimes associated with an area of high pressure.

METEOROLOGICAL OFFICE SERVICES

Weather Bulletins and Gale Warnings

Introduction.

The Meteorological Office provides weather information for vessels operating in the North Sea, the English Channel, the Irish Sea and the North Atlantic seaboard. Regular weather bulletins are issued by radiotelephony and radio telegraphy from Post Office coastal radio stations, and by radio-telephony from BBC stations. Gale warnings are issued as necessary from each of these channels, and facilities are also available for the supply of special forecasts on request.

Gale Warnings.

Gale warnings are issued when mean wind speeds of at least force 8 or gusts reaching 43 knots are expected. The term 'severe gale' implies mean winds of at least force 9 or gusts reaching 52 knots. The term 'storm' implies a mean wind of at least force 10 or gusts reaching at least 60 knots. The term imminent implies within 6 hours of the time of issue; 'soon' implies between 6 and 12 hours: 'later' implies more than 12 hours. These warnings are issued as follows:

(a) **By W/T and R/T from Post Office and Irish Coastal Radio Stations.**

Gale warnings are broadcast by W/T and R/T from coastal radio stations appropriate to the area within which the gale is expected. These stations and areas are listed in the information which follows and the sea areas are shown on the accompanying map.

R/T transmissions are broadcast at the end of the next silence period (from 00 to 03 and from 30 to 33 minutes past each hour) after receipt and also at the next of the following times: 0303, 0903, 1503 and 2103 GMT. The procedure is as follows: On 2182 kHz: the R/T safety signal SECURITE repeated three times, followed by a request for vessels to transfer to the station's working frequency. On the station's working frequency: SECURITE repeated three times, followed by the gale warning. The warning is broadcast first at conversation speed and then repeated at dictation speed.

The date and time of origin are given in each message, of which the following is an example:

'Gale warning 17 June, 0940 GMT. Dover, Wight, Portland, south-westerly gale force 8 imminent.'

(b) **By the BBC.**

Gale warnings are broadcast on BBC radio 2 (200 kHz 1500m) as soon as possible after receipt and are repeated at the following half hour, e.g. a warning received at 1550 will be broadcast as soon as possible and will be repeated at 16.30. In addition gale warnings in force are included within weather bulletins broadcast by this station.

(c) **By visual means.**

See page 108.

Weather bulletins for Shipping – Post Office and Irish Coast Stations.

(a) **BBC radio 2.**

See page 109.

(b) **BBC Radio 4**

See page 110.

(c) **R/T**

See page 111.

Special Forecasts for Shipping on Request.

All forecasts provided under the services which follow are issued by the Central Forecast Office, Bracknell, Berks. Arrangements for obtaining local forecasts are listed elsewhere.

Weather forecasts for any specified period up to 24 hours from the time of issue, accompanied when requested by an outlook for a further 24 hours, may be obtained from the Meteorological Office at any time of the day or night. This service relates not only to the designated coastal forecast areas but also the North Atlantic Ocean between 35°N and 65°N westward to the meridian of 40°W.

The information required may be obtained direct from the Central Forecast Office, Bracknell, by R/T link. The telephone number is Bracknell 20242, extension 2058.

(a) **Forecast issued on request.**

Procedure for yachts at sea.

Normal R/T link call charges are made for weather information obtained direct by R/T.

Procedure for requests originated ashore.

Telephone to the Meteorological Office (Bracknell 20242, extension 2058) or send a prepaid telegram addressed to Metbrack London Telex (Telex 84160), (allowing 20 words for reply, excluding address) requesting forecast.

No charge is made for the latest available forecast providing any telegram is prepaid to allow a reply of 20 words, excluding the address.

(b) **Forecasts required at a later time or date after receipt of the request.**

If a forecast is required to cover a stated occasion, or period in the future, or if the forecast is to be kept under review and subsequent amendments issued, write to the Director General, Meteorological Office, Met. 0.2a, London Road, Bracknell, Berks. RG12 2SZ. Give full details of the service required and the precise conditions necessary for an amendment to be issued, enclosing the appropriate fee, or confirming acceptance of the charge, and stating the address to which the account should be forwarded.

The charge for this service (at the time of going to press) is £1.50 per forecast and £1.00 per amendment message. Cheques should be crossed and made payable to the 'Met. Office H.Q. Public A/C'.

Reports of present weather.

See page 112.

Local weather forecasts.

Mariners and others who have a professional interest can obtain local weather forecasts from the forecast centre nearest to his port, free of charge.

The address and telephone number of the forecast centres nearest to the main ports in Great Britain are given on page 114. Enquirers by telephone should ask for 'Forecast Office'.

Port Meteorological Officers and Merchant Navy Agents.

The helpfulness of these officers to yachtsmen should not be underestimated, although their services are perhaps strictly intended for the benefit of shipmasters and other interested parties. They will invariably provide yachtsmen with meteorological advice on request. In addition they will give barometer checks. It must be remembered that aneroid barometers develop errors over a period, sometimes quite large, and their value is considerably lessened when this occurs. For the price of a telephone call to one of these officers, the yachtsman may obtain a correct barometer reading. Adjustment to an aneroid barometer is simply a matter of turning an adjustment screw on its reverse side. It must, of course, be borne in mind that this service has value only if the aneroid barometer for which a check is required is at sea level and within, say three or four miles of the meteorological office from which a check is requested. Full details of how these officers and agents can be contacted are printed on page 114.

Correction of ships barometers.

In addition to those authorities listed on p.114, the offices on p.115 have tested mercurial barometers, and readings for comparison will be given by the appropriate authority on request. The foregoing remarks relating to the correction of aneroid barometers should be read before application is made.

SHIPPING WEATHER FORECAST AREAS

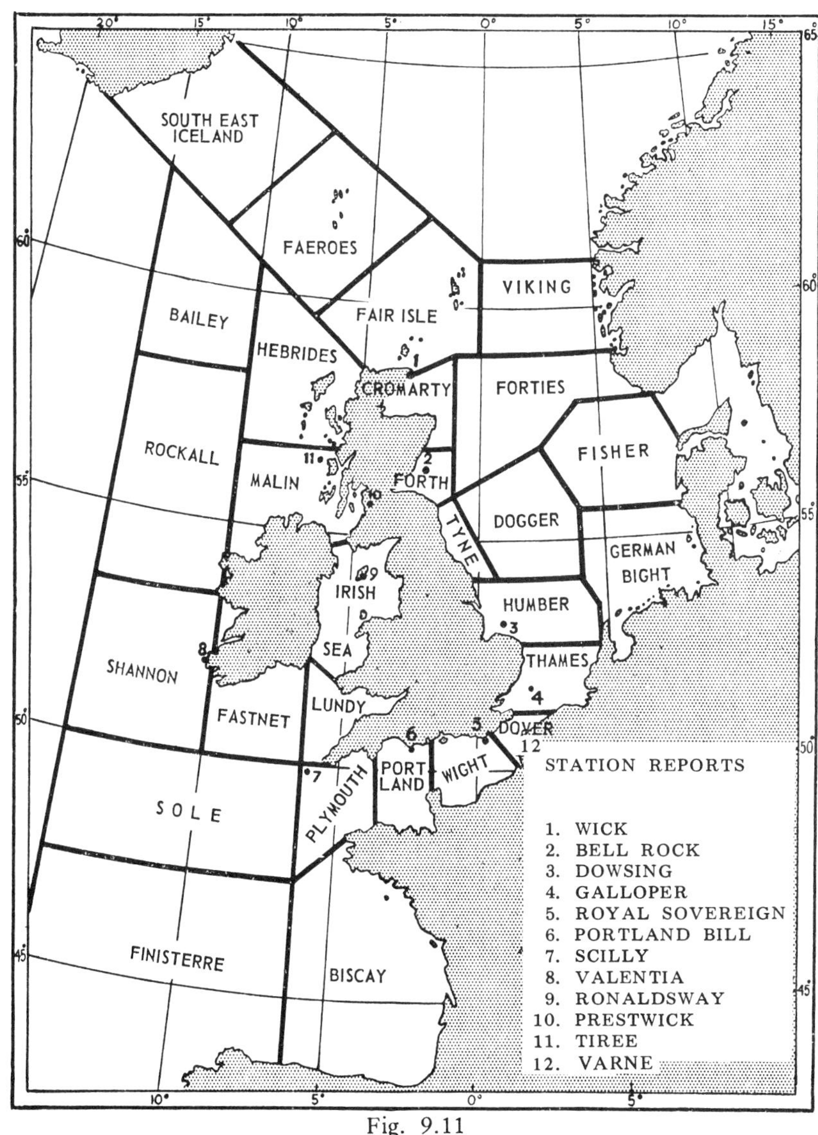

Fig. 9.11

BEAUFORT SCALE OF WIND FORCE

fort le ber	Mean Wind Speed in knots	Limits of Wind Speed in knots	Descriptive Terms	Sea Criterion	Probable Height of Waves in metres*	Probable Maximum Height of Waves in metres*
	Measured at a height of 33 feet above sea level					
	00	Less than 1	Calm	Sea like a mirror.	—	—
	02	1–3	Light air	Ripples with the appearance of scales are formed but without foam crests.	0·1	0·1
	05	4–6	Light breeze	Small wavelets, still short but more pronounced, crests have a glassy appearance and do not break.	0·2	0·3
	09	7–10	Gentle breeze	Large wavelets. Crests begin to break. Foam of glassy appearance. Perhaps scattered white horses.	0·6	1·0
	13	11–16	Moderate breeze	Small waves, becoming longer; fairly frequent white horses.	1·0	1·5
	19	17–21	Fresh breeze	Moderate waves, taking a more pronounced long form; many white horses are formed. (Chance of some spray.)	2·0	2·5
	24	22–27	Strong breeze	Large waves begin to form: the white foam crests are more extensive everywhere. (Probably some spray.)	3·0	4·0
	30	28–33	Near gale	Sea heaps up and white foam from breaking waves begins to be blown in streaks along the direction of the wind.	4·0	5·5
	37	34–40	Gale	Moderately high waves of greater length; edges of crests begin to break into spindrift. The foam is blown in well-marked streaks along the direction of the wind.	5·5	7·5
	44	41–47	Strong gale	High waves. Dense streaks of foam along the direction of the wind. Crests of waves begin to topple, tumble and roll over. Spray may affect visibility.	7·0	10·0
)	52	48–55	Storm	Very high waves with long overhanging crests. The resulting foam in great patches is blown in dense white streaks along the direction of the wind. On the whole the surface of the sea takes a white appearance. The tumbling of the sea becomes heavy and shocklike. Visibility affected.	9·0	12·5
	60	56–63	Violent storm	Exceptionally high waves. (Small and medium-sized ships might be for a time lost to view behind the waves.) The sea is completely covered with long white patches of foam lying along the direction of the wind. Everywhere the edges of the wave crests are blown into froth. Visibility affected.	11·5	16·0
2	—	64 and over	Hurricane	The air is filled with foam and spray. Sea completely white with driving spray; visibility very seriously affected.	14 or over	—

hese columns are added as a guide to show roughly what may be expected in the open sea, remote from land. In enclosed waters, or when near vith an off-shore wind, wave heights will be smaller and the waves steeper.

s.—(1) It must be realised that it will be difficult at night to estimate wind force by the sea criterion.

(2) The lag effect between the wind getting up and the sea increasing should be borne in mind.

(3) Fetch, depth, swell, heavy rain and tide effects should be considered when estimating the wind force from the appearance of the sea.

VISUAL GALE WARNINGS

Gale warnings are sent immediately to Naval and RAF establishments and to coastguard stations and other places where visual signals (cones or lights) are exhibited. The Admiralty publishes details in the appropriate Sailing Directions.

The display of a visual gale warning signal indicates that a gale is expected within 12 hours, or is already in progress, in the coastal sea area on the landward boundary of which the station flying the cone is situated. Thus a cone hoisted at Hartland would indicate a gale warning in operation for the sea area Lundy. (In this context the term "gale" refers to a mean wind of force 8 or above, or a wind gusting to at least 43 knots.)

The cone signal will be lowered when the wind is below gale force, if a renewal of gale-force winds is not expected within 6 hours. Thus, the cone signal is left flying during a temporary abatement of a gale if a renewal is expected.

The North Cone, a cone point upwards (by night, a triangle of lights apex up), is hoisted for gales from any point north of the east-west line. The South Cone, a cone point downwards (by night, a triangle of lights apex down) is hoisted for gales from any point south of the east-west line. When the direction of the gale is expected to change from the northern side to the southern side of the east-west line, the north cone is lowered and the south cone hoisted. Conversely, when the direction of the gale is expected to change from the southern to the northern side of the east-west line, the cone is changed accordingly.

Night signals are displayed only at Southend, Fairlight, Brighton, Polruan, Arbroath, Rame Head (white lights); Workington (red lights); Newhaven (one red, one white light); Portland Naval Base (main signal office), and Falmouth.

Information given by these cone signals is to be regarded only as supplementary to the more detailed weather bulletins for shipping which are regularly broadcast from BBC and Post Office transmitters.

WEATHER BULLETINS FOR SHIPPING

(a) BBC RADIO 2

Weather bulletins for shipping, originated by the Meteorological Office, are broadcast on BBC Radio at the times shown below:

Monday to Saturday:	0033; 0633; 1355; 1755.
Sunday:	0033; 0733; 1155; 1755.

Contents of broadcasts

The broadcasts will include the following items which are broadcast in the order shown:

(i) A statement of the gale warnings in force at the time of issue of the forecasts.

(ii) A general synopsis giving the situation in so far as it affects the area within the next 24 hours, with information as to expected changes within that period.

(iii) Forecasts for the next 24 hours for each coastal sea area, giving wind speed and direction, weather and visibility. The areas will be given in a fixed order (see below). When appropriate, contiguous sea areas may be grouped together.

(iv) The latest reports from a selection of the following stations will be broadcast in this order, the number of stations depending on the time available: Bell Rock Lighthouse, *Dowsing, Galloper* and *Varne* light-vessels, Royal Sovereign Light Tower Portland Bill, Scilly/St. Mary's, Valentia, Ronaldsway, Sule Skerry and Tiree. The elements given will be wind direction (compass points) and speed (Beaufort force), present weather (including "past hour" weather), visibility, and, if available, sea-level pressure and tendency in qualitative terms.

Order of broadcast of areas

Forecasts for coastal sea areas are normally broadcast in the following order:

Viking, Forties, Cromarty, Forth, Tyne, Dogger, Fisher, German Bight, Humber, Thames, Dover, Wight, Portland, Plymouth, Biscay, Finisterre, Sole, Lundy, Fastnet, Irish Sea, Shannon, Rockall, Malin, Hebrides, Bailey, Fair Isle, Faeroes, South-east Iceland.

(b) BBC RADIO 4

Forecasts for inshore waters (up to 12 miles offshore) of England and Wales "until 1800 tomorrow" are broadcast at the end of the London (908, 1484 kHz, 330 m, 202 m), Midland (1088 kHz, 276 m), South and West (1052, 1457 kHz, 285 m, 206 m), Welsh (881 kHz, 341 m) and North (692, 1151 kHz, 434 m, 261 m) BBC Radio 4 programmes at approx. 2345 BST. The forecast of wind, weather and visibility is followed by the 2200 reports of wind direction (compass points) and speed (Beaufort force), present weather, visibility and, if available, sea-level pressure and tendency in qualitative terms from the following stations: Acklington (nr. Newcastle), Gorleston (nr. Yarmouth), Manston (nr. Ramsgate), Portland Bill, Scilly/St. Mary's, Mumbles (nr. Swansea), Aberporth (Cardigan Bay) and Ronaldsway (Isle of Man).

At the end of the Northern Ireland Radio 4 programme (1340 kHz, 224 m) a similar forecast for Northern Ireland inshore waters is given with 2200 reports from Kilkeel (Co. Down), Killough (Co. Down), Malin Head, Machrihanish (Kintyre), Ronaldsway (Isle of Man), Valley (nr. Holyhead) and Orlock Head (nr. Bangor, Northern Ireland).

The forecast for Scottish inshore waters is given in the Scottish Radio 4 programme (809 kHz, 371 m) at approx. 2307 BST on Monday to Friday, 2321 on Saturdays and 2315 on Sundays. Reports are given from the following stations: Machrihanish (Kintyre), Tiree, Stornoway, Wick, Aberdeen (Dyce) and Leuchars.

The forecasts for coastal waters are also broadcast on Radio 4 (VHF); details of frequencies are published in the *Radio Times*.

Post Office and Irish Coastal Radio Stations which broadcast Weather Information

Table 2.—R/T Transmissions

These stations also give weather information on request

Name of station	Position	Working frequency kHz	Working frequency m	Times of weather broad-cast (GMT)	Weather forecast and gale warning areas	Traffic list calling times (GMT)
Wick	58° 26′ N 03 06′ W	1827	164·3	0803 2003	S.E. Iceland, Faeroes, Hebrides, Fair Isle, Viking, Cromarty	0503, 0703, then as (*a*) below
Stonehaven	56 57′ N 02 13′ W	1856	161·6	0833 2033	Forth, Cromarty Forties, Fisher	0133, 0533, 0733 then as (*b*) below
Cullercoats	55 02′ N 01 26′ W	2719	110·3	0803 2003	Tyne, Dogger, Fisher	0303, 0703, then as (*a*) below
Humber	53° 20′ N 00° 17′ E	1869	160·5	0833 2033	Humber, German Bight	0333, 0733, then as (*b*) below
North Fore-land	51° 22′ N 01° 25′ E	1848	162·4	0803 2003	Thames, Dover, Wight	0103, 0503, then as (*a*) below
Niton	50° 35′ N 01° 17′ W	1834	163·6	0833 2033	Portland, Wight	0133, 0533, then as (*b*) below
Land's End	50° 07′ N 05° 40′ W	1841	163·0	0803 2003	Lundy, Sole, Plymouth, Biscay, Finisterre	0303, 0703, then as (*a*) below
Ilfracombe	51° 11′ N 04 07′ W	2670	112·4	0833 2033	Lundy, Fastnet	0333, 0733, then as (*b*) below
Portpatrick	54° 51′ N 05° 07′ W	1883	159·3	0833 2033	Irish Sea, Malin	0133, 0533, then as (*b*) below
Oban	56 28′ N 05 23′ W	2740	109·5	0803 2003	Malin, Hebrides, Bailey, Rockall	0303, 0703, then as (*a*) below
Valentia	51° 56′ N 10 21′ W	1827	164·3	0833 2033	Shannon, Fastnet	0333, 0733, then as (*b*) below

(*a*) 0903, 1103, 1303, 1503, 1703, 1903, 2103, 2303, GMT
(*b*) 0933, 1133, 1333, 1533, 1733, 1933, 2133, 2333, GMT

WEATHER BULLETINS FOR SHIPPING

Reports of Present Weather

Mariners requiring reports of actual weather conditions prevailing at specified places around the coast of the British Isles may obtain such reports by telephone from any of the stations in the following list. (Such reports only apply to present weather in the immediate locality of each station and do not include forecasts nor information concerning other areas.)

The various types of stations are distinguished as follows:

Meteorological Office ... ... Met.O.
Naval Meteorological Service ... ... M.O.S. (N)
Coastguard Stations ... ... C.G.
Lighthouses ... ... L.H.
Signal Station ... ... S.S.
Harbour Master's Office ... ... H.M.O.

See over for list of Coastal Stations.

Reports of Present Weather (Cont.)

Coastal Stations from which observations of present weather may be obtained

Name of Station	*Telephone No.*	*Type of Station*
Scilly/St. Mary's	Scillonia 651	C.G.
Lizard	Lizard 444	C.G.
Mount Batten (Plymouth)	Plymouth 42534	Met.O.
Berry Head (Brixham)	Brixham 2156	C.G.
Beer	Seaton 14	C.G.
Portland Bill	Potland 3100	C.G.
Calshot	Fawley 484	S.S.
St. Catherine's Point	Niton 284	L.H.
Thorney Island	Emsworth 2355	Met.O.
Shoreham-by-Sea	Shoreham-by-Sea 2226	C.G.
Newhaven	Newhaven 131	L.H.
Eastbourne	Eastbourne 20634	C.G.
Fairlight (Hastings)	Pett 3171	C.G.
Dungeness	Lydd 236	L.H.
Folkestone	Folkestone 54230	C.G.
Dover St.	St. Margarets Bay 2515	C.G.
Sheerness	Sheerness 3025	S.S.
Shoeburyness	Shoeburyness 2271	Met.O.
Walton-on-Naze	Frinton-on-Sea 5518	C.G.
Aldeburgh	Aldeburgh 2779	C.G.
Gorleston	Gt. Yarmouth 63444	C.G.
Spurn Point	Spurn Point 283	C.G.
Flamborough Head	Flamborough 203	C.G.
Whitby	Whitby 2107	C.G.
Tynemouth	North Shields 72691	C.G.
Seahouses	Seahouses 274	C.G.
St. Abbs Head	Coldingham 287	L.H.
Usan (Montrose)	Montrose 1	C.G.
Fraserburgh	Fraserburgh 3374	C.G.
Lossiemouth	Lossiemouth 2121	Met.O.
Kinloss (Moray Firth)	Forres 2161 Ext.116	Met.O.
Tarbatness (moray Firth)	Portmahomack 210	L.H.
Wick	Wick 2215	Met.O.
Lerwick	Lerwick 239	Met.O.
Kirkwall (Orkneys)	Kirkwall 2421	Met.O.
Cape Wrath	Scourie 267	L.H.
Stornoway	Stornoway 2256 (Night: 2282)	Met.O.
Rudh Re (Ross and Cromarty)	Gairloch 2481	L.H.
Benbecula (Hebrides)	Benbecula 351	Met.O.
Ardnamurchan (Argyll)	Kilchoan 210	L.H.
Tiree	Scarinish 41	Met.O.
Rhuvaal (Islay)	Port Askaig 202	L.H.
Kildonan (Isle of Arran)	Kildonan 211	C.G.
Ardrossan	Ardrossan 3972	H.M.O.
Prestwick (Firth of Clyde)	Prestwick 78475	Met.O.
Corsewall Point	Kirkcolm 220	L.H.
Portpatrick	Portpatrick 209	C.G.
Mull of Galloway	Drummore 211	L.H.
Carlisle	Carlisle 23422 Ext.440	Met.O.
St. Bee's Head	Whitehaven 2635	L.H.
Point of Ayre	Kirkandreas 238	L.H.
Ronaldsway (Isle of Man)	Castletown 3311 (Night: 3313)	
Ballycastle	Ballycastle 226	C.G.
Bangor (Co. Down)	Groomsport 284	C.G.
Killough	Ardglass 203	C.G.
Kilkeel	Kilkeel 232	C.G.
Fleetwood	Fleetwood 3780	C.G.
Blackpool	Blackpool 43061 (Night: 43063)	Met.O.
Formby	Formby 72903	C.G.
Rhyl	Rhyl 3284	C.G.
Valley (Anglesey)	Holyhead 2288	Met.O.
Porthdynllaen (Caernarvon Bay)	Nevin 204	C.G.
Aberporth (Cardigan Bay)	Aberporth 205/208	Met.O.
Milford Haven	Milford Haven 2343	H.M.O.
Tenby (Monkston Point)	Saundersfoot 2722	C.G.
Mumbles	Swansea 66534	C.G.
Ilfracombe	Ilfracombe 2117	C.G.
Hartland	Hartland 235	C.G.

SPECIAL FORECASTS FOR PORT AREAS

AREA	FORECASTING CENTRE	TELEPHONE NO.
N.E. Scotland	Kirkwall Airport, Orkney Aberdeen Airport Kinloss, Morayshire	Kirkwall 2421 Dyce 2334 Forres 2161
E. Scotland	Pitreavie, nr. Dunfermline	Inverkeithing 2566
N.E. England	Newcastle Weather Centre	Newcastle-upon-Tyne 26453
E. England	Manby, Lincs.	Louth 2145
S.E. England	London Weather Centre	01-836 4311
S. England	Southampton Weather Centre	Southampton 28844
S.W. England	Plymouth	Plymouth 42534
W. England S. Wales	Gloucester	Gloucester 23122
N. Wales	Valley, Anglesey Manchester Weather Centre	Holyhead 2288 061-832 6701
N.W. England	Liverpool Airport Manchester Weather Centre Preston, Lancs.	051-427 4666 061-832 6701 Preston 52628
W. Scotland	Glasgow Weather Centre	041-248 3451
N. Ireland	Belfast (Aldergrove) Airport	Crumlin 339

Port Meteorological Officers and Merchant Navy Agents

Meteorological advice,* corrections to ship's barometers, etc., will be readily supplied by the Port Meteorological Officers or Merchant Navy Agent listed below:

Liverpool	Lieutenant-Commander E. R. Pullan, R.D., R.N.R., Port Meteorological Officer, Room 709, Royal Liver Building, Liverpool L3 1HN. (Telephone: 051-236 6565.)
London	Mr. J. C. Matheson, Master Mariner, Port Meteorological Officer, Movement Control Building, South Side, Victoria Dock, London, E16 1AS. (Telephone: 01-476 3931.)
Bristol Channel (Cardiff)	Mr. D. J. F. Southen, Master Mariner, Port Meteorological Officer, 2 Bute Crescent, Cardiff CF1 6AN. (Telephone: Cardiff 21423.)
Humber (Hull)	Mr. W. G. Cullen, Master Mariner, Port Meteorological Officer, c/o Principal Officer, Dept. of Trade and Industry, Trinity House Yard, Hull HU1 2LN. (Telephone: Hull 36813, Ext. 27.)
Clyde (Glasgow) ...	Mr. H. M. Keenan, Master Mariner, Port Meteorological Officer, 118 Waterloo Street, Glasgow, G2 7DN. (Telephone: 041-248 4379.)
Forth (Leith)	All enquiries to Mr. Keenan above.
Tyne (Newcastle) ...	Captain C. J. D. Sutherland, Merchant Navy Agent, c/o F. B. West & Co., "D" Floor, Milburn House, Newcastle upon Tyne NE1 3DE. (Telephone: Newcastle 23203.)
Southampton	Capt. D. R. McWhan, Port Meteorological Officer, Southampton Weather Centre, 160 High Street below Bar, Southampton SO1 0BT. (Telephone: Southampton 20632 or 28844.)

* Statistical and other enquiries should be addressed to The Director-General, Meteorological Office (Met.O.1a), Eastern Road, Bracknell, Berkshire RG12 2UR (Telephone: Bracknell 20242, extension 2335).

KEY ABBREVIATIONS
METEOROLOGY

OFFICES HAVING TESTED MERCURIAL BAROMETERS

A.D. & Co.	Messrs. Arthur Duthie & Co., Ltd.
B.M.	Berthing-master.
B.T.	Board of Trade.
C.G.	H.M. Coastguard.
C.H.	Custom House.
D.M.	Dock-master.
H.	Havenmaster.
H.M.	Harbour-master.
I.F.	Inspector of Fisheries.
M.M.O.	Marine Manager's Office.
P.I.S.	Port Information Service.
T.N.S.	Thames Navigation Service (Port Information Centre): barometer comparisons can be obtained by V.H.F. R/T.
W.S.	Wharf Superintendent.

Name of Station	*Type of Station*	*Name of Station*	*Type of Station*
Isle of Grain	W.S.	Preston	H.M.
Gravesend	T.N.S.	Formby	C.G.
London (Royal Albert Docks)	B.T.	Eastham	H.M.
Tilbury	B.T.	Liverpool	H.M.
Grimsby...	I.F.	Manchester... ...	H.M.
Hull	P.I.S.	Holyhead	H.M.
Bridlington	H.M.	Milford Haven (Angle Bay Terminal) ...	B.M.
Grangemouth	W.S.	Milford Haven (Esso Marine Terminal)	M.M.O.
Aberdeen	H.M.	Milford Haven ...	H.M.
Oban (Railway Pier) ...	A.D. & Co.	Swansea	D.M.
Finnart, Loch Long ...	H.M.	Cardiff	C.H.
Glasgow (Meadowside Quay)...	D.M.	Newport	D.M.
Ardrossan	H.M.	Avonmouth ...	H.
Heysham	H.M.	Fawley (Esso Marine Terminal) ...	M.M.O.
Fleetwood	H.M. and I.F.		

TABLE FOR CONVERTING BAROMETRIC READINGS IN INCHES INTO MILLIMETRES

Inches	·00	·01	·02	·03	·04	·05	·06	·07	·08	·09
	Millimetres									
27·0	685·8	686·0	686·3	686·6	686·8	687·1	687·3	687·6	687·8	688·1
·1	688·3	688·6	688·8	689·1	689·3	689 6	689·9	690·1	690·4	690·6
·2	690·9	691·1	691·4	691·6	691·9	692·1	692·4	692·7	692·9	693·2
·3	693·4	693·7	693·9	694·2	694·4	694·7	694·9	695·2	695·4	695·7
·4	696·0	696·2	696·5	696·7	697·0	697·2	697·5	697·7	697·9	698·2
·5	698·5	698·7	699·0	699·3	699·5	699·8	700·1	700·3	700·5	700·8
·6	701·0	701·3	701·5	701·8	702·0	702·3	702·6	702·8	703·1	703·3
·7	703·6	703·8	704·1	704·3	704·6	704·8	705·1	705·4	705·6	705·9
·8	706·1	706·4	706·6	706·9	707·1	707·4	707·6	707·9	708·1	708·4
·9	708·7	708·9	709·2	709·4	709·7	709·9	710·2	710·4	710·7	710·9
28·0	711·2	711·4	711·7	712·0	712·2	712·5	712·7	713·0	713·2	713·5
·1	713·7	714·0	714·2	714·5	714·7	715·0	715·3	715·5	715·8	716·0
·2	716·3	716·5	716·8	717·1	717·3	717·5	717·8	718·0	718·3	718·6
·3	718·8	719·1	719·3	719·6	719·8	720·1	720·3	720·6	720·8	721·1
·4	721·4	721·6	721·9	722·1	722·4	722·6	722·9	723·1	723·4	723·6
·5	723·9	724·1	724·4	724·7	724·9	725·2	725·4	725·7	725·9	726·2
·6	726·4	726·7	726·9	727·2	727·4	727·7	728·0	728·2	728·5	728·7
·7	729·0	729·2	729·5	729·7	729·9	730·2	730·5	730·7	731·0	731·3
·8	731·5	731·8	732·0	732·3	732·5	732·8	733·0	733·3	733·5	733·8
·9	734·1	734·3	734·6	734·8	735·1	735·3	735·6	735·8	736·1	736·3
29·0	736·6	736·8	737·1	737·4	737·6	737·9	738·1	738·4	738·6	738·9
·1	739·1	739·4	739·6	739·9	740·1	740·4	740·7	740·9	741·2	741·4
·2	741·7	741·9	742·2	742·4	742·7	742·9	743·2	743·4	743·7	744·0
·3	744·2	744·5	744·7	745·0	745·2	745·5	745·7	745·9	746·2	746·5
·4	746·8	747·0	747·3	747·5	747·7	748·1	748·3	748·5	748·8	749·0
·5	749·3	749·5	749·8	750·1	750·3	750·6	750·8	751·1	751·3	751·6
·6	751·8	752·1	752·3	752·6	752·8	753·1	753·4	753·6	753·9	754·1
·7	754·4	754·6	754·8	755·1	755·4	755·6	755·9	756·1	756·4	756·7
·8	756·9	757·2	757·4	757·7	757·9	758·2	758·4	758·7	758·9	759·2
·9	759·5	759·7	760·0	760·2	760·5	760·7	761·0	761·2	761·5	761·7
30·0	762·0	762·2	762·5	762·8	763·0	763·3	763·5	763·8	764·0	764·3
·1	764·5	764·8	765·0	765·3	765·5	765·8	766·1	766·3	766·6	766·8
·2	767·1	767·3	767·6	767·8	768·1	768·3	768·6	768·8	769·1	769·4
·3	769·6	769·9	770·1	770·4	770·6	770·9	771·1	771·4	771·6	771·9
·4	772·2	772·4	772·7	772·9	773·2	773·4	773·7	773·9	774·2	774·4
·5	774·7	774·9	775·2	775·5	775·7	776·0	776·2	776·5	776·7	777·0
·6	777·2	777·5	777·7	778·0	778·2	778·5	778·8	779·0	779·3	779·5
·7	779·8	780·0	780·3	780·5	780·8	781·0	781·3	781·5	781·8	782·1
·8	782·3	782·6	782·8	783·1	783·3	783·6	783·8	784·1	784·3	784·6
·9	784·9	785·1	785·4	785·6	785·9	786·2	786·4	786·6	786·9	787·1
31·0	787·4	787·6	787·9	788·2	788·4	788·7	788·9	789·2	789·4	789·7
·1	789·9	790·2	790·4	790·7	790·9	791·2	791·5	791·7	792·0	792·2
·2	792·5	792·7	793·0	793·2	793·5	793·7	794·0	794·2	794·5	794·8
·3	795·1	795·3	795·5	795·8	796·0	796·3	796·5	796·8	797·0	797·3
·4	797·6	797·8	798·1	798·3	798·6	798·8	799·1	799·3	799·6	799·8

CHAPTER 10

Collision Regulations

The Regulations are statutorily imposed upon seamen of all nations and they are the instrument by which collision at sea can be avoided. Of course collisions often do occur, and no doubt they will continue to do so. There are two basic reasons for this.

1. Vessels not conforming to those practices and actions which are decreed by the Rules.
2. In certain special circumstances the Rules allow vessels to deviate from the required actions. Masters, or owners, having decided that these exceptional conditions exist, thereafter fail to manoeuvre their vessels in a wise manner.

The latter reason does not necessarily imply incompetence. Seamen are from time to time faced with peculiar, perhaps sudden, circumstances which are fraught with danger. The master of a vessel or the owner of a small pleasure craft may find himself in a situation which causes him to take specific actions which appear seamanlike at the time. Two vessels being involved, and collision occurring, subsequent hindsight will indicate whether one or both vessels were manoeuvred in an unseamanlike manner. If a large vessel is involved this belated wisdom may be provided by a court of law.

Although the precepts of the Rules appear relatively simple, the intelligent interpretation of them is not. Some of the Rules must be read in conjunction with others, yet none can be considered obscure. Drawn up by members of the legal profession, the pure meaning of each word used is absolute. Thus the use of the word 'may' gives the mariner an option: the words 'must' and 'shall' are mandatory.

The complete interpretation of the Rules is the subject of many books and it is interesting to note that, from time to time, a judge's ruling in an Admiralty court has determined how a certain section of the Rules must be interpreted. It will be appreciated that, in British Law, when such a ruling is made, it thereafter becomes a precedent. In interpreting the Rules, therefore, a mariner must be guided on occasion by a court ruling and not by the appropriate section of the Rules. It is fortunate that these cases are not usually a matter of concern for yachtsmen.

Occasionally the Rules are altered slightly to meet the gradual change in types of vessels and technological developments over the years. The last occasion when this occurred was in 1965 when, for the first time, guidance was included for the benefit of seamen navigating vessels fitted with radar.

Yachtsmen spend quite a lot of their time within the limits of one port or another. Invariably byelaws are in force for every port visited. Apart from the general guidance which one would expect to find in them, they often include rules of navigational conduct within a port and they may require vessels to carry extra identification lights and signals. Rarely do byelaws have the effect of negating any part of the collision regulations, yet yachtsmen would do well to familiarise themselves with those of a port which they frequent.

In 1972 the Inter-Governmental Maritime Consultative Organisation (IMCO) drew up new regulations for preventing collision at sea. They are to be brought into force in 1976, and are produced here. At first reading, they could well cause the old hand some dismay as the familiar format which existed for many decades has disappeared. However, when they are studied it will be realised that nothing of real consequence with which the experienced yachtsman is already familiar has been changed. In fact, presentation has been improved. In addition, clear guidelines are included for vessels fitted with radar, the conduct of small sailing vessels in the vicinity of merchant vessels has been given a little more emphasis, the manner in which all vessels should be manoeuvred in, and in the vicinity of, traffic lanes is spelled out clearly and previous 'court rulings' are now written into the Rules. Many other minor facets appear and all of them contribute towards safety at sea generally.

Perhaps above all, the new presentation is more comprehensible to the amateur. The amount of cross reference necessary, always baffling to the inexpert, has been reduced. It is fair to say that mere knowledge of the old Rules was, by implication, insufficient for the professional sailor. He had to study them, interpret them intelligently and ultimately subject himself to examination before he was considered competent to conduct any vessel upon the high seas. It is unrealistic to assume that the new Rules will materially change this aspect. Nevertheless, the writer gains the impression that the degree of application and interpretation necessary has now been reduced. He has little doubt that, in the future, many marine casualities will still be resolved through legal wrangles in Admiralty courts. The impression remains that the international marine lawyers who drew up new Rules have perhaps reduced the travails of their counterparts in courts.

Rule 1

Application

(a) These Rules shall apply to all vessels upon the high seas and in all waters connected therewith navigable by seagoing vessels.

(b) Nothing in these Rules shall interfere with the operation of special rules made by an appropriate authority for roadsteads, harbours, rivers, lakes or inland waterways connected with the high seas and navigable by seagoing vessels. Such special rules shall conform as closely as possible to these Rules.

(c) Nothing in these Rules shall interfere with the operation of any special rules made by the Government of any State with respect to additional station or signal lights or whistle signals for ships of war and vessels proceeding under convoy, or with respect to additional station or signal lights for fishing vessels engaged in fishing as a fleet. These additional station or signal lights or whistle signals shall, so far as possible, be such that they cannot be mistaken for any light or signal authorized elsewhere under these Rules.

(d) Traffic separation schemes may be adopted by the Organization for the purpose of these Rules.

(e) Whenever the Government concerned shall have determined that a vessel of special construction or purpose cannot comply fully with the provisions of any of these Rules with respect to the number, position, range or arc of visibility of lights or shapes, as well as to the disposition and characteristics of sound-signalling appliances, without interfering with the special function of the vessel, such vessel shall comply with such other provisions in regard to the number, position, range or arc of visibility of lights or shapes, as well as to the disposition and characteristics of sound-signalling appliances, as her Government shall have determined to be the closest possible compliance with the Rules in respect of that vessel.

Note:
The writer has always regarded the main content of sub-sections (c) and (e) as the licence by which sundry governments may justify extraordinary positions for navigation lights on aircraft carriers and self-propelled monstrosities. Apart from making a mental note that perhaps once in a lifetime he may encounter such a craft, the yachtsman may as well forget the contents of these sub-sections. He certainly is not going to encounter a convoy but he may, if he is unlucky, encounter a naval fleet on manoeuvres. In this event a degree of complacency is still permissable: a large number of highly competent watchkeepers, spurred to greater efficiency by some ruthless admiral, will nurse him to safety. Fishing fleets when encountered tend to be a law unto themselves and additional lights, give or take a few allowed by the Rules or otherwise, are no less unsettling to the yachtsman than the presence of a fishing fleet itself.

It should be noted that nations may declare separation zones for shipping off their coasts and, being established, all vessels must adhere to the contents of Rule 10.

Rule 2

Responsibility

(a) Nothing in these Rules shall exonerate any vessel, or the owner, master or crew thereof, from the consequences of any neglect to comply with these Rules or of the neglect of any precaution which may be required by the ordinary practice of seamen, or by the special circumstances of the case.

(b) In construing and complying with these Rules due regard shall be had to all dangers of navigation and collision and to any special circumstances, including the limitations of the vessels involved, which may make a departure from these Rules necessary to avoid immediate danger.

Note:
This Rule is one of the most important and it replaces word for word the combined contents of the old Rules 27 and 29.

Subsection (a) is an admonition to mariners, capable of very wide interpretation, which requires him to adopt the ordinary practice of seamen in all circumstances. Blind adherence to the Rules is not sufficient in itself and all seamen must so conduct their vessels that their actions will be judged correct by a competent, conscientious seaman.

The second sub-section is no less important and the reader's attention is drawn in particular to these words, "... including the limitations of the vessels involved ...". It is not just a dredger or an under-powered sludge vessel which has limitations. Amongst others, it includes almost every sailing yacht and many a motor-powered one. A yachtsman, well aware of the limitations of his craft, may decide to take evasive action long before an on-coming merchantman is in close proximity, even though other Rules may adjure him to take actions of a more premeditated nature. He cannot be adjudged wrong if to do otherwise might be to risk craft and life. A mariner can, therefore, depart from the Rules in order to avoid a situation which he assesses as one containing immediate danger, but he must be quite sure that special circumstances demand it before doing so.

Rule 3

General Definitions

For the purpose of these Rules, except where the context otherwise requires:

(a) The word "vessel" includes every description of water craft, including non-displacement craft and seaplanes, used or capable of being used as a means of transportation on water.

(b) The term "power-driven vessel" means any vessel propelled by machinery.

(c) The term "sailing vessel" means any vessel under sail provided that propelling machinery, if fitted, is not being used.

(d) The term "vessel engaged in fishing" means any vessel fishing with nets, lines, trawls or other fishing apparatus which restrict manoeuvrability, but does not include a vessel fishing with trolling lines or other fishing apparatus which do not restrict manoeuvrability.

(e) The word "seaplane" includes any aircraft designed to manoeuvre on the water.

(f) The term "vessel not under command" means a vessel which through some exceptional circumstance is unable to manoeuvre as required by these Rules and is therefore unable to keep out of the way of another vessel.

(g) The term "vessel restricted in her ability to manoeuvre" means a vessel which from the nature of her work is restricted in her ability to manoeuvre as required by these Rules and is therefore unable to keep out of the way of another vessel.

The following vessels shall be regarded as vessels restricted in their ability to manoeuvre:

(i) a vessel engaged in laying, servicing or picking up a navigation mark, submarine cable or pipeline;

(ii) a vessel engaged in dredging, surveying or underwater operations;

(iii) a vessel engaged in replenishment or transfering persons, provisions or cargo while underway;

(iv) a vessel engaged in the launching or recovery of aircraft;

(v) a vessel engaged in minesweeping operations;

(vi) a vessel engaged in a towing operation such as severely restricts the towing vessel and her tow in their ability to deviate from their course.

(h) The term "vessel constrained by her draught" means a power-driven vessel which because of her draught in relation to the available depth of water is severely restricted in her ability to deviate from the course she is following.

(i) The word "underway" means that a vessel is not at anchor, or made fast to the shore, or aground.

(j) The words "length" and "breadth" of a vessel mean her length overall and greatest breadth.

(k) Vessels shall be deemed to be in sight of one another only when one can be observed visually from the other.

(l) The term "restricted visibility" means any condition in which visibility is restricted by fog, mist, falling snow, heavy rainstorms, sandstorms or any other similar causes.

Note:

This Rule is so specific that little explanation is necessary here. Sub-section (f) uses the term "not under command". The expression is sometimes altered by seamen to "not under control", an expression which is perhaps more meaningful to the amateur. The state would exist when for example a vessel's engines have broken down, her steering gear has developed malfunction or, although the vessel is functioning normally, in every way, weather conditions make her unmanageable. A vessel towing may or may not be restricted in her ability to manoeuvre. If she is, then she must exhibit the additional lights described in Rule 27 (b). A precise definition of the circumstances in which she would be restricted is contained in (c) of that Rule.

Part B – Steering and Sailing Rules

Section I – conduct of vessels in any condition of visibility

Rule 4

Application

Rules in this Section apply in any condition of visibility.

Note:

Let not the full import of this ten-word Rule be lost to the reader. There are Rules which apply to vessels in sight of one another, another for vessels when they are not, but Rules 5 to 10 inclusive apply to all vessels in any condition of visibility when underway.

Rule 5

Look-out

Every vessel shall at all times maintain a proper look-out by sight and hearing as well as by all available means appropriate in the prevailing circumstances and conditions so as to make a full appraisal of the situation and of the risk of collision.

Note:

It is this Rule amongst others, which creates in the minds of yachtsmen grave misgivings. Time and again they can encounter merchant vessels obviously flouting its content. How many times have we heard a yachtsman say, "and not a soul was visible anywhere on deck or on the bridge."? There is literally nothing one can do to alter this too frequent state of affairs, apart from recognising the possibility when in the vicinity of merchant vessels.

Not so readily appreciated is the fact that a lookout must be maintained by hearing also. A pleasure craft chugging its way through fog often produces noise which renders a distant fog signal inaudible. To reduce engine noise – and therefore speed – is the implied dictum here but for sundry reasons it is not a popular course. Better perhaps is to stop engines at regular intervals, go forward and listen intently for two or three minutes.

Of course motor-driven merchant vessels have the same problems but, rather than reduce headway to a point when main engine noise is inaudible, one gains the impression that in most cases radar is used as a substitute for ears.

Rule 6

Safe Speed

Every vessel shall at all times proceed at a safe speed so that she can take proper and effective action to avoid collision and be stopped within a distance appropriate to the prevailing circumstances and conditions.

In determining a safe speed the following factors shall be among those taken into account:

(a) By all vessels:

(i) the state of visibility;

(ii) the traffic density including concentrations of fishing vessels or any other vessels;

(iii) the manoeuvrability of the vessel with special reference to stopping distance and turning ability in the prevailing conditions;

(iv) at night the presence of background light such as from shore lights or from back scatter of her own lights;

(v) the state of wind, sea and current, and the proximity of navigational hazards;

(vi) the draught in relation to the available depth of water.

(b) Additionally, by vessels with operational radar:

(i) the characteristics, efficiency and limitations of the radar equipment;

(ii) any constraints imposed by the radar range scale in use;

(iii) the effect on radar detection of the sea state, weather and other sources of interference;

(iv) the possibility that small vessels, ice and other floating objects may not be detected by radar at an adequate range;

(v) the number, location and movement of vessels detected by radar;

(vi) the more exact assessment of the visibility that may be possible when radar is used to determine the range of vessels or other objects in the vicinity.

Note:

In the previous Regulations vessels were adjured to "if necessary, slacken her speed or stop or reverse" in Rule 23 and "moderate speed" in Rule 16 was related only to conditions of restricted visibility. In this Rule all circumstances in which it would be hazardous to proceed at an excessive speed are wisely included. Perhaps sub-section (vi) will mystify the reader. Deep draught vessels with little water under their keels will "feel the ground". Suction, for the want of a more accurate word, will increase their draughts and so they will touch, or nearly touch, bottom and manoeuvrability will be affected.

All instances quoted in the Rule being more or less self-evident, a definition of "safe speed" in thick weather is best included for yachtsmen. It has been defined as that which will allow a vessel to stop within half the visibility range. That is to say that, given visibility of one mile, she should proceed at a speed which will allow her to cease all forward motion within half a mile. In wry theory – depending upon one's sense of humour – if two vessels met end on in these conditions, both would cease forward motion in half the visibility range and so no collision would occur. Perhaps their bows would gently kiss. In dense fog and without the assistance of radar vessels should maintain steerage way only, yet radar-deprived vessels frequently exceed it. "Prove it!", says the miscreant. He knows full well that the writer cannot.

Few indeed are the yachts fitted with radar, and a tiny number of these have the sophisticated radar sets which will materially assist a navigator in arriving at an accurate decision about the course and speed of an approaching vessel. The owner of a radar-fitted craft, whilst having the considerable advantage of obtaining prior warning of other vessels in the vicinity of fog, should never assume complacency.

He should read all that is available about proper interpretation of the intelligence with which his set provides him. And the recent history of marine casualties brought about only through ingenuous elucidation of what a plan position indicator fortells is reason in itself for doing so.

Rule 7

Risk of Collision

(a) Every vessel shall use all available means appropriate to the prevailing circumstances and conditions to determine if risk of collision exists. If there is any doubt such risk shall be deemed to exist.

(b) Proper use shall be made of radar equipment if fitted and operational, including long-range scanning to obtain early warning of risk of collision and radar plotting or equivalent systematic observation of deleted objects.

(c) Assumptions shall not be made on the basis of scanty information, especially scanty radar information.

(d) In determining if risk of collision exists the following considerations shall be among those taken into account.

(i) such risk shall be deemed to exist if the compass bearing of an approaching vessel does not appreciably change;

(ii) such risk may sometimes exist even when an appreciable bearing change is evident, particularly when approaching a very large vessel or a tow or when approaching a vessel at close range.

Note:

Particular attention is drawn to the last sentence in (a) which reads, "If there is any doubt such risk should be deemed to exist." Whilst in no way wishing to minimise the importance of the remaining content of this Rule, the writer suggests that for the yachtsman this excerpt has the greatest substance. Seldom can he carefully watch the compass bearing of an approaching vessel. Reality to him is an on-coming vessel, perhaps with an alert watchkeeper, perhaps not: perhaps with functional radar, perhaps not. She may be steaming at 15 knots or more. In stark reality offshore the yachtsman invariably bows politely to the merchantman, steps aside long before he might bring upon himself a closequarters situation and so allows the other vessel to continue her course whether by the Rules it is right for her to do so or not.

The vessels in Fig. 10.1 are on collision courses. It will be noted that the compass bearings between the vessels remain constant up to the point of collision. Any change of course or speed on the part of only one vessel in each case will destroy the conditions which will produce collision. Inevitably, any such change will cause the compass bearings between vessels to change and so it can be said that, provided the compass bearing appreciably changes, collision will not occur. Let the word "appreciably" be noted: it means a radical change in compass bearing, which must quicken as the range closes. It is not a change of a mere 3 or 4 degrees. Finally, (d) (ii) warns the mariner that the trailing end of a vessel of which he must keep clear might be considerably longer than her navigation lights indicate. See Fig. 10.1 on page 236.

Rule 8

Action to avoid Collision

(a) Any action taken to avoid collision shall, if the circumstances of the case admit, be positive, made in ample time and with due regard to the observance of good seamanship.

(b) Any alteration of course and/or speed to avoid collision shall, if the circumstances of the case admit, be large enough to be readily apparent to another vessel observing visually or by radar; a succession of small alterations of course and/or speed should be avoided.

(c) If there is sufficient sea room, alteration of course alone may be the most effective action to avoid a close-quarters situation provided that it is made in good time, is substantial and does not result in another close-quarters situation.

(d) Action taken to avoid collision with another vessel shall be such as to result in passing at a safe distance. The effectiveness of the action shall be carefully checked until the other vessel is finally past and clear.

(e) If necessary to avoid collision or allow more time to assess the situation, a vessel shall slacken her speed or take all way off by stopping or reversing her means of propulsion.

Note:

(a) uses the word "positve". It means that any alteration of course by one vessel which must avoid another should be bold and decisive, so that her action is clearly apparent to the other. It is plain bad seamanship to delay avoiding action unnecessarily and then to make a minimal alteration. Bad seamanship can cost lives. (b) appears to emphasive the content of the former one. (c) and (d) need no emphasis but reference to (e) must be made here. At least in merchantmen there is often reluctance to reduce speed in clear weather. Of course merchantment ply for profit and so reduced progress implies reduced profit. But what of the merchantman whose watchkeeping engineer is having a whiff of fresh air on the boat deck – and the bridge officer knows it? What of the vessel where antipathy exists between bridge and engineroom and this detestation is carried beyond all sensible bounds, even to the extent of an engineer ignoring the commands of the engineroom telegraph from the bridge? Fantasy? Not so. Fantastic to a yachtsman, certainly.

Rule 9

Narrow Channels

(a) A vessel proceeding along the course of a narrow channel or fairway shall keep as near to the outer limit of the channel or fairway which lies on her starboard side as is safe and practicable.

(b) A vessel of less than 20 metres in length or a sailing vessel shall not impede the passage of a vessel which can safely navigate only within a narrow channel or fairway.

(c) A vessel engaged in fishing shall not impede the passage of any other vessel navigating within a narrow channel or fairway.

(d) A vessel shall not cross a narrow channel or fairway if such crossing impedes the passage of a vessel which can safely navigate only within such channel or fairway. The latter vessel may use the sound signal prescribed in Rule 34(d) if in doubt as to the intention of the crossing vessel.

(e) (i) In a narrow channel or fairway when overtaking can take place only if the vessel to be overtaken has to take action to permit safe passing, the vessel intending to overtake shall indicate her intention by sounding the appropriate signal prescribed in Rule 34(c)(i). The vessel to be overtaken shall, if an agreement, sound the appropriate signal prescribed in Rule 34(c)(ii) and take steps to permit safe passing. If in doubt she may sound the signals prescribed in Rule 34(d).

(ii) This Rule does not relieve the overtaking vessel of her obligation under Rule 13.

(f) A vessel nearing a bend or an area of a narrow channel or fairway where other vessels may be obscured by an intervening obstruction shall navigate with particular alertness and caution and shall sound the appropriate signal prescribed in Rule 34(e).

(g) Any vessel shall, if the circumstances of the case admit avoid anchoring in a narrow channel.

Note:

Subsection (a) demands particular note. When will all yachtsmen instead of a small number obey this dictate in all cases, whether other traffic is present in a channel or not? To "drive on the right" in a narrow channel or fairway should be as natural to him as driving on the left is to him on the roads. He should hug the buoys, the piles, the beacons, the trotts which lie on his starboard side. Short-cuts should not be taken on corners, whether or not the channel is seen to be clear. In wide but busy channels which can create qualms even though the yachtsman holds over to starboard, it is often feasible with his relatively shallow draught, to proceed just outside the channel marks. This area is generally traffic-free and much easier on the nerves.

The word "impede" repeats itself in (b) and (c). It is a word capable of sundry interpretations. A yacht would certainly impede the progress of a large vessel if she held to the middle of the channel when the other vessel was coming up from astern. Indeed, almost any manoeuvre by a sailing craft across and along a channel used by shipping could logically be interpreted as impeding the progress of a large vessel if by so doing the yacht prevented her from making normal safe progress. This similarly applies to power-driven yachts in narrow channels and fairways: they too must hold well over to the starboard side of any channel and keep out of the way of all large vessels and yachts under sail only. The experienced and thoughtful owner of a power-driven yacht will recognise that his conduct could not be otherwise, if his desire is to adopt good seamanship. Whether (d) will ever receive anything more than lip service from large numbers of the yachting fraternity is open to doubt. One has only to watch the thoughtless, irresponsible antics of apparently competent yachtsmen who are crossing shipping channels of the Thames Estuary when large ships in these channels have right of way, or indeed when large, fast ferries must go about their rightful business in Southampton Water to realise that too many yachtsmen do not know what their conduct should be or, if they know, they do not particularly care. Ignorance is bliss to many who take to the water these days, to the horror of the professionals who must conduct their vessels up and down restrictive waterways. The writer can only propound that yachts, whether driven by sails or motors, must give way to, must not impede, must give every consideration to other vessels, be they coasters, tankers, common merchantmen, ferries or naval vessels of almost any size in narrow channels and fairways.

In conclusion, the writer must emphasise that although a channel may be broad to a yachtsman, it may be very narrow to a deep draft merchant vessel. Having entered such a channel she is usually "committed": she MUST traverse the channel. In many cases such vessels can neither stop nor alter course more than a few degrees, and any pilot will aver that it can sometimes be a harrowing undertaking. The yachtsman should ponder these facts. Inexperienced yachtsmen occasionally approach such vessels closely, merely to have a good look at them. They slide into a vessel's blind spots, and down her sides, to the discomfiture and sometimes horror of the pilot.

Rule 10

Traffic Separation Schemes

(a) This Rule applies to traffic separation schemes adopted by the Organization.

(b) A vessel using a traffic separation scheme shall:

(i) proceed in the appropriate traffic lane in the general direction of traffic flow for that lane;

(ii) so far as practicable keep clear of a traffic separation line or separation zone;

(iii) normally join or leave a traffic lane at the termination of the lane, but when joining or leaving from the side shall do so at as small an angle to the general direction of traffic flow as practicable.

(c) A vessel shall so far as practicable avoid crossing traffic lanes, but if obliged to do so shall cross as nearly as practicable at right angles to the general direction of traffic flow.

(d) Inshore traffic zones shall not normally be used by through traffic which can safely use the appropriate traffic lane within the adjacent traffic separation scheme.

(e) A vessel, other than a crossing vessel, shall not normally enter a separation zone or cross a separation line except:

(i) in cases of emergency to avoid immediate danger;

(ii) to engage in fishing within a separation zone.

(f) A vessel navigating in areas near the terminations of traffic separation schemes shall do so with particular caution.

(g) A vessel shall so far as practicable avoid anchoring in a traffic separation scheme or in areas near its terminations.

(h) A vessel not using a traffic separation scheme shall avoid it by as wide a margin as is practicable.

(i) A vessel engaged in fishing shall not impede the passage of any vessel following a traffic lane.

(j) A vessel of less than 20 metres in length or a sailing vessel shall not impede the safe passage of a power-driven vessel following a traffic lane.

Note:

It appears to the writer that this Rule when applied to sailing and motor yachts places channels produced by traffic separation zones in the same category as narrow channels and fairways in the approaches to ports. The yachtsman must not impede – that repetitive word – the passage of larger vessels using separation zones. It is, therefore, logical to assume that the writer's comments which relate to the conduct of small craft in narrow channels and fairways (Rule 9) have equal application in areas where traffic separation zones exist. Then how must a yachtsman conduct his craft in the Dover Strait almost all of which is a separation zone? The implication is that he must give way to all traffic proceeding through the Straits, whether he be crossing the shipping lanes or using them. Obviously it will be sensible to keep to one side or the other of the lanes if he is proceeding through the Straits on passage: firstly, this is wise because it will keep him clear of most through traffic; second, because he will have more freedom to manoeuvre and third, at least he retains some rights of way in the Straits area.

There is emphasis within the Rule upon caution which is to be exercised at the entries and exits to separation zones. This is because some vessels will fan out in sundry directions once clear of them, and so any mariner must be extremely watchful of the movements of other vessels in these areas.

Section II – Conduct of Vessels in Sight of one Another

Rule 11

Application

Rules in this Section apply to vessels in sight of one another.

Note:

To the amateur the message in this Rule is not readily evident. It says in effect that the sundry manoeuvres contained in Rules 12 to 18 inclusive, familiar to most yachtsmen as the means by which collision can be avoided, have no application in thick weather so long as the vessels involved cannot see each other. But as soon as they *can* see each other, even though the range may have closed to less than a few cables before sighting occurs, then Rules 12 to 18 immediately become operative.

Rule 12

Sailing Vessels

(a) When two sailing vessels are approaching one another, so as to involve risk of collision, one of them shall keep out of the way of the other as follows:

(i) when each has the wind on a different side, the vessel which has the wind on the port side shall keep out of the way of the other;

(ii) when both have the wind on the same side, the vessel which is to windward shall keep out of the way of the vessel which is to leeward?

(iii) if a vessel with the wind on the port side sees a vessel to windward and cannot determine with certainty whether the other vessel has the wind on the port or on the starboard side, she shall keep out of the way of the other.

(b) For the purposes of this Rule the windward side shall be deemed to be the side opposite to that on which the mainsail is carried or, in the case of a square-rigged vessel, the side opposite to that on which the largest fore-and-aft sail is carried.

Note:

It must be noted that Rule 12 does not direct a yachtsman to take a particular course of action if he is required to avoid another sailing vessel. Implicit in the Rule is that good seamanship must dictate how avoidance is achieved. In close quarters situations the content of Rule 2 might well apply. Fig. 10.2 (see page 236) indicates three potential collision situations and, according to this Rule, which vessel must give way to the other.

Some misgivings may be experienced when one encounters the sentence in (c) which reads, "... the windward side shall be deemed to be the side opposite to that on which the mainsail is carried ...". The illustration, 10.3 on page 236, should be considered:

Vessel A is running free with the wind right aft. Although in these circumstances her mainsail could be carried on either side, in this case it is being worn to port. By definition, vessel B which is close hauled on port must keep out of the way. If by chance or whim vessel A was carrying her mainsail on the starboard side, *she* would have to give way. It makes no allowance for the ill-mannered yachtsman who deliberately gibes to hold right of way. Some may regard this section of the Rule as less than satisfactory. However, a Rule must be made and this is considered the best. Perhaps the following comments will assist understanding. At night this situation will seldom if ever arise because the requirements of (a) (iii) become operative. Vessel B will see the green light of vessel A and, as she cannot assess on which side the latter is carrying her mainsail, she must keep out of the way.

Although earlier Rules had no doubt to consider the problems of square-riggers, collier-brigs and the like, modern Rules have to take into consideration that sailing vessels today generally have fore and aft rigs and are highly efficient sailing craft in comparison with the sail-propelled merchantmen of yesteryear. In a stiff breeze it is more difficult to manoeuvre a modern yacht running downwind then merely to lay her over on the other tack when beating to windward. There is in this Rule some conformity with racing

Rules, a feature which is considered desirable. Finally, any suggestion that in daylight an inconsiderate yachtsman would deliberately change over his mainsail from port to starboard when running free with the wind right aft has no validity. Apart from the risk of broaching in severe conditions by adopting such a tactic, the Rules deal with the actions of seamen and not of those who would irresponsibly plan to hold the right of way.

Rule 13

Overtaking

(a) Notwithstanding anything contained in the Rules of this Section any vessel overtaking any other shall keep out of the way of the vessel being overtaken.

(b) A vessel shall be deemed to be overtaking when coming up with another vessel from a direction more than 22.5 degrees abaft her beam, that is, in such a position with reference to the vessel she is overtaking, that at night she would be able to see only the sternlight of that vessel but neither of her sidelights.

(c) When a vessel is in any doubt as to whether she is overtaking another, she shall assume that this is the case and act accordingly.

(d) Any subsequent alteration of the bearing between the two vessels shall not make the overtaking vessel a crossing vessel within the meaning of these Rules or relieve her of the duty of keeping clear of the overtaken vessel until she is finally past and clear.

Note:

One must note that this Rule applies whether a vessel is under sail or power and, in the unlikely event of a sailing vessel overtaking a power-driven vessel, the sailing vessel would have to keep out of the way of the other. A vessel does not have to overtake another from more or less astern to be an overtaking vessel. Crossing the other vessel's course, if she approaches from any direction more than 2 points abaft the other's beam, the onus is upon her to keep out of the way. Finally, the overtaking vessel cannot barely overtake the other and then cut across her bows in a risky manoeuvre: Rule 13 applies until she is finally past and clear. See Fig 10.4 on page 236.

Rule 14

Head-on Situation

(a) When two power-driven vessels are meeting on reciprocal or nearly reciprocal courses so as to involve risk of collision each shall alter her course to starboard so that each shall pass on the port side of the other.

(b) Such a situation shall be deemed to exist when a vessel sees the other ahead or nearly ahead and by night she could see the masthead lights of the other in a line or nearly in a line and/or both sidelights and by day she observes the corresponding aspect of the other vessel.

(c) When a vessel is in any doubt as to whether such a situation exists she shall assume that it does exist and act accordingly. (See Fig. 10.5 on page 237).

Note:

Many yachtsmen will recognise this Rule as a condensation of the old Rule 18, "Two power-driven vessels meeting end on or nearly end on". The old Rule and this one have precisely the same meaning but perhaps those who drew up this new-look version considered the former one excessively verbose. (a) and (b) are lucid, definitive and need no explanation here but (c) is new and perhaps some elucidation is desirable. Owners of motor yachts should ponder the following: in the figure, power-driven vessels A and B are approaching one another and let us say that, at the moment of sighting, they are five miles apart. (See Fig. 10.6 on page 237).

It is obvious that vessel A, which is nearly ahead of vessel B, would pass clear if both vessels held their courses. Yet if vessel B assumes that Rule 14 is operative – which she might possibly do – and thereupon alters course to starboard, she will place herself across the bows of vessel A. Vessel A sighting vessel B fine on her starboard bow, may initially assume that she will safely pass across the bows of B and that no risk of collision exists. However, through vessel B altering course to starboard, as the case develops, she will present an unexpected aspect to Vessel A. She will continue to show her red port sidelight to vessel A, although the latter would expect vessel B's lights to change from red to a combination of red and green, and then to green only. Clearly, the safest action for vessel A to take, seeing an unchanging red port sidelight on her starboard bow, is for her to alter course to starboard and so pass under the stern of vessel B. And this is precisely what sub-section (c) directs her to do. The case quoted may appear complex but it is real and the reader will benefit through comprehension. But let him mark this well: the case would never have occurred if vessel B had not acted precipitately. Provided visibility allows, so giving one time to weigh up the situation, it is well to let a case develop and be sure that risks of collision exists.

Rule 15

Crossing Situation

When two power-driven vessels are crossing so as to involve risk of collision, the vessel which has the other on her own starboard side shall keep out of the way and shall, if the circumstances of the case admit, avoid crossing ahead of the other vessel.

Note:

Fig. 10.7 is intended to portray two vessels, A and B which, if they hold their courses as indicated by the hatched lines, will collide at position C. Vessel A has the other on her own starboard side and so she must keep out of the way. It is common practice for vessel A to alter course to starboard, thereby passing under the stern of vessel B, as illustrated. (See Fig. 10.7 on page 237).

When a vessel sights a crossing vessel on her port side and the possibility of collision is deemed to exist then she is required to keep her course and speed by Rule 17, because it is the other vessel which must take avoiding action. Occasionally there is insufficient searoom to enable the "keep-out-of-the-way" vessel to alter course to starboard in the manner described. There is no reason, when circumstances permit, why she should not alter course to port and "take a round turn out of her". That is to say, circling to port, turning right round and eventually returning to her original course, by which time the other vessel will in all probability have passed clear. Another alternative remains: it is to "slacken her speed or take all way off by stopping or reversing her means of propulsion", by Rule 8 (e) and allow the other vessel to pass ahead.

Rule 16

Action by Give-way Vessel

Every vessel which is directed to keep out of the way of another vessel shall, so far as possible, take early and substantial action to keep well clear.

Note:

This is an entirely new Rule. It was included in a different form, yet received less emphasis, in the old Rules. It is bad seamanship to so delay avoiding action that the other vessel is left in doubt whether such action will be taken. It is similarly bad seamanship not to take "substantial action to keep well clear". One must banish from one's mind what the racing fraternity sometimes do; ignore the antics of the tyro in his floating equivalent of a sports car, and just keep well clear. The Rule demands it: the writers adjure it: wisdom dictates it.

Rule 17

Action by Stand-on Vessel

(a) (i) Where by any of these Rules one of two vessels is to keep out of the way the other shall keep her course and speed.

(ii) The latter vessel may however take action to avoid collision by her manoeuvre alone, as soon as it becomes apparent to her that the vessel required to keep out of the way is not taking appropriate action in compliance with these Rules.

(b) When, from any cause, the vessel required to keep her course and speed finds herself so close that collision cannot be avoided by the action of the give-way vessel alone, she shall take such action as will best aid to avoid collision.

(c) A power-driven vessel which takes action in a crossing situation in accordance with sub-paragraph (a)(ii) of this Rule to avoid collision with another power-driven vessel shall, if the circumstances of the case admit, not alter course to port for a vessel on her own port side.

(d) This Rule does not relieve the give-way vessel of her obligation to keep out of the way.

Note:

Sub-section (a)(i) of this Rule is a highly important one and, at least by the amateur, it can be overlooked. When one of two vessels must keep out of the way, it places *equal duty* upon the other vessel to keep her course and speed.

(a)(ii) and (b) appear to say almost the same thing but careful reading of them both will reveal that this is not so. The former allows the "stand on" vessel to disobey the dictate (a)(i) at any range, as soon as it is decided that the other vessel is not going to keep out of the way according to the Rules. The latter directs the "stand on vessel" to take avoiding action if, at any time and in any circumstance, a dangerous close quarters situation with the other develops. The difference between these two sub-sections is perhaps best defined as one of range. "Heads, I win – tails, you lose',, says the mariner. Yes, in effect. In collision cases which are finally settled in court, rarely is the "innocent" vessel accorded no blame whatsoever.

Subsection (c) appears to the writer to be so obvious in terms of good seamanship that it does not merit inclusion in the Rules. His impression is obviously false. Marine experts, with the history of marine casualties before them, have clearly decided that it is essential to make it mandatory that a power-driven vessel shall, yet always with reservations, not alter course to port for a vessel on her own port side.

Rule 18

Responsibilities between Vessels

Except where Rules 9, 10 and 13 otherwise require:

(a) A power-driven vessel underway shall keep out of the way of:

(i) a vessel not under command;

(ii) a vessel restricted in her ability to manoeuvre;

(iii) a vessel engaged in fishing;

(iv) a sailing vessel.

(b) A sailing vessel underway shall keep out of the wayof:

(i) a vessel not under command;

(ii) a vessel restricted in her ability to manoeuvre;

(iii) a vessel engaged in fishing.

(c) A vessel engaged in fishing when underway shall, so far as possible, keep out of the way of:

(i) a vessel not under command;

(ii) a vessel restricted in her ability to manoeuvre.

(d) (i) Any vessel other than a vessel not under command or a vessel restricted in her ability to manoeuvre shall, if the circumstances of the case admit, avoid impeding the safe passage of a vessel constrained by her draught, exhibiting the signals in Rule 28.

(ii) A vessel constrained by her draught shall navigate with particular caution having full regard to her special condition.

(e) A seaplane on the water shall, in general, keep well clear of all vessels and avoid impeding their navigation. In circumstances, however, where risk of collision exists, she shall comply with the Rules of this Part.

Note:

In this day and age, with an abundance of large, fast merchant vessels slicing along and across our seaways, it is perhaps sub-section (a)(iv) of this Rule above any other within the Rules which requires elucidation. The statement is perfectly clear: it is the well known 'steam and sail' rule. Brave is the sailing yachtsman who, encountering a large, fast merchantman and with the possibility of collision with it existing, will stoically maintain his course and speed in the belief that the other will unquestionably take avoiding action. And this in daylight, clear weather and ideal weather conditions. The prudent yachtsman will from the outset consider the possibility that he may have to take avoiding action. He will not leave such action so late that he finds himself in a thoroughly alarming situation.

It is helpful if the off-shore yachtsman knows a little about conditions on the bridge of a merchant vessel. The watch-keeping officer of a well run vessel will keep a good lookout and, seeing a sailing yacht on a collision course with his vessel, he will unquestionably take appropriate avoiding action. But which are the well run vessels? A fairly high degree of reliance may be put upon the actions of the majority of coasting vessels, even though the man at the wheel may be the only person on the bridge at times. But what of the helmsman who dreams his trick away, subconsciously steering quite a good course? These are disturbing reflections. Not infrequently one encounters massive merchant vessels of various nationalities, automatic steering gear obviously engaged and not a soul in sight on the bridge or on the deck. 'So help me', mutters the yachtsman. And well he might.

However, logic must be applied to the vast majority of cases. It dictates that watchkeepers on merchant vessels navigating in home waters are fearful that they may run down a small craft. With the steady increase in recent years of small craft at sea, this fear has increased proportionately. A considerable part of their fear is in the knowledge that they may not see a small craft in sufficient time to take avoiding action. Large vessels are relatively sluggish on the helm and their watchkeepers *must* see a small craft in ample time to enable them to take avoiding action by adequately turning their vessels. Implicit in these remarks are two dictums: yachtsmen should avoid close quarters situations with merchant vessels when ever possible and, at night, they should ensure that their craft will be seen early. The latter one of these is generally the more difficult to apply.

Much has been written about 'blind spots' on merchant vessels. These are areas of sea close ahead of a vessel which, due to her design, are invisible to a watchkeeper on her bridge. Although it is probably true to say that in the majority of vessels blind spots, though present, are inconsequential, in some modern vessels they may extend to two miles and more on forward bearings. In most cases it may be said that if a yachtsman finds himself in a merchant vessel's blind spot, then he has approached that vessel too closely.

In sundry sea areas around our coasts, notably in the English Channel, the Dover Strait and the southern North Sea, traffic separation zones exist. The separation zones produce sea lanes and divide traffic proceeding in opposite directions at focal points of sea traffic. Admiralty charts clearly indicate these zones and the majority of vessels use them – because it is safer to do so – but they are not bound by law to do so. As Rule 10 indicates, in ordinary sea conditions the yachtsman has few if any 'rights' in traffic separation zones and so, if he must cross them, he must do so at or nearly at right angles, and with maximum despatch in the interests of his own safety if for no other reason.

When off-shore a yachtsman should keep his radar reflector hoisted at all times by day and by night, and the higher the better. It is normal practice for merchant vessels to use their radar sets continuously in the seaways surrounding these islands and the presence of a yacht using a radar reflector will be indicated on radar displays. It is well to reflect that the white sails of a yacht can, at long range, be confused with white wave crests and, at night, the relatively poor lights of a yacht may not be visible to a merchant vessel until she is a little too close for peace of mind.

The practice of yachtsmen who, in close quarters situations, illuminate their mainsails to indicate their presence to another vessel must be kept in perspective. At best it is a dim presence which is revealed. Too frequently this illumination of doubtful value is adopted at a moment of time which is rather too late for positive, calculated avoiding action to be taken by a larger vessel. Better by far is the early display of a white pyrotechnic light in these circumstances – although most seem reluctant to use costly flares for safety purposes. Certainly these people have their values mixed but, perhaps nearly as effective, is a powerful white light beamed at the bridge of an oncoming merchant vessel before a tight situation develops. Finally, the reader's attention is drawn to the author's remarks concerning Rule 2. The yachtsman can, and here it is suggested that he does, take evasive action as soon as he decides that a distant vessel may pass him dangerously closely. Such action, which sets aside Rules 17 and 18, can be justified by Rule 2.

The remaining sub-sections of the Rule are self-evident.

Section III – Conduct of Vessels in Restricted Visibility

Rule 19

Conduct of Vessels in Restricted Visibility

(a) This Rule applies to vessels not in sight of one another when navigating in or near an area of restricted visibility.

(b) Every vessel shall proceed at a safe speed adapted to the prevailing circumstances and conditions of restricted visibility. A power-driven vessel shall have her engines ready for immediate manoeuvre.

(c) Every vessel shall have due regard to the prevailing circumstances and conditions of restricted visibility when complying with the Rules of Section I of this Part.

(d) A vessel which detects by radar alone the presence of another vessel shall determine if a close-quarters situation is developing and/or risk of collision exists. If so, she shall take avoiding action in ample time, provided that when such action consists of an alteration of course, so far as possible the following shall be avoided.

 (i) an alteration of course to port for a vessel forward of the beam, other than for a vessel being overtaken;

 (ii) an alteration of course towards a vessel abeam or abaft the beam.

(e) Except where it has been determined that a risk of collision does not exist, every vessel which hears apparently forward of her beam the fog signal of another vessel, or which cannot avoid a close-quarters situation with another vessel forward of her beam, shall reduce her speed to the minimum at which she can be kept on her course. She shall if necessary take all her way off and in any event navigate with extreme caution until danger of collision is over.

Note:

(a) draws attention to the fact that, in addition to typical cases of restricted visibility, danger may exist within a fog bank into which the mariner has not yet entered.

The term 'safe speed' used in (b) has been defined by the writer in his notes relating to Rule 6 on page 120. The manner in which a large number of vessels conform to this requirement may be likened to that in which cars obey the 30 miles an hour law on roads in built-up areas. Yes, they exceed it frequently. The final sentence in (b) is included because some power-driven vessels, when steaming at maximum economical speed, have engines which demand adjustments before they become wholly manoeuvrable.

(c) is self-evident but it is well to remark that, more often than not, range of visibility is somewhat less than the eye estimates in the absence of an object of known range just appearing out of the murk. It is sometimes considerably less. This Rule is headed 'Conduct . . .' but it should be remarked that no specific instructions are given to mariners as to the manner in which they must avoid other vessels. Little imagination is needed to realise that, in fog or similar conditions of restricted visibility, it would be impossible to do so. The edicts of this Rule, coupled with those contained in Rules 5 to 8 inclusive, adjure mariners to adopt specified seamanlike practices. In a court of law they will be judged in error if it becomes apparent that as a consequence of neglect to conform to these Rules, a collision resulted.

The complexities contained in a situation at sea which may be compared with two blindfolded people walking towards each other, emitting regular noises of unvaried volume the while, makes advice here almost irresponsible. Yet with many reservations, the author would aver that if it becomes evident that the fog signal of an approaching vessel remains on a steady estimated bearing and ominously increases in volume, then the best action is to turn at right angles to the bearing and, as our American cousins might say, get the Hell out of it.

Part C – Lights and Shapes

Rule 20

Application

(a) Rules in this Part shall be complied with in all weathers.

(b) The Rules concerning lights shall be complied with from sunset to sunrise, and during such times no other lights shall be exhibited, except such lights as cannot be mistaken for the lights specified in these Rules or do not impair their visibility or distinctive character, or interfere with the keeping of a proper look-out.

(c) The lights prescribed by these Rules shall, if carried, also be exhibited from sunrise to sunset in restricted visibility and may be exhibited in all other circumstances when it is deemed necessary.

(d) The Rules concerning shapes shall be complied with by day.

(e) The lights and shapes specified in these Rules shall comply with the provisions of Annex I to these Regulations.

Notes:

It should be noted that craft of any size must not display lights – deck lights, for example – which can in any way effect the visibility of the prescribed lights for vessels under way or render it difficult for another vessel to determine what prescribed lights are being exhibited.

Rule 21

Definitions

(a) "Masthead light" means a white light placed over the fore and aft centreline of the vessel showing an unbroken light over an arc of the horizon of 225 degrees and so fixed as to show the light from right ahead to 22.5 degrees abaft the beam on either side of the vessel.

(b) "Sidelights" means a green light on the starboard side and a red light on the port side each showing an unbroken light over an arc of the horizon of 112.5 degrees and so fixed as to show the light from right ahead to 22.5 degrees abaft the beam on its respective side. In a vessel of less than 20 metres in length the sidelights may be combined in one lantern carried on the fore and aft centreline of the vessel.

(c) "Sternlight" means a white light placed as nearly as practicable at the stern showing an unbroken light over an arc of the horizon of 135 degrees and so fixed as to show the light 67.5 degrees from right aft on each side of the vessel.

(d) "Towing light" means a yellow light having the same characteristics as the "sternlight" defined in paragraph (c) of this Rule.

(e) "All-round light" means a light showing an unbroken light over an arc of the horizon of 360 degrees.

(f) "Flashing light" means a light flashing at regular intervals at a frequency of 120 flashes or more per minute.

Rule 22

Visibility of Lights

The lights prescribed in these Rules shall have an intensity as specified in Section 8 of Annex I to these Regulations so as to be visible at the following minimum ranges:

(a) In vessels of 50 metres or more in length:

- a masthead light, 6 miles;
- a sidelight, 3 miles;
- a sternlight, 3 miles;
- a towing light, 3 miles;
- a white, red, green or yellow all-round light, 3 miles.

(b) In vessels of 12 metres or more in length but less than 50 metres in length:

- a masthead light, 5 miles; except that where the length of the vessel is less than 20 metres, 3 miles;
- a sidelight, 2 miles;
- a sternlight, 2 miles;
- a towing light, 2 miles;
- a white, red, green or yellow all-round light, 2 miles.

(c) In vessels of less than 12 metres in length;

- a masthead light, 2 miles;
- a sidelight, 1 mile;
- a sternlight, 2 miles;
- a towing light, 2 miles;
- a white, red, green or yellow all-round light, 2 miles.

Note:

The ranges quoted in this Rule are greater than those required by the former Rules but the content of Rule 38 should be noted. Conversion problems have been taken into account and so, for vessels of any type, a minimum of 4 years is given to the owner of any vessel to convert from the requirements of the old Rules to those of the new, provided the keel of his vessel is laid at the time these new Rules are introduced. Needless to say, any vessel at the planning stage when the new Rules are introduced must adhere to the requirements of the new Rules.

Rule 23

Power-Driven vessels underway

(a) A power-driven vessel underway shall exhibit:

(i) a masthead light forward;

(ii) a second masthead light abaft of and higher than the forward one; except that a vessel of less than 50 metres in length shall not be obliged to exhibit such light but may do so;

(iii) sidelights;

(iv) a sternlight.

(b) An air-cushion vessel when operating in the non-displacement mode shall, in addition to the lights prescribed in paragraph (a) of this Rule, exhibit an all-round flashing yellow light.

(c) A power-driven vessel of less than 7 metres in length and whose maximum speed does not exceed 7 knots may, in lieu of the lights prescribed in paragraph (a) of this Rule, exhibit an all-round white light. Such vessels shall, if practicable, also exhibit sidelights.

Note:

Apart from the obvious requirements spelled out here for large vessels generally, the owners of power-driven yachts should pay particular attention to this Rule. The exhortations equally apply to sailing craft which are motoring and not sailing.

Vide (c), the owner of a power craft of less than 7 metres in length which attains a speed of less than 7 knots under full power may, as an alternative to the full requirements, exhibit one all-round white light. She should, if she can, also exhibit sidelights. In this case one is well advised to carry sidelights, in the interests of one's own safety. (c) also says, in effect, that speedboats and other fast craft of this small dimension *must* carry the lights defined in (a) (i), (iii) and (iv), although as stated in Rule 21 (b) sidelights may be a combined lantern and not two separate lights. These same lights must be carried by *all* power-driven yachts between 7 and 12 metres in length, the lights having ranges as defined in Rule 22 (c). If such craft exceed 12 metres in length, the ranges of the lights must conform to Rule 22 (b). Provided they do not exceed 20 metres in length, their sidelights may be exhibited from a combined lantern, vide Rule 21 (b). (See Fig. 10.8 on page 237).

Rule 24

Towing and Pushing

(a) A power-driven vessel when towing shall exhibit:

(i) instead of the light prescribed in Rule 23(a)(i),

two masthead lights forward in a vertical line. When the length of the tow, measuring from the stern of the towing vessel to the after end of the tow exceeds 200 metres, three such lights in a vertical line;

(ii) sidelights;

(iii) a sternlight;

(iv) a towing light in a vertical line above the sternlight;

(v) when the length of the tow exceeds 200 metres, a diamond shape where it can best be seen.

(b) When a pushing vessel and a vessel being pushed ahead are rigidly connected in a composite unit they shall be regarded as a power-driven vessel and exhibit the lights prescribed in Rule 23.

(c) A power-driven vessel when pushing ahead or towing alongside, except in the case of a composite unit, shall exhibit:

(i) instead of the light prescribed in Rule 23(a)(i), two masthead lights forward in a vertical line;

(ii) sidelights;

(iii) a sternlight.

(d) A power-driven vessel to which paragraphs (a) and (c) of this Rule apply shall also comply with Rule 23(a)(ii).

(e) A vessel or object being towed shall exhibit:

(i) sidelights;

(ii) a sternlight;

(iii) when the length of the tow exceeds 200 metres, a diamond shape where it can best be seen.

(f) Provided that any number of vessels being towed alongside or pushed in a group shall be lighted as one vessel,

(i) a vessel being pushed ahead, not being part of a composite unit, shall exhibit at the forward end, sidelights;

(ii) a vessel being towed alongside shall exhibit a sternlight and at the forward end, sidelights.

(g) Where from any sufficient cause it is impracticable for a vessel or object being towed to exhibit the lights prescribed in paragraph (e) of this Rule, all possible measures shall be taken to light the vessel or object towed or at least to indicate the presence of the unlighted vessel or object. (See Fig. 10.9 on page 238).

Rule 25

Sailing Vessels underway and Vessel under Oars

(a) A sailing vessel underway shall exhibit:

(i) sidelights;

(ii) a sternlight.

(b) In a sailing vessel of less than 12 metres in length the lights prescribed in paragraph (a) of this Rule may be combined in one lantern carried at or near the top of the mast where it can best be seen.

(c) A sailing vessel underway may, in addition to the lights prescribed in paragraph (a) of this Rule, exhibit at or near the top of the mast, where they can best be seen, two all-round lights in a vertical line, the upper being red and the lower green, but these lights shall not be exhibited in conjunction with the combined lantern permitted by paragraph (b) of this Rule

(d) (i) A sailing vessel of less than 7 metres in length shall, if practicable, exhibit the lights prescribed in paragraph (a) or (b) of this Rule, but if she does not, she shall have ready at hand an electric torch or lighted lantern showing a white light which shall be exhibited in sufficient time to prevent collision.

(ii) A vessel under oars may exhibit the lights prescribed in this Rule for sailing vessels, but if she does not, she shall have ready at hand an electric torch or lighted lantern showing a white light which shall be exhibited in sufficient time to prevent collision.

(e) A vessel proceeding under sail when also being propelled by machinery shall exhibit forward where it can best be seen a conical shape, apex downwards.

Note:

Anyone familiar with small craft will be equally as familiar with the average yacht builder's interpretations of (a) (i) and (ii). They comprise questionably screened sidelights little removed, in terms of height, from gunwale level and stern lights perhaps 3 or 4 feet above sea level. Sidelights so placed will be seen only intermittently by another craft in sea conditions, due to the common intercedence of wave crests. They will quickly be encrusted with salt when a yacht is taking spray, and so their minimal luminosity will be markedly reduced. One can encounter well-known production craft whose stern lights are sited alongside a transomhung rudder, thereby causing these lights to be invisible over an arc of the horizon of perhaps 30° or 40°. These facts, coupled with others equally as unsatisfactory, may lead the thoughtful yachtsman to one of the following conclusions: in the knowledge that very few yachtsmen sail during the dark hours, many builders consider the navigation lights they provide will suffice for the needs of most: many builders are incapable of interpreting the Rules or of assessing the needs of yachtsmen at sea: some builders are more concerned with building down to a price, instead of up to a standard: others may take the attitude – does it really matter, provided that lights are fitted which the amateur will assume conform to the Rules and which give reasonable safety in clear, calm conditions? Any one of these conclusions is disturbing in itself.

Particular attention is drawn to (b), newly introduced to the Rules. It describes for use in craft less than 12 metres in length a combined lantern carried at the masthead which, through effective screening, comprises starboard and port sidelights and stern light. This lantern has everything to commend it for use on small sailing craft, being so high that it will always be visible to other craft and be well clear of spray. An even better arrangement is a more sophisticated lantern which has, in addition, a brilliant all-round signalling light (vide Rule 36) surmounted by an all-round anchor light of similar style to those provided as standard at this time. These articles are available to yachtsmen from good chandlers. They are similarly available to yachtbuilders. (See Fig. 10.10 on page 238).

Rule 26

Fishing Vessels

(a) A vessel engaged in fishing, whether underway or at anchor, shall exhibit only the lights and shapes prescribed in this Rule.

(b) A vessel when engaged in trawling, by which is meant the dragging through the water of a dredge net or other apparatus used as a fishing appliance, shall exhibit:

(i) two all-round lights in a vertical line, the upper being green and the lower white, or a shape consisting of two cones with their apexes together in a vertical line one above the other; a vessel of less than 20 metres in length may instead of this shape exhibit a basket;

(ii) a masthead light abaft of and higher than the all-round green light; a vessel of less than 50 metres in length shall not be obliged to exhibit such a light but may do so;

(iii) when making way through the water, in addition to the lights prescribed in this paragraph, sidelights and a sternlight.

(c) A vessel engaged in fishing, other than trawling, shall exhibit:

(i) two all-round lights in a vertical line, the upper being red and the lower white, or a shape consisting of two cones with apexes together in a vertical line one above the other; a vessel of less than 20 metres in length may instead of this shape exhibit a basket;

(ii) when there is outlying gear extending more than 150 metres horizontally from the vessel, an all-round white light or a cone apex upwards in the direction of the gear;

(iii) when making way through the water, in addition to the lights prescribed in this paragraph, sidelights and a sternlight.

(d) A vessel engaged in fishing in close proximity to other vessels engaged in fishing may exhibit the additional signals described in Annex II to these Regulations.

(e) A vessel when not engaged in fishing shall not exhibit the lights or shapes prescribed in this Rule, but only those prescribed for a vessel of her length.

Note:

This Rule which replaces the previous Rule 9, has much in common with its predecessor except that it does not include authority to exhibit working lights. In Rule 20 (c) it states that no lights other than those prescribed within the Rules may be exhibited, but if additional lights *are* carried then it must be ensured that they cannot be mistaken for the prescribed lights. Neither must the visibility and character of the latter by impaired by the exhibition of additional lights.

One may agree it is improbable that the inborn habits of vastly experienced fishermen are going to be altered at the stroke of a pen. So the bobbing, brilliant working lights of fishermen about their rightful business may well continue to be the precursory signs that fishing craft are about. It may be said that in many cases it is these lights which will be seen at long range, and the prescribed lights which have greater significance to other mariners will be recognised at a lesser distance. (See Fig. 10.11 on page 238).

Rule 27

Vessels not under Command or Restricted in their Ability to Manoeuvre

(a) A vessel not under command shall exhibit:

(i) two all-round red lights in a vertical line where they can best be seen;

(ii) two balls or similar shapes in a vertical line where they can best be seen;

(iii) when making way through the water, in addition to the lights prescribed in this paragraph, sidelights and a sternlight.

(b) A vessel restricted in her ability to manoeuvre, except a vessel engaged in minesweeping operations, shall exhibit:

(i) three all-round lights in a vertical line where they can best be seen. The highest and lowest of these lights shall be red and the middle light shall be white;

(ii) three shapes in a vertical line where they can best be seen. The highest and lowest of these shapes shall be balls and the middle one a diamond;

(iii) when making way through the water, masthead

lights, sidelights and a sternlight, in addition to the lights prescribed in sub-paragraph (i);

(iv) when at anchor, in addition to the lights or shapes prescribed in sub-paragraphs (i) and (ii), the light, lights or shape prescribed in Rule 30.

(c) A vessel engaged in a towing operation such as renders her unable to deviate from her course shall, in addition to the lights or shapes prescribed in sub-paragraphs (b)(i) and (ii) of this Rule, exhibit the lights or shape prescribed in Rule 24(a).

(d) A vessel engaged in dredging or underwater operations, when restricted in her ability to manoeuvre, shall exhibit the lights and shapes prescribed in paragraph (b) of this Rule and shall in addition, when an obstruction exists, exhibit:

(i) two all-round red lights or two balls in a vertical line to indicate the side on which the obstruction exists;

(ii) two all-round green lights or two diamonds in a vertical line to indicate the side on which another vessel may pass;

(iii) when making way through the water, in addition to the lights prescribed in this paragraph, masthead lights, sidelights and a sternlight;

(vi) a vessel to which this paragraph applies when at anchor shall exhibit the lights or shapes prescribed in sub-paragraphs (i) and (ii) instead of the lights or shape prescribed in Rule 30.

(e) Whenever the size of a vessel engaged in diving operations makes it impracticable to exhibit the shapes prescribed in paragraph (d) of this Rule, a rigid replica of the International Code flag "A" not less than 1 metre in height shall be exhibited. Measures shall be taken to ensure all-round visibility.

(f) A vessel engaged in minesweeping operations shall, in addition to the lights prescribed for a power-driven vessel in Rule 23, exhibit three all-round green lights or three balls. One of these lights or shapes shall be exhibited at or near the foremast head and one at each end of the fore yard. These lights or shapes indicate that it is dangerous for another vessel to approach closer than 1,000 metres astern or 500 metres on either side of the minesweeper.

(g) Vessels of less than 7 metres in length shall not be required to exhibit the lights prescribed in this Rule.

(h) The signals prescribed in this Rule are not signals of vessels in distress and requiring assistance. Such signals are contained in Annex IV to these Regulations.

Note:

(b) is entirely new and should be studied. Firstly, it should be noted that a vessel which is restricted in her ability to manoeuvre must not be confused with a vessel which is constrained by her draught, for which special lights are prescribed in Rule 28. Secondly, it may be recalled that three white lights disposed vertically meant, in the old Rules, that a vessel was engaged in towing and the length of her tow measuring from her stern to the stern of the last vessel towed exceeded 600 feet. It must be appreciated that in the new Rules here quoted, these same three lights retain in broad principle their earlier significance. Nevertheless, worn by themselves they indicate that the towing vessel is in no way restricted in her ability to manoeuvre. If she *is* restricted in her ability to manoeuvre, then she must carry the additional all-round white lights described in this Rule and (c) defines the circumstances in which she shall. (See Fig. 10.12 on page 239).

Rule 28

Vessels constrained by their Draught

A vessel constrained by her draught may, in addition to the lights prescribed for power-driven vessels in Rule 23, exhibit where they can best be seen three all-round red lights in a vertical line, or a cylinder.

Note:

It must not be assumed that only in channels and estuaries is this signal likely to be seen. There are many areas in the open sea around these islands where, due to draughts of some large vessels reaching impressive depths, such constriction will occur.

The three lights will probably have similar luminosity to the sidelights of the vessel wearing them. This likelihood will indicate to a yachtsman that, although he may see the white masthead lights of such a vessel at long range, it will be at a lesser range at which the three meaningful red lights will be sighted. (See Fig. 10.13 on page 239).

Rule 29

Pilot Vessels

(a) A vessel engaged on pilotage duty shall exhibit:

(i) at or near the masthead, two all-round lights in a vertical line, the upper being white and the lower red;

(ii) when underway, in addition, sidelights and a sternlight;

(iii) when at anchor, in addition to the lights prescribed in sub-paragraph (i), the anchor light, lights or shape.

(b) A pilot vessel when not engaged on pilotage duty shall exhibit the lights or shapes prescribed for a similar vessel of her length.

Notes:

To those familiar with the old Rules it will be noted that, somewhat realistically, sailing pilot vessels are no longer taken into account. The flare up light and the intermittent white light which could be used as an alternative have also been excluded.

It must be remembered that a vessel is under way when she is not at anchor or made fast to the shore or aground. She does not have to be making way through the water to be under way. Pilot vessels often drift on their stations and, provided they are engaged on pilotage duty when drifting and stationary, they will carry the distinctive lights. (See Fig. 10.14 on page 240).

Rule 30

Anchored Vessels and Vessels aground

(a) A vessel at anchor shall exhibit where it can best be seen:

(i) in the fore part, an all-round white light or one ball;

(ii) at or near the stern and at a lower level than the light prescribed in sub-paragraph (i), an all-round white light.

(b) A vessel of less than 50 metres in length may exhibit an all-round white light where it can best be seen instead of the lights prescribed in paragraph (a) of this Rule.

(c) A vessel at anchor may, and a vessel of 100 metres and more in length shall, also use the available working or equivalent lights to illuminate her decks.

(d) A vessel aground shall exhibit the lights prescribed in paragraph (a) or (b) of this Rule and in addition, where they can best be seen:

(i) two all-round red lights in a vertical line;

(ii) three balls in a vertical line.

(e) A vessel of less than 7 metres in length, when at anchor or aground, not in or near a narrow channel, fairway or anchorage, or where other vessels normally navigate, shall not be required to exhibit the lights or shapes prescribed in paragraphs (a), (b) or (d) of this Rule.

Upon the customs of large vessels:

It has long been the custom for large vessels at anchor to exhibit deck and working lights. This practice which is a seamanlike one obtained no mention in previous Rules: in effect, vessels were hitherto adopting a practice which was at variance with the exhortation that no vessel must exhibit lights which might impair the recognition or visibility of the prescribed lights. The anomoly has now been rectified by the content of (c). These deck and working lights, numerous and brilliant as they may well be, are frequently the first indication to others that a large vessel is at anchor. As range from such a vessel is reduced, the anchor lights as defined in (a) (i) and (ii) should become recognisable.

It is well to note that, apart from the upper of two anchor lights indicating which is the forward end of such a vessel, in a tideway it gives further valuable information: it registers the direction of tidal flow. This knowledge is useful in itself to the small boat sailor: it behests him to pass the vessel under the low light, because to pass it under the high one might be to sweep a yacht into its anchor cable or across its bows. (See Fig. 10.15 on page 240).

Upon the customs of yachts:

Yachts of 7 metres in length and above must abide by the dictates of this Rule and the all-round white light which yacht builders almost invariably fit on the mast cap of sailing yachts will meet the requirements of (b). Yachtsmen should, and no doubt will, interpret this Rule sensibly. If at anchor in or near a fairway or in open water, clearly it is very much in their interests to display an anchor light. Anchored in a quiet backwash of a seldom-frequented creek, there is little point in so doing. Although by these Rules the untended yachts in serried lines which border the fairways of any of our yachting ports should display anchor lights, local bye-laws usually override the Rules if only because it would be quite impractical for yachts which are often left for weeks at a time to do so.

Rule 31

Seaplanes

Where it is impracticable for a seaplane to exhibit lights and shapes of the characteristics or in the positions prescribed in the Rules of this Part she shall exhibit lights and shapes as closely similar in characteristics and position as is possible.

Part D – Sound and Light Signals

Rule 32

Definitions

(a) The word "whistle" means any sound signalling appliance capable of producing the prescribed blasts and which complies with the specifications in Annex III to these Regulations.

(b) The term "short blast" means a blast of about one second's duration.

(c) The term "prolonged blast" means a blast of from four to six second's duration.

Rule 33

Equipment for Sound Signals

(a) A vessel of 12 metres or more in length shall be provided with a whistle and a bell and a vessel of 100 metres or more in length shall, in addition, be provided with a gong, the tone and sound of which cannot be confused with that of the bell. The whistle, bell and gong shall comply with the specifications in Annex III to these Regulations. The bell or gong or both may be replaced by other equipment having the same respective sound characteristics, provided that manual sounding of the required signals shall always be possible.

(b) A vessel of less than 12 metres in length shall not be obliged to carry the sound signalling appliances prescribed in paragraph (a) of this Rule but if she does not, she shall be provided with some other means of making an efficient sound signal.

Note:

With reference to (a), 12 metres and above is a common dimension for a considerable number of sailing and power-driven craft. A study of Annex III will readily indicate to the yachtsman with this size of craft that for the future, to comply with this Rule, even though his "whistle" may meet the degree of audibility demanded, he is almost certainly going to have to provide his craft with an efficient bell. It is distinctly unlikely that a mouth trumpet, a butane gas fog horn or even a rotary klaxon horn will meet the standard of "whistle" required in the Annex. No doubt manufacturers will for the future recognise and meet the demands of this Rule and Annex III.

By far the greatest number of sailing and power-driven yachts are less than 12 metres in length and the wording of (b) indicates, in the opinion of the writer, that in this class yachtsmen may continue using those items of equipment to make an efficient sound signal which are at present available to them. He is of the unshakeable opinion that devices mentioned in the previous paragraph by which "an efficient sound signal" are said to be capable of being made are in no way efficient. In possession of one of them the yachtsman is lulled into believing that he can adequately indicate his presence to other mariners in fog. He cannot. Particular attention is drawn to Annex III, 1(c), last paragraph, and to the sundry warnings the Admiralty promulgates about the vagaries in the transmission of sound waves in fog. In "close quarters" situations, plights in which a yachtsman will take every step to avoid, these contrivances may well be heard by the other vessel. When noise is non-existant aboard an approaching merchant vessel – an unlikely state of affairs, and a flat calm exists, then the distance at which these inadequate gadgets will be audible may well be increased a little. And that is the best which can be said. "Whistles" activated by air compressors, which consume precious amperes from one's batteries, are the only really efficient fog signals for small craft. The writer tends to feel that, with no intention of appearing lofty, his is a voice in the wilderness.

Rule 34

Manoeuvring and Warning Signals

(a) When vessels are in sight of one another, a power-driven vessel underway, when manoeuvring as authorized or required by these Rules, shall indicate that manoeuvre by the following signals on her whistle:

– one short blast to mean "I am altering my course to starboard";

– two short blasts to mean "I am altering my course to port";

– three short blasts to mean "I am operating astern propulsion".

(b) Any vessel may supplement the whistle signals prescribed in paragraph (a) of this Rule by light signals, repeated as appropriate, whilst the manoeuvre is being carried out:

(i) these light signals shall have the following significance:

– one flash to mean "I am altering my course to starboard";

– two flashes to mean "I am altering my course to port";

– three flashes to mean "I am operating astern propulsion";

(ii) the duration of each flash shall be about one second, the interval between flashes shall be about one second, and the interval between successive signals shall be not less than ten seconds;

(iii) the light used for this signal shall, if fitted, be an all-round white light, visible at a minimum range of 5 miles, and shall comply with the provisions of Annex I.

(c) When in sight of one another, in a narrow channel or fairway:

(i) a vessel intending to overtake another shall in compliance with Rule 9(e)(i) indicate her intention by the following signals on her whistle:

– two prolonged blasts followed by one short blast to mean "I intend to overtake you on your starboard side";

– two prolonged blasts followed by two short blasts to mean "I intend to overtake you on your port side";

(ii) the vessel about to be overtaken when acting in accordance with Rule 9(e)(i) shall indicate her agreement by the following signal on her whistle:

– one prolonged, one short, one prolonged and one short blast, in that order.

(d) When vessels in sight of one another are approaching each other and from any cause either vessel fails to understand the intentions or actions of the other, or is in doubt whether sufficient action is being taken by the other to avoid collision, the vessel in doubt shall immediately indicate such doubt by giving at least five short and rapid blasts on the whistle. Such signal may be supplemented by a light signal of at least five short and rapid flashes.

(e) A vessel nearing a bend or an area of a channel or fairway where other vessels may be obscured by an intervening obstruction shall sound one prolonged blast. Such signal shall be answered with a prolonged blast by any approaching vessel that may be within hearing around the bend or behind the intervening obstruction.

(f) If whistles are fitted on a vessel at a distance apart of more than 100 metres, one whistle only shall be used for giving manoeuvring and warning signals.

Note:

The skipper of a sailing yacht will appreciate it is imperative that he retains the content of this Rule in his memory: and he who skippers a power-driven yacht or pleasure craft must, in addition, conform to its dictates. For both it is a matter of their own safety.

The opening words of this Rule are important and must not be lost to the reader: "When vessels are in sight of one another . . ." Self-evident? Not entirely. Consider two vessels manoeuvring quite close to each other, yet due to fog neither can see the other. Each is anxious to avert collision. The signals described here are not those they must use in such conditions, how ever minimal their distance apart. Yet – the moment they sight each other, or one sights the other, this Rule is immediately operative.

It must also be noted that the signals described are to be given by power-driven vessels *only*. This is by explicit direction in (a) and (b), and by implication in remaining paragraphs. Again by implication in the latter paragraphs, it would appear that the skipper of a sailing craft would not be held at fault if, say, he made sound signals of the character described in the circumstances defined in (d).

Rule 35

Sound Signals in restricted Visibility

In or near an area of restricted visibility, whether by day or night, the signals prescribed in this Rule shall be used as follows:

(a) A power-driven vessel making way through the water shall sound at intervals of not more than 2 minutes one prolonged blast.

(b) A power-driven vessel underway but stopped and making no way through the water shall sound at intervals of not more than 2 minutes two prolonged blasts in succession with an interval of about 2 seconds between them.

(c) A vessel not under command, a vessel restricted in her ability to manoeuvre, a vessel constrained by her draught, a sailing vessel, a vessel engaged in fishing and a vessel engaged in towing or pushing another vessel shall, instead of the signals prescribed in paragraphs (a) or (b) of this Rule, sound at intervals of not more than 2 minutes three blasts in succession, namely one prolonged followed by two short blasts.

(d) A vessel towed or if more than one vessel is towed the last vessel of the tow, if manned, shall at intervals of not more than 2 minutes sound four blasts in succession, namely one prolonged followed by three short blasts. When practicable, this signal shall be made immediately after the signal made by the towing vessel.

(e) When a pushing vessel and a vessel being pushed ahead are rigidly connected in a composite unit they shall be regarded as a power-driven vessel and shall give the signals prescribed in paragraphs (a) or (b) of this Rule.

(f) A vessel at anchor shall at intervals of not more than one minute ring the bell rapidly for about 5 seconds. In a vessel of 100 metres or more in length the bell shall be sounded in the forepart of the vessel and immediately after the ringing of the bell the gong shall be sounded rapidly for about 5 seconds in the after part of the vessel. A vessel at anchor may in addition sound three blasts in succession, namely one short, one prolonged and one short blast, to give warning of her position and of the possibility of collision to an approaching vessel.

(g) A vessel aground shall give the bell signal and if required the gong signal prescribed in paragraph (f) of this Rule and shall, in addition, give three separate and distinct strokes on the bell immediately before and after the rapid ringing of the bell. A vessel aground may in addition sound an appropriate whistle signal.

(h) A vessel of less than 12 metres in length shall not be obliged to give the above-mentioned signals but, if she does not, shall make some other efficient sound signal at intervals of not more than 2 minutes.

(i) A pilot vessel when engaged on pilotage duty may in addition to the signals prescribed in paragraphs (a), (b) or (f) of this Rule sound an identity signal consisting of four short blasts.

Note:

Like every other word within these Rules, the third one here: "near" is not used artlessly. A vessel may be approaching a fog bank and, close within this wall of obscurity, another vessel could be very near. Good seamanship dictates, therefore, that a vessel about to enter such a fog bank must as a precaution indicate its presence by making the appropriate sound signal. Counter argument that she surely should hear the sound signals of the vessel out of sight has no validity. Fog occasionally plays tricks with sound waves and, in any case, one has no means of being certain that she is in fact conforming to the Rules.

The content of this Rule being otherwise self-evident, the author's notes which follow Rule 33 have considerable substance here.

Rule 36

Signals to attract Attention

If necessary to attract the attention of another vessel any vessel may make light or sound signals that cannot be mistaken for any signal authorized elsewhere in these Rules, or may direct the beam of her searchlight in the direction of the danger, in such a way as not to embarrass any vessel.

Note:

Earlier notes have indicated the importance of a tiny yacht being able to draw to the attention of other vessels her presence: this Rule gives her the right to do so. Sound signals capable of being made by most yachts are, due to their inadequacy, best ignored here and comments are confined to visual signals only.

By day

Only an Aldis lamp, or its equivalent, comes within this category. Few yachts carry these daylight signalling devices, so it may be said that the remainder have no practical means by which they can attract the attention of another vessel. If collision is the danger, the yacht must hasten away in the direction which is considered safest.

By night

(a) The "Marinaspec" tungsten halogen, all-round masthead light – in combination with which are sidelights, stern light and anchor light – is, in the opinion of the writer, quite the best for a sailing yacht to attract attention to itself. Its piercing brilliance and its altitude places it in a class on its own.

(b) Certainly an Aldis lamp directed at the bridge of an oncoming vessel is of equal value for use in sailing and power-driven yachts alike. But, as has already been said, few craft carry Aldis daylight signalling lamps.

(c) In the absence of either of these, a powerful hand torch used in the manner described in (b) is a less effective substitute.

(d) Sail illumination by sailing craft is a makeshift in the absence of other means of drawing attention provided the sails are white and illumination is obtained by a means more effective than any torch can provide.

(e) A white flare is, of course, as effective as any other means of attracting attention but it is mentioned last here because, what ever the circumstances, there is generally an unwillingness to use flares for this purpose and they burn for a limited period.

Rule 37

Distress Signals

When a vessel is in distress and requires assistance she shall use or exhibit the signals prescribed in Annex IV to these Regulations.

Note:

The number of distress signals listed in Annex IV must of necessity be severely reduced in the case of small craft at sea. Those which the writer regards as having value are listed below in order of their efficiency:

(a) A signal given by radio-telephony consisting of the spoken word "Mayday". This is far and away more efficient and valuable than any other method. It does not depend upon others seeing it and range potential may vary between 20 and 200 miles, depending upon the power of the transmitter and radio conditions at the time of transmission.

(b) A rocket or parachute flare, or a hand flare, showing a red light. The shortcomings of pyrotechnics will readily be recognised. Poor visibility will drastically reduce their visual range and, in any case, they must be sighted by someone.

(c) A smoke signal giving off purple smoke is most valuable by day but the limitations described in (b) apply here also.

(d) In clear weather, in daylight, slowly and repeatedly raising and lowering arms outstretched can be effective at a range of 2 miles or more. It has value when other vessels are in sight and when, shall we say, engine failure is the cause of distress. One reflects that this signal may well be impractical when in distress in heavy weather.

Visual signals capable of being hoisted on the mast of a yacht are generally of such diminutive dimensinos that they must be regarded as being of small value. The writer realises that the comments here must be of small solace to yachtsmen. Anyone who sails must accept the inherent risks of so doing: it is the spice of the sport. When in distress the yachtsman is facing greater risks than seamen generally, due to his restricted ability to draw attention to his plight.

Part E – Exemptions

Rule 38

Exemptions

Any vessel (or class of vessels) provided that she complies with the requirements of the International Regulations for Preventing Collisions at Sea, 1960, the keel of which is laid or which is at a corresponding stage of construction before the entry into force of these Regulations may be exempted from compliance therewith as follows:

(a) The installation of lights with ranges prescribed in Rule 22, until four years after the date of entry into force of these Regulations.

(b) The installation of lights with colour specifications as prescribed in Section 7 of Annex I to these Regulations, until four years after the date of entry into force of these Regulations.

(c) The repositioning of lights as a result of conversion from Imperial to metric units and rounding off measurement figures, permanent exemption.

(d) (i) The repositioning of masthead lights on vessels of less than 150 metres in length, resulting from the prescriptions of Section 3(a) of Annex I, permanent exemption.

(ii) The repositioning of masthead lights on vessels of 150 metres or more in length, resulting from the prescriptions of Section 3(a) of Annex I to these Regulations, until nine years after the date of entry into force of these Regulations.

(e) The repositioning of masthead lights resulting from the prescriptions of Section 2(b) of Annex I, until nine years after the date of entry into force of these Regulations.

(f) The repositioning of sidelights resulting from the prescriptions of Sections 2(g) and 3(b) of Annex I, until nine years after the date of entry into force of these Regulations.

(g) The requirements for sound signal appliances prescribed in Annex III, until nine years after the date of entry into force of these Regulations.

Note:

It will be apparent to the reader that the changes demanded in vessel generally in the character of their navigation lights are such that reasonable time must be allowed for owners to provide new or altered lights. The time allowed to them is stated here.

ANNEX I

Positioning and Technical Details of Lights and Shapes

1. **Definition**

The term "height above the hull" means height above the uppermost continuous deck.

2. **Vertical positioning and spacing of lights**

(a) On a power-driven vessel of 20 metres or more in length the masthead lights shall be placed as follows:

(i) the forward masthead light, or if only one masthead light is carried, then that light, at a height above the hull of not less than 6 metres, and, if the breadth of the vessel exceeds 6 metres, then at a height above the hull not less than such breadth, so however that the light need not be placed at a greater height above the hull than 12 metres;

(ii) when two masthead lights are carried the after one shall be at least 4.5 metres vertically higher than the forward one.

(b) The vertical separation of masthead lights of power-driven vessels shall be such that in all normal conditions of trim the after light will be seen over and separate from the forward light at a distance of 1000 metres from the stem when viewed from sea level.

(c) The masthead light of a power-driven vessel of 12 metres but less than 20 metres in length shall be placed at a height above the gunwale of not less than 2.5 metres.

(d) A power-driven vessel of less than 12 metres in length may carry the uppermost light at a height of less than 2.5 metres above the gunwale. When however a masthead light is carried in addition to sidelights and a sternlight, then such masthead light shall be carried at least 1 metre higher than the sidelights.

(e) One of the two or three masthead lights prescribed for a power-driven vessel when engaged in towing or pushing another vessel shall be placed in the same position as the forward masthead light of a power-driven vessel.

(f) In all circumstances the masthead light or lights shall be so placed as to be above and clear of all other lights and obstructions.

(g) The sidelights of a power-driven vessel shall be placed at a height above the hull not greater than three quarters of that of the forward masthead light. They shall not be so low as to be interfered with by deck lights.

(h) The sidelights, if in a combined lantern and carried on a power-driven vessel of less than 20 metres in length, shall be placed not less than 1 metre below the masthead light.

(i) When the Rules prescribe two or three lights to be carried in a vertical line, they shall be spaced as follows:

(i) on a vessel of 20 metres in length or more such lights shall be spaced not less than 2 metres apart, and the lowest of these lights shall, except where a towing light is required, not be less than 4 metres above the hull;

(ii) on a vessel of less than 20 metres in length such lights shall be spaced not less than 1 metre apart and the lowest of these lights shall, except where a towing light is required, not be less than 2 metres above the gunwale;

(iii) when three lights are carried they shall be equally spaced.

(j) The lower of the two all-round lights prescribed for a fishing vessel when engaged in fishing shall be at a height above the sidelights not less than twice the distance between the two vertical lights.

(k) The forward anchor light, when two are carried, shall not be less than 4.5 metres above the after one. On a vessel of 50 metres or more in length this forward anchor light shall not be less than 6 metres above the hull.

3. **Horizontal positioning and spacing of lights**

(a) When two masthead lights are prescribed for a

power-driven vessel, the horizontal distance between them shall not be less than one half of the length of the vessel but need not be more than 100 metres. The forward light shall be placed not more than one quarter of the length of the vessel from the stem.

(b) On a vessel of 20 metres or more in length the sidelights shall not be placed in front of the forward masthead lights. They shall be placed at or near the side of the vessel.

4. **Details of location of direction-indicating lights for fishing vessels, dredgers and vessels engaged in underwater operations**

(a) The light indicating the direction of the outlying gear from a vessel engaged in fishing as prescribed in Rule 26(c)(ii) shall be placed at a horizontal distance of not less than 2 metres and not more than 6 metres away from the two all-round red and white lights. This light shall be placed not higher than the all-round white light prescribed in Rule 26(c)(i) and not lower than the sidelights.

(b) The lights and shapes on a vessel engaged in dredging or underwater operations to indicate the obstructed side and/or the side on which it is safe to pass, as prescribed in Rule 27(d)(i) and (ii), shall be placed at the maximum practical horizontal distance, but in no case less than 2 metres, from the lights or shapes prescribed in Rule 27(b)(i) and (ii). In no case shall the upper of these lights or shapes be at a greater height than the lower of the three lights or shapes prescribed in Rule 27(b)(i) and (ii).

5. **Screens for sidelights**

The sidelights shall be fitted with inboard screens painted matt black, and meeting the requirements of Section 9 of this Annex. With a combined lantern, using a single vertical filament and a very narrow division between the green and red sections, external screens need not be fitted.

6. **Shapes**

(a) Shapes shall be black and of the following sizes:

(i) a ball shall have a diameter of not less than 0.6 metre;

(ii) a cone shall have a base diameter of not less than 0.6 metre and a height equal to its diameter;

(iii) a cylinder shall have a diameter of at least 0.6 metre and a height of twice its diameter;

(iv) a diamond shape shall consist of two cones as defined in (ii) above having a common base.

(b) The vertical distance between shapes shall be at least 1.5 metres.

(c) In a vessel of less than 20 metres in length shapes of lesser dimensions but commensurate with the size of the vessel may be used and the distance apart may be correspondingly reduced.

7. **Colour specification of lights**

The chromaticity of all navigation lights shall conform to the following standards, which lie within the boundaries of the area of the diagram specified for each colour by the International Commission on Illumination (CIE)

The boundaries of the area for each colour are given by indicating the corner co-ordinates, which are as follows:

(i) *White*

x	0.525	0.525	0.452	0.310	0.310	0.443
y	0.382	0.440	0.440	0.348	0.283	0.382

(ii) *Green*

x	0.028	0.009	0.300	0.203
y	0.385	0.723	0.511	0.356

(iii) *Red*

x	0.680	0.660	0.735	0.721
y	0.320	0.320	0.265	0.259

(iv) *Yellow*

x	0.612	0.618	0.575	0.575
y	0.382	0.382	0.425	0.406

8. **Intensity of lights**

(a) The minimum luminous intensity of lights shall be calculated by using the formula:

$$I = 3.43 \times 10^6 \times T \times D^2 \times K^{-D}$$

where I is luminous intensity in candelas under service conditions,

T is threshold factor 2×10^{-7} lux,

D is range of visibility (luminous range) of the light in nautical miles,

K is atmospheric transmissivity.

For prescribed lights the value of K shall be 0.8, corresponding to a meteorological visibility of approximately 13 nautical miles.

(b) A selection of figures derived from the formula is given in the following table:

Range of visibility (luminous range) of light in nautical miles D	Luminous intensity of light in candelas for K = 0.8 I
1	0.9
2	4.3
3	12
4	27
5	52
6	94

NOTE: The maximum luminous intensity of navigation lights should be limited to avoid undue glare.

9. **Horizontal sectors**

(a) (i) In the forward direction, sidelights as fitted on the vessel must show the minimum required intensities. The intensities must decrease to reach practical cut-off between 1 degree and 3 degrees outside the prescribed sectors.

(ii) For sternlights and masthead lights and at 22.5 degrees abaft the beam for sidelights, the minimum required intensities shall be maintained over the arc of the horizon up to 5 degrees within the limits of the sectors prescribed in Rule 21. From 5 degrees within the prescribed sectors the intensity may decrease by 50 per cent up to the prescribed limits; it shall decrease steadily to reach practical cut-off at not more than 5 degrees outside the prescribed limits.

(b) All-round lights shall be so located as not to be obscured by masts, topmasts or structures within angular sectors of more than 6 degrees, except anchor lights, which need not be placed at an impracticable height above the hull.

10. **Vertical sectors**

(a) The vertical sectors of electric lights, with the exception of lights on sailing vessels shall ensure that:

(i) at least the required minimum intensity is maintained at all angles from 5 degrees above to 5 degrees below the horizontal;

(ii) at least 60 per cent of the required minimum intensity is maintained from 7.5 degrees above to 7.5 degrees below the horizontal.

(b) In the case of sailing vessels the vertical sectors of electric lights shall ensure that:

(i) at least the required minimum intensity is maintained at all angles from 5 degrees above to 5 degrees below the horizontal;

(ii) at least 50 per cent of the required minimum intensity is maintained from 25 degrees above to 25 degrees below the horizontal.

(c) In the case of lights other than electric these specifications shall be met as closely as possible.

11. **Intensity of non-electric lights**

Non-electric lights shall so far as practicable comply with the minimum intensities, as specified in the Table given in Section 8 of this Annex.

12. **Manoeuvring light**

Notwithstanding the provisions of paragraph 2(f) of this Annex the manoeuvring light described in Rule 34(b) shall be placed in the same fore and aft vertical plane as the masthead light or lights and, where practicable, at a minimum height of 2 metres vertically above the forward masthead light, provided that it shall be carried not less than 2 metres vertically above or below the after masthead light. On a vessel where only one masthead light is carried the manoeuvring light, if fitted, shall be carried where it can best be seen, not less than 2 metres vertically apart from the masthead light.

13. **Approval**

The construction of lanterns and shapes and the installation of lanterns on board the vessel shall be to the satisfaction of the appropriate authority of the State where the vessel is registered.

ANNEX II

Additional Signals for Fishing Vessels Fishing in Close Proximity

1. **General**

The lights mentioned herein shall, if exhibited in pursuance of Rule 26(d), be placed where they can best be seen. They shall be at least 0.9 metre apart but at a lower level than lights prescribed in Rule 26(b)(i) and (c)(i). The lights shall be visible all round the horizon at a distance of at least 1 mile but at a lesser distance than the lights prescribed by these Rules for fishing vessels.

2. **Signals for trawlers**

(a) Vessels when engaged in trawling, whether using demersal or pelagic gear, may exhibit;

(i) when shooting their nets:
two white lights in a vertical line;

(ii) when hauling their nets:
one white light over one red light in a vertical line;

(iii) when the net has come fast upon an obstruction:
two red lights in a vertical line.

(b) Each vessel engaged in pair trawling may exhibit:

(i) by night, a searchlight directed forward and in the direction of the other vessel of the pair;

(ii) when shooting or hauling their nets or when their nets have come fast upon an obstruction, the lights prescribed in 2(a) above.

3. **Signals for purse seiners**

Vessels engaged in fishing with purse seine gear may exhibit two yellow lights in a vertical line. These lights shall flash alternately every second and with equal light and occultation duration. These lights may be exhibited only when the vessel is hampered by its fishing gear.

ANNEX III

Technical Details of Sound Signal Appliances

1. **Whistles**

(a) *Frequencies and range of audibility*

The fundamental frequency of the signal shall lie within the range 70-700 Hz.

The range of audibility of the signal from a whistle shall be determined by those frequencies, which may include the fundamental and/or one or more higher frequencies, which lie within the range 180-700 Hz (± 1 per cent) and which provide the sound pressure levels specified in paragraph 1(c) below.

(b) *Limits of fundamental frequencies*

To ensure a wide variety of whistle characteristics, the fundamental frequency of a whistle shall be between the following limits:

(i) 70-200 Hz, for a vessel 200 metres or more in length;

(ii) 130-350 Hz, for a vessel 75 metres but less than 200 metres in length;

(iii) 250-700 Hz, for a vessel less than 75 metres in length.

(c) *Sound signal intensity and range of audibility*

A whistle fitted in a vessel shall provide, in the direction of maximum intensity of the whistle and at a distance of 1 metre from it, a sound pressure level in at least one 1/3rd-octave band within the range of frequencies 180-700 Hz (± 1 per cent) of not less than the appropriate figure given in the table below.

Length of vessel in metres	1/3rd-octave band level at 1 metre in dB referred to 2×10^{-5} N/m^2	Audibility range in nautical miles
200 or more	143	2
75 but less than 200	138	1.5
20 but less than 75	130	1
Less than 20	120	0.5

The range of audibility in the table above is for information and is approximately the range at which a whistle may be heard on its forward axis with 90 per cent probability in conditions of still air on board a vessel having average background noise level at the listening posts (taken to be 68 dB in the octave band centred on 250 Hz and 63 dB in the octave band centred on 500 Hz).

In practice the range at which a whistle may be heard is extremely variable and depends critically on weather conditions; the values given can be regarded as typical but under conditions of strong wind or high ambient noise level at the listening post the range may be much reduced.

(d) *Directional properties*

The sound pressure level of a directional whistle shall be not more than 4 dB below the sound pressure level on the axis at any direction in the horizontal plane within ± 45 degrees of the axis. The sound pressure level at any other direction in the horizontal plane shall be not more than 10 dB below the sound pressure level on the axis, so that the range in any direction will be at least half the range on the forward axis. The sound pressure level shall be measured in that 1/3rd-octave band which determines the audibility range.

(e) *Positioning of whistles*

When a directional whistle is to be used as the only whistle on a vessel, it shall be installed with its maximum intensity directed straight ahead.

A whistle shall be placed as high as practicable on a vessel, in order to reduce interception of the emitted sound by obstructions and also to minimize hearing damage risk to personnel. The sound pressure level of the vessel's own signal at listening posts shall not exceed 110 dB (A) and so far as practicable should not exceed 100 dB (A).

(f) *Fitting of more than one whistle*

If whistles are fitted at a distance apart of more than 100 metres, it shall be so arranged that they are not sounded simultaneously.

(g) *Combined whistle systems*

If due to the presence of obstructions the sound field of a single whistle or of one of the whistles referred to in paragraph 1(f) above is likely to have a zone of greatly reduced signal level, it is recommended that a combined whistle system be fitted so as to overcome this reduction. For the purposes of the Rules a combined whistle system is to be regarded as a single whistle. The whistles of a combined system shall be located at a distance apart of not more than 100 metres and arranged to be sounded simultaneously. The frequency of any one whistle shall differ from those of the others by at least 10 Hz.

2. **Bell or gong**

(a) *Intensity of signal*

A bell or gong, or other device having similar sound characteristics shall produce a sound presure level of not less than 110 dB at 1 metre.

(b) *Construction*

Bells and gongs shall be made of corrosion-resistant material and designed to give a clear tone. The diameter of the mouth of the bell shall be not less than 300 mm for vessels of more than 20 metres in length, and shall be not less than 200 mm for vessels of 12 to 20 metres in length. Where practicable, a power-driven bell striker is recommended to ensure constant force but manual operation shall be possible. The mass of the striker shall be not less than 3 per cent of the mass of the bell.

3. **Approval**

The construction of sound signal appliances, their performance and their installation on board the vessel shall be to the satisfaction of the appropriate authority of the State where the vessel is registered.

ANNEX IV

Distress Signals

1. The following signals, used or exhibited either together or separately, indicate distress and need of assistance.

(a) a gun or other explosive signal fired at intervals of about a minute;

(b) a continuous sounding with any fog-signalling apparatus;

(c) rockets or shells, throwing red stars fired one at a time at short intervals;

(d) a signal made by radiotelegraphy or by any other signalling method consisting of the group ... --- ... (SOS) in the Morse Code;

(f) the International Code Signal of distress indicated by N.C.;

(g) a signal consisting of a square flag having above or below it a ball or anything resembling a ball;

(h) flames on the vessel (as from a burning tar barrel, oil barrel, etc.);

(i) a rocket parachute flare or a hand flare showing a red light;

(j) a smoke signal giving off orange-coloured smoke;

(k) slowly and repeatedly raising and lowering arms outstretched to each side;

(l) the radiotelegraph alarm signal;

(m) the radiotelephone alarm signal;

(n) signals transmitted by emergency position-indicating radio beacons.

2. The use or exhibition of any of the foregoing signals except for the purpose of indicating distress and need of assistance and the use of other signals which may be confused with any of the above signals is prohibited.

3. Attention is drawn to the relevant sections of the International Code of Signals, the Merchant Ship Search and Rescue Manual and the following signals:

(a) a piece of orange-coloured canvas with either a black square and circle or other appropriate symbol (for identification from the air);

(b) a dye marker.

CHAPTER 11

Safety

The intention in this chapter is not to instruct upon seamanship. Here and there it gives broad guidelines in what may be called the ordinary practice of seamen, but mainly it gives advice upon safety equipment and practice in small craft generally.

Regulations governing safety equipment.

It is perhaps unfortunate that, at a time when there are more small pleasure craft capable of undertaking sea passages than ever before, there is no stipulated minimum amount of safety equipment which must be carried by craft under 45 feet in length.

The Merchant Shipping (Life Saving Appliances) Rules 1965 and the Merchant Shipping (Fire Appliances) Rules 1965 stipulate the appliances which must be carried by all vessels of 45 feet in length and above. Those sections which could possibly relate to craft which come within the scope of this book – vessels between 45 and 70 feet in length – are reproduced in condensed form below.

Recently the Department of Trade and Industry called together many authoritative persons to discuss what steps might be taken to encourage owners of small craft to carry adequate safety equipment, and the practicability of introducing legislation to achieve this end. The meeting high-lighted the practical difficulties in promoting such legislation for the many different types of craft of less than 45 feet in length which are put to widely varying usages. It appears that a compromise resolution resulted: the production of the D.T.I. pamphlet, 'How Safe is your Craft?' to which maximum publicity be given. We have been advised by the D.T.I. that at this time there is no intention to introduce legislation for these craft, but the need for it is kept under constant review.

In the opinion of the authors, the pamphlet 'How Safe is your craft?' is the most valuable and practical publication yet produced on the subject and for this reason it is reproduced in full on pages 143-145.

Department of Trade and Industry requirements for vessels from 45 feet to 70 feet in length.

All such vessels must carry:–

(a) One lifejacket, of a type approved by the Department of Trade and Industry, for every person on board.

(b) A buoyant line, at least 10 fathoms in length.

(c) A minimum of six pyrotechnic signals which meet with Department of Trade and Industry approval. Briefly, these must be parachute distress rocket signals, or red star distress signals which emit two or more red stars at a considerable height.

(d) In a position outside the machinery spaces, a hand pump with a permanent sea connection: a hose with a nozzle of at least ¼ inch in diameter capable of producing a jet of water having a throw of not less than 20 feet which can be directed on to any part of the craft: a spray nozzle suitable for fitting the hose.

(e) The equipment described in paragraph (d) may be substituted by two fire buckets, one of which must be provided with a lanyard, in craft of the following types: fully decked vessels under 50 feet in length and open vessels of less than 70 feet in length.

(f) When fitted with oil-fired boilers or internal combustion engines, two portable fire extinguishers. Such extinguishers must be of an approved type and be designed for extinguishing oil fires.

In addition, if a vessel of the above dimension is engaged on either a voyage to sea in the course of which it is more than 3 miles from the coast of the United Kingdom, or a voyage to sea during the months of November to March, inclusive, she must carry:

(g) One or more liferafts of sufficient aggregate capacity to accommodate the total number of persons on board.

(h) At least two lifebuoys of an approved type, one of which must be fitted with a self-igniting light and a self-activating smoke float.

If a vessel of this dimension does not proceed to sea, or she only proceeds to sea during the months of April to October inclusive, on a voyage in the course of which she is not more than 3 miles from the coast of the United Kingdom, for the requirements outlined in paragraphs (g) and (h), she may substitute:–

(i) Lifebuoys at least equal in number to half the number of persons on board, but she must not carry less than two.

The Merchant Shipping Rules, 1965, mentioned above, are purchasable for a few shillings from H.M.S.O. They include full details of the above summarised requirements, together with complete definitions of the standards which must be achieved before equipment is given Department of Trade and Industry approval.

Safety equipment recommendations.

As will be seen, amongst other counsels which are promulgated from time to time, the Department of Trade and Industry **recommend** - not require - that small craft which proceed to sea or operate in similar conditions, be provided with an approved lifejacket for every person on board. A lifejacket of which the Dept. approves is defined overleaf.

Many publications of note, and organisations such as the Royal Yachting Association, make recommendations relating to safety equipment which is best suited to the needs of small craft generally. Such recommendations are based upon long practical experience and the wise yachtsman will be guided accordingly. Many yacht clubs demand of their members certain safety standards and practices, which can otherwise be defined as good sound seamanship, hence adherence to club rules is frequently a matter of pride.

Personal buoyancy apparatus - lifejackets and personal buoyancy aids. (PBA's)

Before any consideration is given to personal buoyancy apparatus, it is essential that the yachtsman understands the difference between a lifejacket and a personal buoyancy aid (PBA).

A lifejacket.

Halter-like, a lifejacket fits over the head and is usually taped around the waist. It provides most buoyancy at the front, high on the chest, and a lesser amount right round the neck. Made in both adults and childrens sizes, it can save life.

The Department of Trade and Industry approves a lifejacket if it complies with British Standard BS 3595:1969, **provided** it does not entirely depend upon oral inflation. Many lifejackets **do** wholly depend upon oral inflation to meet the British Standards requirements.

BS 3595:1969 requires a lifejacket to be so made that it is capable of providing 35 lb. buoyancy after inflation. This figure becomes more meaningful if one bears in mind that about 12 lb. buoyancy will prevent a person from sinking. When fully inflated - that repetitive condition should be noted - such a lifejacket will allow the wearer to repose in the water in a position which will allow him to breathe freely in moderate waves, even though he may be exhausted or unconscious. Further, it must be capable of turning an unconscious wearer on to his back, so that his face is supported clear of the water.

A personal buoyancy aid (PBA)

The design of a PBA is invariably that of a sleeveless, padded body jacket which is zipped, taped or laced up. Such a garment is intended to be worn at all times when afloat. The majority depend for their buoyancy upon some form of inherent buoyancy such as closed cell foam kapok, air-filled PVC sachets, etc. A few depend upon oral inflation.

This safety device is well-named: it makes no pretence of achieving the qualities of a lifejacket. No British Standard is involved, which some may regard as unfortunate. Nevertheless, the Ship and Boat Builders National Federation - the SBBNF - have themselves declared their own standard for PBA's. It is a high one.

The yachtsman may have confidence in the ability of a PBA giving him a considerable degree of buoyancy in the water, provided it has obtained the SBBNF mark of approval. The standard provides four buoyancies:—

1. Weight range up to 3 stones, possessing 8lb. buoyancy.

2. Weight range between 3 and 6 stones, possessing 12lb. buoyancy.

3. Weight range between 6 and 10 stones, possessing 16lb. buoyancy.

4. Weight range between 10 and 15 stones, possessing 21lb. buoyancy.

A small number of PBA's reach for the high standard required of an approved lifejacket but others fall far short of of it. Even those which are given SBBNF approval may merely meet the standards, or they may markedly exceed it.

Lifejacket or PBA?

The Department of Trade and Industry recommends that, if one intends sailing outside sheltered waters, one lifejacket which conforms to BS 3595:1969 be carried for every person on board. This is authoritative and wise counsel.

The Dept. recognises that in sheltered waters less demanding conditions often exist. Sailing in a river or lake in company with other craft would be a case in point. In these cases it is recommended that, as a minimum precaution, a PBA which conforms to the SBBNF standard be worn. Should a yachtsman require a high degree of safety in all conditions, he should of course wear the type of lifejacket approved by the Department of Trade and Industry.

Practically, the man who cruises offshore should consider providing both types for himself and his crew. The PBA can be worn continuously and the lifejacket donned over the PBA in the case of shipwreck or similar catastrophe. The man who, though not possessing his own craft, often crews for others would be wise to carry his own personal buoyancy apparatus. There is a tendency amongst owners to provide for family members but not for itinerants.

Which type of lifejacket?

The variation in types of lifejacket which conform to the British Standard is considerable. As it is well for the yachtsman to be clear about the advantages and disadvantages of each type, they are listed below.

1. Those having a proportion of built-in buoyancy (closed cell foam, PVC air pockets, etc.), which provides an initial degree of buoyancy on immersion. Thereafter, they must be orally inflated to be wholly effective as a lifejacket.

2. As in 1. above, but fitted with a CO_2 charge which, when triggered, will inflate the lifejacket to maximum buoyancy. The charge may be operated by a ripcord or similar device.

3. Those having no built-in buoyancy which are only capable of achieving the British Standard after complete oral inflation.

4. As in 3. but are inflated by a CO_2 charge which must be actuated manually.

5. As in 3. but inflated partially by mouth and partially by a CO_2 charge.

6. As in 3. but fitted with a gas cylinder which, on immersion in water, automatically inflates the lifejacket.

7. As in 3. but fitted with a gas cylinder which must be manually operated to achieve inflation.

It is not intended to make recommendations here: the desire is to draw to the notice of the reader certain points which he should bear in mind when considering purchase.

It will be appreciated that each of the types listed on page 142. with the exception of the one which automatically inflates itself in the water, requires inflation before the wearer goes overboard. Only by this means can a high degree of safety be assured. But can it be said that the opportunity to inflate a lifejacket will always offer itself when an emergency arises? No doubt because the answer to this question must necessarily be a negative one is the reason why the D.T.I. gives approval only to those lifejackets which have a proportion of built-in buoyancy. (1 and 2 on page 142). These types will give some degree of initial support to a person who finds himself unexpectedly in the sea.

Suddenly finding himself in the water, a person wearing a lifejacket having no built-in buoyancy will, if he is a poor swimmer, probably find himself incapable of orally inflating a lifejacket. This will certainly apply to a non-swimmer, whose panic would probably be such that even the manual operation of a gas device would not occur to him.

The occasional case of a strong swimmer who is unconscious on strking the water cannot be ignored. Wearing an uninflated lifejacket he will certainly drown unless someone goes to his aid. A yachtsman may consider gambling upon the fact that such an occurrence is unlikely to happen.

Automatic inflation would appear to be the simple answer to these disturbing possibilities, yet is one quite prepared to wholly depend upon the proper operation of an automatic device?

The beginner who sees the simple answer to all these problems as being the complete inflation of a lifejacket whenever one is worn has not tried working a boat with the bulk of an inflated lifejacket around his neck and chest. Each yachtsman has to come to terms with himself in connection with the selection and subsequent use of a lifejacket.

Which type of PBA?

Choice of a PBA is somewhat easier than that of a lifejacket. Most types depend upon some form of permanent buoyancy. They are meant to be worn at all times and so they are essentially working jackets. This means that a puncture or a slash can easily be acquired, hence a PBA which depends for its buoyancy upon a small number of air-filled PVC sachets may have its efficiency greatly reduced if one or two were punctured. In normal conditions it may fairly be said that there is little to choose between the various types of 'filling'.

Not all PBA's available meet the exacting standard of the SBBNF but choice should be limited to those types which do achieve it. It will be appreciated that any PBA which depends either wholly or partially upon oral inflation will have all the limitations inherent in lifejackets of similar type.

Markings on lifejackets and PBA's.

A purchaser having decided that he will insist upon an approved pattern of either lifejacket or PBA, should be aware that the type he requires will be clearly recognisable by its markings.

A lifejacket which meets the requirements of BS 3595:1969 should have printed upon it the BS number, the fact that it is a lifejacket, the date of manufacture and instructions for its use. A PBA approved by the SBBNF may not have the above detail upon it but it will clearly state that it is a PBA as opposed to a lifejacket, together with a SBBNF mark of approval.

Care of lifejackets and PBA's.

Any buoyancy apparel is of value only so long as it continues to meet the standards to which it was made. Careless use and unwise stowage can quickly reduce it below these standards.

Makers instructions for care should be followed, an exhortation which particularly applies to apparel which depends entirely upon oral inflation for its effectiveness. In any event it is seamanlike to carry out a thorough annual inspection. It must be remembered that gas cylinders are useless unless they are fully charged, and triggering devices for them may seize up over a long period in sea conditions.

Recommended safety equipment for sea-going pleasure craft of 5·5 metres (18 feet) to 13·7 metres (45 feet) in length overall

PERSONAL SAFETY EQUIPMENT

Safety harness – to BSI specification. One for each person on sailing yachts. One or more on motor cruisers as may be needed when on deck.

Wear a safety harness on deck in bad weather or at night. Make sure it is properly adjusted. Experience has shown, however, that a harness can be dangerous if you go overboard at speeds of 8 knots or more.

Lifejackets – of Department of Trade and Industry accepted type or BSI specification. One for each person.

Keep them in a safe place where you can get at them easily. Always wear one when there is a risk of being pitched overboard.

RESCUE EQUIPMENT FOR MAN OVERBOARD

Lifebuoys – two at least.

One lifebuoy should be kept within easy reach of the helmsman. For sailing at night, it should be fitted with a self-igniting light.

Buoyant line – 30 metres (100 feet) minimum breaking strain of 115 kilos (250 lb)). This too should be within easy reach of the helmsman.

OTHER FLOTATION EQUIPMENT FOR VESSELS GOING MORE THAN THREE MILES OUT, SUMMER AND WINTER:

Inflatable liferaft – of Department of Trade and Industry accepted type, or equivalent – to carry everyone on board. It should be carried on deck or in a locker opening directly to the deck and should be serviced annually; OR

Rigid dinghy – with permanent, not inflatable, buoyancy, and with oars and rowlocks secured. It should be carried on deck. It may be a collapsible type; OR

Inflatable dinghy – built with two compartments, one at least always kept fully inflated, or built with one compartment, always kept fully inflated, and having oars and rowlocks secured.

It should be carried on deck. If the vessel has enough permanent buoyancy to float when swamped with 115 kilos (250 lb) added weight, a dinghy with two compartments may be stowed. In sheltered waters a dinghy may be towed. Check that the tow is secure.

FOR VESSELS GOING NOT MORE THAN THREE MILES OUT IN WINTER (1 NOVEMBER TO 31 MARCH):

Inflatable liferaft or alternatives, as above.

In sheltered waters the summer scale equipment, listed below, may usually be adequate. Liferafts may not be necessary on angling boats operating in organised groups when the boats are continually in contact with each other.

FOR VESSELS GOING NOT MORE THAN THREE MILES OUT IN SUMMER (1 APRIL TO 31 OCTOBER)

Lifebuoys – (30-inch) or **Buoyant seats** – of Department of Trade and Industry accepted type. One for every two people on board.

Lifebuoys carried for 'man overboard' situations may be included. Those smaller than 30-inch diameter should be regarded as support for one person only.

GENERAL EQUIPMENT

Anchors – two, each with warp or chain of appropriate size and length. Where warp is used at least 5.5 metres (3 fathoms) of chain should be used between anchor and warp.

Bilge Pump. Efficient compass – and spare.

Charts – covering intended area of operation.

Distress flares – size with two of the rocket parachute type.

Daylight distress (smoke) signals. Tow-rope of adequate length.

First-aid box – with anti-seasickness tablets.

Radio receiver – for weather forecasts. **Water-resistant torch.**

Radar reflector – of adequate performance. As large as can be conveniently carried. Preferably mounted at least 3 metres (10 feet) above sea level.

Lifeline – also useful in bad weather for inboard lifeline. **Engine tool kit.**

Name, number or generally recognised **sail number** – should be painted prominently on the vessel or on dodgers in letters or figures at least 22 centimetres (9 inches) high.

FIRE-FIGHTING EQUIPMENT

For vessels over 9 metres (30 feet) in length and those with powerful engines, carrying quantities of fuel – two fire extinguishers should be carried, each of not less than 1.4 kilos (3 lb) capacity, dry powder, or equivalent, and one or more additional extinguisher of not less than 2.3 kilos (5 lb) capacity, dry powder, or equivalent, A fixed installation may be necessary.

For vessels of up to 9 metres (30 feet) in length, with cooking facilities and engines – two fire extinguishers should be carried, each of not less than 1.4 kilos (3 lb) capacity, dry powder, or equivalent.

For vessels of up to 9 metres (30 feet) in length, with cooking facilities only or with engine only – one fire extinguisher should be carried, of not less than 1.4 kilos (3 lb) capacity, dry powder, or equivalent.

Carbon dioxide (CO_2) or foam extinguishers of equal extinguishing capacity are alternatives to dry powder appliances. BCF (bromo-chloro-difluoro-methane) or BTM (bromo-trifluoro-methane) may be carried, but people on the boat should be warned that the fumes given off are toxic and dangerous in a confined space, and a similar notice should be posted at each extinguisher point.

Additionally for all craft:

Buckets – two, with lanyards.

Bag of sand – useful in containing and extinguishing burning spillage of fuel or lubricant.

Your craft should have been designed and built with the object of keeping fire risks to a minimum, but a check may be made on such 'built-in' precautions by referring to the Home Office pamphlet 'Fire Precautions in Pleasure Craft' (HMSO, price 12½p).

Recommended safety equipment for pleasure craft of less than 5·5 metres (18 feet) in length overall

Craft of less than 5.5 metres (18 feet) in length overall cover a wide variety – from dinghies and motor cruisers to boats for sea-angling trips, diving and water ski-ing. All are limited in the amount of equipment and the number of people they can carry and there are separate recommendations for them given on the following pages. For deep-sea sailing more than three miles from base and for cruising follow the recommendations, as far as possible, for craft of 5.5 to 13.7 metres (18 feet to 45 feet).

Never overload. The number of people or the amount of equipment a boat can carry is generally shown on a plate fitted by the builder. Sea-angling vessels should be more restricted and the following scale is recommended.

Craft of
4.9 metres (16 feet) to less than 5.5 metres (18 feet): **4 persons**
4.3 metres (14 feet) to less than 4.9 metres (16 feet): **3 persons**
3.7 metres (12 feet) to less than 4.3 metres (14 feet): **2 persons**

Sea-angling from craft of less than 3.7 metres (12 feet) in length is hazardous.

Owners who are going to be at sea more than three miles from base, or whose craft are designed for cruising, should, as far as possible, follow the recommendations for craft of 5.5 metres to 13.7 metres (18 feet to 45 feet).

It is recommended that other craft in this category shall carry the following unless taking part in organised club events with specific safety equipment required.

PERSONAL SAFETY EQUIPMENT

Lifejackets – of Department of Trade and Industry accepted type or BSI specification. One for each person on board.

Alternatively, in sheltered waters, one buoyancy aid, of the Ship and Boat Builders National Federation approved type, for each person on board. Always wear a lifejacket or buoyancy aid when there is a risk of being pitched overboard.

RESCUE EQUIPMENT

Lifebuoy – one, and a 30-metre (100 feet) **buoyant line** (minimum breaking strain of 115 kilos (250 lb)), where practicable.

Alternatively, one Department of Trade and Industry accepted rescue quoit. A second lifebuoy should be carried on motor cruisers and, where practicable, on other craft.

GENERAL EQUIPMENT

Anchor – of sufficient size and with a long enough mooring line or cable, according to the type and size of craft and the possible areas of operation.

A spare anchor and tow-line of 18 metres (10 fathoms) advisable, especially for sea-angling trips.

Efficient bilge pump, and a **bailer** or **bucket** with lanyard (even if the yacht is fitted with a self-bailer).

For powered craft, the bilge pump should be fixed. On other craft a portable bilge pump which can draw water from the sea may be useful for fire fighting.

Paddle or **oar with rowlock** – one at least: two if practicable.

Distress signals – two at least. Even in sheltered waters adequate distress signals should be carried.

Compass – for motor cruisers, angler's craft, dinghy cruising and racing.

First-aid kit.

Water-resistant torch.

Radar reflector – or adequate performance. For craft engaged in sea-angling and cruising in the open sea.

Radio receiver – for craft engaged in sea-angling and cruising in the open sea.

Engine tool kit.

FIRE-FIGHTING EQUIPMENT

One fire extinguisher of not less than 1.4 kilos (3 lb) capacity, dry powder (where fuel is carried), or two if galley is also fitted.

Carbon dioxide (CO_2) or foam extinguishers of equal extinguishing capacity are alternatives to dry powder appliances. BCF (bromo-chloro-difluoro-methane) or BTM (bromo-trifluoro-methane) may be carried, but people on the boat should be warned that the fumes given off are toxic and dangerous in a confined space and a similar notice should be posted at each extinguisher point. A blanket or rug soaked in the sea may also be effective in fighting fires.

Bucket – with lanyard, one, (which may be that used as a bailer).

Your craft should have been designed and built with the object of keeping fire risks to a minimum, but a check may be made on such 'built-in' precautions by referring to the Home Office pamphlet 'Fire Precautions in Pleasure Craft' (HMSO, price 12½p).

ADDITIONAL SAFEGUARD

Yachtsmen making a coastal passage in UK waters are strongly advised to contact the local HM Coastguard station to complete a Coastguard '66' Passage Report Form. This ensures that the Coastguard Service has full particulars regarding the craft, occupants, its equipment and intended voyage, for use should search and rescue action be needed. At his destination, the yachtsman reports his arrival to the nearest Coastguard station. **There is no charge for this service.**

Reprinted from the booklet "How safe is your craft?" with the permission of the Controller of H.M. Stationery Office and the Department of Trade and Industry.

Copies of the booklet can be obtained from: **Information Division, Room 306, Department of Trade and Industry, 1 Gaywood House, Great Peter Street, London SW1P 3LW.**

The use of dinghies.

Unseamanlike practices and negligence are common reasons for the great number of accidents which occur when dinghies are used for ferrying between the shore and privately-owned pleasure craft.

Dinghies of any type have a limited capacity. Frequently there is a tendency to overload if the alternative is to make two journeys to some distant mooring.

In terms of safety, inflatable dinghies are generally preferable to tiny wooden or glass fibre ones. The smaller the dinghy the more dangerous it will be to use.

An owner or skipper should insist that PBA's be worn whenever his dinghy is being used. If it is to be used as a temporary plaything for children he should first find out something of the competence of the children and in any case insist that they wear PBA's. He should provide it with at least one buoyant painter and fit the sculls with lanyards.

The ability to swim.

The ability to swim well is obviously of great importance to anyone who seeks his recreation afloat. The non-swimmer who is intent upon taking to the water would do well to attend a local swimming bath during the winter months.

Obviously the non-swimmer at sea in a small boat must wear a personal buoyancy aid at all times when above decks. The man who foolishly indicates to others that he can swim, when in fact he cannot, is taking an unwarranted risk with his own life and may possibly hazard the lives of others.

Fire precautions.

A great number of serious fires and explosions have occurred in small craft and many of them were attributed to inadequate fittings and to carelessness. The yachtsman who seeks authoritative advice in relation to fire precautions cannot do better than to obtain the pamphlet 'Fire Precautions in Pleasure Craft' obtainable from HMSO, price 12½p. Therein will also be found a bibliography which lists the British Standards publications detailing equipment and practice to which all yachtsmen should adhere.

Use of liquefied petroleum gas.
(Butane, propane, etc.)

These gases are heavier than air and will, when released, fall to the bottom of a compartment even though the bottom is not directly beneath the source of leakage. When freed they tend to diffuse and then, being mixed with air, they form a mixture which is explosive. Although a stenching agent is added to the liquefied gases to facilitate detection of leaks, a concentration at low level may go unnoticed. The gas is lethal when inhaled and therefore asphyxiation is a distinct possibility in a closed compartment where leakage occurs.

In any craft in which a liquefied petroleum gas is used the following precautions are recommended:

(a) Expert advice should be obtained regarding the fitting of a new installation, and upon one which is suspected to have been fitted by persons other than experts. Amongst other things, all gas pipes should be of unbroken drawn copper and joints should be made of a similar adequate material. The use of rubber tubing is highly dangerous.

(b) Although ideally gas containers should be stowed on deck, or in a well ventilated compartment on deck, if stowage below decks is unavoidable, adequate ventilation to a safe area should be provided. Electrical equipment in or near the compartment should be of flame proof construction.

(c) A non-return valve should be fitted in the supply line of each container and, if stowage is in accommodation, the provision for remote closure of the main supply is recommended.

(d) Pressure-reducing valves must be fitted to container valves. Fail-safe devices should be introduced into feed pipes, one of the type which will close a pipe when pressure is lost and another designed to cut off the supply if burner flames are accidentally extinguished.

(e) The provision of gas detecting devices is a wise precaution, and preferably those which are fitted with an automatic alarm system. Regular testing of such equipment is necessary.

(f) If leakage is suspected, every naked light should be immediately extinguished and all motors stopped. Thereafter the source of leakage should be sought using soapy water: never ever a naked flame.

(g) Many yachtsmen cut off the gas supply at the container whenever it is not in use but in any case this precaution should be taken whenever the boat is unattended.

Use of petrol, paraffin and diesel oil.

All three of these will burn fiercely when fed to a fire, but the flash point of each must be taken into consideration. Flash point is the temperature at which a volatile liquid will give off a gas which, when mixed with air, is explosive when ignited. As the flash point of petrol occurs in normal atmospheric temperatures, it is by far the most dangerous. Although the flash point of paraffin is much higher, and that of diesel oil higher still, conditions within a boat can produce high localised temperatures which can reach and exceed their flash point.

Precautions to be taken when fuelling.

The period during and immediately after fuelling has proved to be a highly dangerous one in small craft. Fire and explosion are the hazards. Any leakage or spillage of petroleum spirit will result in the production of vapour. This vapour, being heavier than air, will fall to the lowest point in any compartment or to the bilges. It may travel some distance to reach the lowest point. When the vapour is mixed with air an explosive mixture is produced. This potentially lethal mixture will remain where it settles unless and until adequate ventilation is achieved to remove it.

Paraffin and diesel oil are, of course, less volatile and simple spillage will not normally produce dangerous conditions in a small craft after the manner of petroleum spirit. Nevertheless, they are by no means innocuous. For example, they will become ignited if spilled on a hot exhaust pipe and will feed any existing fire.

The HMSO pamphlet 'Fire Precautions in Pleasure Craft' details the manner in which fuel installations should be designed and the wise yachtsman will obtain it.

When refuelling the following steps should be taken:

1. Stop the engine.
2. Forbid smoking and the exhibition of naked lights.
3. Keep a constant check on the level of fuel in the tank.
4. Immediately clean up any spilled fuel.
5. Thoroughly ventilate the craft for at least 5 minutes before starting up the engine.

Electrical installations.

Short circuits, arcing and overloads are the fire hazards in electrical circuits. Any of these can become a source of ignition of inflammable vapour, the contents of a craft or the craft itself. Properly designed and approved circuits are the only safeguard against mishap.

Small craft which have the means by which lead-acid or nickel-alkali batteries may be charged aboard must beware of an additional danger. Such batteries give off explosive gases when charging. If they are charged in an unventilated compartment and accidental arcing at the terminals occurs, a severe local explosion will result. Obviously, maximum ventilation round charging batteries is essential.

Emergencies.

Emergencies which may beset the yachtsman may be broadly categorised as follows:–

Shipwreck, disablement, fire, explosion
and man overboard.

This section is intended to give advice upon various aspects of disaster and rescue, and means by which assistance may be summoned.

Distress.

A state of danger is usually a matter of degree. Before invoking the assistance of a massive, expensive rescue organisation it is essential to assess whether the degree of distress is such that it cannot be overcome by means within the capability of the crew. The skipper must necessarily be the sole arbiter in this assessment. He may decide, some time before disaster strikes, that catastrophe is inevitable, and assistance must be summoned forthwith.

Distress signals.

Whatever the mode of distress call made, when it is received from or sighted by another vessel, International Law requires that vessel to proceed to the vessel in distress and to render assistance if practicable. Yachtsmen will note that, if distress signals are sighted by them, they too must take similar action. A mariner is absolved from this responsibility if to do so would be to seriously imperil his own craft.

Annex IV of the International Regulations for the Prevention of Collision at Sea (q.v.) enumerates the various means by which distress signals may be made. Some of those listed are not applicable to small craft. Others, such as flag signals, have limited value in that they could go unnoticed.

Naturally, every means of attracting attention should be used, either together or separately, but the following methods are likely to prove most effective in the case of small craft:–

1. **Radio-telephony.**
   Broadcast of the international distress signal 'Mayday' on 2182 kHz. It is essential to give the vessel's name and position in any distress call. Continuous transmissions from the craft in distress will enable shore stations to obtain a fix by radio-direction finding apparatus but this cannot be relied upon.

   On hearing a distress call, all other craft using this working frequency will immediately observe radio silence. In the event air traffic is such that the 'Mayday' call is not heard by others, advantage must be taken of silence periods. During the 3-minute period after every hour and half hour, total radio silence is mandatory. In these periods only distress calls may be made.

   On receipt of a distress call by a shore radio station, whether it is received direct or has been relayed by another vessel, the details are immediately passed to a rescue co-ordination centre. For details of this, see Chapter 19 – H.M. Coastguards.

2. **Pyrotechnic signals.**
   Both by day and by night, pyrotechnics are the most effective visual distress signals. Details of types are given on page 149.

   Such signals may be sighted by any person, whether afloat or ashore. It must not be assumed that persons other than coastguards will not heed the obvious message of red pyrotechnics offshore. A 999 telephone call reporting the sighting of such signals will be relayed to the nearest coastguard station.

   Anxiety and panic produce a desire to let off all one's distress signals in quick succession, yet disciplined and intelligent use is essential. Parachute distress rockets should be fired first, with reasonably long intervals elapsing between each rocket. Hand flares are best preserved to enable rescue craft to pinpoint one's position when approaching lights at night indicate that assistance is on the way.

   Detailed instructions for use are printed on all pyrotechnic signals. All crew members should know how to discharge such signals and, equally important, where they are stowed within the craft.

Forms of rescue.

1. From other vessels and craft in the vicinity.

2. From the Royal National Lifeboat Institution, by lifeboat when offshore and by high speed inflatable power boats when inshore.

3. From the Royal Navy, if vessels are within range. Depending upon availability, helicopters may be used.

4. From the Royal Air Force, through their air/sea rescue services which include helicopters and high speed launches.

The period between the receipt of a distress signal by shore authorities and the arrival of assistance is obviously a variable one. At worst it could be some hours. At best it could be a few minutes when other vessels are close at hand.

In general, small craft are best suited for rendering assistance to other small craft in heavy weather. This does not mean that one can afford to spurn assistance from a large vessel. To effect a rescue a large vessel will in all probability manoeuvre in such a manner that the yacht in distress is brought under her lee. Thereafter a boat may be lowered or scrambling nets provided to enable those in distress to be brought to safety.

Abandon ship - or not?

Experience has proved that, so long as a craft remains afloat, her crew should remain aboard. The overhasty manning of a liferaft is undesirable. In a gale such a raft will be quickly blown down-wind and the task of rescuers will be rendered more difficult.

Where no liferaft is carried the wisdom in remaining aboard as long as possible is more manifest. Death from exposure can occur within the hour in our latitudes and no efficient lifejacket or inflatable dinghy can prevent it.

When it is borne in mind that a liferaft, the canopy of which will provide essential protection from the elements, can support life for days, the reader may consider this a cogent reason for carrying one.

To beach a craft - or not?

In heavy weather the temptation to beach a craft on a lee shore must be avoided, even though the beach may be invitingly smooth. All available evidence indicates that such a measure will prove disastrous to craft and crew. Obviously a seaman must so navigate his craft that lee shore conditions do not become a hazard. Finding himself in this situation, he must make every endeavour to claw to windward and to heave-to until assistance arrives or the weather abates.

It sometimes occurs that a port or haven is located on a lee shore. In difficulties due to heavy weather, a yachtsman may consider that to run for shelter down-wind is preferable to standing off shore. Such action is fraught with dangers. It will probably be found that the sea inshore is wholly unnavigable.

Accepting a tow when disabled.

In heavy weather only small craft are suitable for towing other small craft. Although proceeding at slow speed, a large vessel may well drag a yacht through large seas and foundering could follow. Large vessels cannot give immediate variations in speed. The danger lies in the constant, unrelenting pressure on the towing hawser. Again, in bad weather they are unlikely to be able to steam at a speed which is low enough to allow the craft in distress to ride the seas comfortably.

Having decided to accept a tow, the yachtsman who carries his own towing warp should use it in preference to that of the towing vessel. His warp will be particularly suited to his needs. If a heavy towing hawser is offered by a larger vessel, there is much to be said for bending one's own towrope to that of the other. In a seaway, the longer the towing warp, the less chance there is of it breaking under sudden stress.

To use the base of the mast as a position for securing a towing warp is highly dangerous: a capsize may result. It is unseamanlike to put the eye of a towrope over bitts or a towing bollard. If the towing operation becomes hazardous for any reason, it may be necessary to quickly slip the tow. The eye being used and the hawser being taut, it may be impossible to throw it off. Severence of the hawser may take time which one cannot spare. The wise course is to turn up the towrope on the bitts or towing bollard in such a manner that it can rapidly be eased away and slipped.

The first connection with a towing vessel will probably be by heaving line. A monkey's fist - a plaited ball or round weight - on the end of the line will considerably extend its reach in a high wind. It is customary for the person establishing communication by heaving line to bend his own towing warp on to the heaving line he used. This is of no real consequence so long as hand signals between towing and towed vessel indicate which warp will be used. The possibility of minor accidents in these initial operations is real and controlled speed is essential.

Salvage.

The artless acceptance of a tow from another vessel may result in a salvage claim against the vessel accepting the tow. A salvage claim is unlikely to be made by other amateur seamen but the possibility cannot be wholly ignored. Evidently one must be quite sure that a safe haven cannot be reached by one's own exertions, or with the assistance of a friendly craft. This being ascertained, there is no alternative to acceptance of a tow from a willing stranger.

Salvage agreements are generally made on a 'No cure - no pay' basis and so the towing vessel generally has to take the distressed vessel into a safe refuge for a salvage claim to have validity. Owners would do well to read 'Memorandum on Salvage', an article published in the Royal Yachting Association year book.

Rescue by helicopter.

From the air it will be difficult for a helicopter crew to determine whether a craft is in distress or not, particularly if other similar craft are in the vicinity. Every means of attracting attention from the air is necessary. Pyrotechnics, dye markers and the making of smoke immediately come to mind but any practical device should be used.

The double-lift technique is used by the RAF. A winchman is lowered to the vessel in distress and thereafter rescuer and rescued are winched to safety. One by one the crew will be taken aboard the helicopter.

Obviously the winchman's job is a dangerous one. It is essential to render his vertical descent as free from hazards as possible. A weaving mast is a danger which he usually has to accept, yet evidently he will be lowered as far away from it as possible on the most clear area of deck. The yachtsman can reduce the degree of danger the winchman must face by clearing away or cutting away sails, booms and other paraphernalia.

A violently rolling and pitching craft is an extremely difficult platform on which to alight. A Skipper will probably be able to do little to reduce the movement of his craft but perhaps by sheeting a headsail hard, or by use of the rudder, some small degree of abatement may be achieved.

Fire and explosion.

Fire at sea can be a terrifying experience, whether the sea be calm or otherwise. Other than abandoning ship, one has no means of escape from it. However tiny, a fire must be treated as serious from the outset and every means of extinguishing a blaze must be brought to bear. If a fire is not immediately extinguished, then jettisoning of butane containers and fuel tanks must be carried out, together with preparations for abandoning ship.

If fire occurs in port these advices have equal importance but one crew member, or any other available person, must call the fire brigade.

It is impossible to provide guidelines for action in the event of explosion. Damage may be slight or serious: injuries may be sustained: fire may follow. Prevention of the conditions which will produce explosion is the yachtsman's only defence against it.

Man overboard.

Whether a man who falls overboard is wearing personal buoyancy equipment or not, whether he can swim or not, his life is going to depend to a considerable extent upon the skill and judgement of the helmsman. An immediate requirement is for the craft to be laid alongside the person in the water. This is not intended to be a discourse in seamanship and the manner in which this is achieved must be left to individual helmsmen.

Apart from taking instant action to turn the craft round, the helmsman must throw a lifebuoy towards but not at the man in the water. The self-igniting light which should be attached to the lifebuoy will pinpoint the swimmer at night and pinpoint the lifebuoy for the swimmer. Failing a lifebuoy, a buoyant cushion will assist.

During these initial seconds, the helmsman must also raise the alarm. One hand must be detailed to intently keep his eyes upon the swimmer and to point towards him throughout. Even in daylight a person in the water quickly becomes very difficult to see as distance increases and waves intercede.

A boathook or buoyant heaving line must be extended to the man in the sea as soon as he comes within reach and, having been drawn alongside, the problem of getting him onboard remains. Whether this is an easy task or an extremely difficult one will depend upon his degree of exhaustion. The use of bowlines, tackles, parbuckles and other seamanlike methods provide sundry means of achieving this, yet all hands reaching over the side to grasp his clothing will probably be the method adopted and in fact this is less likely to cause body injury.

He who is a poor or a non-swimmer and is wearing no buoyancy aid may well become a fatality. If another crew member enters the water to go to his aid two deaths by drowning could possibly result. Although the non-swimmer may be quite willing to accept the risks involved in voyaging in small craft at sea, the wise skipper will insist that he either wears a personal buoyancy aid at all times when on deck, or he remains ashore.

Pyrotechnic signals for use by small craft.

The D.T.I. make it mandatory for all vessels over 45ft in length to carry pyrotechnic distress signals. Those between 45 and 70 feet in length must carry a minimum of six, which shall be parachute distress signals complying with D.T.I. requirements, or red star distress signals with similar stipulations attached to them. Basically, the requirements are that such distress signals must ascend to a minimum height, and that they must burn with a stipulated minimum luminosity for a minimum length of time.

Evidently craft under 45 feet in length which make similar voyages should conform to these requirements because the inherent dangers are no less real to them. The writer regards minimum requirements as a quantity below which one's stocks must not fall. From the point of view of safety, a greater quantity is highly desirable.

The Schermuly range of distress signals are widely used by vessels of all dimensions and types. All obtain D.T.I. approval, which is to say that their standard is high, and for yachtsmen they are obtainable in the following waterproof packs:—

1. **Deepwater pack** for vessels 45 feet in length and above:—
   6 rocket parachute flares
   4 red hand flares
   1 buoyant orange smoke signal

2. **Cruiser pack**
   6 rocket parachute flares

3. **Offshore pack**
   2 rocket parachute flares
   3 red hand flares

It is the opinion of the writer that for all small boat sailors who venture to sea, the deep water pack is desirable in the interests of safety and even that should be augmented by a minimum of 4 white hand flares for use at night when desiring to attract the attention of another vessel to one's presence.

CHAPTER 12

Signalling

Sooner or later the yachtsman will find that some form of communication is essential and it is not always convenient to approach within hailing distance of another craft or to go ashore.

He may say to himself that, being familiar with distress signals which he will not hesitate to use if the need arises, he can manage without refinements, but can he? If a shore station calls him using the Morse Code, can he afford to ignore the summons? It may be an urgent message, even a personal one. A single flag displayed by another vessel or a shore signal station may be a message of an urgent nature which is directed to him alone. Does he wish to disregard a signal which may warn him of imminent danger?

Signalling methods.
The various methods of communication at sea, pertaining to small craft, are given below:–

1. **Radio telephony.(R/T).**
Radio telephony is communication by telephone using radio waves instead of telephone wires as the link between two people. It provides the means by which one can speak direct to any vessel carrying R/T equipment, any telephone subscriber on shore and, most important of all, it is by far the most speedy and reliable means of making distress calls in the absence of W/T. Effective range of R/T varies according to the type of equipment carried.

A few years ago the power demands, the cost and the sheer bulk of necessary equipment precluded its use in small craft but this is no longer true. The vast strides which have been made in radio technology are responsible for the change. Although equipment remains costly, the reduced size of modern sets coupled with increased reliability and efficiency makes it suitable equipment for all but very small sea-going craft.

All radio installations on British ships must be licenced. So that he may learn what steps he must take to obtain the necessary sanction to operate R/T equipment, the yachtsman is advised to obtain the HMSO publication, 'Licensing Radio Telephone Apparatus'. It is obtainable from the Post Office, Radio and Broadcasting Department, Wireless Telegraphy Section, Union House, St.Martin's-le-Grand, London, E.C.1.

Operating instructions are provided with all R/T installations but, as is well known, an easily understood jargon and set pattern of procedure is adopted when talking on R/T. This is essential when establishing communication and when passing important messages. Two volumes will provide a yachtsman with the essential information he needs:–

(a) 'Handbook for Radio Operators', published by and obtainable direct from HMSO.
(b) 'Admiralty List of Radio Signals'. Volume 1, Coast Radio Stations, which may be bought from Admiralty chart agents.

2. **The Morse Code transmitted by light.**
One of the most effective means by which yachtsmen can communicate with other vessels and with shore stations is the Morse Code using a signal light. The standard Aldis daylight signalling lamp, battery powered, is ideal for use by them. Such a lamp, purchasable from many yacht chandlers, should be regarded as standard equipment on all sea-going craft. An Aldis lamp has an effective range of many miles during daylight in clear weather. At night a suitable torch will be found to be adequate for short range transmissions but an Aldis will be required for long range transmissions.

The Morse Code which follows includes only the English symbols of the International Code. The full code includes extra symbols to meet the peculiarities in spelling of certain foreign languages but they are extraneous for the general purposes of British yachtsmen.

INTERNATIONAL MORSE CODE

Alphabet

Meaning	Symbol	Meaning	Symbol	Meaning	Symbol
A	.—	*J*	.———	*S*	...
B	—...	*K*	—.—	*T*	—
C	—.—.	*L*	.—..	*U*	..—
D	—..	*M*	——	*V*	...—
E	.	*N*	—.	*W*	.——
F	..—.	*O*	———	*X*	—..—
G	——.	*P*	.——.	*Y*	—.——
H	....	*Q*	——.—	*Z*	——..
I	..	*R*	.—.		

Numerals

Meaning	Symbol
1	.————
2	..———
3	...——
4	....—
5	.....
6	—....
7	——...
8	———..
9	————.
0	—————

Punctuation

Meaning	Sign	Symbol
Fullstop(.) and decimal point	*AAA*	.—.—.—

If it is assumed that a dot is a unit of time, then dashes and space intervals should be made as follows:—

Dot	1 unit of time
Dash	3 units of time
Space between each dash or dot in a letter	1 unit of time
Space between each letter or symbol	3 units of time
Space between each word or group	7 units of time

Only by the adoption of this timing can Morse be made intelligible. A common fault is to make a dot a little too long, and a dash a little too short, so that the receiving station has difficulty in differentiating between them. If lack of practice bedevils he who transmits, it is better by far to shorten the dots and lengthen the dashes, so that confusion cannot possibly arise.

When a letter has been missed in a word, it is often possible to accurately guess what it was from the remaining letters of the same word. It is common practice to spell out numerals in full when precision is essential and amateurs are well advised to adopt this practice at all times.

It is frequently the case that the unpracticed person is able to transmit rather faster than he can receive Morse signals. He must remember to transmit at the same speed as he can receive. This is necessary because it is the custom at sea to reply to a signal at the same speed at which it was sent. Lack of knowledge of this practice can lead to the confusion and exasperation on the part of the yachtsman.

Morse procedure signals.

If disorder is to be avoided when sending and receiving Morse signals by light, or indeed by any other means, a standard procedure must be adopted. The following procedure signals have been adopted internationally and so they should be learned and used. The bar which is placed over certain signs indicates that no pause occurs between letters.

PROCEDURE SIGNALS AND SIGNS

Meaning	*Signs*	*Symbol*
Call for unknown ship and general call	AA AA, etc.	.—.— .—.— etc
Answering sign	$\overline{\text{TTTTTTT}}$, etc.	— — — — — — etc
Erase sign	$\overline{\text{EEEEEEEE}}$	.... etc
Repeat sign	RPT	.—..— —.—
All after	AA	.—.—
All before	AB	.— —...
Word or group between	BN	—...—.
Word or group after	WA	.— —.—
Word or group before	WB	.— — —...
Ending sign	$\overline{\text{AR}}$	.—.—.
From	De	—...
Yes, or previous group should be read in the affirmative	C	—.—.
Message received	R	.—.
Word(plain language) received	T	—
International Code groups follow	YU or INTERCO	—.— —..—
Full Stop and Decimal Point	AAA	.—.—.—

Method of signalling

Let us assume that a yacht named 'Alpha' has a message for another yacht named 'Beta':—

1. **The call.** 'Alpha' will commence by sending the call to 'Beta' which she flashes continuously until it is answered. If 'Alpha' is unaware of the other yacht's name, she will use the general call. Otherwise, she will use the name 'Beta', or 'Beta's' signal letters.

'Beta' having observed the call and being quite ready to receive a Morse message, will reply with the answering sign.

2. **The identification.** If identification is necessary, as would be the case if 'Beta' is unknown to 'Alpha', names or signal letters will be exchanged. 'Alpha' makes De (from) 'Alpha' or her signal letters, whereupon 'Beta' repeats the name or signal letters and follows it with her own name or signal letters. These are then repeated by 'Alpha'.

When both transmitting and receiving crafts are already aware of each other's identities this identification procedure is unnecessary. When more than one message is to be passed, it would be similarly unnecessary to repeat identification after initially establishing identities.

3. **The message.** Each word of the message is then sent separately and 'Beta' must acknowledge receipt of each word by sending T (word received). If a word is not read by 'Beta' she must not acknowledge with T. This is the indication to 'Alpha' that she must send the word again, and yet again if necessary.

4. **The ending.** The message being completed, 'Alpha' sends the ending signal, AR and it is answered by 'Beta' with R. This ends the communication.

Example.

Yacht 'Alpha' wishes to signal yacht 'Beta', who is unknown to her, the following message:—

Can you spare some fresh water please?

'Alpha' transmits		'Beta' receives and makes
AA AA AA AA AA etc.		TTTT etc.
De yacht 'Alpha'		De yacht 'Beta'
De yacht 'Beta'		De yacht 'Beta'
Can		T
you		T
spare	(not received)	—
spare	(not received)	—
spare		T
some		T
fresh		T
water	(not received)	—
water		T
please		T
AR		R

Note: Signal letters comprise a group of four letters — GMUR, for instance—by which a ship, vessel or yacht may be identified when signalling by any method. They are allocated to a vessel by the Registrar General of Shipping and Seamen when it is registered with that authority. Any craft may be registered but, as there is no compulsion for craft plying for pleasure of under 15 tons to do so, rather understandably few small craft are. Signal letters having been allocated to a craft, they are printed in the International Code of Signals. It will be appreciated that signal letters are only meaningful when both craft communicating are in possession of this publication.

5. **Flag Signalling by use of the Inernational Code of Signals.**

The forty individual flags pennants and burgees which make up the International Code of flag signals are illustrated and listed on page 235. It will be noted that each one represents a letter of the alphabet, or a numeral, or it has special significance. Only the book, 'The International Code of Signals' provides the means by which the yachtsman may make full use of this signalling method.

Obviously, the size of the flags will govern the distance at which they will be seen and recognised. Small craft are necessarily confined to the use of small flags, hence their effective range is reduced. One more obstacle remains. The transmission of lengthy signals using code flags is often wholly impractical in small craft, either due to the limitations of the craft or its time consuming nature in a severely confined area.

There remains a potent reason why a yachtsman should possess the full range of International Code Flags. The Code includes single letter signals of a very urgent nature, and others in common use by all vessels. All seamen, both professional and amateur, should know the significance of the single letter signals so that, if necessary, they may take immediate action on sighting them, and themselves display them when needed. These signals, although commonly used in flag signalling, may be made by any other signalling method. For example, if a yachtsman sees the letter 'U' flashed towards him in the Morse Code continuously, he would take it to mean that he is running into danger.

Quarantine signals.

All countries take steps to ensure that no communicable diseases are brought in and so cause an epidemic. Infected ships, aircraft, crews, passengers and ship-borne rats are all capable of transmitting disease. Until such time as port health authorities have satisfied themselves that a vessel which arrives from another country is 'healthy', strict quarantine is enforced, no person is allowed to go ashore and the appropriate quarantine signal must be kept flying. Clearly, quarantine regulations are more stricly enforced when a vessel arrives from a country which is known to have endemic infectious diseases, and they are considerably relaxed in other cases. Yachtsmen would be most unwise to treat lightly the quarantine regulations of any country, including our own, unless the relaxation allowed by local officers is known to them.

The duties of Port Health Officers are often carried out by officers of the Customs and Excise service and so yachtsmen can expect pratique to be granted by these officers in many cases.

Pratique Messages

ZS	My vessel is healthy and I request free pratique.	Q
	*I require health clearance.	QQ
ZT	My Maritime Declaration of Health has negative answers to the six health questions.	
ZU	My Maritime Declaration of Health has a positive answer to question(s) ... (indicated by appropriate number(s)).	
ZV	I believe I have been in an infected area during the last thirty days.	
ZW	I require Port Medical Officer.	
ZW1	Port Medical Officer will be available at (time indicated).	
ZX	You should make the appropriate pratique signal.	
ZY	You have pratique.	
ZZ	You should proceed to anchorage for health clearance (at place indicated).	
ZZ1	Where is the anchorage for health clearance?	
	I have a doctor on board.	AL
	Have you a doctor?	AM

*By night, a red light over a white light may be shown where it can best be seen by vessels requiring health clearance. These lights should ONLY be about two meters (6 feet) apart, should be exhibited within the precincts of a port, and should be visible all round the horizon AS NEARLY AS POSSIBLE.

Signals for Customs and Excise Officers.

There is no specific flag signal by which mariners may indicate that they wish a Customs and Excise officer to board their vessels on arrival in port. The import of a quarantine signal itself precludes the necessity of a special signal.

Yachtsmen must not misconstrue the meaning of a peculiarly British signal. It is the red ensign, knotted at the fly, and flown in a conspicuous position. In British ports it is generally understood that any vessel flying this signal is requesting the attendance of a Customs and Excise officer to release dutiable articles which have already been placed under bonded seal aboard.

National Flags.

The Union Flag.

The Union Flag, often inaccurately called the Union Jack, can never be worn by merchant vessels and yachts of any description.

The White Ensign (See illustration on page 235)

Merchant vessels and the general run of yachts are not allowed to wear the white ensign. Its use is limited to ships of the Royal Navy, the Royal Yacht and vessels belonging to members of the Royal Yacht Squadron.

The Blue Ensign (See illustration on page 235)

Severe restrictions are placed upon the wearing of the blue ensign, either defaced or undefaced, and it can be assumed that any yacht displaying one has obtained a special ensign warrant to do so.

It may be worn by a yacht whose owner is a member of a yacht club which has been granted an ensign warrant by the Ministry of Defence (Navy) and he, through the yacht club, has obtained an ensign warrant for himself. No unregistered yacht and, in any case, no yacht of under 2 tons, may wear a blue ensign.

The Red Ensign (See illustration on page 235)

The red ensign is the correct national flag to wear on any yacht whose owner is British. If a yacht has been registered then this ensign must be worn on all proper occasions. There being no compulsion for a yacht under 15 tons to be registered, the display of the red ensign by an unregistered yacht is not a matter of law, yet the law still requires her to carry one on board.

The wearing of a national flag.

As has been indicated earlier, the vast majority of British yachts which ply for pleasure are under 15 tons, and only a small number of these are registered, hence for this vast armada of small craft the wearing of a national flag is optional.

A national flag has dignity and so it should be treated with decorum and worn with pride. If the owner of an unregistered yacht decides that he will not wear a red ensign, all well and good: he has the option. Nevertheless, if he decides to do so he should resolve to wear it properly. Better no ensign at all than a dirty, bedraggled ensign worn sloppily.

An ensign should be worn:—

1. **In Port.**
   Position. On a special ensign staff right aft, the size being determined by the size of the craft. It should be worn close up, which is to say that it must be hauled up the ensign staff as far as the halliards will allow it.

   Times. Between 25th March and 30th September in British ports, from 08.00hrs. to sunset or 21.00hrs. which ever is the earlier. In winter it should be hoisted at 09.00hrs. the principle being that a national emblem should not be worn during dark hours.

   'Colours' and 'sunset' should be observed at the precise times indicated above. This is a matter for individual owners when not in company with a naval ship or a flag officer of one's yacht club. When either is present, the times of colours and sunset must be taken from the naval ship, or the flag officer. This is done by watching for the hoisting and lowering of the other's ensign.

   It will be found that most near continental countries observe the above times, but in any case it is a matter of courtesy to observe the customs of the country visited.

2. **At Sea.**
   Position. The broad principle is that one's national flag must be worn in the most important position. This remains the aftermost position on a special ensign staff but, when under way, it is not always possible to achieve this for various practical reasons. If, then, this position cannot be obtained, the next most important must be used.

   This position will be the nearest to the most important one, previously mentioned, and it will vary according to the craft. In a single masted yacht it will be two-thirds up the leech of the mainsail. Where a craft has two or more masts and the aftermost is as high as, or taller than, the others, the same position on the after mast may be used. Should the aftermast be shorter than the others, then the ensign should be worn on a special staff at the mizzen-head. The manner of rigging such a staff is portrayed below:—

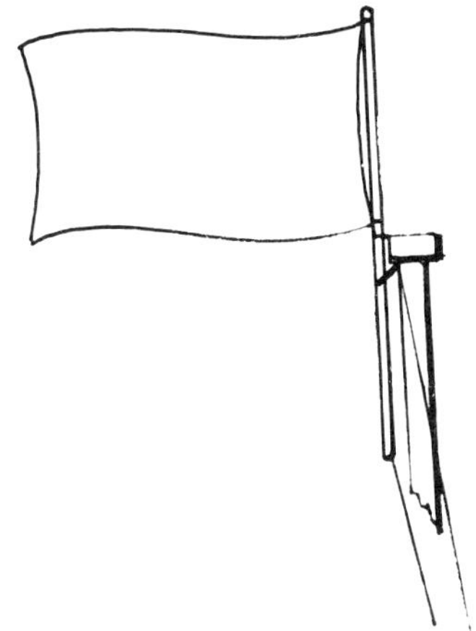

In a power-driven craft which has a single mast, or an aftermast, which is fitted with a gaff (below) then the ensign should be worn on it.

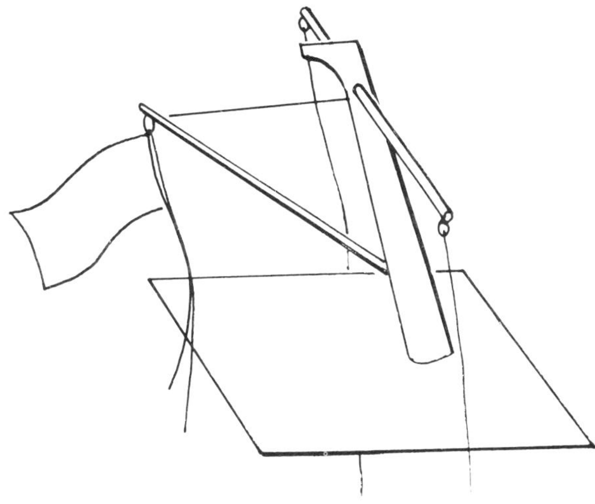

Times. There is no reason why a craft should not display her national colours at all times during daylight at sea, yet for obvious reasons this is not the usual practice. There being sufficient daylight for flags to be seen an ensign should be worn when entering or leaving any port, when passing a man o' war of any nationality, when wishing to indicate one's nationality to any other craft, and when passing any signal station, fort or coastguard station.

3. **Courtesy flags.**
When in a foreign port it is customary, but not compulsory in countries near to our shores, to wear the maritime ensign of the country visited as a matter of courtesy. Port officers in any country are well aware of the implied politeness in a courtesy flag. Through forgetfulness to wear one, foreign port authorities might gain the impression that one has little respect for their country's national emblem. Occasionally this can prove unfortunate.

A courtesy ensign is always smaller than one's own ensign. The usual position for it to be worn is at the starboard yardarm of a single masted vessel, this position being inferior to other positions in which one's own could be worn, yet superior to those to which routine signals might be hoisted.

Vessels with more than one mast should wear it at this position on the foremast, or at the foremast head. It should be hoisted before and lowered after one's own national emblem.

4. **Yacht Club Burgees.**
In port a club burgee should be flown on a staff at the main (or only) masthead. It should be flown at the same times as national colours are exhibited but should be hoisted before, and lowered after, the colours. At sea that guidance which is given for the wearing of ensigns should be observed.

5. **Semaphore.**
Semaphore is a means of communication between two signallers during daylight hours. Short handstaffs, to which are attached square flags, are held at arm's length at varying angles to the body. The angles at which the flags are displayed, either together or separately, represent letters of the alphabet or numerals.

As a means of communication, semaphore is obsolete and no details of the system need be included here.

Hints on care of flags.

The best and most durable flags are made of wool bunting or a more modern cloth which is a wool-nylon mixture. Both are costly but one should not settle for less.

Wind and rain are the two elements which can shorten the life of any flag. Wind will, in time, cause shredding at the fly of any flag. The life of a flag will be considerably extended if the first sign of shredding at a seam is tackled with a needle and bunting thread. Rain will not damage a flag when flying but, if it is put away wet, it will quickly go mildewed and rot will follow. It is better to lash a wet flag to the guardrail and wait for a drying breeze than to stow it away in that condition.

Provided they are dry, flags should be folded once or twice lengthways and then rolled up. A turn round the rolled flag with the flag lanyard and it is ready for stowing away in the flag bag.

CHAPTER 13

Voyaging

Amateur yachtsmen often nurture misconceptions about the men who frequent our seas and the voyages they undertake. So that he may decide for himself where he is going to fit into the offshore community of small boat sailors, the beginner would do well to consider a few comparisons.

Offshore fishermen are almost born to the conditions which exist in our seaways. Their seamanship and their knowledge of our coastlines and seas is such that they seldom need to refer to charts or other navigational aids. The similarity which exists between the average yachtsman and the offshore fisherman lies only in the waters they ply.

Neither can the weekend yachtsman liken himself to deep-sea yachtsmen. There is no comparison between offshore sailing and voyaging across the oceans where small boat sailormen have all the time in the world and about three quarters of its space. To be 100 miles off course in mid-ocean is frustrating and unfortunate. And that is all. It is well to ponder the apparent fact that all skilled ocean voyagers are glad to clear the English Channel.

One must not consider that single-handed sailing in home waters is relatively easy just because some do it superbly. This is a dangerous misconception. If he is to navigate with reasonable assurance over considerable distances, the average yachtsman must take with him at least one other competent person.

It is hoped that these remarks will assist the would-be voyager to identify himself with the countless yachtsmen who realise their own limitations: those who neither overrate nor underrate the sea conditions they face.

Many already have had sufficient sea experience inshore to give them assurance when their departure port dips below the horizon. Those with only smooth water experience would be sensible not to attempt an extended sea passage without first gaining considerable experience offshore, within sight of one's home port. This cannot be gained in a couple of successive Sunday afternoons. All means of fixing position should be practiced, and dead-reckoning positions calculated throughout so that they may be compared with true positions. Experience in making allowances for tidal drift and leeway is essential, particularly on windward courses. These and all other navigational practices described in Chapter 7 can be carried out within sight of familiar land when it does not really matter if calculations are somewhat in error.

The beginner should reflect that although a short passage, or a manoeuvre offshore, may be well within the competence of another yachtsman, it may not be within his.

Seaworthiness.

A craft which puts to sea must be capable of undertaking the intended voyage and able to withstand the rigours of weather to which she may be subjected. She must also be adequately manned and sufficient provision should be made for the safety of her crew. This is basically what is meant by seaworthiness.

The hull-form and design of a craft which is intended for river or harbour use may be wholly unsuited for use at sea. Any small boat sailor who has doubts about the sea-going qualities of his craft should seek professional, or at least, knowledgeable advice. Many craft would be death traps in a nasty sea offshore. It may be said that if a craft has ample strength, possesses good stability, enough free-board, a continuous deck with little top hamper, adequate draft, perhaps a ballast keel, she will probably have sea-going qualities. Most of these are seamen's terms and may need explanation.

If a craft is heeled over due to wave action she must have the ability to return upright fairly quickly. A low distribution of weight usually achieves this. Most sailing and some power-driven craft need additional bottom weight. It may take the form of ballast in the hull bottom or be provided by a ballast keel. These devices provide stability. In terms of seaworthiness fin keels are generally preferable to twin bilge keels. One of the qualities a fin-keeled craft possesses is greater stability. Weight at the bottom of a fin keel gives much more stability to a craft than an equal weight in the bottom of a yacht fitted with bilge keels. When choosing a yacht it is sometimes a matter of balancing the qualities of a fin keel against the usefulness of bilge keels to sit on the ground safely and comfortably.

Freeboard in small craft is the distance between the waterline and deck level. Being heeled over, a vessel adds to her stability increasingly until deck level, or the gunwale, is reached by the sea. Thereafter, although a craft may be fully decked, she will rapidly lose stability and a dangerous situation occurs. Further heeling may lay her over on her beam ends. This is why freeboard is important.

A continuous deck is clearly essential to prevent a craft from becoming awash when waves and heavy spray are breaking over her. Cockpits are intended to take water, but it must not be capable of gaining access to accommodation, dog houses, companionways, wheelhouses. The best designed top hamper in small craft designed for use at sea is low and strongly constructed. Portholes and windows are small and of sufficient strength to withstand heavy seas.

Adequate depth of hull below water level is necessary if a craft is to have a grip on the water at sea. In the case of a sailing yacht this is also essential to prevent her from making excessive leeway. The shape of the hull of a sea-going craft is important too, although discussion of this aspect is not a subject for this book.

Finally, possession of a properly designed sea-going craft is not proof in itself that she is seaworthy. Yachts have been lost through the failure of single defective items, the inadequacy of which could have been found before sailing. Perhaps a worn rudder pintle, a frayed shroud or a defective water closet valve. A craft which is insufficiently provisioned, or has out of date charts or inadequate cooking facilities, or safety equipment which cannot be found when needed, is unseaworthy. Naval instructions to captains of ships sailing outwards commence:— Being in all respects ready for sea — this is seaworthiness.

Crew.

Many factors govern the number of crew which should be borne by any craft. A determining element is the method of propulsion and, in the case of a sailing yacht, sail area. The nature of her passage or cruise is also important. It may fairly be said that, in the case of a typical Bermudian-rigged yacht between 18 and 30 feet in length on an extended cruise, amongst an assorted crew of three or more, there should be a minimum of two, who are capable of both handling and navigating her. When the intention is merely to potter offshore in fine weather, it will generally suffice if the skipper alone has the necessary experience and knowledge. In this latter case watches do not need to be set and the problems are vastly different.

All too frequently it is found that it is the owner/skipper of a sailing yacht who alone is sufficiently accomplished. He has shipped a number of well-meaning and willing family members or friends and has rashly voyaged far. One's only comment can be that he got away with it. His craft was in fact unseaworthy.

The time factor.

The majority of yachtsmen have employment which imposes limitations upon the time they can spend cruising. For example, a man is obliged to plan for a 2 or 3 week holiday, or a free weekend, knowing that he has to return home on a certain day. This necessity can lead the unwary into trouble.

Ideally a yachtsman returns to his terminal port on the day planned. Often this cannot be achieved. If he is excessively anxious he may curtail his adventure and arrive back far too early. Such a decision removes all nagging fears but it can be irritating, particularly to his crew. On the other hand, being eager to extract maximum enjoyment from his far-reaching cruise, he may not leave time in hand for unexpected delays. The weather deteriorating when he should sail for home, he may decide he must sail, although his better judgement indicates otherwise. For the amateur an old saying frequently applies, when in doubt — don't.

When planning a cruise it is sensible to avoid being over-ambitious. Either of the situations described above may be avoided if the itinerary is so planned that one is no great distance away from one's terminal port during the final days of a cruise. As westerly winds are prevalent in home waters, it is well worth while planning on the assumption that the wind will latterly have a westerly slant. In this manner the chances of being faced with a hard beat to windward on the final passage are reduced.

No matter how much he plots and plans the yachtsman can never be sure that he will not be weather bound at some stage in his voyage. Curtailment of a venture is always a possibility. If it occurs at a stage which makes it evident that final return will be delayed, the only course is to send a telegram of apology to one's employers, or take alternative transport home.

Taking advantage of tides.

It is common knowledge that experienced yachtsmen plan passages with the object of obtaining maximum advantage from tidal streams whenever possible. As the speed of a yacht is often little greater than the tidal currents she encounters, this is common sense. To plan in such a manner needs neither great experience nor high intelligence: it just requires a little thought beforehand.

A simple case is that of a yachtsman who intends sailing coastwise on a passage which he estimates will take about 6 hours. It being probable that any tidal stream he experiences will flow for about 6 hours in one direction along the coast, reversing its direction for the following 6 hours, clearly he will time his departure to take full advantage of the favourable stream. Equally, if he notes that tidal streams offshore are going to be athwart his course, on one side or the other, as no assistance from tidal streams can be gained, it is of little consequence when he sails.

More commonly a tidal current strikes one's course at an angle and it does not always occur to the amateur that there may be advantage in sailing at a particular time.

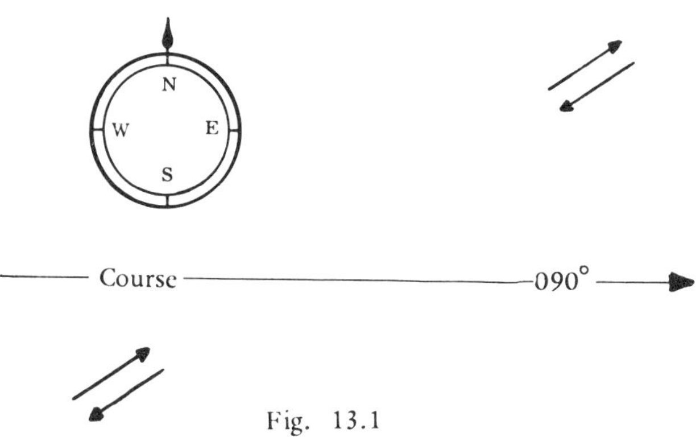

Fig. 13.1

Fig.13.1 portrays the case of the yachtsman whose course is east, in an area where tidal streams flow in either a NE'ly or SW'ly direction. Assuming his passage will have a duration of about 6 hours, it will be to his advantage to sail at the commencement of the NE-going stream. Returning, he will similarly utilise the SW-going stream. If he estimates that passage eastwards will have a duration of about 9 hours - a tide and a half or thereabouts - he will sail at a time which will ensure that he obtains complete advantage of the NE-going stream and, because he cannot do otherwise, accept that for the remainder of the period he will encounter an adverse stream. He will have to take into consideration the period which will elapse between breaking moorings and reaching the open sea, so that he is **outside** when the tidal stream turns in his favour.

During a sea crossing it can occur that two successive tidal streams cancel themselves out, the effect of one stream being to wholly counteract the effect produced by the other. Although many yachtsmen tend to counteract the effect of each stream as it occurs, there is nothing inherently wrong in making no allowance for set throughout such a period. Before adopting this latter method the yachtsman must be sure that the two tidal streams do in fact produce equal and opposite effects. If three tidal cycles will occur during a sea crossing, which in turn will assist and hinder progress, departure should be so timed that advantage is obtained from two and only one is unfavourable.

To make due allowance for set hour by hour in open waters is excessively time-consuming. It is more seamanlike to calculate the mean direction and rate for the whole of one tide, so that a single allowance for set may be made for that tide.

Estuary sailing, particularly in relation to tides, is peculiar and particular. Most familiar navigational methods tend to go by the board and one navigates from buoy to buoy, 'aims off' rather than compute courses to counteract tidal streams and is always acutely aware of height of tide above datum.

Tidal streams flowing along a coast tend to be deflected outwards at headlands and be given an inshore slant in the vicinity of bays. Equally common is a reduction of velocity in bays and an acceleration of rate off headlands. This latter phenomenon sometimes makes it advantageous in an adverse stream to stand offshore a few miles in the vicinity of headlands.

Preparation.

As underwater surfaces fouled by marine growth will markedly reduce the speed of any craft, it is evident that they must be scrubbed clean and perhaps a coat of anti-fouling paint applied before refloating her. This provides an opportunity to check for seaworthiness all underwater fittings and openings.

Equally as important is a thorough examination of all superstructures, masts, fittings, equipment, standing and running rigging, sails and engine. A visual inspection to ascertain the presence on board of all essential equipment and stores items cannot be effectively carried out if check lists have not been previously prepared. Such lists should be used for spares, tools, food stores, cooking equipment, navigational items, safety equipment and personal requirements. A menu which outlines meals for every day of a voyage may seem pernickety in extreme, yet only by this means can the quantity of food needed be estimated.

Assuming that one or more compasses are carried which have recently been checked for correctness, or for which up to date deviation cards are provided, navigational items should be as outlined in Chapter 7. Certain additional equipment for deep-water voyaging is essential:—

1. A means of taking soundings. Even if echo-sounding equipment is carried, a hand leadline is essential in case of failure.

2. Distances sailed being vital information for a navigator, either the old and tried taffrail log must be provided, or more sophisticated electronic distance-recording equipment.

3. A good radio which is capable of receiving BBC weather reports on Radio 2, 1500 metres.

4. An aneroid barometer.

5. Navigation lights.

It must be determined whether existing stocks of charts and navigational publications are adequate for the intended voyage and are up to date. Charts will be needed for an area which is a little larger than that in which it is intended to cruise. This is necessary because the unexpected is always in the offing at sea, and contrary winds or adverse weather may cause one to seek shelter in a haven beyond one's planned cruising limits. In addition to one or more small scale Admiralty charts which cover the whole cruising ground, large scale coastal charts will be needed for coastwise passages. It will be insufficient to provide plan charts only for those ports at which it is intended to call. Unscheduled visits always being a possibility, charts for all or most ports and havens along one's route must be carried.

To avoid unnecessary expenditure on charts, nor yet carry an insufficiency of them, attention is drawn to this subject in Chapter 2. Before making any purchase of charts it is always wise to check whether the Stanford range may be utilised. Their comprehensive style gives them a money-saving potential.

Minimal yet adequate navigational publications are listed below:—

Admiralty Sailing Directions for One's cruising area.

The appropriate Admiralty List of Lights.

Pocket editions of the Admiralty Atlasses of Tidal Streams.

Planning a voyage.

Those who have never voyaged before should plan to potter from port to port coastwise and, although they may consider that such a holiday will be a tepid one, considerable enjoyment will probably result; as well as valuable experience.

The broad outline of a cruise having been decided, it remains to determine what ports may be visited and what routes will be taken. Some sea routes are so self-evident that no expertise is needed to decide them, the Dover-Calais route being a case in point, but others are less easy to determine. The valuable guidance relating to inshore routes, conditions and hazards to be found in the Admiralty Sailing Directions should be studied. Over-printed on Stanford charts are sea routes which yachtsmen may use with confidence.

Having tentatively decided the sea routes to be used they should be drawn on charts and studied closely. Points to consider may be:—

(a) Has sufficient offing been allowed on what may be a lee shore?

(b) Will any one passage be of such duration that it will overtax one's crew?

(c) Does a course line pass through or too near a tide race or overfalls?

(d) Can the cruise be rearranged so that a passage which promises to be a hard beat in the prevailing wind is converted to a long reach?

(e) Is the direct route between points the best, or should one deviate slightly to take advantage of a ready means of fixing position?

This having been done and adjustments having been made if necessary, it will be helpful to discuss the routes with another yachtsman and perhaps benefit from his experience.

It should be borne in mind that adverse winds or inclement weather may intervene at any stage of a cruise, causing an alteration to be made in an itinerary even as late as sailing day. Alternative routes and even an alternative cruise in broad outlines are wise contingencies against dismay and disappointment.

Many people prefer to sail coastwise using a number of short legs. Such a voyage plan is certainly best for a beginner but, if heading for a distant destination, it is time-wasting in the extreme. At every port an entrance must be navigated, a suitable berth found and the yacht brought to harbour trim, the whole procedure being reversed next morning.

The man who already has offshore experience and plans to visit a distant cruising area should consider sailing for it direct. Such an extended passage demands organisation, discipline and good seamanship but it will shake down a crew in a manner which cannot be achieved by the stop/start method. He will reach his goal quickly and have more time in hand at the other end.

Single handed passages.

Adequate competence and stamina being assumed, he who wishes to voyage single-handed in a sailing yacht will find himself limited in his choice of seaworthy craft by two factors. First, by the sail area of a yacht, and therefore by the amount of canvas which he alone must handle. Secondly, by the ability of a yacht to sail herself unattended. This latter quality is essential if a skipper is not to become exhausted by unremitting attention to helm and sails. It is usually found that in a two-masted yacht, a suitable combination of sails can be found by trial and error for most sailing angles. The much more common single-masted yacht is considerably more difficult to balance in this way and would be regarded by most as unsuitable for long single-handed voyages.

Single-handed passages in power-driven craft are a wholly different proposition. Given seaworthiness of craft and reliability of power unit, her range and her speed will determine the length of time her skipper must be at the wheel. By cutting power and lashing the wheel, he will be able to leave the cockpit for brief periods. If he wishes to break off for longer periods he will have to stop engines and let his craft wallow in the trough for a while. Using these methods considerable numbers of small boat sailors have voyaged alone in home waters.

Crew comforts.

If a crew is not to rapidly become listless and exhausted when on passage, hot food and hot drinks are essential. Cold drinks and dry sandwiches are no substitute. If the design of a galley is such that simple hot meals cannot be prepared in adverse weather then the craft is not seaworthy. Previously prepared stews and similar dishes which only need heating are wonderful for morale when one is wet and cold. On a hard beat there is much to be said for heaving-to at meal times so that food may be eaten in relative comfort.

Warmth is similarly essential and each crew member should have at least one complete change of dry clothing available, in addition to a selection of woolly sweaters. For adverse conditions, foul weather suits with hoods are generally preferable to oilskins and sou'westers. They give greater freedom to the wearer and provide better protection against rain and spray. Water trickling down one's neck quickly soaks underclothes and chills the body. A towel wrapped tightly round the neck with the heavy weather gear buttoned hard against it prevents this. The towel gets soaked and the neck becomes wet and uncomfortable, but the body remains warm and dry.

Most people have on occasions slept in the clothes they have been wearing before retiring, so most will know how chilled one can be on rising later. Ashore body warmth can rapidly be induced by a number of methods but afloat in a small craft one can remain chilled for many hours afterwards. When ever conditions allow, the crew should be encouraged to strip off and turn in properly. Apart from the advantage mentioned, it will encourage relaxation and probably sleep.

Seasickness.

Only those who have experienced seasickness can know how it can reduce a person to utter misery and despair. When work is to be done other features reveal themselves: loss of will to do anything; a total lack of interest in anything happening; carelessness, through despondency, for personal safety.

For no apparent reason some are immune to seasickness, others are troubled by it only when boat movement is violent and the remainder would be sick sailing on a millpond. Most become used to motion within a day or two of sailing but this cannot be relied upon. A skipper can have his plans set to nought if a large percentage of his crew is laid low through seasickness, as inevitably there is a limit to that which he can do alone or with the assistance of perhaps one other willing, but inexperienced hand.

With most people, 'seasickness tablets' purchasable at any chemist's shop, are remarkably effective. If a person faithfully follows the directions for taking them, there is a good possibility that freedom from seasickness will be obtained from the outset and, when he becomes used to living with the unfamiliar motion which causes it, the tablets may be discarded. It would be unwise, however, for a sufferer who has overcome seasickness on one passage to assume that he will not be similarly afflicted on the next.

Clearly, a skipper has a duty to ensure that potential sufferers commence medication before sailing outwards and rigidly adhere to directions for taking them afterwards. It is far too late to take seasickness tablets after the onset of nausea and vomiting. Known sufferers who do not know whether the tablets will have an adverse effect upon them would do well to try them at home. Having proved to themselves that the tablets do not produce disagreeable effects, they should take the maximum prescribed dose on voyage.

Watches.

The organisation of the crew during passages of relatively short duration is usually an easy, amicable arrangement of duties between friends and none regards himself being on watch on deck or the watch below. During extended passages it becomes necessary to divide one's crew into watches if general fatigue is not to occur, a state of affairs which reduces awareness and efficiency. With a small crew in the average diminutive yacht it will be found that two watches will suffice, each watch being one of three hours. The skipper should be in charge of one watch and the next most competent crew member in charge of the other.

Although watches may be set on sailing there is an understandable tendency amongst amateurs to excitedly remain on deck, although they should be relaxing during watch below. In the interests of efficiency and safety the skipper has a duty to encourage those whose watch occurs a few hours later to rest below decks. However much faith he places in the crewman who is in charge during his watch below, the skipper would be well advised to be on deck when a landfall is made and he should also ensure that he will be called if at any time the watch on deck is in doubt.

Night navigation.

It is prudent for yachtsmen who have minimal sea experience to confine their passages to daylight hours only. Those who have gained confidence and experience should consider extending their sea passages into dark hours if it is advantageous to do so. Night navigation is very much easier than the average beginner believes, it has many good features, and those who only sail during daylight hours severely restrict the distances they may sail.

At night in clear weather lighthouses, light beacons and lightbuoys can be pinpointed with accuracy at greater ranges than are usually achieved in daylight. The directions in which other vessels are heading are clearly indicated by their navigation lights. These advantages tend to offset the disadvantage of being unable to see unlit features ashore. Leaving a port at night usually presents few problems provided the channel is lit: entering port is less easy for sundry reasons although it is often excessive caution which prompts one to stand offshore until daylight.

Weather.

If foul weather is forecast before departure from any port, whether it is declared imminent or probable within the next day or two, careful consideration must be given to the advisability of sailing. The time required to complete the impending passage may be a governing factor. If it appears evident that the weather will commence deteriorating within a few hours of one's ETA at his next port, it is wisest to cut losses and delay departure. Forecasts remain what they are named and the movement of weather systems are equally as likely to accelerate in movement as they are to decelerate.

Decisions of this nature are often extremely difficult. If it may be helpful, take advice. Sift it, gauge the competence, character, and experience of the man offering it, and then make up one's own mind.

Regular shipping forecasts are transmitted on BBC Radio 2 (1500 m) and, so long as a yacht is at sea, they should be obtained.

Before sailing.

Activity before sailing should be confined to bringing the craft to sea going trim, the yachtsman having already satisfied himself that she is seaworthy in all major respects. It is probable that provisions will be shipped on sailing day and, to avoid muddle at a latter stage in the voyage, simple precautions are desirable. Tins of food inevitably being a considerable proportion of food stores, they must be stowed in a manner which will ensure that they are available in the order needed and in a position well away from the compass. It is well worthwhile marking tins on their ends with one's own special code, the paper labels having an irritating facility for falling off in sea conditions. This is the day on which one must replenish water canisters, check stocks of motor fuel and calor gas, prove the efficiency of engine, navigation lights and all electronic equipment.

An aneroid barometer may cease to read accurately over a long period and so it must be checked and, if necessary, corrected. Means of obtaining a correct barometer reading for comparison are readily avaliable, the details of which are contained in Chapter 11. The adjustment screw in the rear casing of an aneroid turns the pointer on its dial.

The element of danger never being wholly removed from any sea adventure, someone on shore must know:—

When it is intended to sail.
The destination and E.T.A.
What to do if a message of safe arrival is not received within a reasonable period.

For short coastwise passages it will suffice if one's family is kept fully advised, they usually being most interested. Better by far, particularly in the case of an extended cruise, is to advise the coastguard authorities. On page 216 a list of coastguard stations is produced, together with a facsimile of the standard reporting form which outlines the information needed. H.M.Coastguard may be advised in person, by telephone or in writing and there is no charge for the service.

A current weather forecast for shipping is highly important. Details of the various means by which yachtsmen may obtain forecasts will be found in Chapter 9, although the BBC bulletins are those most readily available. If the BBC forecasts produce doubts about the wisdom of sailing, local sea conditions can be obtained by telephone, free of charge, from the nearest Port Meteorological Officer.

Where the intention is to sail for a foreign country, or to the Channel Islands or the Republic of Ireland, the local Customs House or Waterguard Officer should be advised of the intention. H.M. Customs and Excise regulations are explained at the end of this chapter.

Sailing time having been decided, it only remains to efficiently stow or secure every item of movable equipment both above and below decks.

Steering.

The smaller a craft, the more difficult it is to hold it on a precise course in a seaway. Yet whatever the craft, the skill and the unremitting concentration of the helmsman will have a profound bearing upon whether or not good courses are made. The good helmsman is not the man who can steer extremely well; it is he who, possessing that skill, exercises it constantly throughout his trick at the helm.

Assuming a skipper has planned and plotted his courses with great care, he must assume thereafter that for dead-reckoning purposes those courses will be made. Bad steering could on occasion render of small value a subsequent estimation of his dead reckoning position. He has quite enough imponderables with which to contend without his helmsman introducing one more.

For example, more often than not it will be found that a sailing craft, and a power-driven one too in adverse weather, will tend to constantly fall away to one side of the course being steered. Seeing this, the inexperienced helmsman will counteract the movement with the helm and bring the craft back on course. If this action is repeated constantly over a period, it will result in the course actually steered being a few degrees from the required one. It will be a mean course between the required one and the compass point reached before the helmsman decides it is once more time to counteract the movement.

A skipper must ensure that his helmsmen wander off course as much on one side as the other. This is called making the course good. When a tendency to constantly fall away on one side of the course is experienced, one can usually make the course good by bringing the craft back to a compass point **beyond** the required course. When this point is reached the helm is eased and so the boat's head falls away again.

Use of the lead at sea.

As a single simple precursor of the danger of grounding, nothing is more valuable than knowledge of the depth of water beneath one's keel. Sounding equipment, either hand or electronic, should never be regarded as a seaman's aid which need be used only occasionally. So long as soundings can be obtained they should be taken as a routine measure to support or refute the evidence of every navigational process. They assume even greater importance in fog, when closing the land and when position is in doubt.

Making a landfall.

During daylight in summer weather making a landfall, or a port, is frequently quite easy. Nevertheless, like many undertakings, the knowledge of practices adopted by those experienced in them will often simplify matters and, when conditions are less than ideal, perhaps reduce anxiety.

A prior study of a large scale chart of the area is essential, so that a mind picture is retained of all important features. By this means it is possible to visualise with considerable accuracy the probable appearance of a coastline or port. A shoreline is immediately apparent on a chart, yet the land contours associated with it should be studied. Therein will lie the evidence of the shape and height of hills, cliffs, promontories and beaches. Symbols and abbreviations will indicate man-made features which are conspicuous from seaward and probably show the density of buildings in a township or village. Using dividers, one should measure the length of channels, the distances between buoys and the navigable areas in the approaches to a port. One's route into a port or haven having been decided, approach courses should be noted. These seamanlike practices usually preclude anxious moments inshore, when one's own craft and other traffic often demand maximum attention, and time for studying a chart is minimal.

Approaching a coast from seaward, it may be a few hours before features ashore can positively be identified. From the moment of sighting it is natural to make every endeavour to recognise details ashore, yet it is generally prudent to continue one's course until a positive fix or identification is obtained. Dead-reckoning and the evidence of one's compass will probably be more reliable than vague shore outlines.

As a general principle one should make a landfall, or approach a port, at right angles to the coast whenever possible. An oblique approach to an unfamiliar coast or port sometimes leads to grounding. In addition to this aspect, navigational aids in and around a port are usually more easily recognised when approaching directly from seaward. For both reasons it is generally prudent to stand offshore until the position from which one wants to commence the approach is reached. Fig.13.2 indicates such an approach.

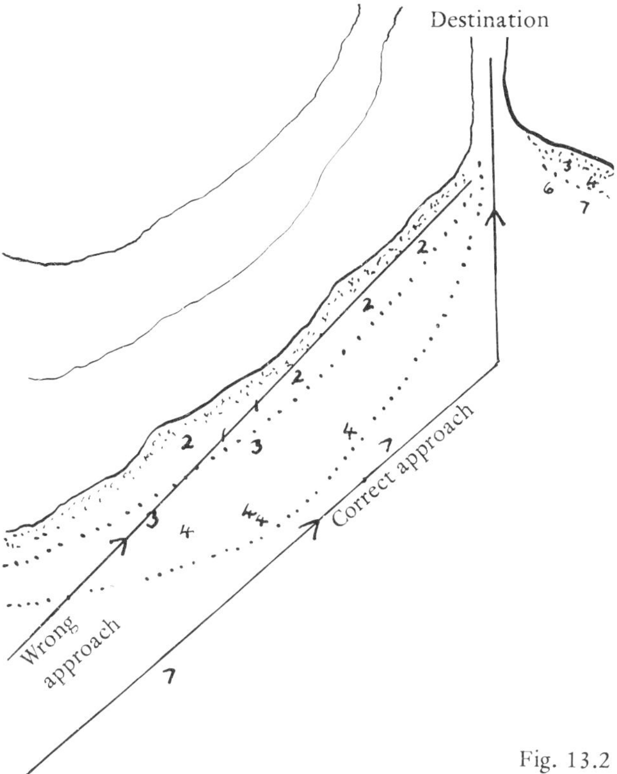

Fig. 13.2

A sailing yacht should be held up to windward of a port, it being easy to drop downwind during the latter stages of an approach, yet difficult to claw to windward from a downwind position in what may be unfamiliar and shallow waters.

When one's destination is on a low-lying coast, it is common practice to shape course for a clearly recognisable navigational feature which is within a few miles of the port, yet it must be said that they are not always available.

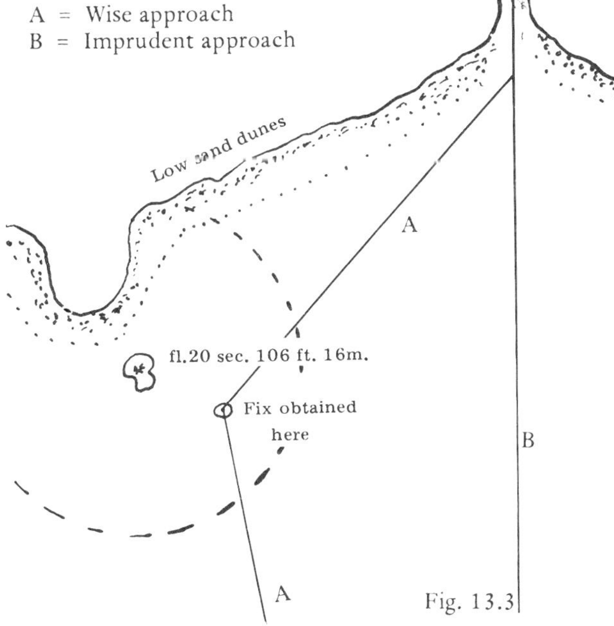

Fig. 13.3

A good fix having been obtained from such an object, course can be re-set shorewards with the assurance that position is not in doubt, even though features on the coast in the vicinity of one's destination may not be recognised until fairly close in.

Landfalls at night do not present the same problems, provided the visibility is good. Yet somewhat in the manner described above, whenever possible course should be so shaped that the yacht is brought within range of a lighthouse, even though it may not be on the direct route to one's destination. This underlines the implied principle that it is better to sail from feature to feature than from port to port. If features and ports are associated, as they often are, so much the better.

Yachtsmen making sea crossings commonly endeavour to arrange a landfall so that it occurs during the hour or two before dawn breaks. Given clear weather they will see any lighthouse at maximum range and so arrive at their destination a few hours later when daylight is assured. This practice is sound and must be judged preferable to an evening landfall when port entry must be made after dark.

No seaman should approach any shore closely when his position is uncertain and danger exists in doing so. Safer by far is to lie to, or to head for the open sea until doubts have been removed.

Navigating small craft in fog.
In fog the thoughts of a yachtsman can become distorted by the fear of two hazards:—

1. That he has badly miscalculated his position.
2. That a large and unsuspecting merchantman will suddenly bear down upon him.

The former can largely be overcome by navigational skill. The latter by reflecting that the chances of being run down, even in a sea lane, are really quite small, provided a good look-out is kept. In any case the fog signal of an approaching vessel is usually heard long before it is alarmingly close.

Position finding in fog.
The section which deals with the calculation of dead-reckoning positions in Chapter 7 should be studied. In clear weather one should always navigate on the assumption that at any moment visibility will be lost. This will ensure that at the onset of fog or reduced visibility one has a position from which to work, the quality of which cannot be improved.

Direction finding equipment has its greatest value in fog. The desire to put faith in any position lines or positions so obtained may tend to override the dictates of good seamanship, and so the limitations of D/F must be kept firmly in mind. Chapter 8 describes these limitations and D/F operation in detail. Here it may be said that if a yacht is well located in relation to surrounding radio beacons, and bearings from them are consistent, fixes so obtained may have a fair degree of reliance put upon them. It remains wise to regard any information obtained from a D/F set as supplementary to, and not as a substitute for, dead-reckoning calculations.

Approaching a coast or a port in fog calls upon more qualities in a yachtsman, than most other evolutions at sea. Fearful of grounding, a timorous yachtsman may heave-to many miles off shore, and within a few hours, probably have less idea of his position than he had before heaving to. A foolhardy one might maintain his course and speed shorewards, probably expecting to see his destination ahead sooner or later. Both overanxiety and recklessness bringing potential danger in their train, in neither case is good seamanship exhibited.

In these conditions the competent yachtsman will have regularly plotted his position from the commencement of his voyage, using every item of information at his disposal to minimise error. Nearing the coast, he will have calculated how long he can maintain his course and speed shorewards without undue risk of grounding. He will take regular soundings, listen for shore fog signals, fairly assess the range at which he may see other vessels or the shore, perhaps glean information from a slight yet perceptible change in the state of the sea, or from the tracks of coastal shipping. His approach might be regarded as foolhardy by the timorous, yet timorous by the foolhardy. If he subsequently fails to make contact with the shore or is unable to fix his position, his actions thereafter will be governed by his judgement. He may decide to continue shorewards for a limited period at low speed, sounding as he goes, or anchor if practicable, or even heave to, head to seaward, and wait for the weather to clear.

Avoidance of collision in fog.

In Chapter 10 it was stated that a yachtsman at sea should display a radar reflector as high as possible both in clear weather and in fog. When a yacht using a radar reflector is in the path of an on-coming vessel operating radar, it can reasonably be assumed that the latter will take avoiding action. Although most vessels are equipped with radar, the worrying fact remains that a yachtsman may encounter one of those which are not so equipped. He has no way of telling, neither can he be sure that the watchkeepers on a radar-equipped vessel have detected the warning blip which will reveal his presence. Extreme caution is essential.

It is wise to assume that a large vessel in fog will not hear a yacht's low-powered fog signal except at very short range. This assumption demands that a yacht takes avoiding action before a close-quarters situation develops. As this is more likely to occur in a sea lane, a yachtsman finding himself in one when fog descends is well advised to commence motor-sailing immediately and head for less hazardous waters.

From the single repetitive note of the fog signal of an on-coming vessel, the yachtsman must decide:

Her range and bearing so long as the fog signal is heard.

Her rate of closing.

Her probable course and speed.

The volume of a fog signal is the only means by which one can guess its range and, bearing in mind the series of cautions outlined in Chapter 3 which are connected with undue reliance upon fog signals, this can be most unreliable. It must be said, however, that the peculiar conditions outlined are infrequently encountered, although it invariably occurs that fog signals upwind are more clearly heard at a distance than those downwind. Bearings are best obtained by pointing towards the fog signals with the arm at full stretch and relating this direction to the compass. A series of bearings should indicate whether or not the bearing is altering appreciably.

Although the volume of a fog signal may steadily increase, if the bearing of it is altering, in all probability the vessel will pass clear. Danger exists when a fog signal remains steady in direction and increases in volume. Faced with these portents a yachtsman's only action can be to sail away at right angles to the bearings with all possible despatch.

The above observations should be read in conjunction with the appropriate Rules in the Collision Regulations and the author's notes therewith. They will be found in Chapter 10.

Coping with heavy weather.

A gale having been forecast, it will invariably be wise for the inexperienced yachtsman at sea to run for shelter before its onset: if he is in port he should delay sailing. This is easy to say but, being at sea, this recommended action is not always possible. A gale may beset him much earlier than the forecast indicated, or he may find himself so far away from a port or haven that he has no option but to ride out the blow. Given a seaworthy craft, it is likely that her ability to weather a gale far exceeds the willingness of her skipper to accept the challenge.

Small craft need plenty of searoom in a gale, the more the better. Consequently, the further a yachtsman removes his craft from a lee shore, the safer he will be. Where necessary he must make every effort to obtain maximum distance from such a shore, snug down his craft and generally prepare for bad weather. At this point he would do well to reflect that his nerves may be tested more severely than his skill. Hard-driven spray sheeting from the weather bow, wind whistling and wailing through the rigging, can lead one to believe that the weather is worse that it actually is.

The wind increasing in velocity, two things inevitably occur: the sails are given greater driving power and the waves increase in size. The craft's movement becomes violent and steering difficult, excessive strain is put on every part of her and she will tend to dig her nose into the seas. A reduction of sail area by reefing and perhaps the removal of unnecessary canvas will at once ease her movement and improve steering qualities. Further increase in wind strength and associated reduction of sail area will bring one to a point when some other action must be taken. It may become evident that the course being steered is not the best in the interests of safety: one may have to heave-to.

In most cases to heave-to is simply to maintain steerage way on a course which will allow a craft to ride oncoming seas most comfortably. A course to windward will generally achieve this, yet to maintain steerage way in a sailing yacht when heading in any direction to windward may be difficult and in some cases almost impossible. The direction to windward could be any course between 3 and 7 points off the wind - say 30° to 80°. Whatever the angle a sailing yacht will be blown downwind at a considerable pace. Power-driven craft usually ride best 2 or 3 points off the wind and, if the wind is not broad on the bow, make little leeway.

There is ample evidence to indicate that a small seaworthy craft of modern design, unable to heave-to in the traditional manner, will probably lie safely if she is allowed to drift, snugged down and with all sails removed — or, as experienced yachtsmen call this condition, under bare poles. This is what is meant by hulling, or lying a-hull. It can be that, given a peculiar condition of foul weather, in any class of small craft, an owner comes to the realisation that he has no alternative but to lie a-hull. Yet the reader must mark this well: in confined waters such as those in which we sail, the small boat owner **must** have sea room to lie a-hull: sea room to leeward, because it is to leeward that danger lies in shore line form. Rock-scraping can be deliciously dangerous in ideal weather conditions but, if the weather changes for the worse, as well it can, one can in effect commit suicide by denying oneself that precious commodity: sea room.

When bowling along on a course to leeward with the wind freshening and a gale forecast from the same direction, dangers exist for the unwary. There is a tendency to believe that one can successfully ride out the blow provided the sail area is progressively reduced as the wind mounts in strength. Doubts can be subdued because one is, in effect, running away from the rising seas and at the same time maintaining desired course. At what point during a gale from a steady direction can one say that the weather will not get worse? In a really heavy stern sea, breaking crests can slew a craft round and, at worst, she may be caught by an overtaking wave which breaks and topples over her. Apart from the swamping effect, the sheer weight of water could smash superstructures. In these conditions it is wise to heave-to on a windward course before these possibilities become realities. One must wait for a lull: an area of less threatening waves which can invariably be found in any condition of sea. Then the craft must be quickly brought round to a windward course and hove-to as outlined above.

To lie-to is a variation of heaving-to. In some yachts it is found that, with minimal canvas and the helm lashed, unattended they will lie steady in a direction perhaps 4 to 7 points off the wind: they will lie-to. It is likely that a yacht in this condition will make slight headway and her windward progress will tend to reduce the considerable leeward drift. The ability to lie-to is more common in ketches and yawls — two masted vessels — but rare in small single-masted Bermudian-rigged yachts. This is basically because the former have two masts on either of which 'storm canvas' can be worn and the balance between helm and sails is more readily achieved. Their greater length and customary deep keels also assist. In a yacht of any design the combination of sail and rudder which will allow it to lie-to will be a matter of experiment, or earlier knowledge of her sailing qualities.

Sea anchors and their use.

A sea anchor is a drogue for use by small craft at sea in heavy weather. The action of the wind is usually to blow a craft rapidly to leeward and, when streamed over the bow, the resistance of a sea anchor will hold the craft's head to wind and sea. A drogue has additional value: a yacht may be blown down wind at any rate up to about 5 knots depending upon wind strength and, with a lee shore not too far away, it may be desirable to check her progress to leeward.

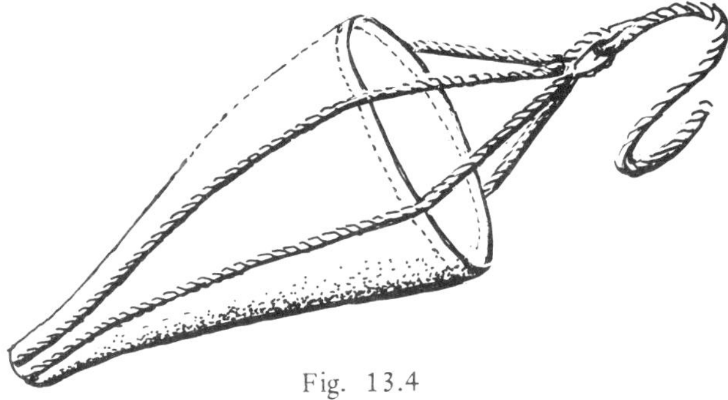

Fig. 13.4

A sea anchor most suitable for use in yachts up to about 30 feet in length is conical in shape and made of heavy canvas. Its mouth is held open by a galvanised iron ring 3 feet in diameter: any lesser dimension will probably reduce its efficiency. A limited amount of water must be allowed to pass through it and so a similar ring about 3 inches in diameter is sewn into its peak. A 4-legged bridle is fitted as shown and sewn down the length of the drogue. The bridle terminates at a metal thimble and to this a warp some 20 fathoms long is attached.

A craft must be being blown downwind at 2 to 3 knots before a drogue can be effective and it is suggested that those who have had little success with one may have overlooked this prime requirement. A sea anchor will reduce but not prevent leeward drift. In open water it may be necessary to hoist a sail to obtain effective leeward progress.

It is improbable that a sea anchor could be used to good effect in a power-driven yacht unless she has top hamper which offers considerable wind resistance. Provided she has power, reduced engine revolutions and the wind perhaps 2 or 3 points on the bow should render a sea anchor unnecessary in heavy weather. A sea anchor might prove of value to such a craft if she had an engine breakdown, or in exceptional conditions when a stern drogue becomes a last resort. Reference to the use of a sea anchor in these bitter circumstances will be found later in this section.

Many text books make reference to a tripping line for use with a sea anchor. This is a light line, one end of which is attached to the peak of the drogue and the other made fast aboard. The line is left slack until it becomes necessary to retrieve the sea anchor. By hauling upon it the drogue is tripped and retrieval made easy. It is the writer's opinion that where yachts are concerned, there is perhaps more theory than practical experience in the use of such a device. If the drogue tends to revolve in the water, as well it may, the tripping line can foul the warp and become entangled with the drogue, thus rendering retrieval a problem at a most inconvenient time. In small craft the weight of a drogue is such that hauling upon the warp renders retrieval within the capability of the average yachtsman. Of course in heavy yachts one must hope that, a tripping line having been used, it trails in the manner desired by skippers.

Lifeboats of the R.N.L.I. sometimes tow a drogue in severe weather, say, when approaching a coast or harbour with a high wind and heavy sea astern. The object, of course, is to keep the lifeboat's stern to wind and sea. Although one can never be dogmatic about a subject such as this, for sundry cogent reasons the average yachtsman is advised against streaming a sea anchor from the stern.

The writer is not unaware that there is a yachting faction which argues that sea anchors are no longer compatible with modern yachting trends; that these general advices are not reconcilable with the handling of small craft in heavy weather. It is emphasised that advices throughout this Companion are intended for the vast community of anonymous yachtsmen who, with family or friends, venture into deep waters. These good people, despite admirable expertise displayed by many, would seldom presume to enter into discussion about the merits and demerits of sea anchors and other nautical topics. The experts, those whose competence commands the admiration of all when racing or cruising in conditions which would daunt the majority, will undoubtedly be guided by their own beliefs and experiences. One would both expect and wish this latter category of yachtsman to do so.

The use of oil to modify waves.

One has only to watch the effect of an oil slick on waves at a harbour mouth to appreciate the potential of oil as a means of drastically reducing the ability of waves to break. Many professional publications recommend its use in heavy weather as a means of modifying waves, yet it is extraordinarily difficult to find a yachtsman who has put it to the test. The writer has merely experimented in a moderate sea.

Thick vegetable oil is recommended but any oil other than paraffin or petroleum spirit should suffice. A constant slight trickle on to the sea is necessary and this is best achieved by the use of a canvas bag, similar to a small hot water bottle. Such bags may be bought from large chandleries. The bag being filled with oil, punctures with a sail needle in its sides will produce the minimal dribble of oil needed. A 1 gallon can of oil may be regarded as ample sea stock for this purpose.

When hove-to in heavy weather, the oil bag should be hung over the weather gunwale and, provided the yacht is making leeway, an oil slick will be left to windward. It is of course to windward that the oil slick is needed. Running before a heavy sea, it has been suggested than an oil bag be hung over the bow and so an oil slick is left astern. The writer reflects that, the yacht speeding downwind, any effective oil slick within 50 yards of the transom will be so narrow that it could have little useful effect upon the waves.

The effect of oil on waves is only apparent in open water and it will not prevent waves from breaking in shoal water and on a sea shore.

Conclusion.

It may be said that there is a recognisable pattern in the state of the sea in gale conditions, both in deep and shallow water, but there are so many unpleasant variations – and combinations of these unpleasantnesses – that one can never fairly say what precise action a seaman must take to counter them. With great wind strength and a particular, peculiar state of sea there can be no book of rules, no wholly satisfactory guide lines, no clear cut answers to a yachtsman's problems. Neither is anyone in a position to say exactly how a particular craft will behave in extreme, or unusual, sea conditions. For example, the wind may be a steady force 8 from a certain direction but if it is gusting to force 10 with associated temporary disturbance of existing sea conditions, it is those gusts and the often dismaying conditions they produce with which he must ultimately contend. Similarly, a force 7 wind against a tidal stream could well produce a state of sea which is more dangerous to a small craft than a force 9 gale in open, tide-less waters. Only when a yachtsman finds himself in an area of severe weather will he learn whether, in particular conditions, he will heave-to, or lie-to, or lie a-hull: whether his craft is safer with a sail to stay her or whether it may prove prudent to run under bare poles. It is not for any of us to deny to an owner any options which might prove useful. Clearly a sea anchor, and oil, are two of these options. They will be carried often and seldom, if ever, used. But if a sea anchor, or an oil bag, or some other device, worked well in a single emergency, that would be enough.

It being the intention in this chapter to outline the basic principles of seamanship in heavy weather, those who wish to learn more of the management of small craft under these conditions can call upon the experience of a large number of expert men and women. Many books written by them describe in detail the manner in which they coped with the worst conditions.

CHAPTER 14

Dover High Water Tables

TIDE TABLES

HIGH WATER DOVER. The times of high water at Dover for each day are listed on a separate card within the book. This card can be pinned to the bulkhead for ease of reference.

HIGH WATER AT A PORT OTHER THAN DOVER. To find the time of high water at a specific port, proceed as follows:

1. Note down the time of high water at Dover for the day in question.
2. Enter the table of tabular port facilities and note down the required port's interval from high water at Dover.
3. The sum of these two times will give the time of high water at the port.

APPROXIMATE TIME OF LOW WATER. First find the time of high water by the methods used in 1, 2 and 3 (above). Add 6 hours 13 minutes to this time to get the time of the next low water.

SPRING RISE AND NEAP RISE. The average Spring Rise (S.R.) and Neap Rise (N.R.) for each port is listed in the section dealing with entrance details.

'TWELFTH' RULE. The amount by which the tide will rise or fall in a given time from high water can be easily reckoned by means of the rough 'Twelfth' Rule as follows:

First hour's rise or fall .... One-twelfth of the Range.
Second hour's rise or fall .... Two-twelfths of the Range.
Three hour's rise or fall .... Three-twelfths of the Range.
Fourth hour's rise or fall .... Three-twelfths of the Range.
Fifth hour's rise or fall.......... Two-twelfths of the Range.
Sixth hour's rise or fall.......... One-twelfth of the Range.

The Range of the Tide is the difference in height between high water and the following low water. Since the level of Mean Low Water Springs is virtually Chart Datum, the Spring Range is virtually the Spring Rise and, knowing this amount, the approximate tide level at Spring Tides can be roughly calculated using the 'Twelfth' Rule (above).

To find the approximate Neap Range, multiply the Neap Rise by two (2) and, from this, subtract the Spring Rise. The resultant is the Neap Range. Again, using the 'Twelfth' Rule the approximate tide level at neaps can be roughly calculated.

IMPORTANT NOTE. It must be appreciated that the predicted levels of both high and low water at any port can only be taken as approximate guides. The level of any tide can be affected by prevailing winds, barometric pressure, outflow from rivers after heavy rain, etc. and may be less or more than predicted.

It is always best to allow a good safety margin when entering port and, if one should run aground, time thus spent will be considerably less on the rising than on the falling tide. It must also be remembered that the safety margin at low water neaps is always greater than that at low water springs.

The times of Spring and Neap tides can be found by studying the heights of high water at Dover. The highest tides denote the periods of Spring Tides.

CHAPTER 15

Port Entrance Information

The following information gives basic details of depth and entrance at the various ports. In general, a standard pattern has been used but, at many east coast ports, where fishing or commercial traffic is the main consideration, the pattern has been altered. This type of port is normally only visited by an occasional cruising yacht; approach is straightforward and the details shown cover the type of docking facility which is available.

A THOROUGHLY UP-TO-DATE CHART MUST ALWAYS BE USED WHEN ENTERING ANY PORT

KENT

RAMSGATE

Depth at entrance. Minimum depth is 5 ft. at MLWS, but this can be reduced after northerly winds. S.R. 16½ ft. N.R. 13 ft.

Entrance Channel. 270 ft. wide. There is a strong cross tide at high water off the entrance, particularly at spring tides.

DOVER

Depth at entrance. There is deep water between the breakwaters at both entrances. S.R. 21½ ft. N.R. 17 ft.

Entrance Channel. The current sets from north to south across the eastern entrance at all times except from 2 hours before to 4 hours after high water. Keep to the north to allow for this and keep ample way on your vessel to pass through the entrance quickly. There are often overfalls due to southerly current and south-west wind. The western entrance often has confused sea and the tides run strongly across it. Yachts should avoid this entrance in strong winds.

Traffic Control Signals for both Western and Eastern entrances—three red balls in a triangle indicates that vessels can leave, and no vessel is to enter or approach the entrance while signal is shown. Two red balls vertical indicates that vessels can enter with permission, and no vessel is to leave or approach the exit while signal is shown. Three red balls vertical means that entrance is closed. Corresponding signals by night are one orange light, two green lights and three red lights vertical.

Irrespective of signals, whether by day or by night, *permission to enter or leave the harbour must be obtained from port control.* Vessels with VHF/RT contact on Channel 12 (156.6 m/cs); other vessels use aldis and signal by morse either SV (I wish to enter port) or SW (I wish to leave port). The Harbour Board Patrol Launch, identified by 'Harbour Patrol' painted on sides will also relay messages. This launch can be identified, at night, by a blue flashing light which it exhibits from the masthead.

FOLKESTONE

Depth at entrance. The inner harbour dries out at MLWS, but has 16 ft. at MHWS. S.R. 21 ft. N.R. 16 ft.

Entrance Channel. There is no entrance channel, the outer harbour opening out into the English Channel. The inner harbour entrance is 100 ft. wide and is marked by a flashing light. No precautions other than depth of water are necessary. A black flag at the signal station prohibits entry.

SUSSEX

RYE

Depth at entrance. The bar dries out at MLWS but yachts drawing up to 4 ft. can enter or leave the harbour during the period 2 hours either side of high water. S.R. 24 ft. N.R. 19 ft.

Entrance Channel. A slight tidal set is experienced across the entrance at the end of the East Pier. During spring tides, the flood runs at about 3 knots, the ebb at about 2½ knots. Near MHWS the west wall skirting and parts of the eastern training wall may become submerged but the beacons clearly mark the channel. By night, the two green leading lights should be used for entering the channel. Pass the red light on the end of the west groyne about a quarter of a cable to port, and then steer up the straight channel on the west side of the eastern training wall which has a white light on its seaward end.

NEWHAVEN

Depth at entrance. 9 to 11 ft. at MLWS with a tide rise of 16 ft. at neap tides and 21 ft. at springs. S.R. 20½ ft. N.R. 16 ft.

Entrance Channel. The transit bearing line leads one in through the centre of the channel to the narrow section between the East Pier and the west side where traffic signals are displayed from the signal mast. These signals are: One red ball (green light by night)—entry but no exit; two red balls (red light by night)—exit but no entry; three red balls (three white lights vertically disposed by night)—port closed.

SHOREHAM

Depth at entrance. 8 ft. MLWS with tidal rise of 14 ft. at neaps and 18 ft. at springs. 8 ft. is the maximum depth immediately after dredging and, as the tidal parts of the port silt rapidly, actual depth at MLWS can be less than this. S.R. 18 ft. N.R. 13½ ft.

Entrance Channel. The entrance channel from the breakwaters to the watch house on the Middle Pier, from whose signal mast traffic signals are exhibited, is 300 ft. wide. At the Middle Pier the channel forks east and west into the Eastern and Western Arms of the Harbour. The Western Arm practically dries out at MLWS and visiting yacht traffic is to the Eastern Arm which is entered by locks. In the entrance channel yachts shall not navigate within 300 yards of any commercial vessel which is navigating in the channel. If, on approaching the watch house on the Middle Pier, the locks are closed the duty officer will direct you to anchor to the eastward of this pier until the locks open.

Traffic Signals for entry, exit or navigation within the harbour are exhibited as follows:

From the signal mast 20 ft. east of the Middle Pier house: Blue flag (blue light by night)—no vessel shall proceed along the Eastern Arm of the harbour for the purpose of leaving, move to another berth in the Eastern Arm or pass into the Western Arm of the harbour; Red diamond shape (quick flashing red light by night)—no vessel shall enter the harbour with a view to proceeding to the Eastern Arm and no vessel outside the harbour entrance shall navigate in such a way as to hinder a vessel leaving; Two blue flags (two blue lights vertically disposed by night)—no vessel shall navigate within the Eastern Arm nor enter the harbour with the purpose of proceeding to the Eastern Arm.

From the mast at the lock: Signals displayed as above, and have the same meaning.

From the mast 40 ft. west of Middle Pier house, and also on the mast at the northern end of Middle Pier: Signals displayed as above, and have the same meaning, *except* that they refer to the Western Arm.

LITTLEHAMPTON

Depth at entrance. From the south end of the West Pier for a distance of 200 ft. to seaward there is only 1 to 5 ft. at MLWS. S.R. 16½ ft. N.R. 13 ft.

Entrance Channel. The entrance channel is marked by two beacons at the seaward end, and then by perches. It is 100 ft. wide at the lighthouse. The flood stream runs in at speeds of up to 5 knots and the ebb at up to 6 knots. When commercial traffic is moving (coasters, dredgers, etc.) all craft must keep out of that part of the channel between South End of West Pier and Ferry Steps. Commercial craft cannot stop their engines between these two points as the tide will set them on to the defence works. When entering, a distance of 20-30 ft. should be kept off the perches or channel markers.

CHICHESTER

Note. Unless one has recent local knowledge, it is important to note that entry must now be made using the conspicuous West Pole Beacon. Also that an up-to-date chart is used as new beacons have been sited in the channels as well as alteration to the buoyage. Many of the buoys are now lighted.

Entry. Chichester Bar lies 7 cables south of Eastoke Point and joins the East and West Pole Sands. These Banks are subjected to frequent changes and the seas break heavily over them when there is a swell. Vessels must therefore give due consideration to the depth of water at the bar, the heights of MHWS, MLWS, MHWN, and MLWN being 16.2, 2.3, 13 and 6 ft. respectively. During calm conditions there should be a depth of about 8 ft. over the bar at half tide. Once inside the entrance the channel divides into two branches, the Emsworth Channel leading northwards, and the Chichester Channel leading towards Chichester and Dell Quay, off which lies the Thorney Channel. All buoys within the harbour are fitted with 'scotchlite' reflectors which are white on starboard hand buoys, red on port hand and red and white on middle ground buoys. They give good reflection to an Aldis or searchlight and several hundred feet reflection to a good torch. Vessels wishing to anchor should do so west of Itchenor in the recognised anchorage west of the Gallon Starting Line. A popular anchorage is just past East Head but vessels should keep clear of the fairway. S.R. 14 ft. N.R. 11 ft.

EMSWORTH

Entry. The channel is marked throughout its length from Mengeham Rithe to Sweare Deep by mean tide level perches which have red can topmarks to port and white diamonds or black cones to starboard. The junctions of Rithes with the main channel are marked by perches which are painted red and white indicating that they are to be left to port, and black and white to be left to starboard for the Main Channel.

There are two main beacons, one marks the S.W. Spit of Pilsey Sands and has a diamond-shaped topmark in black and white with 'Pilsey Sands Spit' in red: the other is sited on the starboard side of the channel, due West of Marker Point.

All these beacons and perches dry out at low water and keel boats should not proceed inshore of them. A tide gauge with a yellow conical topmark is sited at the junction of Mengeham Rithe and Emsworth main channel. A second gauge (unofficial) has been sited on the port telegraph cable marker beacon some 200 yards north of Sweare Deep Point and shows the depth of water over the cill at Emsworth Yacht Harbour.

CHICHESTER YACHT BASIN

Entry. The approach channel into Chichester Yacht Basin is 60 ft. wide and depth varies from 1½ ft. at MLWS to 5 ft. at MLWN. The channel is marked by six starboard hand black beacons, each with a cone topmark, numbered 1 to 6 in 'Scotchlite'. During cross winds, yachts can make fast to any of these beacons or to 10 others which are positioned outside the lock. There is a tide gauge on the lock and on No. 6 beacon. When proceeding along this channel towards the lock keep about 10 ft. away from, and to the north of, the beacons and, when leaving, about 45 ft. to the north of them. Overtaking is not allowed and the maximum speed is 6 knots. The lock is available 24 hours a day and is usually manned from 0700 to 2100 daily and from 0600 to 2200 hours at weekends and bank holidays. Entry to the lock, whether inbound or outbound is controlled by 'WAIT' (red background) and 'ENTER' (green background). Having received the 'ENTER' sign, enter the lock and take up the position as indicated by the Lock Master who will pass down a mooring line to hold you in position. Always keep a turn of this line on a cleat and switch off your engine. When the lock is in a state of 'free flow', the same rules apply for entering or leaving, but a tidal current will be flowing at anything up to 2½ knots.

BIRDHAM

Entry. The Birdham Pool Basin is entered by a lock, but its use is restricted to about 2 hours either side of high water, as the channel almost dries out.

BOSHAM

From the Fairway Buoy a course should be maintained along the narrow channel between the moorings. About 1 cable from Bosham Quay the channel divides and the right-hand fork gives access to a good scrubbing hard at the end of the High Street. This fork is only navigable after three quarters flood, is sparsely marked,a nd local guidance should be sought. The left hand fork leads to Bosham Quay and then on to Burnes Yacht Yard. Bosham Quay practically dries out at MLWS but landing can always be made by dinghy. There is a depth of 8 ft. alongside the quay at MHWN and 12 ft. at MHWS. Application to lie alongisde the quay, from which water is available and there is a 15 cwt. crane, should be made to the Quay Master (Tel. Bosham 3336).

DELL QUAY

The channel to Dell Quay is marked by barrel buoys, port and starboard. At low water there is a depth of 1½ ft. off Copperas Point and from there on it gradually shallows and dries out about 3 cables from the Quay. At half tide, yachts of up to 5 ft. draught can reach or leave Dell Quay. At MHWS there is a depth of 10 ft. alongside.

HAMPSHIRE

LANGSTONE

Depth at entrance. There is a minimum depth of 6 ft. at MLWS approaching and just after the Fairway buoy. At present, dredging on the West Winner keeps the channel open; should this stop, the bar would tend to build up with southerly gales. S.R. 13½ ft. N.R. 10½ ft.

Entrance channel. After passing the Fairway buoy, proceed along the channel between the East and West Winner banks into the harbour, leaving the outer drain light (Qk. Fl. R.) to port. The channel has a minimum depth of 9 ft. at MLWS and has a width of about 800 ft. The flood runs at about 3½ knots; the ebb at 4½ knots.

PORTSMOUTH

Depth at entrance. There is a minimum depth at MLWS of 11 ft. over the Portsmouth Bar, and 8 ft. over the Swashway. S.R. 13½ ft. N.R. 10½ ft.

Entrance Channel. The tides run very strongly in the narrows and a rough sea can be set up during a weather tide.

PORTCHESTER

Entrance Channel. The entrance to Portchester Lake is at the northern end of Portsmouth Harbour and the Portchester channel is marked, port and starboard, by chequered piles. There is a least depth of 8 ft. at MLWS in the channel.

FAREHAM

Entrance Channel. The channel to Fareham is well marked with red port hand and black starboard hand piles. The Reserve Fleet is moored at the entrance to Fareham Lake and this creates unpredictable wind conditions. At the entrance there is a depth of about 30 ft. but the channel gradually shallows and Fareham Creek dries out. Where the channel turns to the west, the depth decreases rapidly and the channel narrows. Care should be taken to observe the channel marks, some of which dry out at low water. At the narrowest part the port and starboard hand piles are discontinued and replaced by a single centre post, which is striped red and white. This post should be passed either side and close to, after which there are many moorings on either side up to Fareham Quay. Care should be taken when turning northwards along the channel as there is a power cable which has 32 ft. of overhead clearance at MHWS. Deep water can be found outside the channel marks in Fareham Lake but there is much debris on the bottom so it is advisable to keep to the channel.

HAMBLE RIVER

Depth at entrance. Least depth of 8½ ft. at MLWS will be found in the entrance triangle formed by Spit Pile and Pile Beacons Nos. 1 & 3. S.R. 12½ ft. N.R. 9¾ ft.

Entrance Channel. The channel is marked by piles: Black with triangular topmarks to starboard and red with can topmarks to port.

I.O.W.

BEMBRIDGE

Entrance. From the North or North East, head for the tide indicator which is sited about 1,000 ft. west of St. Helen's Fort. From the South or East, steer to pass to the northward of St. Helen's Fort and then turn in for the tide indicator. The indicator shows the depth at the shallowest part of the entrance channel and, when there is sufficient water for your draft, follow the buoyed channel carefully. If one is not a regular visitor, it is advisable to check that alterations have not been made to the channel marks as they are subject to alteration with change in channel. S.R. 13½ ft. N.R. 10½ ft.

WOOTTON CREEK

Depth at entrance. There is a depth of 8 ft. at MLWS in the entrance. S.R. 12 ft. N.R. 9¼ ft.

Entrance Channel. Follow the channel, which is dredged to 8 ft. at MLWS, as far as the Ferry Terminal at No. 4 beacon. From this beacon, proceed half-way to the Ferry Pierhead before bearing off to starboard on to the leading marks on the far shore (if proceeding up the Creek). The channel lies close to the starboard moorings (about 3 ft. depth at MLWS to the first bend). Ahead, immediately after the pierhead, is a berthing pool with 2 ft. at MLWS. This is just off the Royal Victoria Yacht Club pontoon. Approach close to the pier to avoid the spit which separates the pool from the channel. At low tide, there is very little water in the upper stretches of the creek towards Wootton Bridge, but a yacht drawing 3½ ft. can navigate as far as the bridge from half-tide onwards. The latter part of the ebb, at springs, runs out through the first reach at up to 3½ knots.

COWES

Channel Depths. There is a minimum depth of 15 ft. at MLWS between the entrance buoys. S.R. 11¾ ft. N.R.9½ ft.

Entrance Channel. The channel varies in width from 500 ft. at the entrance to 250 ft. just before the Red Funnel Pontoon Pier. There is a minimum depth of 8 ft. at MLWS up to the floating bridge between East and West Cowes. The channel is busy with commercial vessels and ferries and small craft should keep clear of it particularly the area between East Cowes Slip and the Pontoon Pier where the ferries manoeuvre. The hovercraft route on the eastern side of the harbour is marked by orange buoys, which cross to the slip on the western side opposite the British Hovercraft factory. In the area east of the channel occupied by moored craft there is a minimum depth of 3 ft. at MLWS between a line from Trinity Wharf to the end of the Shrape Breakwater and the channel.

MEDINA RIVER

Entrance Channel. The Medina River proper is entered through the narrow 250 ft. wide passage at the south end of the harbour where there is a floating bridge ferry continuously crossing to and from. Passage through this narrow section should be made under power, and it is inadvisable to use sail only unless the general conditions are extremely favourable. Beyond the ferry, the river is navigable as far as Newport (approximately 4 miles) with a minimum depth of 6 ft. up to the Folly Inn (approximately 2 miles). From there it gradually reduces to nil at MLWS by the Medina Mill.

NEWTOWN

Depth at entrance. Depth on the bar is 5 ft. at MLWS but north-easterly winds tend to lower the depth. S.R. 9 ft. N.R. 7 ft.

Entrance Channel. The channel is marked by perches and is half a cable wide. The main flood and ebb streams run strongly reaching a maximum of 4 knots at springs. Just inside the entrance, there is a shingle spit which extends from the west shore and which is marked by 3 starboard hand perches. Care should be taken to keep to the east side of the channel opposite the spit.

YARMOUTH

Depth at entrance. Minimum depth of 7 ft. at MLWS in the dredged channel. S.R. 9 ft. N.R. 8 ft.

Entrance Channel. From a position approximately one-third of a cable west of the East Breakwater, a course of S. ¾ W. will take one in through the dredged channel. Fixed green lights, by night, indicate the transit bearing along the channel.

HAMPSHIRE

LYMINGTON

Depth at entrance. The entrance channel is dredged to 7½ ft. at MLWS. S.R. 9 ft. N.R. 6½ ft.

Entrance. The main channel lies more to the west than the east and visitors are advised to keep to the centre of the river marks in the entrance. Ferries run between Lymington and Yarmouth and may serve as a guide to the course of the main channel. From the entrance, the channel up to Lymington is marked by beacons, some of which may be lit during the season for night navigation. Minimum depth in the river is 6 ft. at MLWS.

BEAULIEU RIVER

Depth at entrance. There is a minimum depth at MLWS of between 3 and 4 ft. over the bar. Tidal rise is approximately 8 ft. at neaps and 10 ft. at springs. S.R. 10 ft. N.R. 8 ft.

Entrance Channel. A course of approximately N.W. ¼ W. takes one in over the bar along the transit line of leading beacons, and the entrance piles should be followed carefully round the north-eastern tip of Beaulieu Spit. Once round this bend, the channel is clearly marked by perches, port and starboard. Except for a shallow patch of about 4 ft. north-east of Needs Ore Point and 2 similar patches near Gin's Farm, there is a minimum depth of 5 ft. at MLWS, up to Bucklers Hard.

KEYHAVEN

Depth at entrance. There is a minimum depth from 1½ to 3 ft. over the bar with about a 7 ft. neap rise and about 8 to 9 ft. at springs. S.R. 8½ ft. N.R. 7 ft.

Entrance Channel. Approach along the transit line of the leading beacons, the seaward of which is the first of the line of starboard hand perches along the channel. Starboard hand perches have triangular topmarks, the port hand ones 'X' topmarks. The channel sweeps westerly round the tip of Hurst Point (Northern tip) and the north-westwards and northerly into Keyhaven Lake. Once over the bar, the channel deepens to between 12 and 16 ft. at MLWS to near Mount Lake, where it shallows to about 8 ft. and then gradually shallows up to Keyhaven.

CHRISTCHURCH

Entrance. Depth over the bar is about 1 ft. at MLWS and about 6 to 7 ft. at MHWS. The bar shifts frequently and great care should be taken in entry. Visiting craft can be met at the bar by arrangement with the Quay Superintendent. S.R. 5 ft. N.R. 4 ft.

Entrance Channel. During the summer months port and starboard buoys are placed by the yacht club for the guidance of yachts but the current, particularly during the ebb, runs out very fast and they are liable to drag away from their positions. Once through the narrows of The Run the main channel to Christchurch leads off in a southerly direction and is marked by buoys. Depth varies from 3 to 9 ft.

DORSET

POOLE

Entrance. The tide runs rapidly along the Swash Channel increasing from approximately ¾ knot at the Bar buoy to 4 knots between the Havens. Owing to the double high water in Poole Harbour the tide 'stands' at a high level for nearly 3½ hours. The neap rise and fall is almost negligible and since the tide stands at its highest level for nearly 14 hours in every 24, vessels of small draught can run in and out of the harbour channels at all stages of the tide. S.R. 5½ ft. N.R. 4½ ft.

From the Havens there are two navigable channels marked by buoys; the Eastern or Main Channel, 150 ft. wide with least depth of 12 ft., and the Western (Middle) Channel, 180 ft. wide and least depth of 9 ft. The approach to Poole Quay is via the Little Channel which branches off to the northward from the Main Channel; it is 200 ft. wide with least depth of 12 ft. The channels from the Havens to Poole Quay are well buoyed. To the west of Stakes Buoy, which marks the entrance to Little Channel, is the Wareham Channel. For information on this channel, see the Wareham entry.

WAREHAM

Entrance Channel. The Wareham Channel commences north of Gold Point, and the left hand side of the channel is marked by red and white buoys which must be left to port as well as the line of NATO barges which are moored south-west of Russel Quay. After the last port hand buoy about 5 cables south-south-west of Russel Quay, the channel to the mouth of the River Frome is marked by stakes which are red with a topmark on the port hand and plain black on the starboard hand.

One cable west-north-west of the northern tip of Giggers Island, the channel bends fairly sharply to port and, about 3 cables further on (south-west of Brixe Island) sharply to starboard. Shortly after passing the last port hand buoy depth decreases to 2 to 3 ft. at MLWS, and this depth is maintained to a point 2 cables south-west of Brixe Island where the depth increases to 4 ft. at MLWS, which depth is maintained to Redcliffe where it again decreases to 2 ft., and this depth is maintained to Wareham Quay which has a depth of 3 ft. alongside at MLWS.

High water at Wareham is approximately 1 hour after high water at Poole. The ebb is stronger than the flood, up to 3 knots at springs. During spring tides the first high water is higher than the second, but at neaps the second is higher than the first.

It is not advisable to use this channel at night as there are no lights or useful landmarks.

WEYMOUTH

Depth at entrance. Least depth on the leading marks is 15 ft. at MLWS and this depth is maintained in mid-channel up to within 200 ft. of the Town Bridge, after which it decreases to 6 ft. S.R. 7 ft. N.R. 4½ ft.

Entrance Channel. Width between pier heads is 450 ft. but the 15 ft. channel is only 230 ft. wide and decreases in width towards the bridge. Under normal conditions the average strength of both ebb and flood is about 1 knot.

BRIDPORT

Depth at entrance. Rise and fall of tide approximately 12 ft. at Spring Tide. Part of the entrance channel dries at MLWS. S.R. 12 ft. N.R. 8½ ft.

Entrance. The harbour is formed by two parallel piers, each about 700 ft. long. The entrance width between the pier heads is 50 ft. It is occasionally necessary to scour the harbour basin by opening the sluice gates on the River Brit and it is unsafe to enter while this work is being carried out. No craft should enter the port unless it can take the mud at low water. When the entrance is clear a red flag with a white St. Andrew's Cross is displayed by day, and at night a red light on the West Pier and a green light on the East Pier. When the entrance is not clear, a black ball is exhibited by day. No night signal.

LYME REGIS

Entrance. The entrance should not be attempted at night unless you have local knowledge, nor during strong southerly or easterly winds when the seas are breaking heavily around the piers. Tidal streams run with the coast and are generally weak. There are depths of 6-12 ft. at MLWS about 2 cables eastward of the pierheads, these depths being much less towards Broad Ledge. S.R. 12½ ft. N.R. 8½ ft.

Depth at entrance. Close to the entrance there is a low water depth of 5 ft. at neap tide, 9 ft. at high water neaps and 12 ft. at high water springs. The harbour bar dries out at MLWS, but has a depth of 9-12 ft. at MHWS. There is a depth gauge at the entrance end of the north wall.

DEVON

EXMOUTH

Entrance. Depth on the bar at MLWS can be less than 5 ft. in parts and there is a very dangerous cross sea during onshore winds, particularly when the ebb is strong against the wind. Unless you have local knowledge or can be guided in by a local boat, the crossing of the bar should not be attempted unless the weather is very favourable. S.R. 12½ ft. N.R. 8½ ft.

Entrance Channel. Once over the bar course should be set for a point midway between the first pair of port and starboard hand channel buoys which are almost due west of the Fairway Buoy. From there on the channel is marked by port and starboard hand buoys and one should keep to the centre of the channel between them. The current runs very strongly, particularly in the narrows between Warren Sand and the land on the north side of the channel, reaching a rate of about 5 knots at spring tides and about 3 knots at neap tides.

RIVER EXE

Entrance. The river channel is buoyed as far as Turf Lock which is the entrance to the Exeter Canal. Depth of water at MLWS decreases gradually to about 6 ft. off the lock entrance and to about 3 ft. off Topsham. Above Powderham, the channel is marked by beacons on either side. The Lympstone channel entrance lies to starboard of the black buoy marking the end of the Lympstone Sand spit, and the depth gradually decreases until the channel dries out just short of the harbour where there is a ramp.

TEIGNMOUTH

Entrance. There is 2 to 5 ft. at MLWS over the bar but the entrance should not be attempted during bad weather. The sands on the bar shift periodically and a nasty chop can be set up during onshore winds. Assistance can always be obtained from local fishing boats, other local craft, or the pilot, on entry during bad weather. S.R. 13 ft. N.R. 9½ ft.

Entrance Channel. A small buoy on the bar should be left close to port and once over the bar there is a depth of 7 to 9 ft. at MLWS. Keep the Ness beacon open on the port bow and then bear round to starboard for a point mid-way between Ferry Point and the south shore. When Ferry Point bears 007° (M) haul round to starboard, taking care not to be set onshore by the very strong current which runs in this area. Set course for the nearest quay keeping to the starboard side of the channel where the water is deepest. The salt flats on the south side of the channel are marked by buoys from Shaldon up to the swingbridge.

TORQUAY

Depth at entrance. 18 ft. at MLWS. S.R. 13½ ft. N.R. 10 ft.

Entrance. No channel and the width between piers is 150 ft. No precautions necessary to offset tide or current. Keep to your correct side when entering as there is heavy traffic during the season.

PAIGNTON

Depth at entrance. 14 ft. MHWS, 10 ft. MHWN, dry at MLWS. S.R. 14 ft. N.R. 10 ft.

Entrance Channel. 60 ft. wide and no special precautions are necessary.

BRIXHAM

Depth at entrance. Off the breakwater, 24 ft. Inner Harbour dries out. S.R. 14 ft. N.R. 10½ ft.

Entrance Channel. 3 cables wide and fairway 300 ft. wide. Do not enter the Inner Harbour without permission from the Harbour Master.

RIVER DART TO TOTNES

Approach. The Anchor Stone, off Vipers Quay, should be left to port. This stone, which extends approximately 30 ft. to the west of the white beacon marking the rock, lies 3 cables S.E. of Dittisham. The spring tides run fast over the stone which should be given ample clearance. The channel to the east is wide and deep at all states of the tide but keep clear of the free-running ferry between Dittisham and Greenway Quay.

Depth in River Channel. There is deep water up to Dittisham, after which the minimum depth at MLWS is about 12 ft. to Glampton Quay. From there to Bow Creek the depth gradually decreases to about 2 ft. at MLWS and from there to Totnes to 1 ft. at MLWS.

River Channel. The Flat Owers Sandbank, between Dittisham and Galmpton Creek is unmarked and the main fairway runs to the east of the Sandbank. Keep close to the moorings for the main channel. Between Dittisham and Greenway Quay the channel is 1 cable wide. The ebb runs at approximately 2½ knots and is fastest near Greenway Quay. Flood is maximum at spring tides when it runs at up to 1½ knots. After continuous heavy rain the ebb runs faster than normal, especially in the upper reaches.

DARTMOUTH

Entrance Channel. Just southward of Battery Point is Kitten Rock with 6 ft. of water over it at MLWS and near it is the Checkstone, the outer end of which is marked by a red and white chequered buoy with 'Checkstone' in white letters. The wind can be very fluky in the entrance and sailing vessels may also find difficulty in beating in against a foul tide and head wind, particularly if the wind is light. There are no difficulties for power craft. If entering at night a good lookout should be kept for large mooring buoys in mid-stream. S.R. 15½ ft. N.R. 11½ ft.

SALCOMBE

Entrance. The bar has a minimum depth of 2 to 5 ft. at MLWS. During strong onshore winds, particularly against the ebb out of the river, a confused sea is set up and the bar should not be crossed until at least half-flood. If a southerly gale is blowing a high rough sea is set up which breaks heavily over the bar and when this occurs entrance should not be attempted. S.R. 16 ft. N.R. 12½ ft.

Inside the bar leave the Bass Rock (off Splat Point) to port and the Wolf Rock buoy to starboard. Course should then be altered to starboard to leave the Poundstone to port and the Rocks off Biddlehead and the Ram Rock to starboard. At night the white sector of Sandhill Point Light (008° M.) gives clear passage to apoint N.N.W. of Wolf Rock buoy where the quick flashing leading lights between Ox Point and Pool Point come on transit. This course leads one to the anchorage area.

YEALM RIVER

Entrance Channel. When Wembury Church bears N.E. x N. and the Mewstone W., alter course to E. x N. and maintain this course until the leading beacons south-west of Misery Point come on transit. A course set midway between this transit beacon and the south shore gives the course to the southern end of the bar spit, which has a depth of 4 to 7 ft. at MLWS. When the two leading beacons on the north shore between Season and Warren Points come on transit, steer along this bearing. Once over the bar, follow the centre of the river to the anchorage off Warden Point.

PLYMOUTH

Entrance. The entrance to the Sound can be made through either the west or east channels in both of which there is deep water. The Sound itself has no shallow patches with less than 12 ft. of water at MLWS. Tidal streams are regular, the flood and ebb being of about 6 hours and 10 minutes duration each. The height of rise and fall, however, is affected by the wind. Winds from S.E. to W. increase the flood and retard the ebb while winds from N.W. to E. have the opposite effect. From positions east or west of the breakwater, steer for a position just east of the Melampus buoy and then to the yacht anchorage off Mill Bay Docks. S.R. 16 ft. N.R. 12½ ft.

The St. German's River (at the head of the Hamoaze) has its entrance opposite Bull Point. The river bed undulates but has a minimum depth of 5 ft. at MLWS as far as Earth Hill after which it gradually dries out at MLWS and can only be navigated by dinghies for about an hour on either side of high water. There is good anchcrage in the deep water between Warde Quay and Sandacre Point.

The River Tamar, from Bull Point to Cargreen, has a minimum depth of 5 ft. at MLWS and is well marked for easy navigation. Above Cargreen the channel becomes narrow and tortuous and there are no navigational marks. Local knowledge is advisable if one wishes to proceed beyond Cargreen.

CORNWALL

LOOE

Depth at entrance. The whole harbour, including the entrance, dries at MLWN. S.R. 17 ft. N.R. 13½ ft.

Entrance Channel. The entrance of the harbour is 150 ft. wide between natural rocks on the west-side and the breakwater pier on the east. At springs the tide runs at between 3 and 5 knots. With strong winds from the south-east, seas break heavily over the bar.

FOWEY

Entrance Channel. The channel is not buoyed but deep water extends to within a cable of either shore. Keep well clear of the Punch Cross ledge of rocks which juts out from the eastern side of the entrance. The flood and ebb run at about 2 to 2½ knots but the ebb can exceed this after heavy rain. It is a busy commercial port and yachts must keep clear of cargo vessels in the entrance channel. S.R. 16½ ft. N.R. 13½ ft.

Depth at entrance. Depths of 17 to 22 ft. at MLWS up to Wiseman Point. Southerly gales cause a very confused sea to be set up particularly when the ebb is running out of the river.

River Fowey to Golant, Lostwithiel and Lerryn. From Wiseman Point to Bodmin Pill, the depth gradually decreases until the river dries out. As far as Golant no problems exist for dinghies at high water, but the channels to Lerryn and Lostwithiel are unmarked and tortuous and can only be reached by dinghies of 2 ft. maximum draught and even then only between one hour either side of high water.

MEVAGISSEY

Depth at entrance. There is 10 ft. depth of water at MLWS between the breakwaters but the bottom shelves quickly in all directions and the Inner Harbour dries out completely. S.R. 18½ ft. N.R. 15 ft.

Entrance Channel. Width between the breakwaters is 150 ft. There are rocks close to the East Pier and yachts should keep to the middle of the entrance.

FALMOUTH

Depth at entrance. There is ample depth of water for any size of yacht. Small vessels running for shelter in heavy southerly weather will find the seas less steep if they keep to the deepest part of the channel. S.R. 17 ft. N.R. 14 ft.

Entrance Channel. The Western channel is 3½ cables wide with minimum depth of 20 ft. at MLWS; the eastern channel is 5½ cables wide with minimum depth of 72 ft. at MLWS. Maximum tidal strength is 1½ to 2 knots.

PENRYN

Entrance Channel. The channel, off Greenbank Quay, has a depth of 10 ft. at MLWS but this depth quickly decreases and, after a distance of about 4 cables, the channel dries out. The tide runs at a maximum of 1½ knots during springs and a careful watch must be kept on the tide level to avoid drying out.

ST MAWES

Entrance. When entering, leave the Castle buoy to port. The entrance channel is not buoyed and, as the shores of the Porthcuel River and St. Mawes harbour shelve gradually, deep-draughted boats should keep to the centre of the channel which has a depth of 13 to 15 ft. at MLWS up to Polworth Point. The flood and ebb run at approximately 2 to 3 knots.

RIVER FAL

Mylor Creek. The entrance to this creek is on the west-side of the river channel just north of Pencarrow Point. There is a depth of 4 to 6 ft. at MLWS in the anchorage at Mylor Pool but care should be taken during the approach due to the many sandbanks. The quay at Mylor with its attendant buildings has been turned into a yacht harbour which offers all facilities.

Restronguet Creek. Except for the deep hole at the entrance (just south of Restronguet Point) the creek dries out at MLWS and can only be navigated around the time of high water.

Malpas. Malpas lies at the end of the main navigable river channel which has a depth of 4 to 10 ft. at MLWS from Woodbury Point to Malpas anchorage.

Ruan Creek. The entrance, which dries at MLWS, is on the right-hand side of the river, 1½ miles below Malpas. There is a deep hole just inside the bar to the creek which provides a good anchorage.

Truro River and Truro. The Truro River gradually dries out leaving a very narrow twisting channel as far as Sunny Corner where it completely dries out at MLWS. Truro can only be visited by shallow-draught craft and around the time of high water.

HELFORD RIVER

Entrance. There is deep water in the narrow entrance south of Passage Inn where the width, at MLWS, is about one cable and the shallowest part is just north of Bosahan Point where there is a depth of 10 ft. at MLWS. The northern side of the narrowest part of the entrance, by Passage Inn, has a bank which juts out into the river the end of which is marked by a black conical buoy. Leave this buoy to starboard and make for the anchorage off Navas Creek. S.R. 17 ft. N.R. 14 ft.

PENZANCE

Depth at entrance. 14½ ft. at MHWS; 12½ fr. at MHWN. S.R. 17½ ft. N.R. 14 ft.

Entrance Channel. The entrance gates to the wet docks are usually opened from 2½ hours before, to high water. 2 balls horizontal (2 red lights by night) indicate that the gates are open, 2 balls vertically (red over green lights by night) indicate that the gates are shut.

NEWLYN

Depth at entrance. 11 ft. at MLWS, between the pier heads. S.R. 17½ ft. N.R. 14 ft.

Entrance Channel. No direct channel to the entrance. Width between the pier heads is 15 ft.

ST. IVES

Depth at entrance. The entrance dries at MLWS but has an average depth of 6 ft. at half-tide. S.R. 29 ft. N.R. 20 ft.

Entrance Channel. The entrance between the two piers is wide and no special precautions are necessary.

NEWQUAY

Depth at entrance. The harbour dries out completely at MLWS. The average rise of the tide at the entrance is about 18 ft. S.R. 22½ ft. N.R. 17½ ft.

HAYLE

Depth at entrance. Minimum depth on the bar is 2 ft. at MLWS.

Entrance Channel. Two conical black buoys mark the channel over the bar. The channel has a width of 1½ cables which narrows to ½ cable just before the harbour entrance. During springs, the flood and ebb run from 4 to 6 knots and entrance should only be attempted during the hour before high water when the current is weakest. During strong winds or gales from a north-westerly direction, seas break heavily over the bar which becomes impassable for all vessels.

PADSTOW

Depth at entrance. Minimum depth on the bar is 2 ft. at MLWS but the entrance should not be attempted in any but the calmest sea conditions and, even then, with extreme care. At spring tides the ebb and flood run at between 3 and 4 knots. During strong north-westerly winds the seas break heavily over the bar which becomes impassable. S.R. 22 ft. N.R. 17 ft.

Entrance Channel. As far as St. Saviour's Point, the channel has a minimum width of about 1 cable and, from there to the harbour entrance, gradually narrows to about ¼ of a cable. At MLWS, a craft drawing up to 3 ft. can reach the St. Saviour's Point buoy area. The harbour entrance is marked by red and green fixed lights.

DEVON

RIVER TAW

Depth at entrance. At MLWS there is a depth over the bar of about 6 ft.; 28 ft. at MHWS.

Entrance Channel. The bar buoy at the river entrance is 9 cables south-east of the red and white buoy, and a course of approximately S.E. (by night, leading lights in line) will take one through the channel passing to starboard the Middle Ridge buoy and Outer Pulley buoy, when course should be altered to approximately S. x E. passing the Pulley buoy on the starboard hand. From there on, navigation of the rivers can only be accomplished by using a large scale chart of the area. Entrance, except in an emergency, should only be attempted from 2 hours before to 2 hours after high water. *Special Warning:* Great care must always be taken to counteract the varying and very strong set of the tide (up to 3 knots) in the various channels.

BARNSTABLE AND BIDEFORD

Barnstable is 6 miles up the River Taw, and Bideford 2½ miles up the River Torridge, both from the anchorage at Appledore. The channels to both places are narrow and torturous and are not navigable at MLWS. Between Appledore and Bideford, the banks are constantly changing and frequent changes may be expected in the depths of the channel. The course and depth of the River Taw can change daily and the stakes marking the channel are moved frequently to meet the changing conditions. Because of this, local knowledge is essential before attempting passage to either port and, even then, only around the time of high water.

ILFRACOMBE

Depth at entrance. At the eastern steps, outer harbour, there is a depth of 5 to 6 ft. at MLWS, and 21 to 23 ft. at MHWS. S.R. 28 ft. N.R. 21 ft.

Entrance. The entrance width is about 250 ft., and the tide sets north-west at the north-east face of the pier from 3 hours after high water at between 2 and 3 knots. Signals are shown from the mast when the cross-channel ferries are expected: one red conical shape – ferry berthing on east face of pier; two red conical shapes – ferry berthing on south face of pier.

SOMERSET

WATCHET

Depth at entrance. Dry at MLWS, rising to 9 ft. at MHWN and 19 ft. at MHWS. S.R. 37 ft. N.R. 28 ft.

Entrance Channel. There is no entrance channel as such, but yachts should keep at least 5 cables off the shore until the entrance is well open and then steer direct for the centre between the pier heads. On the ebb tide a strong set is encountered across the entrance, and one should steer well to the east to counteract it. Small craft can enter at half-flood if not drawing more than 3 ft. but, if the wind is fresh from the west when a heavy confused sea can be set up, it is best to wait until at least 2 hours before time of high water. Larger craft should wait nearer the time of high water.

BURNHAM-ON-SEA

Depth at entrance. The bar practically dries out at MLWS, and should not be crossed until after 3 hours of flood tide. S.R. 38 ft. N.R. 28 ft.

Entrance Channel. The flood and ebb both run at up to 5 knots and it is unsafe to cross the bar if the wind is between S.W. and N.N.E. and above force 6 of the Beauford Scale. The drying sandbank, just south of the bar, is marked by a red can buoy with a red flash at night. The leading lights lead in through the channel. After crossing the bar, a black conical buoy is left to starboard and the two buoys marking the edges of the narrow part of the channel between Gore Sands and Stert Flats will be seen about 8 cables ahead. Passing between these 2 buoys a distance of 8 cables will take one to the fork in the channel at the west end of Lark Spit. The right hand channel brings one round to the anchorage off the mouth of the River Brue.

WESTON–SUPER-MARE

Depth at entrance. Practically dries at MLWS. The rise of tide can be as much as 43 ft. at MHWS. S.R. 38 ft. N.R. 29 ft.

Entrance Channel. The entry can be very tricky and local assistance should always be obtained before attempting the passage. It is possible to enter and leave during the 3 hours on either side of high water but deep draughted yachts should wait until 1 hour before high water.

PORTISHEAD

Entrance. Entrance is through the lock which is 66 ft. wide and has a depth of 24 ft. at MHWN; 34 ft. at MHWS. The lock gates are normally open from 2½ hours before to 1½ hours after each high water. S.R. 42 ft. N.R. 32 ft.

AVON

BRISTOL

Depth at entrance. 1 to 2 ft. at MLWS rising to 31.6 ft. at MHWN and 42.2 ft. at MHWS. S.R. 33 ft. N.R. 23 ft.

Entrance Channel. Do not enter the River Avon until 2 hours before high water at Avonmouth. Approach along the line of the South Pier and, when about 1 cable from it, turn to starboard into the river. By keeping well up to the pier end, you avoid the Swash Spit which extends for some distance out from the western side of the river entrance. Make due allowance for the strong set across the entrance. Once inside the river, keep well over to the north side until the leading beacons (lighted at night) are in line when you should alter to starboard and follow a mid-river course. Give commercial traffic plenty of room especially on the bends as they are severely restricted by the depth of water. You should time your arrival to reach the Bristol lock entrance before high water. The tide runs at about 4½ knots during the spring flood and at about 3¼ knots during the ebb.

LYDNEY

Note. If no local knowledge is available, a pilot should be taken from Portishead pilot station. Under no circumstances should the passage be attempted under sail alone.

Approach. Time departure from King Road (off Portishead) to allow for the 15-mile passage to Lydney dock entrance, making allowance for the strength of the tide and the recommended time of arrival off Lydney (see note below). Leave Avonmouth piers to starboard and set course up the main channel (east of the Bedwin Sands) for a position just west of the English Stones No. 1 beacon. Leave this beacon to starboard and steer to leave the No. 2 beacon to starboard. When the No. 2 beacon bears east, alter to bring the Charston Rock Lighthouse dead ahead and, when 2 cables short of this lighthouse, alter to leave Chapel Rock 2 cables to port. Watch out for a strong easterly set in the area of Charston Rock during the flood. When Lyde Rock Lighthouse (by the road bridge on the west side of the channel) bears 4 points on the port bow, alter round to the north-west to leave this rock to port, and when the leading beacons (F. Or.) come on transit, bring them dead astern for the course up the channel west of Oldbury Sands. The tide in this area is very strong so avoid being swept on to the south-west tip of Oldbury Sands. Leave the leading beacons (1 mile south of Wibdon) 2 cables to port, and when they come on transit, bring them dead astern for passage up the channel south of Sheperdine Sands. On this course, the bell buoy marking the northern extremity of the rocks at the northern edge of Oldbury sands will be left to starboard and, when the leading beacons 5 cables east of the buoy come on transit, bring them dead astern for passage up the Sheperdine Sands leaving the 2 black conical buoys to starboard. Passing this buoy bring the leading beacons 8 cables east of it on transit and, when the two leading beacons 5 cables south of the buoy come on transit, bring them dead astern for passage up the channel east of the Saniger Sands and then across the sands to Lydney entrance.

It is not advisable to enter Lydney harbour earlier than 1 hour before high water when there will be sufficient depth of water over the sands. There are 2 piers, the north-east pier being the longer and left to starboard on entry. The spring rate of tide off the north-east pier is 7 knots and, during neaps, 4 knots. It is advisable to swing and stem the tide before making the approach to the dock gates.

Depth at entrance. One hour before high water there is a depth of 8 ft. at neap tides, and 25 ft. at springs. S.R. 33 ft. N.R. 31 ft.

Entrance Channel. The width of the dock entrance to the tidal basin is 33 ft., and to the canal lock entrance 24 ft. A red light is exhibited at night when entry to the port is suspended to allow vessels to leave.

St. PIERRE PILL

Approach. If no local knowledge is available, a pilot should be taken from Portishead pilot station. Under no circumstances should passage be attempted under sail alone. Time departure from King Road to pass through the 'Shoots' (Narrows west of English Stones) about ½ an hour before high water, leaving beacons 1 and 2 about ½ a cable to starboard. Leave Charston Rock close to port as Charston Sands can be safely crossed for about 1½ hours on either side of high water. On the flood tide, make no attempt to leave Charston Rock to starboard as the tide sets very strongly across it. When approaching St. Pierre Pill, make due allowance for the very strong set across the entrance (up to 6 knots). The tide rises 46 ft. at MHWS and 33 ft. at MHWN. See also "Passage notes for the Bristol channel'.

SOUTH GLAMORGAN

PENARTH

Depth at entrance. Basin and harbour dry out at MLWS, but there is sufficient depth of water for craft drawing up to 4 ft. to enter at half-flood. S.R. 37½ ft. N.R. 28 ft.

Entrance Channel. The main channel is 400 ft. wide, and the tidal strength at springs is about 3 knots. Keep well to windward during strong easterly winds. The entrance to the yacht basin is 60 ft. wide, and it is advisable to enter close to the North Pier as the South Pier is derelict and submerged for 1½ hours either side of high water. Its extremity is marked by a post with a yellow topmark.

BARRY

Depth at entrance. 9 ft. at MLWS, and the height variation due to east or west winds rarely exceeds 1 ft. S.R. 36 ft. N.R. 26½ ft.

Entrance Channel. The entrance is between two stone breakwaters which are 350 ft. apart. There is a conspicuous white lighthouse on the west breakwater. Approach with caution as commercial shipping enters and leaves by the same channel. Rise and fall of tide approximately 40 ft. at springs. The lock gates open 4 hours either side of high water.

MID GLAMORGAN

PORTHCAWL

Depth at entrance. The harbour dries out 3 hours on either side of high water, but has a depth of 11 ft. at MHWN and 18 ft. at MHWS. S.R. 29 ft. N.R. 22 ft.

Entrance Channel. There is no tidal effect in the harbour entrance and the approximate width is 40 ft. The channel is open to the south-east and conditions in the channel (and harbour) are bad during strong-easterly winds.

MUMBLES ANCHORAGE

Approach. From the west, the Sir Christopher Shoal, in Oxwich Bay, extends for more than a mile out from the shore, and course should be set well to the southward to avoid it. The Mixon Shoal has a red can bell buoy moored at its southern extremity, and this should be left well to port particularly during weather tides when a heavy confused sea is set up in the area round the shoal. Heavy tide rips also occur off Oxwich Point during spring tides when the rate can reach as much as 5 knots. East of the Mixon, the approach is good for all small craft after flood. See also 'Passage notes for the Bristol Channel'. S.R. 29 ft. N.R. 21 ft.

DYFED

BURRY PORT

Depth at entrance. The outer bar, south-west of Burry Holme, has a least depth of 6 ft. at MLWS. S.R. 27 ft. N.R. 20 ft.

Entrance Channel. The channel between Whiteford and Hooper Sands has a minimum depth of 7 ft. at MLWS in mid-channel, and is approximately 3 cables wide. The channel is not buoyed but the sand banks on either side clearly indicate its direction. If the wind is fresh from a westerly direction a heavy confused sea can be set up at the entrance, and it is advisable to wait until 2 hours of flood have passed before entering. Near Whiteford lighthouse (N.N.W. of Whiteford Point) a strong east-going set will be experienced during most of the flood.

PEMBROKESHIRE

SAUNDERSFOOT

Depth at entrance. Harbour dries out. S.R. 26 ft. N.R. 19 ft.

Entrance. Good anchorage off harbour light while awaiting sufficient depth of water to enter. Yacht drawing about 3½ ft. can enter about half-tide.

Depth at entrance. Dries. S.R. 25 ft. N.R. 19 ft.

Entrance. Anchorage off harbour until sufficient water. Craft drawing about 4 ft. can enter at half-tide.

MILFORD HAVEN

Entrance. The entrance to Milford Haven has been greatly simplified over the past few years, as the Port is now used by some of the largest tankers afloat. In addition to St. Annes Lighthouse, which is on the north side of the entrance to the Haven, there is a system of Day Lights which are used when tankers are approaching. In recent years also, they have built a lighthouse in the centre of the entrance, which has been built on the Mid-channel rocks, and this lighthouse taken in conjunction with St. Annes Lighthouse makes the approach relatively simple.

There are eastern and western channels, each marked by a separate buoyage system, and about four miles from the entrance there is a radar buoy. The entrance to Milford Haven is notorious for tumbling sea in westerly and south westerly winds, but once inside the north shore, the anchorage at Dale is very secure under the old fort, but owing to the depth of water it is not prudent to go further in unless your vessel can take the ground. From Dale to Milford Haven the Channel is well marked by buoys, but these of course are the main channel for 250,000 tonners and there are really no outstanding hazards for the smaller vessel. Once round Esso Pier, which is on the north side, the next bay is Gellyswick. This is the headquarters of the Pembrokeshire Yacht Club, and a little to the east of this bay is the Milford Haven Conservancy Board Jetty, at which you should report if you have not already been met by one of the Conservancy Board Yachts. S.R. 22 ft N.R. 17 ft.

FISHGUARD

Entrance. Fishguard Harbour is enclosed by the North Breakwater and East Breakwater, and is a Railway Harbour and anchorage is prohibited in the harbour north of a line from the Lifeboat house to the Light House on the East Breakwater. There is a depth of 10 ft. at low water for some 300 ft. south of this line, beyond this the area dries out at low water – hard sand. S.R. 15 ft. N.R. 11 ft.

GWYNEDD

ABERDOVEY

Entrance. Aberdovey outer buoy lies 1½ miles west of the estuary entrance and the channel is marked by three starboard hand buoys, the first indicating the bar. The bar has a minimum depth at MLWS of 2 to 4 ft, resulting in a confused sea if the wind is strong. Caution is required under these conditions and crossing should not be attempted at low water in strong winds. S.R. 15½ ft. N.R. 11½ ft.

BARMOUTH

Depth at entrance. About 2 ft. at low water. S.R. 16 ft. N.R. 12 ft.

Entrance. Harbour should only be approached during fine weather.

DYFED

ABERYSTWYTH

Aberystwyth Harbour. Fixed white light on cylindrical black post 18 ft. high and 44 ft. above high water springs. Vis. 10m. 2 fixed red lights near root of pier vis. 3m Lead over Bar 138° true. Depth on Bar 16 ft. 6 in. M.H.W.S.T. Dry L.W.O.S.T. S.R. 15 ft. N.R. 11 ft.

GWYNEDD

PWLLHELI

Entrance. There are no offshore rock hazards or dangers approaching the entrance to Pwllheli harbour and the tidal streams do not run strongly. The entrance to the harbour lies due N.E. of the small promontory known as Gimblet Rock (50 ft. high). The Bar at No. 6 conical buoy at MLWS has a depth of only 1 ft. and yachts can only enter and leave the outer harbour on either side of H.W. (e.g. a yacht drawing 5 ft, can only cross the Bar up to 2½ hours either side of H.W.). S.R. 16 ft. N.R. 12 ft.

CAERNARVON

Entrance. From the West via Bar Channel where least depth of water at MLWS about 5 ft. Channel is buoyed but the buoys are moved without notice to mark changes in the position of the banks. From the East – between Perch Rk and Trwyn Du Lt. House then follow buoyed channel to Menai Suspension Bridge, thence through Swelly Channel and finally buoyed route to Caernarvon. Passage between the Suspension & Tubular Bridges should not be attempted without local knowledge – Tide attains rate of 8 knots at Springs. Best time to navigate Swelly Channel 2 hours before H.W. Liverpool.

ABERSOCH

Depth at entrance. 6 to 8 fathoms.

Entrance. Yachtsmen should pass through St. Tudwals Sound, leaving St. Tudwals West and East islands to starboard, and head for the 'Sandspit' black conical buoy until the village of Abersoch opens up to port. There are no offshore dangers, but care should be taken to avoid the reef that runs for 3½ cables northwards from the West Island. Yachts may pass to seawards of the St. Tudwals Islands but care should be taken to avoid the rocks (Dries 9 ft.) which are situated about 3 cables to the south-eastward of the East Island, and marked by the red can bell buoy.

CONWAY AND CLWYD

Entrance. Approaching from the North West, the yachtsman should look out for the Fairway Buoy, a spherical buoy with R.W.V.S. and no topmark (not lit) followed by No. 2 Buoy and then Nos. 1, 3, and 5 black conical and then No. 4 can buoy and then No. 7 Conical and then Perch Fl. every 5 secs. W.R. sectors (White 076° to 088° Red to 171° White to 319°. Red to 076°). The deepest part of the channel is the northern side and the perch should not be passed too close. Inshore on the other side of the river is a mussel bank which dries at low water springs. When half of Conway bridge is in view then turn and head towards Conway. DO NOT ATTEMPT TO ENTER AFTER HALF TIDE.

Approaching Round Ormes Head do not attempt to head for the perch at the entrance to the estuary outside an hour either side of high water (springs only). Maximum draft will be 6 ft. provided height of tide at Liverpool 25 ft. or more. At any other state of the tide the yachtsman should make for the Fairway buoy and thence follow the buoyed channel as before. The ebb is extremely strong and especially near the perch. S.R. 23 ft. N.R. 18 ft.

ANGLESEY

HOLYHEAD

Entrance. The final entry is from the North-West. The entry to the Harbours is past the breakwater, jutting out in a westerly direction. Beyond the breakwater is the Anglesey Aluminium jetty. The outer harbour is between the breakwater and the jetty. The entrance to the inner Harbour lies beyond the jetty and Salt Island, and is used for cross-channel and car ferry moorings. S.R. 16 ft. N.R. 12 ft.

CHESHIRE

WEST KIRBY

Entrance. Caution must be exercised in approach whether from Welsh Coast or North, as there is the vast West Hoyle Bank facing the estuary mouth but with buoyed deep water channels. "Welshman Cut" running from Wales to Hilbre Island the Welsh Roads a good Westward anchorage at the entrance of the Welsh Channel and the Hilbre Swash feeding into the Wirral channel from Hilbre and buoyed for two miles or so upstream off West Kirby. Parts ebb to four feet at L.W.S. and local advice should be sought from Custodian, Hilbre Island, or from Boatman, West Kirby Sailing Club.

LANCASHIRE

MERSEY

Depth at entrance. 30 ft. over the Bar at low water. S.R. 28 ft. N.R. 22 ft.

Entrance. Entrance to the River Mersey commences at the Bar L.V. and is very well buoyed. A nasty confused sea is set up between Crosby and Formby Light Floats on the Ebb with strong west winds. There are no obstructions in the channel as the river has been recently dredged to take 200,000 ton tankers.

PORT OF LIVERPOOL

Entrance. The approach to the Port is by way of Queens and Crosby Channels which are maintained by dredging and where the least depth is 26 ft. (7.9m) to 28 ft. (8.5m) below Chart Datum. The "BAR" Lightvessel is moored 2.5 miles W. x N. of the seaward entrance to Queens Channel and provides the "landfall" mark for approaching vessels. The hull is painted red and has the word "BAR" in white on each side.

A Racon radar beacon is operated continuously on the BAR lightvessel

The approach channels are marked and buoyed in accordance with the Uniform System of Buoyage – Lateral system. Yachtsmen are warned that training walls constructed of limestone boulders exist on both sides of the channel outside the buoyed limits. Parts of the walls dry and are visible at low water. All mariners are advised not to navigate outside the buoyed channel as serious damage may result from a stranding on the training walls.

The entrance to the River Mersey is marked, in addition to the buoys, by the Rock Lighthouse on the Western side and the North Wall Light on the Eastern side. Both are painted white with red lanterns and the Rock Lighthouse is conspicuous from seaward during daylight. S.R. 28 ft. N.R. 23 ft.

GLASSON DOCK

Entrance. Start from Lune No. 1 buoy (B. & W. conical 3 Fl. every 15 secs.). The channel is straight and wide from here to Abbey Light. On the port hand are red can buoys 2, 4 and 6 (all with radar reflectors). On the stbd. hand are black conical buoys Nos. 3 (Ra. Refl.). 5 (Qk. Fl.) and 7.

The Abbey Light (Fl. every 2 secs.) is left to stbd. Beyond the channel is twisty and narrow. The port hand buoys are 8 ('Braithaven' – Qk. Fl. red), 10 ('Town Scar' – Qk. Fl. red), 12 and 14 (both spherical plastic), 16 (Qk. Fl. red), 18 and 20 (both spherical plastic), 22 (Basil – red can), 24 (Qk. Fl. red and 26 (red can). The stbd. hand marks are Crook Scar Perch (Ra. Refl.) and black conical buoys, 9 (Qk. Fl.) and 11. Keep to the port hand of the channel, but not too close to the marks for, 12 to 22, as these buoys sometimes drift over an underlying training wall. Steer for the dock entrance from 24 or 26.

Beyond Glasson the channel is marked by buoys and perches, but is not lighted. No difficulty should be experienced by small craft keeping in mid channel once past No. 13 buoy (B. conical) which should be left close to stbd. S.R. 28 ft. N.R. 22 ft.

FLEETWOOD

Entrance. Entering Fleetwood from Seaward, pick up Lune Buoy (Double white flash every 10 secs.; Bell. Whistle). Leave this on the Port hand and steer 083°, 4.5 miles to Fairway Buoy (Black conical; white flash every sec.). Leaving this on the Starboard hand alter course 120° for No. 4 buoy (Red can; red Flash), distance 4 cables. (At this point the Flood tide sets strongly to the Eastward.) Leave this close on the port hand and alter course to 177° for No. 6 Buoy (Red can; red Flash) opposite Wyre Light Tower (White flash every 15 secs; bell 1 stroke every 30 secs.). Leave No. 6 Buoy fairly close on Port hand and alter course to about 186° for No. 5 Buoy (Black conical; white flash every sec.). Keep on this course until the leading Lights (Fixed white) come in line, then follow their lead 165° until abreast of No. 9 Buoy (Black conical; white flash every ½ sec.; nautophone blast every 15 secs. in fog), on starboard hand.

Here the course must be altered slightly to starboard in order to leave No. 16 Buoy (red can red flash) on the port hand. Then alter course to Port and follow Fleetwood shore leaving Lifeboat Slipway Dolphin (Fixed Green Light) on Starboard hand. S.R. 28 ft. N.R. 22 ft.

LYTHAM ST. ANNES

Entrance. The yachtsman, approaching from any direction, should head for Gut Gas Buoy and then approach the channel entrance direct leaving Wall End Buoy to starboard. Keep in the centre of the channel until it widens at Salters Buoy. Only cross this bar at about three hours either side of high water. Tide run is very strong during springs, only enter with the flood. Dangerous in strong westerlies. Care must be taken to avoid Salters Bank.

From Salters to Lytham the channel is well marked by perches – these are fixed to stone walls which cover; do not attempt to cross. S.R. 27 ft. N.R. 21 ft.

MORECAMBE

Entrance. Proceed up Heysham Channel past the Harbour Entrance and when the Oil Jetty is abeam change course in a northerly direction for the Gunnel, keeping astern the end of the Oil Jetty in line with the 7th/8th gap of the harbour breakwater for 1¼ miles. You will be out of the Gunnel and in the deep Channel when the Sewer Beacon bears 60M from the Oil Jetty. When in the deep Channel change course to pass the Sewer Beacon to Starboard (White Light on Lattice Tower). Pass Batting Knott (unlit Black Cylinder) to Port, and Stone Jetty (fixed White in Lighthouse) to starboard, keeping clear of fishing lines from Jetty. S.R. 27½ ft. N.R. 22½ ft.

PORT ST. MARY (I.O.M.)

Entrance. Tidal harbour of about 2 acres. Partly enclosed by piers. Vessels proceeding to the inner harbour should give the back of the inner pier a wide berth keeping clear of Little Carrick Rock (unmarked). The inner harbour dries out to firm mud and sand and there is 6 feet of water at the pier head from approx. half flood to half ebb. Maximum rise and fall is about 20 ft. on spring tides but there is little tidal flow within the harbour. There is, however, a strong S-W flow behind the Alfred Pier from half flood to half ebb.

RAMSEY (I.O.M.)

Depth at entrance. Minimum depth in the lower harbour 10 ft. HWNT and 20 ft. HWST. S.R. 23 ft. N.R. 17 ft.

Entrance. Harbour completely dries out to 200 ft. seaward of the pierhead at LWOS. Vessels under 6 ft. draught can enter at half tide. Tide: ebb 3 knots, flood 2 knots.

DOUGLAS (I.O.M.)

Depth at entrance. Minimum depth in outer harbour 12-15 ft. at MLWS. Inner harbour dries out at half-tide. S.R. 22 ft. N.R. 18 ft.

Entrance. Clear with little tide effects. Access to inner harbour at half or full tide barred by swing bridge (Opened on request through Harbour Master). No entry after half-tide for masted vessels. Clearance at HW is 12 ft.

PEEL (I.O.M.)

Depth at entrance. Inner harbour dries out approximately 3 hours either side of LW. S.R. 18 ft. N.R. 14 ft.

Entrance. Should not be attempted in strong N to NW winds. Breakwater LWOST 20 ft. at seaward end, 3½ ft. at inner end. Entrance is clear with no obstructions.

AYR

LOCH RYAN (STRANRAER)

Depth at entrance. 48 ft. decreasing to 13 ft. at southern end. S.R. 9 ft. N.R. 7 ft.

Entrance. Small craft must avoid the sand spit which juts out from the west shore (opposite Cairn Point) and considerably reduces the channel width. There is an anchorage off Stranraer but this is very open to Northerly gales. A more sheltered anchorage is south west of the sand spit called 'The Wig'.

TROON

Depth at entrance. Depth at entrance, 12 ft. S.R. 9 ft. N.R. 7 ft.

Entrance. Steer well up into the harbour and anchor off the shipyard but keep clear of the slipways and dry dock entrances.

GIRVAN

Depth at entrance. About 3 ft. on the bar at low water. S.R. 9 ft. N.R. 7 ft.

Entrance. Entrance is narrow and it is advisable to use the engine. Some 2 cables inside the entrance the channel bends sharply to the southwards and beyond this there is the harbour with about 7 ft. at low water.

PORTPATRICK

Depth at entrance. 6 ft. on bar.

Entrance. Dangerous in strong winds from SW to NW. Steer in between the South and North pier ruins and alter round for the harbour giving a good berth to the drying rock in the north-west corner.

ARDROSSAN

Depth at entrance. 18 ft. at low water. S.R. 9 ft. N.R. 7 ft.

Entrance. Horse Island lies just north of the entrance. End is marked by a beacon. Campbell Rock lies to the south of the entrance. Grinan Rock marked by a red can buoy should be left on the port hand when entering the harbour. Once inside turn sharply to port and anchor in the lee of the breakwater in 12 to 24 ft. of water. Two red lights (two black balls by day) signal entry prohibited.

RENFREW

GOUROCK

Entrance. There are no dangers, the water being deep to close inshore, except in Carowell Bay where yachts should not proceed inshore of a line from the Admiralty Pier and the Bandstand in the Battery Park.

ARGYLL

HELENSBURGH

Entrance. The waters off Helensburgh are free from navigational hazards provided keel boats keep clear of the tidal shallows along the shore. These vary in width from 2 cables along the Helensburgh shore to ½ mile east of Craigendoran Pier. When rounding Rosneath Point care must be taken to keep to the seaward side of Red Buoy No. 24. The tidal stream is fairly strong between Castle Point and Cairndhu Point but elsewhere should not present any problem. S.R. 11 ft. N.R. 9 ft.

CRINAN CANAL

Canal extends from Loch Fyne at Ardrishaig (56° 1′ N., 5° 27′ W.), to Crinan on Loch Crinan (56° 5′ N., 5° 34′ W.), opening into the Sound of Jura; distance 9 miles across Argyllshire, providing sheltered passage to and from the Clyde, 85 miles shorter than exposed voyage round Mull of Kintyre. Vessels up to 800 tons, 300 ft. length and 12 ft. draft, can discharge at Ardrishaig Pier.

Sea locks at either end of the canal admit vessels 100 ft. long, 23 ft. beam and 11 ft. draft into terminal basins at any state of the tide. Vessels 88 ft. long, 20 ft. beam and 9½ ft. draft safely use the canal. There are 15 locks on the canal. Yachtsmen should check whether locks are open on a Sunday.

ISLE OF LEWIS

STORNOWAY

Stornoway lies in a deep loch or bay on E. coast of Island of Lewis, and has an area of 150 acres of anchorage, sheltered from all winds. There is no bar. Depth in entrance 8 fms. LV – Vessels of 12,000 n.r.t. have anchored in the Bay, and vessels of 4,000 n.r.t. have berthed alongside No. 1 pier. General depth of water 18 to 36 ft.; a bottom of sand and mud. There are about 900 yds. of quay wall, 580 yds. wharfage, and a L.W. pier. Depth alongside quay, 13 ft. L.W.O.S.T. for about 700 ft. S.R. 13½ ft. N.R. 9¾ ft.

ORKNEY ISLES

STROMNESS

A safe harbour with three piers, having 12 ft. at L.W.S.T. alongside. 6 fms. entrance and in harbour 20 ft. at quays H.W.S.T. A lifeboat station. Two new leading lights from 1st August to 15th May lead between points of Ness and Holms when in line. S.R. 10 ft. N.R. 7 ft.

SHETLAND ISLANDS

LERWICK

Depth in harbour, or bay, S.T. varying throughout from 10 to 60 ft.; N.T. 4 to 54 ft. S.R. 6 ft. N.R. 4 ft.

Harbour is a capacious landlocked bay on the W. side of Bressay Sound. Victoria Pier, 400 ft. long, 23 ft. alongside L.W.O.S.T., shallowing to 10 ft. Alexandra Wharf, 720 ft. long, 12 to 18 ft. alongside L.W.O.S.T. New extension of wharf 500 ft. long, 23 ft. alongside L.W.O.S.T., shallowing to 12 ft. inner, and forming small boat harbour.

CAITHNESS

WICK

Tidal harbour consisting of Inner and Outer Harbours, and a River Basin. Depth 16½-17½ ft. H.W.S.T., 14-15 ft. H.W.N.T. Quayage about 4,000 ft. Vessels of 260 ft. length and 16 ft. draft can discharge and load. Slipway capable of taking vessels of 90 ft. in length and 240 d.w.t. Entrance between piers very narrow. Busy fishing port with all facilities. S.R. 10 ft. N.R. 8 ft.

INVERNESS

INVERNESS

No difficulties in the approach but a large scale chart of Moray and Beauly Firth must be obtained. Inverness Firth is one of the most sheltered natural harbours in Scotland. Excellent anchorage in Kessock Roads, landlocked and free from swell; depth 5-20 fms. In harbour, vessels partly waterborne at L.W.; ground, soft mud and gravel. No docks. S.R. 16 ft. N.R. 12 ft.

CALEDONIAN CANAL

Canal starts at Clachnaharry, near Inverness, and runs S.W. for 60 miles to Corpach, near Fort William, affording safe passage from North Sea to Atlantic. Length in lochs or lakes, 38 miles; in canal cuttings, 22 miles. There are 29 locks on the canal, which is navigable from dawn to dusk. Total rise and fall, to and from summit level, 100 ft. No Sunday operation, except at sea locks. Vessels up to 13½ ft. draft in fresh water, 35 ft. beam and 150 ft. overall length, can pass through canal. Vessels exceeding that length can be taken up to limit of 160 ft. overall, provided draft is not over 9 ft. Minimum depth in canal, 14 ft. Repairs. Fresh water. Fuel oil by road tanker. Check whether locks are open on Sundays.

BANFF

BUCKIE

A busy fishing port. Entrance channel depth, 19 ft. HWOST with height difference of 11 ft. OST. Four basins with depth of 11 ft. LWOST. Entrance width, 60 ft. Maximum length of vessel accommodated, 250 ft. LOA. Spacious quays for cargo handling with fuel and fresh water. Repair facilities. Radio, Radar and Decca services. Pilots available. S.R. 12 ft. N.R. 10 ft.

ABERDEEN

FRASERBURGH

A busy fishing port. Two tidal harbours, Balaclava Harbour and South Harbour, average depth 16 ft. Faithlie Basin, 11½ ft. LWOST. Quayage, 2½ miles. Maximum size of vessels which can berth – Balaclava Harbour, 280 ft. x 40 ft. S. Harbour, 230 ft. x 38 ft.; Faithlie Basin, 300 ft. x 45 ft. S.R. 11½ ft. N.R. 7 ft.

PETERHEAD

A busy fishing port and the bay, behind the breakwaters, makes an excellent anchorage and port of refuge. Two harbours, 14½ and 7 acres, joined by canal; depth, 12 ft. LWOST. Quayage, 3,860 ft. One graving dock for vessels 185 ft. extreme length. L.V., 305 ft. long, 19 ft. 6 in. draft, 1,040 n.r.t. S.R. 11½ ft. N.R. 7 ft.

ABERDEEN

A busy commercial and fishing port which is entered between the N. & S. breakwaters. Approach should not be attempted when the wind is strong to gale force from the N.E. Port Signal station (on N. Pier) will hail you and allocate a berth. Wet docks are tidal. S.R. 12 ft. N.R. 9 ft.

STONEHAVEN

Small harbour, in the S.W. corner of the bay affords shelter from southerly winds and is the main centre of yachting in the area. The inner harbour dries our. S.R. 14 ft. N.R. 11 ft.

ANGUS

MONTROSE

Annat Bank forms natural breakwater to N. of river mouth. Entrance channel 510 ft. wide, depth 22 ft. HWOST, 17½ ft. HWONT. Dock area, 3¼ acres, dock entrance, 55 ft. wide, depth on sill, 19½ ft. ST, 15 ft. NT. Four berths in dock, total quayage, 1,320 ft. Tidal wharf, 530 ft. long on riverside where vessels lie safely aground. Largest vessels to be docked 3,500 tons d.w. S.R. 15 ft. N.R. 12 ft.

ARBROATH

Bar has approximately 1½-2 ft. at low water. Fishing and commercial port. Tidal harbour, entrance width 100 ft.; depth 15½ ft. OST, 11 ft. ONT; quayage, 1,400 ft. Dock, 2 acres; entrance width, 40 ft. depth on sill, 15½ ft. OST, 12 ft. ONT; quayage, 1,350 ft. L.V. 389 n.r.t., 11 ft. draft. S.R. 16 ft. N.R. 12 ft.

PERTH

RIVER TAY

Entrance should not be attempted unless conditions are favourable. The channel from the fairway buoy is well marked. There are anchorages at Tayport Harbour and in West Ferry Bay. Clearance can be obtained either at the Pilot Station off Broughty Castle or alongside King George Wharf. The tide runs very strongly in the narrows at Broughty Ferry and also alongside the narrow walls. S.R. 17 ft. N.R. 12 ft.

FIFE

KIRKCALDY

A busy commercial port which should not be approached during strong easterly winds. Dock with six quays, depth on sill 21 ft. ST, 15 ft. NT. Entrance width 50 ft. L.V. 2,500 tons d.w., 296 ft. long, 45 ft. beam, 16 ft. draft. S.R. 18 ft. N.R. 12 ft.

E. LOTHIAN

DUNBAR

Entrance practically dries at low water. Victoria Harbour has 16-18 ft. at HWST; 12-14 ft. at N.T. Berth as directed by Harbour Master. S.R. 17 ft. N.R. 13 ft.

BERWICK

GRANTON

Tidal harbour of 121 acres enclosed by breakwaters. Entrance 340 ft. wide, 13 ft. deep LWOST, 30 ft. HWOST West Pier, 3,100 ft. long, deep water berth 23 ft. LW., 40 ft. HW Middle Pier, 3,900 ft. long, depth up to 17 ft. LWST, coaling berth 25 ft. LWST. Rail connections to all berths. L.V. 12,900 g.r.t., draft 22½ ft. at Western Wharf. Vessels up to 5,000 tons with full cargoes of esparto grass and woodpulp are regularly handled at Western Pier. Yachts berth in the eastern side of the harbour. S.R. 18 ft. N.R. 14 ft.

EYEMOUTH

Tidal harbour with 150 ft. wide entrance. Entry should not be attempted during strong easterly winds. S.R. 15 ft. N.R. 12 ft.

BERWICK

The harbour is formed by the lower or sea-reach of the river, which falls into the sea about 1 mile below Berwick Bridge, between a stone pier on the N. and a long low sandy spit, serving as a natural breakwater, on the south. Width of entrance varies, but as a rule is about 300 ft., facing E.S.E. Depth at entrance 4 ft. on sill L.W.S.; Depth on bar, 4 ft. L.W.S.; Vessels of 220 ft. length with max. draught of 13½ ft. and beam of 35 ft. may safely enter the harbour and berth in the Tweed Dock. S.R. 15 ft. N.R. 13 ft.

For details of Harbours on the West coast of Scotland see STANFORD'S HARBOUR GUIDE WEST COAST OF SCOTLAND.

NORTHUMBERLAND

WARKWORTH

Harbour formed by lower reaches of R. Coquet entrance being between two breakwaters 225 ft. apart at entrance. Area of harbour, 20 acres. Depth on bar, 4-6 ft. at LW; 18-20 ft. HWST, 14-16 ft. HWNT; at quays, 9 ft. LW, 22-23 ft. HWST. Quayage about 2,000 ft. L.V. 1,496 tons, 15 ft. 4½ in. mean draft. S.R. 15 ft. N.R. 11 ft.

BLYTH

Entrance. The approach to Blyth from the southward is quite straightforward. Keep about a mile offshore until opposite the south end of Blyth sands. The harbour entrance will now be visible. Head for the lighthouse on the end of Blyth East Pier. Enter on the leading line. The leading lights consist of a white hexagonal tower about 15 feet in height and a square white tower about 35 feet in height. By night the red sector in the tower light on Blyth East Pier covers St. Mary's Island, so long as this light is obscured a vessel entering from the southward will clear all shore dangers.

Approaching Blyth from the northward by day, head for St. Mary's Island Lighthouse until the Sow and Pigs buoy is picked up. Leave it on the starboard hand and head for the fairway buoy in Blyth Bay; when the harbour opens up, enter on the leading line. Approaching Blyth from the northward at night, keep in the white sector of the upper light on Coquet Island, when well to the southward of Newbiggin Point, head for the light on St. Mary's Island. Now watch for the red sector on the lower light on Blyth East Pier; when this light is obscured, head for the fairway buoy in Blyth Bay. This buoy is lighted and may be seen at a distance of at least 2 miles in clear weather. Close the buoy and pick up the two green leading lights; enter on these lights. Blyth harbour is an artificial harbour at the entrance to the River Blyth. It is bounded by the East and West Piers and is dredged to a minimum depth of 24 ft. at low water spring tides. S.R. 14 ft. N.R. 11 ft.

TYNE AND WEAR

PORT OF TYNE

Entrance. The River Tyne is entered between the North and South Piers. Approaching from seaward, vessels should steer a course of 258° true with the Leading Lights in transit ahead and pass between the Pier Heads. Once inside the Piers they should alter course as necessary to keep within the buoyed channel leading to Shields Harbour Reach. This channel is dredged to a depth of 30 ft. below C.D. S.R. 14 ft. N.R. 11 ft.

HARTLEPOOL DOCKS

Entrance. Enter between N. and S. Piers. No hazards. There is good shelter and anchorage in West Harbour for small craft. S.R. 16 ft. N.R. 12 ft.

N. YORKSHIRE

WHITBY

Entrance. The approach to Whitby harbour should be made two hours either side of high water and not when there are strong northerly winds. This entrance, as would be expected, is especially dangerous during the ebb under such wind conditions. Steer between the harbour breakwaters and from this point, close to the port hand breakwater will lead as far as the starboard hand dogleg in the channel. At this point beacons on the East Pier lined up astern lead at 215° M into the Outer Harbour. It is important to observe carefully that one maintains an accurate course. S.R. 16 ft. N.R. 13 ft.

SCARBOROUGH

Entrance. Entry can only be made by visiting craft at about two hours either side of high water, although local boats, knowing their own harbour, would probably extend this to half tide. A black ball is hoisted at the lighthouse masthead when there is a least depth of 12 ft. in the entrance. If it is considered to be dangerous to attempt to enter, a red flag is flown from the same masthead, which prohibits vessels from attempting the passage. S.R. 16 ft. N.R. 13 ft.

HUMBERSIDE

BRIDLINGTON

Harbour, 11 acres, enclosed by two stone piers; North Pier 675 ft. long, South Pier 1,525 ft. long. Harbour dry at LW. Soft mud bottom. L.V. 17 ft. 10 in. draft. Quayage 1,500 ft. S.R. 17 ft. N.R. 13 ft.

RIVER HUMBER

There are good anchorages just inside the Spurn, to the North of the buoyed channel, off Cleethorpes and at Grimsby. The anchorage just inside the Spurn affords excellent shelter from North and South winds. S.R. 20 ft. N.R. 16 ft.

GRIMSBY

Entrance. Proceed up river by way of the Bull L.V. (close by Bull Fort – easily distinguishable) No. 4 Clee Ness Lt. Float and on to No. 6 Lower Burcom Lt. Float. Then make a heading for the Hydraulic Tower (some 360 ft. high), passing the two Fish Dock locks and entering the Royal Basin which is flanked by two piers. The Western of these marks the end of the Grimsby Docks complex and therefore identifies the Royal Dock entrance. At night the entrance to the basin is identified by a double light flashing every 6 secs. on the East pier and on the West pier a white light occulting every 2 secs. The basin can be entered under all weather conditions but is uncomfortable to be in if there are strong northerly or north-easterly winds.

The lock operates 3 hours either side of high water and is usually level for up to 1 hour before high water.

Yachts are advised to ignore the Dock signals, proceed to the lock entrance and hail the lock keeper for instructions. S.R. 20 ft. N.R. 16 ft.

BOSTON

Entrance. Good anchorage in Boston Deeps above the upper Scullridge Buoy in 3 to 5 fms. Ships waiting for the tide to go up river anchor to the southward of High Horn buoy in 4 fms. R. of T. Depth in river below Dock 25 ft. 9 in. at H.W.O.S.T., 19 ft. at H.W.O.N.T. Depth at quays and stages at H.W.O.S.T. 18 ft., at H.W.O.N.T. 11 ft. 6 in. Riverside Quay: 2,640 ft. long. S.R. 22 ft. N.R. 15¼ ft.

NORFOLK

KING'S LYNN

Entrance. A busy commercial port. The channel from No. 1 buoy, although constantly changing is well marked. Anchoring in the river is not recommended due to both current and commercial traffic and one should enter the dock which is open from about one hour before high water. A craft drawing up to 5 ft. can enter the channel just after low water. S.R. 18 ft. N.R. 12 ft.

GT. YARMOUTH

Depth at Entrance. There is a minimum depth of 14 ft. at MLWS in the entrance channel south of the North Breakwater end. S.R. 7 ft. N.R. 6 ft.

Entrance Channel. The entrance channel, between the piers, to the bend is 240 ft. wide and has a minimum depth of 11 ft. at the sides and 14 ft in the centre. The flood runs in at up to 3 knots at springs, and ebbs at up to 3½ knots. During strong easterly winds the depth at the entrance may be less than 14 ft. If proceeding up the River Yare to Breydon Water or the River Bure, it is necessary for sailing craft to lower their masts as there are 2 or 3 bridges to pass under with clearance of 8 ft. maximum at MHWS. Rise of tide is between 6 and 7 ft.

SUFFOLK

LOWESTOFT

Depth at Entrance. 14 ft. at MLWS between the north and south piers. S.R. 7 ft. N.R. 6 ft.

Entrance Channel. The entrance width between the 2 piers is about 200 ft. and, once inside the entrance, the yacht basin will be seen to port of the centre jetty. The Outer Harbour is dredged to 11 ft. at MLWS. Keep a sharp look-out for the many fishing vessels particularly trawlers entering and leaving the port.

SOUTHWOLD

Depth at Entrance. There is a minimum depth of 1 ft. at MLWS on the bar, but conditions can change rapidly during winds from the north-east to east. Any craft proposing to enter should telephone the harbour master 2 or 3 days before their expected time of arrival to obtain the exact depth of water. A red light is exhibited from the breakwater when the harbour is inaccessible. S.R. 8 ft. N.R. 7 ft.

Entrance Channel. Entrance is between the two piers and the spring ebb runs out at up to 5 knots. There is a build up of sand and shingle alongside the north pier which makes the entrance channel between the piers narrow. Entrance should not be attempted until 2 hours before the time of high water. When entering, approach with both piers wide open but keep over to the south pier to avoid the sand and shingle bank against the north pier. Maintain this course until the inner end of the north pier is abeam to starboard, when one should haul over towards the quay side of the channel (to avoid the sand build up on the southern side of the harbour) and then, near Trinity Pier, haul out to mid-channel passing close to the mooring buoys.

If entrance is difficult, a red flag (red flashing light by night) is shown from the north pier. Dredgers periodically operate in the channel and, should one be working, red flags are flown up and down stream from it and also on the dredger. Extra care must be taken as it will have mooring lines stretching across the channel. At MLWS there is a minimum depth of 3 ft. between the piers and up to 10 ft. along the quay.

RIVERS ORE, ALDE & BUTLEY

Depth at Entrance. There is a minimum depth of 4 ft. over the bar at MLWS.

Entrance Channel. Entrance should not be attempted unless one has local knowledge available, as the shingle banks at the entrance shift frequently and, during strong onshore winds, a rough confused sea can be set up in the vicinity of the bar. Without local knowledge, one should heave to off the bar and signal for a pilot from Shingle Street, a distance of about 6 cables. It is also necessary to have a good auxiliary motor available as the tide in the entrance can run at up to 6 knots. The Aldeburgh Yacht Club usually places a small black barrel buoy on the bar during the yachting season and the leading marks over the bar, on the Shingle Street shore, are moved as required to indicate the course of the channel over the bar between the sand banks.

Once over the bar, there is a minimum depth of 13 ft. to Flybury Point, 2¼ miles from the bar, where the bifurcation of the Butley and Ore channels is marked by a black conical buoy on the end of the spit at the south-west end of Havergate Island. The river banks along this stretch are steep-to and the current, both flood and ebb, runs strongly at up to 5 knots. Anchorage is not possible in this stretch of the river.

The shortest passage to Orford or Slaughden is along Main Reach, south of Havergate Island. Main Reach is narrow and the tide still runs strongly. In this reach there is a minimum depth of water at MLWS of 9 ft. The spit, extending north-eastwards from Cuckhold Point is marked by a black can buoy which is left to port for the short passage up to Orford. On this stretch, Orford Castle makes a good landmark but again the banks of the channel are steep-to and there is a depth of not less than 18 ft. although, generally, the depth is nearer 30 ft.

From Orford, the river channel turns fairly sharply to the eastward for about half a mile and then north-easterly and northerly through Raydon and Pigpail Reaches where it changes its name to the Alde. At the north end of Pigpail Reach it narrows slightly before turning north-easterly and northerly to Slaughden. The sides are again steep-to and there is never less than 9 ft. on passage to Slaughden except for one patch of 7 ft. about 4 cables short of Slaughden. At Slaughden, the channel turns sharply westwards and, from there to Iken, is well marked by beacons with red can topmarks to port and black flag topmarks to starboard. As far as Barber Point there is never less than 6 to 7 ft. at MLWS but, from there on, reduces to 3 ft. although there can be as much as 5 ft. in the holes by Iken Cliff.

From Iken to Snape Bridge, the channel practically dries but it is possible for a yacht drawing about 5 ft. to reach Snape Bridge quay around the time of high water.

The Butley River is entered by leaving the black conical buoy off the spit at the west end of Havergate Island to starboard (Flybury Pt. to port) and steering north and then north-east for a distance of 4 cables, when the entrance to the river will be seen to port. Bear off sharply to port into the channel, which has a depth of not less than 6 ft. as far as Butley Ferry, after which it shallows quickly and practically dries out. There is a shallow patch with less than 6 ft. in mid-channel at MLWS about 2 cables inside the entrance.

Instead of turning off to port into the Butley River, one can turn to starboard into Gull Reach (north of Havergate Island) and through to Chantry Point which is only about 4 cables from Orford. This channel has a minimum depth at MLWS of 15 ft., and the deepest water will be found on the western and northern side of the channel.

RIVER DEBEN

Depth at Entrance. 2 to 3 ft. over the bar at MLWS. S.R. 11 ft. N.R. 8 ft.

Entrance Channel. The shingle banks at the entrance shift according to the force and direction of the wind, and the leading beacons and bar buoy are moved accordingly. Unless one has local knowledge, and even that must be recent, due to the frequent changes in channel direction visiting yachtsmen should use the services of one of the 2 pilots available from Felixstowe Ferry. Yachts requiring a pilot should heave to about 2 cables east of the Bar Buoy and signal from there. If there is a strong onshore wind, a rough confused sea is set up in the vicinity of the bar, and entry should not be attempted under any circumstances. Closing the Bar buoy, which is left to starboard, the 2 transit beacons will be seen on the west shore near Tower 'U', and this transit bearing must be followed until about 1½ cables from the nearest transit beacon, when course must be altered to approximately N.½ E. to leave the Bawdsey Ferry Pier (on the east side of the river) fairly close to starboard. In this stretch of the river channel the shingle banks on either side are steep-to, and there is a minimum depth at MLWS of about 4 ft. inside the bar, which deepens to 13 ft. east of the Post Office and to about 40 ft. just off the Ferry Pier. The tide can run at up to 5 or 6 knots and it is essential to have a good auxiliary motor available. Leaving the Bawdsey Ferry to starboard, set course to leave the Horse Sand red and white can buoy close to port, and then follow the course of the river up to Shottisham Reach from where the channel is marked by buoys, stakes and beacons to Woodbridge, a distance of approximately 7 miles from the bar. The river channel has a minimum depth at MLWS of 12 ft. as far as Waldringfield; from there to Methersgate, 8 ft., and then it gradually shallows to about 1 ft. off Woodbridge except in a few places where there are deeper holes. Be careful to avoid the shallow patch, 4 cables S.S.W. of Stoner Point, at the north end of Shottisham Reach, which has 3 ft. at MLWS.

RIVER ORWELL

Entrance to the Orwell. The entrance is 5 cables north-east of Harwich and about the same distance east of Shotley. Leave the Guard buoy close to either port or starboard and the Shotley Spit buoy to port (to clear the shallow water over the spit). From the Stour, leave Shotley Pier and the red buoy (4 cables east of the pier) to port, and set course to pass close south of the Shotley Spit buoy. When this buoy bears north, haul round to port into the Orwell channel.

Depth at Entrance to Orwell. Between Walton and Shotley Spit buoys there is a depth at MLWS of 30 ft. Over Shotley Spit, the water shoals rapidly to the west towards the drying bank off Bloody Point. S.R. 13 ft. N.R. 11 ft.

Orwell River Channel. *Shotley Spit to Ipswich:* From Shotley Spit to Ipswich Docks is a distance of 8½ miles; to Woolverstone, 5½ miles; to Pinmill, 4½ miles and to Levington 3 miles. The channel is buoyed at intervals by lighted buoys as far as Woolverstone and is, on average, about 1½ cables wide. Above this point it narrows to about 300 ft. and is buoyed, port and starboard. Anchoring is not allowed in the channel above Downham Reach except in an emergency, but if anchoring at the side of the channel below this point it is essential to show an anchor light during the hours of darkness, due to the volume of commercial shipping using the port of Ipswich. The flood and ebb run at up to 4 knots and yachts, whether under sail or power, must keep clear of commercial shipping. There is a minimum depth of 19 ft. at MLWS in the river channel to Ipswich.

ESSEX

RIVER STOUR

Stour River Channel. *Harwich to Manningtree:* The river channel runs in a westerly direction and a course of approximately W.½ N. from the Guard buoy will take one along the main channel to a position approximately 2 cables north of the notice board at Stone Point, a distance of 2½ miles. At MLWS this stretch of the river has a minimum depth of 7 ft. and gradually decreases in width from 4 cables at Harwich/Shotley to 2 cables north of Stone Point. There are no navigational marks in the area except the red and white buoy near the west end of Parkeston Quay (where the North Sea Ferries berth).

There are many large mooring buoys on both sides of the channel between Harwich/Shotley and Erwarton Ness and a sharp look-out should be kept in the vicinity of Parkeston Quay for ferries manoeuvring off the berths. From Stone Point to New Mistley, a distance of 3¾ miles, the channel depth at MLWS has a minimum depth of 13 ft. to North Shoal; north of Smith Shoal there is a minimum depth of 2 ft. for a distance of about 4 cables but, in the narrow section close to the drying bank on the north side, there is 7 to 8 ft.

In Ballast Reach there is a minimum depth of 6 to 7 ft. for about 5½s cables, after which the bottom shoals rapidly, and there is then an average depth of 2 to 3 ft. to New Mistley. This 'deep' of 6 to 7 ft. in Ballast Hill Reach is the furthest west point in the river at which a yacht, drawing up to about 5 ft., can lie safely afloat at any stage of the tide.

The channel from Stone Point to New Mistley is clearly marked by buoys, black and white can to starboard and red can to port. There are two main hazards: The Horse, 2 cables N.W. of Stone Point, the eastern end of which is marked by a black and white can buoy (to be left to starboard) and the drying bank 1½ cables N. x W. of Wrabness Point, which is marked by a red can buoy at its eastern end and left to port. From New Mistley to Manningtree the channel is narrow and tortuous and, although marked by port and starboard hand buoys (red to port and black to starboard), should only be attempted with local knowledge. At MLWS there is a depth of 2 to 3 ft. at New Mistley but, from there on the depth gradually decreases and, at Manningtree, the channel practically dries out. It is possible to reach Manningtree on a draught of about 5 ft. near the time of high water, but such craft must be able to take the mud as soon as the tide falls.

HARWICH

Depth at Entrance. At MLWS there is a minimum depth of 23½ ft. in the main channel and 6 ft. in the area of the main channel bounded by a line joining the eastern end of Beacon Cliff Breakwater to the Guard buoy (R.Can, R.Fl.5) except for the area over and surrounding the Cliff Foot Rocks, where there is a minimum depth of 4 ft. S.R. 13 ft. N.R. 11 ft.

Entrance Channel. The entrance channel between Harwich and Felixstowe is about 8½ cables wide and, except for the shallow patch over Cliff Foot Rocks, presents no hazards. The main deepwater channel carries heavy commercial traffic from and to Harwich, Felixstowe and Ipswich, and it is better for yachts to keep to the area west of the main channel. The shallow patch over Cliff Foot Rocks can be avoided, if coming in from the west, by passing within a cable length of Beacon Cliff Breakwater where there is less than 12 ft. depth at MLWS. Tidal strength seldom exceeds 2½ knots but care should be exercised in the area just north of Harwich Shelf when the ebb is running.

HAMFORD WATER & WALTON ON THE NAZE

Depth at Entrance. There is a depth of 4 ft. at MLWS in the vicinity of the entrance just west of the Pye End buoy. S.R. 12 ft. N.R. 10½ ft.

Entrance Channel. From a position approximately 1 to 2 cables west of the Pye End buoy, a course of approximately S.W.½ W. will take one into the channel leaving the Crabb Knoll black conical buoy (4 cables from Pye End buoy) about 1 cable to port. On this course, the first port hand buoy on Pye Sand side of the channel will be seen to port, and the black conical buoy marking the end of the sand spit on the northern side of the channel must be kept fine on the starboard bow. Leave this buoy close to starboard and alter to bring the next port hand buoy (distant, 2 cables) fine on the port bow. Leave this buoy close to port and alter to the southward to bring the next port hand buoy fine on the port bow. Leave this buoy and the next two port hand buoys (all close together) fairly close to port, at which a red and white spherical buoy will be seen practically dead ahead and a red can buoy about 3 points on the port bow. These two buoys mark the east and west spits at the entrance to Walton Creek.

From Crabb Knoll buoy to the Walton Creek entrance there is never less than 20 ft. in the channel centre at MLWS and, at its narrowest part, between the spits, it is about 1 cable wide. To enter Walton Creek, pass midway between the next red can buoy and the post on the west side of the channel. These are the last navigational buoys in the creek but the creek sides are fairly steep-to, and the channel is easily followed. 1½ miles from the entrance Walton Creek dries out but the main creek channel bends round to the west into Twissel Creek.

From Walton Creek entrance to the bifurcation with Twissel Creek there is a minimum depth of 8 ft. at MLWS and, in Twissel Creek, up to 6 ft. for a distance of about 7 cables after which the creek shallows fairly rapidly and practically dries out by the Ford. From the bifurcation with Twissel Creek, Walton Creek dries out at MLWS.

North of the entrance to Walton Creek, Hamford Water flows south-easterly for a distance of just over 1½ miles. There is a minimum depth of 20 ft. up to the entrance to Kirby Creek, and it then gradually shallows to 12 ft. at the entrance to Landermere Creek. On the starboard side, just west of Pewit Island, Oakley Creek bears off to the north. Just inside the entrance to the creek (for about 3 cables) there is a depth of about 6 ft. at MLWS, but the creek channel quickly shallows and practically dries out at MLWS. 3 cables west of Oakley Creek, and on the south side of the water, is Kirby Creek which flows southwards and then eastwards towards Twissel Creek. Up to the point where it narrows and turns east there is a minimum depth of about 6 ft. but, from there on, it quickly shallows and dries out west of the ford. At the west end of Hamford Water, Landermere Creek bears off in a south-westerly direction and has a minimum depth, at MLWS, of about 5 ft. for a distance of about 3 cables along the main creek, after which it shallows and dries out. A branch of the creek bears off westwards and southwards to Landermere Wharf, but this practically dries at low water. At half-tide there is about 3 ft. of water alongside the quay. The tides in Hamford Water run at their strongest in the narrows between the 2 spits just inside the entrance, where they can attain a rate of up to 2½ knots.

RIVER COLNE

Entrance. From the N.W. Knoll buoy a course of N. x W.¼W. will take one up the channel which is buoyed, port and starboard, to Mersea Point. Between the Bar buoy and Channel buoy No. 1 be careful not to be drawn to the east side of the channel where the bottom shoals rapidly. From the Bench Head buoy it is perfectly safe for a yacht drawing up to 6 ft. to haul round to port and set course to leave the red can buoy, the Inner Bench Head buoy, close to port and then alter up the buoyed channel to a position east of Mersea Point.

The area east of Mersea Point is a popular summer anchorage and provides reasonable shelter during westerlies in a good depth of water close to the shore. Depth of water at MLWS is about 35 ft. in the channel off the Inner Bench Head and there is never less than 19 ft. from there to No. 13 buoy where there is 7 to 15 ft. over the spit east of Mersea Point.

BRIGHTLINGSEA

Entrance. Just north of Mersea Point, on the opposite side of the river, is the entrance to Brightlingsea Creek which is marked by a red and white spherical buoy with a cross topmark. Entry is possible by yachts drawing up to 4 ft. and the spherical buoy must be left close to port on a course of N.E.¾ E. when a line of moorings will be seen. S.R. 15 ft. N.R. 12 ft.

PYEFLEET CREEK

Approach. The entrance to Brightlingsea Creek is left to starboard and the wreck buoy to port. Just after passing the wreck the entrance to this creek will be seen to port, and the red can buoy, marking the spit on the northern side must be left to starboard.

BRIGHTLINGSEA TO WIVENHOE

Approach. The River Colne is fairly busy with commercial craft using the port of Colchester and consequently is very well buoyed. If anchoring in the channel an anchor light is essential during the hours of darkness. Depth at MLWS decreases from 20 ft. off the entrance to Pyefleet Creek down to about 5 ft. off Aldboro Point, and this is the furthest point at which most craft can lie afloat at MLWS.

RIVER BLACKWATER

WEST MERSEA

Approach. From the Bench Head buoy steer N.W.¾ W. for 2¾ miles. The coast is flat but the conspicuous buildings north-east of Bradwell give a good bearing, and when the chimneys of these buildings bear W.S.W. haul round to W. x N. On this latter course a tall square beacon with top mark (The Nass) should be sighted fine on the port bow. Just before reaching the Nass a black and white middle ground buoy will be passed to port. There is a minimum depth of 7 ft. at MLWS on the last approach course to the Nass.

Entrance. The entrance channel from the Nass beacon is marked by 2 red port hand buoys and 2 black starboard hand buoys. This channel leads to Mersea Quarters where moorings begin. There is a minimum depth of about 20 ft. at MLWS in the centre of the channel.

TOLLESBURY FLEET

Approach. Tollesbury Fleet leads directly off in a W.S.W. direction from the west end of Mersea Quarters. Both approach and south channels are marked by buoys and withies.

Entrance. The main channel has a depth of 12 ft. at MLWS. Between the buoys marking the entrance to South Channel (East of Great Cob Is.) the depth decreases to 4 to 6 ft. and, on turning south-westwards, the depth increases to 12 ft. and this is maintained to Little Cob Is. where it gradually decreases to 4 ft. at the entrance to Woodrolfe Creek whence it rapidly dries out. Keep to the centre of the South Channel, which is marked by buoys and withies, and pass close either side of the moorings in the channel. Woodrolfe Creek dries out but the bottom is soft mud. There is a tide gauge on the western corner of the entrance to the creek. S.R. 16 ft. N.R. 13 ft.

BRADWELL-ON-SEA

Approach. The approach channel to Bradwell is just over ½ mile west of the conspicuous building on the left-hand side of the entrance to the River Blackwater, just west of the baffle wall which is marked by 2 fixed red lights at each end. This baffle wall can be left to port or starboard, and there is a depth of 26 to 32 ft. north of the wall and 14 ft. on the shore side at MLWS.

Entrance. The entrance to Bradwell Creek is marked by a middle ground buoy with a square topmark. Leave this buoy to starboard and follow the leading marks (painted orange). The tide gauge indicates the depth of water and the channel is dredged to a minimum depth of 5 ft. at MLWOS. The channel is marked by withies on its western side and, on its eastern side by port hand buoys. Where the channel bends to the southward, alter course to port and bring the next pair of leading marks in line and, when the channel turns to starboard, steer towards the marina entrance.

The marina entrance has a tide gauge and the port side of this channel is marked by three port hand buoys. Two leading lights mark the approach through the channel.

STONE ST. LAWRENCE (THE STONE)

Approach. A course of S.W. x W. ¾ W. is maintained along the Blackwater and, when the beacon marking the east end of Thirsted Spit bears N., course should be altered to W.½S. Just over 6 cables along this course the village of Stone will be seen on the northern tip of Ramsey Island.

GOLDHANGER CREEK

Approach. One mile west of the anchorage off Stone is the entrance to Goldhanger Creek, on the north side of the river channel. A black buoy (Channel buoy No. 1) is moored off the end of Goldhanger Spit.

Entrance. The No. 1 black buoy must be left to port, and there is a depth of 1½ to 2½ ft. at MLWS across the entrance.

OSEA ISLAND

Approach. One mile westwards of No. 1 River Channel buoy is the small pier of Osea Island. There is a minimum depth at MLWS of 9 ft. along the centre of the channel, but deep drafted yachts should keep clear of the Barnacle, a shallow patch with minimum depth of about 6 ft. at MLWS, about 1½ to 2 cables east of the pier.

LAWLING AND MAYLAND CREEKS

Approach. The entrance to Lawling Creek is 1¾ cables south of the anchorage off Osea Island pier. No. 2 channel buoy marks the north-east corner of the spit on the western side of the creek entrance.

Entrance. The red can buoy (Channel Buoy No. 2) must be left to starboard and the bar has a depth of about 2 ft. at MLWS.

OSEA ISLAND TO HEYBRIDGE BASIN

Approach. 2½ cables W.S.W. of the anchorage of Osea Island Pier is a black conical buoy (The Doctor) which must be left to starboard. 6 cables W.N.W. of the 'Doctor' are a pair of port and starboard hand buoys and 4 cables west of these two buoys are a second pair. These two pairs of buoys mark the slight bend in the channel before it straightens out to Colliers Reach. From Osea Pier to the first pair of channel buoys there is a minimum depth of 5½ ft. at MLWS, and this is about the most westerly point at which a yacht, drawing 4 ft. can lie afloat at MLWS. 10 cables N.W. of the last pair of channel buoys, the river turns fairly sharply to port and the red buoy, off the northern tip of Northey Island must be left to port as you turn down towards the entrance to Heybridge Basin. Depth at MLWS varies from 3 to 6 ft. as far as the red buoy, and then decreases to about 1½ ft. down to the lock entrance.

HEYBRIDGE BASIN TO MALDON

Approach. The river channel from Heybridge Lock to Maldon practically dries out at MLWS, but it is a pleasant sail when the tide permits and the winding channel is well marked by port and starboard hand buoys. Although it is possible to take the mud at Maldon, it is usually better to take the flood tide up to the town, and then the ebb back to some point in the river where one can lie afloat at low water.

RIVER CROUCH

Entrance. Leaving the Outer Crouch buoy close to starboard a course of W. x S.¾ S. and a distance of 2½ miles will take one to the Inner Crouch buoy. On this course the Crouch buoy should be left close to port. A course of W.½ N. will take one along the main channel to the black barrel buoy which marks the Horse Shoal. This buoy should be left to starboard and course altered to pass close north of the Fairway buoy. There is a least depth of about 20 ft. at MLWS in the main channel except over the Horse Shoal, which has about 3 ft. over it at MLWS. The channel just south of this shoal has a minimum depth of 12 ft. MLWS.

WALLASEA BAY

Approach. The marina at Wallasea Bay is 6 cables west of the town of Burnham-on-Crouch and on the south bank of the river. Minimum depth in the centre of the channel at MLWS is 20 ft.

FAMBRIDGE

Approach. From Wallasea Bay, the river channel flows north-westerly towards Cliff Reach and there are many moorings on both sides of the channel. Off Black Point, the channel turns sharply to port and flows south-westerly and then westerly through Easter Reach and into Raypits Reach where it turns to the north-westwards and westwards into Shortpole and Longpole Reaches. Shortpoles sand bar extends out in a north-easterly direction from Landsend point but, from Burnham to Fambridge Landing (at the westerly end of Longpole Reach) there is never less than 9 ft. in mid-channel at MLWS.

BRANDY HOLE

Approach. Proceeding west for about 9 cables from Fambridge, the river channel curves round fairly sharply to the south into Brandy Hole. Depth at MLWS in the centre of the channel gradually decreases from about 9 ft. west of Fambridge Landing to about 4 ft. at Brandy Hole which is the last point in the river at which a yacht drawing up to just over 3 ft. would remain afloat at any state of the tide.

HULLBRIDGE AND BATTLESBRIDGE

Approach. Leaving Brandy Hole there is a depth of about 3 ft. at MLWS in the centre of the channel and this depth gradually decreases until between Hullbridge and the western end of Long Reach the channel dries out. S.R. 7 ft. N.R. 4 ft.

RIVER ROACH

Entrance. The entrance to the Roach is 11 cables west of the Inner Crouch buoy on the south side of the River Crouch channel. A yellow racing buoy is usually moored off the north-east end of Brankfleet spit during the racing season but it should not be relied on as a navigation mark. East of Brankfleet Spit there is a least depth of 33 ft. in the centre of the channel.

PAGLESHAM REACH

Approach. From Devils Reach, the river channel runs in a direction just north of west and then gradually turns westwards and south-westwards towards Barling Ness. At MLWS, there is a least depth of about 25 ft. in mid-channel off Potton Point, and this depth is maintained for a distance of about 7 cables when the depth gradually decreases to about 7 ft. north of Barling Ness.

Paglesham Creek, which opens out to the north of Paglesham Reach, dries out completely and should only be visited by dinghies on the rising tide.

BARLING QUAY AND ROCHFORD

Approach. From Barling Ness the main river channel runs south-westwards for about 4 cables before turning west and then curving south-westward to Barling Quay which lies on the south bank of the river 1 mile from Barling Ness. Off Barling Ness, depth in mid-channel at MLWS is about 7 ft. and the depth gradually decreases until, off Barling Quay, there is a depth of 2½ to 3 ft.

Above Barling Quay, the river narrows and shallows very quickly and passage should only be attempted near high water and only if local knowledge is available.

POTTON CREEK

Entrance. The entrance to Potton Creek lies just to the north-east of Barling Ness and there is a depth at MLWS of about 10 ft. in the main entrance channel.

KENT

THE MEDWAY TO ALLINGTON LOCK

GARRISON POINT TO ROCHESTER. The minimum depth in the channel at L.W.O.S.T., except for Acorn Patch (near Rochester Bridge) is 14 ft., and the only variations occur when wind and weather conditions cause the tide to fluctuate. The tide varies from 1–2 knots except through the arches of Rochester Bridge and round Gashouse Point where there is a tendency for the tide to surge.

The channel through the various Reaches is well buoyed. Keep to your starboard side. When approaching the jetties at the Isle of Grain, Oakham Ness and Kingsnorth Power Station (all on the starboard bank of the river), keep a sharp lookout for vessels, particularly large oil tankers berthing or unberthing, and keep well out of their way. If making the passage at night, look out for the many unlit buoys in the various Reaches. When rounding Chatham Ness from Chatham Reach allow for the sweep of the flood or ebb tide which could carry your craft in towards the adjacent barge moorings. Acorn Patch, in Bridge Reach, with 8 ft. over it at L.W.O.S.T. is in mid-stream between Strood Pier and Acorn Shipyard slipway. The middle of the centre span of Rochester Bridge has only 20 ft. of headroom at H.W.O.S.T. If proceeding when the tide is at an intermediate stage between high and low water it is advisable to proceed through the Strood Arch.

Commercial craft will be encountered manoeuvring off the riverside wharves and many will be restricted in their movement through towing lighters. It is unwise to consider sailing in the Rochester Port area other than at weekends when there is little commercial traffic moving.

ROCHESTER TO ALLINGTON LOCK. From Rochester Bridge to near Snodland there is plenty of water in mid-stream but it is best to take wide sweeps when rounding the sharper bends. From there on the river gradually dries out at low water and Allington Lock can only operate for about 5 hours over each high water.

MEDWAY CREEKS

STANGATE CREEK. The entrance to this creek is opposite the Isle of Grain tanker jetties and is marked by a red and white spherical buoy moored on the West side. The minimum width of the creek is 1·8 cables and the banks are, for the most part, embanked marshland fronted by mud which dries from 1-11 ft. The minimum width of the channel from one mile below the entrance to Sharfleet Creek to Slaughterhouse point varies from 0.5–1.1 cables and, off Sharfleet Creek, it is 1.3 cables wide. The minimum mid-channel depth in Stangate Creek at L.W.O.S.T. is 11 ft. at a point midway between Slaughterhouse Point and the entrance to Sharfleet Creek. One cable inside the entrance, on the West shore, are the remains of an old pier, which extend out for about a cable; and one cable below the entrance to Sharfleet Creek, on the West side of the channel, is a wreck which is visible at low water. The flood tide runs strongly into the entrance to the Creek.

HALSTOW, TWINNEY AND FUNTON CREEKS. Halstow Creek runs in a S.W. direction for roughly 1 mile to the village of Lower Halstow where there is a small wharf. The mud banks on either side dry up to 10 ft. but there is 8 ft. of water alongside the wharf at H.W.O.S.T. and 5 ft. at H.W.O.N.T.

Twinney Creek is a secondary channel running also to Lower Halstow but taking a slightly longer route.

Funton Creek is an offshoot of Stangate Creek and runs in a South-Easterly direction. Both banks dry up to 10 ft. and there are no jetties or wharves on which to land.

These 3 creeks dry out at about half tide and a yachtsman exploring them must avoid being stranded on a falling tide.

HALF ACRE, RAINHAM, SOUTH YANTLET AND BARTLETT CREEKS. The entrance to Half Acre Creek lies just East of No. 16 Channel buoy. Minimum width is 2 cables and the minimum depth at L.W.O.S.T. is 9 ft. except at the Southern end where it reduces to 4 ft.

Just West of Otterham Fairway buoy is the entrance to Bartlett Creek which has minimum width of 0.8 cables and 1 ft. of water at L.W.O.S.T. Rainham Creek, a continuation of Bartlett Creek, dries out completely at low water.

South Yantlet Creek is entered just West of Otterham Fairway Buoy and its channel is marked by 3 middle ground buoys and one fairway buoy at its Western end. It is only 1 ft. deep in places at L.W.O.S.T. and the Western end dries out. At half tide, a vessel with 6 ft. draught could cross the Western end of the creek. It is not recommended as an alternative passage from Rochester to Sheerness but is useful for passage from Rochester to Bartlett or Rainham Creeks. The tide normally flows in towards Rainham Creek until the marshes between Nor Marsh and the mainland are covered and the tide is diverted into the Medway above Gillingham. During South-Westerly gales, depth in the area can be reduced by as much as 3 ft. and increased, by the same amount, during Northerly gales.

QUEENBOROUGH AND THE WEST SWALE

Approach. From a position off Garrison Point, course should be set direct for the entrance to the Swale. Although the Swale is lit for part of its length for night navigation, strangers to the area should not attempt this passage during the hours of darkness.

Entrance. The entrance is marked by Queenborough Spit lighted beacon and a starboard hand unlit buoy. Both should be passed to the Eastward. S.R. 17 ft. N.R. 14 ft.

WEST SWALE TO KINGSFERRY. The minimum depth in the Swale is 11 ft. at L.W.O.S.T. but during South-Westerly gales the depth of water can be reduced by as much as 3 ft. and, during Northerly gales, increased by the same amount. Minimum channel width is 0.5 cables just downstream from Kingsferry Bridge. Tidal streams are subject to considerable variation and the following information on these is only approximate.

The stream is slack throughout between minus 05 55 to minus 05 25 Sheerness and then starts to run in from the Medway and the Thames (East Swale). These inflowing streams meet near Fowley Island but this position is subject to fluctuation during gales or spring tides and they can meet as far west as Elmley. The flood continues until plus 00 05 Sheerness when the stream turns at Elmley and runs out through the East Swale. From this time until plus 01 15 Sheerness runs into the West Swale from the Medway. Between Long Point and Sheerness the stream turns and flows into the Medway from plus 01 05 Sheerness. The maximum spring tide flood rate is 3½ knots near Kingsferry and the maximum ebb (4 knots) occurs near the same point.

Passage through the Swale is straightforward provided one keeps to the centre of the channel. Horse Shoal, marked by an unlit buoy, should be passed to the southward and, just west of Horse Shoal, care should be taken when rounding Long Point where the river turns sharply through approximately 160°. Allow for the sweep of the tide round Long Point and keep a sharp lookout for commercial traffic which is unable to deviate from its course. Kingsferry Bridge has a lifting centre span with a width of 90 ft. between piers. Minimum clearance, when the span is raised horizontally is 114 ft.; 30 ft. when the span is down.

THE EAST SWALE

Approach. Entering from the Thames, passage can be made either through the Hamgat, North of Columbine Shoal, or in through Whitstable Bay. The latter approach is clearly marked with buoys, and the Northern end of Pollard Spit is marked by the Pollard Spit Buoy.

POLLARD SPIT TO KINGSFERRY. Except for a shallow patch of 4–5 ft. just East of Harty Hard, the channel is deep to Spitend. From there to Elmley the minimum depth at low water is 1 ft. and from there to the bridge 8 ft. No difficulty should be experienced on passage from No. 5 to No. 1 Channel buoys. Between No. 4 and 3 buoys keep to the south side of the channel to avoid the Fowley Bank. After passing No. 1 buoy, keep to the Northern side of the channel and pass close South of the notice board which marks the pipeline. Then make for a point just North-West of the Lillies and then follow the channel up to the Bridge.

When approaching Ridham and Grovehurst Docks keep watch for any commercial vessels which may be manoeuvring out into the stream and give them a wide berth.

EAST SWALE CREEKS

FAVERSHAM CREEK. The entrance to this creek is 4 cables downstream from Harty Hard and marked by a red and white spherical buoy. The channel into the creek is well marked and yachts of up to 7 ft. draught can enter on a good spring tide. At L.W.O.S.T. there is a depth of 0–1 ft. Yachts of up to 2 ft. draught can enter at half-tide. S.R. 17 ft. N.R. 14 ft.

OARE CREEK. This creek is entered from the Faversham Channel and yachts of up to 6 ft. draught can enter on a good spring tide. At L.W.O.S.T. the channel dries out but yachts of up to 1½ ft. draught can enter at half-tide.

CONYER CREEK. Approaching from the East, steer through the South deep from a point 4 cables West of No. 5 Channel buoy. This channel is not marked except for a black post 4 cables, S.E. by S. off Spitend Point and a white post on the mainland, 2 cables S.S.E. of the black post. One mile along this channel are mooring buoys and you should steer for these moorings and then for the creek entrance which is marked by 4 switches. These switches must be left to starboard and boats must keep between the stakes marking the channel or they will run aground. The stakes marking the 30 ft. wide channel show triangular topmarks to starboard and round topmarks to port. On a good spring tide, yachts of up to 6 ft. draught can enter but the creek practically dries out at L.W.O.S.T. At half-tide vessels up to 2 ft. draught can enter. If entering for a short time and intending to sail on the same tide, your yacht should be turned round before going alongside.

Leaving the creek, to avoid the passage back to No. 5 Channel buoy, if it is your intention to proceed further up the Swale, you can steer direct from the entrance switches for a point midway between Fowley Island and the small islet just west of it and, when through this, set course for No. 3 Channel buoy.

It is essential to check with the Boat Yards that there will be sufficient depth of water for your draught on the rising tide before attempting to use this West channel to No. 3 buoy. At L.W.O.S.T. there is a depth of 0 ft. in the west channel and 3 ft. in the South deep.

MILTON CREEK. This creek has a busy traffic in barges carrying mostly sand and, since these vessels are arriving and departing at all times, it is not advisable for yachts to enter. The fairway is extremely narrow; barges have to stop to pass each other and any yacht using the channel would be at risk and severely restrict the commercial operations.

WHITSTABLE

Approach. Whitstable Bay, at L.W.O.S.T., is very shallow and shoals lie off the approaches.

If coming in from the Thames, Columbine Shoal is marked by the Columbine Spit Buoy but there are depths of 2 ft. at L.W.O.S.T. North-West of the buoy. Course should be set to pass just North of the Columbine Buoy and then altered round for the Whitstable Street buoy and down to the anchorage. From the Swale, the Pollard Spit buoy should be passed to starboard and then haul round for the anchorage. From the East, pass the Whitstable Street buoy to port and then haul down. The flood and ebb tides in the anchorage run at speeds of up to 2½ knots maximum.

When anchoring, remember that commercial shipping will be entering/leaving the harbour when there is sufficient depth of water, so anchor well clear of the fairway between the harbour entrance and the Whitstable Street buoy.

Entrance. The harbour dries out at L.W.O.S.T. but can take vessels of up to 11 ft. draught at M.H.W.N.T. S.R. 16 ft. N.R. 13 ft.

MARGATE

Entrance. Harbour is tidal and dries out at L.W.O.S.T. Yachts are able to enter from half flood to two hours after high water. At high tide there is 10 ft. average depth except during Southerly gales when the height is retarded. 500 yards West of the main pier and running out North-East for ¼ mile are the Nayland Rocks. When approaching the entrance keep well up to the West side of the main pier. S.R. 15 ft. N.R. 12 ft.

EUROPEAN PORTS

IJMUIDEN

Depth at entrance. 52 ft. at MLWS.

Entrance. The Outer Harbour is entered between 2 breakwaters which, at their seaward end are 1,300 ft. apart. Two new breakwaters are being constructed as well as other large construction works, and due to this, fairways, buoys and lights are being constantly altered so that care must be taken when entering this part of the harbour.

About 10 cables inside the breakwaters the harbour divides into northern and southern channels which lead to Ijmuiden Docks and to the various lock entrances to the North Sea Canal (see Amsterdam entry). Yachts take the northern channel for a distance of about 5 cables and then turn to an easterly course when the entrance to the small locks will be seen about 5½ cables ahead. S.R. 74. N.R. 6 ft.

HOOK OF HOLLAND

Yachts are no longer permitted to enter the Hook of Holland. Entry is now south through the Goerce Channel and thence north via the Voorne Canal.

AMSTERDAM

Entrance. Passage to the port of Amsterdam is by way of the North Sea Canal which is entered through the lock at Ijmuiden. The canal is 443 ft. wide at the bottom and 49¼ ft. deep. It is lighted at night, is navigable under all conditions and has no tides or currents. The distance from the locks at Ijmuiden to the West Harbour at Amsterdam is 9 miles and, to the Eastern Harbour, 14 miles.

About 8 miles along the canal, the docks of Zaandam will be seen on the port hand and those of the West Amsterdam Harbour will commence on the starboard hand. The harbour channel now starts to curve to the south-east with a long curving breakwater on the starboard side, and about a mile further on from the end of this breakwater, the yacht harbour will be seen on the port side (by the commercial vessels buoy moorings).

FLUSHING

Depth at entrance. 35 ft. at MLWS. S.R. 15 ft. N.R. 13 ft.

Entrance channel. The entrance between the fixed red and green lights on the ends of the breakwaters is 1,500 ft. wide and the locks into the inner harbour are approximately 1,000 ft. along to port from the western breakwater end. There is a minimum depth of 17 ft. at MLWS in the lock. Depth in the Inner Harbour is kept at a constant 20 to 24 ft. Once through the lock, steer straight ahead for the end of the big dock, and the Yacht Harbour will be seen on the starboard hand of the cut which leads to the lock's entrance for the canal to Middleburg and the Delta. While waiting for the lock gates to the Inner Harbour to open, yachts can make fast alongside the piling of the western breakwater arm.

BRESKENS

Depth at entrance. 15½ ft. at MLWS, with tidal range of 12 to 15 ft. S.R. 16 ft. N.R. 13 ft.

Entrance. The entrance is between two breakwaters and allowance should be made for the tidal set when making for the mid-point between them. At night, there is a sectored light on the western breakwater and a fixed red light on the eastern one. Keep within the green sector until the light is abeam and then haul round for the entrance.

TERNEUZEN

Depth at entrance. 20 ft. at MLWS. S.R. 16 ft. N.R. 14 ft.

Entrance Channel. Distance between the breakwaters is about 120 ft. and allowance for the tide must be made when hauling round from the channel to pass between the breakwaters.

ZEEBRUGGE

Depth at entrance. 26 ft. at MLWS. S.R. 16 ft. N.R. 13 ft.

Entrance. The harbour is formed by a long curving breakwater on the west side along which are the commercial deep-water berths. When entering keep a sharp lookout for merchant vessels which may be leaving the breakwater berths and give them priority of movement and a wide berth. Approach the harbour entrance from the east on a course roughly parallel to the north-east end of the breakwater and, when you sight the two buoys marking the channel between these buoys, head for the opening of the Inner Dock. The yacht club and facilities are in the first dock whose opening is on your left-hand side just before the Bruges Canal lock entrance.

OSTEND

Depth at entrance. 18 ft. in mid-channel at MLWS under all weather conditions. S.R. 17 ft. N.R. 12 ft.

Entrance Channel. Minimum width, at entrance, is 230 ft. and no special precautions are necessary.

Traffic Signals: 3 cones, no exit; cone and two balls, no entry; two cones and a ball, no entry or exit.

NIEUPORT

Depth at entrance. Minimum depth is 10 ft. at MLWS. S.R. 17 ft. N.R. 13 ft.

Entrance Channel. The fairway lies in a N.W./S.E. direction, is about 262 ft. wide, and is protected by pile piers. The entrance between the two piers is marked, at night, by a green light on the west pier and by a red light on the east pier. The flood stream runs in at about 2 knots and the ebb at about 1½ knots. When commercial or naval vessels are entering or leaving, yachts must keep out of the entrance channel and obey the signals on the pier head. These signals are: 3 cones (red, white, red lights by night) – no exit; cone and 2 balls (red, white, red lights by night) – no entry; 2 cones and one ball (green, white, red lights by night) – no entry or exit.

DUNKIRK

Depth at entrance. 26-27 ft. MLWS. S.R. 19 ft. N.R. 15 ft.

Entrance. Many deep-draughted merchant ships use the port and every yacht manoeuvring in the roadstead or approaching the entrance between the breakwaters must give them a wide berth as their movement is severely restricted by the depth of water. Yachts arriving in the roadstead should advise their arrival to the Port Captain on Channel 12, VHF if equipped to do so. For those yachts not equipped with radio, enter only when a vertical signal (Red, White, Red) is shown on the north side of the signal tower on the West Mole. All yachts must keep within 33 ft. of the breakwater heads when entering, and also keep within this distance off the east breakwater when making for the yacht basin which is in the west corner of the Avant Port. They must remain in the north-east corner of the Nouvel Avant Port if a merchant vessel is coming out of the lock.

GRAVELINES

Depth at entrance. 1½ ft. at MLWS and 19½ ft. at MHWS. S.R. 19 ft. N.R. 16 ft.

Entrance Channel. The river dries at MLWS and entry is only possible during 3 hours on each side of high water. Keep slightly to the western side of the channel when passing between the breakwaters and then keep more to the eastern side of the channel as it silts towards the western breakwater side.

CALAIS

Depth at entrance. Minimum depth is 15 ft. at MLWS. S.R. 22 ft. N.R. 18 ft.

Entrance Channel. Entrance width between the breakwater heads is 300 ft. The tide sets fairly strongly across the entrance (up to 2 knots) until within 20 yds of the heads. No special precautions are necessary, but course should be maintained down the centre of the channel until well into Avant Port, as the channel dries out on the starboard side off Fort Risban.

BOULOGNE

Depth at entrance. Minimum depth of 33 ft. at MLWS between the breakwaters. S.R. 29 ft. N.R. 23 ft.

Entrance Channels. Width between the breakwater heads is approximately 1,600 ft. No difficulties at entrance, but once inside the breakwaters a course should be steered to make for the Southern Jetty extension at the Inner Harbour entrance to avoid the sandbanks to the northern side which dry out at MLWS.

Harbour Signals: The signal station displays the following signals at night: Two green and one yellow lights or two red and one yellow lights indicate that a small vessel or tow is entering or leaving; entrance or departure should therefore be made with caution while carefully observing the Collision Rules. If green, yellow and red lights are displayed then exit and entrance are forbidden. If in doubt and your vessel is equipped with VHF, call 'Le Dispatching' on channel 12.

ST. VALERY SUR SOMME

Depth at entrance. There is a depth, at MLWS, of 15 ft. at the landfall buoy and about 12 ft. at the outer channel buoy. S.R. 32 ft. N.R. 26 ft.

Entrance Channel. The seaward end of the channel is marked by a red and white conical buoy marked A1. Its position varies with the changes in the flow of the channel bed but it can usually be found within the sector 040°-120° of the landfall buoy and distant 1 to 2 miles from it. The channel, except in the pools, practically dries out at MLWS, and the bottom is sand and mud. The depth at high water varies with the wind and tide; an easterly wind having the effect of reducing the depth by about 1½ ft. The 10-mile channel is marked by 50 buoys and can be navigated from 3 hours before to one hour after high water. The surface can get rough in winds over force 5 but presents no danger.

DIEPPE

Depth at entrance. There is a minimum depth of 13 ft. MLWS between the breakwaters. S.R. 30 ft. N.R. 23 ft.

Entrance Channel. Entry is possible in all weathers and at all times. The current runs across the entrance at up to 2 to 3 knots and allowance must be made for this when entering. Once inside the entrance keep a minimum distance of 6½ ft. off the quays to avoid the quay aprons which uncover at low tide.

Traffic signals: Entry and departure of the car ferries is indicated by the following signals; Green flag or light — exit forbidden; red flag or light — entry forbidden; green and red with pendant — exit and entry forbidden.

Before entering or leaving the inner port channel make sure that no ferries or other commercial craft are already in the channel. A dredger may also be operating in the channel and both it and its cables must be given a wide berth.

FECAMP

Depth at entrance. 8 ft. at MLWS outside the breakwaters, and 5 ft. at MLWS between the breakwaters. S.R. 26 ft. N.R. 21 ft.

Entrance Channel. The entrance channel is between the two breakwaters and care should be taken to keep up towards the north breakwater as there is a drying patch at MLWS off the end of the southern breakwater. Channel between the breakwaters is approximately 100 ft. wide.

LE HAVRE

Depth at entrance. There is deep water both in the approaches and the channel. Depth, 50 ft. at MLWS. S.R. 25 ft. N.R. 21 ft.

Entrance Channel. The new channel lies in a 107° (T.) direction to the mid-point between the breakwaters. The flood tide runs in towards the harbour entrance at up to 1.6 knots and allowance must be made for its effect when manoeuvring through the breakwaters. Winds are predominantly from north to north-west.

TROUVILLE

Depth at entrance. The entrance dries out and entry can only be made during the interval before and after high water. For a yacht drawing 4 ft. entry can be made 3 hours before to 4½ hours after MHWS, and from 2½ hours before to 4 hours after MHWN. S.R. 25 ft. N.R. 20 ft.

Entrance Channel. When there is sufficient water to enter, keep to the middle of the channel between the jetties. The yacht harbour is closed by gates which open about 1½ hours before and close about 2 hours after the 'stand' of high water. The 'stand' of the tide in the Seine Bay is shown for the months of June to September in a special table printed by the Yacht Club.

OUISTREHAM

Depth at entrance. Depth of water in the channel is indicated by the following signals on the lock head: Circular sign or white light — over 16½ ft.; rectangular sign or red light — 3¾ — 16½ ft.; triangular sign or green light — 8 in. — 3¾ ft. S.R. 25 ft. N.R. 20 ft.

Entrance. When there is sufficient water to enter, pass just east of Nos. 1, 3 and 5 buoys and then steer to pass just west of No. 4 buoy and then towards the lock. At night, the two red lights give the transit bearing into the channel which is marked by buoys and beacons. It should be noted that the buoys are moved to meet changes in the channel.

Traffic Signals: The movement of vessels is governed by the following signals displayed at the jetty head and from the Port Office: Green flag (green, white, green lights) — entrance permitted to vessels in the roads: red flag (red, white, red lights) — entrance forbidden; green and red flags (3 red lights) — all movement forbidden.

A 95 ft. pontoon is situated at the west end of the new dock for the use of yachts waiting for the lock to open. The lock gates open approximately 3 hours either side of high water and, when the lock gates are open, a strong current flows through the lock pit. Yachtsmen should have bow and stern mooring ropes ready for use and these should be long enough to reach the bollards on the lock. In the large lock, where the current is particularly strong, engines should be used.

CHERBOURG

Depth at entrance. Both entrances are accessible to any size of yacht at any state of the tide and there are no locks or gates. S.R. 20 ft. N.R. 15 ft.

Entrance Channel. The entrance channel to the inner roads and yacht harbour is near the mid-point of the southern part of the Outer Roads. It is free from current effect and has sufficient depth of water for any size of yacht.

BRAYE

Entrance. Lies between the breakwater and Bibette Head. Care must be taken to avoid the sunken end of the breakwater which extends in a N.N.E. direction for about 3 cables. S.R. 21 ft. N.R. 16 ft.

ST. MALO

Entrance Channel. From the Grand Jardin lighthouse, the tide runs fairly strongly in the channel, up to 3 knots during the flood and up to 2 knots on the ebb. Minimum ebb in the main channel is 24 ft. at MLWS up to the port entrance.

The lock is open from 2 hours before to 2 hours after high water and yachts must give way to merchant vessels who have preference in docking. Lock signals are as follows: Red flag (red light by night) – entrance prohibited; red and green flags (red and green lights by night) – entrance and departure prohibited; green flag (green light by night) – departure prohibited; red and green flags plus another flag or pennant (2 red and one green or two green and one red lights by night) – entrance and departure prohibited except for specially authorised vessels; International Code Flag 'P' – both gates open.

Should you arrive when the lock is closed, there is plenty of anchorage space in the river just south of the middle bank by the lock. Yachts waiting for entry may, if there is room, use the Chambre de Commerce et d'Industrie mooring buoys just outside the lock near the approach channel. S.R. 39 ft. N.R. 29 ft.

GOREY

Entrance. The harbour entrance dries at 10 ft. (3m), and vessels should anchor in the vicinity of the red mooring buoy about 2 cables eastward of Gorey Pierhead until there is sufficient water to enter. The berths on mud and sand, alongside the pier dry from 10-15 ft. (3m. to 4½m). S.R. 34 ft. N.R. 25 ft.

SARK

CREUX HARBOUR. Approaching from Jersey or south about from Guernsey, pass close east of La Conchee Rock and direct for the harbour entrance. The approach transit is Pt. Robert Lighthouse in line with the white mark on the end of Creux Pier, Pass close to Les Laches Rock. There is a mooring buoy off the harbour entrance and there is no run of tide shoreward of the buoy. Inside the harbour between the crane and the steps there is a least depth of 10 ft. at L.W.N.T. The harbour should not be approached if the winds are strong from a southerly direction.

MASELINE. Maseline Harbour lies just north of Creux and can be approached by passage between the Pinnacle and Burons, if going north from Creux Harbour. Approaching from the South, however, the normal course is to pass just east of the Burons and then haul round for the end of the pier passing south of the Founiais. If the wind is from the north east, the harbour is very exposed and a nasty chop is set up at low water. It should not be approached under these conditions.

Note. Both harbours are very congested during the summer months and visiting craft are not allowed to lie alongside the quays.

OTHER ANCHORAGES. Depending on the prevailing wind, there are good anchorages in La Greve Bay and in the bays by Point Chateau.

ST. PETER PORT

Depth at Entrance. Minimum 18 ft. at MLWS but there can be variations of up to 1½ ft. due to weather and barometric variations. S.R. 29 ft. N.R. 22 ft.

Entrance. The width between the breakwaters is 600 ft. and the tide flows across the entrance at approximately 2 knots. Priority of movement is given to commercial vessels. These are indicated by Pier Head Mast Signals: 2 black balls (green light at night), vessel entering; Red flag (red light), vessel departing.

On arrival report at North Pier Head. Give name of boat and last port of call and obtain mooring instructions. Yachts from continental ports show "Q" flag until boarded by Customs.

CHANNEL ISLANDS MARINA (GUERNSEY)

Entrance. Immediately after passing through the 60 ft. wide entrance, a sharp turn to the south should be made to clear the green breakwater buoy to starboard. The entrance channel dries 5 ft. so the tide level should be obtained over the sill at the time of approach. Tide gauges indicating the depth of water are placed both inside and outside the entrance channel. High water at the Marina is - 4H.31m on H.W. Dover, or + 16m on H.W. St. Helier. There is at least 4 ft. in the entrance at neap tides but, during springs, entry is restricted to 3 or 4 hours on either side of H.W. Should there be insufficient depth of water to enter, a yacht may moor to the buoy adjacent to the North Head. There is no cross current within 200 yards (182 m). of the entrance. S.R. 29 ft. N.R. 22 ft.

ST. HELIER

Signals for entering and leaving. A green light permits entry and prohibits exit. A red light prohibits entry and permits exit. Both lights mean that the harbour is closed both ways. A yellow metal flag or flashing amber light is exhibited from the control station indicating that vessels under power and of less than 82 feet overall length may disregard the light signals and enter or leave harbour, keeping to starboard as far as practical between the pierheads. Maximum speed 5 knots.

The Harbour Master requests that visiting yachts lying in St. Helier Harbour fly flag 'P' on the day of their intended departure. This will assist the authorities to deal expeditiously with arriving yacht movements.

Depth at entrance. 9 ft. at MLWS. S.R. 36 ft. N.R. 29 ft.

Entrance Channel. The width of the channel varies from just over half a cable to one cable and, due to the numerous rocks, it is essential to keep to the leading marks. On spring tides, from 2½ hours before high water to high water, the tidal stream runs in a northerly direction at about 1 knot across St. Helier Harbour Pierheads. Harbour speed limit in St. Helier is a maximum of 5 knots.

GRANVILLE

Depth at entrance. 13 ft. between red and green lights at MHWN. S.R. 42 ft. N.R. 31 ft.

Entrance Channel. The harbour dries out but a yacht drawing up to 6 ft. should have no difficulty in entering from 4 hours before to 4 hours after MHWN.

The inner harbour lock opens from approximately one hour before to one hour after high tide. The tide will be found to be setting westerly at between ½ and 1½ knots during the period when it is possible to enter. Width of the entrance is approximately 75 ft. When the lock gates open fishing vessels entering or leaving transit the lock at high speed, and it is advisable for yachts to wait for about 10 minutes before making for the lock. Possible to dry out on legs in the north part of outer harbour.

Lock gate signals: cone (point up) – tide rising; cone (point down) – tide falling (cone is lowered half way 10 minutes before lock closes); three cones (green white green lights vertical at night) – exit forbidden; cone, ball, cone (red white red lights vertical at night) – entrance forbidden.

LEZARDRIEUX

Depth at entrance. 19 ft. at MLWS. S.R. 33 ft. N.R. 25 ft.

Entrance. The river is well buoyed, port and starboard, and there are also beacons marking isolated dangers. Depth in the river varies from 19 ft. in the lower reaches to 10 ft. at Lezardrieux, both at MLWS. The current is variable and runs at speeds of up to 4 knots.

PAIMPOL

The anchorage is sheltered from all winds with depth of water from 6 ft. (1.8m) minimum. Bottom is sand and gravel. There is a rock covered by 9 ft. (2.8m) of water at low water at the intersection of the Denou and Jument Channels.

Entrance Channel. From the anchorage, first follow the approach transit (see above) and then follow the buoyed channel to the entrance. There are oyster beds on the south side of the channel and the northern side tends to silt. The bend in the channel where it turns into the lock entrance is very clearly marked but sailing craft will find this section difficult in strong westerly winds and must use their engine. During the rising tide a counter current sets south on to the jetty at speeds of between ½ and 2 knots depending on weather conditions. This current ceases when the water level has reached about 32¾ ft. (10m). The inner channel to the lock dries to 13 ft. (4m) and the rest of the harbour dries to 16½ ft. (5m). Yachts can pass through the lock 1½ hours either side of high water. S.R. 34 ft. N.R. 25 ft.

CHAPTER 16

Port Facilities

KEY

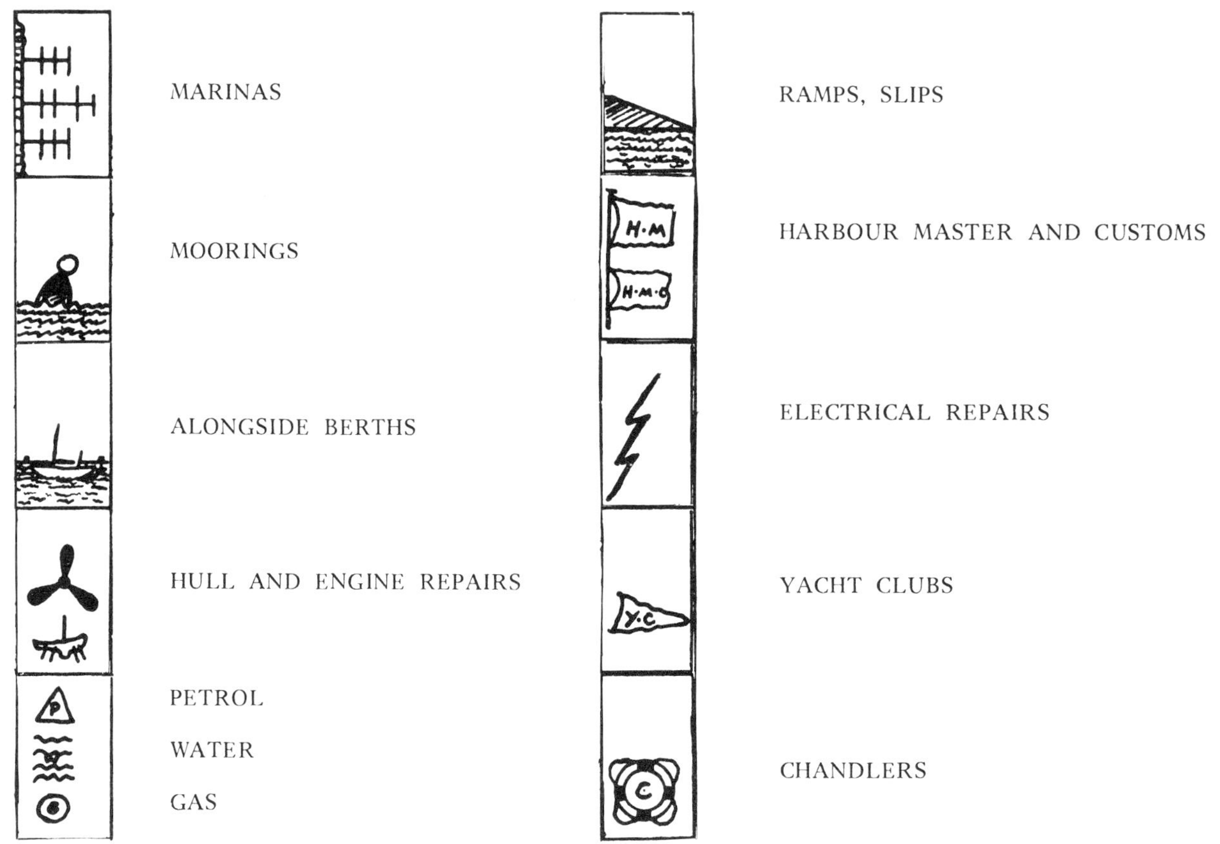

*Indicates availability.

PLACE	INTERVAL FROM H.W. DOVER	CHART REFERENCE					P		H·M H·M·C		Y·C	C
	H M											
KENT												
River Medway	+ 01 - 56	Stanford 5,8	3	*	*	*	* * *	*	* *	*	8	*
Queenborough	+ 01 - 56	Stanford 5,8,H1		*	*	2	* * *	2	* *	1	1	4
East Swale	+ 01 - 56	Stanford 5,8	1	*	*	*	* * *	*	*	*	4	*
Whitstable	+ 01 - 41	Stanford 5,8		*		2	* * *	1	* *	*	1	4
Margate	+ 01 - 19	Stanford 5,8		*	*	1	* * *	1	* *	1	2	2
Ramsgate	+ 00 - 52	Stanf'd 1,5,9,19,H1	1	*	*	5	* * *	2	* *		1	2
Dover		Stanford 1,9,19,H1		*	*	2	* * *	1	* *	2	1	3
Folkestone	– 00 - 07	Stanford 1,9,19,H1		*	*	2	* * *	1	* *	1	1	4
SUSSEX												
Rye	– 00 - 05	Stanford 1,9,19,H1		*	*	4	* * *	1	* *	2	1	5
Newhaven	– 00 - 01	Stanford 1,9,H1	1	*	*	4	* * *	3	* *	2	1	5
Shoreham	– 00 - 02	Stanford 1,9,H1		*	*	2	* * *	several	* *	1	2	3
Littlehampton	+ 00 - 20	Stanford 1,9,H1	1	*	*	8	* * *	3	* *	1	2	5
Chichester Harb: –	+ 00 - 15	Stanf'd 1,9,10,11,H2										
Emsworth	+ 00 - 27	Stanford 10,11,H2	1	*	*	4	* * *	2	* *	1	2	1
Chichester Yacht Basin	+ 00 - 15	Stanford 10,11,H2	1	*	*	1	* * *	1	* *	1	1	1
Birdham	+ 00 - 15	Stanford 10,11,H2	1	*	*	1	* * *	2	* *	1	1	1
Bosham	+ 00 - 15	Stanford 10,11,H2		*		3	* * *	1		1	1	5
Dell Quay	+ 00 - 15	Stanford 10,11,H2		*		1	* * *	1		1	1	4
HAMPSHIRE												
Langstone	+ 00 - 22	Stanford 10,11,H2		*		2	* * *	1	* *	1	4	2
Portsmouth	+ 00 - 14	Stanford 11,H2	1	*	*	2	* * *	1	* *	3	3	2
Porchester	+ 00 - 12	Stanford 11,H2		*		1	* * *				1	1
Fareham	+ 00 - 10	Stanford 11,H2		*		2	* * *	1		1	2	3
Hamble River	+ 01 - 30	Stanford 11,H2	4	*	*	7	* * *	several	* *	1	5	6
ISLE-OF-WIGHT												
Bembridge	+ 00 - 09	Stanford 1,2,11,H2		*	*	4	* * *	several	*	1	3	1
Wootton	+ 00 - 20	Stanford 1,2,11,H2		*		5	* * *	1	*	1	1	3
Cowes	+ 00 - 20	Stanford 2,11,H2	2	*	*	6	* * *	7	* *	2	7	6
Medina River	+ 00 - 30	Stanford 2,11,H2	1	*	*	*	* * *	2		1		1
Newtown	+ 01 - 08	Stanford 2,11,H2		*		1		1	*			
Yarmouth	– 00 - 28 + 00 - 58	Stanford 2,11,H3		*	*	7	* * *	3	* *	1	1	1
HAMPSHIRE												
Lymington	– 00 - 19 + 01 - 20	Stanford 2,11,12,H3	2	*	*	6	* * *	2	* *	1	2	7
Beaulieu River	– 00 - 13 + 01 - 41	Stanford 2,11,H3	1	*	*	4	* * *	4	*	1	1	3
Keyhaven	– 00 - 22 + 01 - 00	Stanford 2,11,12,H3		*		3	* * *	1	*	1	2	2
Christchurch	– 02 - 13 + 01 - 17	Stanford 2,12,H3		*	*	9	* * *	8	*	1	2	10

PLACE	INTERVAL FROM H.W. DOVER	CHART REFERENCE					P		H·M H·M·C		Y·C	C
	H M											
DORSET												
Poole	{ − 02 - 34		1									
	{ + 00 - 50	Stanford 2,12,15,H3		*	*	30	* * *	several	* *	4	8	16
Wareham	+ 01 - 50	Stanford 12,15,H3		*	*	2	* * *	1		1	1	1
Weymouth	− 04 - 39	Stanford 2,12,H3		*	*	9	* * *	2	* *	1	2	7
Bridport	− 05 - 03	Stanford 2,12,H3		*		2	* * *	1	* *	*		
Lyme Regis	− 04 - 55	Stanford 2,12		*		1	* * *	1	* *	*	2	2
DEVON												
Exmouth	− 04 - 53	Stanford 2,12,H4		*		7	* * *		* *	*	2	3
Exeter	− 04 - 45	Stanford 2,12,H4				7	* * *	1	* *	*	3	8
Teignmouth	− 05 - 11	Stanford 2,12,H4		*		5	* * *		* *	*	2	5
Torbay (Torquay, Paignton)	− 05 - 08	Stanford 2,12,H4		*	*	5	* * *	1	* *	*	3	4
Brixham	− 05 - 10	Stanford 2,12,H4		*		4	* * *	1	* *	*	*	4
Totnes	− 04 - 45	Stanford 2,12,H4		*		2	* * *		* *	*	2	3
Dartmouth	− 05 - 15	Stanford 2,12,13,H4	2			5	* * *	1	* *	*	2	5
Salcombe	− 05 - 38	Stanford 2,12,13,H4		*		10	* * *	1	* *	*	2	7
Yealm River	− 05 - 37	Stanford 2,13,H5		*		2	* * *	1	* *	*	1	2
Plymouth	− 05 - 49	Stanford 2,13,H5	1	*	*	9	* * *	1	* *	*	9	7
CORNWALL												
Looe	− 05 - 53	Stanford 2,13,H5		*		5	* * *	1	* *		1	1
Fowey & Polruan	− 05 - 55	Stanford 2,13,H5		*	*	6	* * *	1	* *	*	3	4
Mevagissey	− 05 - 55	Stanford 2,13,H5		*		1	* * *	1	* *		2	2
Falmouth & Penryn	− 05 - 59	Stanford 2,13,H6		*	*	12	* * *	1	* *	*	2	3
Truro	− 05 - 51	Stanford 2,13,H6		*		8	* * *	1	* *		3	6
Helford River	− 00 - 42	Stanford 2,13,H6		*		3	* * *		* *	*	1	2
Mounts Bay (Penzance, Newlyn)	− 05 - 50	Stanford 2,13,H6		*		3	* * *	1	* *		3	3
Newquay	− 05 - 43	Stanford 2,13,H6					* * *	*	*		1	
Padstow	− 05 - 36	Stanford 2,13,H6		*	*	1	* * *	2	* *		1	1
St. Ives	+ 05 - 47	Stanford 2,13,H6		*	*		* * *		*			*
Hayle	+ 06 - 02	Stanford 2,13,H6	1	*	*	*	* * *	*	* *	*		*
DEVON												
Bideford	− 05 - 04	Stanford 14,H6		*	*	*	* * *	*	* *	*	*	*
Ilfracombe	− 05 - 10	Stanford 14,H6		*	*	1	* * *	*	* *	*	2	3
SOMERSET												
Minehead	− 05 - 21	Stanford 14		*	*		* * *	*	* *		1	1
Watchet	− 04 - 32	Stanford 14		*			* * *	*	* *			
Burnham-on-Sea	− 04 - 34	Stanford 14		*		2	* * *		* *		1	
Weston Super Mare	− 04 - 13	Stanford 14		*		1	* *	*	*		3	1
Portishead	−	Stanford 14		*	*	1	* *	*	* *		2	
GLOUCESTERSHIRE												
Bristol	− 03 - 50	Stanford 14		*	*	5	* * *	*	* *	*	3	4
Upper Severn Estuary	+ 05 - 45	Stanford 14		*				*	*		1	

PLACE	INTERVAL FROM H.W. DOVER	CHART REFERENCE					P		H·M H·M·C		Y·C	C
	H M											
GLAMORGANSHIRE												
Penarth	– 04 - 26	Stanford 14		*	*	2	* * *	*	* *	*	2	1
Barry	– 04 - 44	Stanford 14		*	*	2	* * *	*	* *	*	1	2
Porthcawl	– 05 - 08	Stanford 14		*		2		*	* *		2	2
Mumbles	– 05 - 01	Stanford 14		*		various	* * *	*	*		3	2
CARMARTHENSHIRE												
Burry Port	– 05 - 11	Stanford 14		*			* * *	*	* *		2	1
PEMBROKESHIRE		Admiralty										
Saundersfoot	– 05 - 15	Chart 1167,1076		*		1	* * *	*	* *		1	1
Tenby	– 05 - 22	Chart 1167,1076		*	*	2	* * *	*	* *		1	1
Milford Haven	– 05 - 08	Chart 2878,3274		*	*		* * *	*	* *			
		3275,2877		*		2	* * *	*	* *		1	2
Fishguard	– 04 - 05	Chart 1484,1410		*		1	* * *	*	* *		1	1
CARDIGANSHIRE												
Aberystwyth	– 03 - 30	Chart 1484, 1972		*			* * *	*	* *		1	1
MERIONETH												
Aberdovey	– 03 - 12	Chart 1484, 1972		*	*		* * *	*	* *		1	1
Barmouth	– 03 - 05	" 368, 1484, 1971		*		1	* * *	*	* *		2	1
CAERNARVONSHIRE												
Pwllheli	– 03 - 14	Chart 1971		*	*	3	* * *	*	* *		2	2
Abersoch	– 02 - 19	Chart 1971		*		2	* * *	*	*		1	2
Caernarvon	– 01 - 20	Stanford 17		*	*		* * *	*	* *		2	
ANGLESEY												
Holyhead & Trearodur Bay	– 00 - 50	Stanford 17		*		2	* * *	*	* *		2	2
CAERNARVONSHIRE												
Bangor	– 00 - 26	Stanford 17		*	*	1	* * *	*	*	*	1	2
Conway & Deganwy	– 00 - 29	Stanford 17		*		6	* * *	*	*		2	3
CHESHIRE												
Hoylake & West Kirby		Stanford 17		*		4	* *	4	*		2	5
LANCASHIRE												
Liverpool	+ 00 - 04	Stanford 17		*		6	*	*	* *	*	2	5
Lytham St. Annes	00 - 00	Stanford 17		*			* * *	2	*		2	4
Blackpool & Fleetwood	+ 00 - 20	Stanford 17		*	*	3	* * *		*	*	2	5
Morecambe & Heysham	+ 00 - 05	Stanford 17		*		1	* * *	2	* *		1	1
ISLE OF MAN												
Port St. Mary	+ 00 - 08	Stanford 17		*			* * *	*	* *		1	
Douglas	00 - 00	Stanford 17		*	*		* * *		* *	*	1	1
Peel	+ 00 - 08	Stanford 17		*	*	*	* * *	1	* *	*		*
Ramsey	+ 00 - 08	Stanford 17		*	*		* * *		* *		1	

PLACE	INTERVAL FROM H.W. DOVER	CHART REFERENCE					P		H·M H·M·C		Y·C	C
	H M											
WIGTOWN												
Stranraer	+ 00 - 50	Stanford 18		*		*	* * *		* *	*	*	*
AYRSHIRE												
Troon	+ 00 - 50						* * *	*		*	2	*
Girvan	+ 00 - 45	Stanford 18		*	*	*	* * *	*		*	*	*
Port Patrick	+ 00 - 11						* * *			*	*	*
Ardrossan	+ 00 - 49			*		*	* * *		* *	*	*	*
RENFREWSHIRE												
Gourock	+ 01 - 08	Stanford 18		*		1	* * *	*	* *		2	*
ARGYLL												
Hellensborough	+ 01 - 10	Stanford 18		*		*	* * *	*		*	2	*
Crinan Canal				*	*	*	* * *	*		*		*
LEWIS IS.												
Stornoway	– 04 - 15	Admiralty Chart 512		*	*	*	* * *	*	* *	*	1	*
ORKNEY IS.												
Stromness		Chart 2568		*	*	*	* * *	*	* *	*		*
SHETLAND IS.												
Lerwick		Chart 3814		*	*	*	* * *	*	* *	*		*
CAITHNESS												
Wick	+ 00 - 10	Chart 1462		*	*	*	* * *	*	* *	*		*
INVERNESS												
Inverness	+ 01 - 10	Chart 1784		*		*	* * *	*	* *	*	1	*
Caledonian Canal		Chart 1791										
BANFF												
Buckie	+ 01 - 00	Chart 1462		*	*	*	* * *	*	* *		1	*
ABERDEEN												
Fraserburgh	+ 01 - 00	Chart 1462		*	*	*	* * *	*	* *	*		*
Aberdeen	+ 02 - 25	Chart 1446		*	*	*	* * *	*	* *	*		*
KINKARDINE												
Stonehaven	+ 02 - 35	Chart 1438		*		*	* * *	*	* *	*	1	*
ANGUS												
Montrose	+ 03 - 00	Chart 1438		*	*	*	* * *	*	* *	*	1	*
Arbroath	+ 03 - 15	Chart 1438		*	*	*	* * *	*	* *	*	1	*
PERTH												
River Tay	+ 03 - 40	Chart 1481		*	*	*	* * *	*	* *	*	1	*
FIFE												
Kirkaldy	+ 03 - 25	Chart 137			*	*	* * *	*	* *	*		*
E. LOTHIAN												
Dunbar	+ 03 - 10	Chart 114A		*	*	*	* * *	*	* *	*	1	*

PLACE	INTERVAL FROM H.W. DOVER	CHART REFERENCE					P		H·M / H·M·C		Y·C	C
	H M											
BERWICK		Admiralty										
Granton	+ 03 - 25	Chart 3724		*	*	*	* * *	*	* *	*	1	*
Eyemouth	+ 03 - 29	Chart 137		*	*	*	* * *		*	*		
Berwick	+ 03 - 37	Chart 111, 1192		*		2	* * *	1	* *		1	2
NORTHUMBERLAND												
Warkworth	+ 04 - 10	Chart 1170, 1721		*		*	* * *	*	* *	*		*
Blyth	+ 04 - 29	Chart 1626		*		2	* * *	*	* *	*	1	1
DURHAM												
Tynemouth	+ 04 - 35	Stanford 20		*		1	* * *	1	* *	*	2	2
Hartlepool	+ 04 - 37			*		2	* * *		* *	*	2	3
YORKSHIRE												
Whitby	+ 05 - 01	Stanford 20		*	*	5	* * *	*	* *	*	1	2
Scarborough	+ 05 - 27			*		5	* * *	1	* *	*	1	2
Bridlington	+ 05 - 42			*		2	* * *	*	* *	*	1	2
Humber	− 05 - 45			*		*	* * *	*	* *	*	*	*
LINCOLNSHIRE												
Grimsby	− 05 - 35	Stanford 20		*		*	* * *	1	* *	*	4	*
Boston	− 04 - 53		*	*	*	*	* * *	*	* *	*	2	4
NORFOLK												
Kings Lynn	− 04 - 55	Stanford 20			*	*	* * *		*	*		1
Gt. Yarmouth & Gorleston-on-Sea	− 02 - 19	Stanford 3,19	*		*	4	* * *	3	* *		2	4
SUFFOLK												
Lowestoft & Oulton Broad	− 01 - 44	Stanford 3,19		*		4	* * *	4	* *	*	5	3
Southwold	− 01 - 16	Stanford 3,19		*		2	* * *	1	* *		1	1
Aldeburgh	− 00 - 24	Stanford 3		*		1	* * *	1	*		2	2
Woodbridge	+ 01 - 06	Stanford 3,5		*		6	* * *		*		3	3
Waldringfield	+ 00 - 46	Stanford 3,5		*		2	* * *	1	*		1	2
Felixstowe Ferry	+ 00 - 26	Stanford 3,5		*		2	* * *		*	*	1	2
Ipswich	+ 00 - 59	Stanford 3,5		*		4	* * *		* *	*	1	4
Pin Mill	+ 00 - 45	Stanford 3,5		*		3	* * *	*	* *		2	2
Woolverstone	+ 00 - 45	Stanford 3	*	*	*	1	* * *	*	* *		1	1
Levington	+ 00 - 44	Stanford 3	*	*	*	*	* * *	*		*		
ESSEX												
Harwich	+ 00 - 24	Stanford 3,5		*		2	* * *	1	* *	*	2	2
Frinton-on-Sea & Walton-on-the-Naze	+ 00 - 42	Stanford 3,5		*		2			*	*	1	4
Clacton-on-Sea	+ 00 - 31	Stanford 5						*	*		3	

PLACE	INTERVAL FROM H.W. DOVER	CHART REFERENCE										
	H M											
ESSEX												
Brightlingsea	+ 00 - 48	Stanford 4, 5		*		10	* * *	1	* *	*	2	1
Wivenhoe & Rowhedge	+ 00 - 54	Stanford 4, 5		*		4	* * *		* *	*	1	3
West Mersea	+ 00 - 53	Stanford 4, 5		*		4	* * *	1	*	*	2	3
Tollesbury & Goldhanger	+ 01 - 08	Stanford 4, 5	1	*		4	* * *	2	*	*	3	1
Maldon	+ 01 - 28	Stanford 4, 5		*		6	* * *	*	* *	*	3	4
Mayland, Maylandsea, & Stone	+ 01 - 30	Stanford 4, 5		*		2	* * *		*		3	2
Bradwell-on-Sea	+ 01 - 15	Stanford 4, 5	1	*		6	* * *	*	*		5	7
Hullbridge on Crouch & South Woodham Ferrers	+ 01 - 31	Stanford 4, 5		*		1	* * *	*	*	*	5	1

PLACE	INTERVAL FROM H.W. DOVER	CHART REFERENCE					P		H·M / H·M·O		Y·C	C
	H M											
EUROPEAN PORTS												
Ijmuiden	+ 03 - 52	Stanford 19	1			*	* * *	*	* *	*		*
Amsterdam		Stanford 19	1	*	*	*	* * *	*	* *	*	*	*
Flushing	+ 02 - 03	Stanford 1, 19	1	*	*	*	* * *	*	* *	*	1	*
Breskens	+ 02 - 20	Stanford 1, 19	1	*	*	*	* * *	*	* *	*	1	*
Ternuizen	+ 02 - 39	Stanford 1, 19	1	*	*	*	* * *	*	* *	*	2	*
Zeebrugge	+ 01 - 33	Stanford 1, 19	1	*	*	*	* * *	*	* *	*	1	*
Ostende	+ 00 - 49	Stanford 1, 19	1	*	*	*	* * *	*	* *	*	2	*
Nieuport	+ 00 - 54	Stanford 1, 19	1	*	*	*	* * *	2	* *	*	2	*
Dunkirk	+ 00 - 45	Stanford 1, 19	1	*	*	*	* * *	*	* *	*	1	*
Gravelines	+ 00 - 36	Stanford 1, 19			Limited	*	* * *	*	* *	*		*
Calais	+ 00 - 18	Stanford 1, 19	1	*	*	*	* * *	*	* *	*	2	*
Boulogne	– 00 - 07	Stanford 1, 19	1	*	*	*	* * *	*	* *	*	2	*
St. Valery Sur Somme.	– 00 - 44	Stanford 1	1	*	*	*	* * *	*	* *	*	1	*
Dieppe	+ 00 - 20	Stanford 1	1	*	*	*	* * *	*	* *	*	1	*
Fecamp	– 00 - 53	Stanford 1	1	*	*	*	* * *	*	* *	*	1	*
Le Havre	– 01 - 16	Stanford 1	1	*	*	*	* * *	*	* *	*	1	*
Trouville	– 01 - 49	Stanford 1	1	*	*	*	* * *	*	* *	*	1	*
Ouistreham (Caen).	– 01 - 43	Stanford 1	1	*	*	*	* * *	*	* *	*	1	*
Cherbourg	– 03 - 17	Stanford 1, 2, 16	1	*	*	*	* * *	*	* *	*	1	*
Braye	– 04 - 11	Stanford 2, 16		*		*	* * *		* *	*	1	*
St. Malo	– 05 - 11	Stanford 2, 16	1	*	*	*	* * *	*	* *	*	1	*
Gorey	– 04 - 45	Stanford 2, 16				*	* * *		* *		1	
St. Peter Port	– 04 - 42	Stanford 2, 16	1			*	* * *	*	* *	*	2	*
Channel Is. Marina	– 04 - 42	Stanford 2, 16	1	*	*	*	* * *	*	*	*		*
St. Helier	– 04 - 47	Stanford 2, 16	1	*	*	*	* * *	*	* *	*	3	*
Granville	– 05 - 02	Stanford 2, 16	1	*	*	*	* * *	*	* *	*	1	*
Paimpol	– 05 - 15	Stanford 2, 16		*	*	*	* * *		* *	*		*
Lezardrieux	– 05 - 14	Stanford 2, 16	1	*	*	*	* * *	*	*	*	1	*

CHAPTER 17

Admiralty Notices to Mariners

The following extracts from Admiralty Notices to Mariners are particularly relevant to yachtsmen and should be studied in detail.

General Arrangements for Search and Rescue (SAR)

The radio watch on the international distress frequencies which certain classes of ships are required to keep when at sea is one of the most important factors in the arrangements for the rescue of people in distress at sea. Since these arrangements must often fail unless it is possible for ships to alert each other or to be alerted from shore for distress action, every ship fitted with suitable radio equipment should make its contribution to safety by guarding one or other of these distress frequencies for as long as is practicable whether or not required to do so by regulation.

To supplement the efforts of ships at sea most maritime countries maintain a life-saving service for the rescue of people in distress around their coasts. The organisation of SAR measures vary from country to country, but coast radio stations always play an important part by guarding the international distress frequencies so that in the event of a distress signal being heard they can alert ships in the vicinity of the casualty and notify the proper shore authorities.

When a ship or aircraft is in distress off the coasts of the United Kingdom, assistance may be given not only by ships in the vicinity but also by the following authorities:–

(i) *Coast Radio Stations* operated by the Post Office. There are eleven of these, all of which keep continuous watch on the distress frequencies of 500 kc/s and 2,182 kc/s except Oban which watches on 2,182 kc/s only. There is also a long distance radio station with practically a world-wide range at Burnham/Portishead in Somerset. When a radio distress signal is received by a Coast Radio Station, it is transmitted on both distress frequencies to ships at sea and various authorities ashore are also notified, including H.M. Coastguard who initiate the appropriate SAR measures. Radio distress calls and distress traffic have absolute priority. During a distress incident no transmissions are allowed from any ship or Coast Radio Station which may interfere with the transmission or reception of signals connected with the rescue, the only exception being messages from or to any other ships overtaken by distress during the same period.

(ii) *H.M. Coastguard,* which is the authority responsible for initiating and co-ordinating the search and rescue measures for all vessels in distress off the coast of the United Kingdom. The area over which this responsibility extends approximates closely to that which can be reached by long range aircraft capable of operating up to 1,000 miles from the shore, and is bounded by latitude 43° and 68° North, by longitude 30° West and by the coastline of Western Europe or 8° East, whichever is nearer to the coastline of the United Kingdom.
The Coastguard maintains continuous visual, and radio listening watch on 2,182 kc/s, at 48 stations, 31 of which are designated as Coastguard Rescue Headquarters, the remaining 17 being sited where there is a large volume of coastal and fishing traffic or exceptional navigational hazards. There are some 80 intermediate stations where watch is kept during predictably busy times of the day and in bad weather (when wind is Force 6 or more). In addition there are 170 Auxiliary Watching Stations, which keep visual watch in bad weather. All these stations have Rescue Equipment, in addition to about 80 Rescue Stations which do not keep watch.

(iii) *The Royal National Life-boat Institution,* which is a private organisation supported entirely by voluntary contributions, maintains 137 life-boats round the coast of the United Kingdom, the Republic of Ireland, the Isle of Man and the Channel Islands. In addition it has an operational fleet of about 100 inshore rescue boats. There are also two 70-foot steel life-boats undergoing evaluation trials but available for rescue purposes. Every life-boat is equipped with a radio set which operates on the distress frequency of 2,182 kc/s. When launched on service a life-boat can listen to distress traffic on that frequency and can also make use of this and other medium frequencies, if necessary, for direct speech to other vessels or shore installations concerned with SAR operations. Life-boats are also equipped with an AM/UHF radio telephone which enables them to communicate direct with Service SAR Helicopters. More than two thirds of the life-boats are also fitted with FM/VHF for communication with the Coastguard and certain harbour and other authorities. The coxswain of the life-boat is kept informed by radio telephone either directly from the Coastguard or through the appropriate Coast Radio Station. Half of the inshore rescue boats are similarly fitted with FM/VHF. Life-boats of the Royal National Life-boat Institution are now fitted with a quick-flashing blue light exhibited from the masthead, showing at least 120 flashes every minute.

(iv) *The Royal Navy* which assists casualties by means of ships and aircraft, including helicopters.

(v) *The Royal Air Force* which, operating through the Rescue Co-ordination Centres at Edinburgh and Plymouth, is responsible for providing rescue facilities for Service and civil aircraft in and around the United Kingdom, but also, so far as Service requirements and operational practicability permit, assists ships in distress by means of aircraft.

(vi) *Air Traffic Control Centres* which are often the first to receive information about aircraft in distress. All commercial and many private aircraft are able to communicate with these centres by radio, and, in certain circumstances, are under an obligation to do so. They may be requested to assist in the search for a casualty at sea by keeping a look-out along or near their normal routes, by reporting the position of the casualty if they should find it and, if possible, by guiding ships to the rescue.

(vii) *Lloyd's* who are informed of casualties by the Coast Radio Stations and are responsible for notifying ocean-going tugs.

(viii) *Officers of the Fishery Departments* who inform the Coastguard of fishing vessels which are missing or overdue.

The nature of the action taken by these Authorities when a casualty happens or is imminent depends on whether a ship or an aircraft is involved, the position of the casualty and the circumstances in which it occurs. For example, if a vessel becomes stranded on the coast, the Coastguard may be forewarned by seeing the vessel drifting towards the coast, or they may observe distress signals fired from the vessel, or her plight may be reported to them by a Coast Radio Station which has received a distress message from her. The Coastguard will at once inform the local Secretary of the Royal National Life-boat Institution, who will decide whether or not to launch, and the Coastguard will also muster the local company of the Coastguard Auxiliary Service with its rescue equipment and send it as quickly as possible to the scene of the casualty. The Coastguard might also decide to ask for a helicopter from the R.A.F. or send a radio-equipped rescue vehicle to obtain a first-hand report. If, however, a ship is in distress perhaps some distance from the coast and sends out a distress call, other ships hearing the distress call will at once go to her assistance. The Coast Radio Station which hears the distress call will cause it to be re-broadcast on both distress frequencies, thus ensuring that both radiotelephone ships in the area are alerted for action, and will also inform the Coastguard, the appropriate Area Flag Officer and Lloyd's. The Coastguard will inform the local Secretary of the Royal National Life-boat Institution and, if it seems likely that aircraft assistance will be of value, will also notify the appropriate Rescue Co-ordination Centre. The local Area Flag Officer will decide whether or not to assist by despatching either naval vessels or naval aircraft. Tug companies, on being notified of the casualty by Lloyd's, may decide to send tugs. The Coast Radio Station will keep the authorities informed of all signals received from the casualty and from vessels, including life-boats, going to her assistance.

In the case of an aircraft casualty at sea, the first intimation that the aircraft is in trouble will normally be received by an Air Traffic Control Centre which will pass the information to the appropriate Rescue Co-ordination Centre. The latter is responsible for the despatch of rescue aircraft and helicopters, and will inform the appropriate Area Flag Officer, and also the Coastguard if it is thought that Royal National Life-boat Institution life-boats may be able to assist or that a broadcast message to shipping is required.

It will be seen that the circumstances attending a casualty vary considerably and the speed with which rescue measures can be taken depends on a rapid, yet careful, appreciation of the situation by those concerned, particularly by the authorities who have to initiate search and rescue action. Generally, H.M. Coastguard is the authority ashore which initiates and keeps in touch with SAR measures for ships in distress off the coasts of the United Kingdom, while the R.A.F. Rescue Co-ordination Centres perform a similar function in relation to aircraft casualties. However, although much can often be done by the shore authorities, the co-ordination and direction of operations at the scene of the casualty will at times be a matter primarily for the Master of the distressed vessel or the Master of another ship going to her rescue, or the Pilot of a search and rescue aircraft. The degree to which reliance must be placed on those at the scene will usually depend on the distance from the coast at which the casualty occurs; the further from the coast, the greater the reliance on co-ordination on the spot.

Guidance for masters on the assistance to be given during emergencies at sea is contained in a Merchant Ships Search and Rescue Manual (MERSAR), obtainable from Inter-Governmental Maritime Consultative Organization, 104 Piccadilly, London W1V 0AE, Price 50 new pence.

Minelaying and Minesweeping Exercises

In the North Sea, English Channel and waters around the British Isles a harmless, non-explosive practice mine which lies on the bottom and may eject a red, green or white flare to the surface is now extensively used. Vessels engaged in mine hunting carry, vertically, a red ball, white diamond and red ball signals by day and, by night, red, white, red all round lights. These lights are in lieu of the lights prescribed in Rule 2 (*a*) (i) and (ii) and Rule 7 (*a*) of the International Regulations. In the vicinity of these light-draft rubber dinghies may be operating from which divers are working. These small craft display, by night, two red lights 6 feet apart horizontally in addition to the lights required by Rule 7.

Visual signals used between shore stations in the United Kingdom and ships in distress

In the event of a ship being in distress off or stranded on the coast of the United Kingdom, the following signals should be used by life-saving stations when communicating with her, and by the ship when communicating with life-saving stations.

(*a*) Replies from life-saving stations or maritime rescue units to distress signals made by a ship or person:—

Signals	*Signification*
By day. – Orange smoke signal or combined light and sound signal (thunderlight) consisting of three single signals which are fired at intervals of approximately one minute . .	"You are seen – assistance will be given as soon as possible."
By night. – White star rocket consisting of three single signals which are fired at intervals of approximately one minute	(Repetition of such signals shall have the same meaning.)

If necessary the day signals may be given at night or the night signals by day.

(*b*) Landing signals for the guidance of small boats with crews or persons in distress:—

Signals	*Signification*
By day. – Vertical motion of a white flag or the arms or firing of a green star-signal or signalling the code letter "K" (— - —) given by light or sound-signal apparatus . . . . By night. – Vertical motion of a white light or flare, or firing of a green star-signal or signalling the code letter "K" (— - —) given by light or sound-signal apparatus. A range (indication of direction) may be given by placing a steady white light or flare at a lower level and in line with the observer	"This is the best place to land."
By day. – Horizontal motion of a white flag or arms extended horizontally or firing of a red star-signal or signalling the code letter "S" (- - -) given by light or sound-signal apparatus . . . . By night. -- Horizontal motion of a white light or flare or firing of a red star-signal or signalling the code letter "S" (- - -) given by light or sound-signal apparatus	"Landing here highly dangerous."
By day. – Horizontal motion of a white flag, followed by the placing of the white flag in the ground and the carrying of another white flag in the direction to be indicated or firing of a red star-signal vertically and a white star-signal in the direction towards the better landing place or signalling the code letter "S" (- - -) followed by the code letter "R" (- — -) if a better landing place for the craft in distress is located more to the right in the direction of approach or signalling the code letter "L" (- — - -) if a better landing place for the craft in distress is located more to the left in the direction of approach . . . . By night. – Horizontal motion of a white light or flare, followed by the placing of the white light or flare on the ground and the carrying of another white light or flare in the direction to be indicated or firing of a red star-signal vertically and a white star-signal in the direction towards the better landing place or signalling the code letter "S" (- - -) followed by code letter "R" (- — -) if a better landing place for the craft in distress is located more to the right in the direction of approach or signalling the code letter "L" (- — - -) if a better landing place for the craft in distress is located more to the left in the direction of approach . .	"Landing here highly dangerous. A more favourable location for landing is in the direction indicated."

(*c*) Signals to be employed in connection with the use of shore life-saving apparatus:—

Signals	*Signification*
By day. — Vertical motion of a white flag or the arms or firing of a green star-signal . . . . By night. — Vertical motion of a white light or flare or firing of a green star-signal	In general — "Affirmative". Specifically — "Rocket line is held." "Tail block is made fast." "Hawser is made fast." "Man is in the breeches buoy." "Haul away."
By day. — Horizontal motion of a white flag or arms extended horizontally or firing of a red star-signal . . . . By night. — Horizontal motion of a white light or flare or firing of a red star-signal	In general — "Negative." Specifically — "Slack away." "Avast hauling."

(*d*) Signals to be used to warn a ship which is standing into danger:—

Signals	*Signification*
The International Code Signals U or NF The letter U (· · —) flashed by lamp or made by foghorn, or whistle, etc.	"You are running into danger".

If it should prove necessary, the attention of the vessel is called to these signals by a white flare, a rocket showing white stars on bursting, or an explosive sound signal.

Co-operation between a ship's crew and H.M. Coastguard in the use of rocket rescue equipment

Should lives be in danger and your vessel be in a position where rescue by the rocket rescue equipment is possible, a rocket with line attached will be fired from the shore across your vessel. Get hold of this line as soon as you can. When you have got hold of it, signal to the shore as indicated in paragraph (*c*).

Alternatively, should your vessel carry a line-throwing appliance and this is first used to fire a line ashore, this line will not be of sufficient strength to haul out the Whip and those on the shore will, therefore, secure it to a stouter line. When this is done, they will signal as indicated in paragraph (*c*). On seeing their signal, haul in the line which was fired from the vessel until the stouter line is on board.

Then, when the rocket line is held, make the appropriate signal to the shore (paragraph (*c*)) and proceed as follows:—

(1) When you see the appropriate signal, i.e. "haul away", made from the shore, haul upon the rocket line until you get a tail block with an endless fall rove through it (called the "Whip").

(2) Make the tail block fast, close up to the mast or other convenient position, bearing in mind that the fall should be kept clear from chafing any part of the vessel, and that space must be left above the block for the hawser. Unbend the rocket line from the Whip. When the tail block is made fast and the rocket line unbent from the Whip, signal to the shore again (as in paragraph (*c*)).

(3) As soon as this signal is seen on the shore a hawser will be bent to the Whip, and will be hauled off to the ship by those on shore. Except when there are rocks, piles or other obstructions between the ship and the shore, a bowline will have been made with the end of the hawser round the hauling part of the whip.

(4) When the hawser is got on board, the bowline should be cast off. Then, having seen that the end of the hawser is clear of the Whip, the end should be brought up between the two parts of the Whip and made fast to the same part of the ship as the tail block *but just above it and with the tally board close up to the position to which the end of the hawser is secured* (this will allow the breeches buoy to come right out and will facilitate entry to the buoy).

(5) When the hawser has been made fast on board, unbend the Whip from the hawser and see that the bight of the Whip has not been hitched to any part of the vessel and that it runs free in the block. Then signal to the shore (as in paragraph (c).

(6) The men on shore will then set the hawser taut, and by means of the Whip will haul off to the ship the breeches buoy into which the person to be hauled ashore is to get. He should sit well down in the breeches buoy and when he is secure, signal again to the shore as indicated in paragraph (*c*) above, and the men on shore will haul the person in the breeches buoy to the shore. When he is landed the empty breeches buoy will be hauled back to the ship. This operation will be repeated until all persons are landed.

(7) During the course of the operations should it be necessary to signal, either from your ship to the shore, or from the shore to your ship, to "Slack away" or "Avast hauling" this should be done as indicated in paragraph (*c*).

It may sometimes happen that the state of the weather and the condition of the ship will not admit of a hawser being set up; in such cases a breeches buoy will be hauled off by the Whip which will be used without the hawser.

The system of signalling must be strictly followed. It should, however, be noted that the rescue operation, as a whole, will be greatly facilitated if signal communication (by semaphore or flashing lamp) is established between the ship and the shore or life-boat). The large majority of Coastguard Rescue Companies and life-boats have trained signalmen.

All women, children, passengers, and helpless persons, should be landed before the crew of the vessel. Masters and crews of stranded vessels should bear in mind that success in landing them by the rocket rescue equipment depends, in a great measure, upon their own coolness and attention to the instructions laid down.

A mounted glazed poster with illustrations – suitable for display in the Chart Room – can be obtained on application to the Clerk of Stationery, Board of Trade, Forms Store, Eileen House, Newington Causeway, London S.E.1.

Sea Rescues by helicopter

The main type of helicopter used for SAR duties in the United Kingdom is the Whirlwind, which at short ranges from the coast can rescue up to 8 persons at any one time. Helicopter rescue is not normally undertaken over the sea at night, or when the wind exceeds 45 knots.

When a distress message is received either visually or by radio from a ship in distress, steps taken by the rescue authorities ashore may include asking the nearest R.A.F. Rescue Co-ordination Centre, to despatch a helicopter to assist in the rescue.

Once the helicopter has become airborne, the speed with which it locates the ship and the effectiveness of its work depends to a large extent on the co-operation of the ship herself.

From the air, especially if there is a lot of shipping in the area, it is very difficult for the pilot of a helicopter to pick out the particular ship he is looking for from the many in sight, unless that ship uses a distinctive distress signal which can be clearly seen by him. One such signal is the orange coloured smoke signal carried in the life-boats. This is very distinct from the air. A well trained Aldis lamp can also be seen except in very bright sunlight when the life-boat heliograph could be used. The display of these signals will save valuable time in the helicopter locating the casualty, and may mean all the difference between success and failure. It is not suggested, of course, that the Aldis lamp need necessarily be used to pass messages in Morse.

It is essential that the ship's position should be given as accurately as possible if the original distress signal is made by radio. The bearing (magnetic or true) and distance from a fixed object, like a headland or lighthouse, should be given if possible. The type of ship and colour of hull should be included if time allows. The search and rescue helicopters, whose maximum radius of action is 90 miles, carry Decca equipment, and therefore a Decca fix is most useful to them.

Because of their operational limitations, helicopters should not be unnecessarily delayed at the scene of the rescue. Every effort should be made to provide **a clear stretch of deck or hatchway and to mark this area with a large letter "H" in white,** prior to the arrival of the helicopter. All loose articles, equipment, garbage containers etc. must be secured or cleared from the transfer area, as the down-wash (normally about 40 knots) will surely dislodge them.

Paper, rags and tarpaulins are particularly prone to involuntary disembarkation, and can cause an accident by being ingested into the helicopter intakes. A helicopter will approach the ship from astern and come to the hover over the cleared area, heading into wind. In order that the helicopter pilot and crewman may have as large an area of the ship as possible on which to operate consistent with the helicopter remaining heading into wind, the ship should steam at a constant speed heading 30° to starboard of the prevailing wind direction. If this is not possible the ship should remain stationary head to wind. If these conditions are met the helicopter can lower on to or lift from the clear area, the maximum length of the winch cable being about 50 ft. **On no account should the strop on the end of the winch cable, when lowered to the vessel, be secured to any part of the vessel or allowed to become entangled in any rigging or fixtures.** If the ship cannot comply with these conditions the helicopter may be able to lift a man from a boat towed astern on a long painter. If the vessel is on fire and making smoke it is of advantage to have the wind two points off the bow. In all cases an indication of wind direction is useful. Pennants and flags are acceptable for this purpose and possible smoke from the galley funnel, provided that there is not too much smoke.

The helicopter winch wire carries a static charge of electricity and should not be touched without rubber gloves.

Helicopters are well practised in rescuing survivors from either a deck or the sea and two methods are employed. These are:–

(1) The survivor, whether on deck or in the water, is rescued by means of the strop. The crewman is lowered from the helicopter together with the strop which is secured around the survivor's back and chest, and both are winched up into the helicopter.

(2) If a survivor on a deck is injured to the extent that the use of a strop around his back and chest would aggravate the injury or cause suffering, a crewman is lowered on to the deck with a Neil-Robertson stretcher. The survivor is placed in the stretcher, strapped in in such a manner that it is impossible for him to slip or fall out, and both stretcher and crewman are winched up into the helicopter. If possible, the helicopter will be carrying a doctor who will be lowered to the deck and will assist the survivors as necessary.

The helicopter pilot and crewman are professionals in these methods of rescue and well intentioned assistance from either the survivor himself or third parties in securing survivors invariably results in delays. Assistance should therefore only be given if specifically requested by the crewman.

Helicopters are fitted with V.H.F. and U.H.F. R/T. They cannot work on the M.F. frequencies. If a ship wishes to send a life-saving message to a helicopter which is coming to its assistance, and is unable to do so by visual means or V.H.F., the message should be sent by radio through the nearest Coast Radio Station, addressed to the Coastguard. On receipt the Coastguard will pass it to the R.A.F. Rescue Co-ordination Centre or station controlling the helicopter.

Almost all R.N.L.I. life-boats are, in addition to their M.R. equipment, now fitted with V.H.F. to enable the coxswain to speak direct to a helicopter working with the life-boat on a rescue service. If therefore a life-boat is known to be in the vicinity of a ship the message for the helicopter from the ship should be passed on M.F. (2,182 kc/s) to the life-boat for transmission to the helicopter. Ships without radiotelephony but with radiotelegraph facilities should pass the message to the Coast Radio Station.

If from the ship in trouble it is observed that the helicopter is going to pass by, or is on a course which will take it away, continued use should be made of visual distress signals, and at the same time, if fitted with radio, the fact reported to the Coastguard stating the present bearing and distance of the helicopter. The Coastguard will pass this information to the helicopter through its R.A.F. Rescue Co-ordination Centre or station controlling the helicopter.

It is well to be advised of the particular dangers to be recognised when working with helicopters in respect of their rotors. As indicated previously, helicopters keep clear of any obstructions such as masts, since any contact by them with the main rotor, and particularly the tail rotor, is disastrous for the helicopter. Similarly, when survivors are landed from the helicopter they must observe closely the instructions given by the crew since there is an ever present danger of walking unwittingly into the tail rotor. This warning may appear to be overstating the obvious, yet it is surprising how simply and how often it is done.

Aircraft casualties at sea

Distress Communications

Visual Signals. An aircraft may indicate it is in distress by firing a succession of red pyrotechnic lights, by signalling "S.O.S." with signalling apparatus or by firing a parachute flare showing a red light. Navigation markers dropped by aircraft at sea, emitting smoke, or flames and smoke, should not be mistaken for distress signals. Low flying is not in itself an indication of distress.

An aircraft which has located another aircraft in distress may notify ships in the vicinity by passing a message in plain language by signalling lamp using the prefix "XXX." It may also give the following signals, together or separately, to attract a ship's attention:—*(a)* a succession of white pyrotechnic lights, *(b)* the repeated switching on and off of the aircraft's landing lights and *(c)* the irregular repeated switching on and off of the aircraft's navigational lights. If it wishes to guide a ship to the casualty or survivors it will fly low round the ship or cross the projected course of the ship close ahead at a low altitude opening and closing the throttle or changing the propeller pitch. It will then fly off in the direction in which the ship is to be led. British pilots are instructed to rock their aircraft laterally when flying off in the direction of the casualty. The ship should acknowledge receipt of this signal and of messages passed by signalling lamp by a succession of "T's" in the Morse Code. It should then either follow the aircraft or indicate by visual or radio means that it is unable to comply. The procedure for cancelling these instructions is for the aircraft to cross the wake of the surface craft close astern at a low altitude, opening and closing the throttle or changing the pitch.

In order to take advantage of the greater visibility of pyrotechnics by night, searching aircraft will fly a creeping-line-ahead type of search, firing off green pyrotechnics at 5-10 minute intervals and watching for a replying red from the survivor.

Survivors from crashed aircraft in rubber liferafts may give the following visual distress signals:—

(1) Fire pyrotechnic signals emitting one or more red stars, or orange/red smoke.

(2) Flash a heliograph.

(3) Flash SOS or other distinctive signal by hand torch or other signalling lamp. Some liferafts may show a steady or a flashing light.

(4) Blow whistles.

(5) Use fluorescein dye marker giving an extensive bright green colour to the sea around the survivors.

(6) Fly a yellow kite from the liferaft to support the aerial for the emergency radio transmitter.

Radio signals. Radio is not carried by all civil aircraft. If, however, an aircraft transmits a distress message by radio, the first transmission is made on the designated air/ground route frequency in use at the time between the aircraft and the appropriate ground station, normally an Air Traffic Control Centre (A.T.C.C.). The aircraft might be asked by the A.T.C.C. to change to another frequency, possibly on another H.F. route frequency or on the civil aeronautical emergency frequency of 121·5 Mc/s in the V.H.F. band. If the aircraft is unable to contact the ground station on the route frequency, any other available frequency may be used in an effort to establish contact with any land, mobile or direction-finder station. In addition, if time permits and the aircraft is so equipped, the distress call is made on the international distress frequency 500 kc/s.

There is close liaison among shore stations, including Air Traffic Control Centres, Rescue Co-ordination Centres, Coast Radio Stations and H.M. Coastguard, and merchant ships will ordinarily be informed of aircraft casualties at sea by broadcast messages from the Coast Radio Stations made on the international distress frequencies of 500 kc/s and 2,182 kc/s. Ships may, however, become aware of the casualty by:–

(1) picking up an SOS message from an aircraft in distress which is able to transmit on 500 kc/s or by intercepting a distress signal from an aircraft using radiotelephony on 2,182 kc/s.

(2) by hearing and being able to D.F. on the radiotelegraphy signal on 500 kc/s from the hand-operated emergency transmitters carried by survival liferafts, or

(3) by picking up a message from a search and rescue aircraft.

Action taken to render assistance

All information concerning aircraft in distress at sea in waters surrounding the United Kingdom is passed to the R.A.F. Rescue Co-ordination Centre in whose area of responsibility the casualty has occurred or is likely to occur. Aircraft will then be sent, if necessary and practicable, to search for and fix as accurately as possible the position of the casualty. Although these aircraft will carry droppable survival equipment the survivors must normally be rescued by naval and merchant ships or life-boats of the Royal National Life-boat Institution. Nevertheless, it is possible that survivors will be picked up by SAR helicopters.

Aircraft usually sink quickly (i.e. within a few minutes) and ships making for an aircraft in distress should consequently steam at full speed.

Every endeavour will be made to give merchant ships an accurate position of an aircraft casualty or liferaft. An aircraft will, if practicable, be kept over survivors at least during daylight hours, until they are rescued. When given such a fix the ship should at once consult any other ships in the neighbourhood on the best procedure to be adopted, as is the practice in the case of casualties to ships; the ship going to the rescue should answer the station sending the broadcast and give her identity, position and intended action.

If a merchant ship should pick up an SOS message direct from an aircraft in distress, she should act as indicated in the immediately preceding sentence and also relay the message to the nearest Coast Radio Station. Moreover, a merchant ship which has received an SOS message direct from an aircraft in distress and is going to the rescue should take a bearing on the transmission, and inform the Coast Radio Station or other vessels in the vicinity of the call-signal of the distressed aircraft and the time at which the distress message was received, followed by the bearing and time at which the signal ceased.

Action to be taken when survivors are picked up

A survivor from an aircraft casualty at sea who is picked up by a ship may be able to give information which will assist in the rescue of other survivors. Masters are therefore asked to put the following questions to rescued survivors of an aircraft casualty and to communicate the answers to a Coast Radio Station. They should also give the position of the rescuing vessel and the time when the survivor was picked up.

(1) Did you bale out or was the aircraft ditched? What was the time and date?

(2) If you baled out, at what altitude?

(3) How many others did you see leave the aircraft by parachute?

(4) How many ditched with the aircraft?

(5) How many did you see leave the aircraft after ditching?

(6) How many survivors did you see in the water?

(7) What flotation gear had they?

(8) What was the total number of persons aboard the aircraft prior to the accident?

(9) What caused the emergency?

Action to be taken when an aircraft is forced to "ditch" (alight on the sea)

The captain of a distressed aircraft will be materially assisted in locating a ship if the latter:–

(1) Transmits homing bearings to the aircraft, or (if so requested) transmits signals enabling the aircraft to take its own bearings;

(2) By day makes black smoke;

(3) By night directs a searchlight vertically.

Ditching an aircraft is difficult and usually dangerous. A ship which knows that an aircraft intends to ditch should, if practicable, try to provide a lee of calm water. This may be achieved by any means at the Master's discretion, such as steering on a circular course through 360 degrees, with the addition, if possible, of an oil "slick".

The Captain of an aircraft normally sits on the port side of the cockpit, and thus has better visibility on that side. An aircraft will therefore usually ditch on the starboard side of a ship and heading into wind, although, when seas are running high, it may be expected to attempt to land along the trough of the seas. In the absence of a pre-arranged plan, the ship should steam into wind and assume that the aircraft will ditch on her starboard side. Helicopter captains sit on the starboard side of the aircraft and would, therefore, normally ditch on the port side of a ship heading into wind.

If it is dark, the ship should illuminate the sea as much as possible by searchlight on the side upon which the aircraft is expected to ditch. Care should be taken not to dazzle the pilot who might otherwise lose control of his aircraft at a critical moment. It will help the pilot considerably if flame floats or preferably, in view of the danger of petrol coming into contact with them, battery operated floats are laid line astern to indicate the direction of the suggested alighting area. Six floats should be laid at 200-yard intervals.

The ship's Master should, if possible, tell the Captain of an aircraft which is going to ditch the general weather conditions, including wind speed and direction visibility, state of sea and swell, approximate cloud base, and barometric pressure.

A land plane may break up immediately on striking the water, and liferafts may be damaged. The ship should therefore have a life-boat ready for launching, and if possible boarding nets should be lowered from the ship and heaving lines made ready in the ship and the life-boat. Survivors of the aircraft may have orange lifejackets, water torches and whistles.

The method of picking up survivors from liferafts must be left to the judgment of the captain of the ship carrying out the rescue operation.

The drift rate of a liferaft would normally be expected to exceed that of a ship, so that with the ship to windward, the liferaft might drift away from the ship unless some suitable means were available to catch the liferaft and hold it alongside. This might involve the ship having to repeat the whole procedure of coming alongside again. However, if the ship was stopped long enough for her full drift rate to develop, this rate should exceed that of the liferaft which would decrease as the lee afforded by the ship increased. On the other hand, ships of low freeboard would not afford much protection in any seaway, and the drift rate of the liferaft might not be arrested, and heavy seas washing over the lee side would make it difficult to take survivors onboard. Another point to be considered is the lack of manoeuvrability once a ship is stopped.

With the ship to leeward, there should be no difficulty in keeping the liferaft alongside, but with heavy seas running, there is the risk of the liferaft being dashed against the ship's side, and greater difficulty in taking survivors onboard.

It should be borne in mind that Military aircraft are often fitted with ejection seat mechanism, the position of which is indicated by a red solid triangle. The mechanism is activated by black and yellow striped handles. All handles or knobs, switches, etc. coloured red and with black and yellow stripes should *not* be touched, as the consequences of so doing may be injurious or even fatal to both rescuer and rescued.

Firing practice and exercise areas.

Firing and bombing practices, and defence exercises, take place in a number of areas off the coasts of British Commonwealth and Colonial Territories as well as in foreign waters.

In future, and in view of the responsibility of range authorities to avoid accidents, limits of practice areas will not as a rule be shown on navigational charts and descriptions of areas will not appear in the Sailing Directions. They will, however, be shown in Home Waters on a new series of 6 small scale charts called the PEXA series. Such range beacons, lights and marking buoys as may be of assistance to the Mariner, or targets which might be a danger to navigation, will, however, be shown on navigational charts and, when appropriate, mentioned in Sailing Directions.

Lights will be mentioned in the Admiralty List of Lights.

The principal types of practices carried out are:—

(*a*) *Bombing practice from aircraft.*
Warning signals usually shown.

(*b*) *Air to air, and air to sea or ground firing.*
The former is carried out by aircraft at a large white or red sleeve, a winged target, or flag towed by another aircraft moving on a steady course. The latter is carried out from aircraft at towed or stationary targets on sea or land, the firing taking place to seaward in the case of those on land.
As a general rule, warning signals are shown when the targets are stationary, but not when towed targets are used.
All marine craft operating as range safety craft, target towers or control launches for wireless controlled targets will display, for identification purposes, while in or in the vicinity of the danger area, the following markings:—

(1) A large red flag at the masthead;

(2) A painted canvas strip, 6 feet by 3 feet, with red and white chequers in one-foot squares, on the fore deck or cabin roof.

(*c*) *Anti-aircraft firing.*
This may be from A.A. guns or machine guns at a target towed by aircraft as in (*b*) above, a pilotless target aircraft, or at balloons or kites. Practice may take place from shore batteries or ships.
Warning signals as a rule are shown from shore batteries. Ships fly a red flag.

(*d*) *Firing from shore batteries or ships at sea at fixed or floating targets.*
Warning signals usually shown as in (*c*)

(*e*) *At remote-controlled craft.*
These craft are 68 feet in length and carry not under control shapes and lights, as well as normal navigation lights. Exercises consisting of surface firing by ships, practice bombing, air to sea firing

and rocket firing will be carried out against these craft or targets towed by them.

A control craft will keep visual and radar watch up to approximately 8 miles and there will be cover from the air over a much greater range to ensure that other shipping will not be endangered.

(*f*) *Rocket and Guided Weapons firing.*

These may take the form of (*b*), (*c*) or (*d*) All such firings are conducted under Clear (Air and Sea) Range procedure. Devices are generally incorporated whereby the missiles may be destroyed should their flights be erratic.

Warning signals are usually shown as in (*c*).

Warning signals, when given, usually consist of red flags by day and *red fixed* or *red flashing* lights at night. The absence of any such signal cannot, however, be accepted as evidence that a practice area does not exist. Warning signals are shown from shortly before practice commences until it ceases.

Ships and aircraft carrying out night exercises may illuminate with bright *red* or *orange* flares.

CAUTION. A vessel may be aware of the existence of a practice area from PEXA Charts, Local Notices to Mariners or similar method of promulgation and by observing the warning signals or the practice.

The Range Authorities are responsible for ensuring that there should be no risk of damage from falling shell-splinters, bullets, etc., to any vessel which may be in a practice area.

If, however, a vessel finds herself in an area where practice is in progress, she should maintain her course and speed but, if she is prevented from doing this by the exigencies of navigation, it would assist the Range Authority if she would endeavour to clear the area at the earliest possible moment. Furthermore, if projectiles or splinters are observed to be falling near the vessel, all persons on board should take cover.

Fishermen operating in the vicinity of firing practice and exercise areas may occasionally bring unexploded missiles or portions of them to the surface in their nets or trawls. These objects may be dangerous and should be treated with great circumspection and jettisoned immediately, no attempt being made to tamper with them or bring them back for inspection by Naval Authorities.

It is realised that the foregoing provisions do not apply in all respects in all countries. It is not, however, intended to repromulgate by Admiralty Notice information received about firing practice or exercise areas in foreign waters.

Areas are only in force intermittently or over limited periods, and local promulgation or warnings by radio, visual signals or Notices should be such that they will come to the attention of those whose co-operation or instruction is intended.

The foregoing provisions do not apply to Submarine Exercise areas, the existence of which, when known, are indicated on charts and in the Sailing Directions.

Seismic surveys are being undertaken in various parts of the world in connection with exploration for oil and gas. It is seldom practicable to publish details of the areas of operation except in general terms and vessels carrying out seismic surveys may therefore be encountered without warning.

There are several methods of carrying out such surveys:—

(1) **Single-boat operation.**

The survey craft tows a recording line about 1-2 miles long from the stern and shooting lines up to 3,000 feet long on either side. The recording line is usually submerged but the end may be marked by a buoy. The shooting lines usually float. Charges do not exceed 50 lbs.

(2) **Two-boat operation.**

The recorder vessel tows the recording cable and the shooting vessel the shooting cable. Both vessels move in the same direction and the shooting vessel may be stationed anywhere alongside the recording cable or up to 1,500 feet astern of it. Lengths of cables and charges are similar to those used in Single-boat operations. In certain cases a Marker vessel may be stationed at the end of the recording cable.

(3) **Velocity-Profile operations.**

The recorder and shooting vessels towing cables as in (2) start at positions 4-5 miles apart. They move on opposite courses towards and past each other until each has reached the other ship's starting position. Charges up to 200 lbs are fired.

(4) **Refraction Method.**

This is the same as (3) except that the initial distance apart is 10-12 miles. An alternative method is for the shooting vessel to remain in one position and fire charges up to 2,000 lbs, the recorder vessel being up to 30 miles distant.

Survey vessels generally carry the signals described in Rule 4(*c*) of the Regulations for Preventing Collisions at Sea (1960), i.e. at night 3 lights in a vertical line, the highest and lowest red and the middle white; by day 3 shapes in a vertical line, the highest and lowest being red balls, the middle a white diamond. They may carry the signals PO and IR (International Code). The shooting vessel may carry signal B (International Code) or at night a single red light in addition.

Survey vessels are unable to manoeuvre freely and Masters should therefore give them a wide berth (say 2-2½ miles).

They often keep radio silence if charges are fired by radio so as to avoid any uncontrolled firings. Vessels being called by light by a survey vessel should therefore answer by the same means and not by radio or radio telephone.

The charges are contained in various types of can, cylinder, cardboard tube or polythene bag, which are not marked as dangerous. Unexploded charges which have been recovered by vessels should be jettisoned immediately.

With reference to paras. 1, 2 & 3 above, the use of "air" or "gas" guns in lieu of dynamite charges has recently been introduced and either method may be employed.

Information concerning submarines

Part I Warning Signals

(a) Visual signals

(1) Mariners are warned that considerable hazard to life may result by the disregard of the following warning signals, which denote the presence of Submarines:

> British vessels fly one of the two International Code Group N.E.2. to denote that Submarines, which may be submerged, are in the vicinity. Vessels are cautioned to steer so as to give a wide berth to any vessel flying either of these signals. If from any cause it is necessary to approach her, vessels should approach at low speed until warning is given of the danger zone by flags, semaphore or megaphone, &c., a good lookout being kept meanwhile for Submarines whose presence may be only indicated by their periscopes or snorts showing above water.
>
> A Submarine submerged at a depth too great to show her periscope, may sometimes indicate her position by releasing a "smoke candle" which gives off a considerable volume of smoke on first reaching the surface. Her position may sometimes be indicated by red-and-white or red-and-yellow buffs or floats, which tow on the surface close astern.

(b) Pyrotechnics and Smoke Candles

(2) The following signals are used by a submerged Submarine in a Submarine exercise area.

Signal	*Signification*
One *red* pyrotechnic light, or smoke, repeated as often as possible.	Keep clear. I am carrying out emergency surfacing procedure. Do not stop propellers. Ships are to clear the area immediately and stand by to render assistance.
Two *yellow* pyrotechnic lights, or two *white* or *yellow* smokes, 3 minutes apart.	Keep clear. My position is as indicated. I intend to carry out surfacing procedure. Do not stop propellers. Ships are to clear the immediate vicinity.

It must not be inferred from the above that Submarines exercise only when in company with escorting vessels.

(3) Under certain circumstances warnings that Submarines are exercising in specified areas may be broadcast by a General Post Office radio station.

Part II Navigation Lights

(4) Submarines may be met on the surface by night, particularly in the vicinity of the following ports:

> Thames Estuary, Portsmouth, Portland, Plymouth, Barrow, Liverpool, Londonderry, Forth and Clyde Areas.

(5) The steaming and bow lights of H.M. Submarines are placed well forward and very low over the water in proportion to the length and tonnage of these vessels. In particular, the forward steaming light may be lower than the side lights and the after steaming light may be well forward of the mid-point of the submarine's length. Overtaking lights are placed very low indeed and may at times be partially obscured by spray and wash. They are invariably lower than the side lights. In the case of nuclear submarines much of the hull between the conning tower, or fin, and the overtaking or anchor light is submerged or awash. While at anchor by night they can, therefore, be confused with two separate vessels of less than 150 feet in length.

(6) The overall arrangement of submarines' lights are therefore unusual and may well give the impression of markedly smaller and shorter vessels than they are. Their vulnerability to collision when proceeding on the surface and the fact that some submarines are nuclear powered dictates particular caution when approaching them. United States Submarines only, are fitted with an amber quick flashing light situated six feet above the after steaming light. This additional light is for use as an aid to identification in narrow waters and areas of dense traffic. It should not be confused with a similar light used by British hovercraft.

Certain Submarines of the Royal Navy will shortly be fitted with quick-flashing amber anti-collision lights. These lights will flash at between 90 and 105 flashes per minute and, due to the configurations of the various classes, will be fitted 3 to 6 feet above or below the steaming light.

Sunken Submarine

A bottomed submarine, unable to surface, will try to indicate her position by the following methods:

(a) *Releasing an Indicator Buoy.* The cylindrical buoy, painted with high visibility paint called "International Orange", has a light which flashes twice every second in the centre of the top and there is also a ring of "cat's-eye" reflectors round the top. The buoy carries a vertical whip aerial and has marked on it a serial number which is affixed under the word "Forward" or "Aft" to denote which of the buoys on the submarine has been released. They are also fitted with an automatic transmitting radio which operates on 4,340 kc./s and transmits the serial number (three times);

S.O.S. (six times); SUBSUNK (three times) and Long Mark (once). Message is transmitted twice during a period of four minutes followed by a six-minute silence period.

(b) *Firing yellow or white smoke candles,* on hearing the approach of surface vessels. The yellow candles burn for about five minutes and the white for about fifteen minutes.

(c) Pumping out oil.

(d) Blowing out air.

The sighting of such a buoy should be reported immediately by the quickest available means and the report should include the number of the buoy. Any vessel finding such a buoy should stay in the area of the buoy and stand by to pick up survivors. To inform the occupants of the submarine that help is at hand, small charges may be dropped, the echo sounder can be run, or the underwater section of your hull may be banged on with a hammer.

Sonobuoys are dropped by aircraft to detect submerged submarines and must not be confused with submarine indicator buoys. If in doubt, approach and check that it is in fact an indicator buoy before reporting it.

Flexible Oil Barges

The attention of Mariners is drawn to the development of towed flexible oil barges now commonly known as "DRACONES". These barges consist of a sausage-shaped envelope of strong woven nylon fabric coated with synthetic rubber. Since they float by reason of the buoyancy of their cargo, usually oil and petroleum products, they are almost entirely submerged. A typical tow would be 200 feet long on a 100-fathom tow line.

Following a recent recommendation made by I.M.C.O. (Intergovernmental Maritime Consultative Organization) the United Kingdom has decided that the signals to be displayed by "Dracones" and the vessels towing them will be changed. The signals promulgated for "Dracones" in Admiralty Notices to Mariners 2265(T) of 1963 will not be applicable as from 1st December, 1964.

With effect from 1st December, 1964, the signals which will be displayed are as follows:

By Day — The vessel towing will exhibit, where it can best be seen, a black diamond shape. The Dracone, or the last Dracone if there is more than one in line will tow a float also exhibiting a black diamond shape, thus indicating the extremity of the tow.

By night– The vessel towing will exhibit, in addition to the normal towing lights, where it can best be seen, an all round blue light visible at a distance of at least two miles, and the float towed by the Dracone, or the last Dracone if more than one is in line, will exhibit an all round white light visible at a distance of at least two miles.

Air Cushion Craft (Hovercraft)

Hovercraft can be wholly or partially supported by a self-generated air cushion underneath the hull. Present-day craft can proceed fully waterborne, partially airborne but with keels or sidewalls remaining in the water, or fully airborne a few inches off the water.

In the first two cases the craft have similar characteristics. to shallow draft vessels. In the last case they can operate over land or water and are capable of high speeds up to 80 knots and are windborne (i.e. susceptible to wind effects). In an emergency all Hovercraft can stop extremely quickly by alighting on the water.

Because of the capabilities of the Hovercraft outlined above, they shall, when at sea, in general keep well clear of all vessels and avoid impeding their navigation. In circumstances, however, where they are unable to take timely steps to keep clear of vessels, or where risk of collision exists, they will proceed at a moderate speed having regard to the existing circumstances and comply with the International Regulations for Preventing Collisions at Sea as if they were powerdriven vessels.

Because of the noise of operation of some types of Hovercraft, sound signals may not be given by them, and they may not be able to hear sound signals made by ships.

In addition to the general conditions set out above, Hovercraft will also observe such other conditions in specific areas as may be promulgated in local Notices to Mariners.

Deep Draught Vessels

In deep water channels where they are unable to manoeuvre without risk of grounding very large ships should show the following signals so that they can be recognised and avoided by smaller craft:

By day; a black cylinder, 1m. long and ½m. in diameter, displayed where it can best be seen.

By night; three red lights vertically disposed 2m. apart visible all round the horizon at a distance of two miles. These are in addition to the normal steaming lights.

Note: These signals in no way absolve a vessel from acting in accordance with the collision regulations, or with local by-laws.

Identification Signal

When operating other than as a displacement vessel, air cushion craft (Hovercraft) operating off the coasts of the United Kingdom will display, in addition to the lights required by the International Regulations for Preventing Collisions at Sea, an amber flashing light, flashing at approximately 60 times per minute and of such a character as to be visible all round the horizon at a distance of at least 5 miles.

This light will be exhibited in all weathers from sunset to sunrise. It may also be exhibited from sunrise to sunset in restricted visibility or in other circumstances when it is deemed necessary.

Attention is drawn to paragraph 6 of Admiralty Notices to Mariners 8/64 which indicates that an orange quick flashing light may be displayed by United States submarines when on the surface at night, as an aid to identification in narrow waters and areas with dense traffic.

CHAPTER 18

Customs Procedure

Yachts and other private craft sailing for, and returning from, overseas (including the Channel Islands and the Republic of Ireland) are subject in general to the same regulations as other foreign-going ships. The Commissioners of Customs and Excise do not, however wish to impose any undue restriction upon the movement of private craft and are therefore prepared to relax certain of the normal controls. The essential requirements are set out below.

Warning.—A yacht or other private craft is liable to Customs search in the same way as any other ship. Any craft carrying prohibited or uncustomed goods is liable to forfeiture and the persons concerned to heavy penalties.

DEPARTURES

Licences

1. (a) *General*—The Small Craft Regulations, 1953, require the licensing of any vessel of less than 40 tons register which it is intended shall proceed outside a distance of:—

(i) twelve nautical miles seaward from that part of the coast of England which is between North Foreland and Beachy Head, or

(ii) thirty-six nautical miles seaward from any other part of the coast of the United Kingdom.

(b) *Exemption from licensing*—Yachts and similar pleasure craft are exempt from these licensing requirements provided the Commissioners are satisfied the vessel is used exclusively for pleasure by the owner.

In addition to actual use by the owner himself, the qualification about exclusive use for pleasure by the owner may be taken to cover use, provided this is without remuneration to the owner, by:—

(i) anyone acting under the direction of the owner, or

(ii) with the consent of the owner, dependent members of the owner's family or his bona fide guests.

whether or not the owner is actually on board at the time. A vessel will not be regarded as being used exclusively for pleasure by the owner if it is hired, chartered or operated in any way other than as provided above.

The term "owner" may be taken to include any part-owner whose interest is properly registered or, in the case of a vessel owned by a properly constituted yacht club and hired out to club members, any member of the club. "Tons register" means the vessel's net tonnage ascertained according to the regulations of the Merchant Shipping Acts, 1894 to 1965.

(c) *Licence Applications*—Application for a licence should be made, in writing, by the owner or the person under whose direction the vessel will be used to the Collector of Customs and Excise for the place at which it is usually based or from which it is intended to operate. The application should contain:—

(i) particulars of the vessel;

(a) name,

(b) how propelled,

(c) if registered, number, year and port of registry,

(d) tons register,

(e) name of master,

(f) name and address of owner;

(ii) name and address of person under whose direction the vessel will be used;

(iii) period for which licence is required;

(iv) purpose for which licence is required;

and should be signed by the applicant.

A licence will be issued without payment for such period as the circumstances require (e.g., for the voyage or for the period of hire or charter) but will lapse automatically should there be any change in the ownership of the craft. A lapsed licence is to be surrendered to the Collector from whom it was obtained, and if the new owner requires another licence a fresh application should be made. The licence must always be carried on board and shown, on request, to any Customs Officer.

Notice of intended departure

2. The date of intended departure from the United Kingdom should be notified, as far in advance as possible, to the Customs official *at the Customs Office nearest to the place of departure.* The name, place of registration and tonnage of the vessel, the intended destination and the name of the owner or master should also be given.

Shipment of stores

3. In general no restriction is placed upon the shipment of reasonable quantities of foodstuffs, fuel and other stores unless they are goods on which duty is chargeable or upon which drawback is claimed. The shipment of duty-free stores is normally restricted to vessels of 40 tons net register or more but, subject to certain conditions, such stores may be shipped on yachts or other private craft of less than 40 tons register departing for a port beyond certain limits (viz. south of Brest or north of the north bank of the Elbe). Prior application is necessary and information about the procedure for shipping stores may be obtained at any Custom House. If shipment of duty-free stores, or the reshipment of surplus duty-free stores previously landed, is authorised the vessel must be entered outwards and cleared at the Custom House.

Cargo

4. No goods other than bona fide stores may be shipped unless all the relative Customs, export licensing and other requirements are met.

Immigration Regulations

5. All persons not of British nationality need the permission of an Immigration Officer to embark. It is the responsibility of the owner or master of the vessel to make sure that permission is obtained.

ARRIVALS

Notification of arrival

6. All private craft arriving from abroad, including those from the Channel Islands and the Republic of Ireland, whether dutiable stores are carried on board or not, are subject to Customs, Public Health and Home Office (Immigration Department) requirements. Accordingly arrival must be notified by exhibiting the appropriate signal in a conspicuous position on the craft until such time as it is boarded by a Customs Officer. The signals are:—

(a) by day-the international code flag "Q".

(b) by night—a red light over a white light, the lights being not more than six feet apart.

When cruising in home waters with dutiable stores under seal the ensign with a knot tied in it should be hoisted on arrival at any British port.

Customs duty on yachts and other private craft

7. Yachts and other private craft of less than 80 tons gross arriving in the United Kingdom from abroad are all potentially liable to Customs duty; but vessels built in the United Kingdom and other vessels shown to have previously departed from the United Kingdom (except vessels temporarily imported by visitors from abroad) are usually re-admissible free of duty. Duty may, however, be chargeable on any repairs or alterations (other than ordinary running repairs) carried out abroad and particulars of any such repairs and alterations must be declared in Section B of Form C.142A (see paragraph 8).

The owner or master of a British yacht, etc. returning to the United Kingdom after a trip abroad must therefore, when so required, satisfy the Customs officer on arrival as to the title of the vessel to free re-admission.

In order to facilitate the identification of British yachts, etc., of less than 80 tons gross returning from temporary visits abroad, owners are advised to enter their vessels with the Customs prior to departure from home waters on Form X.S.29 in duplicate, and to obtain a certificate thereon from the Customs Officer. The duplicate Form X.S.29 may be retained for use as a Customs Pass to cover further temporary exits and re-entries. Copies of the form may be obtained from the nearest Custom House.

If a person resident in the United Kingdom buys a yacht or other private craft while abroad or if a yacht or other private craft is brought to this country on or for sale, or for hire, to anyone in the United Kingdom, the vessel must be produced to the Customs officer on arrival and full details of the transaction (actual or prospective) declared.

British registration of a vessel does not in itself establish title to duty-free admission into the United Kingdom.

Importation of goods

8. Goods, including stores, brought in a private craft, whether obtained abroad or shipped from bond, and all hydrocarbon oils, irrespective of origin, must be declared to the Customs Officer. Declaration Forms C.142 and C.142A, which are used for this purpose, may be obtained from any Custom House. Many goods are subject to licensing control and are liable to duty and/or Purchase Tax. Failure to declare goods may render the persons concerned liable to heavy penalties.

Stores and equipment

9. Dutiable stores may not be used duty-free while cruising in home waters. If however, the owner of a private craft finds it necessary for the victualling of his vessel when so cruising to use sealed dutiable stores, the Commissioners will raise no objection provided their officers are informed on arrival at the next port of call (the appropriate signal being hoisted) and all duties due on the quantities consumed are paid immediately.

When private craft are laid up any dutiable stores should normally be cleared on payment of duty but, exceptionally, arrangements may be made either for the temporary deposit in the Queen's Warehouse or for their retention on board under Customs seal for future use. In this case the owner or master is required to give suitable security.

Duty may be charged on any equipment of the craft, wholly or partly of foreign origin, which is landed in the United Kingdom.

Immigration Regulations

10. All persons who are not of British nationality, and also Commonwealth citizens to whom Section 1 of the Commonwealth Immigrants Act applies, need the permission of an Immigration Officer to land when they arrive from outside the United Kingdom, the Channel Islands, the Isle of Man or the Republic of Ireland. It is the responsibility of the owner or master to make sure that permission is obtained.

Currency Regulations

11. There is no restriction on the importation of any currency notes, including United Kingdom bank notes.

The above information is produced by permission of H.M. Customs and Excise.

CHAPTER 19

H.M. Coastguard

H.M. Coastguard is the only co-ordinater of civilian S.A.R. (Search and Rescue) in the United Kingdom. There are some 180 centres placed around our shores.

Coastguards keep watch, both visual and radio-listening, particularly during bad weather, from modern stations and lookouts which are strategically sited along our coastline. Although their overall duties are numerous, their main task is to help ships and other craft which get into difficulties. With the ever-increasing numbers of pleasure craft sailing in both coastal and short-sea waters, these services are in demand more than ever before.

As soon as he sees a distress flare or is otherwise alerted, e.g., by a Mayday or S.O.S. signal from a Post Office Radio Station with which Department there is complete liaison, a fully-trained Coastguard can take immediate action. On his own responsibility, he must decide whether the rescue operation can be handled by local resources or that a full-scale air-sea rescue is called for. He must, as deemed necessary, alert R.N.L.I. lifeboats or inshore rescue craft; R.A.F. or R.N. helicopters; breeches buoy apparatus; etc.

Local Cruises and Coastal Passages. The reporting systems now in use are designed to provide the Coastguard with the best possible information to enable them to initiate a S.A.R. operation in the quickest and most effective manner possible. Form CG66A covering Local Surveillance and Form CG66B, Passage Surveillance (Pink Form to Coastguard, White Form to Agent) are detailed on page 217 together with an explanation on the use of each. **This Service is Free.**

Note. These services must have the full co-operation of the yachtsmen and they must report Arrivals and Departures to the nearest Coastguard Station. Also any change in the proposed voyage.

Yachts proceeding to French Channel ports can take advantage of the scheme and they must report their Arrival/ Departure to the French authorities. Obviously, on cross channel passages and out-of-sight of land, such craft cannot be kept under visual surveillance.

Addresses and telephone numbers of H. M. Coastguard Rescue Headquarters Stations:

Lerwick, Shetland (76)
Kirkwall, Orkney (3268)
Wick, Caithness (2332)
Stornoway, Isle of Lewis (13)
Peterhead, Aberdeenshire (3563)
Aberdeen (23312)
Fifeness, Fife (Crail 236)
Seahouses, Northumberland (274)
Tynemouth, Northumberland (NorthShields 72691)
Whitby, Yorkshire (2107)
Flamborough Head, Yorkshire (Flamborough 203)
Cromer, Norfolk (2507)
Gorleston, Norfolk (Great Yarmouth 63444)
Walton-on-Naze, Essex (Frinton-on-Sea 5518)
Deal, Kent (3232)
Shoreham-by-Sea, Sussex (2226)
Needles, Isel of Wight (Freshwater 2265)
Wyke Regis, Dorset (Weymouth 4105)
Brixham, Devon (2156)
Hartland, Devon (235)
Falmouth, Cornwall (314481)
St. Just, Cornwall (657)
Mumbles, Glamorgan (Swansea 66534)
St. Anne's, Pembrokeshire (Dale 218)
Holyhead, Anglesey (2051)
Formby, Liverpool, Lancashire (Formby 72903)
Portpatrick, Wigtownshire (209)
Southend, Campbeltown, Argyll (Southend 232)
Ballycastle, Co. Antrim, N. Ireland (226)
Bangor, Co. Down, N. Ireland (Groomsport 284)
Ramsey, Isle of Man (3255)

If you own, or hire, a yacht or boat you should complete Card CG 66A and send it to the Coastguard. This will ensure that the details of your craft and safety equipment are immediately available should you ever be in distress. These cards are available from all Coastguard Stations, yacht clubs, harbour masters, etc.

CG 66 A LOCAL SURVEILLANCE	Issuing Authority	Club or Association	Name of Craft
Type of Craft		Usual base, mooring and activity	
Length			
Colours: Hull Topsides Sail		Usual local operating area(s)	
Sail Number			
Special identification features		Is the following equipment carried? Anchor Lights Compass Life jackets	
Speed and endurance under power		Owners name address and telephone No.	
Life raft type and Serial No.			
Radio HF/MF VHF			
Distress signals		Date	Signature
For official use only			

For coastal passages or a long voyage, you should complete card CG 66B, and send it to the Coastguard. A copy of this card should be given to a relative or friend ashore who can alert the Coastguard if there is reason to believe that you are overdue. By dispatching further cards during your voyage, you will keep both the Coastguard and your relative or friend up to date with your progress.

CG 66B PASSAGE SURVEILLANCE	Issuing Authority	Master and Club or Association		Name of Craft
Type of Craft		PASSAGE INFORMATION		
Length		PORT	Estimated Date and Time	
			Arrival	Departure
Colours: Hull Topsides Sail				
Sail Number		Further Intentions		
Special Identification features				
Speed and endurance under power		Name Address and Telephone number of Agent with whom duplicate has been lodged		
Life raft type and Serial No.				
Radio HF/MF VHF				
Distress signals				
No. of persons on board		Date	Signature	
For official use only				

CHAPTER 20

Relevant Tables

COMPASS CONVERSIONS

NORTH
000°
360°

Points		3 figure
N	-	360°
N x W	-	$348\frac{3}{4}$°
NNW	-	$337\frac{1}{2}$°
NW x N	-	$326\frac{1}{4}$°
NW	-	315°
NW x W	-	$303\frac{3}{4}$°
WNW	-	$292\frac{1}{2}$°
W x N	-	$281\frac{1}{4}$°
W	-	270°

Quadrantal		3 figure	Quadrantal		3 figure
N	-	360°	N	-	000°
N 5° W	-	355°	N 5° E	-	005°
N 10° W	-	350°	N 10° E	-	010°
N 15° W	-	345°	N 15° E	-	015°
N 20° W	-	340°	N 20° E	-	020°
N 25° W	-	335°	N 25° E	-	025°
N 30° W	-	330°	N 30° E	-	030°
N 35° W	-	325°	N 35° E	-	035°
N 40° W	-	320°	N 40° E	-	040°
N 45° W	-	315°	N 45° E	-	045°
N 50° W	-	310°	N 50° E	-	050°
N 55° W	-	305°	N 55° E	-	055°
N 60° W	-	300°	N 60° E	-	060°
N 65° W	-	295°	N 65° E	-	065°
N 70° W	-	290°	N 70° E	-	070°
N 75° W	-	285°	N 75° E	-	075°
N 80° W	-	280°	N 80° E	-	080°
N 85° W	-	275°	N 85° E	-	085°
W	-	270°	E	-	090°

Points		3 figure
N	-	000°
N x E	-	$011\frac{1}{4}$°
NNE	-	$022\frac{1}{2}$°
N E x N	-	$033\frac{3}{4}$°
NE	-	045°
N E x E	-	$056\frac{1}{4}$°
ENE	-	$067\frac{1}{2}$°
E x N	-	$078\frac{3}{4}$°
E	-	090°

WEST 270°

EAST 090°

Points		3 figure
W	-	270°
W x S	-	$258\frac{3}{4}$°
WSW	-	$247\frac{1}{2}$°
SW x W	-	$236\frac{1}{4}$°
SW	-	225°
SW x S	-	$213\frac{3}{4}$°
SSW	-	$202\frac{1}{2}$°
S x W	-	$191\frac{1}{4}$°
S	-	180°

Quadrantal		3 figure	Quadrantal		3 figure
W	-	270°	E	-	090°
S 85° W	-	265°	S 85° E	-	095°
S 80° W	-	260°	S 80° E	-	100°
S 75° W	-	255°	S 75° E	-	105°
S 70° W	-	250°	S 70° E	-	110°
S 65° W	-	245°	S 65° E	-	115°
S 60° W	-	240°	S 60° E	-	120°
S 55° W	-	235°	S 55° E	-	125°
S 50° W	-	230°	S 50° E	-	130°
S 45° W	-	225°	S 45° E	-	135°
S 40° W	-	220°	S 40° E	-	140°
S 35° W	-	215°	S 35° E	-	145°
S 30° W	-	210°	S 30° E	-	150°
S 25° W	-	205°	S 25° E	-	155°
S 20° W	-	200°	S 20° E	-	160°
S 15° W	-	195°	S 15° E	-	165°
S 10° W	-	190°	S 10° E	-	170°
S 5° W	-	185°	S 5° E	-	175°
S	-	180°	S	-	180°

Points		3 figure
E	-	090°
E x S	-	$101\frac{1}{4}$°
ESE	-	$112\frac{1}{2}$°
SE x E	-	$123\frac{3}{4}$°
SE	-	135°
SE x S	-	$146\frac{1}{4}$°
SSE	-	$157\frac{1}{2}$°
S x E	-	$168\frac{3}{4}$°
S	-	180°

SOUTH
180°

DISTANCE OFF BY VERTICAL ANGLE

dist. in miles	height in metres 10	20	30	40	50	60	70	80	90	100
	vertical angle									
	° ′	° ′	° ′	° ′	° ′	° ′	° ′	° ′	° ′	° ′
0.1	3 05	6 10	9 12	12 11	15 06	17 56	20 42	23 21	25 54	28 21
0.2	1 33	3 05	4 38	6 10	7 41	9 12	10 42	12 11	13 39	15 06
0.3	1 02	2 04	3 05	4 07	5 08	6 10	7 11	8 11	9 12	10 12
0.4	0 46	1 33	2 19	3 05	3 52	4 38	5 24	6 10	6 55	7 41
0.5	0 37	1 14	1 51	2 28	3 05	3 42	4 19	4 56	5 33	6 10
0.6	0 31	1 02	1 33	2 04	2 34	3 05	3 36	4 07	4 38	5 08
0.7	0 27	0 53	1 19	1 46	2 12	2 39	3 05	3 32	3 58	4 24
0.8	0 23	0 46	1 10	1 33	1 56	2 19	2 42	3 05	3 28	3 52
0.9	0 21	0 41	1 02	1 22	1 43	2 04	2 24	2 45	3 05	3 26
1.0	0 19	0 37	0 56	1 14	1 33	1 51	2 10	2 28	2 47	3 05
1.1	0 17	0 34	0 51	1 07	1 24	1 41	1 58	2 15	2 32	2 49
1.2	0 15	0 31	0 46	1 02	1 17	1 33	1 48	2 04	2 19	2 34
1.3	0 14	0 29	0 43	0 57	1 11	1 26	1 40	1 54	2 08	2 23
1.4	0 13	0 27	0 40	0 53	1 06	1 19	1 33	1 46	1 59	2 12
1.5	0 12	0 25	0 37	0 49	1 02	1 14	1 27	1 39	1 51	2 04
1.6	0 12	0 23	0 35	0 46	0 58	1 10	1 21	1 33	1 44	1 56
1.7	0 11	0 22	0 33	0 44	0 55	1 05	1 16	1 27	1 38	1 49
1.8	0 10	0 21	0 31	0 41	0 52	1 02	1 12	1 22	1 33	1 43
1.9	0 10	0 20	0 29	0 39	0 49	0 59	1 08	1 18	1 28	1 38
2.0	0 09	0 19	0 28	0 37	0 46	0 56	1 05	1 14	1 23	1 33
2.1	0 09	0 18	0 27	0 35	0 44	0 53	1 02	1 11	1 19	1 28
2.2	0 08	0 17	0 25	0 34	0 42	0 51	0 59	1 07	1 16	1 24
2.3	0 08	0 16	0 24	0 32	0 40	0 48	0 56	1 05	1 13	1 21
2.4	0 08	0 15	0 23	0 31	0 39	0 46	0 54	1 02	1 10	1 17
2.5	0 07	0 15	0 22	0 30	0 37	0 45	0 52	0 59	1 07	1 14
2.6	0 07	0 14	0 21	0 29	0 36	0 43	0 50	0 57	1 04	1 11
2.7	0 07	0 14	0 21	0 27	0 34	0 41	0 48	0 55	1 02	1 09
2.8	0 07	0 13	0 20	0 27	0 33	0 40	0 46	0 53	1 00	1 06
2.9	0 06	0 13	0 19	0 26	0 32	0 38	0 45	0 51	0 58	1 04
3.0	0 06	0 12	0 19	0 25	0 31	0 37	0 43	0 49	0 56	1 02
3.1	0 06	0 12	0 18	0 24	0 30	0 36	0 42	0 48	0 54	1 00
3.2	0 06	0 12	0 17	0 23	0 29	0 35	0 41	0 46	0 52	0 58
3.3	0 06	0 11	0 17	0 22	0 28	0 34	0 39	0 45	0 51	0 56
3.4	0 05	0 11	0 16	0 22	0 27	0 33	0 38	0 44	0 49	0 55
3.5	0 05	0 11	0 16	0 21	0 27	0 32	0 37	0 42	0 48	0 53
3.6	0 05	0 10	0 15	0 21	0 26	0 31	0 36	0 41	0 46	0 52
3.7	0 05	0 10	0 15	0 20	0 25	0 30	0 35	0 40	0 45	0 50
3.8	0 05	0 10	0 15	0 20	0 24	0 29	0 34	0 39	0 44	0 49
3.9	0 05	0 10	0 14	0 19	0 24	0 29	0 33	0 38	0 43	0 48
4.0	0 05	0 09	0 14	0 19	0 23	0 28	0 32	0 37	0 42	0 46
4.1	0 05	0 09	0 14	0 18	0 23	0 27	0 32	0 36	0 41	0 45
4.2	0 04	0 09	0 13	0 18	0 22	0 27	0 31	0 35	0 40	0 44
4.3	0 04	0 09	0 13	0 17	0 22	0 26	0 30	0 35	0 39	0 43
4.4	0 04	0 08	0 13	0 17	0 21	0 25	0 30	0 34	0 38	0 42
4.5	0 04	0 08	0 12	0 16	0 21	0 24	0 29	0 33	0 37	0 41
4.6	0 04	0 08	0 12	0 16	0 20	0 24	0 28	0 32	0 36	0 40
4.7	0 04	0 08	0 12	0 16	0 20	0 24	0 28	0 32	0 36	0 39
4.8	0 04	0 08	0 12	0 15	0 19	0 23	0 27	0 31	0 35	0 39
4.9	0 04	0 08	0 11	0 15	0 19	0 23	0 27	0 30	0 34	0 38
5.0	0 04	0 07	0 11	0 15	0 19	0 22	0 26	0 30	0 33	0 37
	32.8	65.6	98.4	131.2	164.0	196.8	229.7	262.5	295.3	328.1
	height in feet									

DISTANCE OF THE SEA HORIZON & FEET/METRE CONVERSIONS

height in feet	metres	dist. miles	height in feet	metres	dist. miles
3.3	1	2.08	167.3	51	14.9
6.6	2	2.95	170.6	52	15.0
9.8	3	3.60	173.9	53	15.1
13.1	4	4.17	177.2	54	15.3
16.4	5	4.66	180.4	55	15.4
19.7	6	5.10	183.7	56	15.6
23.0	7	5.51	187.0	57	15.7
26.2	8	5.88	190.3	58	15.8
29.5	9	6.24	193.6	59	16.0
32.8	10	6.58	196.8	60	16.1
36.1	11	6.91	200.1	61	16.2
39.4	12	7.21	203.4	62	16.4
42.7	13	7.51	206.7	63	16.5
45.9	14	7.78	210.0	64	16.6
49.2	15	8.06	213.3	65	16.8
52.5	16	8.32	216.5	66	16.9
55.8	17	8.58	219.8	67	17.0
59.1	18	8.83	223.1	68	17.2
62.3	19	9.05	226.4	69	17.3
65.6	20	9.30	229.7	70	17.4
68.9	21	9.53	232.9	71	17.5
72.2	22	9.75	236.2	72	17.7
75.5	23	9.98	239.5	73	17.8
78.7	24	10.18	242.8	74	17.9
82.0	25	10.40	246.1	75	18.0
85.3	26	10.61	249.3	76	18.2
88.6	27	10.81	252.6	77	18.3
91.9	28	11.00	255.9	78	18.4
95.1	29	11.20	259.2	79	18.5
98.4	30	11.39	262.5	80	18.6
101.7	31	11.6	265.7	81	18.8
105.0	32	11.8	269.0	82	18.9
108.3	33	11.9	272.3	83	19.0
111.5	34	12.1	275.6	84	19.1
114.8	35	12.3	278.9	85	19.2
118.1	36	12.5	282.1	86	19.3
121.4	37	12.7	285.4	87	19.4
124.7	38	12.8	288.7	88	19.5
128.0	39	13.0	292.0	89	19.7
131.2	40	13.2	295.3	90	19.8
134.5	41	13.3	298.6	91	19.9
137.8	42	13.5	301.8	92	20.0
141.1	43	13.7	305.1	93	20.1
144.4	44	13.8	308.4	94	20.2
147.6	45	14.0	311.7	95	20.3
150.9	46	14.1	315.0	96	20.4
154.2	47	14.2	318.2	97	20.5
157.5	48	14.4	321.5	98	20.6
160.8	49	14.5	324.8	99	20.7
164.0	50	14.7	328.1	100	20.8

height in metres	feet	dist. miles	height in metres	feet	dist. miles
0.30	1	1.15	15.54	51	8.20
0.61	2	1.62	15.85	52	8.28
0.91	3	1.99	16.15	53	8.36
1.22	4	2.30	16.46	54	8.44
1.52	5	2.57	16.76	55	8.52
1.83	6	2.81	17.07	56	8.59
2.13	7	3.04	17.37	57	8.67
2.44	8	3.25	17.68	58	8.74
2.74	9	3.45	17.98	59	8.82
3.05	10	3.63	18.29	60	8.89
3.35	11	3.81	18.59	61	8.97
3.66	12	3.98	18.90	62	9.03
3.96	13	4.14	19.20	63	9.11
4.27	14	4.30	19.51	64	9.19
4.57	15	4.45	19.81	65	9.26
4.88	16	4.60	20.12	66	9.33
5.18	17	4.73	20.42	67	9.40
5.49	18	4.87	20.73	68	9.47
5.79	19	5.01	21.03	69	9.54
6.10	20	5.14	21.34	70	9.61
6.40	21	5.26	21.64	71	9.67
6.71	22	5.39	21.94	72	9.74
7.01	23	5.51	22.25	73	9.81
7.31	24	5.62	22.55	74	9.88
7.62	25	5.74	22.86	75	9.94
7.92	26	5.86	23.16	76	10.01
8.23	27	5.97	23.47	77	10.07
8.53	28	6.08	23.77	78	10.14
8.84	29	6.18	24.08	79	10.20
9.14	30	6.30	24.38	80	10.27
9.45	31	6.40	24.69	81	10.33
9.75	32	6.50	24.99	82	10.40
10.06	33	6.60	25.30	83	10.46
10.36	34	6.70	25.60	84	10.52
10.67	35	6.80	25.91	85	10.59
10.97	36	6.90	26.21	86	10.65
11.28	37	6.99	26.52	87	10.71
11.58	38	7.09	26.82	88	10.77
11.89	39	7.17	27.13	89	10.83
12.19	40	7.27	27.43	90	10.89
12.50	41	7.36	27.74	91	10.95
12.80	42	7.44	28.04	92	11.01
13.11	43	7.54	28.35	93	11.07
13.41	44	7.62	28.65	94	11.13
13.72	45	7.70	28.96	95	11.19
14.02	46	7.79	29.26	96	11.25
14.33	47	7.88	29.56	97	11.31
14.63	48	7.96	29.87	98	11.37
14.93	49	8.04	30.17	99	11.42
15.24	50	8.12	30.48	100	11.48

SPEED — TIME — DISTANCE TABLE

time in minutes	speed in knots 0.5	1.0	1.5	2.0	2.5	3.0	3.5	4.0	4.5	5.0	5.5	6.0
	distance in nautical miles											
1	0.01	0.02	0.03	0.03	0.04	0.05	0.06	0.07	0.08	0.08	0.09	0.10
2	0.02	0.03	0.05	0.07	0.08	0.10	0.12	0.13	0.15	0.17	0.18	0.20
3	0.03	0.05	0.08	0.10	0.13	0.15	0.18	0.20	0.23	0.25	0.28	0.30
4	0.03	0.07	0.10	0.13	0.17	0.20	0.23	0.27	0.30	0.33	0.37	0.40
5	0.04	0.08	0.13	0.17	0.21	0.25	0.29	0.33	0.38	0.42	0.46	0.50
6	0.05	0.10	0.15	0.20	0.25	0.30	0.35	0.40	0.45	0.50	0.55	0.60
7	0.06	0.12	0.18	0.23	0.29	0.35	0.41	0.47	0.53	0.58	0.64	0.70
8	0.07	0.13	0.20	0.27	0.33	0.40	0.47	0.53	0.60	0.67	0.73	0.80
9	0.08	0.15	0.23	0.30	0.38	0.45	0.53	0.60	0.68	0.75	0.83	0.90
10	0.08	0.17	0.25	0.33	0.42	0.50	0.58	0.67	0.75	0.83	0.92	1.00
11	0.09	0.18	0.28	0.37	0.46	0.55	0.64	0.73	0.83	0.92	1.01	1.10
12	0.10	0.20	0.30	0.40	0.50	0.60	0.70	0.80	0.90	1.00	1.10	1.20
13	0.11	0.22	0.33	0.43	0.54	0.65	0.76	0.87	0.98	1.08	1.19	1.30
14	0.12	0.23	0.35	0.47	0.58	0.70	0.82	0.93	1.05	1.17	1.28	1.40
15	0.13	0.25	0.38	0.50	0.63	0.75	0.88	1.00	1.13	1.25	1.38	1.50
16	0.13	0.27	0.40	0.53	0.67	0.80	0.93	1.07	1.20	1.33	1.47	1.60
17	0.14	0.28	0.43	0.57	0.71	0.85	0.99	1.13	1.28	1.42	1.56	1.70
18	0.15	0.30	0.45	0.60	0.75	0.90	1.05	1.20	1.35	1.50	1.65	1.80
19	0.16	0.32	0.48	0.63	0.79	0.95	1.11	1.27	1.43	1.58	1.74	1.90
20	0.17	0.33	0.50	0.67	0.83	1.00	1.17	1.33	1.50	1.67	1.83	2.00
21	0.18	0.35	0.53	0.70	0.88	1.05	1.23	1.40	1.58	1.75	1.93	2.10
22	0.18	0.37	0.55	0.73	0.92	1.10	1.28	1.47	1.65	1.83	2.02	2.20
23	0.19	0.38	0.58	0.77	0.96	1.15	1.34	1.53	1.73	1.92	2.11	2.30
24	0.20	0.40	0.60	0.80	1.00	1.20	1.40	1.60	1.80	2.00	2.20	2.40
25	0.21	0.42	0.63	0.83	1.04	1.25	1.46	1.67	1.88	2.08	2.29	2.50
26	0.22	0.43	0.65	0.87	1.08	1.30	1.52	1.73	1.95	2.17	2.38	2.60
27	0.23	0.45	0.68	0.90	1.13	1.35	1.58	1.80	2.03	2.25	2.48	2.70
28	0.23	0.47	0.70	0.93	1.17	1.40	1.63	1.87	2.10	2.34	2.57	2.80
29	0.24	0.48	0.73	0.97	1.21	1.45	1.69	1.93	2.18	2.42	2.66	2.90
30	0.25	0.50	0.75	1.00	1.25	1.50	1.75	2.00	2.25	2.50	2.75	3.00
31	0.26	0.52	0.78	1.03	1.29	1.55	1.81	2.07	2.33	2.58	2.84	3.10
32	0.27	0.53	0.80	1.07	1.33	1.60	1.87	2.13	2.40	2.67	2.93	3.20
33	0.28	0.55	0.83	1.10	1.38	1.65	1.93	2.20	2.48	2.75	3.03	3.30
34	0.28	0.57	0.85	1.13	1.42	1.70	1.98	2.27	2.55	2.83	3.12	3.40
35	0.29	0.58	0.88	1.17	1.46	1.75	2.04	2.33	2.63	2.92	3.21	3.50
36	0.30	0.60	0.90	1.20	1.50	1.80	2.10	2.40	2.70	3.00	3.30	3.60
37	0.31	0.62	0.93	1.23	1.54	1.85	2.16	2.47	2.78	3.08	3.39	3.70
38	0.32	0.63	0.95	1.27	1.58	1.90	2.22	2.53	2.85	3.17	3.48	3.80
39	0.33	0.65	0.98	1.30	1.63	1.95	2.27	2.60	2.93	3.25	3.58	3.90
40	0.33	0.67	1.00	1.33	1.67	2.00	2.33	2.67	3.00	3.33	3.67	4.00
41	0.34	0.68	1.03	1.37	1.71	2.05	2.39	2.73	3.08	3.42	3.76	4.10
42	0.35	0.70	1.05	1.40	1.75	2.10	2.45	2.80	3.15	3.50	3.85	4.20
43	0.36	0.72	1.08	1.43	1.79	2.15	2.51	2.87	3.23	3.58	3.94	4.30
44	0.37	0.73	1.10	1.47	1.83	2.20	2.57	2.93	3.30	3.67	4.03	4.40
45	0.38	0.75	1.13	1.50	1.88	2.25	2.62	3.00	3.38	3.75	4.13	4.50
46	0.38	0.77	1.15	1.53	1.92	2.30	2.68	3.07	3.45	3.84	4.22	4.60
47	0.39	0.78	1.18	1.57	1.96	2.35	2.74	3.13	3.53	3.92	4.31	4.70
48	0.40	0.80	1.20	1.60	2.00	2.40	2.80	3.20	3.60	4.00	4.40	4.80
49	0.41	0.82	1.23	1.63	2.04	2.45	2.00	3.27	3.68	1.08	1.10	1.00
50	0.42	0.83	1.25	1.67	2.08	2.50	2.92	3.33	3.75	4.17	4.58	5.00
51	0.43	0.85	1.28	1.70	2.12	2.55	2.98	3.40	3.83	4.25	4.68	5.10
52	0.43	0.87	1.30	1.73	2.17	2.60	3.03	3.47	3.90	4.33	4.77	5.20
53	0.44	0.88	1.33	1.77	2.21	2.65	3.09	3.53	3.98	4.42	4.86	5.30
54	0.45	0.90	1.35	1.80	2.25	2.70	3.15	3.60	4.05	4.50	4.95	5.40
55	0.46	0.92	1.38	1.83	2.29	2.75	3.21	3.67	4.13	4.58	5.04	5.50
56	0.47	0.93	1.40	1.87	2.33	2.80	3.27	3.73	4.20	4.67	5.13	5.60
57	0.48	0.95	1.43	1.90	2.38	2.85	3.32	3.80	4.28	4.75	5.23	5.70
58	0.48	0.97	1.45	1.93	2.42	2.90	3.38	3.87	4.35	4.83	5.32	5.80
59	0.49	0.98	1.48	1.97	2.46	2.95	3.44	3.93	4.43	4.92	5.41	5.90
60	0.50	1.00	1.50	2.00	2.50	3.00	3.50	4.00	4.50	5.00	5.50	6.00

SPEED — TIME — DISTANCE TABLE

time in minutes	speed in knots												
	6.5	7.0	7.5	8.0	8.5	9.0	9.5	10.0	11.0	12.0	13.0	14.0	15.0
	distance in nautical miles												
1	0.1	0.1	0.1	0.1	0.1	0.2	0.2	0.2	0.2	0.2	0.2	0.2	0.3
2	0.2	0.2	0.3	0.3	0.3	0.3	0.3	0.3	0.4	0.4	0.4	0.5	0.5
3	0.3	0.4	0.4	0.4	0.4	0.5	0.5	0.5	0.6	0.6	0.7	0.7	0.8
4	0.4	0.5	0.5	0.5	0.6	0.6	0.6	0.7	0.7	0.8	0.9	0.9	1.0
5	0.5	0.6	0.6	0.7	0.7	0.8	0.8	0.8	0.9	1.0	1.1	1.2	1.3
6	0.7	0.7	0.8	0.8	0.9	0.9	1.0	1.0	1.1	1.2	1.3	1.4	1.5
7	0.8	0.8	0.9	0.9	1.0	1.1	1.1	1.2	1.3	1.4	1.5	1.6	1.8
8	0.9	0.9	1.0	1.1	1.1	1.2	1.3	1.3	1.5	1.6	1.7	1.9	2.0
9	1.0	1.1	1.1	1.2	1.3	1.4	1.4	1.5	1.7	1.8	2.0	2.1	2.3
10	1.1	1.2	1.3	1.3	1.4	1.5	1.6	1.7	1.8	2.0	2.2	2.3	2.5
11	1.2	1.3	1.4	1.5	1.6	1.7	1.7	1.8	2.0	2.2	2.4	2.6	2.8
12	1.3	1.4	1.5	1.6	1.7	1.8	1.9	2.0	2.2	2.4	2.6	2.8	3.0
13	1.4	1.5	1.6	1.7	1.8	2.0	2.1	2.2	2.4	2.6	2.8	3.0	3.3
14	1.5	1.6	1.8	1.9	2.0	2.1	2.2	2.3	2.6	2.8	3.0	3.3	3.5
15	1.6	1.8	1.9	2.0	2.1	2.3	2.4	2.5	2.8	3.0	3.3	3.5	3.8
16	1.7	1.9	2.0	2.1	2.3	2.4	2.5	2.7	2.9	3.2	3.5	3.7	4.0
17	1.8	2.0	2.1	2.3	2.4	2.6	2.7	2.8	3.1	3.4	3.7	4.0	4.3
18	2.0	2.1	2.3	2.4	2.6	2.7	2.9	3.0	3.3	3.6	3.9	4.2	4.5
19	2.1	2.2	2.4	2.5	2.7	2.9	3.0	3.2	3.5	3.8	4.1	4.4	4.8
20	2.2	2.3	2.5	2.7	2.8	3.0	3.2	3.3	3.7	4.0	4.3	4.7	5.0
21	2.3	2.5	2.6	2.8	3.0	3.2	3.3	3.5	3.9	4.2	4.6	4.9	5.3
22	2.4	2.6	2.8	2.9	3.1	3.3	3.5	3.7	4.0	4.4	4.8	5.1	5.5
23	2.5	2.7	2.9	3.1	3.3	3.5	3.6	3.8	4.2	4.6	5.0	5.4	5.8
24	2.6	2.8	3.0	3.2	3.4	3.6	3.8	4.0	4.4	4.8	5.2	5.6	6.0
25	2.7	2.9	3.1	3.3	3.5	3.8	4.0	4.2	4.6	5.0	5.4	5.8	6.3
26	2.8	3.0	3.3	3.5	3.7	3.9	4.1	4.3	4.8	5.2	5.6	6.1	6.5
27	2.9	3.2	3.4	3.6	3.8	4.1	4.3	4.5	5.0	5.4	5.9	6.3	6.8
28	3.0	3.3	3.5	3.7	4.0	4.2	4.4	4.7	5.1	5.6	6.1	6.5	7.0
29	3.1	3.4	3.6	3.9	4.1	4.4	4.6	4.8	5.3	5.8	6.3	6.8	7.3
30	3.3	3.5	3.8	4.0	4.3	4.5	4.8	5.0	5.5	6.0	6.5	7.0	7.5
31	3.4	3.6	3.9	4.1	4.4	4.7	4.9	5.2	5.7	6.2	6.7	7.2	7.8
32	3.5	3.7	4.0	4.3	4.5	4.8	5.1	5.3	5.9	6.4	6.9	7.5	8.0
33	3.6	3.9	4.1	4.4	4.7	5.0	5.2	5.5	6.1	6.6	7.2	7.7	8.3
34	3.7	4.0	4.3	4.5	4.8	5.1	5.4	5.7	6.2	6.8	7.4	7.9	8.5
35	3.8	4.1	4.4	4.7	5.0	5.3	5.5	5.8	6.4	7.0	7.6	8.2	8.8
36	3.9	4.2	4.5	4.8	5.1	5.4	5.7	6.0	6.6	7.2	7.8	8.4	9.0
37	4.0	4.3	4.6	4.9	5.2	5.6	5.9	6.2	6.8	7.4	8.0	8.6	9.3
38	4.1	4.4	4.8	5.1	5.4	5.7	6.0	6.3	7.0	7.6	8.2	8.9	9.5
39	4.2	4.6	4.9	5.2	5.5	5.9	6.2	6.5	7.2	7.8	8.5	9.1	9.8
40	4.3	4.7	5.0	5.3	5.7	6.0	6.3	6.7	7.3	8.0	8.7	9.3	10.0
41	4.4	4.8	5.1	5.5	5.8	6.2	6.5	6.8	7.5	8.2	8.9	9.6	10.3
42	4.6	4.9	5.3	5.6	6.0	6.3	6.7	7.0	7.7	8.4	9.1	9.8	10.5
43	4.7	5.0	5.4	5.7	6.1	6.5	6.8	7.2	7.9	8.6	9.3	10.0	10.8
44	4.8	5.1	5.5	5.9	6.2	6.6	7.0	7.3	8.1	8.8	9.5	10.3	11.0
45	4.9	5.3	5.6	6.0	6.4	6.8	7.1	7.5	8.3	9.0	9.8	10.5	11.3
46	5.0	5.4	5.8	6.1	6.5	6.9	7.3	7.7	8.4	9.2	10.0	10.7	11.5
47	5.1	5.5	5.9	6.3	6.7	7.1	7.4	7.8	8.6	9.4	10.2	11.0	11.8
48	5.2	5.6	6.0	6.4	6.8	7.2	7.6	8.0	8.8	9.6	10.4	11.2	12.0
49	5.3	5.7	6.1	6.5	6.9	7.4	7.8	8.2	9.0	9.8	10.6	11.4	12.3
50	5.4	5.8	6.3	6.7	7.1	7.5	7.9	8.3	9.2	10.0	10.8	11.7	12.5
51	5.5	6.0	6.4	6.8	7.2	7.7	8.1	8.5	9.4	10.2	11.1	11.9	12.8
52	5.6	6.1	6.5	6.9	7.4	7.8	8.2	8.7	9.5	10.4	11.3	12.1	13.0
53	5.7	6.2	6.6	7.1	7.5	8.0	8.4	8.8	9.7	10.6	11.5	12.4	13.3
54	5.9	6.3	6.8	7.2	7.7	8.1	8.6	9.0	9.9	10.8	11.7	12.6	13.5
55	6.0	6.4	6.9	7.3	7.8	8.3	8.7	9.2	10.1	11.0	11.9	12.8	13.8
56	6.1	6.5	7.0	7.5	7.9	8.4	8.9	9.3	10.3	11.2	12.1	13.1	14.0
57	6.2	6.7	7.1	7.6	8.1	8.6	9.0	9.5	10.5	11.4	12.4	13.3	14.3
58	6.3	6.8	7.3	7.7	8.2	8.7	9.2	9.7	10.6	11.6	12.6	13.5	14.5
59	6.4	6.9	7.4	7.9	8.4	8.9	9.3	9.8	10.8	11.8	12.8	13.8	14.8
60	6.5	7.0	7.5	8.0	8.5	9.0	9.5	10.0	11.0	12.0	13.0	14.0	15.0

FACTORS FOR CALCULATING **RUNNING FIX** * TO GIVE DISTANCE OFF WHEN ABEAM

ANGLE BETWEEN COURSE MADE GOOD and FIRST BEARING

Change of Bearing	16°	18°	20°	22°	24°	26°	28°	30°	32°	34°	36°	38°	40°	42°	44°	46°	48°	50°
20	.47	.56	.64	.73	.83	.92	1.02	1.12	1.22	1.32	1.43	1.53	1.63	1.73	1.83	1.92	2.02	2.11
22	.45	.53	.61	.69	.78	.87	.96	1.05	1.14	1.23	1.32	1.42	1.52	1.61	1.69	1.78	1.86	1.95
24	.44	.51	.58	.66	.74	.83	.91	.99	1.08	1.17	1.25	1.34	1.42	1.50	1.58	1.66	1.74	1.81
26	.42	.49	.56	.64	.71	.79	.87	.95	1.03	1.11	1.18	1.26	1.34	1.42	1.49	1.56	1.63	1.70
28	.41	.47	.54	.61	.68	.76	.83	.90	.98	1.05	1.13	1.20	1.27	1.35	1.41	1.47	1.54	1.60
30	.40	.46	.52	.59	.66	.73	.80	.87	.94	1.01	1.07	1.14	1.21	1.27	1.34	1.40	1.45	1.51
32	.39	.45	.51	.57	.64	.70	.77	.83	.90	.96	1.03	1.09	1.15	1.21	1.27	1.33	1.38	1.43
34	.38	.44	.49	.56	.62	.68	.74	.80	.87	.93	.99	1.05	1.11	1.16	1.22	1.27	1.32	1.36
36	.37	.43	.48	.54	.60	.66	.72	.78	.84	.89	.95	1.01	1.06	1.11	1.16	1.21	1.26	1.30
38	.36	.42	.47	.53	.58	.64	.70	.75	.81	.86	.92	.97	1.02	1.07	1.12	1.16	1.20	**1.24**
40	.36	.41	.46	.50	.57	.62	.68	.73	.78	.84	.89	.94	.99	1.03	1.08	1.12	1.16	**1.19**
42	.35	.40	.45	.49	.56	.61	.66	.72	.76	.81	.86	.91	.95	.99	1.04	1.07	**1.11**	1.14
44	.34	.39	.44	.48	.54	.59	.64	.69	.74	.79	.83	.88	.92	.96	1.00	**1.04**	1.07	1.10
46	.34	.39	.43	.47	.53	.58	.63	.67	.72	.77	.81	.85	.89	.93	**.97**	1.00	1.03	1.06
48	.33	.38	.43	.47	.52	.57	.61	.66	.70	.75	.79	.83	.86	**.90**	.93	.97	.99	1.02
50	.33	.37	.42	.46	.51	.56	.60	.64	.69	.73	.77	.80	**.84**	.87	.90	.93	.96	.98
52	.32	.37	.41	.45	.50	.54	.59	.63	.67	.71	.75	**.78**	.82	.85	.88	.90	.93	.95
54	.32	.36	.41	.44	.49	.53	.57	.61	.65	.69	**.73**	.76	.79	.82	.85	.88	.90	.92
56	.32	.36	.40	.44	.48	.52	.56	.60	.64	**.67**	.71	.74	.77	.80	.83	.85	.87	.89
58	.31	.35	.39	.44	.47	.51	.56	.59	**.62**	.66	.69	.72	.75	.78	.80	.82	.84	.86
60	.31	.35	.39	.43	.47	.50	.54	**.58**	.61	.64	.67	.70	.73	.76	.78	.80	.82	.83
62	.31	.34	.38	.42	.46	.50	**.53**	.57	.60	.63	.66	.69	.71	.74	.76	.77	.79	.80
64	.30	.34	.38	.42	.45	**.49**	.52	.56	.59	.62	.64	.67	.69	.72	.74	.75	.77	.78
66	.30	.34	.37	.41	**.45**	.48	.51	.54	.57	.60	.63	.65	.68	.70	.71	.73	.74	.75
68	.30	.33	.37	**.40**	.44	.47	.50	.53	.56	.59	.62	.64	.66	.68	.69	.71	.72	.73
70	.29	.33	**.36**	.40	.43	.46	.49	.52	.55	.58	.60	.62	.64	.66	.68	.69	.70	.71
72	.29	**.32**	.36	.39	.43	.46	.49	.51	.54	.57	.59	.61	.63	.64	.66	.67	.68	.68
74	**.29**	.32	.36	.39	.42	.45	.48	.50	.53	.55	.57	.59	.61	.63	.64	.65	.66	.66

Change of Bearing	52°	54°	56°	58°	60°	62°	64°	66°	68°	70°	72°	74°	76°	78°	80°	82°	84°	86°	88°	90°
20	2.19	2.17	2.35	2.43	2.49	2.56	2.61	2.66	2.71	**2.75**	2.78	2.80	2.82	2.83	2.84	2.83	2.82	2.80	2.78	2.75
22	2.02	2.10	2.16	2.23	2.29	2.34	2.39	2.44	**2.48**	2.51	2.53	2.55	2.56	2.57	2.57	2.56	2.55	2.53	2.51	2.48
24	1.88	1.95	2.01	2.06	2.12	2.17	2.21	**2.25**	2.28	2.30	2.33	2.34	2.35	2.35	2.35	2.34	2.33	2.30	2.28	2.25
26	1.76	1.82	1.87	1.92	1.97	2.01	**2.05**	2.08	2.11	2.13	2.15	2.16	2.17	2.17	2.16	2.15	2.13	2.11	2.08	2.05
28	1.65	1.71	1.76	1.80	1.84	**1.88**	1.91	1.94	1.96	1.98	2.00	2.00	2.01	2.00	2.00	1.98	1.96	1.94	1.91	1.88
30	1.56	1.61	1.65	1.70	**1.73**	1.76	1.79	1.82	1.84	1.85	1.86	1.87	1.87	1.86	1.85	1.84	1.82	1.79	1.76	1.73
32	1.48	1.52	1.56	**1.60**	1.63	1.66	1.69	1.71	1.72	1.73	1.74	1.74	1.74	1.73	1.72	1.71	1.69	1.66	1.63	1.60
34	1.41	1.45	**1.48**	1.52	1.54	1.57	1.59	1.61	1.62	1.63	1.63	1.63	1.63	1.62	1.61	1.59	1.57	1.54	1.52	1.48
36	1.34	**1.38**	1.41	1.44	1.47	1.49	1.51	1.52	1.53	1.54	1.54	1.54	1.53	1.52	1.51	1.49	1.47	1.44	1.41	1.38
38	**1.28**	1.31	1.34	1.37	1.39	1.41	1.43	1.44	1.45	1.45	1.45	1.45	1.44	1.43	1.41	1.39	1.37	1.34	1.31	1.28
40	1.23	1.26	1.28	1.31	1.33	1.34	1.36	1.37	1.37	1.37	1.37	1.37	1.36	1.34	1.33	1.31	1.28	1.26	1.23	1.19
42	1.17	1.20	1.23	1.25	1.27	1.28	1.29	1.30	1.30	1.30	1.30	1.29	1.28	1.27	1.25	1.23	1.20	1.17	1.14	1.11
44	1.13	1.15	1.18	1.19	1.21	1.22	1.23	1.24	1.24	1.24	1.23	1.22	1.21	1.19	1.18	1.15	1.13	1.10	1.07	1.04
46	1.08	1.11	1.13	1.14	1.16	1.17	1.17	1.18	1.18	1.17	1.17	1.16	1.14	1.13	1.11	1.08	1.06	1.03	1.00	.97
48	1.04	1.06	1.08	1.10	1.11	1.12	1.12	1.12	1.12	1.12	1.11	1.10	1.08	1.06	1.04	1.02	.99	.97	.93	.90
50	1.01	1.02	1.04	1.05	1.06	1.07	1.07	1.07	1.07	1.06	1.05	1.04	1.02	1.01	.98	.96	.93	.90	.87	.84
52	.97	.99	1.00	1.01	1.02	1.02	1.03	1.02	1.02	1.01	1.00	.99	.97	.95	.93	.90	.88	.85	.82	.78
54	.94	.95	.96	.97	.98	.98	.98	.98	.97	.96	.95	.94	.92	.90	.88	.85	.82	.79	.76	.73
56	.90	.92	.93	.93	.94	.94	.94	.93	.93	.92	.90	.89	.87	.85	.83	.80	.77	.74	.71	.67
58	.87	.88	.89	.90	.90	.90	.90	.89	.88	.87	.86	.84	.82	.80	.78	.75	.72	.69	.66	.62
60	.84	.85	.86	.86	.87	.86	.86	.85	.84	.83	.82	.80	.78	.76	.73	.70	.67	.64	.61	
62	.82	.82	.83	.83	.83	.83	.82	.82	.80	.79	.77	.76	.74	.71	.69	.66	.63	.60		
64	.79	.79	.80	.80	.80	.79	.79	.78	.77	.75	.74	.72	.69	.67	.64	.62	.59			
66	.76	.77	.77	.77	.77	.76	.75	.74	.73	.71	.70	.68	.65	.63	.60	.57				
68	.74	.74	.74	.74	.74	.73	.72	.71	.69	.68	.66	.64	.62	.59	.56					
70	.71	.71	.71	.71	.71	.70	.69	.68	.66	.64	.62	.60	.58	.55						
72	.69	.69	.69	.68	.68	.67	.66	.64	.63	.61	.59	.57	.54							
74	.66	.66	.66	.66	.65	.64	.63	.61	.59	.57	.55	.53								

(DISTANCE RUN BETWEEN BEARINGS) × FACTOR = DISTANCE OFF ABEAM.

The factors tabulated in **bold type** are those which apply when the second bearing is the beam bearing. The left hand upper part of the table therefore pertains to ante-beam fixes, and the right hand lower part to post-beam fixes.

IMPORTANT NOTE: The distance off abeam obtained by applying the factors given in the above table to the distance sailed between bearings depends for its accuracy on knowledge of the course and distance made good, i.e., a) either there being no cross current or leeway, b) or, where cross current and leeway are known, they are applied to the course and speed of the ship's heading to produce the course and speed made good for entry into the table.

It should be appreciated that there can be a substantial difference between course made good at low speeds in even moderate cross setting currents.

APPROXIMATE COASTAL DISTANCES
IN NAUTICAL MILES

HARBOURS etc.	Cowes	Dover	Dublin	Galway Bay	Greenock	Leith	Menai Strait	Newhaven	Plymouth	Sunk Lt. V.	Swansea	Tyne Piers	Owner's Harbour
Cowes	-	110	390	496	532	500	403	54	120	156	298	395	
Dover	110	-	500	605	641	390	510	57	228	46	407	284	
Dublin	390	500	-	352	176	500*	80	444	275	546	169	542*	
Galway Bay	496	605	352	-	330	991	380	550	390	651	360	890	
Greenock	532	641	176	330	-	387*	194	586	430	687	325	425*	
Leith	500	390	500*	991	387*	-	488*	447	617	344	645*	103	
Menai Strait	403	510	80	380	194	488*	-	455	293	546	174	535*	
Newhaven	54	57	444	550	586	447	455	-	172	103	352	341	
Plymouth	120	228	275	390	430	617	293	172	-	274	192	512	
Sunk Lt. V.	156	46	546	651	687	344	546	103	274	-	453	238	
Swansea	298	407	169	360	325	645*	174	352	192	453	-	689	
Tyne Piers	395	284	542*	890	425*	103	535*	341	512	238	689	-	
Aberdeen	520	408	415*	507*	307*	85	410*	465	630	362	561*	140	
Amsterdam	270	160	660	765	804	373	657	216	385	132	572	278	
Belfast	480	590	110	314	90	415*	130	534	375	636	260	467*	
Calais	127	22	512	623	657	395	529	74	245	55	420	292	
Cape Wrath	681	570	365	410	303	254	357	627	620	524	518	308	
Casquets	79	166	347	455	496	556	337	108	80	212	254	450	
Cobh	330	430	160	224	319	817	175	374	210	476	169	716	
Dundee	501	391	472*	996	351*	50	475*	448	618	345	619*	112	
Dunkirk	148	40	527	640	680	408	535	94	264	55	450	307	
Elbe Lt. V.	431	320	820	925	703*	405	818	377	547	278	732	355	
Falmouth	151	258	250	352	395	648	253	203	38	304	160	542	
Fastnet	344	455	202	150	370	841	230	400	236	501	210	740	
Flushing	197	87	587	692	731	405	584	143	314	81	500	307	
Hook of Holland	229	118	618	723	760	367	615	175	340	93	528	284	
Lands End	178	282	212	317	358	670	212	227	66	328	123	557	
Le Havre	95	115	439	558	585	505	442	78	173	160	353	403	
Lizard	158	262	235	343	384	652	225	207	47	308	142	556	
Ostende	169	60	555	660	705	391	555	115	290	62	468	288	
Salcombe	102	206	292	399	443	596	290	151	19	252	203	500	
Spurn Point	295	184	675	789	531*	205	680	241	414	140	586	110	
St.Catherine's Pt.	25	110	388	495	538	500	390	53	119	156	298	382	
St. Malo	145	225	378	483	524	615	378	172	133	271	289	509	
Start Point	96	200	295	405	446	590	290	145	25	246	205	495	
Torquay	89	194	312	411	462	584	305	139	45	240	223	488	

Distances to or from North Sea Ports which are marked thus * are via the Caledonian Canal, all others are via the English Channel. Distances to or from Cape Wrath are by the shortest practicable route.

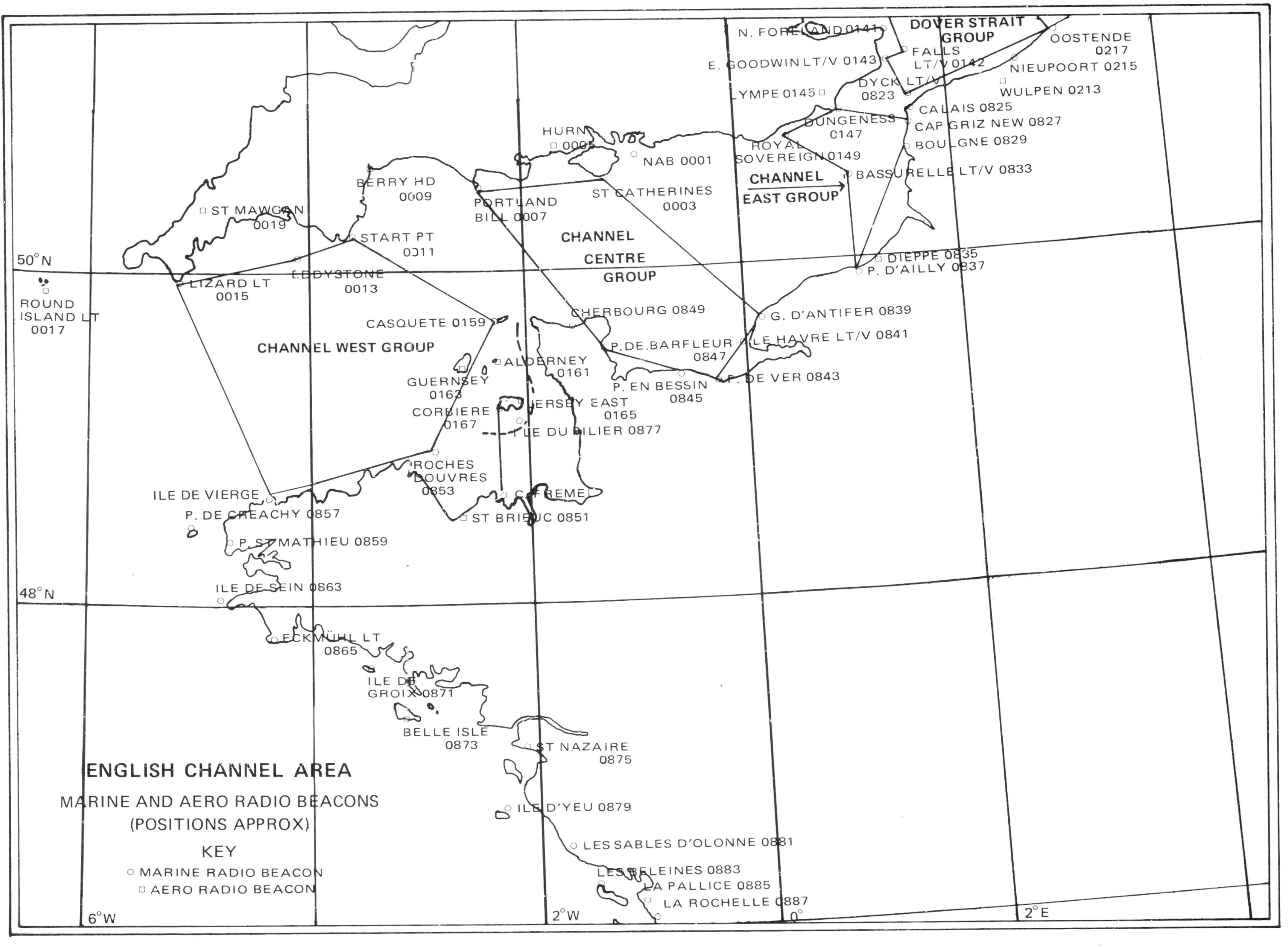
ENGLISH CHANNEL AREA
MARINE AND AERO RADIO BEACONS
(POSITIONS APPROX)
KEY
MARINE RADIO BEACON
AERO RADIO BEACON
DOVER STRAIT GROUP
N. FORELAND 0141
E. GOODWIN LT/V 0143
FALLS LT/V 0142
OOSTENDE 0217
NIEUPOORT 0215
WULPEN 0213
DYCK LT/V 0823
LYMPE 0145
CALAIS 0825
CAP GRIZ NEW 0827
DUNGENESS 0147
BOULGNE 0829
ROYAL SOVEREIGN 0149
BASSURELLE LT/V 0833
CHANNEL EAST GROUP
HURN 0005
NAB 0001
ST CATHERINES 0003
PORTLAND BILL 0007
BERRY HD 0009
ST MAWGAN 0019
START PT 0011
EDDYSTONE 0013
LIZARD LT 0015
ROUND ISLAND LT 0017
CHANNEL CENTRE GROUP
DIEPPE 0835
P. D'AILLY 0837
G. D'ANTIFER 0839
LE HAVRE LT/V 0841
CHERBOURG 0849
P.DE.BARFLEUR 0847
P. DE VER 0843
P. EN BESSIN 0845
CASQUETE 0159
CHANNEL WEST GROUP
ALDERNEY 0161
GUERNSEY 0163
JERSEY EAST 0165
CORBIERE 0167
ILE DU PILIER 0877
ROCHES DOUVRES 0853
C. FREMEL
ST BRIEUC 0851
ILE DE VIERGE
P. DE CREACHY 0857
P. ST MATHIEU 0859
ILE DE SEIN 0863
ECKMÜHL LT 0865
ILE DE GROIX 0871
BELLE ISLE 0873
ST NAZAIRE 0875
ILE D'YEU 0879
LES SABLES D'OLONNE 0881
LES BALEINES 0883
LA PALLICE 0885
LA ROCHELLE 0887
50° N
48° N
6° W
2° W
0°
2° E

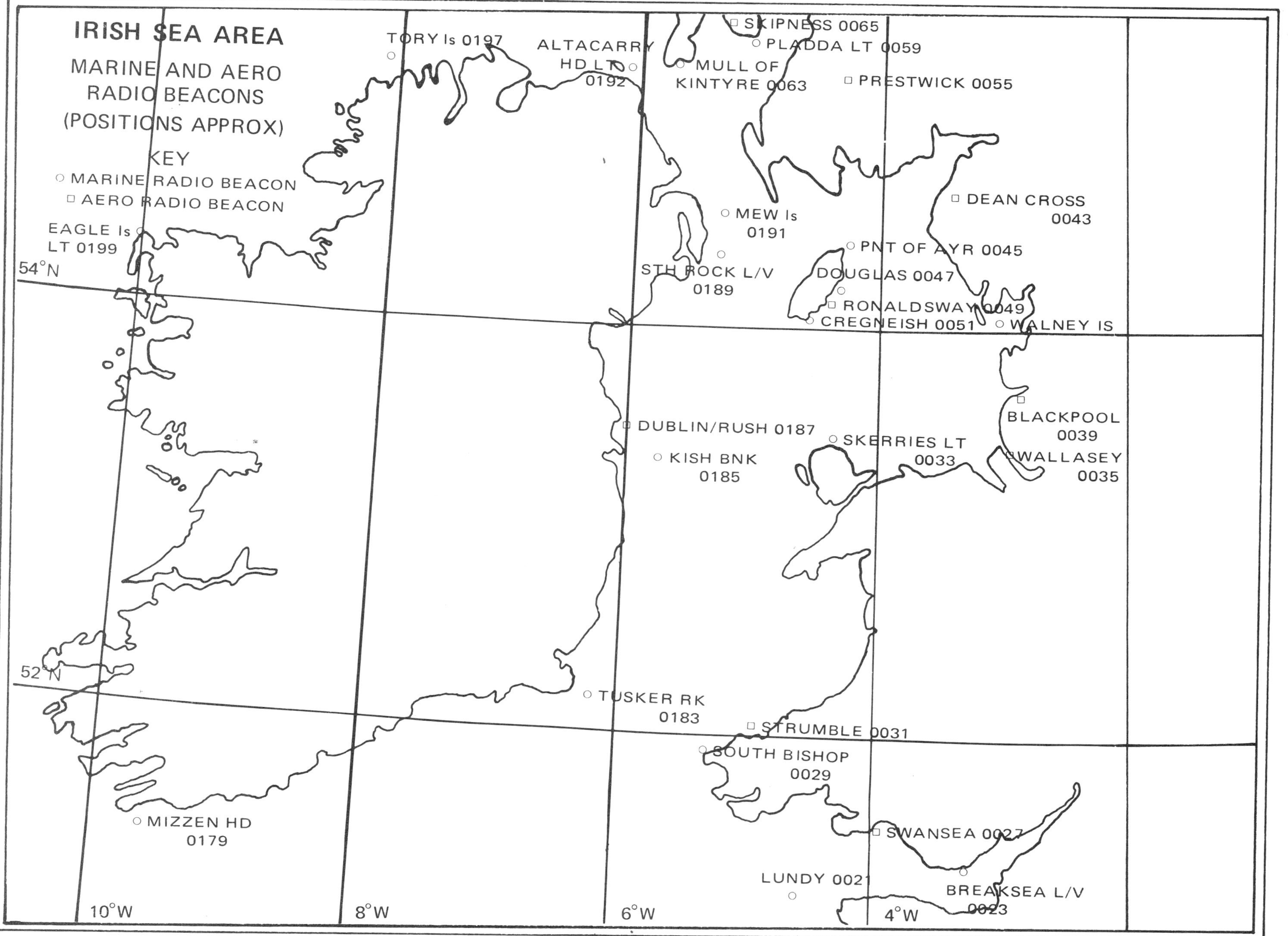
IRISH SEA AREA
MARINE AND AERO RADIO BEACONS (POSITIONS APPROX)
KEY
MARINE RADIO BEACON
AERO RADIO BEACON
EAGLE Is LT 0199
TORY Is 0197
ALTACARRY HD LT 0192
SKIPNESS 0065
PLADDA LT 0059
MULL OF KINTYRE 0063
PRESTWICK 0055
DEAN CROSS 0043
MEW Is 0191
PNT OF AYR 0045
STH ROCK L/V 0189
DOUGLAS 0047
RONALDSWAY 0049
CREGNEISH 0051
WALNEY IS
BLACKPOOL 0039
DUBLIN/RUSH 0187
SKERRIES LT 0033
WALLASEY 0035
KISH BNK 0185
TUSKER RK 0183
STRUMBLE 0031
SOUTH BISHOP 0029
MIZZEN HD 0179
SWANSEA 0027
LUNDY 0021
BREAKSEA L/V 0023
54°N
52°N
10°W
8°W
6°W
4°W

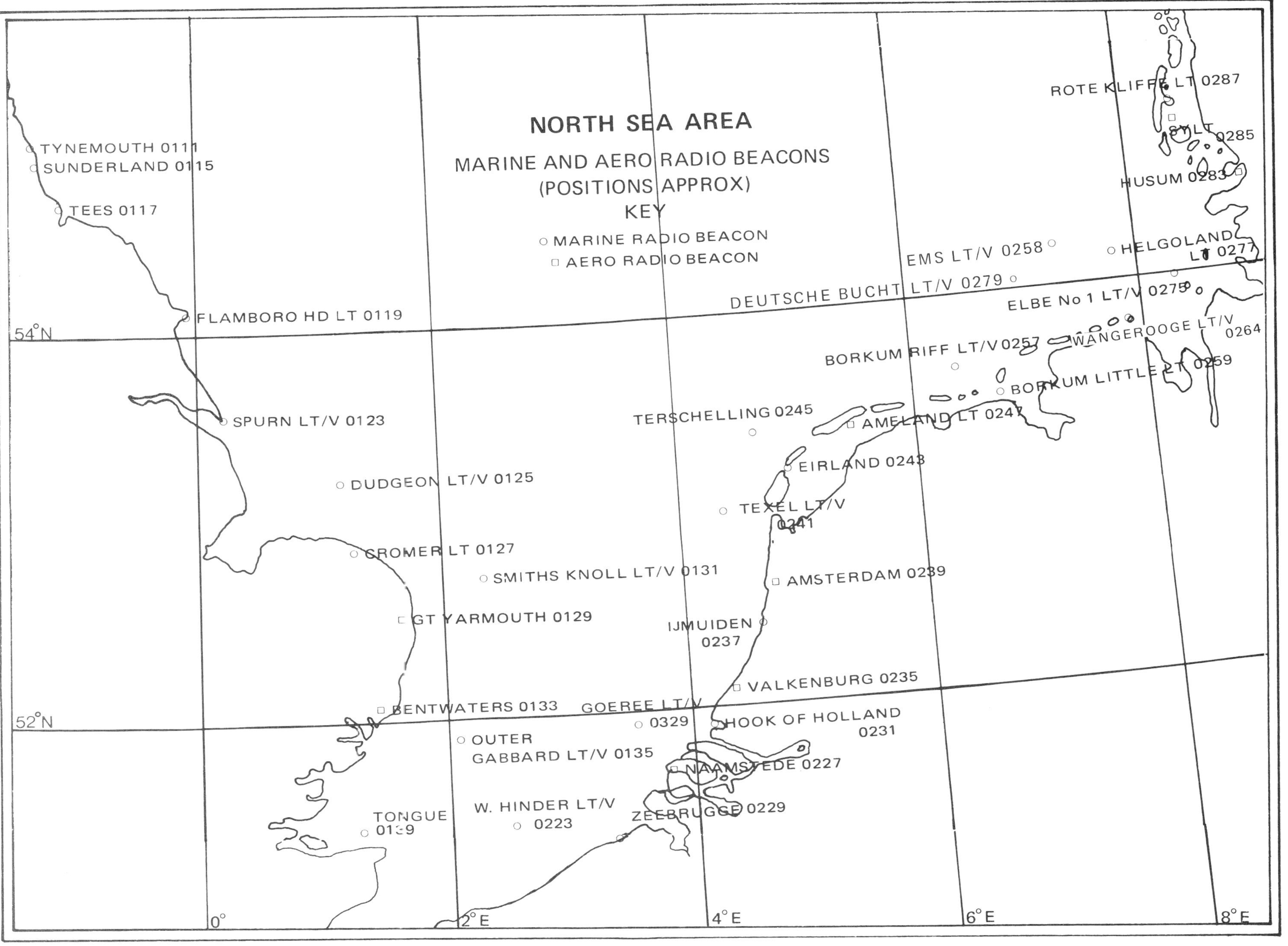
NORTH SEA AREA
MARINE AND AERO RADIO BEACONS
(POSITIONS APPROX)
KEY
MARINE RADIO BEACON
AERO RADIO BEACON
TYNEMOUTH 0111
SUNDERLAND 0115
TEES 0117
FLAMBORO HD LT 0119
SPURN LT/V 0123
DUDGEON LT/V 0125
CROMER LT 0127
SMITHS KNOLL LT/V 0131
GT YARMOUTH 0129
BENTWATERS 0133
GOEREE LT/V 0329
OUTER GABBARD LT/V 0135
W. HINDER LT/V 0223
ZEEBRUGGE 0229
NAAMSTEDE 0227
HOOK OF HOLLAND 0231
VALKENBURG 0235
IJMUIDEN 0237
AMSTERDAM 0239
TEXEL LT/V 0241
EIRLAND 0243
TERSCHELLING 0245
AMELAND LT 0247
BORKUM LITTLE LT 0259
BORKUM RIFF LT/V 0257
WANGEROOGE LT/V 0264
ELBE No 1 LT/V 0275
DEUTSCHE BUCHT LT/V 0279
EMS LT/V 0258
HELGOLAND LT 0277
HUSUM 0283
SYLT 0285
ROTE KLIFFE LT 0287
54°N
52°N
0°
2°E
4°E
6°E
8°E

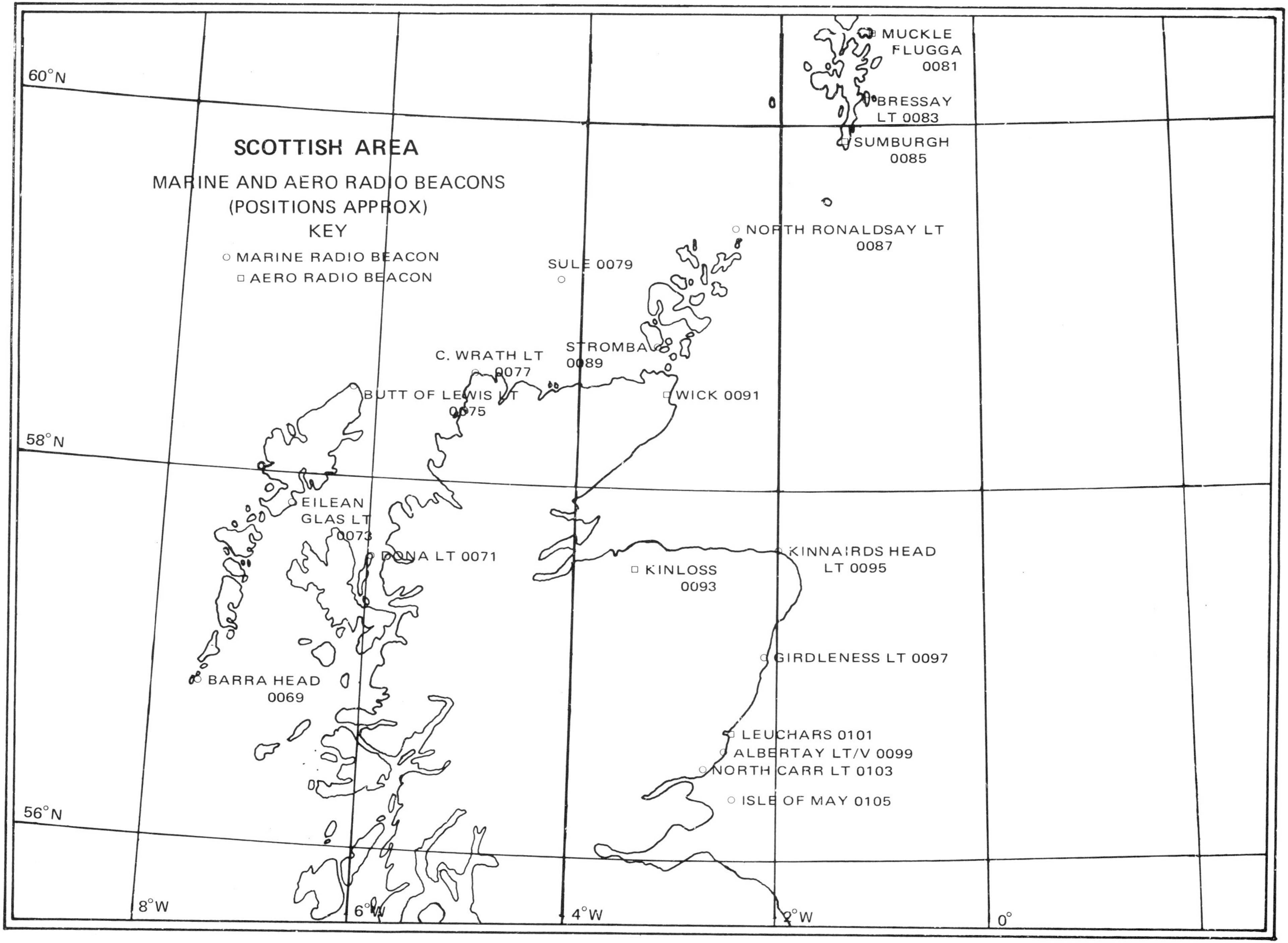

SCOTTISH AREA

MARINE AND AERO RADIO BEACONS
(POSITIONS APPROX)

KEY

○ MARINE RADIO BEACON
□ AERO RADIO BEACON

INDEX

LATERAL SYSTEM OF BUOYAGE

BUOY	SHAPE	TOPMARK	LIGHT
STARBOARD HAND		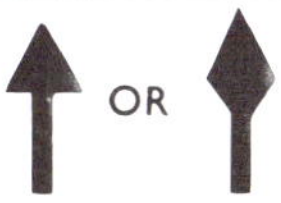 OR	1, 3 & 5 GP. FL. WHITE
PORT HAND		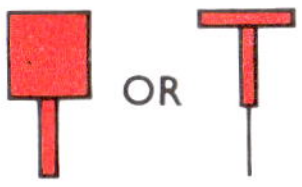 OR	2, 4 & 6 GP. FL. WHITE or 1, 2, 3 or 4 GP. FL. RED
MIDDLE GROUND MAIN CHANNEL TO THE RIGHT MAIN CHANNEL TO THE LEFT CHANNELS OF EQUAL IMPORTANCE		 OUTER INNER OUTER INNER OUTER INNER	FLASHING RED or WHITE DISTINCTIVE
STARBOARD HAND WRECK	 WRECK		GP. FL. (3) GREEN
PORT HAND WRECK	 WRECK		GP. FL. (2) GREEN
EITHER HAND WRECK	 WRECK		OCC. GREEN
LANDFALL or MID-CHANNEL		 SHAPE OPTIONAL	FL. DISTINCTIVE
DANGER ZONE (U.K.COAST)	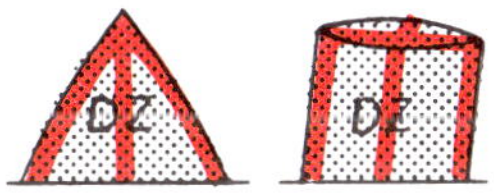 DZ DZ	PRACTICE AREA 	
SPOIL GROUND	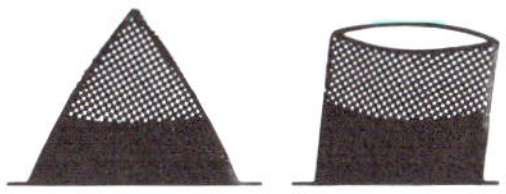	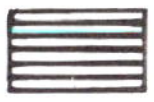 BLUE  YELLOW	
WATCH BUOY	 WATCH	QUARANTINE AREA 	
ISOLATED DANGER	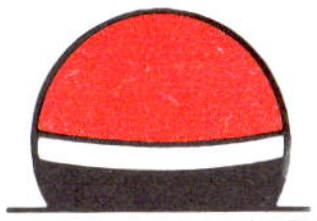	 OR OR	FL. WHITE or RED

CARDINAL SYSTEM OF BUOYAGE

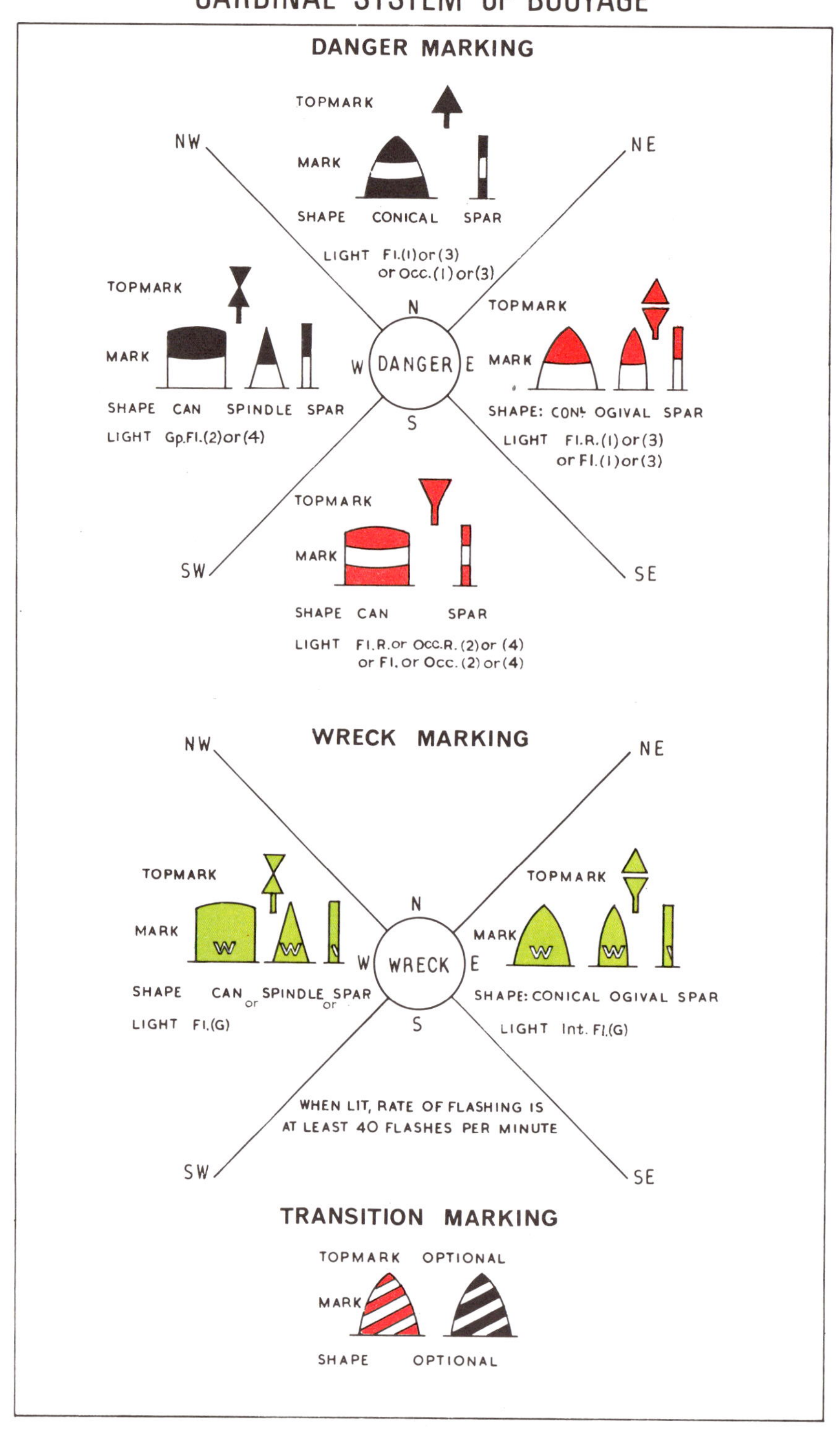

INTERNATIONAL CODE OF SIGNALS (FLAGS)

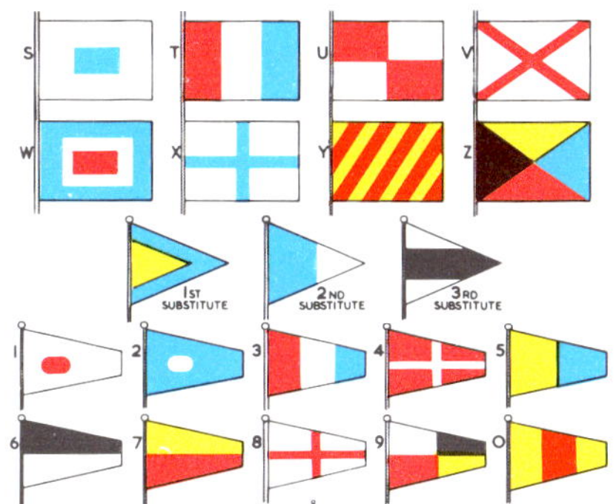

A I have a diver down; keep well clear at slow speed.

*B I am taking-in or discharging or carrying dangerous goods.

C **Yes** (affirmative or "The Significance of the previous group should be read in the affirmative").

*D **Keep clear** of me—I am manoeuvring with difficulty.

*E I am altering my course to **Starboard.**

F I am **disabled.** Communicate with me.

G I require a pilot. (When made by fishing vessels operating in close proximity on the fishing grounds it means "I am hauling nets".)

*H I have a **pilot** on board.

*I I am altering my course to **Port.**

J I am on fire and have dangerous cargo on board, keep well clear of me.

K I wish to communicate with you.

L You should **stop** your vessel instantly.

M My vessel is stopped and making no way through the water.

†N **No** (negative or "The Significance of the previous group should be read in the negative").

O **Man overboard.**

P In harbour: All persons should report on board as the vessel is about to proceed to sea.
At sea: May be used by fishing vessels to mean "My nets have become fast upon an obstruction".)

Q My vessel is **healthy** and I request free pratique.

‡R No signal.

*S My engines are going **astern.**

T **Keep clear of me. I am engaged in pair trawling.**

U You are running **into danger.**

V **I require assistance.**

W **I require medical assistance.**

X **Stop** carrying out your intentions and watch for my signal.

Y I am **dragging** my **anchor.**

Z **I require a tug.** When made by fishing vessels operating in close proximity on the fishing grounds it means: "I am shooting nets".

† This signal may only be given visually or by sound. For voice or radio transmission the signal should be NO.
‡ No single letter signals have been allocated to these letters as these already have a meaning in the Collision Regulations.
* These letters may only be made in compliance with the requirements of the International Regulations for Preventing Collisions at Sea.

NATIONAL FLAGS

The White Ensign

The Blue Ensign

The Red Ensign

DIAGRAMS ON COLLISION REGULATIONS

Fig. 10.1

Fig. 10.3

Vessel A must keep out of the way of vessel B in each case.

Fig. 10.2

Although vessel A is crossing the course of vessel B, vessel A is approaching from a direction more than 22½° abaft the beam of vessel B: vessel A is, therefore, an overtaking vessel and must keep out of the way.

Fig. 10.4

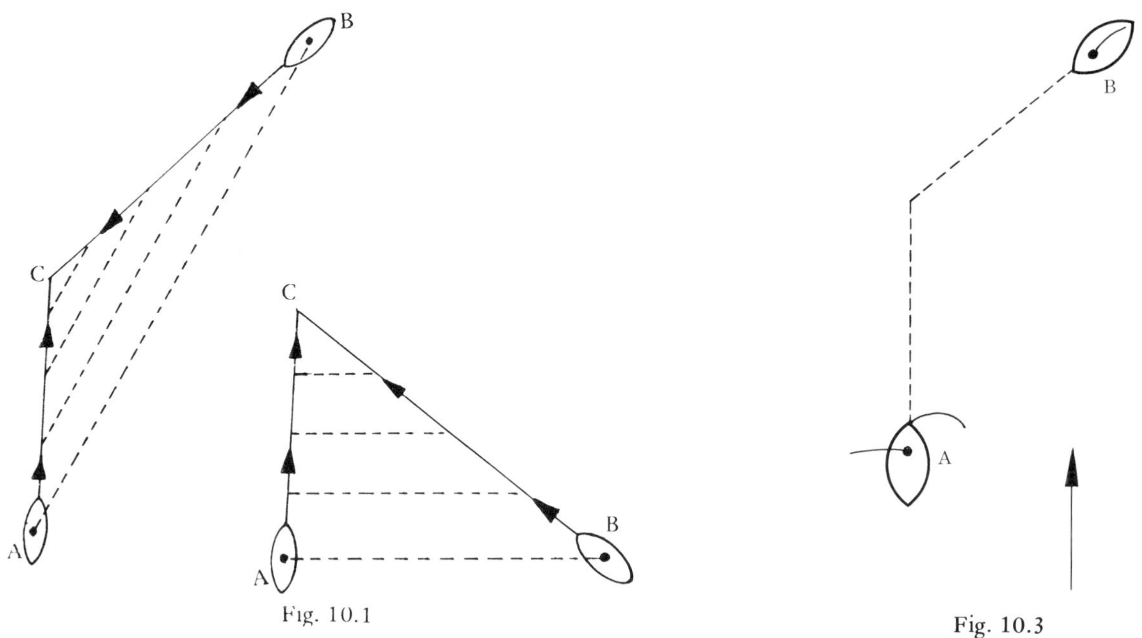

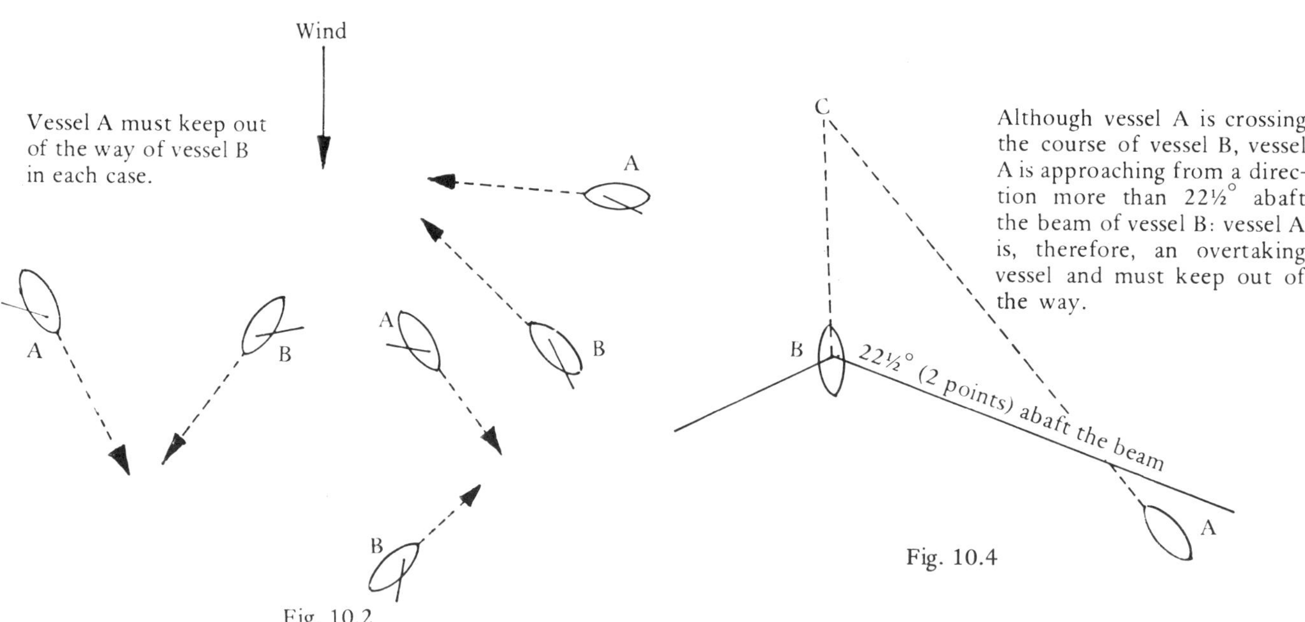

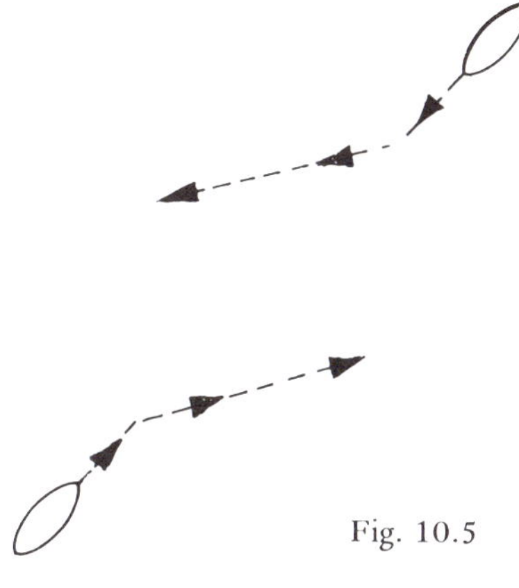

Fig. 10.5

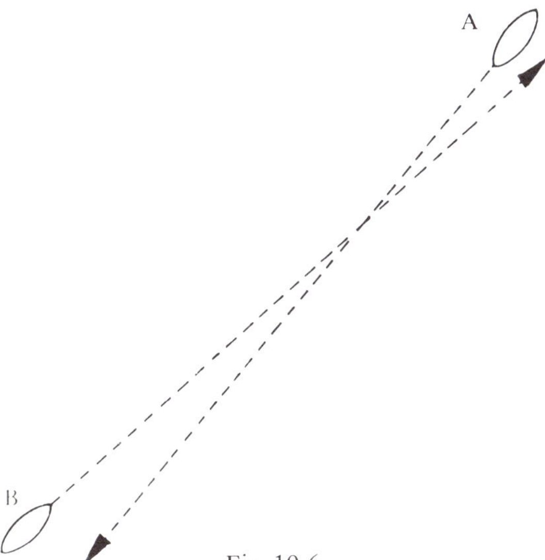

Fig. 10.6

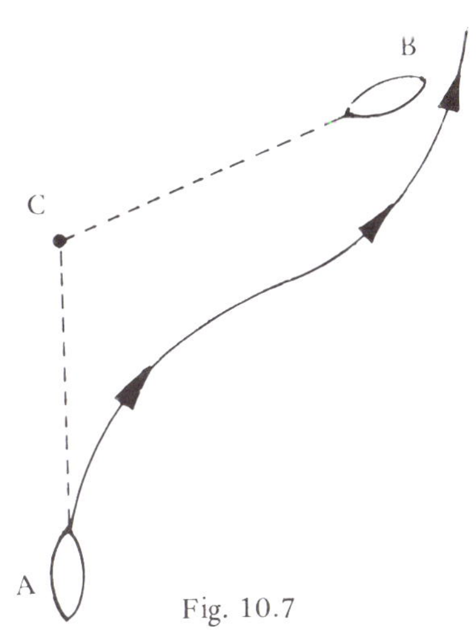

Fig. 10.7

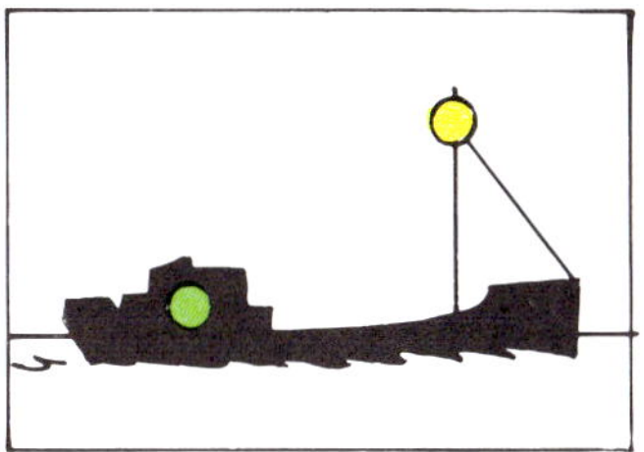

Power-driven vessel under 50 metres

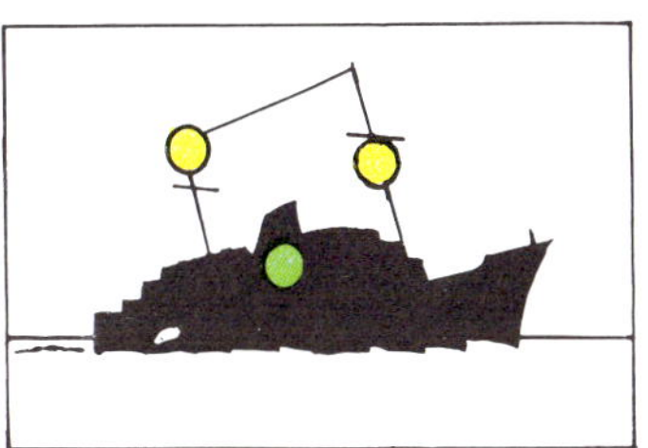

Power-driven vessel over 50 metres

Power-driven vessel over 50 metres. Stern light is also shown.

Fig. 10.8

Power-driven vessel towing another vessel, the length of the tow not exceeding 200 metres.

Power-driven vessel towing another vessel, the length of the tow exceeding 200 metres.

A vessel being pushed ahead by a power-driven vessel.

Fig. 10.9

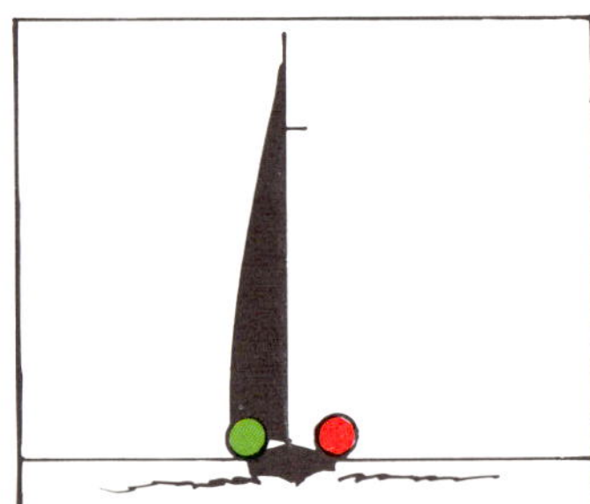

Sailing craft under way, bows on.

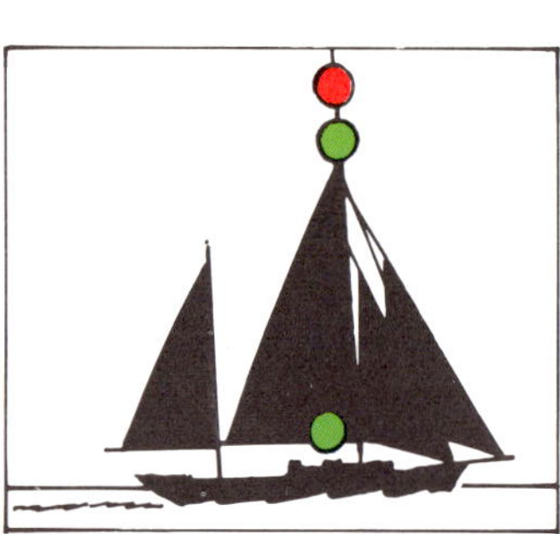

Sailing craft under way displaying the optional masthead lights.

Fig. 10.10

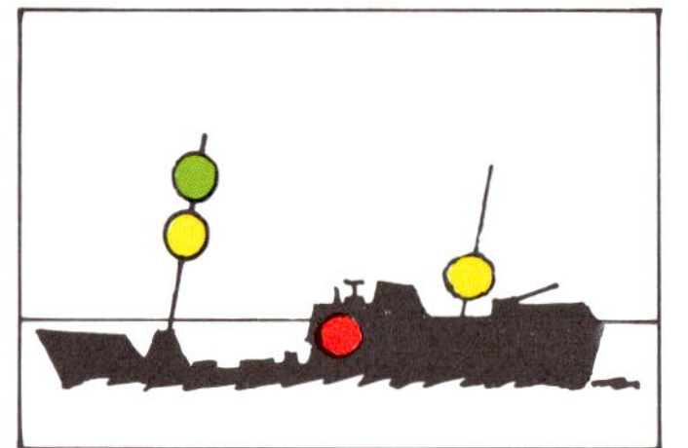

Trawler trawling and making way. Showing optional steaming light.

Vessel engaged in fish

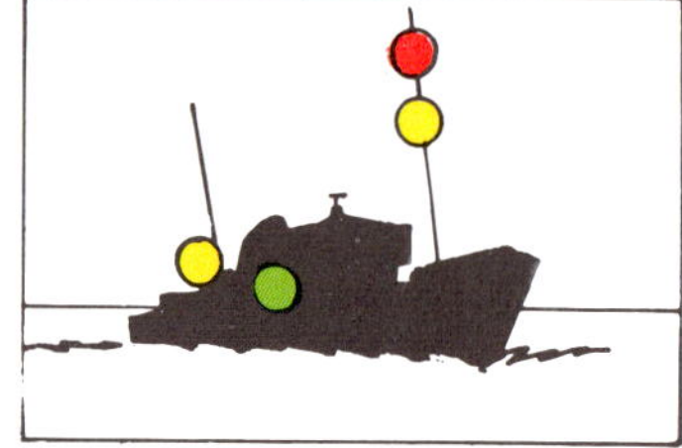

Fishing vessel making way and having gear extending more than 500 feet.

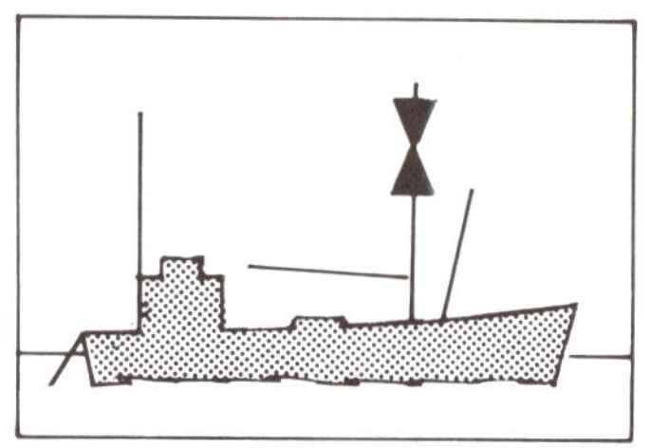

Vessel engaged in fishing.

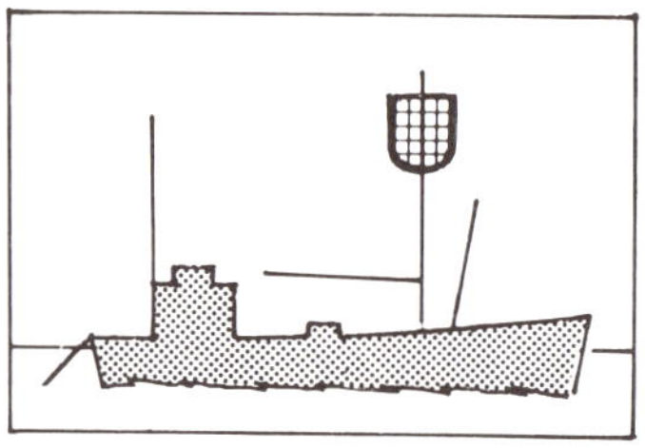

Vessel of less than 20 metres engaged in fishing.

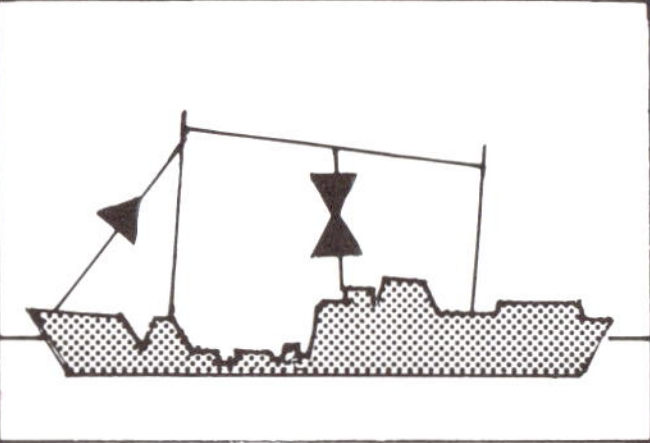

Fishing vessel with outlying gear extending more than 500 feet.

Fig. 10.11

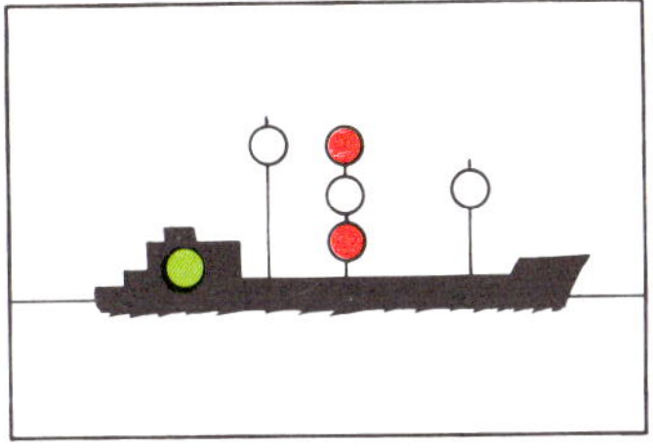

Vessel exceeding 50 metres in length making way through the the water.

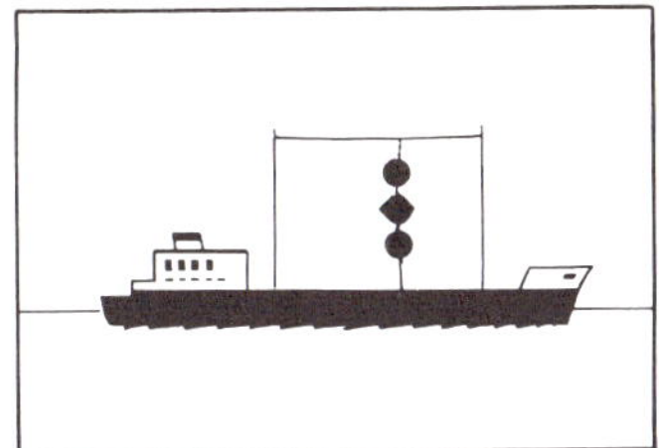

By day.

Vessel not under command.

Vessel not under command, under way and making way through the water.

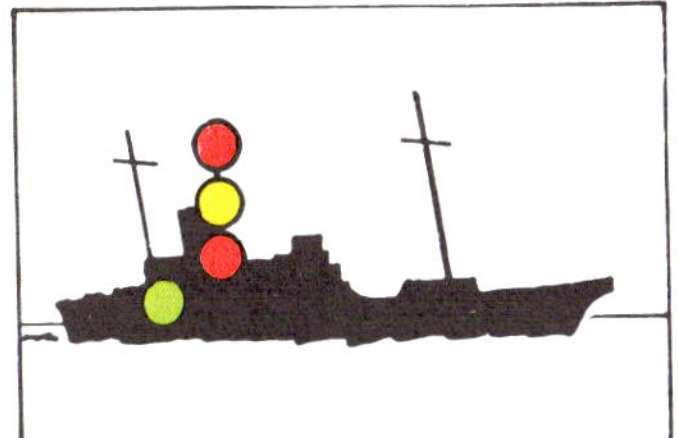

Vessel engaged in laying or picking up a telegraph cable, etc. etc., under way and making way through the water.

Fig. 10.12

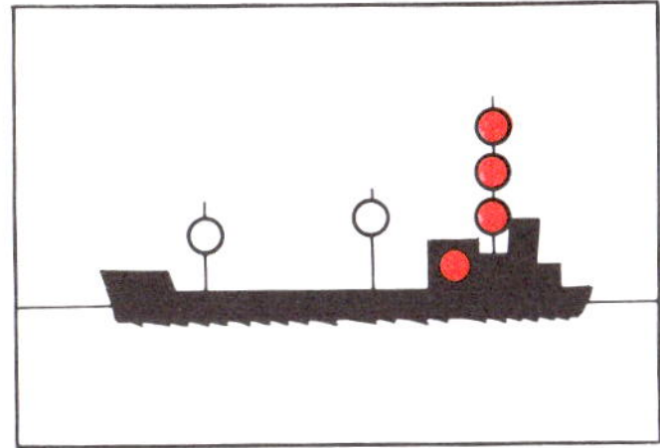

Fig. 10.13.

Power-driven pilot-vessel on station and under way.

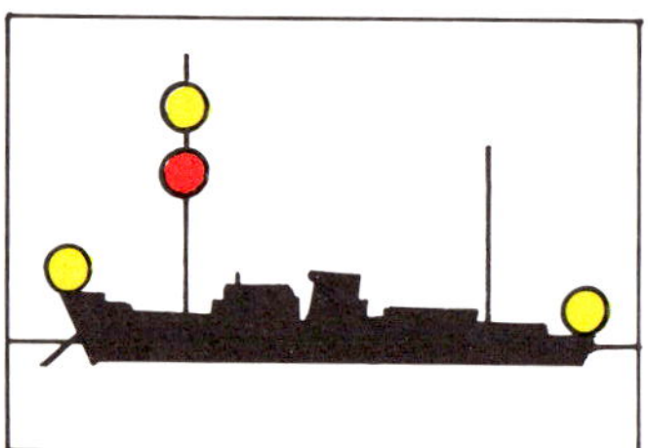

Power-driven pilot-vessel on station and at anchor.

Fig. 10.14

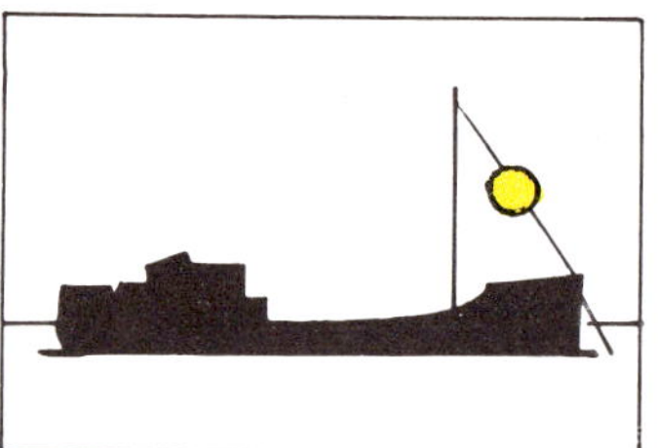

Vessel over 50 metres long at anchor.

Vessel over 50 metres long at anchor

Vessel at anchor.

Fig. 10.15